I0796586

Helion & Company Limited
Unit 8 Amherst Business Centre
Budbrooke Road
Warwick
CV34 5WE
England
Tel. 01926 499 619
Email: info@helion.co.uk
Website: www.helion.co.uk
Twitter: @helionbooks
https://helionbooks.wordpress.com/

Front cover photo: one of three or four F-35Cs of the US Navy's Test and Evaluation Squadron VX-9, equipped with experimental 'mirror' coating. (USN)
Front cover artwork: an F-35I Adir of the No. 140 Squadron, Israeli Air-Space Force during combat operations of the 'Seven Fronts War' of 2023-2025. (Artwork by Tom Cooper)
Rear cover artwork top: The first prototype of the brand-new B-21 Raider strategic bomber designed for the US Air Force, a type that is near-certain to strongly complement operations of US and allied F-35s for decades to come. (Artwork by Tom Cooper)
Rear cover artwork bottom: first revealed to the public in late 2024, the first prototype of the Chengdu Aerospace Corporation's three-engined heavy fighter-bomber system, probably designated J-36, represents the most challenging potential adversary of the F-35. (Artwork by Tom Cooper)

Designed and typeset by Mach 3 Solutions (www.mach3solutions.co.uk)
Cover design Paul Hewitt, Battlefield Design (www.battlefield-design.co.uk)

ISBN: 978-1-804519-40-0

British Library Cataloguing-in-Publication Data
A catalogue record for this book is available from the British Library

CONTENTS

Abbreviations and Acronyms 2

1 A Primary Fighter for the Post-Cold War Era 2
2 One Program For All Services 17
3 Operationalising the F-35 36
4 Deployments and Operations 53
5 Mission Scope: A Fighter Relied on for Every Role 69
6 The Pentagon and Lockheed Martin: Acquisitions, Sustainment, and Flaws 93
7 Powering the F-35 110
8 The F-35 as Part of a Global Fighter Program 122
9 Threat Environment: The F-35 in a Future War 141
10 Into the Sixth Generation Era: The Future of the F-35 and Supporting Programs 157
11 Evaluation 170

Bibliography 179
Endnotes 179
About the Author 194

Note: In order to simplify the use of this book, all names, locations and geographic designations are as provided in *The Times World Atlas*, or other traditionally accepted major sources of reference, as of the time of described events.

ABBREVIATIONS AND ACRONYMS

AESA	active electronically scanned array
AETP	Adaptive Engine Transition Program
AWACS	Airborne Warning and Control System
AI	artificial intelligence
ALIS	Autonomic Logistics Information System
ASTOVL	Advanced Short Takeoff Vertical Landing
CAS	close air support
CIA	Central Intelligence Agency
CTOL	conventional take-off and landing
DARPA	Defense Advanced Research Projects Agency
DoD	Department of Defense
EABO	Expeditionary Advanced Base Operations
EMALS	Electromagnetic Aircraft Launch System
EOTS	Electro-Optical Targeting System
ERAM	Extended Range Attack Munition
GAO	Government Accountability Office
IASF	Israeli Air & Space Force
IFF	Identification Friend or Foe
IOC	Initial Operating Capability
IOT&E	Initial Operational Test & Evaluation
IRST	infrared search and track
JASDF	Japan Air Self-Defense Force
JSF	Joint Strike Fighter
MACE	Mission Affordable Capacity Effector
MCAS	Marine Corps Air Station
NATF	Naval Advanced Tactical Fighter
NATO	North Atlantic Treaty Organization
NGAD	Next Generation Air Dominance
PACAF	Pacific Air Forces
PESA	passive electronically scanned array
PLAAF	People's Liberation Army Air Force
RCS	radar cross section
RoCAF	Republic of China Air Force
STOVL	short take-off and vertical landing
TR-3	Technology Refresh 3
UAE	United Arab Emirates
UAV	unmanned aerial vehicle
U.S.	United States
USAF	United States Air Force
USSR	Union of Soviet and Socialist Republics
VMFA	Marine Fighter Attack Squadron
VTOL	vertical take-off and landing

1

A PRIMARY FIGHTER FOR THE POST-COLD WAR ERA

Origins of Stealth

The history of the development of aircraft optimised for evading enemy radars is almost as old as the use of radars itself, with the de Havilland Mosquito multirole combat aircraft having been commissioned from November 1941, and using plywood panelling to provide a limited ability to evade radar detection. Research into radar absorbent materials from the early Cold War years subsequently facilitated the development of aircraft using more advanced materials that did not significantly compromise flight performance. The service entry of the U.S. Air Force's (USAF) SR-71 and Central Intelligence Agency's (CIA) A-12 strategic reconnaissance aircraft in 1966 and 1967 were major milestones in this development, with the latter combining advanced radar absorbent materials with a 'plasma stealth' effect created by a cesium-based radar-absorbing exhaust plume.[1] CIA efforts under Project Rainbow to develop a more effective radar evading design for the A-12 notably failed, however, while an abysmal accident rate among other issues meant that the aircraft had to be removed from service just a year after being commissioned.[2]

U.S.-led efforts to develop means of penetrating Soviet airspace initially focused heavily on the ability to fly at altitudes beyond the reach of enemy air defences. This approach had proven successful during the Pacific War, when the B-29 bomber's ability to operate at heretofore unseen altitudes had been a major contributor to its survivability against Japanese air defences. While the B-29 subsequently proved highly vulnerable to even small numbers of Soviet-built fighters in the skies over Korea, the U-2 spy plane was designed to fly over twice as high at 22,300 metres, at which altitudes American radars were unable to track it. Soviet radars, however, caused considerable amazement within the Pentagon by demonstrating the ability to track U-2s throughout their flight paths, which combined with major advances in missile technologies allowed an S-75 surface-to-air missile system to shoot down a U-2 flown by CIA pilot Gary Powers on 1 May 1960. Subsequent efforts focused on developing aircraft that could combine extreme altitudes with very high speeds, with the A-12 and SR-71 designed to operate at over Mach 3, while the B-70 bomber had a similarly impressive flight performance and made its first demonstrator flight on 21 September 1964.

Much as had been the case for the U-2, a growing consensus quickly emerged in the mid-1960s that the rate of advances in Soviet air defence capabilities would leave high and fast flying penetration aircraft obsolete before they could enter service. Soviet air defence technologies were consistently found to be advancing much faster, and did so at a small fraction of the cost of American programs to develop offensive systems. The Soviet MiG-25 interceptor and S-200 air defence system were both well within their performance parameters to hit America's new Mach 3+ aircraft, while even the older S-75 system which had brought down multiple U-2s, had also damaged two CIA A-12s flying at altitudes of over 24,000 metres and at speeds well exceeding Mach 3 over North Vietnam in October 1967.[3] The system would years later in August 1981 come close to achieving the same against an SR-71 over North Korea. With the costly B-70 bomber expected to be highly vulnerable before it even entered service, development was terminated in 1969 and further programs to secure survivability through very high speeds were not pursued.

A subsequent approach to penetrating Soviet and allied airspace would focus on the ability to fly at extremely low altitudes. This shielded aircraft against radar detection at longer ranges, as the conforming of radar waves to the earth's curvature meant the lower altitude an aircraft flew at, the shorter the distances at which it could be detected. Flying very close to the earth also created clutter, among which it could be very difficult for airborne radars to pick out a target. The Subsonic Low-Altitude Bomber study for the future of strategic penetration of enemy airspace was among the assessments which favoured such an approach, leading to the development of the F-111 strike fighter and B-1B bomber which entered service from 1967 and 1986 respectively. It also influenced the development of low flying cruise missiles such as the BGM-109A Tomahawk, AGM-86 and AGM-129. The survivability advantages provided by this approach, however, would also prove to be limited.

The Soviet Union quickly developed a network of short-range air defence systems down to the level of handheld infrared guided systems, which left low-flying aircraft highly vulnerable. This worsened as the first Soviet look-down shoot-down radars were introduced on the MiG-23M fighter from 1976, a year after the first USAF fighter, the F-15, had done so. Such radars quickly proliferated across the Soviet fleet, leaving low flying aircraft exposed. In 1981 the Soviet Air Defence Forces introduced the MiG-31 interceptor, which carried the world first, and for the next two decades the only, electronically scanned array radar built for air-to-air combat the N007, which was also by far the world's largest radar carried by a tactical combat aircraft. The radar allowed vast areas 200 kilometres wide to be scanned near instantaneously, tracking targets 50 metres off the ground and thousands of metres above the Armstrong Limit simultaneously. The MiG-31's development was considered a primary factor in the cancellation of the B-1A bomber program in 1980, and the subsequent decision to cut production of the B-1B to just 100 aircraft.[4] With the much-improved new MiG-31M scheduled for service entry in the mid-1990s, and with smaller radars using similar technologies set to proliferate widely in the Soviet and allied fleets, hopes for low altitude penetration of Warsaw Pact airspace were effectively ended.

Where flying up and over enemy air defences at extreme speeds, or evading them with terrain-hugging flight profiles, both proved increasingly unviable, a revolutionary third approach had the potential to provide the ability to fly directly through them at regular speeds and altitudes. As observed in a publication by the Centre for a New American Security: 'If Americans were to penetrate Soviet air defences, they were no longer going to be able to go either higher and faster or lower. They would need to disappear altogether.'[5] Where the first approach had been focused on an ability to evade missiles, and the second on the ability to exploit weaknesses in radar coverage, the new third approach focused on building aircraft with intrinsic properties that allowed them to thwart enemy targeting radars even if flying right into their kill zones. This would be achieved not only with the development of new generations of radar absorbent coatings and materials, but also by positioning the surfaces of the aircraft so radar waves struck at close to tangential angles, and far from any right angles to edges, to reduce the radar returns by several orders of magnitude.

The amount of radar energy a body reflects back to its source is referred to as the radar cross section (RCS), with a lower cross section making an aircraft more difficult for radars to detect, track or lock onto. While stealth aircraft with reduced radar cross sections are far from invisible to radars, particularly those which operate in longer wavebands, they are only detectable at shorter ranges and, most importantly, difficult for radars, and particularly the small high frequency radars on anti-aircraft missiles, to lock on to. The advantages this can provide in all manner of missions, whether for air-to-air combat, air defence suppression, anti-shipping, or even bombing runs with gravity weapons, are tremendous. Although radar-guided weapons systems would be specifically designed to target low RCS aircraft, even these would do so with far more difficulty and over far shorter ranges than they would be able to against high RCS targets.

MiG-31 interceptor. The appearance of this aircraft with revolutionary new sensor and beyond visual range targeting capabilities was an important factor strengthening the consensus that development of aircraft emphasising low observability to enemy radars was vital. (Fedor Leukhin)

A B-1B during low altitude bombing run. The bomber's survivability for penetration flights into enemy airspace was in serious question since before its entry into service. While it benefitted from very limited radar-cross-section reductions, its emphasis on low altitude opreations to evade targeting was not considered viable due to advances in Soviet air defence capabilities. (USAF)

Reductions to an aircraft's radar cross section can be achieved through changes to the airframe shape, as well as through altering structures of airframe elements, and in particular the contacts between covering, hatches, and moving and fixed parts of the airframe. Use of radar absorbent materials and coatings are a third major means of reducing RCS. Early efforts to develop aircraft with reduced radar cross sections were made during the 1950s, after the Soviet Air Defence Forces demonstrated the ability to track U-2s throughout their flight paths. The CIA in response requested aerospace manufacturer Lockheed investigate ways to reduce the radar cross section of its aircraft, with the U-2's successor the A-12 benefitting from a reduction of two orders of magnitude. The D-21 reconnaissance drone developed in parallel to the A-12 achieved an RCS reduction of another order of magnitude.[6] Although both aircraft had to be quickly retired due to reliability issues, they pioneered important advances in stealth technologies. The SR-71 also saw advances made during its development, with the program manager at Lockheed, Paul Martin, stating that it was for this program that the firm 'first developed aircraft shaping methods, radar absorbing structural edges, radar absorbing coatings, and other design features that greatly reduced the SR-71's radar signature.'[7]

One of the most influential early studies on the potential to shape an airframe to minimise radar returns was conducted by a leading scientist at the Moscow Institute of Radio Engineering, Pyotr Ufimtsev, who in 1962 published the paper: Method of Edge Waves in the Physical Theory of Diffraction. He identified that the shape of an object could influence how it appeared to a radar far more than its size, meaning a large object, such as a strategic bomber, could be made as difficult to detect as a golf ball if properly shaped. Ufimtsev further succeeded in mathematically predicting the scattering of electromagnetic waves from three-dimensional objects. His paper was republished in English by the U.S. Air Force Foreign Technology Division in 1966, and would later be credited with sparking a revolution in American combat aviation.

Where early efforts to develop stealth technologies had focused heavily on high value strategic aircraft, this would change from the early 1970s. The October 1973 Arab-Israeli War highlighted the vulnerability of American fighters to Soviet air defences, with the Israeli Air Force losing 109 aircraft in the conflict's first 18 days primarily to ground based systems supplied by the USSR to Egypt and Syria.[8] Some Western estimates were significantly higher, indicating dozens of losses on the first day alone.[9*] While the F-4E which formed the backbone of the Israeli Air Force was by far the most capable fighter in the Western world, the fact that Arab states lacked any of the USSR's newest and most capable systems, and had far fewer layers in their air defence networks than the Soviets did, and much less capable aircraft, only made the need for major improvements to fighters' survivability appear all the more urgent. The performance of Soviet air defences in the conflict was widely credited with stimulating efforts to develop fighter-sized aircraft with advanced stealth capabilities, lest the Western Bloc's fighter fleets be subjected to tremendous losses in a potential engagement.[10] This marked the beginning of the formation of a consensus that stealth would be imperative for fighters to be survivable in future, particularly for offensive penetration missions, as radar and missile

* The much higher mobility and more advanced targeting systems demonstrated by new generations of Soviet air defence systems, in particular the 2K12, was singled out by Israeli ambassador to the United States Simha Dinitz, who informed State Secretary Henry Kissinger: 'we suffered very heavy casualties ... from the SAM-6s [2K12] which were very effective against our planes.' U.S. Chief of Naval Operations Thomas Moorer commented on the 2K12: 'yes, for two reasons. They're mobile and [the Israelis] can't find the launchers. Also, we have never been able to get sufficient information about them to develop any good countermeasures.' (Ginor, Isabella and Remez, Gideon, *The Soviet-Israeli War, 1967–1973: The USSR's Military Intervention in the Egyptian-Israeli Conflict*, Oxford, Oxford University Press, 2017 (p. 345).)

The Lockheed A-12, which served in the CIA fleet for a year from 1967-1968, was one of the first aircraft designed with limited radar cross section reductions. (Lockheed Martin)

technologies improved. This consensus would continue to strengthen for over half a century into the 2020s.

In 1974 the Defense Advanced Research Projects Agency (DARPA) requested proposals for a fighter-sized aircraft with stealth capabilities. Where stealth had provided only a secondary contribution to the survivability of the A-12, D-12 and SR-71, which relied overwhelmingly on their speeds and altitudes, the new aircraft would rely on stealth as its primary means of ensuring survivability. This posed a number of new challenges, and led Lockheed to draw heavily on Pyotr Ufimtsev's work. The program marked the firm's return to the fighter industry after a ten year absence, and leveraged its unique experience developing aircraft with stealth capabilities for CIA programs.

Under the Have Blue program, Lockheed's Skunk Works division built two technology demonstrator aircraft with unique faceted surfaces intended to deflect radar waves away from a radar receiver. They had highly-swept wings and inward-canted vertical stabilisers. The first of the demonstrators made its first flight on 1 December 1977, and the second on 20 July 1978. Both were lost to crashes within 13 months of their first flights, although the program was considered a major success with both demonstrators showing that more extreme radar cross section reductions were indeed possible. The development of fly-by-wire control systems, which was pioneered by the F-16 fighter, was critical to allowing highly unconventional aircraft designs to fly. Such systems used flight control computers to conduct thousands of measurements per second, and utilised this data to automatically manipulate control surfaces in order to counter deviations from the pilot-set flight path.

The development of stealth aircraft was publicly announced by Defense Secretary Harold Brown at a Pentagon news conference on 22 August 1980, at which time he stated regarding the technology's promise: 'It is not too soon to say that by making existing air defence systems essentially ineffective, this alters the military balance significantly.'[11] Efforts to develop a specially shaped fighter with a reduced radar cross section were pursued in parallel to efforts to achieve reductions in the infrared, visual, contrails, engine smoke, acoustic, and electromagnetic signatures. Particularly important was the development of new generations of much quieter radars with low signatures, limiting an adversary's ability to home in on them when active and thus reducing the possibility that they would give away the aircraft's position. Also important was the reduction of heat emissions in order to limit adversaries' ability to use infrared sensors as an alternative to radars for detection and targeting. Major reductions across all these types of observable signatures, radar cross section foremost among them, came to define stealth aircraft and promised to revolutionise the survivability of aviation assets. The technology's promise was such that it quickly came to be expected that all future American manned combat jets would be built around a focus on stealth technologies.

Developed with a design closely based on the technology demonstrators of the Have Blue program, the F-117 in 1983 entered service as the world's first stealth fighter, and for over 30 years would remain the only stealth fighter optimised for air-to-surface missions. Its designation as a fighter, however, was decided on to attract better pilots within the Air Force, with its total lack of air-to-air capabilities and very limited flight performance and pilot visibility meaning an attack (A) or bomber (B) designation would otherwise have been considered more representative of its role and capabilities.[12] The F-117 was designed from the outset in the expectation that it would both help soften enemy air defences and deliver early tactical nuclear strikes. The rapid advances in Soviet air defence capabilities made this particularly vital, with the introduction of systems such as the S-200D, the S-300 and the MiG-31 interceptor, having left older aircraft such as the B-52H and B-1B bombers and F-111 strike fighters with little chance of penetrating Warsaw Pact airspace.

Despite the promise of its stealth technologies, the F-117 proved to be highly problematic, with its operational costs being wholly unaffordable for even medium-scale procurement. This constrained serial production to just 59 aircraft. Its flight performance was by far the poorest in the world, leaving it overwhelmingly dependent on stealth and highly vulnerable should it be detected. Its capacity for just 2,300 kilograms of ordnance, or under 10 percent of its take-off weight, made it one of the most inefficient fighter designs in the world in this respect. Had it not been for advances in precision guidance technology, which served as a major force multiplier for bombing operations, the aircraft would have been near useless for non-nuclear missions. With advances in Soviet air defence technologies by the mid-1980s fuelling growing concerns that even next generation stealth aircraft planned to enter service in the 1990s

F-117A fighters at Wright-Patterson Air Force Base. (USAF)

could be effectively detected and targeted, the F-117's utility in a great power war was considered highly limited from the outset.[13]

When deployed for combat operations in the Gulf War in 1991, the F-117 formed a core part of the public relations campaign that sought to portray the United States as the undisputed leading power in the post-Cold War era. While the aircraft did prove capable against Iraqi air defences, however, this largely reflected the severe limitations of the Iraqi network, which could only manage 20-40 hostile aircraft at a time, lacked any remotely comprehensive coverage, relied on mostly ageing equipment, and other than a small number of P-12, P-18 and Nanjing radars did not have sensors optimised to detecting stealth targets.[14] The old and highly centralised network was not well suited to enduring the powerful U.S.-led electronic warfare attacks launched against it.[15] Early claims of the F-117's successes were nevertheless later proven to be exaggerated, with the aircraft frequently failing to neutralise their targets.[16]

Following the Have Blue program and the initiation of the F-117's development, the rival aircraft manufacturer Northrop, which had lost to Lockheed in its pitch for the stealth fighter, was instructed to undertake a study for the development of a much larger deep penetration stealth aircraft which eventually became the B-2 intercontinental range bomber. The program would mark a major leap in the advancement of stealth technologies, with the new bomber designed to retain a very low radar cross section from all sides and in a much wider range of radar wavebands. This was achieved in large part by pioneering the use of computer-aided design and manufacturing technologies, with the bomber's tailless 'flying wing' design, although highly unsuitable for fighters due to its severe limitations on flight performance, also being optimal for its stealth requirements. Compared to the F-117, the B-2 was significantly more difficult to detect or track despite being over five times the size, while its more efficient design could allocate a proportion of its weight approximately twice as large to weapons carriage. Where the F-117 straddled the line between a demonstrator and a service aircraft, and represented something of a stopgap until stealth technologies further matured, the B-2 was from the outset envisaged to have a much larger production run. Production was planned at 132 bombers, which was more than twice the number of F-117s built, despite the aircraft costing several times as much. The B-2 entered service from 1997, 14 years after the F-117.

The development of the F-117 and B-2 represented major landmarks in the maturing of stealth capabilities the waning years of the Cold War, and among manned aircraft they remain to date by far the most heavily reliant on stealth for their survivability. While many of the technologies developed for the B-2 would be further improved and used in a number of secretive flying wing drone programs, most famously the CIA's RQ-170, the early 21st century would also see the first stealth aircraft enter service with genuinely competitive fighter-like flight performances, including high manoeuvrability and supersonic speeds. This was made possible as technological advances significantly reduced the compromises needed for an aircraft to have advanced stealth capabilities. With these new aircraft having primarily tactical rather than strategic roles, they were not developed under 'black' or 'grey' programs as the F-117 and B-2 had respectively been.

America's First Fifth Generation Fighter: The F-22 Raptor

The first formal requirements document for America's first fifth generation fighter program were drawn up in January 1973, six months after the first fourth generation fighter built for the U.S. Air Force, the F-15 Eagle, had made its first flight. By the early 1980s a number of new technologies applicable to fighter design had begun to reach required maturity, with advances in composite materials and lightweight alloys, advanced flight control systems, and a range of technologies related to propulsion systems and avionics, all expected to be at the heart of what distinguished the next generation. Under what formally came to be designated the Advanced Tactical Fighter program, the Air Force published its first request for information in May 1981, and its second the following month, with design concepts subsequently being provided by defence contractors. It was projected at the time that the fighter would enter service as the first fourth generation fighters were nearing the end of their service lives, with an initial operating capability scheduled for 1993-1994. A final request for proposals was released to industry on 18 May 1983, just five months before the F-117 formally entered service. Stealth technology had by this time become a central driver of the new fighter's design, with an amendment to the proposal on 23 May placing a much greater emphasis on stealth features.[17]

The B-2 Spirit bomber was the world's first strategic bomber with a very low observable design, and was developed to penetrate deep into heavily defended Soviet airspace. (U.S. DoD)

As work on the Advanced Tactical Fighter's development progressed, United States government sources came to define the following eight features as prerequisites for a combat aircraft to be considered fifth generation: use of a stealth airframe with internal carriage of missiles and significant reductions to both radar cross section to infrared signature; active electronically scanned array (AESA) radars; sensor fusion; advanced data links and network-centric warfare capabilities; sophisticated electronic warfare suites with advanced Digital Radio Frequency Memory jammers and electro-optical defensive systems; long range multiband electro-optical targeting systems; advanced glass cockpits; the ability to reach supersonic speeds without using engine afterburners otherwise known as a supercruise capability.

The requirements of fighter programs consistently responded to the challenges of their times, with the Advanced Tactical Fighter being no exception. It was thus notable that from January 1973, when the first formal requirements document for the program was drafted, up to 1980, air-to-air combat had not even been explored as part of the aircraft's mission package. This would change drastically over the following years, however, beginning in April 1980 when a new Program Management Directive for Combat Aircraft Technology was issued, and reoriented the program towards a focus on air dominance.[18] Although the program's first Request for Information in May 1981 had placed equal emphasis on air-to-air and strike missions, by 1982 the program had already become heavily focused on the former at the expense of the latter. Intelligence on the development of Soviet MiG-29 and Su-27 fourth generation fighters, including satellite footage of their respective Product 9-01 and T-10 prototypes at the Ramenskoye Flight Test Centre, was a factor stimulating this change.[19] Both fighters would enter service in the early-mid 1980s, and proved to have of significant advantages over their fourth generation counterparts in Western fleets.

In May 1986 Secretary of the Air Force Edward Aldridge decided that the choice of design for the ATF program would be based on a fly off between technology demonstrators, rather than solely on studies of paper proposals. Of five firms that submitted proposals, including Boeing, General Dynamics, McDonnell Douglas, Lockheed Martin and Northrop Grumman, the designs of the final two were selected. The two firms had by far the greatest experience developing stealth aircraft due to their respective work on the F-117 and the B-2. The first fifth generation fighter technology demonstrators, the Northrop Grumman YF-23 and Lockheed Martin YF-22, first flew in August and September 1990.[20]

From the outset the YF-23 appeared to be the more promising design, and comfortably outperformed the YF-22 in all areas other than manoeuvrability. Although still comfortably exceeding the requirement for combat manoeuvrability. It had a larger weapons capacity, a lighter wing loading, superior low observable specifications, and was also found to be more readily adaptable to proposed deep strike and interdiction missions, to which Lockheed Martin's design would prove particularly poorly suited.[21] The circumstances of the time, however, led the Air Force to favour the YF-22, as not only had the end of the Cold War reduced the perceived imminent need for the most capable fighter possible – which had been the case during the preceding F-15's development – but a gradual contraction of defence budgets made a more conservative lower risk design favourable. Where the YF-23 looked like an aircraft out of science fiction, the YF-22 and the F-22 fighter it was developed into looked, as observed in *Air Force Magazine*, 'like a more angular version of the F-15C Eagle it was designed to replace.'[22]

The lack of peer-level competition after the Cold War would affect not only the selection of a design for the first fifth generation fighter program, but also the selection of an engine. The Joint Advanced Fighter Engine saw the firms Pratt & Whitney and General Electric develop the rival F119 and F120 engines to prototype stages, with both flown on the YF-22 and YF-23 demonstrators. The F120 was considered the more advanced and innovative design, and although slightly heavier, it had greater room to accommodate future thrust

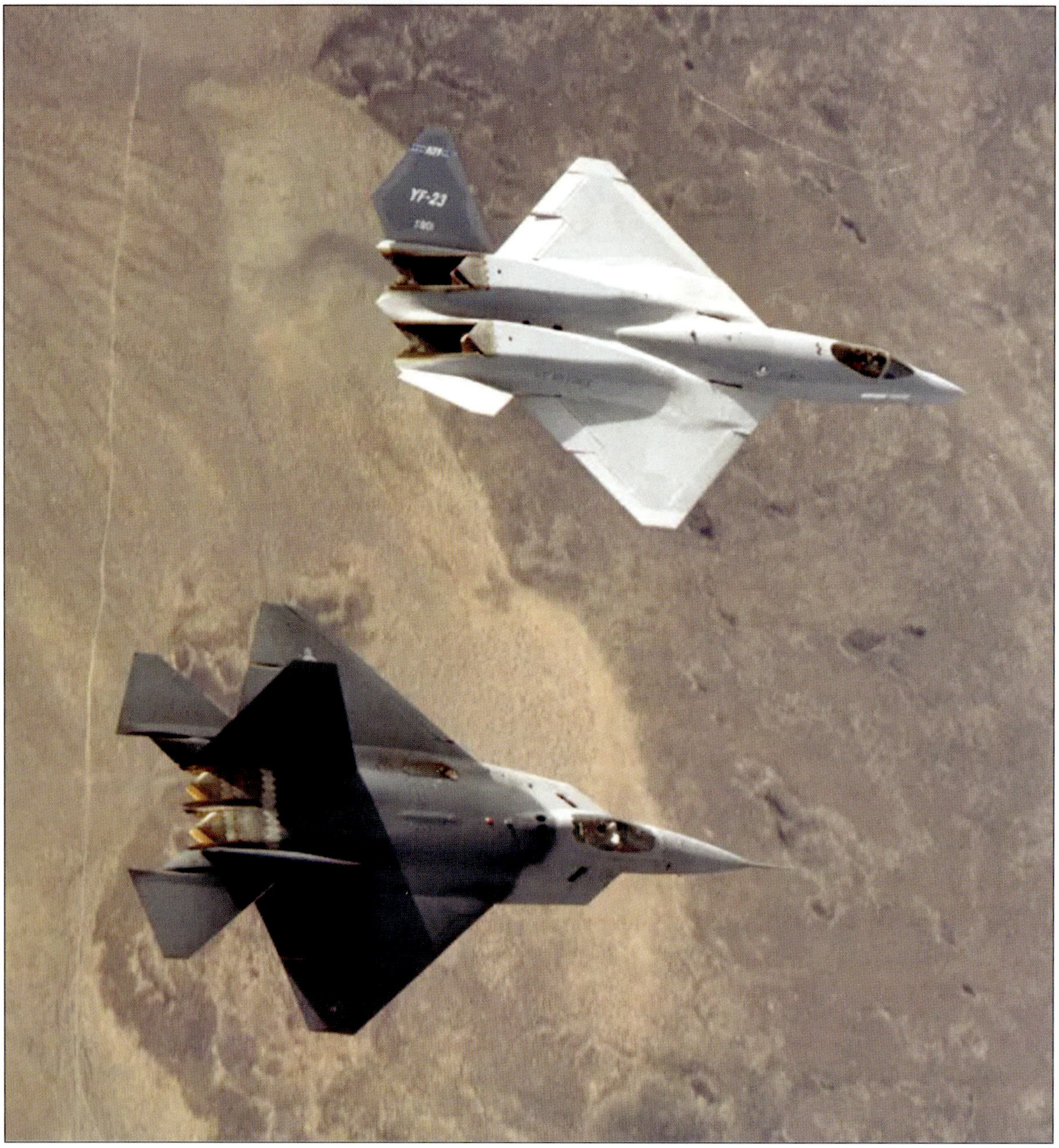

The Northrop-Grumman YF-23 as seen during its flight-testing. (U.S. DoD)

YF-23 and YF-22 side-by-side during the Advanced Tactical Fighter competition flight demonstration phase. (USAF)

One of the YF-23 prototypes during flight testing. The aircraft's design was in many ways more ambitious, and although it comfortably outperformed the YF-22 in all major areas other than manoeuvrability, it also posed a number of greater risks and was expected to be significantly more costly. The decision not to select the YF-23 as the basis for developing the Advanced Tactical Fighter would have very significant implications for the subsequent program to develop a lighter counterpart to the aircraft of the Joint Strike Fighter program. (U.S. DoD)

upgrades and excelled at high-altitude, high speed operations. Much like the YF-22, the F119 was a much more conservative design that was selected mainly because it presented less technological risk – a choice that likely would have been different had the Cold War still been ongoing and the threat of Soviet air superiority still appeared imminent.[23]

Despite being undermined by the end of the Cold War, the Advanced Tactical Fighter program made many considerable achievements. The F-22 fighter's airframe set new standards for high use of advanced composite materials, while its F119 engine introduced high-pressure turbine blades made from single-crystal superalloys, and was able to achieve a very low bypass ratio of 0.30. This facilitated the high thrust needed to meet requirements for flight performance, specifically supercruise. The powerplant generated 25 percent more thrust than the F-15's F100, which was not only sufficient to compensate for the F-22's much greater weight than its predecessor, but also facilitated much improved manoeuvrability and sustained supersonic flight without afterburners at speeds of over Mach 1.5. The fighter was the first in the Western world to use thrust vectoring engines, and while still far less manoeuvrable than the Russian Su-37 that first flew in 1997, its manoeuvrability was comparable to the top Russian production fighter the Su-30MKI which entered service in 2002. F-22 pilots would highlight into the 2020s that the manoeuvres the aircraft could perform were not possible for any other Western fighter, with the aircraft's ability to remain controllable while surpassing the critical lift limit and losing altitude remaining unique in the Western world.[24] Where the F-117's performance attributes other than stealth had all been unremarkable, the F-22 brought industry into a new generation of stealth in which compromises to other areas would not need to be anywhere near as extreme, as the fighter combined a much lower radar cross section than the F-117 with supermanoeuvrability, a supercruise capability, and a degree of sensor fusion.

The F-22's AN/APG-77 was one of the first electronically scanned array radars carried by a fighter. The Soviet MiG-31 had been the first to do so in 1981, followed nineteen years later by the United States, which in 2000 retrofitted APG-63(V)2 radars onto a squadron of eighteen experimental F-15C/Ds operated by the 3rd Fighter Wing based at Elmendorf Air Force Base in Alaska. It was followed by France in 2001 with the Rafale's RBE2 radar, and Japan in 2002 with the F-2's J/APG-1 radar. The last fighter program to adopt an electronically scanned array radar was the joint German, British, Spanish and Italian Eurofighter, which until 2019 was produced with a mechanically scanned array radar, the Captor, that had long since been considered obsolete.

Electronically scanned array radars are not only far more reliable and less susceptible to jamming, but also facilitate a much wider range of electronic warfare techniques, are significantly more powerful and efficient, and can scan much faster than those with mechanically scanned arrays. While mechanically scanned array radars rely on a single continuous radio beam, electronically scanned array radars emit multiple intermittent beams from hundreds of discrete individual electronically steered emitters, which can: scan almost instantaneously, narrowly aim at multiple objects to simultaneously track targets, search for other possible targets, track friendly missiles, and send commands to multiple missiles to intercept multiple targets. Electronically scanned array radars are also considerably more powerful and efficient. The F-22 could thus simultaneously track and engage targets operating just 50 metres off the ground and others in near space, up to 28,000km above sea level.

One of the YF-22 prototypes as seen while firing an AIM-120A advanced, medium-range air-to-air missile (AMRAAM) during flight testing in the 1990s. (U.S. DoD)

While early electronically scanned array radars used passive electronically scanned arrays (PESA), the APG-63(V)2, J/APG-1 and AN/APG-77 were the first with active electronically scanned arrays. AESA radars have the further advantage of being able to scan more precisely and send out radio waves at different frequencies in multiple directions simultaneously, which is especially important for electronic warfare. Their radar signatures are also significantly lower, making it more difficult for potential adversaries to use their emissions to home in on the aircraft they belonged to, with this being particularly vital for stealth aircraft and highly complementary to reductions in radar cross section. Alongside its stealth airframe and powerplant, the F-22's position as the first American fighter produced with an electronically scanned array radar was among its most defining features.

After the USSR's disintegration in December 1991, issues of complacency and budget cuts that had surfaced when the Cold War ended only worsened. The defence sector and broader American industrial base contracted sharply over the following decade, while the F-22's capabilities were heavily watered down with several key subsystems removed. The aircraft failed to deliver improved performance in those areas in which the Air Force assessed the F-15 as most deficient,[25] and cost 276 percent as much per airframe as initially planned – at $412 million up from just $149 million.[26] With pre-production costs reaching more than double the initial estimates, the fighter's development time initially estimated at nine years took nineteen.[27] Delays to meeting minimal testing criteria were such that the fighter was rushed into production years before these were met,[28] with an initial operating capability achieved over a decade behind schedule in December 2005.[29]

Compared to the F-15, the F-22 entered service with a shorter range, much poorer availability rates, lower reliability, much lower versatility, much greater difficulty incorporating upgrades, and many more performance issues. A key requirement for the Advanced Tactical Fighter program was that it would be easier and cheaper to maintain than the F-15, which the Air Force was assured as late as 1999 would be the case.[30] The fighter's actual maintenance needs were in fact far higher with conservative estimates placing the F-22's hourly operational costs at well over double the F-15's – over $68,000 compared to $29-32,000.[31] The man hours needed to service the fighter for every hour in the air were similarly far higher for the F-22, with the discrepancy making it not only economically unviable as a successor to the F-15, but also ensuring that a far lower proportion of an F-22 fleet would be operable at any time compared to an F-15 fleet of the same size.

Excessive operational costs and maintenance needs resulted in very poor mission capable rates well below those of either Cold War era fighters or 21st century foreign competitors, and were a major factor in the decision to cancel over 75 percent of planned production aircraft.[32] One Air Force report highlighted 'maintenance troubles' and 'unexpected shortcomings' with serviceability,[33] while the very large suite of ground support equipment needed limited where and how the fighter could operate. Issues with breakdowns, poisonous effects on pilots' lungs – known as 'Raptor Cough' – caused by 'a "mosaic" of interrelated cockpit equipment issues,'[34] and problematic avionics and computer architecture,[35] among several others, sharpened the contrast to the F-22's famously successful Cold War era predecessors the F-15 and F-4. As Lockheed Martin's F-22 program chief Sherman Mullin noted after his retirement, regarding the procurement system which produced a fighter that proved so problematic: 'the system is totally broken and everybody knows it.'[36]

With the fighter program failing to provide a viable successor to the F-15, the decision to terminate Raptor production was finalised and approved by congress in 2009. The production line, in Marietta, Georgia, closed in 2011, less than six years after the first aircraft entered service. The F-15, by contrast, would remain in production and on order by the USAF into the latter half of the 2020s, over 50 years after it entered service in 1975, with greater perceived cost effectiveness facilitating continuous orders which in turn allowed the aircraft to be modernised incrementally over time. The result was that F-15s produced in the 2020s had far more advanced avionics and sensors than the F-22. Only 177 production F-22s were ever built, alongside 18 test and development airframes, where 750 were initially planned for the Air Force with further orders from the Navy expected.[37] Compared to the F-15, which would see a production run of over 1800 aircraft, the new fighter developed at far greater cost to replace it saw less than 10 percent of the production airframes completed. Although the Advanced Tactical Fighter program successfully produced the first fighter of a new generation, the F-22's wide ranging shortcomings increasingly led the program to be viewed as having failed to achieve its primary goals.

In May 2021 longstanding suspicions that the Air Force would condemn the F-22 to an early retirement were confirmed, with the

U.S. Air Force F-22 Raptor. The Air Force initially planned to procure 750 of the aircraft, allowing the F-15C/D fleet to fully be retired from service, while production and incremental modernisation between batches continued into the 2020s in parallel to production of the F-35. Not only were over 75 percent of planned production numbers cut, all Block 10 and Block 20 fighters were not expected to ever be made combat capable. (Rob Shenk)

fighter set to be outlasted in service by several decades by the F-15 and other Cold War-era fighter types which had proven much less troublesome.[38] Deputy chief of staff for Air Force futures Lieutenant General Samuel Clinton Hinote explained at the time that the fighter suffered from 'limitations' that 'we can't modernise our way out of,' referring to the Raptor as a '1990s – and even late 1980s – design' – an age often masked by the fact that it only became fully operational in the second half of the 2000s due to development delays. Hinote singled out growing parts obsolescence as a particular issue, with the closure of production lines for over a decade making this more difficult to address.[39] The first F-22s to be retired would be less than one third of the way through their service lives, even without

An F-15C (foreground) and an F-22 of the 433rd Weapons Squadron. In contrast to the F-15, which has seen a production run of over half a century, the final decision to terminate F-22 production was given less than four years after it entered service, ensuring that the aircraft would play a much smaller role in the fleet and no role in the air forces of American strategic partners, and thus guaranteeing that a greater burden would be placed on both the F-15 and on the newer F-35. (USAF)

counting the possibility of life extensions through refurbishment, meaning the USAF was ridding itself of the aircraft decades earlier than necessary. The F-22's mission capable rates of around 50 percent, which were by far the lowest in the American fighter fleet, were expected to begin to improve slightly as the first aircraft were retired, allowing the decommissioned fighters to be cannibalised for much needed spare parts.[40] While F-22s were being retired the Air Force simultaneously continued to purchase new F-15s at over $100 million per airframe, indicating a strong preference for the older aircraft and serving as perhaps the clearest indicator of the newer fighter's failings.

Joint Strike Fighter

Until the 1970s the U.S. Air Force had been able to afford procuring the most capable fighter type available to form the backbone of its fleet, with third generation F-4D/E Phantoms having been fielded in very large numbers despite being the largest, most complex, and most expensive fighters of their time. This changed, however, with the introduction of the F-15 from 1975. After the Soviet MiG-25 had demonstrated its outstanding high-altitude flight performance under combat conditions during reconnaissance missions over Israel and the Israel-occupied Sinai Peninsula from 1971, serious concerns regarding the capabilities of interceptor variants of the aircraft had forced serious revisions to the F-15's performance requirements, which had the effect of making it significantly more costly to procure and sustain. The result was the need for a lighter fighter, the F-16, to be procured in large numbers as part of a high-low combination, with the aircraft carrying a smaller radar and fewer weapons, having a lower thrust/weight ratio, and being restricted to a shorter range and lower altitude ceiling.

Much like the F-15, the F-22 was also envisioned from the outset to require the development of a lighter and less costly counterpart to facilitate wider modernisation of the Air Force's fleet to a fifth generation level. After initiating the development of programs that produced the world's first three manned stealth aircraft the F-117, the B-2, and the F-22, the Air Force had in the 1980s initiated a fourth program, the Multi-Role Fighter, to provide a lighter single engine counterpart to the Advanced Tactical Fighter, which could also be considered the direct successor to the F-16. The budgetary restrictions of the post-Cold War era, however, would lead to a decision in the 1990s to cancel the program, and instead develop the aircraft under a multi-service program to meet the requirements of the Air Force, the Marine Corps and the Navy. Where the program goals of the F-22, the F-15 and the F-16 during development had been relatively straightforward, insofar as that the fighters were intended to meet the requirements of a single service with well defined mission scopes to directly succeed specific aircraft from preceding generations, the next fighter program would be considerably more complicated.

In 1983 a DARPA program began assessing the technologies available which could be used to design and manufacture a 'replacement for the AV-8 Harrier II' operated by the Marine Corps, with a specific requirement for supersonic capabilities. While the Harrier had been designed for vertical take-off and landing (VTOL), this capability had excessively limited its weapons carrying capacity, leading the aircraft to consistently conduct short take-off and vertical landings (STOVL), which would be the primary requirement for its successor. The program, known as Advanced Short Takeoff Vertical Landing (ASTOVL), quickly evolved into a joint development effort with the United Kingdom, as the British Armed Forces, for which the Harrier had originally been developed, also sought a STOVL-capable successor.

In parallel to the ASTOVL program and the Air Force's Multi-Role Fighter, the Navy required a next generation successor to its A-6 Intruder long range strike fighter – an aircraft which after its introduction in 1963 had seen extensive use in the Vietnam War. The Navy had in 1983 initiated the Advanced Tactical Aircraft program to meet these requirements, with McDonnell Douglas awarded a contract the following year. The resulting A-12 Avenger II strike fighter was scheduled to enter service in the mid-1990s, with the Navy expected to purchase 620 of the aircraft, and the Marines 238, which would all primarily operate from the Navy's

An F-35A accompanied by the fighter it was foremost designed to replace the F-16C, both operated by the 544th Fighter Wing based at the Luke Air Force Base. (USAF)

supercarriers. The Air Force also considered purchasing up to 400 A-12s to replace the F-111 as its primary long-range strike fighter, providing a heavier and more sophisticated counterpart to the F-117.[41] Deploying a high endurance and very low observable strike fighter from carrier groups was set to be a game changer for their offensive potential. Nevertheless, the A-12's revolutionary and unconventional design, the significant secrecy surrounding its development, and most importantly the end of the Cold War in 1989 which significantly reduced the operational requirements for carrier groups, between them led to a decision by the Department of Defense in 1991 to cancel development as a cost saving measure. The $57 billion weapons program was the largest ever to be terminated by the Pentagon.

With the A-12 having been expected to cost $96 million per fighter, following the program's termination the Navy initiated the Advanced-Attack (A-X) program in 1991 to develop a lighter and more affordable stealth fighter to replace the A-6.[42] The service in parallel pursued development of a successor to the F-14 under the Naval Advanced Tactical Fighter (NATF), which as its name implied was expected to derive many of its technologies from, and potentially be a variant of, the Air Force's Advanced Tactical Fighter program that had produced the F-22. Development of a navalised F-22 variant was projected to cost $8.5 billion through to the end of prototype stages, although providing a predicted 40 percent savings over a standalone Navy program, and additional life cycle savings through common systems with the Air Force. Production was initially projected at 546 aircraft, before being cut to 384 aircraft, and eventually being cancelled as the F-22 proved highly problematic.[43] The possibility of acquiring a carrier based variant of the F-117, namely the F-117N pitched by Lockheed Martin in 1995, was also decided against.[44] This left the Navy very heavily reliant on the A-X program, and meant the aircraft would need to be capable of air-to-air combat, fleet defence against enemy bombers, and deep penetration strikes. The addition of secondary requirements for an air-to-air capability to the A-X program led it to be re-designated the A/F-X in 1991.

With the Marines and Air Force's respective ASTOVL and Multi-Role Fighter stealth fighter programs ongoing, DARPA and the Navy in 1993 initiated the Common Affordable Lightweight Fighter program. This was intended to bring together requirements for a common lightweight combat jet that prioritised low costs and maintenance needs, with separate ground based, carrier based and STOVL variants for the Air Force, Navy and Marines respectively, with the British Royal Navy co-developing the Marine variant. In doing so, it was intended primarily to provide a successor to their respective fleets of F-16s, F-18s and Harriers. While a common fighter for the Air Force and Navy was far from unprecedented, the requirement that it produce a STOVL variant was something no joint program had done before due to the significant design changes required to accommodate such capabilities, and added considerable complications.

Key to gaining Air Force support for the Common Affordable Lightweight Fighter were efforts by Lockheed Martin to persuade the service that the aircraft could integrate a range of technologies from the Advanced Tactical Fighter program to make it an effective lighter counterpart to the F-22. Chief Aeronautical Scientist and Chief Engineer of the Skunk Works Paul Bevilaqua was widely credited with playing a central role in this.[45] The appeal of this would grow as the Advanced Tactical Fighter program failed to provide an aircraft with lower operational costs and maintenance needs than the F-15, instead producing one with close to double the costs, meaning it could only be procured in very small numbers. This ensured that should the Air Force seek to widely field stealth fighters, it would need to rely more heavily on a lighter counterpart to the F-22. A further important factor was that after the end of the Cold War and USSR's disintegration, a significant contraction in the number of operational fighter units, and the significantly lower flying rates for the F-16 fleet meaning they would last far longer than expected, made sharing development costs and production lines with two other services highly welcome as an alternative to pursuing the Multi-Role Fighter program alone. The fact that the Advanced Tactical Fighter program's development costs had also run significantly over budget in the 1990s placed a further strain on the Air Force's finances.

Following the USSR's disintegration, deep cuts to defence spending and a shift in requirements for a highly uncertain post-Soviet era left the future orientation of the U.S. Armed Forces in question, and placed the Department of Defense under severe budgetary pressure. On 23 February 1993, the Department initiated a formal bottom-up review of military forces and modernization plans intended to develop a strategy for post–Cold War defence planning, which was focused on the ability to fight and win two near simultaneous major regional conflicts comparable to the Gulf War. In September 1993 it was announced that following the review, the Air Force's Multi-Role Fighter and the Navy's A/F-X had been cancelled as separate programs, with work on both brought together into the new Joint Advanced Strike Technology program, which was intended to develop requirements, mature technologies, and demonstrate concepts for a next generation fighter. Subsequently in October 1994, under orders from Congress, the Joint Advanced Strike Technology program was merged with the Marines and Royal Navy's ASTOVL program. This joint program would in May 1996 be named the Joint Strike Fighter (JSF) program.

Developing fighters for three services under one joint program had been favoured from the outset, in the expectation that increasing commonality would both make the services more interoperable, and reduce program costs. As observed by executive vice president of the JSF program in the early 2010s, Larry Lawson: 'We're going to save money in production because Henry Ford had it right. The cost is tied to the numbers that you build.'[46] Economies of scale were expected to make relatively small numbers of STOVL and carrier based fighters much more cost effective due to commonalities with a conventional variant that was in demand in far greater numbers, driving down costs of development and production for all three variants.

From its outset, a combination of factors primarily including issues with the Advanced Tactical Fighter and budget cuts following the end of the Cold War left the U.S. Armed Forces heavily dependant on the Joint Strike Fighter program. The cancelled A-12, its successor the A-X, the retiring A-6, the soon to be retired F-14, the F-14's cancelled successor the NATF, and the F-18, would all be replaced by the aircraft in the Navy alone, as would the Marines' cancelled ASTOVL program and the Air Force's cancelled Multi-Role Fighter program and their respective Harriers and F-16s. Shortcomings with the Advanced Tactical Fighter, meanwhile, meant that the new lighter aircraft would be relied on to form a larger portion of the Air Force's fleet and to shoulder a greater burden for air superiority missions.

The Joint Strike Fighter program's conventional take-off variant, later designated the F-35A, was intended to replace the F-16, and later also the A-10 ground attack jet, in the U.S. Air Force, and a wide range of other jets including F-4s, F-15s and F-18s in the fleets of America's strategic partners. Deep cuts to F-22 procurements also led the F-35A to increasingly be seen as the only viable replacement for Cold War era F-15C/D and F-15E fighters in the USAF, with a significant portion of both fleets set to be replaced by the much smaller and lighter new stealth aircraft. With the F-22 initially lacking an air-to-ground capability, and never able to carry high diameter ordnance such as B61 nuclear bombs or any air-to-surface missiles, the F-35A was also relied on to serve as a direct replacement for the F-117 as a short ranged nuclear-capable stealth bomber.

The Joint Strike Fighter program's STOVL variant, later designated the F-35B, was designed primarily for the Marine Corps and the British Royal Navy, while also having potential appeal to foreign clients seeking to deploy them either from small carriers without arresting gear, as would be the case for Italy and Japan, or from small makeshift airfields as was the case for Singapore. The aircraft would primarily replace the Harrier, although the much smaller discrepancy between its combat performance and those of non-STOVL aircraft compared to the Harrier allowed it to appeal to a much wider range of clients. The aircraft could thus also replace conventional land-based fighters such as British Tornados and Singaporean F-16s.

The Joint Strike Fighter program's carrier-based variant, later designated the F-35C, was designed to replace a range of naval aircraft, primarily the F-18C/D, F-18E/F and remaining EA- 6B electronic warfare planes, while also replacing part of the Marine Corps' small fleet of F-18C/Ds that deployed from the Navy's nuclear-powered supercarriers. It also restored some of the capabilities lost with the retirement of the A-6 and F-14 after they were retired without replacement in the 1990s and 2000s. The aircraft was not expected to gain significant interest from overseas clients due to the very limited number of foreign countries operating conventional aircraft carriers with arresting gear, none of which were clients for American fighter aircraft.

Developing a fighter for three services was unprecedented, with joint programs by the Navy and Air Force themselves being rare. The Navy had refused to adopt the F-111 in the 1960s despite the aircraft initially being planned for both services. The YF-17 was rejected by the Air Force in 1974 in favour of what later became the F-16, with its derivative, the F-18 Hornet, only later being selected to serve in the Navy and Marines. The Navy had rejected multiple proposed carrier-based F-16 variants pitched in 1974-1975 that would have increased commonality with the Air Force and allowed for joint development of future variants. Although the F-4 did fly for all three services, it was initially developed for the Navy, and was only later adopted in separate variants by the Air Force and Marines. This was in part due to its significant advantages over other available fighters, but also due to Defense Secretary Robert McNamara's pressure on the services to adopt a unified fighter for many of the same reasons that they would be pressed to jointly develop the Joint Strike Fighter 30 years later. The opportunity to implement common training and tactics environment across all three services, and in allied fleets, could for the first time enable reductions in expensive training and support infrastructure. It could also allow much greater burden sharing across all services as none would be left behind due to inferior configurations.

The scale of the JSF program meant the aircraft had connections to most of the main American third and fourth generation fighter types. The fighter would directly replace the third generation F-5 in the Swiss Air Force, as well as its heavier counterpart the F-4 in the fleets of South Korea, Japan, Greece, and originally Turkey. It directly replaced F-15s, F-16s, F-18s and Harriers in the United States and allied states such as Finland, Italy, Japan and Australia, as well as the A-10 attack jet in the USAF. The F-35's stealth capabilities built on those developed for the F-117 and F-22 programs, and integrated a number of subsystems that had initially been intended for the F-22 such as distributed aperture systems. It directly replaced the F-117 as America's only nuclear-capable stealth fighter. The fighter even had some connection to the venerable F-14, with the decision to retire the aircraft far ahead of schedule in 2006 taken in the expectation that F-35Cs would be entering service in little over half a decade later as the primary fighter in carrier air wings. Australia's decision to retire the Vietnam War era F-111 strike fighter in December 2010, too, was taken in the expectation that F-35s would replace them within half a decade.

A New Threat Environment in the Post-Cold War Era

In contrast to the F-15, F-16 and F-22, which had all been developed with a strong focus on air-to-air combat, the Joint Strike Fighter, as the program's name implied, was conceptualised as an aircraft intended to primarily serve in air-to-ground roles. As the first major fighter program of the post-Soviet era, the elimination of the USSR as a leading high tech economy with a cutting edge combat aviation sector limited the perceived possibility of a peer level challenge to American air superiority re-emerging. Consequentially, advanced ground-based air defence systems emerged as the leading challenge to which program requirements were tailored, with the development and operation of these systems being far more affordable than advanced fighters, and being pursued with promising results by post-Soviet Russia, China and North Korea.

From 1949 until the end of the Cold War, the Soviet defence sector for four decades proved capable of producing combat jets that posed peer level challenges to their American counterparts in air-to-air combat across each generation. This made the ability to tackle Soviet fighters a priority, until the country disintegrated. The first generation MiG-15 had left all Western fighters other than the F-86 Sabre obsolete over the skies of Korea, with the USAF leadership and its veteran pilots having widely concluded that the MiG had overwhelming superiority.[47] USAF Lieutenant Colonel Earl J. McGill, an expert on the air war in Korea, concluded it was 'more than capable of beating the best the West put up against it,'[48] adding that 'the MiG's superior performance left the 86s far behind ... the MiG-15 was a machine well ahead of its day.'[49] Shortly before being shot down and killed by a MiG over Korea, America's greatest ace, F-86 pilot George A. Davis Jr. had written to his wife lamenting very high losses among pilots, stressing that 'things can't go on like they are' and that MiG-15s 'are so much better than the Sabres.'[50]

Although the USSR significantly curtailed its investment in tactical combat aviation programs from the mid-1950s, the country's fighters and interceptors proved capable of more than holding their own against their American counterparts in the second and third generations. In their sole engagements with American F-104s, Soviet MiG-21s demonstrated the ability to comfortably outmatch them when deployed by Pakistan and India respectively in 1971.[51] In the third generation the Soviet MiG-25 interceptor was considered to undisputedly have a grater combat potential than the F-4E, with Iraqi MiG-25PDs credited with a kill ratio of 13:1, against Iranian F-4D/Es and F-5E/Fs during the Iran-Iraq War.[52] The aircraft's armaments, speed, altitude, and its powerful Smerch-A radar provided major advantages, with the sensor pioneering the use of two wavebands simultaneously making it virtually jam-proof – a feature which particularly impressed American analysts when the first gained access to it in 1976.

Moving into the fourth generation, the top Soviet air superiority fighter the Su-27 Flanker posed major new challenges to Western fleets, with a significantly higher thrust/weight ratio than any

Western fighter,[53] vastly greater manoeuvrability at low speeds,[54] and blended body-fuselage layout generating greater lift with a smaller wing area that saved structural weight while generating less drag.[55] The aircraft combined an unprecedentedly high mileage per gallon at all altitudes, with allocation of a 50 percent greater proportion of its internal capacity to fuel carriage than the F-15 and a specific fuel consumption 25 percent lower.[56] When the Cold War ended the consensus in the West on the Su-27's primacy in air-to-air combat quickly strengthened,[57] with the head of the USAF Tactical Air Command General Joseph Rallston informing Congress in 1995: 'we do not need an intelligence effort to realise the Su-27s ascendancy over the F-15 in agility and power.'[58] USAF Chief of Staff General Michael Ryan observed in 2002 that if pilot quality were equal, the Flanker could reliably outperform the F-15.[59] Project personnel working on the F-22 similarly stated: 'The Russians are hot fighter jocks and the MiG-29 and Su-27 are hotter than anything we have in our inventory,' referring to the latter as 'the top gun at the moment.'[60] Perceptions of the Flanker's primacy were further strengthened by the results of simulated air battles, and in 1992 pilots from a Russian Air Force Su-27 unit visiting the home of the USAF First Tactical Fighter Wing at Langley Air Force Base proved capable of tackling multiple F-15s simultaneously. They did so even when starting a mock fight at a disadvantage with the Eagles on their tails.[61] Separate tests of the Su-27's R-73 air-to-air missile, which had high off-boresight targeting capabilities not seen on any Western fighter, consistently concluded that it provided tremendous advantages.[62]

While countering the Su-27 had been considered the primary requirement for the Advanced Tactical Fighter program, the USSR's disintegration ended the perceived threat. Not only did the Russian Air Force contract to a small fraction of its prior size and effectively end new fighter procurements, but training standards diminished to an extreme degree, with most fighter units' pilots failing to spend sufficient time in the air to meet minimal safe flying standards, let alone to pose a serious challenge in air-to-air combat. While Russian Su-27 pilots had won overwhelmingly in simulated engagements with USAF F-15s in 1992, by 2000 American pilots were expected to prevail by a very considerable margin in any similar engagements.

Where the Soviet Union had made rapid progress towards developing a promising fifth generation fighter to succeed the Su-27 under the Izdeliye 1-42 program, known colloquially as the MiG 1.42, the state's disintegration slowed and eventually ended development work. The extreme contraction of the Russian economy and sharp deterioration in education, high tech and industry, gradually turned the country from a leader in fighter aviation into a laggard. While Russia would produce a number of impressive fighters for export, most notably the Su-27-derived Su-30MKI to meet Indian requirements, this was achieved primarily by completing programs that had reached mature stages in the Soviet era. Once momentum from Soviet era R&D efforts was expended, Russia appeared set to cease being a leading competitor in fighter aviation, which became increasingly clear in the 2020s as the standing of its top fighters diminished. Where the first MiG 1.42 regiment had been expected to enter service from 2001, Russia would only operationalise its first fifth generation fighter regiment in the year 2024, with its Su-57 being far less impressive for its time than new generations of Soviet fighters had been. Decline was not only qualitative, but also quantitative, and from 1992 to the turn of the century the Russian air and air defence forces' fleet of fighters and interceptors contracted by 82 percent to just 1,230 aircraft,[63] before declining further to just 720 aircraft in 2020.[64] Pilot flight training hours, although improving in the 2000s, remained below U.S. or Chinese standards, while the armaments on existing fighters would quickly fall behind the cutting edge, with no major procurements of post-Cold War air-to-air missile designs made until the mid-2010s.

As Russian fighter aviation ceased to pose a peer level challenge, the Joint Strike Fighter program focused heavily on countering challenges from ground-based air defence systems. Although Russia quickly lost its Soviet era lead in fighter aviation, its standing in air defence technologies remained world leading well into the new century, with technologies and complete systems being widely proliferated to potential American adversaries from China and North Korea to Algeria and Syria. Despite being less versatile and restricted to covering smaller areas than combat aircraft, operating ground-based systems and training their crews incurred only a very small fraction of the costs of equivalent fighter or interceptor units. This made them highly attractive for countries seeking to asymmetrically defend against much larger and more advanced air fleets.

General chaos and sharp economic and industrial decline caused by the dissolution of the USSR resulted in repeated and lengthy postponements in the development of the next generation of Russian-designed combat aircraft. Although the MiG 1.42 design passed the Soviet Air Force's review in 1991 with flying colours, the first demonstrator airframe only made its maiden flight in February 2000, nine years behind schedule, by which time continuation of the program was considered far from viable. (Pavel Vanka)

The termination of the MiG 1.42 program, and refocusing of resources towards developing the much less ambitious Su-57 fighter, marked a highly unfavourable turning point for the standing of Russian fighter aviation. After sustained delays, the first full Su-57 squadron regiment was formed only in 2024, but is still not operational, 23 years after the first MiG 1.42 regiment was scheduled to have been formed. As the fifth generation era dawned, Russia for the first time since the 1940s would not field fighters with peer level capabilities to their most advanced American counterparts. (Sukhoi Design Bureau)

Ground-based air defences were one of very few areas that received substantial continued investment in Russia in the 1990s despite economic and industrial crisis. Their perceived importance grew proportionally as training top tier fighter pilots became unaffordable, and as the country's fifth generation fighter programs were abandoned. While early variants of the S-300 system which entered service from 1978-1992 had been unable to provide long-range area defence,[65] with the original S-300P having an engagement range of just 70 kilometres, the system began to play a much greater role with the introduction of the S-300PM from 1992. The new variant's 48N6 missile combined a 195km engagement range with a sufficiently compact size to be launched in fours from a mobile transporter erector launchers, allowing the system to combine high mobility with a wide area defence capability. As the first system in the world able to deploy multiple missile types simultaneously, the S-300PM was considered sufficiently distinct that it and its successors received the new NATO designation SA-20, where the older S-300P/PS series had been designated SA-10.[66] Its successor, the S-300PM-2, operationalised from 1997, introduced a range of improvements, including superior radar and electronic warfare systems and greater autonomy for individual firing units. This paved the way to development of the highly ambitious S-300PM-3, which for marketing purposes was re-designated S-400.

Entering service in 2007, the S-400 could detect large aircraft up to 600km away, and used multiple networked radars operating in different wavebands to achieve a high degree of situational awareness, including against stealth targets. The system was much more mobile, had far superior electronic warfare capabilities, and demonstrated a 250km engagement range even against targets flying at over Mach 8,[67] with this being extended to 400km from 2018.[68] Much as the F-35 would absorb the large majority of Pentagon funding for procurement of manned tactical combat jets from the mid-2010s, the Russian Defence Ministry from 1992-2022 spent more than twice as much procuring S-400s as it did procuring fighters, and significantly more than spending on all other air defence systems combined. While the F-35 was by the late 2010s produced on a far larger scale than any other fighter type worldwide, by that time the opening of multiple new facilities for S-400 production had also made it by far the most mass produced long range air defence system worldwide, with 5-6 battalions' worth delivered per year.

The McDonnell-Douglas A-12 Avenger II strike fighter had been developed to provide the U.S. Navy with its first stealth aircraft, and replace the A-6 long range strike fighter. The program's cancellation occurred at the time of massive cuts to defence spending, marking the beginning of an era in which different U.S. services experienced growing cost-overruns with projects related to future combat aircraft. (U.S. DoD)

Unlike during the Cold War, when the U.S. Air Force had faced the possibility of engaging close to a dozen or more states with cutting edge Soviet-supplied fighters or interceptors, in the early 21st century the primary challenge to American control of the skies was the proliferation of S-400s and other advanced Russian air defence systems. While S-400s had been exported to six countries by the mid-2020s, many more benefitted from imports of other advanced air defence systems and, in the cases of North Korea and China in particular, from technology transfers to support their own development of similarly advanced systems. In contrast to the Soviet era, when the latest American fighters had consistently been compared to their most advanced Soviet counterparts, the F-35's capabilities would primarily be compared to those of the S-400, with its ability to tackle the system and its surrounding network seen as one of the most important measures of its performance.

Reflecting the realities of the post-Cold War era, the F-35 was designed with an unprecedented focus on strike operations, and placed a much greater emphasis on electronic warfare capabilities than all preceding multirole fighters. Its weapons bays were much deeper than those of the F-22 allowing it to carry higher diameter beyond visual range weapons, including missiles optimised to seeking and destroying air defence sites. Developed with electronic intelligence and network centric warfare capabilities that were entirely unprecedented, the aircraft was very well optimised for locating mobile enemy air defence systems, with their ability to quickly change location, or 'shoot and scoot,' having long been a primary contributor to their high survivability. Although less heavily specialised and more versatile than the preceding F-117 and A-12 strike fighters, the F-35's air-to-air capabilities were still secondary and largely defensive, contrasting sharply with the F-15, F-16 and F-22.

2

ONE PROGRAM FOR ALL SERVICES

Development

As had been the case for the Advanced Tactical Fighter program under which the F-22 was developed, the decision on which firm's design would be selected for the Joint Strike Fighter program was made based on a competition between technology demonstrators, rather than solely on a study of paper proposals. Unlike the Advanced Tactical Fighter program, however, there was no fly off between the demonstrators, and other than take-off and landing capabilities flight performance was not a significant part of testing. This reflected the fact that the program placed a much lower emphasis on flight performance from the outset, and was not intended to pioneer new levels of speed or manoeuvrability as the preceding fifth generation program had.

Contracts for development of this first stage of the program were signed on 16 November 1996, with Lockheed Martin and Boeing subsequently developing the rival X-35 and X-32 demonstrators. Lockheed Martin was from the outset seen to have a significant advantage, having already developed both of the United States' prior stealth fighters. The firm's position to develop a vertical landing capable variant had also been strengthened considerably through acquisitions of technical data from the Soviet Yak-41 program. Due to the requirements for three separate variants of the Joint Strike Fighter, the competition between demonstrators was particularly complicated, with both designs being assessed on their performance in all three variants. Lockheed Martin's X-35 saw a dedicated carrier based variant built, the X-35C, while a conventional take-off variant was designed to be convertible later in the testing program into a vertical landing variant, the X-35A/B. Boeing's X-32 meanwhile saw a dedicated short take-off and vertical landing (STOVL) variant built, the X-32B, while the second demonstrator, the X-32A/C, demonstrated conventional and carrier based take-off capabilities.

The first X-32 demonstrator made its maiden flight on 18 September 2000, followed by the first X-35 on 24 October 2000. The X-35 was widely likened to a smaller F-22, and closely resembled the YF-22 demonstrator. The X-32 used a distinctive delta wing design and chin mounted air inlet, which was expected to provide greater airflow and increase manoeuvrability at high angles of attack, while also giving the aircraft a particularly distinctive appearance. Central to Boeing's pitch was that its aircraft would be easier and cheaper to produce, and was a simpler design with lower operational costs.

A primary advantage of the X-35 was its short take-off and vertical landing capabilities, with its separate lift fan fed by an intake

Side-by-side comparison of the two technology demonstrators developed for the Joint Strike Fighter program: the Boeing X-32 (left), and the Lockheed Martin X-35. (USAF)

The X-35B demonstrator hovers over Edwards Air Force Base. (USAF)

behind the cockpit and swivelling exhaust system. This design closely resembled that of the Yak-41, and far outperformed the X-32's more traditional Harrier-like direct lift vectored thrust approach. The X-32's STOVL capabilities required significantly greater design compromises, and notably caused hot air from the exhaust to be recirculated into its intake, reducing thrust and causing persistent overheating issues. The aircraft could not perform STOVL at all at Edwards Air Force Base in California due to the thin air at the high altitude location. Its test pilot Commander Phillip Yates recalled that the demonstration of the discrepancy in STOVL capabilities was a turning point in the program. He further highlighted that 'the Lockheed design was pretty close to what they submitted' for their proposed production design, while Boeing's was still far off.[1] The most conspicuous example was that the X-32 demonstrators used a delta wing design, while the final production model shown on paper and in mockups had a more conventional wing.[*] A major factor in this discrepancy between the two programs was the significant head start that Lockheed Martin gained due to its experience developing the F-22, including already having built and extensively operated two YF-22 demonstrators.

Both the X-32 and the X-35 met the requirements for the Joint Strike Fighter program. On 26 October 2001 the X-35 was selected as the winner of the competition, with the contract for System Development and Demonstration awarded to Lockheed Martin. Unlike in the Advanced Tactical Fighter program, under which the more capable design with greater demonstrated potential was widely considered to have been the one overlooked in favour of a more conservative one, the X-35 was near unanimously considered the superior design. The decision caused almost no controversy.[†]

On 7 July 2006, the USAF announced that the F-35 would be designated Lightning II, honouring both Lockheed's 1940s P-38 Lightning propeller driven fighter, as well as the English Electric Lightning fighter jet developed in the late 1950s. The first post-demonstrator flight aircraft, number AA-1, was unveiled that day, and made first flight five months later on 15 December 2006. Eighteen fighters would be built for the F-35 Integrated Test Force, including eight STOVL F-35Bs, five conventional take-off F-35As and five carrier take-off F-35Cs. The first F-35B flew on 11 June 2008, and first conducted a vertical landing on 18 March 2010. The first F-35C flew on 6 June 2010. Early test aircraft, although not designated prototypes, were not production representative, with the concurrency approach under which the F-35 was developed (see Chapter 3) leaving a less distinct division between prototypes and production aircraft.

Information Superiority: The F-35 as an Elevated Sensor and Flying Computer

Beyond the F-35's stealth capabilities, a leading feature distinguishing the aircraft from other Western fighters is its avionics suite, which facilitates the collection, sharing and processing of vast quantities of intelligence in ways that no fighter before it has ever come close to. As observed by former Pacific Air Forces Vice Commander

* Compared to serial production aircraft, the X-35's forward fuselage was 130mm shorter, with later expansion accommodating more mission avionics. The X-35's horizontal stabilisers were 51mm farther forward, with the later move backwards intended to retain balance and control once the forward fuselage was lengthened. The demonstrator's divertless supersonic inlet was also four sided and 762mm farther forwards, where that on the production fighter was three sided. Its fuselage section also had a top surface that was 25mm lower along the centerline, with the change made to accommodate internal weapons storage. Overall, however, the demonstrator's design was similar to that of the production aircraft.

† It was notable that had Northrop Grumman's YF-23 program been selected for the Advanced Tactical Fighter program in 1991, the firm would have been far more likely to be selected to produce a technology demonstrator for the JSF, with the lighter single engine fifth generation fighter potentially having looked like a 'smaller F-23' rather than a 'mini-F-22' as it was at times referred to. The Advanced Tactical Fighter program thus had a significant influence on the Joint Strike Fighter program.

X-35 demonstrator flying over Edwards Air Force Base. (USAF)

Lieutenant General David Deptula, regarding how F-35s differed from preceding fighter types, they 'are not fighters ... they are flying sensor-shooters that have the ability to act as information nodes in a combat cloud – a universe if you will – made up of platforms, not just airborne but also operating at sea and on land, that can be networked together.'[2] The F-35's avionics suite was designed to place it at the crux of this network, and represented a much greater leap forward compared to the F-22's avionics, than the F-22's avionics had compared to late Cold War era aircraft.

The tremendous advances in information centric warfare capabilities realised by the F-35 program represented the culmination of a decades long transformation which began in the Vietnam War, during which the U.S. Armed Forces had conducted the largest air campaign in military history. The campaign saw the first widespread use of electronic warfare, first use of air power to take and hold ground without infantry support, the first computerised bombing, and the first use of communications satellites were to support air operations. It also stimulated new innovations which would culminate in a wide range of capabilities materialising many years later, ranging from new robotic information regimes, to a wide range of new drone capabilities.

The Vietnam War saw the USAF pioneer the combination of rapid sharing of data and significantly enhanced surveillance and precision strike capabilities to create sophisticated kill chains. The required technologies were still in their infancy at the time, however, and billions of dollars of investment in surveilling the Ho Chi Minh Trail resulted in unequivocal failure as the Air Force was found to have significantly overstated its successes – with CIA assessments of these claims being among the most damning. Nevertheless, the efforts made to build a kill chain using vast arrays of sensor assets, from acoustic listening devices parachuted to treetops, to specially developed new drone types, which would provide targeting data to F-4 fighters with laser guided bombs, allowed a vision to form which would begin to mature in the late 1980s.[3] Commander of U.S. forces in Vietnam General William Westmoreland elaborated on this vision as follows:

> On the battlefield of the future, enemy forces will be located, tracked and targeted almost instantaneously through the use of data links, computer assisted intelligence evaluation, and automated fire control. With first round kill probabilities approaching certainty, and with surveillance devices that can continually track the enemy, the need for large forces to fix the opposition physically will be less important ... I see battlefields or combat areas that are under 24 hour real or near time surveillance of all types. I see battlefields on which we can destroy anything we locate through instant communications and the almost instantaneous application of highly lethal firepower. I see a continuing need for highly mobile combat forces to assist in fixing and destroying the enemy ... Our problem now is to further our knowledge—exploit our technology, and equally important — to incorporate all these devices into an integrated land combat system.[4]

The F-35 was the culmination of this vision in manned tactical combat aviation, and was designed to facilitate precision strikes at the core of a vast and seamlessly integrated network.

A top view of the Boeing X-32 demonstrator aircraft. The shortcomings of the aircraft's lift fan system were a primary factor in favour of its rival, the X-35. (USAF)

The F-35's primary sensor is its AN/APG-81 multi-mode X-band AESA radar, which uses a slightly upward canted array to reduce reflectivity, and can scan to plus or minus 60 degrees off-boresight. The radar was developed as a derivative of the F-22's AN/APG-77, and introduced new features for air-to-ground operations including high resolution mapping, multiple ground moving target indication and tracking, and a range of new electronic warfare features. Although significantly more sophisticated than AN/APG-77, which had first been operationalised in the 1990s, by the late 2010s the AN/APG-81's capabilities were nevertheless considered far from outstanding compared to those of other American and Chinese fighters such as the F-15EX, F-18E Block 3, J-20 and J-16. It is thus among the less remarkable features in the aircraft's avionics suite, although this is set to change in the second half of the 2020s as it is replaced by the new AN/APG-85.

Since most pilots transitioning to the F-35 had previously only operated fighters with mechanically scanned array radars, even with the AN/APG-81 the F-35's radar was the area where experienced pilots perceived some of the greatest discrepancy between the aircraft's performance and those of their previous fighters.[5] The F-35's much larger size than its direct predecessor the F-16 allowed it to carry a significant larger radar, with the AN/APG-81's estimated weight of around 220 kilograms being approximately 60 kilograms heavier compared to 135 kilograms for the most advanced F-16 radar the AN/APG-83. This was nevertheless approximately one third smaller than the F-15's AN/APG-82 radar, and well under half the size of the radars on modern Flanker variants such as the Chinese J-16 and Russian Su-35. It was slightly smaller than the F-22's AN/APG-77 with approximately 16 percent fewer transmitting/receiving modules.

Serving as a secondary sensor on the F-35, the AN/AAQ-37 Distributed Aperture System is a highly unique subsystem that gives the aircraft a distinct situational awareness advantage over other Western fighters. Six diamond-shaped windows embedded throughout the airframe house electro-optical sensors as part of this system, and by covering all directions they allow pilots to observe their surroundings 360 degrees around the aircraft, including through the bottom, using their helmets. This ability to 'see through' the aircraft is facilitated by the F-35's unique helmet, called the Helmet Mounted Display System, which houses two small projectors just above the pilot's forehead to allow pilots to visualise data inputs from the system. This serves to eliminate blind spots, which is particularly valuable for visual range combat. The system further facilitates the detection and tracking of enemy missiles, including launch point detection, and the cueing of countermeasures, as well as the detection and tracking of enemy aircraft and cueing for air-to-air munitions and infrared tracking systems, while further providing imagery for cockpit displays and pilot night vision.

The benefits of the AN/AAQ-37 were effectively summarised by Russian defence analyst Vladimir Tuchkov as follows: 'It is the pilot's helmet, which makes the aircraft "transparent." That is, visibility is not limited by the cockpit windows. The whole panorama of the surrounding area is displayed in the pilot's visors, in both the visible and the infrared spectrum. Monitoring the pilot's head and eye movements, the computer provides the necessary panoramic viewpoint and provides the pilots with tips, and manages targeting.' Tuchkov indicated that a lack of such a system on the Russian Su-57 fifth generation fighter was a leading disadvantage faced by the aircraft, with this also hindering the F-22's combat potential compared to the F-35 and to rival Chinese fighters with similar systems.[6]

The F-35 further benefits from the integration of a chin-mounted electro-optical targeting system (EOTS), which serves as both an infrared search and track (IRST) system and as a laser designator. It was the world's first sensor to combine forward-looking infrared search and track functionality with a precision air-to-air and air-to-surface targeting capability. Considerable design attention was paid to ensure that the EOTS would not compromise the fighter's radar

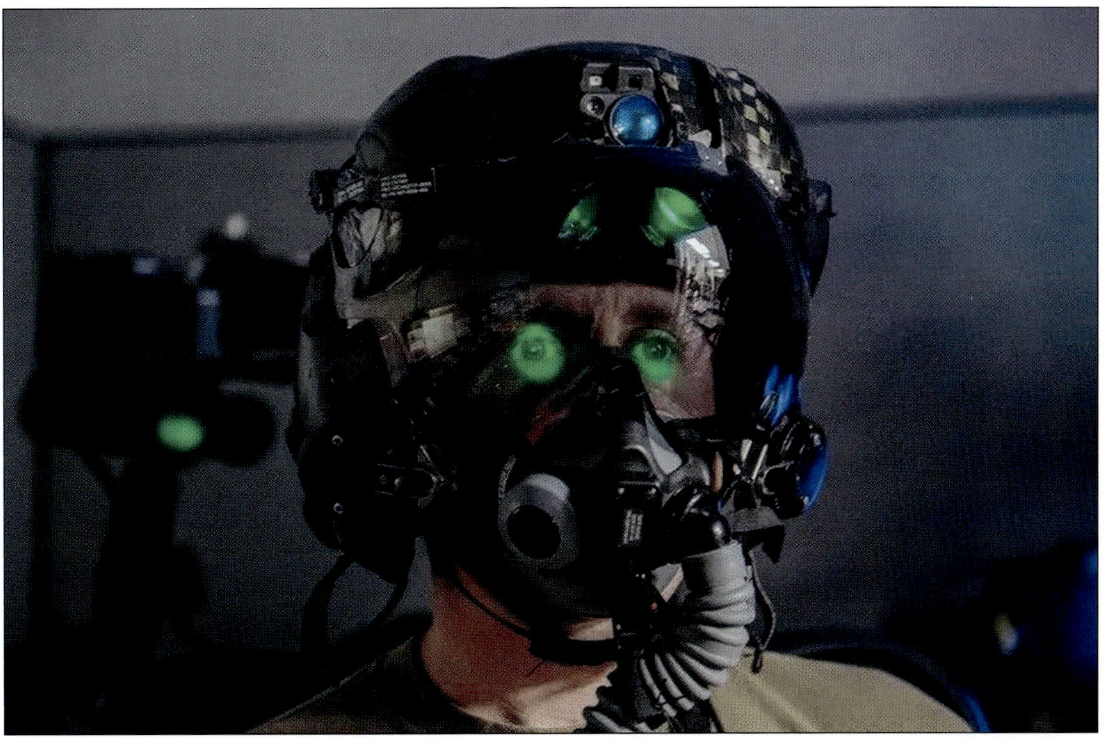

A technician of the U.S. Air Force posing for a photo to demonstrate the F-35's highly-complex Generation III helmet-mounted display. (USAF)

cross section, with the sensor integrated into the fuselage with a durable sapphire window and linked to the aircraft's integrated central computer through a high-speed fibre-optic interface. This ensures both maximum stealth and very low drag, contrasting to fourth generation fighters which carry such systems on external pylons.

IRSTs had been fielded on all new Soviet frontline fighters from 1982, and were gradually adopted on frontline American fighters from the mid-2010s, with the F-35 being the first followed by new variants of the F-15 and F-18. Such systems allow fighters to maintain a degree of situational awareness without using their radars, with the lack of radar emissions being highly complementary to the stealth capabilities provided by the F-35's low radar cross section. The fact that fifth generation stealth technology reduces radar cross section to a much greater degree than it does heat emissions make IRSTs valuable as a means to track and target other stealth aircraft at medium ranges. Notably, plans to integrate an IRST onto the F-22 in the 1990s were cancelled as one of a wide range of cost cutting measures, despite F-22 pilots having attested to the significant boost to air-to-air capabilities which this otherwise would have provided.[7]

One of the most distinguishing features of the F-35 is its tremendous capacity to 'suck up electronic signals,' as several sources referred to it, and automatically classify and geolocate them.

A close-up view at the front section of an F-35A, revealing details of its cockpit and the EOTS-sensor installed under the nose. (USAF)

Chinese People's Liberation Army Air Force J-20S twin seat fifth generation fighter with electro-optical targeting system clearly visible below nose, resembling that of the F-35. (Chinese Internet)

Passive antennas embedded across many of the fighter's edges were designed to feed signals information to its computers. Slight time delays between when signals hit different antennas allow onboard computers to automatically determine the azimuth and range to the emitter – a process known as interferometry – which can be used to provide target-quality coordinates on the source of the radio frequency emitter. This forms a part of the F-35's Radar Warning Receiver and Electronic Support Measures suite, and provides electronic intelligence capabilities that are unprecedented for a multirole fighter. Information is not only displayed to pilots, but is also shareable with other assets by data link, and is all stored and downloaded after each mission. Flights of F-35As flying in wide formations, often tens of kilometres from one another, and linked through the system's multifunction advanced data link, can exchange and pair the azimuth traces of detected threat emissions to facilitate more accurate calculation of their locations, as the accuracy of the target location increases markedly as the angular difference increases between two points.

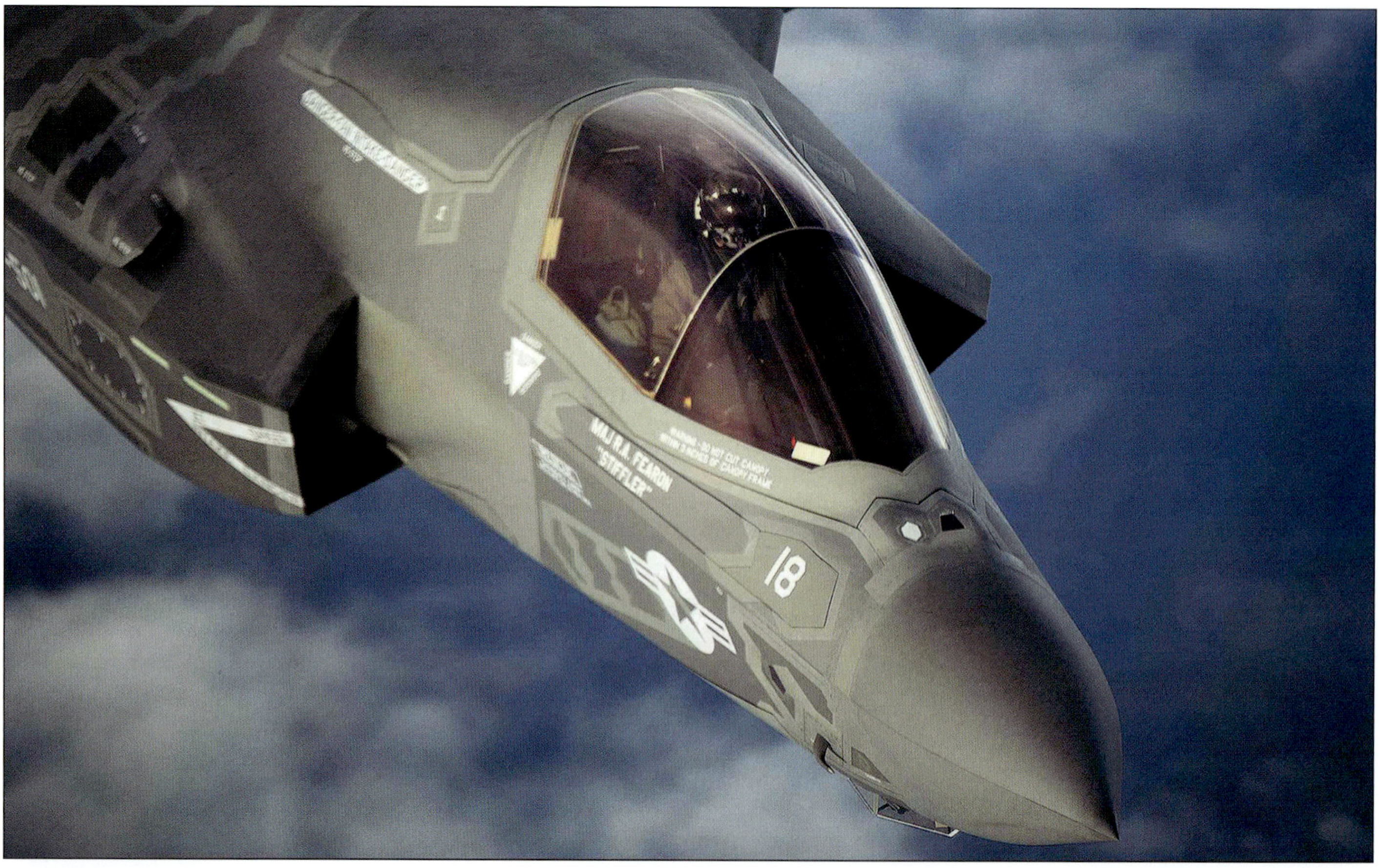

The 'business end' of an F-35A. Notable is an array of antennas installed in front and around the front section of the cockpit, as well as on upper edges of the intakes. (USAF)

The F-35's electronic intelligence capabilities are one of the most significant contributors to its survivability and its offensive capabilities, and allow personnel to determine the locations of potential threats and make more informed decisions on how to engage. While aircraft on penetration missions would usually follow carefully planned flight paths into enemy territory, using trajectories where surface-to-air missile and radar coverage is weakest, the F-35's ability to provide pilots with a continuous stream of intelligence allows flight paths to be revised as the threats the fighter faces change minute-to-minute. For a fighter conceptualised for penetration strikes into heavily defended enemy airspace, these capabilities were intended to help ensure that engagements with hostile air defence systems occurred on the terms chosen by the American pilots. The extent to which the F-35 surpasses previous fighters, including the F-22, in its ability to gather electronic intelligence, had fuelled predictions since long before the aircraft entered service that it could be deployed on dedicated intelligence gathering missions including in peacetime. This was unprecedented for a multirole fighter, and was a mission usually assigned to dedicated intelligence aircraft such as the RC-135 and EP-3E. The ability to rely on a ubiquitous frontline fighter for high end electronic intelligence gathering missions is a revolutionary development, and ensures that America and its allies will maintain far greater awareness of enemy activities on frontiers ranging from the Korean Peninsula to the Kerch Strait. For many services which lack significant fleets of dedicated electronic intelligence aircraft, such as the U.S. Marine Corps and the Polish Air Force, the implications of the F-35's new capabilities have an even more transformative impact.

Summarising the revolutionary improvements in situational awareness achieved by the F-35's sensor suite, retired U.S. Marine Corps Lieutenant Colonel Dave Burke, who had flown F-22s and F-35s for over seven years, observed: 'If you take all the sensors on the F-35, and draw them out in how far they would reach and how wide a band they would reach and what bands they're in, and lay them down and compare them to any other fighter in the world, to include the F-22, the amount of available information in different bands, in different bandwidths, in different regimes, is infinitely greater in an F-35. You have so much more information.' The impact of this was significantly greater when combined with the F-35's tremendous network centric warfare capabilities, with Burke observing that 'then through fusion you're sharing and collaborating with all the other airplanes out there. It is impossible if you are a fourth gen perspective to understand without seeing it from the inside how much more awareness that you have.'[8]

The Multifunction Advanced Data Link developed specifically for the F-35 provides an unprecedented capacity to seamlessly share data as part of wider networks. As observed by Air Force Chief of Staff General David Goldfein, the F-35 'starts talking in the network before the pilot even climbs the ladder. It starts comparing information, it starts placing symbology on the visor of the pilot. That symbology is replicated not only in the displays but across the network of everywhere it's joined.' He cited this network-centric capability in particular to stress that operating the aircraft required 'a completely different mindset' to the older F-117 stealth fighter.[9] As otherwise observed by Italian Air Force Chief of Staff General Luca Goretti regarding the unprecedented network-centric capabilities which the data link system played a key role in facilitating: 'The F-35 has to be considered not only an aircraft, but it has to be considered a node of data information… So we use that aircraft to change completely the mindset of the people. It is no longer an aircraft to fly but actually is a data machine available in the air for everyone.'[10]

The Multifunction Advanced Data Link allows F-35s to transmit data to other aircraft that used the older Link 16 high-speed digital data link system. More significantly still, it allows F-35s to communicate between themselves and with other more modern assets using frequencies that are considerably more challenging for enemy signals intelligence to intercept. F-35 squadron commanders would observe that unlike flights of F-16s, in which wingmen operated around 1.5 kilometres away from each other, F-35 wingmen during operations over wide areas would maintain distances five to twenty times as far, allowing a unit to work closely together while being much more widely dispersed.[11] The ability to operate in very wide flights was also important to making full use of F-35 units' aforementioned ability to optimise joint signals intelligence collection capabilities.*

The ability to share data with other fighters using their older Link 16 systems allowed the F-35 to serve as a major force multiplier for legacy fleets, tremendously boosting the situational awareness of aircraft in its network. Fourth generation pilots would widely attest to the massive boost to situational awareness seen when flying alongside networked F-35s. This complemented the benefits provided by the stealth fighter's 'very impressive' electronic warfare support.[12] As observed by USAF F-35 pilot instructor Major Justin Lee: 'In the F-35, we're the quarterback of the battlefield — our job is to make everyone around us better ... Fourth-gen fighters like the F-16 and F-15 will be with us until at least the late 2040s. Because there are so many more of them than us, our job is to use our unique assets to shape the battlefield and make it more survivable for them.'[13]

U.S. Air Force Lieutenant Colonel Tucker Hamilton was among the sources to assess that the F-35's unique combination of stealth, electronic intelligence gathering and intelligence sharing capabilities was a leading strength that made it particularly revolutionary, observing:

> It absorbs, and most importantly disseminates information like no platform in the history of aviation. So that is kind of the game changer. Unlike the F-22 which absorbs a lot of information, but has a harder time disseminating on that side, the F-35 absorbs even more, and when I say absorbs – it is taking the electromagnetic spectrum and absorbing a lot of information about what is going on around it. And then it has a unique capability to communication certain things about that electromagnetic spectrum to other players in the field. That could be other F-35s, or it could be an AWACS [Airborne Warning and Control System], or it could be a boat, or it could be other people that are connected in with and have the ability to connect in to the data link. And so it is just a really big game changer in regards to information dissemination.[14]

One of the most significant challenges in developing the F-35's avionics suite was the development of an analysed cross-referenced picture combining inputs from the fighter's radar, electro-optical, infrared, and passive sensors, as well as the same sets of sensors deployed by multiple other fighters in a flight. This picture forms

* The Multifunction Advanced Data Link was briefly considered for integration onto the F-22 as part of an upgrade package, which would have gone a long way towards bridging the discrepancy with the F-35 in situational awareness and network-centric warfare capabilities. These plans were cancelled in 2010 to reduce costs. This was the latest of many planned subsystems that were never integrated onto the F-22 for this reason, and as a result the aircraft would continue to only be able to transmit sensitive data to other F-22s, which seriously limited its usefulness in the era of network-centric operations.

a collective multiple perspective picture totally incomparable to anything seen on the F-22 or other preceding fighters, with the combining of four cutting edge sensor systems with the Multifunction Advanced Data Link being one of the F-35's most distinguishing advantages over other Western combat jets.

A key facilitator of the F-35's ability to provide pilots with very large quantities of data is its revolutionary means of displaying information. The fighter's cockpit was designed by a team of former military aviators led by Lockheed Martin's chief pilot-vehicle interface engineer Mike Skaff, a former USAF F-16 pilot. Its revolutionary new layout distinguishes it from all previous aircraft including the F-22. Skaff referred to it as 'the most naked cockpit we've ever built,' at the centre of which are two adjacent 8- by 10-inch touch screens which between them form an 8- by 20-inch display. Pilots can use touch, voice commands, or one of the cockpit's very small number of buttons and switches, to call up, organise or share flight and mission data, and to utilise advanced guided weapons. Eric Branyan, who led the team which developed the F-35's mission systems, observed regarding their functioning: 'We take all these sensors, put it on an 8-by-20 piece of glass, and put a God's-eye view in front of that pilot that says "Here's where all the good guys and the bad guys are. Help the good guys, shoot the bad guys."'[15] As otherwise explained by Air Force F-35 pilot instructor Major Justin Lee: 'In the F-16, each sensor was tied to a different screen ... often the sensors would show contradictory information ... The F-35 fuses everything into a green dot if it's a good guy and a red dot if it's a bad guy— it's very pilot-friendly. All the information is shown on a panoramic cockpit display that is essentially two giant iPads.'[16] [*]

Where previously fighters operating complex guided weapons, and particularly those equipped for both air-to-air and air-to-surface missions, usually accommodated both a pilot and a weapons systems officer in tandem seats, the F-35 requires a single pilot to do the same, while also processing heretofore unseen quantities of information. Its unprecedented complexity for a fighter made it critical to streamline the data provided, and to automate flight as much as possible. While the pioneering of fly-by wire controls on the F-16 in the late 1970s had been a major milestone in this regard, the F-35's flight control computers, with over 10 million lines of software code, took this much further and did most of the flying. A control stick located on the right side of the cockpit and a throttle located on the left both operated electronically instead of mechanically. Thus, as noted by Mike Skaff, F-35 pilots could concentrate on being combat tacticians.[17†] Commander of the USAF Air Combat Command General Mark Kelly highlighted that the high levels of automation of the fighter's sensor suite and data sharing capabilities allowed pilots to focus on managing data and the fighter's electromagnetic signature, projecting that this would increasingly be a primary focus for pilots moving into the next generation.[18] Former Navy pilot Tony Wilson summarised the evolution of pilots' roles transitioning to the new generation as follows: 'As we moved into fourth-generation fighters like the F-16, we moved from being pilots to being sensor managers. Now, with the F-35, sensor fusion allows us to take some of that sensor management responsibility off the pilot's hands, allowing us to be true tacticians.'[19] To further simplify flight, the F-35 lacked a heads up display beneath its canopy, with all information usually shown there instead being visible on the inside of the pilot's helmet visor alongside data inputs from the aircraft's distributed aperture systems. As summarised by USAF Lieutenant Colonel Tucker Hamilton: 'When you look out where you would traditionally see a heads-up display, you see a heads-up display but its all displayed in your helmet.'[20]

For an F-35 pilot, the fighter's rapid automatic processing of data from the aircraft's active and passive sensors and data links, which receive information from satellites, warships, drones, ground radars, AWACSs, and a wide range of other assets, ensure an unprecedented level of situational awareness. This is particularly apparent when the aircraft are deployed near the frontlines with potential adversaries, with Israeli Air and Space Force Chief of Staff General Tal Kelman referring to the F-35A's situational awareness as follows in June 2016 shortly after the first fighters were delivered: 'At 5,000 feet, the whole Middle East is there for you in the cockpit. You see things, it's inconceivable. American pilots who visit us haven't seen anything like it, because they fly over Arizona or Florida, and here they suddenly see the [entire] Middle East as a combat zone – the threats, the different players, at both close range and long range. Only then do you grasp the enormous potential of this machine. We're already seeing it with our eyes.'[21] [‡]

The Standard Variant: F-35A

The F-35 was designed with a wing-tail configuration, with flight control surfaces including leading-edge flaps, flaperons, rudders, and all-moving horizontal tail stabilators, as well as leading edge root extensions running forwards to the air inlets. Its fixed diverterless supersonic air inlets use a bumped compression surface and forward-swept cowl to shed the boundary layer of the forebody away from the inlets, which form a Y-duct for the engine. The fighter's sleek blended wing-body shape and smooth, curvilinear surfaces, sharply angled edges, and the chine line running around its fuselage, all help to minimises its radar cross section. The lines and contours of the aircraft's exterior, the composite panels and parts on its body, and the radar absorbent materials coating the entire airframe, are primary contributors to stealth, alongside the AN/APG-81 designed

* A number of sources would dispute the simplicity of the cockpit, with USAF pilot Justin Lee, who contributed to developing a syllabus for training F-35 pilots, observing that the small number of buttons masked a much higher level of complexity. 'The switches are very similar to the F-16, only each switch also goes down. So you have that z-axis. You have, like, short pushes, long pushes. People don't understand just how many commands you can do with these, with the hands-on throttle and stick, you can literally do thousands of different commands. Each button goes forward, back, left, right, long pushes, short pushes, and then we have multiple Master Modes that completely change all the buttons. So just getting a handle on all of that, so that you're fluent and able to think in F-35 took me about a year.' He added that this only became more complex as upgrades made the fighter more advanced. ('F-16s to F-35s to YouTube with "Hasard" (ep. 167),' *Fighter Pilot Podcast*, 20 May 2023.)

† Commander of the USAF 356th Fighter Squadron Lieutenant Colonel Ryan Worrell similarly observed regarding the benefits of much higher levels of automation that compared to the F-16, the F-35 'brings a lot more sensor [situational awareness] and a lot more automation into how the sensors provide information to the pilot so that I'm no longer running the radar. I'm no longer trying to manage where my radar is looking to get the correct aspect on something. There's still some pieces to that, but it's much more about what decisions the pilot [is] making in the cockpit now. That has changed how we started to train our four-ships and our wingmen.' (Altman, Howard, 'The Intricacies Of F-35 Operations Over The Frigid Alaskan Frontier,' *The War Zone*, 11 August 2022.)

‡ The F-35's tremendous situational awareness advantage would be similarly highlighted by personnel from other units newly converted from Cold War era aircraft. An example was commander of the USAF 34th Fighter Squadron Lieutenant Colonel George Watkins, who observed after his squadron participated in Red Flag exercises in 2017: 'I've had four of my [F-35A] pilots come back from missions, guys who have flown the F-15 and F-16 at Red Flag for years, and tell me "This is amazing. I've never had this much situational awareness while I'm in the air. I know who's who, I know who's being threatened, and I know where I need to go next." You just don't have all of that information at once in fourth-generation platform.' (Garbarino, Micah, 'F-35A proving its worth at Red Flag combat exercise,' *388th Fighter Wing official website*, 3 February 2017.)

to emit a minimal radar signature, and the F135 engine designed to minimise its heat signature.

Thirty-five percent of the F-35A airframe's weight is made up of composite materials, primarily bismaleimide and composite epoxy materials. Later production lots have also included carbon nanotube-reinforced epoxy. The fighter has a combat weight of approximately 20.5 tons, a wing loading of 428 kilograms per square metre, and span loading of 1.93 tons per metre. It has a thrust-to-weight ratio of 0.87 with a standard weapons load and full internal fuel load, with this rising to 1.07 when the internal fuel load falls to 50 percent. With a wing sweep of 34°, and a power-to-frontal area ratio of 17.9 newtons per square centimetre on its engine, the aircraft has very low instantaneous and sustained turn rates. A sustained turn rate of only around 11 degrees per second is less than half as fast as the F-22. Acceleration and transient performance are also low.

While the F-35's most distinct technological advances over the F-22 were in its avionics, significant advances in composite material technologies allowed major structural segments which had been made of metal in complex areas on F-22 be built from composite structures on the F-35. This had significant positive implications for the fundamental structural characteristics of the airplane, and served as an important facilitator of improved stealth capabilities. Stealth capabilities had been extremely costly to maintain on the F-117 when it first entered service, before improving significantly over the type's service life. The F-35's own stealth airframe was designed to be much more efficiently maintainable than either the F-117 or F-22, in addition to the maintenance advantages of being a much smaller aircraft than the F-22 and having only a single engine. An example of a design choice intended to mitigate the negative effects of stealth technologies on maintainability was the placing of 86 percent of all avionics behind panels with non-low observable seals, which allowed panels to be opened and closed for maintenance of these avionics without the need for stealth re-coating or cure time.

Like all stealth aircraft, the F-35 is required to carry all weaponry internally. Unlike the F-22, however, its primary role as a strike fighter means that its weapons bays were designed to accommodate high diameter air-to-surface ordnance including cruise missiles and 1000-kilogram bombs. While being a key facilitator of a reduced radar cross section, the F-35's carriage of weapons internally also helps to reduce drag and improve flight performance.

Notwithstanding the increases in aircraft weights of each successive generation, the F-35 is considerably heavier relative to other fighters of its generation than the preceding 'low' fighters in USAF 'high-low' combinations, the F-16 and F-5, were in their respective eras. Furthermore, unlike its two predecessors, the F-35's range is longer than that of its larger heavyweight counterpart the F-22 – where the F-16 and F-5 where very comfortably outranged by their respective 'high' heavyweight counterparts the F-15 and F-4. The F-16 and F-5 were particularly prized for their high manoeuvrability, especially at low speeds, and were designed with a focus on visual range air-to-air combat, in contrast to the F-35, which has a flight performance that is far from exceptional and was designed with a focus on air-to-ground missions and beyond visual range engagements. Thus, although the F-22's design generally followed the trends set by its third and fourth generation predecessors, the F-35's design was a much more radical departure from many of these.

Primary contributors to the F-35's relatively heavy weight were the requirements for a particularly large avionics suite, which ensured that while the F-5 and F-16 had very poor situational awareness relative to the F-4 and F-15, the discrepancy between the F-35's radar size and that of the F-22 would be far smaller. Its avionics are disproportionately heavy for an aircraft of its size, earning it the informal name of the 'flying computer.' These design choices reflected the broader trend in Western thought particularly in the post-Cold War era that superiority in stealth, sensors, data links, missiles, and electronic warfare capabilities superseded the need for a high speed or manoeuvrability. The F-35's disproportionately large and deep

A top-view at an F-35A of the U.S. Air Force demonstrating its manoeuvrability during a public display. (USAF)

weapons bays for an aircraft of its size are a further major contributor to its weight, and reflect its primary role as a strike fighter.

The F-35A also has an unusually high fuel fraction for a Western fighter at 0.38 of its total weight, with an internal capacity of 8,400 kilograms of fuel. This was considered necessary due to the particularly high specific fuel consumption of its F135 engine at 0.9 lb/lb/hour (91.77 kg of fuel per kN of thrust per hour) – where 0.75 is otherwise considered standard for 21st century fighter engines. The combination of disproportionately high fuel carriage and a particularly fuel hungry engine results in a fighter with a 1,093 kilometre combat radius with a standard weapons load, which is less than half that of China and Russia's J-20 and Su-57 fifth generation fighters, but still high by standards of Western fighters surpassing the F-16 or F-22.[22] The F-35C variant carries a little over 8 percent more fuel at 9,100 kilograms, accommodating the extra capacity in its larger wings, which provides a slightly longer range, but also negatively impacts its thrust/weight ratio. The naval fighter has a combat radius of 1,100 kilometres,[23] allowing it to closely match the range of the F-18E/F it was designed to replace. By contrast, the F-35B carries 29 percent less fuel than the F-35A at just 5,940 kilograms, which alongside the very high fuel consumption rates needed for short take-off and vertical landing limit its combat radius to just 833 kilometres.[24] Lower fuel carriage does not positively impact the F-35B's thrust/weight ratio, as the weight of the fuel is heavily compensated for by the added weight of vertical lift fans.

Despite many aspects of the F-35's flight performance being far from remarkable, it does have notable strengths. F-35 pilots have reported that the fighter can achieve higher angles of attack than its predecessor the F-16, which had faced significant limitations in this respect.[25] The fighter was reported to perform particularly well at high angles of attack.[26] Its acceleration to reach Mach 1 speeds was also reportedly faster than that of any other American fighter type, including the F-22, although at over Mach 1 acceleration was less outstanding.[27] This feedback contrasted sharply with predictions by Air Force pilots in the mid-2010s that the fighter would suffer from particularly poor acceleration and an abysmal turn rate.[28] Pilots who had flown both aircraft nevertheless consistently rated the F-35's instantaneous and its sustained turn rates as inferior to those of the F-16, and far inferior to those of the F-15, with the same being the case for its ability to recover airspeed. The F-35 was, however, assessed to have superior responsiveness at low speeds, and a superior stack/scissors performance, than both of the older aircraft.[29] The fighter's flight performance was not overwhelmingly inferior to that of the F-16, but neither was it a significant improvement as had previously consistently been the case when moving into new generations in the past.

The F-35A is the only variant of the fighter with a gun built into its airframe, while the F-35B and C can carry separately developed GPU-9/A external gun pods on their centrelines. The GAU-22/A Gatling gun is integrated inside the F-35A's left wing, and adds 104.3 kilograms of weight in addition to the weight of its 182 rounds. With only enough rounds for four seconds of fire, the gun's limitations were a significant source of controversy when the F-35A was suggested for close air support rounds (see Chapter 5). Questions were widely raised regarding whether this capability was worth the significant added weight. For the F-35B and F-35C, although efforts were made to ensure that both variants' gun pods' external enclosures were stealthy, they still increased the aircraft's radar cross sections significantly, which alongside the additional weight increased the appeal of operating the aircraft without their guns for the majority of missions.

The F-35A can be most easily visually distinguished from other variants by its boom refuelling receptacle port on the top of its airframe, and its gun blister on its upper port side. The lack of either the extended foldable wings seen on the F-35C, or the lift fan behind the cockpit seen on the F-35B, are other conspicuous identifiers. As by far the most widely used F-35 variant, a small number of sub-variants of the F-35A have been developed with minor changes made to meet the requirements of various clients. These include the Israeli F-35I, which integrates a number of the client's avionics subsystems, and Norwegian F-35As which have parachute systems to facilitate short landings on icy runways. On 27 December 2021, it was confirmed that Lockheed Martin was developing a new F-35 sub-variant for an anonymous client.[30]

A U.S. Air Force F-35A firing its GAU-22/A gun. (USAF)

The Second Variant: Supercarriers and the F-35C

Since the end of the Second World War, the U.S. Navy has remained unrivalled among the naval services around the world in the potency of its aviation capabilities. When the Cold War ended in 1989 its fleet of combat aircraft was organised into 79 operational squadrons, which were distributed among 13 operational carrier air wings. The Cold War era fleet combined multiple highly specialised types, which in 1989 included 26 squadrons of F-14s which served as interceptors and air superiority fighters, 14 squadrons of versatile F-18A/B medium weight multirole fighters, 28 squadrons of A-6 and A-7 attack jets, and 11 squadrons of EA-6B electronic attack jets. Deep spending cuts following the end of the Cold War led the Navy to standardise its fleet around an enlarged and enhanced variant of the F-18, the F-18E/F Super Hornet, and its electronic attack derivative the E/A-18G Growler. The Super Hornet and Growler proved straightforward and affordable to develop and operationalise, while their conservative operational costs and maintenance needs relative to the combat jets they were replacing, in particular the A-6 and F-14, ensured significant savings over time. The Super Hornet was far less capable in strike roles than previously envisaged A-6 and A-7 successors were expected to be, nor as potent in air-to-air combat as an F-14 successor was expected to be, and was significantly lighter and shorter-ranged than either of the planned new aircraft. It was nevertheless considered sufficient for the requirements of the post-Cold War era.

Compromises to the performances of carrier air wings were significant, and while an F-14 successor was expected to allow them to control much wider areas of surrounding airspace, the F-18E/F had only 50 percent of the F-14's capability to deliver a fixed set of ordnance on target. This cut carriers' area of influence by 77 percent when transitioning from the F-14 to the Super Hornet.[31] Compared to the much longer ranged A-12, which would have introduced advanced stealth capabilities, the F-18E/F was even more restricted. Despite these limitations, the Super Hornet's performance was from the late 2010s gradually enhanced, with notable improvements including the integration of the AN/APG-79 AESA radar, stealth coatings, infrared search and tracking systems, and AIM-183 long range air-to-air missiles. The integration of hypersonic weapons is also expected by the end of the 2020s.[32] The F-18E/F was considered a stopgap to simplify carrier operations, replace ageing airframes, and reduce operational costs, until the fleet could be standardised around a high-low combination of the F-35C and a larger much long ranged sixth generation fighter.

Like its predecessors, the F-35C was designed for catapult-assisted take-off and barrier arrested recovery operations from aircraft carriers, and for compatibility with the respective steam and electromagnetic catapult systems on the Navy's Nimitz- and Gerald Ford-class supercarriers. The systems provide aircraft with considerable energy upon launch, allowing them to take off over short distances and with larger weapons and fuel loads. Their success would lead the Navy from the mid-2020s to consider development of ground based catapult systems for the F-35C to improve its short airfield performance.[33]

By far the most conspicuous difference between the F-35C and the other two variants is the wing, which at 13.1 metres has a 22.4 percent larger span. The resulting wing area of 62.06 square metres is 45.2 percent greater than the other variants. Larger wings make the F-35C the heaviest variant of the fighter, with an empty weight 18.7 percent greater than that of the F-35A at around 15,800 kilograms. Wings not only house more fuel, but also improve the aircraft's manoeuvrability, which is particularly valuable for positioning for arrested landings on carrier decks. The F-35C's ability to carry out more strenuous manoeuvres is nevertheless limited, with the airframe designed to only endure g forces up to 7.5, compared to the 9g limit for most 21st century fighter types including the F-35A. Despite its wide wingspan, the F-35C occupies far less space in storage due to its foldable wingtip sections. Its landing gear, including twin-wheel nose gear, is significantly stronger than those of other variants due to the stresses imposed by catapult assisted take-offs and arrested landings.

The Navy is notably less heavily invested in the F-35 program than the Air Force or Marine Corps for multiple reasons. Where the two other services made relatively few fighter procurements after the turn of the century, with delays to the F-35's development causing crises in both services as much of their Cold War era fleets aged past their initially expected retirement dates (see Chapter 6), the Navy alone continued to invest in acquisitions of '4+ generation' F-18E/Fs and E/A-18Gs. The tremendous scale on which the Navy procured

A Grumman F-14B (foreground), accompanying its successor: the McDonnell-Douglas/Boeing F/A-18E Super Hornet, as seen in 2005 – one year before the F-14 was withdrawn from operational service with the U.S. Navy. (U.S. Navy – USN)

An F-35C of the Strike Fighter Squadron 147. The squadron was the first to attain an initial operating capability with the aircraft. (USN)

the two aircraft, far exceeding any service in the Western world's acquisitions of any post-Cold War fighter type, was the primary factor that placed it in a strong position to bide its time on F-35 procurements. By the time the first F-35Cs entered service in 2018, the Navy had already acquired 560 F/A-18E/Fs and 131 EA-18Gs – for a total of 691 enhanced fourth generation combat jets.[34] Super Hornet production for the Navy would continue up to 2027, which was interpreted as an indication of the service's continued scepticism regarding the F-35C's capabilities and readiness for high intensity operations. The last order for 17 additional F-18E/Fs was placed on March 18, 2024.[35]

From the early 2010s major increases to F-18E/F orders and work on a sixth generation carrier based fighter between them appeared to have the potential to seriously limit the room in the Navy's fleet for the much delayed F-35C. Some assessments went so far as to claim that development of the F-35C had been unnecessary from the outset; with the F-35B providing a sufficient carrier-based stealth fighter capability until a sixth generation fighter was ready for service. This overlooked multiple key factors, however, including the F-35B's far more limited combat potential and range, its far higher procurement and operational costs, and the fact that it could not benefit from the catapult launch systems on American supercarriers. While Marine Harrier jets had deployed from Nimitz-class carriers in the past, the far greater heat levels omitted by the F-35B would have made accommodating the aircraft far from straightforward and required extensive and costly modifications to the 100,000 ton ships.

Although there were strong arguments for the development of both the F-35B and the F-35C, if the Pentagon were forced to choose between the two, it is likely that the F-35C would have been prioritised. With ten to twelve nuclear powered supercarriers in service, their viability for high intensity operations against modern adversaries was seriously at risk if continuing to deploy only fourth generation fighters. Marine carrier aviation had played very limited roles in prior American military campaigns, while a significant proportion of Marine air units were to deploy F-35Cs from Nimitz- and Gerald Ford-class supercarriers. For the Navy, by contrast, the F-35C represented its entire investment in fifth generation combat aviation. The Marine Corps' decision in February 2025 to deeply reduce planned F-35B procurements and acquire more F-35Cs further strengthened the consensus that the carrier-based variant was likely to be a more significant contributor to warfighting capabilities in a near peer conflict scenario.

Prevailing post-Cold War trends in the American defence sector indicated that the Navy would come to depend on the F-35C far more than the service initially anticipated, due to the high likelihood of delays to the development of the service's sixth generation fighter under the F/A-XX program (see Chapter 10). The House Appropriations Committee was among the sources to indicate that F/A-XX would likely be no less problematic and prone to delays than the F-35, and that investment in the older aircraft should be sustained accordingly. It highlighted the precedent set by the delays and shortcomings that had affected the F-35C itself, which had forced the Navy to invest much more heavily than expected in F-18E/F procurements.[36] The possibility of a significant rise in F-35C orders increased from the mid-2020s as the future of the F/A-XX began to appear increasingly uncertain, with major delays potentially leading the F-35C to be acquired to replace older Super Hornets from the mid-late 2030s, by which time its capabilities would have been improved significantly. By making large-scale procurements much later on, the Navy would be acquiring F-35s that were on average much less troublesome and much more capable than those from earlier production lots.

The Third Variant: Marine Air Power and the F-35B

Multiple fighter programs throughout the Cold War and since have had both ground and carrier-based variants, with adaptations comparable to those made to the F-35A to produce the F-35C, or vice versa, being far from uncommon. Notable examples included the F-4B Phantom II, developed into the F-4C/D/E land-based variants; the Soviet Su-27K that emerged as a carrier-based version of the Su-27; and the Chinese J-11 which was developed into the carrier-based J-15. In the 1990s the U.S. Navy had similarly considered commissioning a carrier-based variant of the F-22s as a replacement for the F-14.[37]

One of the most outstanding aspects of the F-35 program was that an additional variant with a third, separate take-off and landing capability was pursued, namely the F-35B designed for short take-off and vertical landing (STOVL) developed primarily to meet the requirements of the U.S. Marine Corps. Modifications required for STOVL were far more complex and demanding than those required

A row of F-35C fighters of the Strike Fighter Squadron 147, as seen on the deck of the aircraft carrier USS *Carl Vinson* in 2019. (USN)

for conventional carrier operations. Although the possibility of developing STOVL or vertical take-off and landing (VTOL) aircraft had gained significant attention from the dawn of the jet era, with extensive testing done in several countries from the 1950s, the significant sacrifices to combat potential required to achieve this limited the appeal of operationalising such aircraft. Prior STOVL/VTOL fighter types were thus few and far between, with the only two to have entered service being the British Harrier, including its enhanced derivative jointly developed with the U.S. the AV-8B Harrier II, and the Soviet Yak-38. These had been designed from the outset as specialised VTOL capable aircraft, rather than as variants of a pre-existing aircraft under a joint program. The major design compromises required for their take-off and landing capabilities made them by far the least capable fighters in production in their respective eras, with development of variants for conventional take-offs never having been considered.

As the first operational fighter capable of vertical landings, the Harrier was notably not conceptualised as a carrier-based aircraft, but rather to be able to deploy near the frontlines in Central Europe. There the ability to operate without airfields was expected to be highly prized in the event of a full-scale war with the Warsaw Pact. The cancellation of the British Malta-class and Queen Elizabeth-class carrier programs in 1945 and 1966, however, meant that should the Royal Navy continue to field fighters on carriers, they would need to be deployed from the very light 22,000-ton Invincible-class carriers, which would require a vertical landing capability. Initially intended as helicopter carrying escort cruisers, primarily for anti-submarine warfare, the three small ships commissioned from 1980 were far from optimally sized to deploy fixed wing aircraft. After the retirement of the last Audacious-class aircraft carrier HMS *Ark Royal* in 1979, Invincible-class ships would provide Britain's only carrier aviation capability for the next four decades. This resulted in significant investments being made in vertical landing capable fighters. In 1978, nine years after the original Harrier entered service, the Sea Harrier was introduced for the Invincible-class.

The limitations of the Harrier and Yak-38 were such that neither was initially conceptualised with a significant air-to-air combat capability, with both lacking radars. The two fighter types nevertheless provided valuable experience operating VTOL aircraft, allowing Britain and the Soviet Union to develop more capable new generations of aircraft with similar take-off and landing capabilities with the intention of commissioning them in the 1980s and 1990s.

Unlike the United Kingdom, which developed the Harrier II as an improved variant of the original aircraft, the Soviet Union developed an entirely new and highly promising VTOL fighter, the Yak-41, which first flew in March 1987. With the country having been working on the development of a VTOL fighter since the 1940s,[38] the Yak-38 which had joined the Soviet Navy in 1976 had been considered a stopgap to acquaint the service with VTOL aircraft and fixed wing carrier operations until the Yak-41 was ready. As a newer much more capable aircraft, its flight performance was entirely unrivalled among VTOL fighters, and it quickly set a dozen world records.[39] The Yak-41's capabilities, which included an option for ski jump assisted STOVL take-off, led the USSR to be assessed in the 1990s to be 15-20 years ahead of the world in its VTOL/STOVL technologies. The aircraft's scheduled service entry in the mid-1990s was set to represent a culmination of almost half a century of efforts to develop a VTOL/STOVL fighter with a genuinely competitive

Two AV-8B Harrier II fighters – the final variant of this family of combat jets originally designed and developed in the United Kingdom – as seen in the process of landing aboard of one of the amphibious warfare ships of the U.S. Navy. (USN)

combat performance, and would have introduced a vertical landing capable supersonic fighter two full decades before any other country could.[40] Beyond the Yak-41, a more manoeuvrable successor with stealth capabilities, the Yak-43, had begun development in 1983, with both expected to be increasingly widely fielded in the Soviet Air Force and Navy.[41] Following the USSR's disintegration, however, the two programs were terminated in the early 1990s.

While the Soviet Union had been well placed to finance development of a clean sheet new VTOL aircraft alone, the United Kingdom's interest in further programs was stimulated primarily by demand from the United States. The U.S. Department of Defense invested in joint development of the Harrier II primarily due to the Marine Corps' requirement to field a fighter capable of deploying both from makeshift airfields and from amphibious assault ships such as the eight 40,000 ton Wasp-class vessels that entered service from 1989.

Much like the U.S. Air Force's creation as a separate service from the Army, independent Marine aviation had its origins in the aftermath of the Second World War. A key turning point in the perceived need for Marine aviation was the Battle for Guadalcanal in the Solomon Islands, where the Marines' lack of support from naval aviation resulted in significant losses to Japanese air strikes. As observed by official Marine historian Ben Kristy: 'The lesson learned was that the U.S. Marine Corps needed to be able to bring its air power with it over the beach because the large-deck Navy aircraft carriers might not always be there.'[42] As early 1958, the Corps had a written requirement for a fixed-wing high performance VTOL/STOVL aircraft, which was intended to deploy from the short runways of amphibious assault ships, as well as from 100 foot concrete patches as small as tennis courts that could be quickly installed near the frontlines to serve as makeshift airfields.[43] Such aircraft could thereby provide air support to amphibious landings even without carriers or airfields nearby, and were thus well suited to how the Marines operated. 'USMC [Marine Corps] interest in a working V/STOL [VTOL/STOVL] attack aircraft outstripped the state of aeronautical technology,' Kristy observed, with American experimentation with such aircraft proving catastrophic, as every single STOVL and VTOL prototype built from 1946 to 1966 crashed.[44]

The Marine Corps leadership's continued perception of a need for STOVL or VTOL fighters, and the failure of domestic industry to make meaningful progress with development, resulted in considerable interest when the Harrier entered service in the British Royal Air Force. With distinctive swept back and downward wings, and four rotating engine nozzles that could pivot downwards to provide vertical lift, the highly unusual aircraft quickly made a strong impression. Marine pilot Colonel Thomas H. Miller, who was one of the first two Americans to fly the Harrier, stated afterwards: 'If I had my way, I'd have a squadron of those things tomorrow.'[45] 114 of the ground based radarless variant were purchased from the United Kingdom, with these entering service from January 1971 under the designation AV-8A Harrier. Their time in service was short, with the last of the aircraft retired in 1987.

After significant delays and opposition from the U.S. Navy, a memorandum of understanding was belatedly signed in August 1981 between British Aerospace and McDonnell Douglas for the joint development of a new enhanced variant of the Harrier, with the Pentagon including the aircraft in its annual budget from that year. The Harrier II was thus jointly developed by McDonnell Douglas and British Aerospace, and unlike its predecessor it was developed for STOVL as well as VTOL, rather than purely the latter. The former take-off mode entailed using vertical lift from the Harrier's downward facing nozzles to supplement the lift generated by flight surfaces as the aircraft moved along a short runway, rather than relying exclusively on vertical lift for take-off. This reduced the burden on the lift fan, and thus facilitated significantly higher take-

A prototype of the Yak-41 vertical takeoff and landing fighter in landing configuration. The aircraft's layout was unique and revolutionary, and would significantly influence the F-35B. (Ken Videan)

off weights. Entering service from 1985-2003, the Marine Corps would receive 397 Harrier IIs, which were designated AV-8B.

While the fielding of a STOVL fighter revolutionised how Marine air power could operate, the practical benefits were limited due to the Harrier's significant performance limitations and design issues. With a propensity for rolling over and slamming into the ground, the AV-8A suffered 31.77 accidents per 100,000 hours, with 58 percent of the fleet, or 66 of the 114 aircraft, destroyed in accidents as a result. It was accordingly dubbed the 'Widow Maker' within the Corps. The AV-8B Harrier II, although improving on its predecessor's very poor safety record, still proved far from reliable, with an accident rate of 11.44 per 100,000 flight hours by the early 2000s – more than twice that of the F-16 and 3.5 times that of the F-18. The aircraft had by 2002 suffered more than 300 accidents and 900 less serious incidents. By the time of the Iraq War one third of the fleet had been destroyed in 143 separate noncombat accidents, killing 45 Marines, and leading it to be termed the 'most dangerous airplane flying in the U.S. military today.'[46]

Beyond its reliability issues, the Harrier II's combat capabilities proved highly constrained, with other aircraft consistently favoured to perform the same missions. During the Gulf War in 1990-1991 makeshift forward air strips were never set up, while the aircraft's range proved insufficient to operate effectively from distant airfields or assault ships, meaning even the provision of five to ten minutes of close air support would have been difficult to achieve. The aircraft carried too little ordnance, and proved highly vulnerable to gunfire and handheld surface-to-air missiles, leaving it poorly suited for close air support. 'It's the most vulnerable plane that's in service now,'

An F-35B Accompanied by a Spanish Navy AV-8B+. (Armada)

concluded Franklin C. Spinney, who evaluated tactical aircraft for the Pentagon, adding: 'You can't hit that thing without hitting something important.'[47] The hot thrust-producing nozzles at the heart of the aircraft's fuselage created a particularly high heat signature, which was especially dangerous for a close support aircraft which faced a primary threat from short ranged heat-seeking missiles. The aircraft's loss rate was more than double that of other major combat aircraft, with five Harriers shot down despite the small number of sorties flown. As analyst at the Center for Strategic and International Studies Anthony Cordesman thus concluded: 'The AV-8B simply wasn't competitive in terms of range, payload, survivability, target acquisition [or] communications capability.'[48]

Not only was the Harrier's performance highly constrained, but its vertical-flight controls and the minimal lift and manoeuvrability of its tiny wings made it difficult to fly, while its logistical demands were much higher than those of other fighters or than the Air Force's A-10 close air support jets. As noted by former Secretary of the Navy John F. Lehman Jr., the aircraft 'turned out to be grossly more expensive' than expected, highlighting that the accident rate made operations especially costly.[49] A special report on the aircraft by the *Los Angeles Times* accordingly stressed that it 'required an enormous transport and supply operation to keep it provisioned with bombs, fuel, parts and distilled water for cooling the engine, a far cry from its originally stated mission of operating from remote locations.' The report concluded that the Harrier II was 'a plane bedevilled by mechanical problems and maintenance mistakes.'[50]

After its performance limitations were made clear in the Gulf War, Harriers were sidelined from contributing to the invasion of Afghanistan, with those based on the assault ship USS *Peleliu* conducting manoeuvres over the Arabian Sea. Harrier pilot Captain Matthew Parker recalled of his time on the *Peleliu*: 'Other squadrons were going north to the war and we were flying south for more training ... It was very frustrating.'[51] 'This is the sort of conflict in which Harrier proponents typically would expect to see the Harrier prominently used, especially early on ... I don't think it's lost on many people that the Harriers were not the first airplanes used in that war,' recalled military aviation analyst for the Congressional Research Service Christopher Bolkcom.[52] Commenting on the Harrier's combination of a very high accident rate and limited practical combat utility, Philip E. Coyle, who served as the Pentagon's chief weapons tester from 1994 to 2001, concluded in 2002: 'If the Harrier had been decisive many times in battle, we would all still regret horribly the tragedies of the pilots who have been killed, but at least you'd be able to say that the Harrier made a difference. What makes this situation so difficult is that we just don't have that kind of battlefield record to support the accidental deaths.'[53]

While the Harrier's time in service had been marred by both tragedies and combat shortcomings, the introduction of the F-35B promised to revolutionise the capabilities of Marine aviation. The deficiencies of the Harrier meant that, for the Marine Corps' fighter units, the F-35's introduction would provide a far greater boost to their combat capabilities that it did for the Navy or Air Force, which had fielded much more robust fourth generation fleets. As the Western world's first clean sheet successor to the Harrier, which had first flown in 1967, the F-35's third and most unusual variant the F-35B would not only provide a generational improvement in capabilities, but also far greater reliability and a much greater range of practical uses. Furthermore, unlike the Harrier and Yak-38, but much like the cancelled Yak-41, the F-35B was a truly multirole fighter with avionics, weaponry and a flight performance which allowed it to effectively conduct high intensity operations other than close air support. Not only was it able to hold its own against modern fighters in the Navy and Air Force in ways Harriers never could, but the aircraft could also be expected to have a significant advantage in air-to-air combat against the large majority of challengers, largely due to the scarcity of fighters with fifth generation level capabilities. Where the Harrier had had negligible air defence suppression capabilities, those of the F-35B were at the opposite end of the performance spectrum and truly world leading.

The F-35B was the first aircraft to enter service using a lift fan, which at around 135 centimetres in diameter, and with two counter-rotating blades, was installed horizontally in a large ducted hole behind the cockpit to provide downward thrust for take-offs and landings. A large rear-opening door behind the F-35B's cockpit was designed to open to expose the fan shortly before take-off and landing, while following take-off or landing the fan would disengage and the door would close to ensure a low radar cross section. Further contributing to downward thrust, the F-35B's F135-PW-600 engine was designed to swivel 90 degrees downwards during take-off and landing, with its thrust combined with that of the lift fan totalling more than 160kN (36,000 pounds). Two smaller streams of exhaust, funnelled down ducts to a small nozzle under each wing, each provide approximately 8.9 kN (2,000 pounds) more lift, although their primary purpose is to help balance and control the aircraft with vectored thrust during take-off and landing. With the engine swivelling into a conventional rear facing position after take-off, while the lift fan disengages, the aircraft transitions to fixed wing lift in forward flight.* The revolutionary advances in STOVL/VTOL technologies which the F-35B was the first aircraft to fully operationalise would pave the way for a range of other programs to be considered, with a notable example being a runway-independent special operations VTOL transport which by the mid-2020s had a flight demonstrator under development by Boeing under a DARPA program.[54]

The F-35B became the first fighter to operationalise a lift fan in 2015 primarily due to the termination of the Yak-41 program, which had been set to enter service two decades prior, and the Yak-43 which would have entered service around a decade prior, with both Soviet jets having been designed with lift fans. It was thus notable that the Yak-41's R79V-300 afterburning turbofan nozzle significantly influenced the design of the F135-PW-600.[55] The use of a large exhaust nozzle behind the engine that could swing down 90 degrees to generate vertical thrust, and was supplemented by two jet engines behind the pilot which were only used for vertical flight, was one of the Soviet fighter's most defining features which it had pioneered. By comparison, the Harrier achieved vertical lift by swinging down four nozzles. The single large exhaust nozzle of the Yak-41 was far more efficient during flight, allowing it to retain VTOL capabilities with significantly less compromises to other aspects of its performance. A partnership between Lockheed Martin and the Yak-41's developer Yakovlev was announced on 6 September 1992, under which the former would provide $385-400 million to develop three new prototypes and an additional static aircraft to test improvements in design and avionics. The arrangement was made public in June 1994.

* The extra weight from the lift fan and the shaft was insignificant compared to the benefits provided by the extra thrust, while the fact that no combustion was used meant that the exhaust from the lift fan was much colder, and thus would not significantly affect the ground environment. This also reduced requirements for the main engine to contribute to STOVL with its own thrust, where on the Harrier the engine had been the sole source of thrust. As a result, the engine could be conventionally sized to the requirement of up-and-away thrust as was necessary to achieve transonic acceleration.

F-35B assigned to Marine Strike Fighter Squadron 122 in landing configuration, with the doors for its lift-fan open, and its main engine's exhaust swivelled downwards. (U.S. Marine Corps - USMC)

Other than the use and positioning of a lift fan and integration of a 90 degree swivelling engine, the F-35B's design heritage from the Yak-41 was most prominent in the tail arrangement. The Soviet fighter had a tail split into a twin boom arrangement to allow the engine to be placed closer to the airframe's centre of mass, allowing it to better facilitate vertical take-offs and landings. The F-35's tail arrangement was less pronounced but very similar. Where the Harrier's engine had been located in the centre of the fuselage, the Yak-41 and F-35B's arrangements avoided not only the flight performance inefficiencies that this caused, but also the major increases to heat signature that had long made the British-designed jets vulnerable. This arrangement had been far ahead of its time, and had no equivalent anywhere else in the world.

While the flight decks of Wasp-class assault ships extended to 258 metres, just 16 percent of the 2,500 metres the F-35A needed to take off, the F-35B could take off from runways measuring just 182 metres. If using a ski jump, it could do so from 138 metre runways. Despite being designed for carrier operations, the F-35B was not designed with folding wings, which while helping to reduce weight, forced designers to reduce the wingspan to just 10.7 metres – the very widest that the elevators and parking areas on amphibious assault ships could accommodate. The aircraft is also approximately 10 centimetres shorter than the F-35A and C variants, and 3 and 12 centimetres smaller than the two other variants respectively. Not only is its turn rate far lower than that of the F-35C, but its manoeuvrability is affected by a g force limit of just 7g, compared to 7.5g for the F-35C and 9g for the F-35A. The complexities of the lift fan and swivelling engine also make the aircraft far more costly to operate and more maintenance intensive than either of the other variants, contributing to the already significant difficulties of keeping stealth fighters combat ready. Unlike the Harrier II and Yak-41 which were designed to be capable of both short and vertical take-offs, the F-35B was not designed for VTOL, with its much greater weight preventing it from taking off vertically while carrying a combat load.

The two other leading shortcomings with the F-35B are its much lower fuel capacity, which at 6,120kg is close to 20 percent below that of the F-35A, as well as its lower weapons carrying capacity at just 6,800kg, compared to the F-35A and C variants' 8,200kg. The planned discrepancy in the sizes of the three variants' main weapons bays had previously been larger, before a decision was made in 2003 to enlarge the F-35B's bay for greater commonality with the other variants, albeit at the expense of a weight increase of close to 1,000 kilograms. This in turn forced a major redesign to ensure the aircraft was still STOVL capable. The F-35B's smaller main weapons bays nevertheless still became a particularly significant shortcoming when 'Sidekick' missile racks were introduced onto the F-35A and F-35C with the Block 4 upgrade, which increased their air-to-air missile payloads from four to six. The F-35B's inability to incorporate this upgrade significantly widened the gap in air-to-air combat capabilities between it and the other variants, with a number of air-to-surface missile types introduced with the Block 4 upgrade such as the AGM-88G and MACE also being incompatible with the fighter (see Chapter 5). If operating in non-stealth mode, the F-35B's two outboard weapon stations are restricted to carrying 38 percent less ordnance compared to the F-35A and F-35C at 680 kilograms, rather than 1,100 kilograms. Despite these shortcomings, the discrepancy between the F-35B's capabilities and those of the F-35A are very significantly smaller than those seen between the Harrier and fourth generation fighters such as the F-16 and F-18, with the F-35B's far more efficient configuration for STOVL than its predecessor taking a far smaller toll on performance, and resulting in a significantly higher standing among fighters of its time than the Harrier had.

While the F-35B was by far the most impressive and unusual variant of the Joint Strike Fighter, the design trade-offs needed to facilitate STOVL in many cases also detrimentally influenced the F-35A and F-35C variants as well. This fuelled widespread criticisms of the decision to develop STOVL aircraft as part of a joint program when it accounted for under 15 percent of the fighters planned for procurement. As summarised by observers at *The War Zone*: 'it's short-take-off and vertical landing requirement dictated the design of the F-35 overall, handicapping its carrier-based and conventional counterparts in the process.'[56] Senior Research Fellow for Airpower and Technology at the Royal United Services Institute Justin Bronk referred to the issue as the F-35's 'design compromises from the fact that short take-off and vertical landing was required by the Marine Corps version,' adding that 'that did push choices in terms of the shape of the aircraft and some of the internal layout' which were not ideal had a STOVL variant not been part of the program.[57] This argument was summarised as follows by American military aviation writer Tyler Rogoway, who observed that the F-35A and C:

> [P]aid a huge price aerodynamically and conceptually in order to include the short take-off and vertical landing requirement into the Joint Strike Fighter's basic design. In the name of commonality, the F-35B, with its huge box-like central lift fan, along with its complex drivetrain and downward swivelling exhaust nozzle, basically handicapped the aerodynamics, and in essence the very concept, of its more conventional Navy and Air Force brethren. In other words, some would say that the F-35 was built as a STOVL aircraft first, and then adapted to a standard and carrier fighter second, instead of the other way around. The F-35B design demand of lifting twenty plus tons, near vertically, on a pillar of thrust, are simply so consuming that they compromised the potential performance, and to some degree the cost, of the other two more traditional, less 'engineering challenged' F-35 variants. Oddly enough, the Marine's F-35B order only represents about 14% of the DoD's total F-35 buy, yet the other 86% of aircraft will be handicapped by the F-35B's unique design requirements. When the JSF's baseline design was finally locked, the aircraft was left with a massive fuselage cross-section, as well as a single engine with a huge circumference. This, along with many other STOVL related design results, gave the more numerous A and C versions of the jet an airframe that is far less than optimal given their basic sub-design's goals.[58]

The Marine Corps was by a significant margin the greatest beneficiary of the F-35's development as a joint tri-service program, and with by far the smallest budget for fighter procurements of the three services, developing a high performance STOVL-capable fifth generation fighter, even if doing so jointly with British support and funding, would have been very far from viable. Had the F-35 been developed jointly for the Air Force and Navy's requirements alone, however, it not only would have been far less complex and difficult, but would likely have also provided both services with fighters that were overall significantly more capable. The two services could thus be seen to be subsidising Marine aviation at their own expense.

Where STOVL was considered a very niche capability in the era of the Harrier and Yak-38, the F-35B's much more respectable overall performance for its time raised the possibility of aircraft with such capabilities being fielded much more widely. Much as the original Harrier has been built for the Royal Air Force, rather than the Royal Navy, so too had the Yak-41 been intended not only for the Soviet Navy, but also for the Air Force's frontline fighter units to ensure some combat jets could operate if airfields were destroyed. The F-35B, too, was intended not only to deploy from amphibious assault ships, but also from makeshift airfields. The Marine Corps and the air forces of Italy, the United Kingdom, Japan and Singapore ordered the aircraft specifically for such operations, while the Israeli Air and Space Force and the Republic of China Air Force also considered the aircraft for this purpose.

Pairing advances in STOVL technologies with a world leading fifth generation fighter program made the F-35B by far the most revolutionary F-35 variant. Although major sacrifices to the wider program were made to see the F-35B developed, which its limited service in the Marine Corps' small air wing made difficult to justify, the possibility remains that the value attributed to its capabilities will significantly increase its importance in the fleet and its planned deployment numbers. One leading factor which could increase the perceived value of the F-35B would be its adoption by the U.S. Navy, as the service faces the possibility of moving away from exclusive reliance on 100,000 ton supercarriers and procuring smaller lower cost carriers to better disperse its investments. It was confirmed in March 2020 that under the Future Carrier 2030 Task Force study the Navy was considering restricting procurement of the Gerald Ford-class supercarrier to four ships, rather than the planned ten, with the vessels costing two to three times as much as the Cold War era Nimitz-class ships at over $17 billion each.[59]

Investment in smaller carriers had long been advocated as an alternative under a 'distributed lethality' concept, with a study by the Centre for Strategic and Budgetary Assessments commissioned by Congress in 2017, and a Senate Armed Services Committee White Paper published earlier that year, being among the sources to do so.[60] Smaller ships such as the 45,000 ton America-class were considered

An F-35B operated by the Marine Fighter Attack Squadron 121 secured on the deck of the amphibious assault ship USS *Wasp*. (USN)

A front view of an F-35B landing onboard a Wasp-class amphibious assault ship. (USMC)

a leading alternative, reducing the fleet's vulnerability to strikes by adversaries' increasingly advanced anti-shipping assets. A shift to relying on such ships had the potential to significantly expand the overall role of the F-35B in the U.S. Armed Forces. As observed by professor at the U.S. Naval War College Angus Ross, adopting a modification of the Marines' 'Lightning Carrier' would 'generate crucial operational flexibility for the Navy.'[61] This possibility had been speculated as early as 1992, when after the USSR's disintegration one senior Navy official observed that if the service was not permitted by post-Cold War budgets to keep its large supercarrier fleet, it may need to consider other alternatives. 'If ASTOVL [Advanced STOVL] is viable, then you will be able to put your aviation at sea on a different type of carrier,' he commented at the time.[62]

Beyond the Navy, there also remains a significant possibility that a future high intensity war between world leading militaries, such as a new inter-Korean conflict, could demonstrate the ability of missile and drone forces to leave conventional fighters like the F-35A near unusable by striking airbases, and thus raise the perceived value of the F-35B for ground based operations. Indeed, in the late 1990s senior Pentagon acquisition officials argued that the Air Force procure the F-35B variant, asserting that it provided 'a capability that would let the Air Force operate from shorter, rougher fields, thus moving closer to the battlefield and providing wider deployment and basing options.'[63] At the time, however, the F-35B was projected to cost only $3 to $7 million more than the F-35A, while the extent of its performance shortcomings compared to the A variant were not yet known.[64]

Writing in *Airpower Journal* earlier that decade, USAF Major Jeffrey Prater asserted that an advanced STOVL fighter could provide unprecedented mobility, permitting the Air Force to abandon the 'archaic concept of hardening air bases deep in the theatre rear area for survivability, while at the same time putting the machines closer to the battle.'[65] In 2023, Italian Air Force Chief of Staff Lieutenant General Luca Goretti notably justified his service's decision to procure a small number of F-35Bs on the basis that there were 'many short airfields around the world,' with the fighter's capabilities ensuring that it could 'be relevant everywhere in the world.' 'If you consider also what's happening in Ukraine, airfield dispersion can be maybe one day the only way to protect your high-value assets,' he concluded.[66] Following Italy, Japan, Singapore, and the United Kingdom, the possibility remained significant that the air forces of more countries could follow suit in procuring the F-35B.

With the F-35A's range seen as a leading shortcoming in the Pacific theatre in particular,[67] the F-35B's appeal, despite its even shorter range, due to its greater options for forward basing may well grow, particularly as concerns have continued to mount regarding the growing vulnerability of American air bases.[68] As the Air Force has responded to emerging challenges to the security of its bases by placing a growing emphasis on Agile Combat Employment for the F-35A, which involves preparing to quickly redeploy fighters to and from unconventional locations away from major airfields, introducing the F-35B would have a transformative impact on its ability to do so. Although, the F-35B's future remains heavily dependant on its service record in the Marine Corps, however, which deployed the aircraft particularly extensively for austere airfield and small carrier operations, indications from the mid-2020s that the fighter was not meeting expectations, and the Corps' curtailing of its investment in the fighter from 2025, boded ill for prospects for its wider adoption by other services (see Chapter 4).

3

OPERATIONALISING THE F-35

Testing the F-35

A central factor shaping the F-35 program's development, and setting it apart from fighter programs of the Cold War era, was the decision to place the aircraft in production while it was still in very early testing. Beginning production at such stages, or even before testing had begun, was a process referred to as concurrency, and was intended to accelerate the introduction of multiple major new assets in the early 21st century. The F-35 thus entered production on a significant scale well over a decade before testing had reached stages that would previously have been considered satisfactory to allow this. Although the aircraft would only be approved for full-scale production in March 2024 after meeting Pentagon requirements for readiness, a full 12 years behind the program schedule set in the early 2000s, in practice this had little impact on production rates, which had long since already reached full-scale levels.

The concurrency approach would be widely criticised for its highly detrimental effects on multiple programs beyond the F-35, with critics referring to it as: 'The idea that a weapons manufacturer, aided by computer modelling, modern material science and other fragmented improvements in design and construction techniques realised over the last 20 years, can design something so complex yet so perfect on the first try, that testing it is more of a formality than a necessity.' By investing in this approach, noted aviation journalist Tyler Rogoway, 'the DoD, defence contractors and Congress suddenly believed that they could collectively field game changing weapons that were flawless right out of the box, even though they have never really done such a thing before.'[1] Undersecretary of Defense for Acquisition, Technology and Logistics Frank Kendall as early as 2012 referred to it outright as 'acquisition malpractice,' and to the process as 'putting the F-35 into production years before the first test flight.' He stated that the Pentagon had made 'optimistic predictions' that advanced design tools, simulations and modelling would ensure that only minimal problems would emerge when the aircraft was in testing. That 'was wrong and now we're paying the price,' he said, adding that the F-35 represented a particularly extreme case of transitioning from development to production too early. 'It should not have been done. But we did it,' Kendall concluded, although by then it was already too late to contain the fallout from these errors.[2] While it remains open to speculation the extent to which the concurrency approach was a direct result of post-Cold War complacency, the full extent of the consequences would only gradually become apparent over the following decade.

As a result of concurrency the line between prototype aircraft and serial production aircraft was much less well defined than in previous programs. 189 early production F-35s suffered from such widespread issues that they were not expected to ever be made viable for actual combat.[3] With the bulk of these flawed models being usable exclusively for training, while in many cases the costs of addressing their issues

The first U.S. Air Force F-35A in flight before landing at Eglin Air Force Base in July 2011. Its pilot, Lieutenant Colonel Eric Smith, was the first qualified F-35 pilot in the Air Force. (USAF)

exceeded those of buying entirely new aircraft, Air Force officials by the early 2020s increasingly questioned whether it was cost effective to finance their sustainment, or whether they should be retired several decades early.[4] Having been rushed into high rate production, issues affecting early batches of F-35s were serious and wide ranging. One of the most significant examples was revealed on 30 January 2019, when the contents of the Office of the Director of Operational Test and Evaluation's 2018 annual review of the F-35 program were first reported. The review revealed the results of durability testing data, which indicated that the service lives of early production F-35Bs could be as low as 2,100 flight hours due to serious structural problems with the aircraft – compared to an expected service life of 8,000 hours. This could force the service to begin grounding jets, or retiring them permanently, as early as 2026, after only around a decade in service.[5]

Beyond issues with the airframes themselves, problems with the software of early production models were significant enough, and the costs of fixing them to become combat capable so immense, that the Joint Program Office considered forgoing these upgrades altogether. Only fighters with Block 3 standard software were intended to be combat capable, with preceding generations of software having been intended for use in testing only. The issue was made all the more serious by the fact that the number of aircraft delivered with Block 2B software was far greater than expected, with 108 of these non-combat capable jets procured by the Pentagon each of which would required 150-160 modifications to reach the most basic Block 3 standard – Block 3i.[6]

By the mid-2010s the target for completing the F-35's development test phase was set for October 2017. This goal from the outset appeared unviable, with the program in mid-2014 reported to be only 60 percent through development testing.[7] From 2016 there were strong signs that the F-35 Joint Program Office was aware that this goal was highly unlikely to be met, and the target date for completion was subsequently delayed to January 2018. Key contributors to delays included issues with preparing a fully verified mission data load for fighters with the latest Block 3F software, expected delays to accuracy tests of bombs and missiles, and open deficiencies causing shortfalls in fielding Block 3F capabilities.

On 11 April 2018 the F-35 flew its final developmental flight test, effectively capping off the development phase of the program. Eleven years of developmental flight testing included more than 9,200 sorties, the accumulation of over 17,000 flight hours, and the execution of more than 65,000 test points to verify the design, durability, software, sensors, weapons capability and performance for all three F-35 variants. Lockheed Martin's Vice President and General Manager of the F-35 Program Greg Ulmer called it the 'most comprehensive, rigorous and the safest developmental flight test program in aviation history.' The development test phase was thus a nearly 12-year-long effort which cost approximately $60 billion dollars. To place this figure in perspective, the entire F-22 program was assessed after its completion to have cost little over $67 billion, including all costs of development, testing and production of 199 demonstrator, test, and service airframes, despite significant cost overruns in all of these areas.[8]

Although the F-35's completion of its development test phase had been significantly delayed, delays would have been considerably greater had the Joint Program Office (JPO) not significantly watered down requirements to achieve this major program milestone, including by controversially deleting a number of important test points. The JPO thus avoided the appearance of further delays by lowering standards. Commenting on this process and its implications with concern, analysts at *The War Zone* noted at the time:

> Perhaps more worrying is the fact that, despite gathering data on more than 65,000 test points, the F-35 program only met this much delayed SDD [System Development and Demonstration] flight test schedule by deleting additional test points and accepting potentially flawed data. According to DOT&E [Director Operational Test & Evaluation], significant numbers of test flights involved aircraft with earlier editions of the critical, but troublesome onboard mission software, among other things, which may not reflect the actual capabilities of the stealth fighters as they exist now.[9] *

The Project on Government Oversight criticised the JPO's decision as arbitrary and not reflecting actual progress in the program, asserting: 'Instead of completing the presently planned development work, the Program Office is now proposing to substitute a vaguely defined F-35 upgrade program called "continuous capability development and delivery (C2D2)" ... the proposed plan is just a way to hide major development delays and cost overruns while facilitating increased annual production buys of incompletely developed F-35s.' This was seen as necessary as the program had 'entered an unprecedented seventeenth year of continuing redesign, test deficiencies, fixes, schedule slippages, and cost overruns,' and was still far from the 'finish line.'[10] Shifting a greater burden of testing to the Continuous Capability Development and Delivery program had again moved the goalposts to mask the extent of delays, allowing the System Development and Demonstration phase to be concluded by reducing the requirements to do so. The latest annual report from the Director, Operational Test & Evaluation criticised the plan as 'not executable due to inadequate test resources' in the rapid timelines proposed.[11]

In December 2018 the F-35 began its Initial Operational Test & Evaluation (IOT&E) phase, three months behind the most recent and already much delayed schedule, by which time the course of the program had cemented a consensus among analysts that further significant delays were highly probable. IOT&E was conducted by the Pentagon's independent testing office, and would fully assess the readiness of the three F-35 variants for actual combat, including confirming that they met not only performance requirements, but also maintenance requirements, and that production was being carried out efficiently. This testing represented the final part in the F-35's System Development and Demonstration phase, after which the aircraft could formally begin full-scale production.

On 18 October 2019, the Pentagon's acquisition executive announced that the Department of Defense would refuse to clear the F-35 for full-rate production, meaning that the IOT&E phase would continue into the next decade. The Pentagon had previously intended to approve full-rate production by the end of 2019. Under Secretary of Defense for Acquisition and Sustainment Ellen Lord told reporters that the Department of Defense would have to defer this by up to 13 months.[12] A key contributor to delays was that the Joint Simulation Environment, which was relied on to conduct evaluations of the F-35 in a range of simulated high-threat scenarios, faced serious and persistent delays in development through the late 2010s and into the early 2020s.[13]

---

* The shifting of goalposts to mask the extent of delays was far from unprecedented within the F-35 program. A notable prior example was the JPO's watering down of the Block 3 standard, which was supposed to be fully functional, to develop the interim limited capability Block 3i software suite, followed by the Block 3F – F standing for 'final.' This significantly reduced the appearance of delays in reaching the Block 3 standard by lowering the standards that needed to be met with the addition of Block 3i.

In November the Pentagon's director of operational testing, Robert Behler, stated that the F-35 continued to fall short of full combat readiness targets, and elaborated on some of its most significant prevailing issues. Despite some progress on reliability issues, all three versions were breaking down 'more often than planned,' while none were meeting their five key 'reliability or maintainability metrics.' A key challenge was the mean flight hours between critical failure, in which the F-35's progress lagged by 'a large margin.' 'The operational suitability of the F-35 fleet remains at a level below service expectations ... The results show that neither the F-35B nor F-35C currently is on track to meet ORD [Operational Requirements Document] reliability or maintainability requirements when they attain flight-hour maturity,' he stated, adding that the fighter had not been 'able to meet any of the ORD's full reliability or maintainability requirements for mature aircraft,' and that all variants were taking longer than expected to fix after each breakdown.[14] The Pentagon on this basis denied Lockheed Martin permission to begin full-scale production of the F-35.

In October 2020, spokeswoman for the office of Under Secretary of Defense for Acquisition and Sustainment Jessica Maxwell announced that the final decision on certifying the F-35 for full-scale production had again been delayed by a year. Instead, 'production of the F-35 will continue in [low-rate initial production] in accordance with Congressional authorization and appropriation.' It had previously been expected that full-scale production would begin in March 2021.[15] Continued delays authorising full-scale production caused growing concern regarding the state of the program, with analysts at *The War Zone* summarising: 'the continued failure to complete IOT&E — and in turn trigger a full-rate production decision — means that question marks will continue to hang over the viability of the jet, especially in the kinds of high-end warfare scenarios in which the F-35 is anticipated to fight for decades to come.'[16]

As commented by analysts at *Defense News*: 'The Pentagon is already buying the F-35 in numbers that would qualify as full-rate production for most aircraft procurement programs,' with 134 F-35s delivered to all clients in 2019. Regarding full-scale production, they observed: 'the milestone is considered an important show of confidence in the maturity of the program; it signifies that the aircraft has been fully tested in operational conditions.' This raised further controversies regarding the concurrency process, with full-scale production proceeding in all but name despite the aircraft's capabilities failing to meet requirements.[17]

Operationalising the F-35B: A Controversial Process

On 20 November 2012, the 3rd Marine Aircraft Wing equipped with F-18C/D Hornet fighters was re-designated as Marine Fighter Attack Squadron 121 (VMFA-121), with this designation reflecting the new roles it would fulfil as the first operational F-35 squadron in the United States Marine Corps and the world. Three years later on 31 July 2015 the Commandant of the Marine Corps General Joseph Dunford declared that the F-35B had gained an Initial Operating Capability with VMFA-121 following a five-day operational readiness inspection. The commandant stated at the time that he had full confidence in the F-35B's ability to support Marines in combat, with ten F-35Bs in the Block 2B configuration at the time fielded by the squadron.[18] While Lockheed Martin had by that time delivered around 150 F-35s to the Air Force, Marines, Navy and foreign clients, these were the sole 10 aircraft in service.

Significant controversy surrounded the decision to declare VMFA-121's F-35Bs as operationally capable while they still relied on Block 2B software, with this not only seriously limiting the aircraft's manoeuvrability and sensors, but also leaving them compatible with just three different weapons – a 500-pound laser-guided bomb, a 2,000-pound GPS-guided bomb and the AIM-120 radar-guided air-to-air missile. The fighters had no weapons for visual range air-to-air combat, with even the F-35B's gun taking a further five years to be made ready, nor did they have any beyond visual range air-to-surface or anti-ship weapons.

The declaration of an initial operating capability for the F-35B became significantly more controversial after the contents of a memo from the Director of Operational Test and Evaluation obtained through the Freedom of Information Act revealed the true state of the fleet, and highlighted that the aircraft were very far from being operationally viable. While a demonstration of the F-35B's performance on the amphibious assault ship USS *Wasp*, Operational Test One, was hailed by officials as a rebuttal to the program's critics,[19] according to the DOT&E report this was not an actual operational test 'in either a formal or an informal sense of the term.' The test 'did not — and could not — demonstrate that Block 2B F-35B is operationally effective or suitable for use in any type of limited combat operation, or that it was ready for real-world operational deployments, given the way the event was structured.' Operational testing required conditions closely matching those that would realistically be seen in combat operations.[20]

F-35A from early production batches as seen in markings it wore at the time the IOT&E began in late 2018. (USAF)

The DOT&E report highlighted the extent to which personnel had difficulties keeping six F-35Bs flight worthy for the brief demonstration, which included having to substitute one F-35B with another 'due to a fuel system fault that would have been impractical to fix at sea given the maintenance workload.' Unlike in an actual operational scenario, over 20 additional aircraft that would make up the rest of the Air Combat Element were kept off deck, while combat mission systems were absent either because they were not cleared for use or were simply not installed. Software unavailability meant nose apertures for the infrared Distributed Aperture System, night vision camera, and several radar modes on many of the aircraft were all unavailable, with this not expected to be resolved until 2017 at the earliest when Block 3F software became available.[21]

The DOT&E report further observed that software degradations which would need to be addressed in combat 'were often ignored during this event, as long as the aircraft were able to safely conduct the event's limited training objectives.' Issues with the radio, radar, and the Electro-Optical Targeting System were notably not included as part of potential maintenance work orders, as maintenance crews 'made no attempt to fix these during this detachment.' Furthermore, the fighters would not be cleared to carry any ordnance during the supposed operational test.[22] As concluded by analysts at the *Project on Government Oversight*: 'the number of mechanical and electronic maintenance problems during this short period of time, and on such a highly publicised event, is remarkable,' highlighting that DOT&E revelations regarding the test made it appear to be 'no more than a PR exercise.'[23]

The ten F-35Bs were never able to achieve the planned number of flight hours on any day of the exercise, and on the worst days achieved just 16.6 percent and 24 percent of intended time in the air. The fighters were consistently rendered Non-Mission Capable due to accidents, in one case after an aircraft's very first flight, and 50 to 66 percent of them were often out of service forcing planned missions to be cancelled. One of the six aircraft, BF-37, could fly only one actual mission, with even its sole brief flight ending in an emergency diversion to Marine Corps Air Station Cherry Point. The majority of flights were made by just two of the aircraft, BF-23 and BF-38, as they were the only ones in the ten-fighter squadron which could remain airworthy.

During the test no less than 80 embarked contractor personnel from Lockheed Martin, Pratt & Whitney, and Rolls Royce all needed to be on hand onboard the USS *Wasp* for maintenance support – none of which would be available under actual combat conditions. The unreliability of the Automatic Logistics Global Sustainment system forced the Marines to use non-operationally representative supply system workarounds, including for basic tasks such as fuelling the fighters. Despite its basic nature, the exercise required 'several ad hoc supply actions to obtain spare parts … that could not have been accomplished in a timely or a practical manner when operationally deployed' – including extraordinary runs for parts using MV-22 aircraft specially on hand specifically for this purpose.* 'This level of support should not be expected as normal for combat deployments once away from the continental United States,' the report noted, highlighting that without supplies consistently being flown in by helicopter, F-35s could not have been restored from Non-Mission Capable status as they frequently were. DOT&E concluded that even with these tremendous advantages that were far from representative of combat conditions, 'it was difficult for the Marines to keep more than two to three of the six embarked jets in a flyable status on any given day.' Actual combat conditions would make this 'substantially tougher.'[24]

As concluded in a *Project on Government Oversight* report in September 2015, citing the revelations from the DOT&E report: 'It's clear that the F-35B's IOC declaration does not establish that any necessary combat capabilities have actually been achieved. It simply establishes that the Joint Strike Fighter Program Office and the Marine Corps were doggedly determined to reap the public relations benefits of meeting their artificial IOC deadline — even if in name only — no matter what.'[25] It would not be until 2019, four years later and 19 years after the F-35's first demonstrator flight, that the aircraft would gain something resembling an initial operating capability, albeit still far below the requirements of combat readiness. Misleading declarations of the F-35B's combat readiness were notably not isolated to the particular variant, with the F-35A's deployment for exercises indicating a degree of readiness being dismissed by analysts at 'P.R. Stunts' aimed at 'shoring up the F-35's image,' on the basis that key features were still barely functioning or missing entirely.[26] Highly misleading declarations regarding the F-35 program's progress would continue to be made as it faced serious issues throughout its development and modernisation.[27]

F-35B First Deployments: Precision Bombing From Korea to Afghanistan

In January 2017 Marine Fighter Attack Squadron 121's ten F-35Bs, operating within the 3rd Marine Aircraft Wing, began their first operational deployment, which was the first ever for an F-35 unit. Nine days after departing from their home base at Marine Corps Air Station (MCAS) Yuma in Arizona, they arrived at Marine Corps Air Station Iwakuni in Yamaguchi Prefecture, Japan. The deployment occurred three months after the unit's pilots and maintainers participated in Developmental Test III and the Lightning Carrier Proof of Concept Demonstration aboard the amphibious assault ship USS *America*, which was intended to ensure they could operate the F-35B in harsh sea conditions.[28]

The first foreign deployment of F-35s positioned the aircraft optimally not only to support the broader Pivot to Asia initiative aimed at prioritising America's military presence in the Western Pacific, but also more specifically to support the new Donald Trump administration's efforts to convey shows of force to North Korea, as longstanding tensions between Pyongyang and Washington came to a head that year. On 30 August 2017, four of VMFA-121's F-35Bs would be deployed for their first show of force near North Korean airspace, escorting a pair of B-1B strategic bombers, before dropping live GBU-32 Joint Direct Attack Munitions, the largest bomb the F-35B's smaller weapons bays could accommodate, at the Pil-sung training range in South Korea. When taxiing out for departure from MCAS Iwakuni, images published by the Pentagon showed that the aircraft were equipped with live AIM-120 missiles on their inner internal hard points, which was interpreted by some analysts as an attempt to further intimidate Pyongyang.[29] The operations ultimately failed to deter North Korea from completing development of an intercontinental range nuclear missile deterrent that year, which

* For example, one F-35B needed a replacement fuel boost pump. None were available on board, so one was flown in from Norfolk Naval Air Station on an MV-22. Maintainers attempted to install the replacement part, but they found it had been damaged at some point either before or during transport. Three more identical parts were later transferred to ensure at least one undamaged part would be available. Logistics issues were exacerbated by 'numerous errors' with related data, including missing files and inconsistencies between home station and deployed files. Technicians were forced by the sheer size of the files to process them using civilian wireless internet off base, after which Lockheed Martin database administrators corrected it.

An F-35B operated by the Marine Fighter Attack Squadron 121 during a deployment to the Marine Corps Air Station Iwakuni, Japan, on 2 February 2017. (USMC)

placed the country in a strong position to pursue de-escalation on favourable terms the following year. With the country's airspace being among the most densely defended in the world, the lack of a meaningful stealth fighter strike capability with high diameter ordnance, in large part due to the major delays the F-35 program faced, was widely criticised as having weakened Washington's hand in the conflict.

In June 2016 Marine Attack Squadron 211 was re-designated as Marine Fighter Attack Squadron 211, and transitioned from AV-8B Harrier II to the F-35B. The change in designation reflected the fact that the Harrier was an attack jet, while the F-35 was a multirole fighter aircraft which would allow the unit to operate in a much wider range of roles. As the Marine Corps' second F-35B squadron, VMFA-211 would primarily deploy from amphibious assault ships, with two of its fighters conducting the first deck landing qualifications on the Wasp-class ship USS *Essex* in August. Wasp-class and newer America-class ships were designed long before the F-35B was tested, and due to the far greater heat levels given off by the aircraft during take-off and landing compared to the Harrier, both ship classes required extensive modifications to accommodate them. These modifications could take over ten months to complete, and required deep restructuring to move lighting, ventilation, piping, wiring, mechanical systems, and a range of other subsystems deeper below flight decks to insulate them from the F-35B's engines.

The need for extensive modifications to the new America-class ships, which were built specifically to deploy F-35Bs, was widely criticised as a negative consequence of the concurrency approach. With the heat given off by the fighter's engines far exceeding expectations earlier in the program, a number of analysts asserted that it would have been far cheaper and less time consuming to build the carriers only after the fighter's design had been fully finalised.[30] The F-35B's far greater heat emissions also prevented it from operating from Nimitz- and Gerald Ford-class supercarriers alongside the F-35C, in contrast to the Harrier which had on a small number of occasions done so alongside the F-18C/D.

Four F-35Bs operated by the Marine Fighter Attack Squadron 121 accompanied by three Republic of Korea Air Force F-15Ks. (ROKAF)

Two years after VMFA-211 transitioned to operate the F-35B, the USS *Essex* on 10 July 2018 departed Naval Base San Diego for a deployment to the Middle East under the Fifth Fleet, marking the first deployment of American-operated F-35s to the region. It had been widely speculated that this deployment would see the U.S. Armed Forces make their first use of the F-35 in combat, likely for attacks on the remnants of the Islamic State terror group. On 25 September, VMFA-211 was confirmed to have conducted reconnaissance missions over or near Somalia, with its F-35Bs reportedly having been ready to respond to any requests for close air support that U.S. forces in the country may have made.[31] This occurred amid ongoing conflict in Somalia's southern regions, which the Pentagon had designated the previous year as an area of active hostilities. The USS *Essex* was at the time sailing off the coast of the Horn of Africa where its air wing was due to conduct a routine training exercise. With the Harrier having had relatively negligible reconnaissance capabilities and a much lower endurance, operations in Somalia demonstrated how the F-35B had totally transformed the mission scope for amphibious assault ships. While Marine Expeditionary Units were particularly well optimised to responding to such regional crises, they had never had fighters capable of supporting these operations in a remotely comparable way. The F-35B's maiden deployment from such a ship also demonstrated the value of being able to rapidly redeploy, and to do so from a vessel much smaller than a supercarrier.

On 27 September it was announced that VMFA-211, deploying from the *Essex*, had conducted strikes against a fixed target in Afghanistan 'in support of ground clearance operations,' with the operation deemed a success by the ground force commander.[32] With the F-35 still considered incapable of striking moving targets, the kinds of target the aircraft's first bombing raid could be launched against were limited. Deploying new fighters for limited air strikes against non-state actors with little to no air defence capabilities allowed them to be declared to be combat tested with no more cost and risk than a training operation, with the F-22 having similarly seen its first combat operation four years prior in September 2014 striking an Islamic State command and control building. France would similarly burnish the credentials of its Rafale fighter in 2011, after ten years of persistent failures to market it for export, by declaring it to be combat tested after strikes on Libya – something which Vietnam War era F-4Es could have done due to the negligible resistance faced. The British Royal Air Force, meanwhile, could claim to have gained its first kill in air-to-air combat in over 70 years in December 2021, when a Eurofighter shot down a 'small hostile drone' deployed by jihadist insurgents in Syria.[33] Post Cold War fighters' lack of meaningful combat testing was most prominently illustrated by the circulation of an edited image of an F-22 showing a balloon kill marking in February 2023, after the aircraft shot down a Chinese weather balloon, which marked the only air-to-air operation in the air superiority fighter's more than 17 years in service.[34] Even more so than the F-35, use of the F-22 for strikes on Islamist militant groups, which any other American fighter could have done equally effectively, was seen as highly wasteful and faced criticism both externally and within the Air Force.[35] It mirrored the similar maiden combat use of the F-117 during the U.S. invasion of Panama in December 1989 to strike an empty field outside a barracks building, with the declaration that the aircraft had been utilised in combat then used to deflect criticism from the costly program.[36]

The absence of opportunities for meaningful combat testing was in many respects advantageous for the troubled F-22 and F-35 programs, since both could without significant risk be declared to have achieved Initial Operating Capabilities at times when their development was far less mature than had been the case for their Cold War era predecessors. This was done in confidence that beyond air strikes on undefended and non-moving targets, the requirement to participate in more difficult operations that seriously tested their combat potentials was highly unlikely to emerge for several years. The F-15 and F-16, by contrast, were very intensively combat tested within a few years of entering service, reflecting the much more intense nature of global conflict in the Cold War era.

An F-35B from Marine Fighter Attack Squadron 211 launches from the flight deck of Wasp-class amphibious assault ship USS *Essex* on August 30, 2018. (USN)

Deploying ten F-35Bs, Marine Fighter Attack Squadron 211 flew approximately 100 combat sorties over Afghanistan, Iraq and Syria over a period of 50 days while operating under the Fifth Fleet, averaging one sortie every five days per fighter. This contingent was larger than usual, which was speculated to have been required to compensate for the F-35's still very low availability rates and the high possibility of bugs and maintenance issues. Wasp-class carriers were typically expected to deploy approximately six F-35Bs, with the extra four being accommodated at the expense of MV-22 and CH-53E transport helicopters. Nevertheless, the ships could also be configured to serve entirely as aircraft carriers for the fighters, in which case each could deploy up to 20 F-35Bs – a configuration referred to as the Lightning Carrier. Where this had been far from desirable when the Marine Corps had relied on the Harrier, the combat capabilities and range of which were very limited, the F-35B made the fielding of amphibious assault ships as lighter aircraft carriers highly viable. The difficulties and inefficiencies of operating both STOVL fighters and helicopters simultaneously from an assault ship, which during the era of the Harrier was found to be nearly impossible at night, created a further incentive to form more specialised air wings.[37]

Reflecting the new realities of operating amphibious assault ships as aircraft carriers, the Wasp-class' successor, the America-class, was designed from the outset with a greater emphasis on such operations. Displacing approximately 45,000 tons, the ships were 11 percent larger, while the first two had much expanded aviation facilities at the expense of sacrificing their well decks used for amphibious landings. U.S. Navy amphibious assault ships were much larger than the aircraft carriers deployed by most countries, with continental Europe's largest aircraft carrier the nuclear powered ship *Charles de Gaulle* being lighter than America-class assault ships at 42,500 tons. The F-35B's potential to transform this fleet into a second aircraft carrier fleet if required was seen to be a primary factor in the America-class fleet being planned at 11 ships, where the Wasp-class had been planned at just eight. The much greater versatility and combat potential that air wings of 6-20 F-35Bs provided considerably increased the ships' importance to the Navy.

The Wasp-class amphibious assault ship USS *Essex* with six F-35B fighters on deck, alongside rotary wing aircraft. Based on the earlier Tarawa-class, these vessels were designed to operate significantly larger air wings. (USN)

F-35B Lightning II, operated by the Marine Fighter Attack Squadron (VMFA) 211, parked on the flight deck of Wasp-class amphibious assault ship USS *Essex* (LHD 2) on 4 Sept 2018. (USN)

The Wasp-class' ability to operate as an aircraft carrier was highlighted at the time of the F-35B's first deployment in the Middle East. Amphibious Squadron 1 Operations Officer Lieutenant Commander David Mahoney, for one, observed: 'We're definitely changing the way amphibs are employed, especially on the blue side – we're no longer just the trucks that carry Marines that we used to be ... the Amphibious Ready Group is now becoming almost like a mini Carrier Strike Group [CSG], where as part of the warfare concept we were executing many of those duties that would normally reserve to a CVN [nuclear-powered aircraft carrier].' Regarding how this changed Wasp-class and America-class ships' position in the fleet, he added: 'We are being treated as a CSG in a lot of respects: you can see that layered defence, so we were always bringing in destroyers to help work with us.' He would particularity stress that the F-35B's introduction significantly changed the Navy's mindset for how the assault ships could be used.[38]

Further elaborating on the shift, 13th Marine Expeditionary Unit (MEU) Commanding Officer Colonel Chandler Nelms observed: 'The aircraft we had before was predominantly a close-air support weapon, so for any type of air threat we were relying either on the naval surface force ship or we were relying on purple (joint) air to provide that top cover for anti-air warfare.' By contrast, with the F-35B's introduction, he observed: 'We now have an all-mission-capable aircraft that's also capable of stealth operations and has fantastic sensors at the disposal of the MEU commander when I'm doing ship-to-shore operations or ashore operations, but also at the disposal of the commodore as he seeks to maintain maritime and air superiority. So the difference is vast.' Comparing F-35B operations from amphibious assault ships to traditional carrier operations, he added:

> [W]e have limitations on an amphibious ship that's unlike a carrier. So we don't have the number of aircraft and we don't have the flight window of a carrier – we can't do 24-hour operations, we don't have 60 aircraft on the flight deck, we have a much smaller number. But when applied, when you want that capability, it's there. And we can do very high-end things for limited durations in our tasking, whether it's in the maritime environment or the littoral environment ship-to-shore.[39]

On 11 October 2018, a month into the USS *Essex's* deployment to the Middle East, the warship was confirmed to have entered the Strait of Hormuz, where the presence of American warships had long been a particularly sensitive issue for Iran. It was thus far from ideal that when the *Essex* entered the Persian Gulf on what should have been a show of force, its F-35Bs were all grounded due to the discovery of a faulty fuel tube inside the aircraft's engine – one suspected of having contributed to the 28 September crash of an F-35B near Marine Corps Air Station Beaufort. The *Essex* was subsequently aggressively shadowed by Iranian patrol boats.

On 12 December the USS *Essex* began joint exercises in the Arabian Sea with the Nimitz-class supercarrier USS *John C. Stennis*, which had just arrived in the region. This included an in-flight refuelling of an F-35B from one of the *Stennis*' F-18F fighters. The following month the assault ship sailed to the Pacific, anchoring off the coast of Phuket, Thailand, on 24 January, before pulling into Apra Harbor, Guam, on 8 February, and concluding its deployment on 1 March. This marked the end of the first ever F-35 carrier deployment, which had been extended by a month to reach 234 days.

Although Block 2B standard F-35Bs were capable of making very low intensity contributions to overseas operations, the aircraft's availability rates continued to further seriously limit their value to the U.S. Armed Forces. Figures released in early 2019 revealed that the average number of fully mission capable Marine F-35Bs had over the past two years never exceeded 25 percent, falling to 12.9 percent

A pair of F-35Bs from the Marine Fighter Attack Squadron 211, 13th Marine Expeditionary Unit, underway over Afghanistan in September 2018. (USAF)

in October 2017, and a year later staying at 12-13 percent. Combat operations from the USS *Essex* saw F-35Bs fly an average of one sortie every three days. This compared poorly to fourth generation aircraft, such as the F-16, F-15 and A-10, which had demonstrated the ability to fly more than one sortie per day. The A-10, which had consistently had the highest combat readiness rates, had during its first combat deployment been able to fly 420 percent as many sorties daily as the F-35B had.[40]

Operationalising the F-35A and First Deployments

On 2 August 2016, the Air Force announced that an Initial Operating Capability for the F-35A had been attained, with fighters operated by the 34th Fighter Squadron of the 388th Fighter Wing based at Hill Air Force Base in Utah declared operational. Established in 1944, and having operated F-16s from 1979–2010, the unit had been disbanded for five years before being reactivated in 2015, and receiving its first two F-35As on 2 September that year.[41]

Much as had been the case with the Marines, the Air Force's requirements for declaring an Initial Operating Capability were far lower than they had been for previous fighter types, with the goalposts for this major program milestone having been shifted significantly, minimising the appearance of delays. The Air Force had at the beginning of the decade intended to declare IOC only when full Block 3 software and capabilities were operationalised. This was intended to be achieved no later than October 2016. The Block 3 standard, although still highly constrained, was considered sufficient to allow the aircraft to perform its full range of missions. Delays, however, meant that the capabilities initially envisaged for Block 3 would not be reached until 2018 at the earliest.

In February 2012 the head of the Air Combat Command General Mike Hostage erased the Air Force's timeline set in 2010 for declaring the F-35A's IOC, replacing it with a new plan that was 'not date driven' and did not require full Block 3 software as a precondition for IOC. This plan was subsequently revised, however, with a new deadline for IOC set at December 2016. With the F-35A's software expected to still be far from reaching the Block 3 standard by that time, due to significant delays to the program, the Air Force created a new software standard – Block 3i standing for 'interim'. This left the aircraft little more combat ready than the Block 2B Marine F-35Bs, and able to conduct only very basic ground-attack missions, and even these only in undefended airspace.[42]

Two factors led the Air Force to revise this plan, and rather than wait for Block 3 software to become available, arbitrarily create the Block 3i milestone with a new deadline. The first factor was that the House of Representatives on 18 May 2012 wrote language into the 2013 National Defense Authorization Act requiring the Pentagon to set deadlines for bringing the F-35 into service. The second, highlighted in the Air Combat Command's official history for 2013, which was obtained two years later by Freedom of Information Act, was that the Air Force leadership were worried that the absence of a firm deadline for war-readiness would hurt the F-35's export prospects. 'Too much of a delay could discourage partners from buying or participating at all,' it was observed. 'However, the Air Staff made it clear that they wanted to avoid "F-22 déjà vu" by sacrificing capabilities to meet timeline pressures.' While a 2018 date was considered achievable for integrating full Block 3 software, which came to be known as Block 3F, 'Hostage began to realise the overall negative repercussions associated with waiting,' with his concerns reinforced by feedback from lawmakers.[43]

As summarised at the time by analysts at *The War Zone*: 'the F-35 program has chronically shared an absurdly bright view of the F-35's progress, even though the facts have suggested otherwise ... declaring IOC with the aircraft still so immature is really just ... a PR move.' The F-35 was 'pushed to operational status long before testing has concluded. In fact, the jet has not even started operational testing, which has been pushed back to early 2018,' while reports of its deployments and operations overseas, all of them at very low intensity, were 'not indicative of the aircraft's developmental state.'[44] The effective moving of the IOC goalposts for public relations purposes was otherwise effectively summarised as follows by analysts at *War is Boring*:

> To satisfy Congress while also reassuring the dozens of countries that had invested in, or might invest in, the Joint Strike Fighter program, Air Combat Command proclaimed that its F-35A version of the new warplane would be war-ready no later than December 2016. But there was a catch — one that the Air Force has not been keen to publicise. In order to meet the end-of-2016 deadline, the flying branch had to badly water down the F-35 ... The jet fighter that the Air Force plans to debut sometime before January 2017 is a weak version of itself. One that by the military's own admission won't be capable of reliably winning a high-tech battle.[45]

In August 2016, as the first USAF F-35s were declared operational, the head of the Air Combat Command General, Herbert Carlisle, stated regarding future plans for the 34th Fighter Squadron: 'I would like to deploy it to both the European and the Pacific theatre in the not-too-distant future, so I would say within 18 months I think I'll try to get to both those theatres.'[46] Eight of the 34th Fighter Squadron's F-35s were briefly deployed to RAF Lakenheath in the United Kingdom in April 2017, marking the first USAF F-35 deployment to the continent. Two of the fighters were then flown on a training mission to Ämari Air Base in Estonia. The first operational deployment subsequently began in November, when a dozen F-35As and 300 airmen from the 34th Fighter Squadron began a six-month deployment to Kadena Air Base, Okinawa, which was one of the most high profile facilities due to its proximity to the Taiwan Strait. This represented the U.S. Pacific Command's first operational tasking for the F-35A, following the deployment of Marine F-35Bs under the command ten months prior.[47]

In September 2017 the 34th Fighter Squadron received the first Block 3F F-35As, with the upgraded software package then delivered to the 61st, 62nd, and 63rd Fighter Squadrons – three specialised training units at Luke Air Force Base in Arizona. This milestone was referred to by Lockheed Martin as providing F-35s with 100 percent of the software required for full warfighting capability, including data link imagery, full weapons, and embedded training.[48] The software allowed pilots to manoeuvre their fighters without artificial restrictions on g force, and improved targeting systems, situational awareness, and network centric warfare capabilities. It also allowed for employment of a wider range weapons intended for the aircraft – although still short of all weapons envisaged which many sources had erroneously reported at the time. Multiple issues were also resolved, most notably that of individual targets depicted by the radar, the distributed aperture system, the Electro-Optical Targeting System, and other onboard and off-board systems being displayed to pilots as multiple separate targets, which was a problem that had been consistently raised by pilots.[49]

Although Lockheed Martin and the Air Force both touted Block 3F software as providing 'full combat capability,' delivery of aircraft

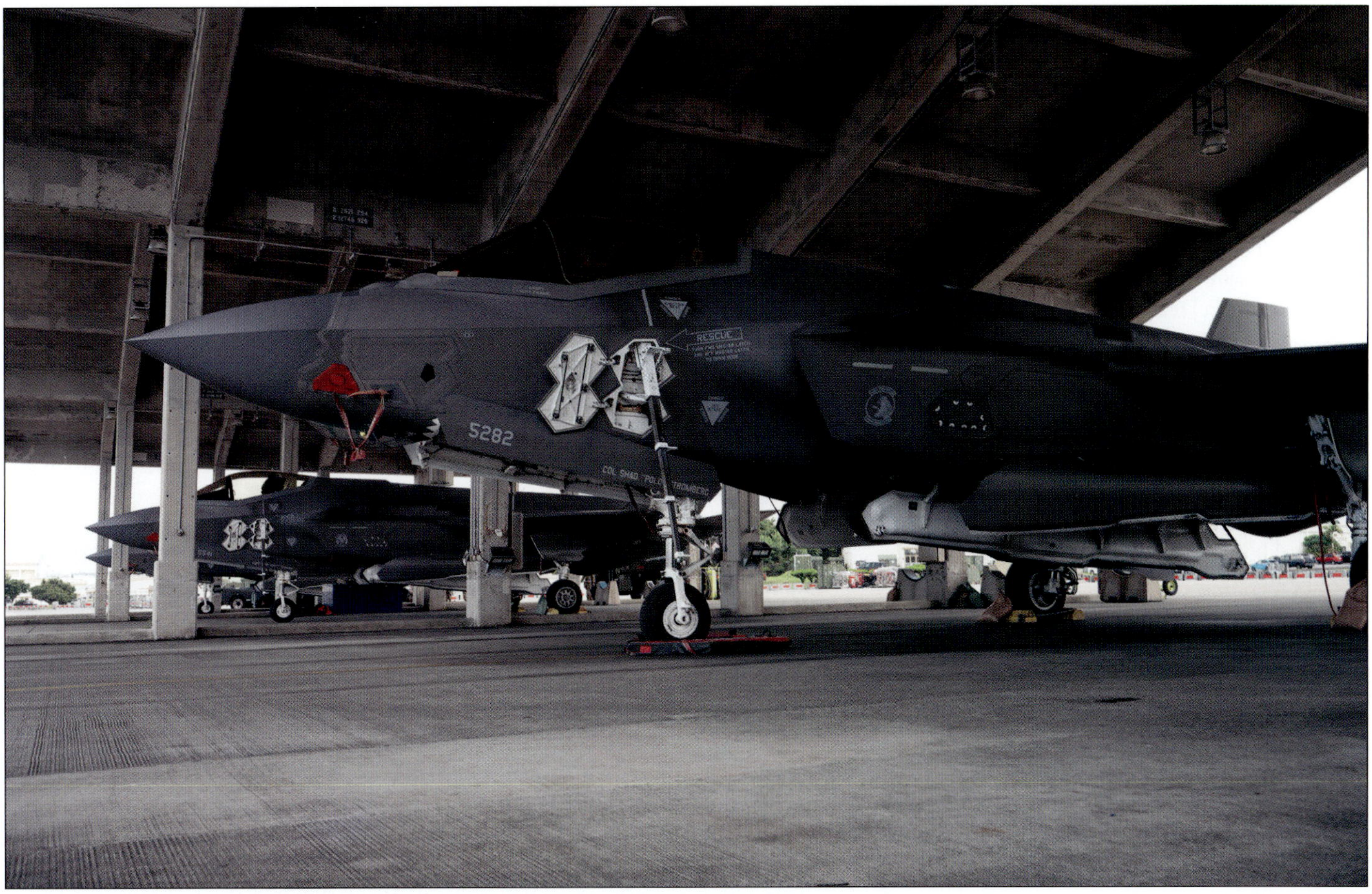

F-35As operated by the 34th Fighter Squadron under a shelter at Kadena Air Base, Japan. The squadron would rotate through the strategically located facility frequently particularly from late 2022. (USAF)

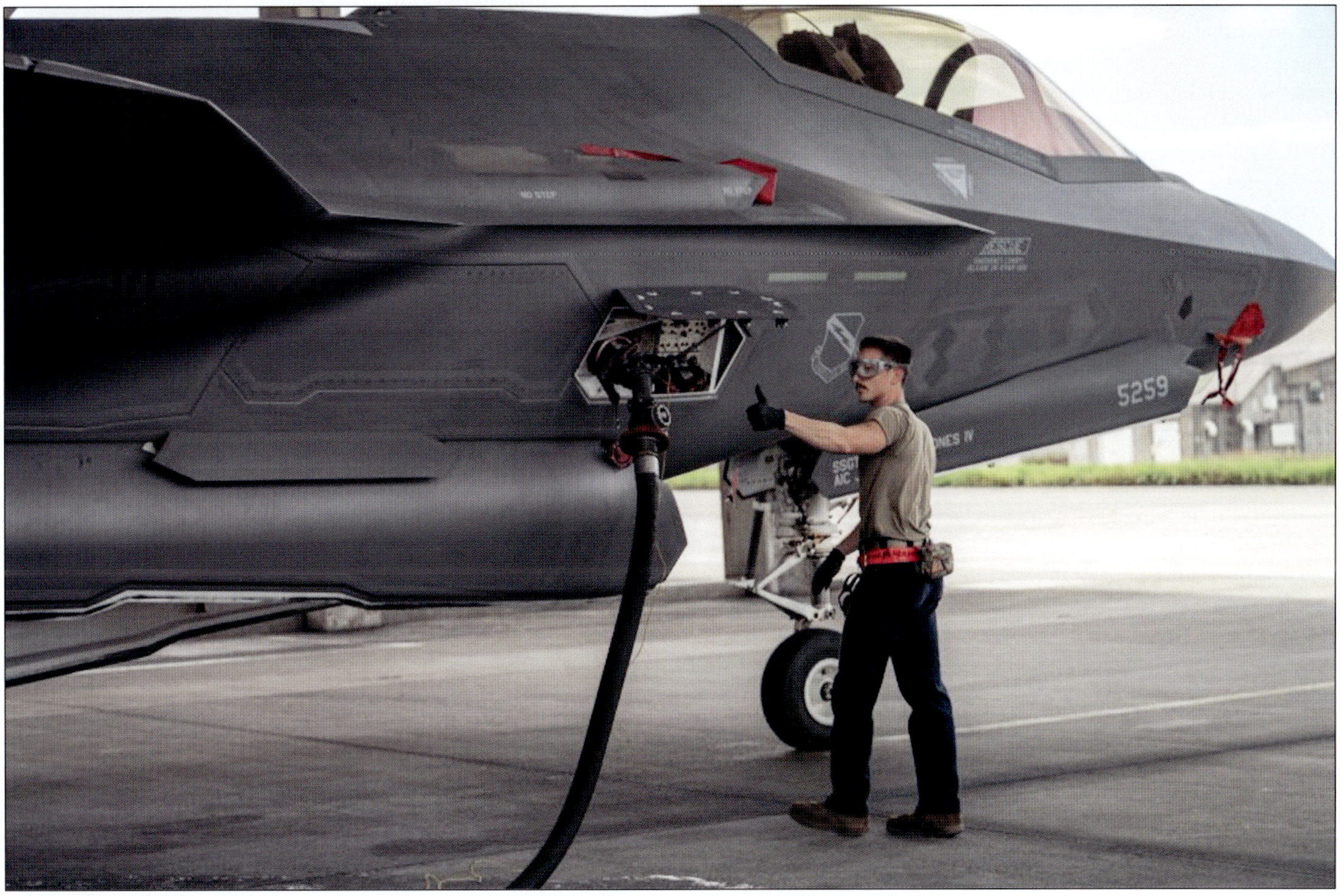

34th Fighter Squadron crew chief Airman 1st Class Gunnar Luna refuels an F-35A at Kadena Air Base, Japan. (USAF)

with this software was far from synonymous with the software completing proper testing, and there remained dozens of known deficiencies at the time when deliveries began.[50] Prevailing issues ranged from hypoxia-like symptoms suffered by F-35A pilots, not unlike the 'Raptor cough' that had affected F-22 pilots,[51] to an insufficient ability to share and display information either to the pilot, to other F-35s or to different assets within its network (see Chapter 6).[52] Although the Block 3F software package was installed, it would only be tested in an Initial Operations Test and Evaluation from December 2018, and would take many more years to be confirmed ready to allow the F-35 to enter medium or high intensity combat.

Operationalising the F-35C

On 28 February 2018 the Commander of Naval Air Forces Vice Admiral DeWolfe Miller III and the U.S. Marine Corps Deputy Commandant for Aviation Lieutenant General Steven Rudder jointly announced that the F-35C 'met all requirements and achieved an Initial Operating Capability,' thus meeting the Pentagon's long held goal of reaching this milestone before the end of the year.[53] Data on F-35 operations made available in early 2019, however, highlighted that the F-35C's status as a operational fighter remained seriously in question. While all F-35 variants' availability rates were poor, those of the F-35C were exceptionally so with an average of only around two percent of the fleet being fully mission capable at any given time. Assessing new data on the aircraft a year after it was declared to have achieved an IOC, the Project on Government Oversight concluded that the F-35C 'continues to dramatically underperform in crucial areas including availability and reliability, cyber-vulnerability testing, and life-expectancy testing.' 'The Navy is pushing ahead with the aircraft in spite of evidence that it is not ready for combat and could therefore put at risk missions, as well as the troops who depend on it to get to the fight,' it further observed.[54] Although less extreme than the case of the Marine Corps' declaration of an Initial Operating Capability for the F-35B, the discrepancy between the F-35C's declared capabilities, and the actual status of the fleet, was very significant.*

On 27 August 2018, F-35Cs were first deployed to launch from, land on, and manoeuvre around the flight deck of an aircraft carrier, namely the Nimitz-class supercarrier USS *Abraham Lincoln*, as part of operational testing. The carrier required a number of modifications, including adding classified spaces and installing more robust jet blast deflectors to be able to accommodate F-35Cs, as was the case for all Nimitz- and Gerald Ford-class ships. The F-35C deployment onboard the *Abraham Lincoln* was intended to assess how the aircraft 'integrates with the ship, how it interoperates with communications, data links, other aircraft, and then how we conduct the mission and tie into the other aircraft that are conducting that mission and how effective they are when they do it.'[55] Less than four months later, on 12 December 2018, officials declared that the first F-35C unit, Strike Fighter Squadron 147, had received its Safe for Flight designation, meaning it had become qualified for carrier landings and launches.[56] This paved the way for the aircraft to be evaluated for an Initial Operating Capability, which was declared to have been attained on 28 February 2019.[57] †

On 2 August 2021, the F-35C began its first ever operational deployment onboard an aircraft carrier, when the Nimitz-class supercarrier USS *Carl Vinson* departed from San Diego with the 10 stealth fighters from Strike Fighters Squadron 147 onboard, alongside some of the newest F-18E/F fighters in the Navy. The *Carl Vinson*'s air wing was unusual in that it included seven rather than five EA-18G electronic attack aircraft and five rather than four E-2D airborne warning and control systems, which alongside the F-35s formed what was referred to as the 'air wing of the future.' Much like the maiden overseas deployment of the F-35B, Washington's central focus on the Pacific, and on China in particular, made deployments to the region a priority for the most capable naval assets, with the strike group led by the *Carl Vinson* remaining in the region under the Tokyo-based 7th Fleet for the entirety of its 262 day deployment. Plans to deploy under the 5th Fleet in the Middle East were cancelled. This was the 'first deployment in a long time where the aircraft carrier and the strike group has stayed in the South China Sea, in the Philippine Sea, and in the 7th Fleet [area of responsibility],' according to 3rd Fleet Commander Vice Admiral Steve Koehler, who stressed that this was 'indicative of the competition amongst great powers. In the end, to compete, you've got to be on the court to win. And you all spending all that time in the 7th Fleet AOR [area of responsibility] is indicative of that competition.'[58]

The *Carl Vinson's* deployment reflected how the operations of carrier groups changed as the U.S. returned to an era of great power competition, with the F-35C, as the only carrier based fighter of the latest generation, being vital in supporting this change. Commanding Officer on the *Carl Vinson* Captain P. Scott Miller observed to this effect that compared to deployments under the 5th Fleet around the Middle East, deployments under the 7th Fleet in East Asia were: 'more of a mission of presence and being prepared to project power if required, as opposed to an active operational power projection mission.' 'There's a different shift in mindset for sure when you know you're going to go drop bombs… in a long-running conflict, [compared to] operating in or near specifically the [South China Sea] and not wanting to do that but needing to be prepared to respond in an appropriate manner at any moment,' he added.[59] While the F-18E/F had been developed for the post-Cold War era, and was an optimal workhorse for the era of the War on Terror, against China, which fielded its own highly sophisticated fifth generation fighter fleet, the F-35C's presence was critical.‡

The strike group's commander, Rear Admiral Dan Martin, would similarly elaborate regarding the shift in how carrier groups operated:

* Alongside performance issues, the F-35C also suffered from variant-specific manufacturing difficulties, with deliveries facing further delays in 2019-2020 as full-scale production was again postponed due to undisclosed 'production issues.' This led the Joint Program Office to dedicate a new assembly line to addressing the delays. (Trimble, Steve, 'JPO Dedicates Assembly Line To Fix U.S. Navy F-35C Delays,' *Aviation Week*, 23 January 2020.)

† To help support these operations, the Navy had on 12 January 2017 activated Strike Fighter Squadron 125, which had been disbanded since 2010, to serve as its first F-35C Fleet Replacement Squadron – a unit dedicated to providing training to services operating the class as it had previously done for the F-18. The unit received its first F-35Cs on 25 January.

‡ 'Once you even get close to the South China Sea, you can bank on Chinese ships coming out to meet you and escort you in,' Miller further noted, adding regarding the experience gained: 'All these sailors and all these young officers learned how to operate with a persistent presence of the PRC, day and night, so that meant standing alert, watches are fully energised throughout the night. And they figured out the resiliency piece of always being on edge, of moving the strike group quickly, keeping your speed up and being unpredictable.' (Eckstein, Megan, 'Three takeaways from the US Navy's first F-35C deployment,' *Defense News*, 15 February 2022.)

An F-35C of the Strike Fighter Squadron 147 in the process of touch-down for an arrested landing aboard the aircraft carrier USS *Carl Vinson* in late 2021. (USN)

> This deployment, I think, showcased what would be a paradigm shift in the way that the aircraft carrier and the strike group deployed ... Since I was a young lieutenant, we've been going to 5th Fleet and flying close air support missions for the Marines and the SEALs and Army on the ground, with air supremacy. This is just a complete change, with a near-peer competitor, with activity that is in the air, on the surface of the sea and below the surface of the sea. You have to shape the air wing to best handle that activity.[60]

The commander added that an expansion of the Navy's fighter squadrons from 14 to 20 aircraft could be important to supporting this. Regarding the F-35C, he observed: 'It's a brand-new aircraft with advanced sensors, so we like to pair that with a Growler to complement each other. And when you fly around that theatre ... they pull so much into the cockpit; the sensors onboard can see activity that other aircraft cannot.' He particularly emphasised the value of deploying E/A-18Gs to support F-35C operations, adding: 'we're advocating for more [Growlers] because we saw the value of that aircraft in theatre.'[61] It was noted that although the F-35C's dimensions were considerably smaller than those of the F-18E/F, the stealth fighter required significantly more support equipment, which caused some initial difficulties with deck space.

The F-35C's first deployment proceeded far from smoothly, and on 28 January 2022 the Navy confirmed the authenticity of leaked footage showing one of the aircraft crashing into the South China Sea after a landing mishap during routine flight operations.[62] The fighter was seen adding power and rapidly moving its flight control surfaces just before passing over the carrier's stern. The pilot and six sailors were injured during the incident. The loss of the aircraft caused serious concerns due to the possibility that ships from an adversary state could be the first to recover it, forcing the Navy closely survey the surrounding waters until a specialised salvage vessel arrived to recover it.

Following the loss of an F-35C during landing, further concerns were raised by the emergence of footage on the Pentagon's Defense Visual Information Distribution Service showing significant corrosion and rust on the fighters of Strike Fighter Squadron 147. The images were publicised on 29 January 2023, shortly before the USS *Carl Vinson* concluded its eight month deployment and returned to San Diego on February 14, and had been taken earlier in the month when the carrier had been underway in the Philippine Sea. The images indicated that the Navy had failed to maintain the aircraft and their notoriously sensitive radar absorbent skins, which had significant implications for their stealth capabilities. Reddish-brown lines and blotches covered most of the fighters' centre fuselages, wings, and tail surfaces and other upper surfaces, with the condition of lower surfaces not being shown. It remained uncertain whether this had affected the airframes themselves or only their stealth coatings.

Maintaining the radar-absorbent coatings of stealth aircraft had been a leading challenge since the F-117 first entered service, and was far more difficult at sea where the climate accelerated corrosion and facilities were relatively minimal. This was initially expected to be a leading challenge for the Navy operating the A-12 carrier based stealth fighter before its development was cancelled, with similar challenges expected for the F-35C despite the service having touted its 'minimal low observable maintenance, even in the harshest shipboard conditions.'[63] The rusting of F-35Cs on the USS *Carl Vinson* was notably far from isolated, and followed a broader and growing trend of key naval assets being seen rusting when returning from sea,[64] including Zumwalt-class stealth destroyers.[65]

With the F-35C being the only variant acquired for operation by two separate services in the U.S. Armed Forces, the Marine Corps received their first two of the aircraft on 21 January and 31 January 2020. After attaining Safe for Flight operations certification on 20 March, the Marine F-35Cs were announced on 1 December to have gained an Initial Operating Capability under Fighter Attack Squadron 314 (VMFA-314). This unit had previously been the first in the Corps to transition to F-18C/D Hornet, which it operated for 38 years from 1982, and before that had been the first to transition to the F-4 in 1961. Commissioning the F-35C was vital to allowing the Corps to continue its fighter operations from the Navy's nuclear powered supercarriers. VMFA-314 was the second F-35C squadron to be operationalised after Strike Fighter Squadron 147 in the Navy. The squadron's executive officer, Lieutenant Colonel Duncan French, highlighted 'the F-35C's unique capabilities, compared to the F-35B,' stressing its importance for Marine combat projection capabilities.[66]

VMFA-314 was declared fully operational in July 2021, and subsequently made its maiden carrier deployment from 3 January the following year onboard the USS *Abraham Lincoln*, alongside three Navy F-18E/F and one E/A-18G squadrons. The supercarrier would remain at sea for over seven months, returning on 11 August, and operated primarily in the Western Pacific. Rear Admiral J.T. Anderson, the commander of Carrier Strike Group, stressed that operations in the area 'were important to send a signal to China, North Korea, Russia of our commitment to the region,' elaborating: 'We spent a lot of time manoeuvring around not only the Philippine Sea, but also in the South China Sea and well as the East China Sea. And the dynamic manoeuvre wasn't just exclusively manoeuvring around to avoid certain things, but it was also that that's our best way of being able to compete in that space, as well as provide a strong presence throughout the region.'[67] The difficulties of adapting from 5th Fleet operations near the Middle East to the much more competitive climate under the 7th Fleet was again emphasised by commanders, as was the value of the lessons learned from the USS *Carl Vinson's* deployment a year prior.[68] Officials again stressed the value of the F-35C's capabilities, with Admiral Anderson emphasising 'the tremendous capability that the aircraft provides from an ability to generate information, the sensors that it has onboard, as well as its ability to distribute that information, not just to other aircraft but to the rest of the force.'[69]

U.S. Navy F-35C accelerating before takeoff from the USS *Carl Vinson*. (USN)

Photograph shows the F-35C that crashed into the sea while attempting to land on board the USS *Carl Vinson* on 24 January 2022. The photograph was verified by the 7th Fleet, U.S. Navy. (OedoSoldier)

Right: A top view at an F-35C of the Strike Fighter Squadron 147 parked in front of the island of the USS *Carl Vinson*. Traces of grease, rust and corrosion can be seen prominently on its spine. (USN)

Below: F-35Cs operated by Strike Fighter Squadron 147 about to launch from USS *Carl Vinson*, and also suffering from rust. (USN)

Consequences of Delays to F-35 Procurement

The F-35 was scheduled at the turn of the century to gain an initial operating capability in 2010, allowing it to replace fourth generation fighters which would begin to be retired throughout the decade. The aircraft's imminent service entry was consistently cited to support major cuts to the troubled F-22 program, on the basis that a much more reliable, versatile and cost effective fifth generation fighter would soon be available in much greater numbers.[70] It was also consistently cited as justification for ending acquisitions of fourth generation fighters, particularly by the Air Force. A notable example was Defense Secretary Robert Gates's projection in 2009 regarding the size of the fleet to justify the decision taken that year to end F-22 production: 'By 2020, the U.S. is projected to have nearly 2,500 manned combat aircraft of all kinds. Of those, nearly 1,100 will be the most advanced fifth generation F-35s and F-22s. China, by contrast, is projected to have no fifth generation aircraft by 2020.' This indicated a fleet of close to 900 F-35s by that year, where in reality only 318 were in service – 207 in the Air Force, 28 in the Navy and 83 in the Marine Corps.[71]

The degree to which the F-35 was relied on, not only as the fighter which would form the backbone of the Air Force's next generation as the F-16's successor, but also as the only fighter of its generation for the Navy, the Marine Corps, or for the remainder of the Western world, meant the fallout from delays to its development and procurement were nothing short of devastating. As the Chinese People's Liberation Army Air Force received its first fifth generation fighters in 2016, four years earlier than Secretary Gates had projected, and from 2022 accelerated acquisitions significantly, the U.S. Armed Forces by then

J-20 fifth generation fighter in yellow primer from the first serial production batch. The image was released on National Day, September 2016, shortly after the first deliveries to the Chinese People's Liberation Army Air Force, and five months before the type's entry into service. (机外停车 Rabbit on Weibo)

fielded just 660 fifth generation fighters. Worsening this was the fact that approximately forty percent its F-35s in service at the time, or 189 aircraft, were highly troubled early production models that were not expected to ever be made viable for high intensity combat. These were expected to fly for small fractions of their intended service lives due to structural defects, which made the discrepancy in numbers significantly narrower still.[72]

Not only were initial production models highly flawed, but across the fleet the extent of delays meant that many of the F-35's subsystems were far less cutting edge than they had been intended to be when they entered service. Examples ranged from the fighter's electro-optical targeting system, which by the mid-2010s was much less advanced than those of many fourth generation fighters, to the AN/APG-81 radar, which had to be phased out of production early.[73]

Serious delays to F-35 procurements required services that had ordered the aircraft to invest in the modernisation and life extension for older fourth generation fighters. The rising costs of procuring and sustaining new F-35s, however, was at the same time consistently cited as a factor forcing the Pentagon to make serious cuts to funding for the operation and upgrading of its fourth generation aircraft. Thus, as delays in developing and fielding the F-35 increased the need for fourth generation aircraft, its major cost overruns, particularly in terms of sustainment at the same time, reduced the funds available for fourth generation aircraft. The result was a shift between cutting life extension and upgrade programs for fourth generation fighters as the F-35's cost overruns became apparent, to then increasing investment in these programs as the full extent of delays to the F-35 program became increasingly clear.

Notable early examples of affected programs were the Service Life Extension Program and the Combat Avionics Programmed Extension Suite which were planned in the 2010s for 300 F-16s that had been procured in the 1990s. The former program involved replacing significant portions of their basic structures, while the latter involved the integration of new radars, defensive systems, communications equipment and digital monitors. The costly upgrades cost around one fifth as much per fighter as buying a new F-16 built to a similar standard. The need to finance the F-35's significant cost overruns was cited as a major factor in the Air Force's decision in 2013 to terminate both programs.[74]

Cuts to funding for the fourth generation fleet to accommodate the F-35 program's major cost overruns would continue to mount, with multiple sources citing the need for additional funding for the F-35 as a central factor in the Pentagon's decision to accelerate the decommissioning of nearly 500 A-10s, F-15s, F-16s and F-18s between 2007 and 2012 without replacement. This represented 15 percent of the country's entire fighter fleet.[75] The need to make cuts to accommodate the F-35's cost overruns would subsequently continue to be cited to justify the early retirement of older fighters as F-35s began to enter service, despite new F-35s replacing only a fraction of the aircraft being retired. A notable example was the first ever USAF facility to receive F-35As, Hill Air Force Base in Utah, where the Air Force in April 2015 argued in a memo to the House Armed Services Committee that retirement of A-10s was needed to ensure adequate funding for the new aircraft. This faced stiff opposition in Congress due to the A-10's perceived importance to the service's commitment to provide close air support to the Army. Where retirement of A-10s was not politically feasible, the Air Force instead moved to retire F-16s at the Hill Air Force Base early to accommodate the F-35's costs.[76]

By the mid-2010s, tremendous delays and cost overruns affecting the F-22 and F-35, and procurement rates of both at just fractions of planned levels, made it increasingly apparent that fourth generation fighters would need to play a much larger role in the Air Force into the 2030s and beyond than had originally been envisaged. As these aged, their operational costs and maintenance needs rose steeply. The issue gained growing attention from 2023, by which time the Air Force's F-15s and the bulk of its F-16 fleet had served

F-16C/D fighters operated by the 388th Tactical Fighter Wing permanently deployed at Hill Air Force Base, pictured here in 1990 during temporary deployment to Saudi Arabia. (USAF)

long beyond their planned service lives averaging thirty-eight and thirty-two years old. The much smaller rate of F-35 procurements than projected ensured that the average ages of the fourth generation fighters were set to continue to increase unless the older airframes were simply retired without replacement.

The ageing of the fourth generation fleet, and the lack of favourable options for its retirement, left a growing majority of the Air Force's fighter units out of date, which was particularly dangerous as adversaries fielded new generations of advanced air defence systems and '4+' and fifth generation fighters in growing numbers. More seriously still, however, as fighters aged their operational costs and maintenance needs rose, while availability rates fell. This had highly detrimental impacts not only on overall fleet availability, but also on training. Lieutenant General Joseph Guastella was among several figures in the Air Force leadership to highlight that the fleet's rising age was taking a serious toll on crews' flying hours.[77] 'We're on a collision course,' he stressed, warning that fighter force readiness could 'fall off a cliff.' This issue was only exacerbated by the fact that units which had transitioned to the F-22 or F-35 suffered from much lower availability rates and far higher maintenance needs, despite the airframes being new and lacking the decades of wear that affected fourth generation aircraft.[78] The Air Force was thus stuck between aircraft that had once been maintenance friendly but had been excessively worn out by flying far longer than intended, and newly delivered aircraft that were far from maintenance friendly from the outset, and would only become more problematic as they aged.

At the time of the publication of a Mitchell Institute policy paper addressing the issue, which was co-authored by General Guastella in June 2023, former U.S. Pacific Air Forces Vice Commander Lieutenant General (ret.) David Deptula was among the figures to highlight that Chinese pilots, flying fighters which were on average several decades newer, were getting more flying hours than their USAF counterparts. Additional training 'makes a difference,' he stressed, with this giving the Chinese fleet an important edge in better preparing itself for warfare at a fifth generation level.[79] This also had implications for potential clashes with more minor adversaries. While Russian fighter pilots, for example, had far less flight training hours than their Soviet predecessors, the fall in American training hours was gradually narrowing the previously large discrepancy that had favoured the USAF.

The highly problematic and much delayed introduction of the F-35, as well as the delayed and sharply reduced acquisitions of the F-22, would stimulate efforts to modernise older fourth generation fighters, while also fuelling calls for resumed procurement of these older types of aircraft. This contrasted sharply with the introduction of fourth generation fighters, which had provided a leading argument against investments in the modernisation of fighters from the preceding generation. In the 1970s and 1980s a number of ambitious modernisation programs had been developed for the USAF's primary type of third generation fighter the F-4E Phantom, many of which were highly comprehensive including the integration of entirely new armaments, engines and avionics. Similar proposals were also developed for the Soviet MiG-23ML, MiG-25 and MiG-27, and in some cases by foreign operators such as the joint Israeli-U.S. F-4-2000. The development of fourth generation successors, however, which were not only much more capable, but also far more cost effective to operate, provided a primary argument against the modernisation of older aircraft. The increase in interest in fourth generation fighters in the 2010s and 2020s thus reflected poorly on the states of the fifth generation programs.

The fuelling of support for plans to invest significantly in the modernisation and life extension of fourth generation fighters as a direct result of the F-35's delays, reduced procurement and availability rates, and major procurement and sustainment cost overruns, closely mirrored the way deep cuts to F-22 procurement stimulated reinvestment in the legacy F-15C/D fleet, which was forced to serve decades longer than expected. Work to integrate modern avionics onto the F-15C/D, including AN/APG-63(V)3 AESA radars, began in 2007,[80] while in the mid-2010s a life extension and modernisation program was planned for 179 aircraft. The final cost of this proposal, however, which stood at between \$30 and \$40 million per aircraft, was considered unacceptably high, with Air Combat Command chief General Mike Holmes stressing that increasing procurement of new aircraft, namely F-35s, was a more cost-effective alternative.[81]

The F-15 life extension program highlighted that the modernisation of older fighters to compensate for cuts or delays to

U.S. Air Force F-15C and F-35A fighters in formation. Repeated reductions in procurement of F-35s, and prior deep cuts to F-22 procurements, ensured that the F-35A would serve alongside a much larger fleet of F-15s and F-16s than had previously been planned. (USAF)

fifth generation fighter procurements was often not a cost-effective option. Not only did these old aircraft suffer from rising operational costs and falling availability rates, but the modernisation packages themselves often far exceeded the total costs which foreign countries paid to procure more advanced new fighters from production lines. To place the $30-40 million cost of F-15 modernisation in perspective, Russia's most costly fighter type, the fifth generation Su-57, had a flyaway cost in the early 2020s of just $35 million, although this varied depending on dollar-rouble exchange rates.[82]

On 7 June 2017, Northrop Grumman announced that it had received a contract to integrate the AN/APG-83 AESA radar onto 72 Air National Guard F-16s.[83] Mass production of the new radar had been financed by an order for 144 for the Republic of China Air Force in 2016, later reduced to 139, as part of upgrades to bring its F-16A/B fighters to the F-16V '4+ generation' standard.[84] The radar would ensure F-16s remained viable for air defence duties, with far higher situational awareness, greater electronic warfare capabilities, lower susceptibility to jamming, and an ability to guide new generations of beyond visual range air-to-air missiles such as the AIM-120D and AIM-260.

Two years later in June 2019 it was reported that the USAF was considering options to extend the service lives of up to 841 Block 40/42 and Block 50/52 F-16C/D fighters from 8,000 hours to more than 13,800 hours. This represented a major increase from prior plans announced in April to comprehensively modernise just 340 F-16C/Ds and increase their service lives to 12,000 hours. Although not improving combat performance, each service life extension cost less than $500,000 per F-16, making it a highly attractive means to maintain the number of operational squadrons despite not addressing the issue of their growing obsolescence. Plans to extend the lives of such a large number of F-16s, which would allow them to fly to the year 2040 and beyond, contributed to a growing consensus

An F-16C leads an F-15EX, an F-15E, and an F-15C of the 85th Test and Evaluation Squadron and the 40th Flight Test Squadron. The development and procurement of the F-15EX, and the significant levels of funding for life extension, modernisation and operations for the other three types, were direct results of the shortcomings of the F-35 and F-22 programs. (USAF)

that the Air Force was seriously reconsidering plans to procure the 1,763 F-35A that it officially still stated its intention to procure. Had F-35A procurements been intended to proceed as planned, the need for life extension of the F-16 fleet on such a large scale would have been highly questionable.

In parallel to the Air Force's decision to perform much wider life extensions across the F-16 fleet, the U.S. Navy made a near simultaneous decision to invest in life extension for F-18E/F and EA-18G aircraft, while modernising a number of the former to the Block 3 standard. While the Air Force would resume procurements of F-15s in 2020, almost two decades after it ended, to help make up for the severe fighter shortage that resulted from the F-22 and F-35 programs' shortfalls, the Navy would extend production of the F-18E/F, which had initially been intended to conclude in 2015. The announcement of this decision closely coincided with the F-35C's service entry. Production would be extended by a full twelve years, ending only in 2027, with all F-18E/Fs produced in that time being acquired by the Navy. The last extension, from 2025 to 2027, was announced on 21 March 2024, just days after the F-35 had been approved for full-scale production.[85] While the F-35C was very far behind schedule on deliveries, F-18E/F procurement allowed the Navy to age out its older F-18C/Ds without suffering from a major increase in the average age of its fighters. This decision came at a cost, however, and ensured that the Navy would rely on older fourth generation fighters to form a far greater portion of its fleet into the 2040s than the Air Force did. Expanded F-18E/F procurement was a direct consequence of major delays to the F-35 program.

The Marine Corps faced a similar situation to the Air Force, as it had also ended the procurement of fourth generation fighters in the 2000s, which left it with few options to respond to delays in procuring F-35s. The Corps was in 2016 revealed to be resorting to cannibalising retired F-18s in Boneyard storage for spare parts, as well as a museum.[86] The effect on availability rates was devastating, with roughly 70 percent of its ageing F-18C/D fleet left unable to fly at any given time – just 87 of the Corps' 276 aircraft.[87] After the end of procurements in 2000, the Iraq War and War on Terror had taken a particular toll on the Marine fleet, and worn the F-18s out, which made their replacement even more urgent. This may have partly explained the Corps' greater willingness to rush troubled F-35Bs into service despite the significant issues the aircraft still suffered from.

4

DEPLOYMENTS AND OPERATIONS

Japan

After hosting the first permanent overseas deployment of F-35s with the arrival of Marine Fighter Attack Squadron 121 in January 2017, Japan would quickly come to host a concentration of the fifth generation fighters wholly unparalleled worldwide. By the middle of the 2020s, it was the only country that hosted permanent deployments of all three variants of the fifth generation fighter by the U.S. Armed Forces, which was something no other country was expected to do for the foreseeable future.

On 9 September 2021, it was announced that a second U.S. Marine Corps F-35B squadron had achieved an initial operating capability in Japan, with Marine Fighter Attack Squadron 242 transitioning to the aircraft from the F-18D Hornet.[1] The squadron was declared fully operational in May 2022, bringing the total number of F-35Bs at Marine Combat Air Station Iwakuni to 32, with 16 aircraft from each squadron.[2] In parallel to the Marine Corps, F-35s would form a rapidly growing portion of the Air Force's fighter fleet in Japan, with units in the country prioritised for receipt of the new aircraft. In October 2022, the service announced that F-15C/D fighters, which had been permanently based at Kadena Air Base on Okinawa for 43 years, would belatedly be withdrawn. The F-15 had been the most capable fighter fielded by any Western air force when first deployed, replacing the previous elite of the USAF the F-4. Previously, the aircraft had expected to be replaced by the F-22 in the 2010s, before issues with the fifth generation program fully surfaced. Rotational deployments of F-35s, F-22s, F-15Es and F-16s were thus initiated to facilitate the withdrawal of F-15C/Ds from Kadena, with this considered a stopgap measure until a new fighter type could be selected for permanent deployment.

On 28 March 2023, F-35As from the 355th Fighter Squadron based at Eielson Air Base in Alaska arrived at Kadena Air Base on rotational deployment. The U.S. Pacific Air Forces reported at the time regarding these rotations: 'The next batch of F-15s will depart Kadena in phased movements over the coming months. Departures will occur once sufficient deployed forces are in place and operational to ensure no gap in steady-state fighter presence.' Eight months later on 20 November, F-35As from the 4th Fighter Squadron arrived at Kadena from Hill Air Force Base in Utah.[3] The fighters would return to the United States in April 2024, before again returning to Kadena on 1 November that year. Rotational deployments would continue, with the 355th Fighter Squadron's F-35As confirmed on 4 November 2024, to have returned to Kadena,[4] followed less than two months later by F-35As from the 134th Expeditionary Fighter Squadron.[5]

The lack of a successor to the F-15C/D to deploy to Kadena, which was the closest U.S. or allied air base to the strategically vital Taiwan Strait, was a legacy of the shortcomings of the F-22 program, with the allocation of F-35s for rotational deployments there representing one example of the F-35 'picking up slack' for the previous fifth generation program. While a permanent deployment of F-35s was speculated as a possibility, the fighter's much shorter range than the F-15, low availability rates, and limited suitability for air superiority missions made it far from ideal. Remaining questions regarding the future of the fighter presence at Kadena were answered on 3 July 2024, when the Pentagon confirmed that the 48 F-15C/Ds would be replaced by a permanent deployment of 36 new F-15EX fighters. The slow rate of procurement of the fighters, however, meant that this was not expected to materialise for several years, despite Kadena being prioritised to host the first operational active-duty F-15EXs. The delivery of these aircraft, fighters 15 through 51, would only

A close-up view at the front section of an F-35B operated by the Marine Fighter Attack Squadron 242. The squadron was the second in the Corps to be permanently deployed in Japan, as a result of a broader prioritisation of deployments of the fifth generation fighters in the country by the Marines, Navy and Air Force. (USMC)

begin from the second half of 2025. This ensured that rotational deployments of F-35s and older fighters would continue to be relied on to make up the shortfall in numbers for some years.

Thirty-six F-15EXs provided a far greater combat capability than 48 F-15C/Ds had, particularly when considering that there would likely be many more F-15s available for operations at any given time due to the newer aircraft's far higher availability rates, which would more than compensate for a 25 percent cut in numbers. The latest figures for availability rates when the planned permanent deployment of the F-15EX was announced showed that the new aircraft were mission capable 86 percent of the time, compared to just 33 percent for the F-15C, with rates for the latter improving the following year as the most worn out airframes in the fleet were retired.[6] Nevertheless, the lack of a fifth generation successor to the F-15 ensured that, while the U.S. Air Force had previously enjoyed a vast capability advantage over Chinese air units the last time the fighter type on permanent deployment had changed, its closest air unit to Taiwan would now rely on fighters that lacked the advanced fifth generation capabilities needed to match top performing Chinese fighters such as the J-20.

With no fifth generation fighters at Kadena, F-35s deployed elsewhere in Japan were expected to shoulder a heavier burden in the event of a conflict with the Chinese mainland. As the selection of the F-15EX for the new permanent deployment was announced, it was also confirmed that 36 F-16CMs permanently deployed by the 35th Fighter Wing at Misawa Air Base would be replaced by 48 F-35As, thus compensating for the reduction in the number of fighters at Kadena. These specialised F-16s were heavily optimised for suppression or destruction of enemy air defences, and while the F-35s replacing them would not be modified for this role, it would be reflected in their armaments and training.

Since Japan did not operate the F-16, phasing the fighter type out in favour of the F-35A would increase commonality with local forces. The F-35A would provide a significantly more potent air defence suppression capability than the F-16CM, while also being far more versatile allowing it to perform more effectively in other roles. Fighter units in Japan faced three of the world's most capable air defence networks, those of China, Russia, and North Korea, with the latter two countries relying very heavily on ground based systems to compensate for their lack of peer level fighter capabilities.

In August 2024, the U.S. Navy forward deployed F-35C fighters operated by Strike Fighter Squadron 147 to Marine Corps Air Station Iwakuni, joining the 36 F-35Bs already based at the facility, and replacing the F-18E/F Super Hornets from Strike Fighter Squadron 115 that were previously based there. The fighters would join Carrier Air Wing 5 which was permanently based in Japan. This made Japan the first and only country to host permanent foreign F-35 deployments by all three services.

With 147 F-35s having been ordered for the Japan Self-Defense Force (see Chapter 8), and with further American permanent and rotational F-35 deployments to the country expected to continue to be announced, the concentration of F-35s in Japan was unrivalled in its intensity. The unique challenges to American air dominance posed by China's defence sector and its armed forces, which were heavily focused in Northeast Asia, were consistently cited as a primary factor stimulating this, with the J-20 fighter program in particular leaving any fighter type other than the F-35 at a steep disadvantage. Japan was set to similarly be prioritised to host the USAF's first E-7 airborne warning and control systems, with unplanned orders for these aircraft in 2022 having been justified largely on the basis that they were needed to maintain situational awareness against China's advanced fifth generation fighters.[7]

Japan is set to remain at the crux of the F-35's presence in the Western Pacific, with not only the United States, but also other Western Bloc states seeking to support the Pivot to Asia initiative, prioritising the country for deployments of the aircraft. A key landmark in these deployments was the first arrival of Italian Air Force F-35As in Japan on 4 August 2023, with four fighters arriving at the Japan Air Self-Defense Force's Komatsu Air Base in Ishikawa Prefecture. After the enactment of the Japan-Australia Reciprocal Access Agreement on 13 August, the first Australian F-35s arrived in Japan on 30 August for joint exercises. A year later, on 22 August

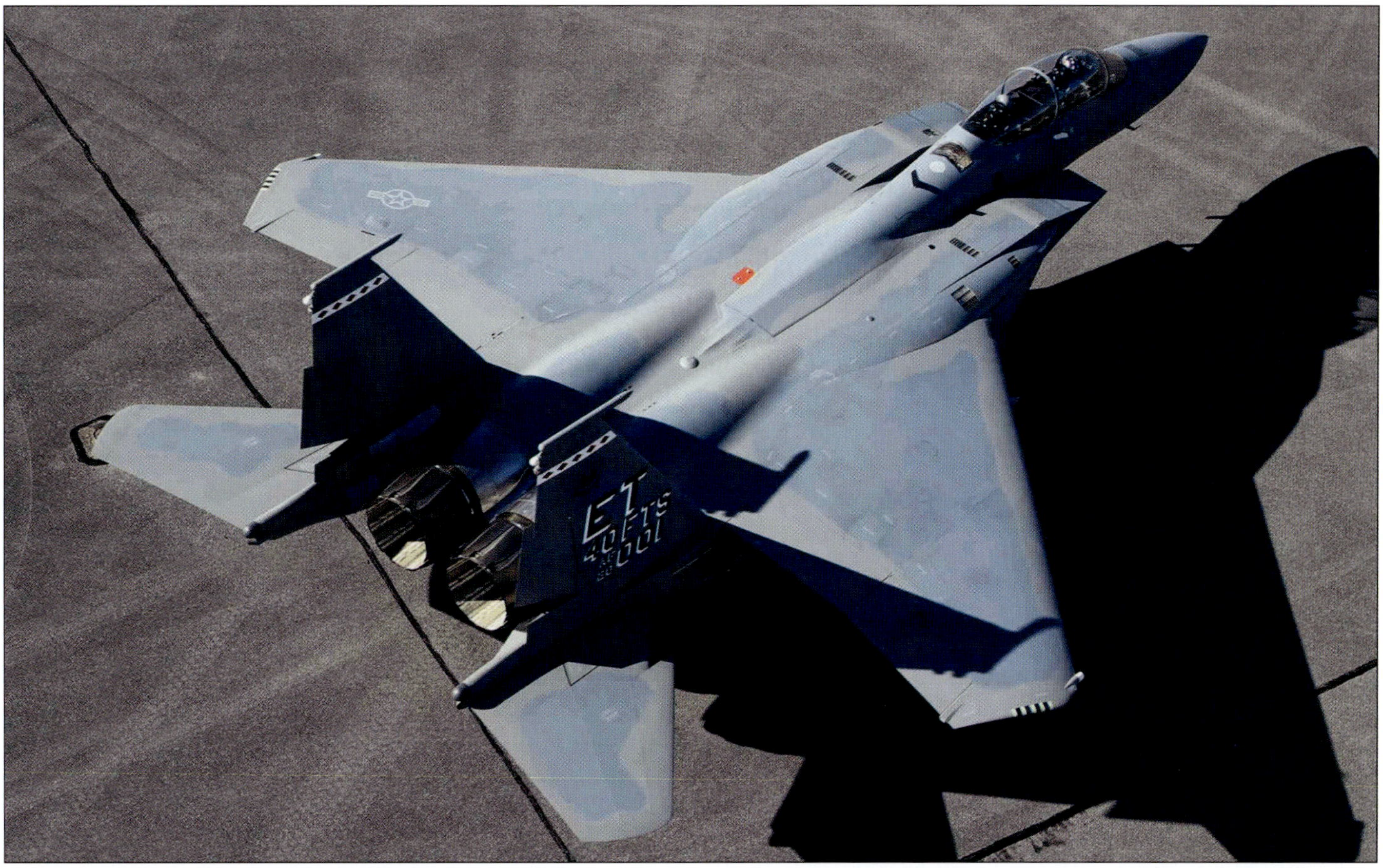

The first F-15EX as seen on arrival at Eglin Air Force Base in March 2021. Although the new F-15 was a twin seater based on the F-15E Strike Eagle, the Air Force flew the aircraft like F-15Cs and made no operational use of their rear cockpits, which reflected their primary purpose of serving as interceptors and air superiority fighters in the Air National Guard and at Kadena Air Base respectively. The decision to acquire the F-15EX, rather than increasing orders for the F-35, caused significant controversies within the Air Force. (USAF)

2024, the Italian Navy aircraft carrier *Cavour* and frigate *Alpino* made a port call at the Yokosuka Base, with *Cavour* carrying eight F-35Bs alongside seven Harrier IIs. At a time when Japan was preparing for its first F-35B carrier deployments, the Italian Navy's sharing of information on F-35B operations from small carriers was expected to be highly prized.

Italian Navy Rear Admiral Giancarlo Ciappina confirmed at the time of the *Cavour's* deployment that Japanese naval and air force officials would be hosted on the carrier to 'follow the activity with the F-35B.' Defence Minister Guido Crosetto also visited Japan and boarded the carrier, stating regarding plans to work with Japan's navy: 'We are talking about ships and aircraft from different

The joint F-35B component including Navy and Air Force aircraft in the Italian Navy aircraft carrier *Cavour* in the Pacific. (Italian Navy)

countries preparing to operate, should the need arise, as if they are all part of the same force.' Crosetto claimed that the carrier's visit 'was not a matter of sending a message to China or North Korea,' which was precisely the rationale which analysts had widely attributed to the deployment.[8] After Italy, other NATO members were expected to also prioritise Japan for F-35 deployments, with the Dutch ambassador to Japan, Gilles Beschoor Plug, in December 2024 confirming plans to deploy F-35As to the country in 2026, citing the growing power of Chinese and North Korean forces as a leading cause for concern.[9] The United Kingdom and Germany were poised to be among the first to follow suit, with a significant possibility emerging that over half a dozen Western Bloc states could frequently rotate F-35s through Japanese facilities.

Korea

Beyond Japan, the broader Pacific would also be prioritised for deployments of F-35s for many of the same reasons. Alongside China, North Korea would be a primary target of many of the major deployments made, with the first foreign deployments to the region in 2017 having been largely aimed at the country during a period of particularly high tensions. The 35th Fighter Wing at Misawa Air Base that specialised in air defence suppression was expected to play particularly central role in a Korean conflict, due to the extreme density and fast growing sophistication of North Korea's air defence network. Continued advances in North Korean strike capabilities, including the operationalisation of increasingly advanced ballistic missiles, rocket artillery systems, and methods of special forces insertion, was expected to continue to influence the U.S. Armed Forces' decision not to make a permanent F-35 deployment in South Korea due to the vulnerability of airbases on the country. F-35s permanently stationed in Japan and Alaska would instead by depended on for temporary deployments to South Korea, with the fighter's range allowing it to fly sorties against North Korean targets from Japan where bases were less vulnerable.

Following the end of the administration of South Korean President Moon Jae-in in May 2022, which had from 2018 opposed major exercises simulating conflict with North Korea, the new Yoon Suk-yeol administration would support a rapid escalation of such exercises. These came to frequently involve large numbers of USAF and Marine Corps F-35s. Shortly after the inauguration of Yoon's administration, on 5 July 2022 six USAF F-35As of the 356th Fighter Squadron arrived from Eielson Air Force Base, Alaska, to Kunsan Air Base on South Korea's west coast, marking the first American fifth generation fighter deployment to the country in five years. Flying approximately 40 hours and 30 sorties, their exercises focused on increasing interoperability with local air units, including Republic of Korea Air Force F-35As which also participated.[10]

A major landmark in the renewal of F-35 exercises in Korea was the initiation of the Vigilant Storm 23 drills on 31 October 2022 in which four F-35Bs operated by Marine Fighter Attack Squadron 242 participated after temporarily deploying to Kunsan Air Base. Over 100 American military aircraft took part in the exercises, alongside South Korean F-35As, with the two fleets flying 1,600 mock sorties against simulated North Korean targets. This made them the largest air exercises ever on the peninsula.[11] The Foreign Ministry in Pyongyang slammed the exercises as 'an aggression-type war exercise with the basic purpose of hitting strategic targets of the Democratic People's Republic of Korea,' stressing: 'Nowhere in the world can we find a military exercise with an aggressive character like the joint military exercise held by the United States and its followers in terms of duration, scale, content and density.'[12]

While North Korea had specifically protested South Korean procurement of F-35s as far from conducive to peace on the peninsula,[13] the aircraft's optimisation for air defence suppression missions and penetration strikes, including using tactical nuclear warheads, made their deployments appear a particularly serious threat. With U.S. military planning since the 1950s having placed a strong emphasis on the importance of tactical nuclear strikes if engaging North Korea's formidable ground forces, which was reiterated by senior military officials in the 1990s in particular, the F-35's position as the only nuclear armed stealth fighter could make it particularly critical in a new Korean War.[14] The fighter's combination of advanced stealth capabilities and an ability to deliver high diameter penetrative conventional and nuclear bombs against North Korea's particularly large network of deeply fortified targets made it invaluable.

North Korea's ground based air defence network had remained among the densest in the world since the 1960s, and uniquely fortified its assets underground using lifts to allow them to appear, fire, and then withdraw.[15] Significant improvements to this network were

A pair of the Marine Fighter Attack Squadron 121's F-35Bs dropping JDAMs with training warheads during their deployment to South Korea. (ROKAF)

made from the late 2010s, beginning with the operationalisation of the Pyongae-5 system in 2017 after close to 20 years of development, which provided a broad equivalent to the Russian S-300PM-1/PM-2. This system was seen as a stopgap until the operationalisation of the more advanced Pyongae-6 system some time in the early 2020s. It was followed by continued development and testing of new types of surface-to-air missiles for the system.[16] The rate of improvements to North Korea's ground based air defence network continued to make its airspace one of the most challenging that American aircraft could potentially be tasked with penetrating. This made the F-35's world leading air defence suppression capabilities appear particularly valuable. Signs from late 2023 of North Korean interest in procuring advanced Russian fighter aircraft, in particular the Su-57, which led experts to make detailed assessments of the ways Moscow could seek to circumvent the UN arms embargo on its neighbour, also raised the possibility that F-35s would be relied on more heavily to counter the country's future fighter capabilities.[17]

Pacific

From the early 2010s preparations for possible wartime operations in disputed regions of the South China Sea gained growing importance in the U.S. Marine Corps, with the service highly valuing the F-35B for thoroughly transforming how it could employ air power in the theatre. The fighter for the first time provided Marine Expeditionary Strike Groups deploying from amphibious assault ships with an aircraft capable of deep strike, air defence suppression, counter-air, advanced penetrating reconnaissance and advanced electronic intelligence far into highly contested territory, which were all missions for which the Harrier had been poorly suited. The ability to penetrate deeper into well defended enemy airspace provided options for the Marines to use the aircraft to suppress enemy air defences, both kinetically and through jamming, or to escort MV-22 Osprey rotary wing transports to their targets, which significantly increased their potential reach. The F-35B allowed amphibious assault ships to combine a highly formidable offensive air capability with a potent ground assault capability, posing a fundamentally new kind of threat to American adversaries that had particularly significant implications in the Pacific.

Marine plans to operate the F-35B in the Pacific to launch offensives into areas covered by China's advanced Anti-access area denial assets were elaborated in 2018 by retired Marine Lieutenant Colonel David Berke. These plans relied heavily on using the fighter's STOVL capabilities to operate from makeshift airfields and even minor atolls across the Pacific. 'You can fly the F-35B literally anywhere. If your traditional places of operation are unavailable the F-35B can be there,' Berke stated, adding: 'Find me 600 feet of flat surface anywhere in the world, and I can land there.' He compared the F-35B to the A-10 in its ability to operate from short runways or dirt roads, noting that the Marines could use their MV-22 and CH-53 helicopters to airlift supplies and set up small makeshift airbases.

The operations described by Berke were termed Expeditionary Advanced Base Operations (EABO), and were elaborated on in the 2019 Marine Aviation Plan as follows:

> EABO is a future naval operational concept that mitigates peer competitors' anti-access / area denial capability by creating a more survivable, resilient, and persistent forward- postured force. The EABO concept is designed to re-establish the force credibility required to have a deterrent effect. Using key maritime terrain in the vicinity of close and confined seas … EABO sustains and advances the inside force's ability to leverage the lethality of the outside force. The EABO concept is comprised of low-signature, mobile, relatively low-cost capabilities operating in expeditionary and temporary locations. These capabilities provide the joint force commander with the ability to target and strike the adversary while also making up the backbone of an active maritime defence-in-depth. EABO provides … sea denial options by using advanced bases to position and operate joint aircraft. All six functions of Marine aviation can be executed through the

U.S. Marines load AIM-120 air-to-air missiles onto an F-35B during an exercise. (USMC)

> use of mobile and expeditionary EABs. By using all available basing options, Marine aviation can expand the reach and lethality of the joint force commander.[18]

Key obstacles to successfully setting up makeshift bases for F-35B operations were the aircraft's high maintenance requirements particularly for its stealth coatings, its high fuel consumption which placed a significant burden on logistics, and its short range which was a major limiting factor over the vast distances of the Pacific. Indeed, even before the fighter's significant exceeding of intended maintenance and fuel consumption requirements became known, the immense logistical difficulties of operations described by Berke were seen to be prohibitive. Marine Harrier pilot Major Ben D. Hancock thus argued in an early paper on the F-35B:

> The Marine Corps does not have enough equipment to supply significant amounts of fuel and ammo to manoeuvre units. Relying almost exclusively on aviation to supply forward bases will place an enormous burden on already limited vertical lift capability ... the difficulty of dispersion to forward sites is the problem of command and control and logistics. Aircraft have a constant demand for fuel. And if you want to use the aircraft in combat, you need to be able to supply it with ordnance, spare parts, maintenance support, water and food for the troops, and security or force protection. Operating jet aircraft from dispersed sites is a big logistical challenge.[19]

Marine aviation's focus on EABO was closely in line with the priorities of the Corps' deep overhaul announced in March 2020, which increased its focus on lighter more mobile assets that could be utilised effectively in the Pacific, while divesting all tanks and the majority of artillery. In contrast to the post-Cold War era, when planned operations consistently assumed technological and firepower superiority, the prospects of engaging a Chinese force that was fighting much closer to home, was technologically on par, and had vastly more firepower, resulted in a focus on greater mobility and flexibility by the Marines to fight asymmetrically. The kind of makeshift facilities which Marines trained to rapidly establish to operate F-35Bs were thus increasingly colloquially termed 'guerrilla airfields.'

After over five years of experience training to launch EABO in the Pacific using F-35Bs, the Obsidian Iceberg test events were launched in January 2023 to further improve this capability, and again drew attention to Marine Corps' plans for the STOVL fleet. Operational Test Director of Marine Corps Operational Test and Evaluation Squadron One, which carried out the tests, Lieutenant Colonel Robert Guyette, elaborated at the time regarding their purpose: 'It's about the F-35 executing sustained combat operations from places that, quite honestly, the enemy's not gonna expect us to be operating from.'[20]

Elaborating on the challenges and requirements for EABO, Guyette would observe in December 2024 during exercises simulating these operations: 'Once we get there, we're going to have to protect ourselves, and we're going to minimise our time in any one place. We're going to have to be able to strike from that place and then pack up and then fight our way back out.' He recalled asking personnel 'to shift their mindset from a hangar or a ship, where we have everything we could ever want, into this kind of field environment where they're aggressively conserving materials and doing without a lot of creature comforts that we normally have.' 'They know we're not going to have hangars. We're not going to have all of our nice equipment like at home. It'll be compromised, destroyed, or we're going to have to move away from it when the time comes,' he added.[21] Observing Marine EABO exercises in the Pacific first hand in January 2025, analysts at *The War Zone* noted: 'All of the squadrons that participated showed an extraordinary ability to get maintenance done with far fewer tools and equipment than they would normally have at MCAS Yuma.'[22]

China and North Korea's missile strike capabilities against targets within their own region were from the 2010s wholly unrivalled by those of other potential American adversaries, with Russian investments in tactical missiles with ranges over 500 kilometres

F-35B operated by the Marine Fighter Attack Squadron 122 conducts expeditionary advanced base operations on simulated narrow roads. (USMC)

F-35B operated by the Marine Fighter Attack Squadron 242 launches from the USS *America* in the Philippine Sea on 25 May 2025. (USN)

remaining limited even after the INF Treaty's suspension in 2019. Even in the Middle East, where Iran acquired large arsenals of increasingly advanced drones and medium range ballistic and cruise missiles, not only were Iranian delivery options much less diverse, but it also lacked nuclear or chemical warheads. The growing consensus on the potency of Chinese strike capabilities was effectively summarised by Defense Secretary Pete Hegseth, who stressed two months before being sworn into office that the U.S. would lose its 'whole power projection system' in the first 20 minutes of a war. 'If 15 hypersonic missiles can take out our 10 aircraft carriers in the first 20 minutes of a conflict, what does that look like?' he stated.[23] This remained a central factor in the high importance that was attributed to EABO and the F-35B when planning for conflict in the Pacific.

Alongside the Marine Corps, the Air Force and Navy have sought to improve their ability to operate from austere airfields in the Pacific, although the inherent design limitations of the F-35A and F-35C prevented them from doing this in a comparable way.[24] Efforts to adapt naval aviation units to such operations capitalised on the F-35C's arresting hooks, with arresting gear from December 2020 tested for installation on ground based runways to allow the aircraft to make very short landings much as they did on carriers.[25] From July 2024, it was confirmed that options were being considered to develop a derivative of the Gerald Ford-class supercarrier's Electromagnetic Aircraft Launch System (EMALS) for integration onto small airfields on land to facilitate short take-offs by F-35Cs.[26]

Following reports of continued difficulties in employing F-35Bs for EABO, a major turning point in the Marine Corps' plans for its fighter fleet was announced in February 2025, namely that planned F-35B procurements had been reduced by 21 percent from 353 to 280 aircraft. Funds were to be reallocated to F-35C procurements, which would be increased by 109 percent from 67 to 140 fighters. This raised serious questions regarding the Marines' successes employing the F-35B for EABO, and left significant grounds for speculation that the aircraft's failure to perform as envisaged may have led the service to sharply refocus towards more traditional carrier-based air power.[27] This also had significant implications for the future of the America-class amphibious assault ship program, the large-scale planned procurement of which was influenced by plans to operate the vessels as carriers for the F-35B.

Europe

The U.S. Armed Forces made their first F-35 deployment to Europe on 15 April 2017, when the USAF 388th Fighter Wing transferred eight F-35As from Hill Air Force Base in Utah, to Royal Air Force Lakenheath in the United Kingdom. Two of the fighters made brief forward deployments to Ämari Air Base in Estonia on 25 April and to Graf Ignatievo Air Base in Bulgaria on 28 April. The training deployment concluded on 7 May, with the fighters returning to the United States after having flown 76 sorties. From that time, the U.S. Air Force would periodically make temporary deployments of the F-35A to European bases for a range of purposes, primarily for deterrence missions and participation in exercises. The service's ability to conduct such forward deployments was increased significantly from 1 October 2021, when the first American F-35 squadron was permanently stationed in Europe with the reactivation of the 495th Fighter Squadron at Royal Air Force Lakenheath in the United Kingdom. The first of the squadron's 27 F-35As began to arrive at the facility two months later.

From early 2022, USAF F-35 deployments in Europe were expanded in response to concerns of an impending Russian invasion of Ukraine, with F-35As of the USAF 388th Fighter Wing and the Air Force Reserve's 419th Fighter Wing forward deployed from Hill Air Force Base to Germany's Spangdahlem Air Base on 16 February. Their perceived importance would grow after Russian-Ukrainian hostilities escalated into a full-scale war on 24 February, with the fighters being allocated missions that leveraged the intelligence collection capabilities of their unique avionics suites. This made the F-35 squadrons active participants in the Russian-Ukrainian

F-35A fighters and airmen from the 388th Fighter Wing after landing at Spangdahlem Air Base, Germany, on February 16 2022. (USAF)

F-35A being pulled into a near-vertical climb by Colonel Craig Andrle. (USAF)

War, and supplemented NATO members' deployment of a wide range of non-kinetic assets to bolster the Ukrainian War effort, ranging from Starlink communications terminals to surveillance satellites and airborne warning and control systems.[28]

Reflecting a leading strength of the F-35's sensor suite, a primary mission of USAF F-35A units in Europe was to collect electronic intelligence by operating in proximity to Russian forces, with a particular focus on Russia's ground based air defence systems. Data collection opportunities became particularly valuable as these Russian systems began to see medium and high intensity combat use, which in many cases was their first ever such employment. The S-400, for example, which formed the backbone of Russia's air defence network, saw its first confirmed combat use on 5 March 2022.[29] Elaborating on the role of F-35s operating over Eastern Europe, 388th Fighter Wing Commander Colonel Craig Andrle stated in an interview in April 2023: 'We weren't crossing the border. We're not shooting anything or dropping anything. But the jet is always sensing, gathering information. And it was doing that very, very well ... We had all hoped it was going to work like it's supposed to, but then to see it actually perform very, very well in that role was great.' He added that the F-35s faced challenges when encountering Russian long-range air defence systems, noting: 'We're looking at an SA-20 [NATO designation for the S-300PM series]. I know it's an SA-20. Intel says there's an SA-20 there, but now my jet doesn't ID it as such, because that SA-20 is operating, potentially, in a war reserve mode that we haven't seen before.'[30]

Despite dating back to the mid-1990s, the S-300PM series posed challenges due to their ability to disguise their signatures and counter electronic warfare measures from air defence suppression aircraft. This capability was considerably further refined on newer systems such as the S-300V4, S-400 and S-500. Intelligence collected on how these systems did so could potentially be of significant value in the event of a conflict with Russia, where warfare in the electromagnetic spectrum was expected to be at least as important as that waged using kinetic weapons. The F-35's ability to collect electronic intelligence in ways that no fighter ever had before, in many ways comparably to a dedicated electronic warfare aircraft, made it an ideal asset in this regard.

Although Russian forces' medium and high intensity air defence operations provided an invaluable opportunity for intelligence collection, operating the F-35's sensors within the range of Russian air defence systems also created a risk that valuable intelligence on the fighter would fall into Russian hands. As observed by 388th Operations Group Commander Colonel Brad Bashore regarding F-35 operations in Eastern Europe: 'We don't have a ton of weapons where we can decimate the entire space. We're sharing data and making sure that everybody has awareness – surface-to-air and air-to-air – of what's out there in the environment ... They're doing the same thing that we're doing. We just looked at each other.' There was 'no direct interaction and nothing that was unprofessional on either side,' he added.[31]

Operations targeting Russian air defence systems were the closest U.S. or allied F-35s came to high intensity combat by the middle of the 2020s. They were accordingly specifically cited by Singaporean Minister of Defence Ng Eng Hen in March 2024 to justify a decision to procure the F-35A. 'In recent activities, the United States has mobilised its F-35s to identify the deployment of Russian anti-aircraft missile systems within Ukraine. The gathered intelligence is subsequently disseminated to NATO countries,' he stated at a session of the Parliamentary Committee on Public Procurement. This was quickly followed by a response from the Pentagon, which issued confirmation 'that the U.S. does not fly F-35s in Ukraine' – a claim which Minister Ng had never implied.[32] The F-35 could participate in the conflict, including potentially providing valuable intelligence to Ukrainian and other friendly forces, without crossing into the physical war zone.

The escalation of conflict in Ukraine had a transformative effect on F-35 operations in Europe, albeit a gradual one. In early May 2023, following Finland's formal accession to NATO the previous month, it was confirmed that Washington and Helsinki were involved in negotiations for a Defence Cooperation Agreement, which according to Finnish media would allow the United States to set up extensive military infrastructure in the country to facilitate forward deployments of the F-35.[33] Signed on 18 December 2023, it was speculated by a number of analysts that the agreement was intended as a first step towards turning Finland into a central hub of USAF F-35 operations on the continent alongside the United Kingdom and Germany. The fact that the Finnish Air Force not only had 64 F-35As on order, but also in November 2023 ordered its first U.S.-Israeli David's Sling long range air defence systems, ensured American F-35s would not only be highly interoperable with local forces, but that facilities hosting them would also be particularly well protected.[34]

Finland's accession to NATO effectively doubled the length of the NATO-Russian land border, placing significant further pressure on Russia's already stretched defences, with the concentration of large numbers of F-35s on Finnish soil having the potential to further exacerbate this. Alongside large investments in ground-based air defences, Russia's ability to counter the F-35 depended very heavily on its ballistic and cruise missile strike capabilities against bases hosting the aircraft, with notable examples including the Iskander-M, Kinzhal and Oreshnik ballistic missile systems and the Zircon cruise missile. Facing this threat, F-35 units deployed in Finland were expected to place a particularly high emphasis on the ability to make dispersed deployments from specially reinforced highways, with this capability first being demonstrated by the Royal Norwegian Air Force on 21 September 2023, during joint exercises with the Finnish Air Force.[35] This capability was subsequently demonstrated by USAF F-35As during Baana 24 exercises in Finland on 4 September 2024.[36]

The ability to deploy F-35As away from major airbases had first been tested abroad by the USAF in the Middle East in 2019, and was referred to as an Agile Combat Employment. The general resurgence in the Air Force's focus on this capability was further stimulated by the lessons from the Russian-Ukrainian War, as Ukraine's MiG-29 and Su-27 fighters' ability to operate away from major airbases proved critical to their ability to continue to fly sorties with a much reduced risk of being targeted on the ground.[37] The USAF began its first ever Pacific exercises employing F-35As from austere runways at Guam's Northwest Airfield in February 2021, with exercises including 'hot pit' refuelling with their engines still running. F-35A squadrons training on the United States mainland would also increasingly focus on these kinds of operations.[38] Unlike the MiG-29, the Su-27, or the F-35B, however, the F-35A was not particularly well optimised to operating away from major airfields, and required runways to be in pristine condition and any roads it flew from to be specially hardened, which was a costly investment that few countries made.

As F-35s formed a rapidly growing portion of the fighter fleets of European states, the aircraft would increasingly see temporary deployments to bases in Eastern Europe for air policing operations. Examples included Italy's deployment of F-35As to Ämari Air Base in Estonia in April 2021 to support NATO's Baltic Air Policing mission, which was followed a month later by the type's first close encounter with a Russian Su-30SM fighter over the Baltic Sea. The stealth fighters were equipped with Luneberg reflectors to prevent Russian forces from collecting intelligence on their airframes' stealth features. In April 2022, the Royal Netherlands Air Force deployed its own F-35As for air policing from Graf Ignatievo Airforce Base in Bulgaria, while the British Royal Air Force began its first air policing missing using F-35Bs in August 2024 with a deployment to Keflavík Air Base in Iceland. The U.S. Air Force would itself continue to make temporary F-35A deployments to forward locations across Europe, often coinciding with periods of rising tensions, with the 48th Fighter Wing permanently based at RAF Lakenheath relied on particularly heavily to do so.

An F-35A operated by the 34th Fighter Squadron conducting 'hot pit' refuelling at Mountain Home Air Force Base, Idaho. A 'hot pit' refuelling enables aircraft to refuel without turning off their engine, within just 13 minutes. (USAF)

The Arctic

Although making far fewer headlines than other locations for F-35 deployments, the U.S. Air Force's fifth generation fighter contingent in Alaska was not only the most significant in the United States, but also among the most important in the world. Located closer to Tokyo than to Honolulu, Eielson Air Base would serve as a hub of F-35 operations not only for the defence of Alaskan airspace, but also for the projection of power into East Asia, with stealth fighters from the facility relied on heavily for deployments to the region both in peacetime for exercises, and in wartime to quickly reinforce the hundreds of U.S. and allied F-35s already based there. The importance which proximity to East Asia granted F-35 units at Eielson was highlighted by commander of the 354th Fighter Wing, Colonel David Berkland, who stressed that the fighters could move 'rapidly to the AOR [area of responsibility],' including to austere locations with minimal logistics in place. 'We can really, in a single fighter sortie, range to just about any AOR in the Northern Hemisphere pretty easily,' he stated.[39] Referring to Alaska as 'the greatest air space in the world to train for fifth generation tactics against advanced threats, both on the air and on the ground,' Colonel Berkland on a separate occasion alluded to the territory's optimal position to project power into both the Pacific and the Arctic. 'Gen. Billy Mitchell talked about it in the 1930s, that whoever holds Alaska, holds the world. So the strategic importance of competing and securing our nation's interests, which were there then, remains as much now as ever,' he noted as the last two F-35s arrived under his command.[40]

The first pair of F-35As arrived at Eielson Air Force Base on 21 April 2020, where they would serve under the 354th Fighter Wing permanently deployed at the facility. The fighter wing received all 54 fighters in just two years, with the last two fighters arriving on 15 April 2022. These aircraft were split between the 355th Fighter Squadron and the 356th Fighter Squadron. With temperatures at the facility falling to close to 40 degrees below freezing, and not infrequently below minus 50 degrees, accommodating F-35s and approximately 3,500 personnel required an expansion of the facility costing over $500 million, and included the construction of 36 new buildings and 54 housing units.

A pair of F-35A fighters operated by the 354th Fighter Wing underway over the snow-covered landscape of Alaska. (USAF)

The extreme climate at Eielson placed a considerable strain on operations, with Colonel Berkland stating to this effect: 'All of our mission-important people that are out there on the flight-line operating, clearing the snow and ice around the clock, they have to operate in those environments. They have to maintain vehicles in that environment, in those conditions, so it is a challenge ... Before our pilots can fly here in the winter months.'[41] Other officers highlighted that Alaska's position 'kind of at the end of the logistics train for most of our parts and supplies' meant replenishing equipment could take considerably longer than it would for fighter units based elsewhere.[42]

Alaska hosted by far the greatest concentration of fifth generation fighters in the United States, and alongside the 355th and 356th squadrons at Eielson, Joint Base Elmendorf-Richardson located farther south near Anchorage hosted the 3rd Fighter Wing, under which the 90th Fighter Squadron and the 525th Fighter Squadron between them deployed 24 F-22s. Regarding the frequent exercises between F-35s and F-22s, commander of the 356th Fighter Squadron at Eielson Lieutenant Colonel Ryan Worrell observed: 'We can easily integrate with the Raptors down from the south. So we do integration on a quarterly basis with the Raptors on the JPARC ... I mean, we call the bros down the street and ... we can train with a single sortie, so that's a big advantage of being here in Alaska.'[43*]

* Also based at Eielson, F-16s flew under the 18th Aggressor Squadron established in August 2007, which in February 2024 was redesignated as the 18th Fighter Interceptor Squadron. This designation was last used during the Cold War, and denoted the unit's renewed focus on air defence. Its new duties were expected to help take pressure of F-35s and F-22s. While fifth generation fighters were needed for Pacific operations, they were not considered as vital for homeland defence against Russian bombers, which were not expected to receive fifth generation fighter escorts until well into the 2030s. Although being much less costly to operate and far easier to sustain at high availability rates, however, the ageing F-16 Block 30s in the squadron were among the least capable fighters in the Air Force.

F-35A and F-16 Fighters operated by the 354th Fighter Wing in formation during a readiness exercise at Eielson Air Force Base, Alaska. (USAF)

Alongside temporary deployments to the Pacific, F-35s based in Alaska were also relied on to deploy elsewhere in the Arctic. On 15 January 2023, F-35s operated by the 356th Fighter Squadron made their first ever deployment to Pituffik Space Base, formerly Thule Air Base, in Greenland, where they would remain for the next 16 days as part of North American Aerospace Defense Command (NORAD) exercise Operation Noble Defender. Located 1,200 kilometres north of the Arctic Circle, Pituffik represented the northernmost known base facility of the U.S. Armed Forces. Having been built in secret at the start of the Cold War to serve as a staging ground for nuclear attacks on the Soviet Union, Russian government sources expressed concern at the 'comprehensive modernisation' of the facility 'including radar systems worth billions of dollars' and 'airfield infrastructure for F-35 fighter jets, which are capable of carrying nuclear weapons.'[44] The F-35's limited range, however, meant it had negligible utility for dropping nuclear bombs on Russian territory from the facility.

The Arctic theatre received growing attention from the Pentagon from the late 2010s, with the rapid build-up of an F-35 presence in Alaska helping to place Washington in a strong position to make an expanded territorial claim on 19 December 2023 to approximately 1 million square kilometres of seabed, which included tremendous quantities of Arctic mineral and energy resources. This claim was made just 12 days after the commander of the Russian Navy, Admiral Nikolay Yevmenov, stressed that 'the collective West is ramping up efforts to impede Russia's economic activities in the Arctic.'[45] Following Sweden's accession to NATO three months later, seven of eight states with Arctic territories were now NATO members, with all except Sweden and Iceland having ordered F-35s.

The Arctic was by the early 2020s estimated to house 90 billion barrels worth of untapped oil and 44 billion barrels of liquid natural gas, accounting for 22 percent of the world's estimated undiscovered fossil fuels. With the Arctic Ocean losing 13 percent of its ice each decade, these resources were set to be increasingly exposed, as were key rare earth mineral deposits which were of tremendous strategic value to both Russia and to adversary NATO member states that staked claims to the region. Beyond the benefits of claiming resources for itself or its allies, the U.S. military presence was expected to be utilised to limit Russia's ability to make economic gains from the region, with Russian-claimed Arctic territories estimated to have $2 trillion dollars worth of rare earths. Notable examples included terbium and dysprosium, vital for the production of military assets such as radar and sonar systems. Russia by the early 2020s had developed over 200 oil wells in the Arctic, with the region generating 20 percent of the country's GDP. This figure was set to continue to increase as Arctic resources became an increasingly important driver of Russian growth.[46]

A further source of the Arctic's strategic importance was the exposure of the North Sea Route through Russian territory, which with support from Russian icebreaker ships offered an alternative for shipping from Asia to Europe that was 40 percent shorter than transiting through the Malacca Strait and Suez Canal. For Russia's strategic partner China in particular, this was highly valued as an alternative to transiting shipping through waters dominated by Western navies. Russia's own shipping through the North Sea Route increased by 31,400 percent in the 2010s, from 100,000 tons in 2010 to 31.5 million in 2019. With the build-up of forces across key Chinese trade routes having been a central focus of the Obama administration's Pivot to Asia initiative from the early 2010s, in order to provide Washington with options to launch distant blockade operations of its primary geopolitical rival, the ability to also threaten trade across the North Sea Route had considerable strategic value.[47] *

* China's military presence in the Arctic was notably not insignificant, with the country designating itself as a Near Arctic State, and investing heavily in bolstering Russia's position in the region. A major landmark in the expansion of Chinese military activities occurred on 24 July 2024, when Chinese H-6 bombers were first confirmed to have been deployed to Russian bases to conduct joint patrols near Alaska. The H-6s and Russian Tu-95s

An F-35A of the 354th Fighter Wing taking-off from Elmendorf Air Force Base in full afterburner. (USAF)

Top view of a Russian Aerospace Forces MiG-31BM interceptor. (Russian MOD)

The high priority which the Russian Defence Ministry gave its defences in the Arctic, combined with the region's geopolitical significance, made the deployment of F-35s a priority for the U.S. and many of its allies. On 21 July 2020, the U.S. Department of the Air Force released its first ever Arctic Strategy, which particularly emphasised that Russia was 'developing an integrated network of air defence, coastal missile systems, and early warning radar to secure its northern approaches,' highlighting that 'no other country has as much permanent military presence above the 66th parallel.' Russia's considerable investments in refurbishing airfields and infrastructure across the region and constructing new military facilities gained particular attention.[48] The Russian Arctic was prioritised for deployments of many of the country's most high profile new aerial warfare systems, such as S-400 and S-500 long range air defence systems and MiG-31BM interceptors, with some assets such as the Tor-M2DT and Pantsir-SA air defence systems having been specifically developed for Arctic conditions. The PAK DP next generation interceptor, like the MiG-31 it was developed to replace in the 2030s, was also intended to be heavily focused towards Arctic operations, although consistent delays to the program raised questions regarding whether it would ever materialise.[49]

The Arctic retains the potential to become a new centre of U.S.-Russian hostilities, with Moscow focusing a far greater portion of its military potential in the region than the United States ever has. The region could thus emerge as a main focus for F-35 deployments second only to the Western Pacific, particularly as Russia has expanded its network of regional airbases considerably and appears poised to deploy a larger interceptor fleet there. Although F-35s are expected to retain a technological edge over Russian combat jets, Russia's fielding of interceptors heavily tailored to Arctic conditions, and which carry radars and missiles several times the size of the

entered Alaska's Air Defence Identification Zone, and were intercepted by USAF F-35s, F-16s and Canadian F-18s. Beyond the significant options Chinese aircraft were likely to be granted for temporary basing in Russia, the growing ranges of new Chinese combat aircraft, and the country's rapidly expanding aerial refueling capabilities, also made operations into the region from domestic airbases appear increasingly viable.

F-35's own, makes the balance of power in the air in many ways less unfavourable to Moscow than it is in other theatres.

Middle East

The U.S. Air Force first deployed F-35s to the Middle East on 15 April 2019, after aircraft from the 388th and 419th Fighter Wings flew from Hill Air Force Base to Al Dhafra Air Base in the United Arab Emirates. The airmen involved in this landmark deployment had previously been deployed to RAF Lakenheath and Kadena Air Base in 2017. The deployment allowed USAF F-35As to participate in combat for the first time, with the aircraft on 30 April striking an Islamic State tunnel network and weapons cache in Iraq, seven months after Marine Corps F-35Bs had first seen combat in September 2018. As the F-35's first ever short-notice foreign deployment, the fighters were for the first time used to practice Agile Combat Employment outside the United States, which entailed operating from small forward airstrips closer to the targets than the main airfield. Commander of the 34th Fighter Squadron Lieutenant Colonel Aaron Cavazos observed regarding the importance of this aspect of F-35 operations:

> Successfully implementing split operations was the biggest takeaway for us ... To be able to bed down in a forward location means that we now have unpredictability against potential adversaries. They are so used to us showing up in country, staying in the same place for half a year, doing the same things and leaving. They know it. We know it. Now we proved we can be more agile. That principal can carry over operationally to other regions and any potential adversaries there.[50]

Deploying for extended periods, and implementing the first ever Agile Combat Employment abroad, posed a number of unique challenges, with the lead production superintendent of the 34th Aircraft Maintenance Unit, Senior Master Sergeant Westley Calloway, observing: 'We had to think creatively to solve logistics and communication challenges, because in a lot of ways we're writing the playbook. But once those chains are established, we were able to maintain the health of our fleet and complete every task asked of us.'[51]

F-35As and their airmen would continue to rotate rapidly into and out of Al Dhafra, with F-35As of the 34th Fighter Squadron deploying to the facility in October 2019, and departing eight months later in June 2020. F-35s from the 388th and 419th Fighter Wings would make a second much longer deployment to Al Dhafra on 16 November 2019, the former unit just two weeks after it had

Above left: A 380th Air Expeditionary Maintenance Group crew chief meets an F-35A pilot at Al Dhafra Air Base in the United Arab Emirates in April 2019 during the fighter type's first ever deployment in the Middle East. (USAF)

Above right: A pilot from 4th Expeditionary Fighter Squadron performs a preflight check on an F-35A in April 2019, at Al Dhafra Air Base. (USAF)

Left: An F-35A pilot assigned to the 4th Expeditionary Fighter Squadron performs a performance check in preparation for the first combat sortie in the U.S. Air Forces Central Command area of responsibility on 26 April 2019 at Al Dhafra Air Base, United Arab Emirates. (USAF)

left the region. It would then again return to Hill Air Force Base in May 2020. In August 2020, after a 16 month continuous presence of USAF F-35s, Lieutenant Colonel Cavazos reported regarding their operations: 'We were doing everything from strafing in close air support, which wouldn't normally compute in your brain with the capabilities a fifth generation fighter brings, to running maritime escort for Carrier Strike Groups in the span of a single day.'[52] The experience was 'a confidence booster' which would improve how F-35 personnel trained after returning to the United States, he added, noting regarding the significance of the deployment for the fighter's integration into service: 'Operationally, we're becoming our own F-35 community. We aren't a hodgepodge of pilots from other airframes anymore.'[53]

The first ever short-notice deployment of F-35s occurred amid rising tensions between Washington and Tehran, which would culminate in the Iranian shoot-down of a USAF RQ-4A Global Hawk in or near its airspace on 20 June, and the CIA assassination by air strike of Iran's most influential military officer Major General Qasem Soleimani in Iraq on 3 January the following year. The deployment was part of a much broader military build-up aimed at demonstrating resolve to Tehran, which included deployments of B-52H bombers, F-15C/D and F-15E fighters, and F-22s to the region in mid-2019 among a wide range of other assets. Iran's total lack of modern manned combat aircraft, and heavy reliance on surface-to-air missile systems for its defence, made deployments of F-35s well optimised to countering such networks a particularly potent show of force. The director of the Air Force's F-35 Integration Office, Brigadier General David Abba, commented regarding the deployment's timing: 'It is no surprise that the aircraft were deployed during periods of heightened tension within the Middle East ... All I can tell you on that is that our aircrew and our jets were ready to respond on a moment's notice, should the order have been given for anything, for any additional missions to be executed.'[54]

The detection capabilities of Iran's air defence network were significantly improved in 2019 with the acquisition of the Russian Rezonans-NE long-range radar system. A number of sources speculated that the procurement may have been an emergency measure and the delivery expedited specifically in response to mounting tensions and deployments of American stealth jets. The delivery was confirmed in August 2020 by deputy CEO of the Rezonans research centre, Alexander Stuchilin, who observed regarding the system's use to detect F-35s in the region: 'At the beginning of 2020 this radar identified U.S. F-35 planes and tracked them … The radar's personnel were transmitting information, including the routes of F-35 flights, in clear, thus confirming that it was reliably tracking the planes. For this reason, the opponent did not commit any irreparable actions that might have caused a big war.'[55] Considering the close proximity of F-35s based in Abu Dhabi

Two F-35As from the 421st Expeditionary Fighter Squadron, as seen while rolling down a taxiway at Al Udeid Air Base in Qatar on 5 September 2023. (USAF)

A Rezonans-NE radar, as operated by the Russian Aerospace Forces. Iran acquired four slightly different sets, named Ghadir in local service. (VPK)

to Iran, this was far from impossible. Russia had invested heavily in developing and fielding advanced long waveband radar systems with very long ranges to provide awareness of enemy aircraft over extreme distances, although the ability to detect F-35s hundreds of kilometres away fell far short of providing a means to effectively target them even at a small fraction of these distances.

F-35s would continue to be deployed to the Middle East into the 2020s. As part of a broader surge in the presence of American combat jets, USAF F-35As were on 26 July 2023 deployed to an unknown location in the region under the 421st Air Expeditionary Squadron, with the Marine Corps near simultaneously deploying F-35Bs to the region on the carrier USS *Bataan*, while the Air Force made new deployments of F-16s and A-10s. The deployments were seen as a show of force both to Iranian forces in the Persian Gulf and to Russian forces in Syria, at a time when tensions with both states were high. The F-35s were subsequently withdrawn in late September, after which Commander of the U.S. Air Forces Central Command Lieutenant General Alexus Grynkewich strongly implied that their deployments had led the Russian Aerospace Forces to cease flying fighters over U.S. forces in Syria or releasing flares in the paths of American drones.[56]

As F-35As of the 421st operated deep inside Syrian airspace, Damascus and Moscow were both deterred from responding to these violations, with Commander Grynkewich observing regarding the benefits of their presence: 'What the F-35s did is they gave us additional capacity,' allowing the Air Force to 'continue doing the missions we were doing up in Iraq and Syria and elsewhere in the region, and increase what we were doing in support of the Navy doing basically combat air patrols over the Straits of Hormuz.' He added that the deployments of new air and naval units 'deterred Iran from taking any actions against maritime shipping.'[57] The withdrawal of the F-35s reportedly occurred just hours before the outbreak of hostilities between Israel and Palestinian paramilitaries in the Gaza Strip on 7 October.

Beyond the United Arab Emirates, F-35s were also hosted at Al Udeid Air Base in Qatar and at Shahid Muwaffaq Al Salti Air Base in Jordan. Following the United Arab Emirates' Chinese-mediated rapprochement with Iran from early 2023, Abu Dhabi's imposition of restrictions on the use of its territory for bombing missions in the region was considered a key factor in the USAF's decision to redeploy F-35s and other key aviation assets from the country to Qatar in May 2024.[58]

Following this outbreak and escalation of war in the Middle East from October 2023, the presence of USAF F-35As in the region would, over the next two years, correspond closely to the state of tensions and hostilities between Iran and Israel, with expanded deployments made in April and November 2024 and in June 2025, as active hostilities broke out between the two states. The U.S. Armed Forces' active hostilities with Yemeni Ansurullah Coalition forces from October 2023, and the continued frustrations faced by efforts to neutralise the paramilitary group's air defences, led both Navy and Marine F-35Cs to also be employed for strikes on targets in Yemen, as well as for air-to-air operations against local drones. Marine Fighter Attack Squadron 314's F-35C strikes against parliamentary forces in Yemen in November 2024 marked the first combat mission flown by the Corps' supercarrier-based stealth fighters. Ansurullah Coalition air defences would on at least one occasion come close to shooting down an F-35, after achieving multiple successes against fourth generation fighters and a range of American drone types, highlighting the threat which even relatively basic infrared guidance systems could pose to stealth aircraft.[59]

F-35As from the 421st Expeditionary Fighter Squadron arriving at Al Dhafra Air Base in the United Arab Emirates in May 2020. (USAF)

A pair of F-35As from the 388th Fighter Wing on the tarmac at the Muwaffaq Al Salti Air Base in Jordan. (USAF)

5

MISSION SCOPE: A FIGHTER RELIED ON FOR EVERY ROLE

Close Air Support: the Questionable Mission

The F-35 was designed as a highly versatile multirole fighter, and much like almost all other 21st century fighter types it is capable of air-to-air, air-to-ground and anti-shipping engagements at both visual and beyond visual ranges, as well as performing a range of electronic warfare techniques to support kinetic attacks using missiles and bombs. Unusually, however, the aircraft was also intended to replace two types of American combat jet heavily optimised for close air support (CAS) missions – namely the A-10 Thunderbolt II and the AV- 8B Harrier II fielded by the Air Force and Marine Corps respectively.

The Pentagon defines close air support as 'air action by fixed-wing and rotary-wing aircraft against hostile targets that are in close proximity to friendly forces and requires detailed integration of each air mission with the fire and movement of those forces.'[1] CAS missions traditionally involve low altitude low speed flight over the battlefield to employ bombs and cannon to supplement the firepower of armour and artillery units on the frontlines. Aircraft specifically designed for such roles are commonly colloquially referred to as 'flying tanks,' and in most cases benefit from armour protection and parts redundancy in ways that fighters do not, allowing them to brave enemy fire with slow low altitude flight. Such aircraft need to have high endurances to be able to loiter over ground units for extended periods, and often carry many more cannon rounds than other fighters due to these weapons' high utility for CAS missions.

The performance requirements for traditional close air support aircraft were in many respects complete opposites to those of the Joint Strike Fighter program. The F-35 had no armour protection leaving it vulnerable to even lower calibre gunfire. Its very high operational costs and maintenance requirements, and high production costs made losses difficult to replace, contrasting sharply with the A-10 and other aircraft of its kind which were consistently the least costly and most maintenance friendly manned combat jets in any fleet that fielded them. The F-35's endurance was also far too low for it to support ground units for extended periods as the A-10 and its foreign equivalents could. Its lower weapons payload would also mean close to twice as many F-35 sorties would be needed to provide comparable support, and possibly significantly more.

The A-10 could carry a much more diverse array of munitions, including multiple types of precision-guided rockets, missiles and bombs, while the F-35 not only had a much more limited range of CAS optimised weapons, but also could not carry different kinds of ordnance on its underwing pylons and in internal weapon bays at the same time. This meant it could not be equipped to optimally engage multiple types of target. While the A-10's GAU-8 seven barrel 30mm gun was among the most powerful deployed by any combat jet, the F-35A's GAU-22 four barrelled 25mm gun was significantly less outstanding, with the fighter carrying just 182 rounds, sufficient for just four seconds of fire, compared to 1,174 rounds carried by the A-10.

A stealth fighter and a close air support aircraft were on complete opposite ends of the spectrum among manned tactical combat jets, which made the marketing of the Joint Strike Fighter program as a solution to the growing age of the A-10 fleet appear to be one of its most unusual aspects. This nevertheless played an important role in winning support for the F-35's development despite significant cost overruns and delays, on the basis that it would obviate the needed for a separate new program for a dedicated CAS aircraft. Before the F-35, options previously considered to replace the ageing A-10 included a heavily modified and up-armoured F-16 derivative, designated the A-16, and the much lighter Israeli Lavi which was specifically designed for CAS. The former was considered insufficiently well armoured, however, and the latter never entered production due to the program's collapse.[2]

The F-35's viability, or lack of it, in serving as a direct replacement to the A-10 was expected to be highlighted by Air Force testing from 5-12 July 2018, which specifically compared the two aircraft's close air support capabilities. A 48-page report on the test was belatedly completed by Pentagon's Director, Operational Test and Evaluation four years later, although the publicly released version was so heavily redacted that very little was revealed.* Tests were conducted in low and medium threat air defence environments, and evaluated close air support, forward airborne control, and combat search and rescue capabilities. Pilots flying A-10s could engage targets significantly more accurately, could fly closer to their targets due to greater armour protection and much higher systems redundancy, and reported a 'significantly lower workload' in airborne forward air controller missions than those flying F-35s, which was particularly notable when considering the new fighter's very high levels of automation. The entire subsequent section was redacted, however, so it was unclear how significant this issue was.[3] The A-10 proved to be more effective despite being handicapped by test conditions that prevented it from using its superior digital communications capabilities to coordinate with friendly assets, with this restriction partially levelling the playing field in favour of the F-35 which lacked a similar communications capability.

An assessment by the Project on Government Oversight concluded regarding the results of testing that the Air Force's leadership 'fought to hide them completely for years,' highlighting that 'the information they did release does not paint a very positive picture of the F-35's ability' to replace the A-10. Indeed, the tests comparing the two aircraft were only conducted due to extensive lobbying efforts, including from staff at POGO, which resulted in a congressional mandate for the Air Force to carry them out. POGO reports further highlighted that even before the report's release, 'it became immediately clear that the tests were designed to make the F-35 look as good as possible' resulting in clear 'shortcomings of the

* A heavily censored version was released in October 2023 following a Project on Government Oversight Freedom of Information Act request for a copy in April 2022, which was ignored until legal action was taken to force the Air Force to release it.

Arkansas Air National Guard A-10C firing an AGM-65 air-to-surface missile at a firing range at Davis-Monthan Air Force Base. (USAF)

testing program.'[*] 'Had the F-35 come out as the winner, there can be little doubt that a clear, declarative statement to that fact would have prominently appeared in the opening paragraph of the report,' it concluded, with the report's authors conceding that the F-35 did not perform as expected in a CAS role.[4]

Even if the F-35 was operationally just as capable as the A-10 in providing CAS, not only was it cost prohibitive to use the stealth fighter for such roles, but its very low availability rates and high maintenance requirements would also significantly reduce the support available for ground units. While it was clear that the F-35 was far more limited as a CAS aircraft, however, there were still strong arguments for replacing the A-10 fleet. By the 1980s the viability of traditional close air support aircraft was increasingly limited by advances in low-altitude air defence systems, including at the lowest level man-portable infrared guided missile systems. These emitted no radar signatures, which made them particularly difficult to locate. Although aircraft flying at higher speeds and altitudes, or engaging targets from longer ranges, had high survivability against such systems, those flying close to their targets at low altitudes, as the A-10 and similar aircraft were designed to do, were highly vulnerable.

* The test's key shortcomings were summarised by POGO as follows: 'A close air support test should involve large numbers of ground troops in a highly fluid combat simulation in varied terrain, across many days. It should test the pilot's ability to spot targets from the air in a chaotic and ever-changing situation. The test should also include a means of testing the program's ability to fly several sorties a day, because combat doesn't pause to wait for airplanes to become available.' The test met none of these conditions. Ground forces were absent and testing relegated solely to a desert environment where targets had no cover, making provision of support straightforward even for aircraft with limited capabilities. Tests were designed without ever consulting the Air Force's resident experts on close air support, and relied on 'unrealistic scenarios that presuppose an ignorant and inert enemy force.' Former A-10 pilots were chosen to fly the F-35s to 'minimise the impact' of shortfalls in F-35 pilot training for CAS. (Grazier, Dan, 'Close Air Support Fly-Off Farce: F-35 Versus A-10 Fly-Off Tests Designed to Mislead,' *POGO*, 10 July 2018.) (Grazier, Dan, 'F-35 and A-10 Close Air Support Flyoff Report,' *POGO*, 30 October 2023.)

A key facilitator of the gradual transformation in how close air support was provided were the advances in precision guidance capabilities for air-to-surface weapons, which allowed aircraft to engage targets much closer to friendly armour or infantry using course correcting bombs and missiles from higher altitudes and at greater distances. Preceding the era of precision guided weapons, in conflicts such as the Korean War the only means of ensuring sufficient accuracy when engaging ground targets near friendly forces was to fly very low and slowly, which was done using aircraft such as the Air Force's A-1 Skyraider and Navy and Marines' F4U Corsair. These operated similarly to how the A-10 would in the Cold War's later years.

Although close air support traditionally entailed a mission profile akin to that of a 'flying tank,' flying low with armour protection as A-10s did, new precision guidance capabilities made the means by which such support could be provided increasingly diverse. Major advances in these technologies and in low altitude surface-to-air capabilities closely coincided, and increasingly limited the importance of aircraft like the A-10 not only in potential high intensity 'Great Power Conflicts,' whether in Korea or in Eastern Europe, but also in low intensity conflicts such as the Taliban Insurgency, where less specialised aircraft such as F-16s could support infantry adequately well. Indeed, it emerged as a point of contention between senior Pentagon officials and prominent lawmakers in the 2010s whether strategic bombers such as the B-52H and B-1B could provide CAS, although with precision guided weapons both bombers did so extensively in Afghanistan – albeit at the price of wearing out their airframes in ways that were far from cost effective.[5] As a result by the 2010s, although the United States was not in conflict with any state adversaries, A-10s were relied on for only around 20 percent of CAS missions – a figure which would further diminish considerably if facing a modern adversary with sophisticated anti-aircraft capabilities.

The shift in how close air support was provided was seen not only in the United States, but also abroad. China's last manned CAS aircraft, the Q-5, entered service seven years before the A-10 in 1970,

A U.S. Marine Corps F-35B inverted, showing the installation of the GPU-9/A gun pod. While podded variants of the GAU-22/A are available for both the F-35B and F-35C, differences in the outer mold-line fairing mean that they are unique to each variant. (USMC)

An F-35A from the 388th Fighter Wing dropping a GBU-31 JDAM precision guided bomb. Advances in precision guidance capabilities have allowed a wide range of tactical and strategic aircraft to provide close air support from safer ranges, speeds and altitudes. (Scott Wolff)

and was retired from service in 2017 without a direct replacement. In contrast to the United States and Russia, China's output of combat jets increased drastically in the 30 years after the Cold War, as had the diversity of types in production, meaning that loss of a specific type of aircraft, namely low flying CAS jets, was against the general trend. This indicated that a manned dedicated CAS aircraft was no longer perceived to be necessary. The People's Liberation Army Air Force and Navy would instead rely on fighters such as the JH-7 to provide CAS with guided bombs. Although Chinese fighters trained for low altitude bombing using non-glide bombs, this required close coordination with nearby special forces to provide warning of enemy efforts to engage using man-portable air defence systems.[6]

Russia's own CAS aircraft, the Sukhoi Su-25, which was the closest foreign analogue to the A-10, similarly demonstrated serious limitations in how it could be employed. Although only a single aircraft was lost during counterinsurgency operations in Syria in the late 2010s, shot down by Turkish-backed Islamist paramilitaries on 3 February 2018, the aircraft had to be deployed cautiously throughout the campaign due to insurgents' use of man-portable air defence systems. Su-25s would see significant losses both when deployed by the Ukrainian Air Force against Eastern Ukrainian separatist groups that decade, and in the 2020s when Ukrainian Su-25s, as well as unmanned aircraft with similar roles such as the Turkish Bayraktar, proved unable to effectively provide close air support against Russian forces.[7]

From 2023 Russian close air support was increasingly provided by Su-34 strike fighters and other fighter types deploying a range of precision guided glide bombs, which proved much more effective than traditional CAS aircraft and could supplement artillery support with very large-scale attacks. This approach provided a favourable alternative to using Su-25s, which were expected to suffer unsustainable losses to Ukrainian air defences if deployed for low altitude short range attacks. As glide bombs played an increasingly central role in Russian tactical applications of its air power in the conflict, this provided a strong indication of the future of CAS. Where Su-25s had been likened to 'flying tanks,' precision guided glide bombs made the Su-34 operate as something of a 'flying precision artillery' system. As one of the only high intensity wars between major state militaries since the 1990s, this was one of multiple aspects of the Russian-Ukrainian War that was observed closely worldwide to provide insight into how warfare was evolving, including applications of air power against adversaries with significant air defence capabilities.

Russia's shift towards the use of multirole fighters with glide bombs provided an important indication of why replacing the A-10 with the F-35 may not significantly undermine close air support capabilities, despite the new aircraft's many shortcomings when evaluated as a traditional CAS aircraft. The F-35 was not well suited to loitering or flying low or slow, but advances in precision guided weaponry and the demonstrated effectiveness of precision guided glide bombs, even with Russia's more limited guidance capabilities, allowed any modern multirole fighter to provide effective close air support. This was again demonstrated during Israeli operations in the Gaza Strip from 2023, when F-35s provided close air support using precision guided bombs in close coordination with ground forces, although unlike in Ukraine, the almost total lack of enemy

Part of the wreckage of a Russian Aerospace Forces Su-25 close air support aircraft shot down during the first two weeks of Russian-Ukrainian hostilities in February-March 2022. (Ukrainian social media via Military Watch Magazine)

Russian Aerospace Forces Su-34 dropping a glide bomb during hostilities with Ukraine. (Russian Telegram Channels via Military Watch Magazine)

Glilde bomb in flight after being dropped by a Su-34. (Russian Telegram Channels via Military Watch Magazine)

air defences made such operations highly straightforward.[8] The F-35 did have a number of drawbacks, most notably its much lower endurance and weapons load and its very low availability rates and high maintenance needs, although these shortcomings affected its suitability for all roles, including as a replacement for the F-16 and F-18 among others, rather than its suitability for CAS specifically.

The U.S. Air Force had recognised the diminishing usefulness of traditional CAS aircraft in high intensity conflicts as early as the 1980s, and after beginning efforts to retire the A-10 within a decade of the type's service entry, the service renewed these efforts after the Gulf War in 1991, and again in the 2010s as F-35 production began. These efforts were consistently blocked by Congress largely due to the Army's support for keeping the A-10 in service.[9] The Air Force's dispute with lawmakers over the A-10 at times grew highly contentious, to the extent that a scandal erupted in 2015 after an Air Force general suggested to his subordinates that defending the A-10 to lawmakers was tantamount to treason.[10]

The Air Force was found to have gone as far as to doctor and otherwise cherry pick data to present the A-10 in an especially poor light,[11] and to suppress a prominent documentary highlighting the aircraft's importance,[12] while cutting funding for important upgrades and life extension, and burying requirements it had drafted for a possible successor that could have challenged the F-35A for funding.[13] Other notable moves against the A-10 by the Air Force included attempting to circumvent legislation barring the aircraft's retirement in 2015 by putting them into backup status, which it was forced to reverse after an outcry from lawmakers,[14] and three years later using creative accounting techniques to stealthily sideline a larger portion of the fleet in ways that were less noticeable to lawmakers.[15] The Air Force leadership consistently argued that the aircraft were not survivable against modern air defences. The service also worked to close the gap in targeting capabilities between the F-35's ageing Electro-Optical Targeting System and the modern podded targeting systems on the A-10C by integrating similarly advanced targeting systems on F-35s produced at the Block 4 standard onwards.

Criticisms of the A-10's survivability applied significantly more so to the AV-8B Harrier II, which despite also having been designed for CAS, lacked the armour, systems redundancy and firepower of its Air Force counterpart. This made it far easier to justify its replacement with the F-35B. The growing risks to close air support aircraft, and diminishing perceived need for them as precision guided munitions rapidly improved, resulted in a significant reduction in the utility of the Marines' Harriers before their retirement, as seen most clearly during in the 2000s during the invasion and subsequent counterinsurgency operations in Afghanistan. As summarised as early as 2002 in an award winning special report on the aircraft by the *Los Angeles Times*: 'Advancing technology of laser-guided missiles and bombs has allowed all combat planes to fly at higher altitudes. In the process, the Harrier has become less relevant.'[16]

A counterargument to the diminished utility of dedicated CAS aircraft is that airmen in a well armoured low flying combat jet would be no more at risk facing infantry with advanced man-portable surface-to-air missiles than personnel in tanks and other armoured vehicles would be against infantry with modern man-portable anti-tank missiles. Furthermore, while tanks carry three-to-four personnel, CAS aircraft like the A-10 carry just one. The fact that the procurement cost of an A-10 was comparable to that of an M1 Abrams tank only further strengthened this argument.

While there were arguments to be made that continued use of the A-10, or development of a direct successor intended to be operate in much the same way, could make military sense, for political and public relations purposes it was not desirable. The psychological and public relations impact of losing manned combat jets was significantly greater than that of losing ground vehicles, with this having been a leading factor in the reluctance to deploy these aircraft against well defended enemy ground forces while tank crews were placed at similar risk. This was seen clearly in Ukraine in 2022, when the United States refused to supply A-10s to the Ukrainian Air Force specifically due to 'the worrying prospect of dozens of American-made planes falling to the ground in flames without having done anything to help Ukraine's war effort' – as summarised by *The Telegraph*.[17] Aviation was a leading remaining strength of American industry, and air power was particularly central to U.S. power projection and to all its major military successes since the Second World War, which made it particularly vital to avoid high risk operations for manned combat aircraft, such as their use as 'flying tanks,' due to the high possibility of negative psychological and reputational repercussions.

A potentially optimal solution to the retirement of the A-10, the F-35's limitations in serving as a direct replacement, and the ongoing debate regarding utility of traditional CAS aircraft, was the

F-35A (front) and A-10C. The F-35 was not considered well suited to loitering and low altitude strafing like the aircraft it was designed to replace, but like all modern multirole fighters, could still provide effective close air support using a wide range of precision guided weapons from higher altitudes. (USAF)

development of an unmanned successor to the A-10. This would be able to engage enemy ground forces at low altitude without either putting a pilot at risk or threatening to cede a psychological victory. Such an aircraft would be significantly cheaper to develop and operate than a manned equivalent, while phasing pilots out of a position where they were at greatest risk. It could be highly complementary to the F-35 in a CAS role, and even serve as a 'wingman' to it, with rapid advances in the autonomy of unmanned aircraft potentially facilitating use of a high calibre gun much as the A-10 did.

Although the F-35 was envisaged from the outset to provide close air support, it is able to do so in much the same capacity as the F-16 or Su-34, and not in the most traditional sense of the role which was never at all viable for the aircraft. While its shortcomings as a CAS aircraft have been a significant source of criticism, the evolution of the mission has meant phasing out the A-10 for a more general unspecialised aircraft was in line with prevailing trends. The primary issue the fleet will face, however, is that the F-35's very low availability rates and high maintenance needs, combined with its more limited weapons carrying capacity, will limit the availability of CAS as more units transition to the aircraft. The Air Force's growing interest in acquiring a lighter, simpler and more maintenance friendly fighter to complement the F-35 (see Chapter 6), however, could see this second fighter type allocated CAS roles, allowing the F-35 fleet to focus on other missions which make greater use of its advanced capabilities.

Nuclear Strike: The Most Destructive Mission

Fielding the second largest nuclear arsenal in the world, although the United States has consistently deployed significantly fewer nuclear warheads than Russia on its strategic and tactical ballistic missile arsenals, the country has maintained a considerable lead in the deployment of tactical nuclear warheads from fighter-sized aircraft. While the F-35 program's role in transitioning the bulk of the American fighter fleet to field fifth generation level capabilities had been referred to as a 'disruptive game-changer,' and as a strategic rather than a tactical investment,[18] this was arguably most clear when considering the program's consequences for U.S. and allied nuclear strike capabilities.

Alongside the suppression of enemy air defences, a primary mission for the world's first stealth fighter the F-117 was to deliver nuclear strikes against Warsaw Pact targets such as ground force concentrations and military bases using B57 and B61 bombs. The Advanced Tactical Fighter program that followed was initially intended to produce a much longer ranged, stealthier and less maintenance intensive aircraft with a secondary air-to-ground capability with both conventional and nuclear weapons. Expectations that the F-22 would be modified to be able to launch nuclear attacks, as well as to carry radar evading air-to-ground weapons, persisted into the second half of the 2000s.[19] This failed to materialise, however, with the F-22's inherent limitations leaving it as the only fighter type in the American inventory without a nuclear strike capability. Lockheed Martin would pitch using the fighter for a nuclear strike role in 2008 as part of an effort to forestall the imminent decision to further cut and then permanently end production of the aircraft. Thomas Christie, who had served as the Pentagon's chief weapons tester for four years up to February 2005, dismissed this proposition as 'amazing' and 'grasping at straws,' with the wide-ranging issues that had emerged with the F-22 leaving little possibility of such investments being made.[20]

Despite the end of the Cold War, tactical nuclear bombs had remained vital not only to planned campaigns against nuclear weapons states, but also when considering possible attacks on non-nuclear adversaries. One of the most notable examples in the 1990s was the possibility of nuclear strikes should hostilities with North Korea escalate, which was considered vital to compensate for the country's conventional advantages. U.S. Army Lieutenant (ret.) General John Cushman summarised one of the primary arguments as follows in 1994: 'just as the United States considered nuclear first use an option against an overwhelming Warsaw Pact advantage in Europe, it must in all realism consider that option on the Korean peninsula today, if the alternative is the loss of Seoul and a long and costly refight of the Korean War.' He proposed use of eight tactical warheads of approximately 100 kiloton yield 'against selected troop and other military targets north of the DMZ [inter-Korean demilitarised zone].' Concerns that the U.S. Armed Forces may not be able to decisively win a conventional war led to a greater importance being attributed to tactical nuclear capabilities.[21]

Following the F-117's retirement in April 2008, the F-22's lack of a nuclear strike capability, and F-35's significant development delays, left the Air Force without a means of delivering nuclear gravity bombs using stealth fighters. The shortfall was exacerbated by the cancellation of 115 of the 135 planned serial production B-2 stealth bombers, and the fact that the remaining 20 suffered from very low availability rates among other issues, which left the Air Force's tactical nuclear strike capabilities far from sufficient even in the context of relatively low geopolitical tensions in the 2000s. These limitations were used to further argue for investment in the F-35 program.

The F-35's certification for deployment of nuclear weapons was scheduled to closely coincide with the operationalising of the B61-12 tactical bomb, a 320-kilogram weapon that famously cost more to produce than its weight in gold. The bomb was specifically sized to be accommodated in the F-35's internal weapons bays, and is prized for its ability to significantly vary its yield without modifications, providing significant versatility to engage a wide range of possible targets. Its minimum yield is 300 tons, less than the estimated size of the Beirut ammonium nitrate explosion in August 2020, while the maximum is 50,000 tons, 3.3 times as large as the Little Boy bomb used on Nagasaki. The bomb's significantly higher precision than older B61 variants, and its ability to be primed to detonate with low yields, was seen to make it unprecedentedly 'usable' on the battlefield despite the prevailing taboo against nuclear weapons use.

Combining world leading stealth and electronic warfare systems with a very high degree of situational awareness, the F-35's tremendous improvement in penetrative capabilities over all previous fighters makes its deployment as a nuclear-armed strike fighter a game changer for America's offensive nuclear capabilities. The fact that the F-35 would serve as U.S. Armed Forces' primary fighter across dozens of forward bases, over a dozen carriers, as well as in the fleets of all its nuclear sharing partners, and several prospective partners for future nuclear sharing agreements, makes the potential nuclear threats it can pose particularly difficult to predict. Where the F-117 had been a niche asset, with just 59 built, fleets of thousands of F-35s, the large majority of which would be fielded by states which arm them with nuclear weapons, pose an entirely new kind of threat to adversaries.

On 24 November 2020, the U.S. Air Force for the first time released footage of an F-35 dropping a test B61-12, after a simulated nuclear strike was launched at the Tonopah Test Range in Nevada on 25 August. The bomb included functional non-nuclear components and simulated nuclear components, and hit its target 42 seconds after being dropped. This was the first test to exercise all systems, including mechanical, electrical, communication and release, which made it a major landmark in the integration of the B61-12 with the F-35. A little over three years later, on 9 March 2024, the F-35A was officially certified to carry the B61-12. Spokesman for the F-35 Joint Program Office Russ Goemaere stated regarding this milestone in the fighter program: 'The F-35A is the first 5th generation nuclear capable aircraft ever, and the first new platform (fighter or bomber) to achieve this status since the early 1990s,' adding that the development provided all of NATO with a 'critical capability' and supported Washington's 'extended deterrence commitments.'[22]

The addition of the B61-12 to the F-35's arsenal had significant implications not only for the United States, but also for at least five of the fighter's foreign operators due to nuclear sharing agreements. These agreements saw countries that hosted USAF facilities where B61s were deployed train to employ these weapons using their own fighters; the intention being that the bombs be transferred to the hosting countries in the case of a great power war for near immediate use. Thus although the Netherlands, Belgium, Germany, Italy, and Turkey were not nuclear weapons states, the ability to carry out nuclear strikes was a core mission for which their fighter units trained, and significantly influenced their decisions regarding fighter procurements.

Nuclear sharing was considered controversial. Some of the dangers were summarised as follows in 2008, before the British House of Commons Defence Committee, as part of an assessment of the future of NATO and European defence: 'There are concerns that this arrangement undermines, and possibly contravenes, Articles I and II of the NPT [Treaty on Non-Proliferation of Nuclear Weapons] ... a nuclear sharing arrangement that may have had some logic in the pre-NPT and cold war world is now a source of weakening for the NPT, as it offers a rationale to other states to pursue a similar programme. NATO's nuclear sharing programme could now be used as an excuse by China, Pakistan or any other nuclear-armed nation to establish a similar arrangement.'[23] The tremendous enhancement of sharing partners' nuclear strike capabilities provided by the F-35, to which Germany transitioned from the Tornado, and all others from the F-16, further exacerbated these concerns. The fact that the United States had a wide range of partners capable of sharing its nuclear warheads and acquiring its stealth fighters, where China and Russia lacked remotely comparable networks of partnerships since the disintegration of the Warsaw Pact, meant that little could be done to proportionately respond either to nuclear sharing, or to the proliferation of F-35s intended to serve as nuclear delivery platforms.[24]

Eighty-three days after USAF F-35As were certified to employ B61-12 bombs, the Royal Netherlands Air Force (RNLAF) became the first partner in a nuclear sharing agreement to operationalise B61s in an F-35A squadron. The RNLAF announced on 1 June that F-35s operated by 313 Squadron had fully taken over the nuclear attack role from F-16s, elaborating: 'The Dutch transition from the F-16 to the F-35 for the nuclear role within NATO was initiated many years ago. In the last couple of years, the F-35 underwent a comprehensive testing and certification process for the nuclear role of the Netherlands. The RNLAF already started using the F-35 for conventional tasks ... NATO's nuclear deterrence is essential to the security of the Alliance, and therefore also to the security of the Netherlands.'[25] F-35As in Belgium and Italy, followed by Germany, and Turkey should it receive the aircraft, were expected to follow suit. In the United States itself, certification for the F-35B and F-35C was expected to occur in the following years. Dutch F-35As were the first to participate as nuclear strike aircraft in NATO nuclear war drills, namely Exercise Steadfast Noon in October 2024, with such exercises expected in future to see F-35s from multiple countries simulate nuclear attacks together.

As part of a broader response by Washington and many of its European allies to the escalation of tensions with Moscow, and the outbreak of full-scale war between Russia and Ukraine in February 2022, the tactical nuclear arsenal in Europe received renewed attention. This had significant implications for the future capabilities of the F-35 fleet. In August 2023, the Federation of American Scientists published a detailed assessment of reported preparations by the USAF to re-establish its forward deployed nuclear arsenal at RAF Lakenheath in the United Kingdom, where they were expected to equip two new F-35A squadrons.[26] The deployment of the warheads was confirmed in February 2025 to have been completed.[27] On 16 June 2024, NATO Secretary General Jens Stoltenberg confirmed that the U.S. was 'modernising their gravity bombs for the nuclear warheads they have in Europe and European allies are modernising the planes which are going to be dedicated to NATO nuclear mission.' He added that the alliance was holding talks on the deployment of more nuclear weapons in Europe, stating that the bloc needed to show its nuclear arsenal to the world. 'I won't go into operational details about how many nuclear warheads should be operational and which should be stored, but we need to consult on these issues. That's exactly what we're doing,' he stated, citing primary challenges from China, Russia and North Korea.[28]

By the mid-2020s the possibility appeared significant that more nuclear sharing agreements would allow more countries' F-35 fleets to launch nuclear attacks in wartime, with chairman of the Joint Chiefs of Staff nominee Dan Caine on 1 April 2025 stating that the United States was ready to consider entering into nuclear sharing agreements with more of the country's NATO allies.[29] After the completion of B61-12 deployments to RAF Lakenheath, British Minister of State for Defence Maria Eagle on 9 June confirmed that procurements of F-35A fighters specifically for nuclear strike roles were planned.[30] It was subsequently confirmed on June 24 that a new nuclear sharing agreement would be implemented to partially restore the second arm of the United Kingdom's nuclear triad.[31] The possibility of further nuclear sharing agreements affecting other F-35 fleets had been raised multiple times, in particular with Poland, Japan, South Korea and Australia. Polish Prime Minister Mateus Morawiecki stated on 30 June 2023 that his country was seeking to enter such an agreement,[32] while Japan's highly influential former Prime Minister Shinzo Abe had on 27 February the previous year called for his country to consider a similar sharing agreement.[33] Agreements involving South Korea and Australia had widely been speculated and called for in the two countries.[34]

While the U.S. moved to enhance its forward deployed nuclear arsenal, in parallel to expanding forward deployments of F-35s and continuing deliveries of the fighters to nuclear sharing partners, the Pentagon on 27 October 2023 also announced plans to develop a new variant of the B61 – the B61-13. This would be produced in smaller numbers, and would have a maximum yield seven times that of the B61-12 at approximately 350 kilotons. The bomb was designed to 'provide the President with additional options against certain harder and large-area military targets,' and appeared set to provide the F-35 with a truly strategic level of firepower. 'The B61-13 would take advantage of the current, established production capabilities supporting the B61-12, and would include the modern safety, security, and accuracy features of the B61-12,' a Pentagon press report explained.[35] The following month *Newsweek* highlighted that the new bomb would allow a single F-35 to kill over 310,000 inhabitants of the Russian capital Moscow on

An F-35A of the 461st Flight Test Squadron, as seen while releasing a mock B61 nuclear bomb during testing. (USAF)

one sortie, or over 360,000 inhabitants of the more densely populated city of St Petersburg.[36] This highlighted how threatening expanding deployments of by far the world's most capable penetration strike fighter, and of its nuclear warheads, was to potential adversaries, particularly Russia, North Korea and China, especially as these missions could be launched with little warning by almost any of the thousands of F-35s set to be deployed around the world.

The versatility of the F-35's nuclear arsenal had the potential to grow beyond the B61-12 and B61-13, with the USAF Nuclear Weapons Center mentioning potential 'future variants' of the B61 in January 2025. A successor to the B61-11 with a similarly reinforced outer shell for penetration of enemy fortifications was one notable possibility. Alongside the United States and its nuclear sharing partners, Israeli-built nuclear bombs of unknown designation and payload are also widely thought to have been integrated with the country's F-35s, with the country's unique ability to install its own software and weapon systems domestically onto the fighter meaning this can be done while maintaining Washington's plausible deniability.[37]

Ballistic Missile Defence

In the early 1970s the F-14 fighter became the first combat jet in the world to demonstrate a limited ability to shoot down incoming missiles, although its use of a mechanically scanned array radar restricted its ability to engage widely dispersed targets, or to maintain situational awareness while engaging. The Soviet MiG-31 interceptor would later that decade pioneer a more revolutionary missile defence capability, and demonstrated the ability to shoot down low diameter low flying cruise missiles over significant ranges, even if its targets were tens of kilometres apart. The MiG-31's capabilities caused considerable amazement in the Western world, and would not be replicated abroad for two decades.[38] The shift from mechanically scanned array to electronically scanned array radars was key to facilitating this change, and by the time the F-35 entered service such capabilities had become the norm among fighters. The F-35's smaller radar, shorter range and more limited missile carrying capacity relative to the F-15, however, means it is far from the best optimised aircraft in the American inventory for missile defence, for which advanced stealth capabilities are considered to be of relatively limited value.

Beyond cruise missile defence, the possibility has repeatedly been raised of the F-35 pioneering a new capability for tactical combat jets to also contribute to defence against ballistic missile attacks, although the realisation of such a capability is set to pose significantly greater technological challenges. Alongside air defence suppression, ballistic missile defence emerged as a high priority challenge for the U.S. Armed Forces after the end of the Cold War, with ballistic missile systems' asymmetric value in engagements with larger U.S. and allied forces making them highly prized by potential adversaries such as North Korea, Russia, Iran and Syria. The capabilities of such systems were in many ways complementary to those of ground based air defence systems that these countries also came to heavily rely on for an asymmetric defence. Thus for the F-35 program, an ability to make major contributions to ballistic missile defence, alongside the fighter's already highly refined ability to combat advanced air defence networks, would further optimise it to meet the main challenges of the post-Cold War era.

In 2014 the F-35 reached an important landmark during testing by successfully tracking a missile launch and transmitting tracking data using its data link. After four years of further testing, in August 2019 an F-35 transmitted live tracking data on a test strategic missile launch to the U.S. Army's Integrated Air and Missiles Defense Battle Command System.[39] The F-35's role as an elevated sensor linked into missile defence networks was further refined in subsequent testing.[40] Beyond the fighter's role as a sensor platform, however, the use of air-launched weapons to shoot down incoming ballistic missiles was a potential game changer for American ballistic missile defence capabilities. In April 2018 it was confirmed that such a role was being planned for the F-35, with director of the Missile Defense Agency General Samuel Greaves predicting at the time that the fighter would be ready for such operations by 2025. He described it as 'if not a game changer, then a significant contributor to future ballistic missile defence.'[41] Congressman Duncan Hunter at the time boasted that the F-35's existing AIM-120 air-to-air missile could be used for such a role, stating: 'You can shoot down missiles coming out of North Korea in the boost phase with CAPs [Combat Air Patrols] of F-35s and AMRAAMs [AIM-120 Missiles], and I've got a map to show it.' The ability to target ballistic missiles in their boost phases was ubiquitous to almost all modern fighters, however, with aircraft having only very narrow windows to do so, and under most circumstances being required to operate deep inside enemy airspace to target missiles in such a way. To be able to contribute more meaningfully to ballistic missile defence, a new missile type capable of engaging targets farther along in their trajectories would be needed.

An F-35B assigned to the 461st Flight Test Squadron of the U.S. Air Force, as seen while launching an AIM-120C during separation testing. (USAF)

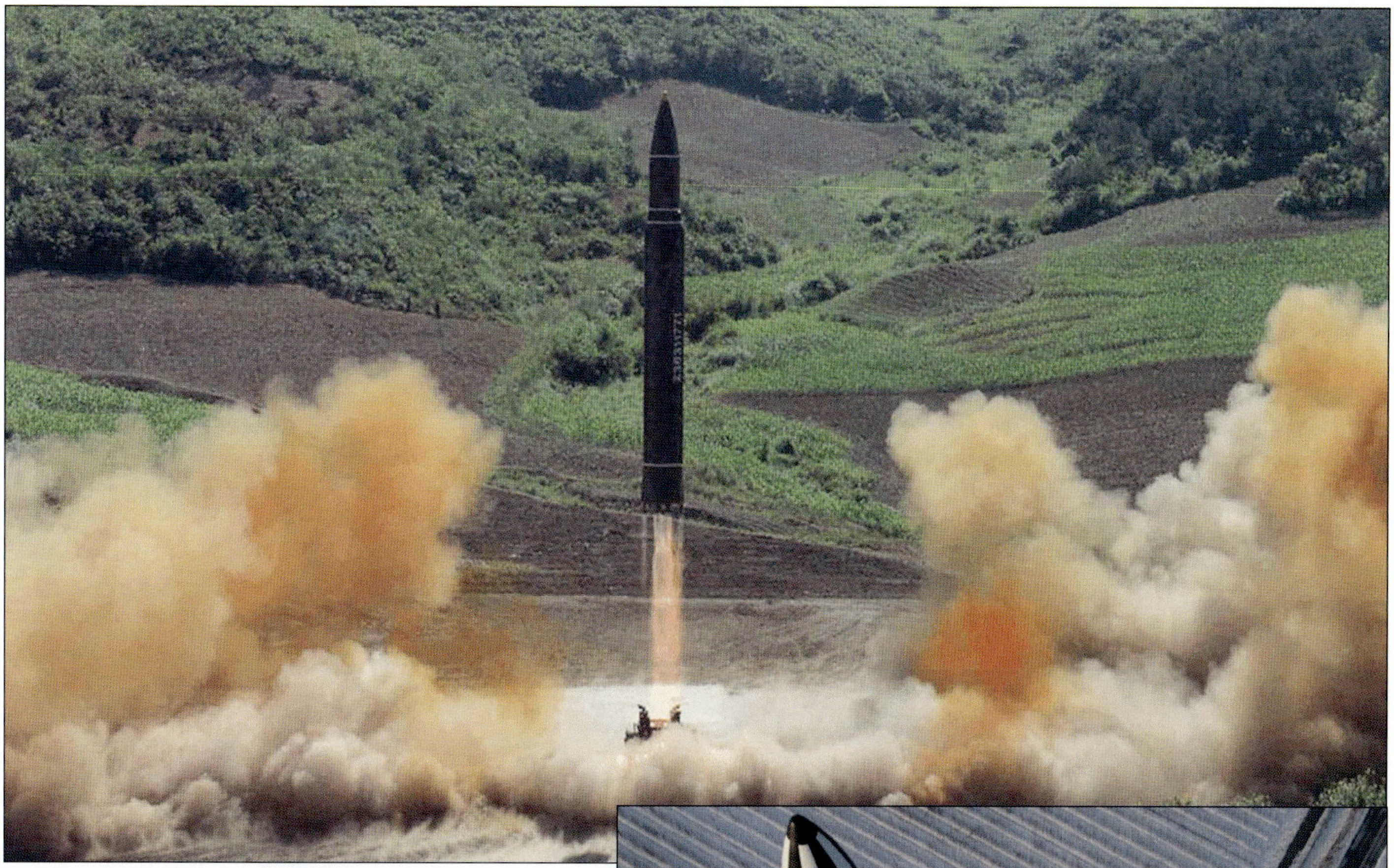

First test-launch of the Hwasong-14 ballistic missile on 4 June 2017, which was North Korea's first confirmed successful launch of an intercontinental range ballistic missile (above). This was followed by multiple newer ICBM classes, including the Hwasong-18 in 2023 which was the country's first to use a solid fuel composite (pictured right). The solid fuel engine significantly reduced preparation time before launch, posing greater challenges to any potential efforts to neutralise them before firing. (Korean Central News Agency)

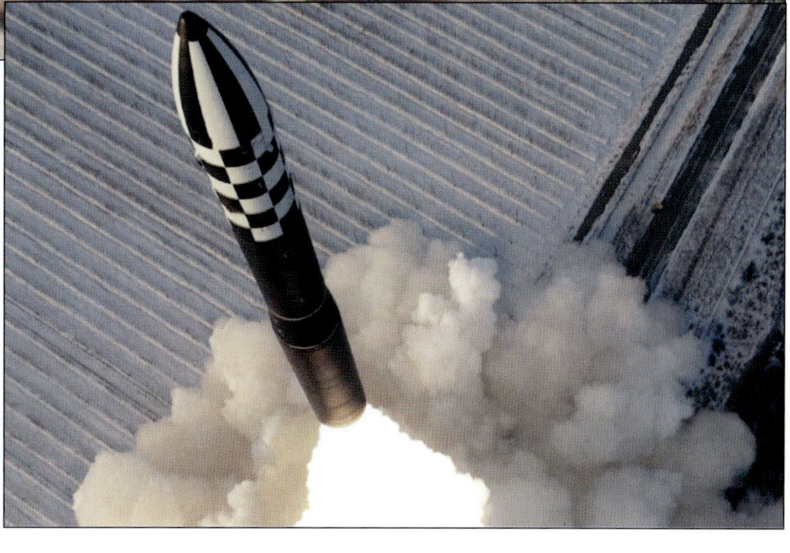

The possibility of developing a new missile type for the F-35 to widen the window in which it could intercept ballistic missiles in the boost phases was considered a significant possibility from the mid-2010s. Nevertheless, the F-35 was far from the optimal fighter for such a role, with its climb rate, altitude ceiling, speed and weapons carrying capacity, all being far more limited than previous aircraft designed to engage high speeds high altitude targets. The Soviet MiG-25 and MiG-31, which were designed to operate well above the Armstrong Limit, cruise at speeds exceeding Mach 2, and carry oversized missiles too large for regular fighters, had the most optimal performance characteristics for intercepting ballistic missiles in their boost phases, while among Western aircraft the F-15 was by far the most well suited. Nevertheless, the F-35 retained the advantage of truly global deployments, placing the fighters near many of the key launch sites of potential ballistic missile attacks against U.S. and allied targets – from the Persian Gulf to Eastern Europe, the Arctic and the Korean Peninsula. There thus remained a not insignificant possibility of a specialised missile being developed for the fighters for missile defence roles, with this potentially allowing F-35s to play a role in the broader Golden Dome missile defence initiative that has placed a renewed emphasis on targeting ballistic missiles before or shortly after launch.

Alongside a new type of missile, the integration of a compact solid-state airborne laser weapon onto the F-35 has been raised by analysts as a possible facilitator of anti-ballistic missile operations since the mid-2010s.[42] Lasers leave no time lag after firing for targets to evade or activate countermeasures, and may allow fighters to engage more targets per sortie than they could with a limited missile arsenal, and to do so at a much lower cost per shot fired. The lack of a time lag was highly valued for anti-ballistic missile roles, and had the potential to widen the windows for interception while avoiding many of the complexities that came with shooting down fast missiles with other missiles. The fact that laser weapons required a large amount of energy to be effective, however, was expected to significantly delay their integration onto fighter-sized aircraft.

Beyond ballistic missile defence, laser weapons had significant applications for air-to-air combat and air-to-surface attacks. Head of the Air Force Special Operations Command Lieutenant General Brad Webb in 2017 summarised the potential benefits of an airborne laser weapon for strike missions as follows: 'Without the slightest bang, whoosh, thump, explosion or even aircraft engine hum, key targets are permanently disabled ... The enemy has no communications, no escape vehicle, no electrical power and no retaliatory ISR [intelligence, surveillance and reconnaissance].'[43] The importance of such weapons was further highlighted in April 2024, when the USAF made its first ever fighter deployment to neutralise a large-scale drone attack. F-15Es involved in the operations were seriously constrained by their limited missile carrying capacities when engaging large numbers of low value Iranian drones, which had been launched to strike targets in Israel.[44] A laser could be particularly beneficial for the F-35 due to the additional constraints imposed on its missile payload by the size of its internal weapons bays.

The F-35 was throughout the 2010s and early 2020s expected to be one of the world's first fighters to integrate a laser weapons system, with the USAF's Self-protect High Energy Laser Demonstrator (SHiELD) program having been pursued to facilitate this. Initiated in 2016, the program goal was to test a laser weapon on a fighter. On 27 May 2024, however, it was confirmed that the program had been terminated after eight years of work without achieving its goal, and with 'no plans for further testing and evaluation.'[45] The program's failure was far from isolated, with the Army having disclosed earlier that month that it was facing major hurdles integrating a laser weapons system onto its Stryker vehicles. Two months prior on 19 March the USAF had announced that work to integrate a laser weapon onto the AC-130J gunship had also been terminated without success after nine years under development.[46]

While a laser weapons system would provide important new capabilities for air-to-air and air-to-surface missions, the F-35's ability to perform ballistic missile defence was particularly heavily reliant on advances in the integration of such a system. The high

Even when armed with a total of 12 AIM-120 air-to-air missiles, like this F-15EX of the Air Force 53rd Fighter Wing, the air-to-air payloads of F-15s were considered far from sufficient to effectively counter large swarms of low value attack drones. The AIM-120's cost is also close to two orders of magnitude more than that of many of the drone types it would be relied on to shoot down in such scenarios. (USAF)

perceived importance of ballistic missile defence, signs of significant progress in China to develop airborne laser weapons for its own fighters, and the growing need for low cost capabilities to counter large drone swarms, between them raise the possibility that work towards developing a laser for the F-35 with anti-air and anti-ballistic missile applications will continue to receive funding, despite the failings of other laser weapons programs.

Air Superiority: The Unintended Mission

Throughout its development and early years in service, significant questions were raised regarding the F-35's performance in air-to-air combat. The fighter's bulky appearance and stubby wings made it appear set to fly far more like a 'brick' F-4 than a sleek F-15 or F-16. Member of the self-dubbed 'Fighter Mafia', and former special assistant at the Office of the Secretary of Defense, Pierre Sprey, who claimed to have played a central role in the design of the F-16, would in the early 2010s gain considerable publicity for his interviews claiming the aircraft had a poor turn rate and lacked of manoeuvrability, while particularly highlighting the very small wing area of the F-35A and B variants.[47] The credibility of Sprey's assertions was widely questioned. Nevertheless, many more credible sources would point to the fact that the F-35 was indeed not well optimised for air-to-air combat. USAF Chief of Staff General Mark Welsh, for one, stated that the F-35 'was never designed to be the next dog fighting machine. It was designed to be the multipurpose, data-integration platform that could do all kinds of things in the air-to-ground arena including dismantle enemy, integrated, air defences. It had an air-to-air capability, but it was not intended to be an air-superiority fighter. That was the F-22.'[48] USAF Combat Command Chief General Mike Hostage similarly warned: 'If I do not keep that F-22 fleet viable, the F-35 fleet frankly will be irrelevant. The F-35 is not built as an air superiority platform. It needs the F-22.' This was similarly asserted on the basis that the F-35's air-to-air capabilities were wholly insufficient to face a peer level enemy air force without support from a better optimised air superiority fighter.[49] The U.S. Air Force in the 1990s argued that for the F-35 to be relied on without the F-22 fleet, it would have to be redesigned presumably to improve its air-to-air performance.[50] *

While it was clear that the F-35 was not optimised for air-to-air combat, the fighter would quickly prove to be highly capable of outperforming fourth generation fighters, including those developed specifically for air superiority missions. An early indication of the tremendous advantages which fifth generation fighters retained over their fourth generation predecessors was provided by the F-22's simulated engagements with F-15s and F-16s preceding and shortly after its formal entry into service. F-22s gained overwhelming victories in these engagements. Captain John Teichart, an F-22 pilot who flew F-15s against the F-22 in simulated combat, reported regarding his adversary's advantage: 'Its like clubbing baby seals its so easy.' Pilot Captain Jeremy Durtsch who also participated similarly referred to the F-22's advantage as 'clubbing baby seals.'[51] Although designers of the F-15 and F-16 had placed a far greater emphasis on air-to-air performance than the F-35's had, the technological discrepancy between the aircraft was expected to more than compensate for this and provide the F-35 with tremendous superiority.

An early indication of the advantage the F-35A retained over its direct predecessor the F-16 was provided by the Royal Norwegian Air Force's first F-35 pilot Major Morten Hanche, who in 2015 compared the newly delivered fighter's performance with that of the F-16 which he had previously flown. Hanche observed:

> So how does the F-35 behave in a dogfight? The offensive role feels somewhat different from what I am used to with the F-16. In the F-16, I had to be more patient than in the F-35, before pointing my nose at my opponent to employ weapons; pointing my nose and employing, before being safely established in the control position, would often lead to a role reversal, where the offensive became the defensive part. When I push the stick forward; the F-35 reacts immediately, and not delayed like the F-16 ...
>
> The F-35 provides me as a pilot greater authority to point the nose of the airplane where I desire. (The F-35 is capable of significantly higher Angle of Attack than the F-16. Angle of Attack describes the angle between the longitudinal axis of the plane – where nose is pointing – and where the aircraft is actually heading – the vector). This improved ability to point at my opponent enables me to deliver weapons earlier than I am used to with the F-16, it forces my opponent to react even more defensively, and it gives me the ability to reduce the airspeed quicker than in the F-16.[52]

Hanche's statement provided an important early indicator of the F-35A's advantages even in an area where the aircraft was most criticised, its flight performance, relative to the famously nimble F-16.

In January 2017 the F-35 made its first demonstration of its air-to-air combat capabilities at the U.S. Air Force's premier air combat exercises, Red Flag, held at Nellis Air Force Base in Nevada. F-35As from the 388th and 419th Fighter Wings were deployed to Nellis on 20 January, with exercises beginning three days later. Initial reports indicated that mock engagements between the new F-35s and fourth generation fighters resulted in a 15-1 kill ratio favouring the F-35s, although Vice Commander of Air Combat Command Lieutenant General Jerry D. Harris subsequently characterised the kill ratio as 20-1.[53] 34th Fighter Squadron commander and F-35A pilot Lieutenant Colonel George Watkins observed: 'The first day we were here, we flew defensive counter-air and we didn't lose a single friendly aircraft. That's unheard of.'[54] †

Significant questions were raised regarding the conditions under which mock engagements took place, with F-22s having been

* U.S. Air Force F-35A pilot Major John Searcy in 2019 summarised as follows how differences in mission between the F-35 and F-22 were reflected in flight performance: 'The F-35, they made design decisions that they knew going in that they would not achieve that same level of maneuverability, but as we're complementing the Raptor which is our air dominance fighter, we were designed for a different mission set, so more of the suppression of enemy air defences, or destruction of enemy air defences, or just long range strike and air interdiction. So we were designed more as that multi-role fighter as opposed to an air dominance fighter. And so while the Raptor as a fifth gen is more manoeuvrable than a fourth gen fighter, the F-35 is not.' ('4th vs 5th Gen Fighters,' *Fighter Pilot Podcast*, 12 January 2019.)

† Critics of the F-35 throughout the 2010s claimed that the aircraft's air-to-air performance would be limited by its less than outstanding aerodynamic performance, citing the fact that its sustained turn rate and other areas of flight performance had been downgraded below the program's original specifications. As early as 2013, however, Royal Australian Air Force Air Marshal Geoff Brown dismissed such criticisms on the basis that the F-35's combination of stealth and situational awareness were far more important in modern air-to-air engagements. 'The ability to be in a cockpit with a God's-eye view of what is going on in the world was such an advantage over a fourth-generation fighter,' he stated. 'The difference in the situational awareness in our two cockpits was just so fundamentally different. That is the key to fifth-generation. That is where I have trouble with the APA analysis.... To me that is key: it is not only stealth; it is the combination of the EOS and the radar to be able to build a comprehensive picture.' ('The F-35's Air-to-Air Capability Controversy,' *Defense Industry Daily*, 16 May 2013.)

An F-35A from the 388th Fighter Wing, as seen while releasing an AIM-120C air-to-air missile. (USAF)

heavily involved in the exercises on the side of the F-35, fuelling speculation that the kill ratio may have referred to a joint effort by the two fighter types.[55] Other questions regarding the circumstances of the engagements were wide ranging. Had simulated combat been carried out using visual range missiles only, for example, the F-35 would have had an overwhelming advantage over older fourth generation fighters that lacked helmet mounted sights and off-boresight targeting capabilities. Chinese and Russian fourth generation fighters were all capable of high off-boresight targeting, meaning overwhelming victories for the F-35s against fighters without such capabilities would mean little in practical terms. With the F-35 program urgently in need of better press, the possibility could also not be discounted that the exercises, or a part of them, had been scripted to advantage the new fighters and thus generate favourable headlines.

The fact that the U.S. Air Force did not field '4+ generation' fighters, unlike the U.S. Navy and the fleets of most of America's leading potential adversaries, provided favourable conditions for the F-35 to achieve entirely one sided results. Had exercises seen modern fourth generation fighters with infrared search and tracking systems, AESA radars, high off-boresight targeting capabilities and modern data links fielded, the F-35's victories may well have been far less overwhelming. The fact that the Air Force would in 2018 begin to seriously consider placing orders for F-15EX '4+ generation' fighters, while the Navy continued into 2024 to expand orders for F-18E/F Block 3 '4+ generation' fighters, indicated that the F-35's advantages may well have been less extreme than sensationalist headlines of 20:1 kill ratios indicated.

Preceding Red Flag 2017, exercises cited to demonstrate the F-35's combat readiness or its enhanced combat performance were widely criticised by agencies such as the Government Accountability Office, after multiple separate investigations found them to have been heavily scripted in the stealth fighter's favour. Many more minor exercises simulating air-to-air engagements saw interpretations of the little information regarding the F-35's performance vary widely, with the exercises often demonstrating far less than headlines made it appear. In June 2016, for example, seven F-35As deployed to Mountain Home Air Force Base in Idaho for operational tests alongside F-15Es of the 366th Fighter Wing. F-35As were reported to have suffered 'zero losses' in simulated engagements with the F-15s, which was interpreted by some sources as an 8:0 kill ratio. There was no indication that the F-15s shot back, however, and it appeared more likely that stealth fighters were intended to neutralise eight ground targets in an area defended by F-15s and, while successfully evading the enemy fighters, did not actually engage them. While evading the F-15s may have been a notable achievement – although depending on the setting of the exercise it may not have been – the record of reporting on the F-35's performances in exercises indicated that if the stealth aircraft had achieved shoot-downs, it would likely have been reported as such specifically.[56]

The F-35's performance at Red Flag 2017 appeared to do little to shift the consensus among informed sources regarding its flight performance, which was significantly more critical than named officers' statements to the press would indicate. Aviation journalist at *The War Zone* Tyler Rogoway in July 2017 summarised the prevailing spectrum of informed reports on the matter based on his own direct contacts. His findings were in line with widespread reports that the fighter had a flight performance considered mediocre at best, and was not expected to perform well in visual range engagements in particular, but that it had achieved unprecedented levels of automation that made it easier to fly within the limits that it could be flown. He observed:

Milliseconds after being released from the lower weapons bay of an F-35C (assigned to the U.S. Navy's flight test squadron VX-9), the motor of this AIM-120C is activating. Clearly visible under the outboard underwing pylon is an AIM-9X short-range air-to-air missile. (USN)

A Boeing infographic showing components of the F-18E/F Block III package, and other planned upgrades for the Super Hornet, bringing the aircraft up to a '4+ generation' level. The Navy would continue to invest heavily in procuring these aircraft while placing only limited orders for the F-35C, indicating that the older aircraft continued to be seen as cost effective and viable. (Boeing)

> I have heard directly from crews from both branches that have flown against the F-35 in training manoeuvres or are close (as in very) to the program. Their comments have ranged from 'good enough I think' to 'she's a pig but who cares I don't plan on seeing the enemy up close in it' to 'we need new jets OK, and this is what they are giving us.' I have never heard a rave review directly from anyone about the F-35's kinematic performance or agility. On the brighter side, by all accounts the pilots say the airplane is easy to fly generally speaking, which is great because it allows them to concentrate on the tactical aspects of the mission and not on aviating.[57]

In January 2019 new Red Flag exercises saw F-35As of the 4th Fighter Squadron deployed by inexperienced pilots gain highly favourable kill ratios against experienced airmen in fourth generation fighters. Since the Red Flag exercises in 2017, F-35s had integrated Block 3F software that brought them significantly closer to being fully operational. Colonel Joshua Wood, who participated in the exercises, recalled the following regarding their performances:

> I've never seen anything like it before. This is not a mission you want a young pilot flying in. My wingman was a brand new F-35A pilot, seven or eight flights out of training. He gets on the radio and tells an experienced, 3,000-hour pilot in a very capable fourth-generation aircraft: 'Hey bud, you need to turn around. You're about to die. There's a threat off your nose.' The young pilot then 'killed' the enemy aircraft and had three more kills in the hour-long mission. Even in this extremely challenging environment, the F-35 didn't have many difficulties doing its job, that's a testament to the pilot's training and the capabilities of the jet.[58]

The results of Red Flag indicated that with the F-35's functions heavily automated, its performance advantages over fourth generation fighters were such that they could more than compensate for tremendous discrepancies in pilot experience levels.* While this report provided one of the most significant insights into the F-35's performance in air-to-air combat, the fact that the fighter's automation could so heavily make up for a lack of experience also had important implications for the fleet's capabilities as services around the world were forced to reduce flight training hours due to the aircraft's low availability rates and high operational costs. The fact that the F-35 was so potent even in the hands of a pilot 'seven or eight flights out of training' indicated that concerns regarding the impact of flight training reductions on combat capabilities may well have been misplaced. Nevertheless, it remains uncertain to what extent this would apply if F-35s faced peer level fifth generation fighters, and whether pilot experience could still play a central role if aircraft had a smaller technological gap between them, or whether automation had reached a stage that piloting skills had become a relatively minor secondary factor.

The F-35 was notably not the only new stealth fighter that had the results of its simulated combat with fourth generation fighters reported, with a Chinese J-20 in September 2020 reported to have confronted targets approaching from all directions while flown by a novice pilot, and scored 17 kills for zero losses.[59] Much like in the U.S. Air Force, older fighters in the Chinese fleet, such as the Su-27SK which were technologically around 30 years behind, provided opportunities for a new stealth fighter to gain overwhelming victories which could deliver headlines that were highly favourable to the program. As was the case with the F-35's reported victories, the circumstances of the engagements, and the extent to which they may have been scripted, remained uncertain. The report that the J-20 pilot had just 100 hours of experience in the aircraft mirrored reports from the USAF of novice F-35 pilots comfortably outperforming seasoned veteran flyers in fourth generation aircraft, highlighting the growing degree to which technological discrepancies appeared to more than compensate for differences in pilot skills.[60] Nevertheless, much like in the United States, the fact that China's air force and navy continued to invest heavily in acquiring large numbers of enhanced fourth generation fighters, such as the J-15B and J-16, indicated that they were not as overwhelmingly inferior as a first reading of the results of exercises may have indicated.

Advanced fourth generation fighters like the F-18E/F Block 3, J-16 and J-10C, which were equipped with AESA radars several times as powerful as the sensors of the Cold War era, as well as infrared tracking systems, modern data links, and training in counter stealth tactics, had a much greater chance of challenging fifth generation aircraft like the J-20 and F-35. Some limited stealth capabilities of their own, and much more capable PL-15 and PL-16 missiles with inertial AESA radar guidance, were other important capabilities the J-16 and J-10C had, but advances in radar technology and data sharing capabilities were likely to be the most significant in making fifth generation aircraft's advantages less extreme. Thus although the F-35 and J-20 would have a strong advantage, these very high end fourth generation aircraft were still expected to be challenging to tackle, in contrast to the 'baby seals' position more basic fourth generation aircraft were in.

While there were no reports of F-35s carrying out major simulated exercises against very high performing fourth generation fighters, such as the F-15EX, the J-20 notably had. In January 2022 the *Global Times* reported that the J-20s of the Northern Theatre Command 'started the year with intensive mock combat training sessions' against J-16s and other fighter types, and entered combat with a handicap by using Luneburg lenses which nullified their stealth capabilities. The result was a close fight, as both the J-20s and the J-16s were able to evade multiple simulated missile attacks by pulling high g manoeuvres after at one point firing simultaneously on one another. Some two-versus-two mock combat lasted more than an hour. The fifth generation fighters managed to prevail using performance advantages other than stealth, although reports indicate that the results of engagements were close. Where the J-20 had one of the world's most impressive flight performances, however, and was designed as an air superiority fighter, questions remained regarding how the F-35 would have fared under similar circumstances.

J-20s on a separate occasion engaged J-16s in night-time exercises without luneberg lenses, the results of which were described as follows by the brigade's commander Senior Colonel Li Ling: 'During air combat at night, the J-20 takes advantage of its stealth capability, carries out beyond-visual-range combat missions and plays the role of a commander in the air, taking initiatives in combat.' At least one mock engagement saw J-20s engage J-16s two-on-two. Experts cited by the *Global Times* highlighted that these exercises would give pre-fifth generation units experience in tackling fifth generation targets, with lessons learned against the J-20 likely being applicable against F-35s and other stealth targets.[61] The J-20 reportedly 'took advantages of its stealth and attack capabilities and realised the tactical goals of finding the enemy first, firing missiles first, breaking away from combat first and destroying the target first,' according to state media reports.[62] The J-20s were nevertheless spotted and targeted at range by their adversaries on at least one occasion, although they managed to evade. The fact that J-16 procurements continued on a large scale long afterwards indicated that the fighter, despite being among the most expensive in the world, was still seen as a cost-effective investment, and that high performing fourth generation fighters were not as overwhelmingly outmatched as many reports supporting the F-35 program would indicate.

While the F-35's viability to combat the most capable Chinese fifth generation fighters remains a far more contentious issue, the question also arises as to its standing should it face a heavily enhanced fourth generation fighter like the J-16. Although not produced on the same scale as the J-20, the J-16's numbers were estimated to have surpassed 350 fighters in mid-2024,[63] which was almost the exact number of operational F-35As in the U.S. Air Force.[64] This made the J-16 by far the most numerously commissioned heavyweight fighter type by a single air force anywhere in the world since the turn of the century. While the unknown factors in such an engagement remain considerably more than the known ones, available information can provide a number of indications.

A central factor in a possible engagement would be the supporting assets on either side, as if there were airborne warning and control systems and other supporting sensor platforms within range, the J-16 could potentially benefit much more as these helped bridge the discrepancy in situational awareness with the F-35. Although

* Providing further insight into the F-35's performance at Red Flag 2019, 1st Lieutenant Landon Morris, a new F-35A pilot, recalled: 'With stealth, the F-35 can get closer to threats than many other aircraft can. Combined with the performance of the fused sensors on the F-35, we can significantly contribute to the majority of the missions. As this aircraft matures, we continue to see it be a significant force-multiplier in a threat-dense environment. Red Flag was a success for us and has made our younger pilots more lethal and more confident.' (Garbarino, Micah, 'Hill Airmen, F-35 a lethal combo at Red Flag,' *388th Fighter Wing Official Website*, 15 February 2019.)

A J-20 as seen during the 2018 Zhuhai Airshow with PL-10 short-range air-to-air missiles in firing poistion and an open main weapons bay. (Wang Weidong, via China Military Online)

Chinese People's Liberation Army Air Force J-16 fighters. This high performance fourth generation fighter has proven capable of going head-to-head with fifth generation fighters during combat testing, and is fielded in similar numbers to the F-35A in the U.S. Air Force. (央广军事 on Weibo)

the J-16's radar was well over twice as large as the AN/APG-81, and was considered similarly sophisticated, this would likely be far from sufficient to compensate for the vast discrepancy in stealth capabilities favouring the F-35, meaning the J-16 would struggle to track the F-35 at anywhere near its maximum effective targeting range without support. The F-35's AN/APG-81 radar would likely prove sufficient to lock onto a J-16 well beyond maximum targeting range without support.

In beyond visual range combat with a fighter with avionics as advanced as the J-16's, the F-35's primary advantage would be its stealth capabilities. The F-35's electronic warfare capabilities may also provide an edge, as the capabilities of the J-16's own EW suite remain unknown. The J-16 would have the advantage of a higher missile payload, the ability to launch missiles at higher speeds and from higher altitudes allowing them to travel significantly farther, and a greater ability to conduct evasive manoeuvres at all ranges. Within visual ranges a stealth configured F-35 would face a tremendous disadvantage against the large majority of potential adversaries, primarily not due to its limited flight performance, but rather to the fighter's lack of high off-boresight targeting capabilities due to an inability to carry the AIM-9X missile internally. Pilots would thus be forced to physically point their fighters' noses towards their targets, rather than cuing missiles against a wide plane of threats using helmet mounted sights. Even against relatively basic Soviet high off-boresight targeting capabilities operationalised in the mid-1980s, this would leave the F-35 at an overwhelming disadvantage, as has been consistently demonstrated in testing. Combined with the J-16's manoeuvrability advantages and cutting edge PL-10 missiles, this would ensure any such engagements are extremely one-sided.

Should the F-35 deploy AIM-9X missiles on its external wing pylons for a visual range engagement, the fighter's distributed aperture system would provide a significant advantage that would help to compensate for the J-16's much greater manoeuvrability. Such a configuration, however, would nullify the F-35's primary advantage in beyond-visual-range engagements, and is considered highly unlikely to be adopted for most high intensity engagements. The F-35 is thus the only fifth generation fighter forced to choose between a world leading beyond visual range air-to-air performance, and a respectable visual range performance, unlike the J-20 or F-22 which can be equipped for combat at all ranges while conserving stealth. The inability to carry the AIM-9X under the large majority of circumstances makes the fighter among the most vulnerable in visual range combat, and represents a leading shortcoming of the F-35 in terms of its air-to-air performance.

Should the new American AIM-260 air-to-air missile prove sufficiently reliable to allow the F-35 to avoid a visual range fight, the fighter would likely have a significant advantage over the J-16 under most circumstances, but not necessarily an overwhelming one. Such capable fourth generation fighters are very few and far between outside China, however, with the only fighters boasting comparable performances to J-16 being the J-15B and the F-15EX. With the large majority of potential adversaries relying on Russian fourth generation fighter aircraft, even the most capable of which are significantly less potent than the J-16 or F-15EX, the F-35 is likely to be sufficient to ensure a tremendous edge against adversaries using non-Chinese aircraft, including the Russian Aerospace Forces itself.

The F-35 is not a fighter well optimised for air-to-air combat, with most challengers able to manoeuvre better, carry more ordnance, cruise faster, launch missiles from higher altitudes, and carry larger radars. The baseline Su-27S which first entered service in 1984 is no exception. Nevertheless, these aspects of air-to-air combat are increasingly secondary in their importance, with the F-35 expected to retain overwhelming superiority against all but the most capable '4+ generation' fighters at beyond visual ranges, and over these a narrower but still significant edge. The fighter's electronic and network centric warfare capabilities, its stealth features, and the sophistication of its radar and missiles, are among the leading factors ensuring such an advantage. While the F-35's advantages over rival fighters are much more pronounced in its air-to-ground and air defence suppression capabilities, if able to avoid visual range engagements it will still represent one of the world's foremost fighters for air-to-air combat. Its ability to do so depends on the reliability of a number of technologies, among them its Identification Friend or Foe (IFF) systems and AIM-260 missiles.

Scripted Engagements

While the issue of engagements being scripted to favour the F-35 have been mentioned multiple times, as the fighter program further matured into the mid-2020s, and controversies surrounding it abated, it was not unheard of for more extreme cases of engagement scripting to occur – albeit not favouring the fighter but rather handicapping it. A notable case was revealed in June 2024, when USAF F-35A pilot Captain Patrick Pearce and German Eurofighter pilot 1st Lieutenant Alexander Grandt discussed a one-on-one mock engagement at Ramstein Air Base, using paper planes on video to elaborate on their manoeuvres. This provided a perfect example of how mock engagements could be scripted to create a result that was very far from representative of the actual discrepancy in capabilities between two aircraft, in this case advantaging Grandt's Eurofighter in what would otherwise inevitably be an extremely one-sided encounter.

Regarding the engagement, the two pilots recalled that neither knew what kind of adversary they would face, with each only given a slip of paper detailing a location in the air to fly to before engaging in visual range combat. The scenario allowed the Eurofighter to benefit from its 'little bit more thrust,' according to Grandt, with the aircraft able to win by getting behind the F-35 and achieving a simulated gun kill. 'You can just feel it in the pit of your stomach,' Pearce said, saying it's 'like man, this guy just won the fight.'[65]

With both pilots instructed to engage within visual range at a set location, the F-35's most significant advantages, its stealth capabilities and situational awareness, were effectively nullified. This was alluded to by Lieutenant Grandt, who stated that in a realistic scenario the F-35 would 'probably kill me beyond visual range even before I knew he was there.'[66] The Eurofighter, alongside the Gripen, was one of the very last fighter types in the world to transition from mechanically to electronically scanned array radars in production, doing so only from 2019. With the F-35's world leading electronic warfare suite designed to be able to jam similarly advanced fighters, successful jamming against the effectively obsolete Captor radar used by German Eurofighters was a near certainty. This combined with the F-35's stealth capabilities and its vastly greater network centric warfare capabilities would have ensured an overwhelming discrepancy in beyond visual range engagements, and left little prospect of a Eurofighter pilot having much idea where its target was.

Within visual ranges, the fact that neither party was permitted to use missiles for simulated kills prevented the F-35 from exploiting the significant advantages its distributed aperture system provided for targeting. Thus not only did the exercise demonstrate how the results of simulated combat could be highly misleading, but the constraints in place highlighted precisely the areas of the F-35's performance that gave it its primary advantages. The conditions that allowed Grandt's Eurofighter to prevail, by making low speed manoeuvrability a premium, would have similarly allowed a Soviet MiG-29 from 1982, which had even greater low speed manoeuvrability, to prevail consistently against the F-35. Pearce and Grandt's engagement thus served as an effective example of how misleading reports on simulated engagements could be, while also highlighting the primary factors that gave the F-35 its comfortable advantage over most fourth generation fighters.

Taking Over the F-22's Role

Much like the F-15 and F-16, the F-22 and F-35 were from their development stages closely linked as part of a high-low pairing from the same generation, with the technologies developed, numbers produced, and performances demonstrated by each having significant implications for the other. Significant improvements to the F-16C/D's combat capabilities from the late 1980s with the introduction of new avionics and the first beyond visual range missiles, for example, were key to allowing the USAF to make deep cuts to its fleet of F-15 air superiority fighters after the USSR's disintegration in 1991. By contrast, serious delays to the F-22's development, deep cuts to the number of F-22s planned culminating in a termination of production in 2011, followed a decade later by plans for the type's very early retirement, seriously disrupted plans for the phasing out of the Air Force's Cold War era fighter fleet. This in turn placed far greater pressure on the F-35 as the service's only other next generation fighter. With the F-22 having been expected to succeed the F-15 not only in the USAF, but also in the fleets of a number of strategic partners such as Japan and Israel, these countries were also forced to rely much more heavily on the F-35.

As a direct result of the significant shortcomings of the F-22 program, the F-35 came to be relied on as America's top fighter for air-to-air combat. A primary factor in this was the vast discrepancy in avionics between the two aircraft, with the F-22's computer architecture, radar and other key technologies having completed development in the 1990s, while the F-35 was not only a decade newer, but was being incrementally modernised over much a longer production run. While other fighters in high-low combinations, such as the F-4 and F-5 or F-15 and F-16, had been produced and modernised in parallel, ensuring they remained at comparable technological levels, this was far from the case for the F-22 and F-35, and ensured the latter would gain a strong and growing advantage. The growing discrepancy in avionics by the early 2020s increasingly appeared to more than compensate for the F-22's considerably superior flight performance, larger radar and higher weapons carriage.

The F-22's evolution differed greatly from projections made even in the late 2000s, with USAF Brigadier General Major Paul Moga, then an F-22 pilot, having stated in 2008:

> I would say based on all on all of the things I've read and all of the things I've heard, we are at least a couple of decades away from having to really face a significant or viable fifth generation threat. When that technology finally catches up to where the United States is today, guess what, the Raptor is going to evolve. The Raptor two decades from now that some kid's going to be flying, and I'm going to be sitting at my desk, is going to be nothing like the Raptor that's flying right now. Its going to, it would kick the snot out of it.[67]

Projections at the time, one year before orders were given for the termination of production, were that distributed aperture systems and helmet mounted sights would be among the upgrades the aircraft would receive.[68] Had the F-22 followed the paths of the F-15 and the F-4, with a long production run ensuring incremental updates to both the airframe and avionics, its standing against other fifth generation fighters the mid-2020s would have been considerably higher.

Providing insight into the advantages the F-35 retained, F-22 pilot Captain Patrick Bowlds in 2021 observed after flying simulated combat against the newer fighters that they 'have better detection capabilities kind of against everybody just because of their new radar and the avionics they have.' 'It definitely adds a level of complexity,' he noted.[69] Although its radar was smaller, the discrepancy in sophistication, combined with the F-35's next generation data link system, distributed aperture system and EOTS ensured an overwhelming situational awareness advantage, with the F-22 lacking any of these features. Beyond these factors, while a primary advantage of the F-4 and F-15 over their lighter counterparts had been their far longer ranges, the F-22's range was far the shortest in the world for a fighter of its size, and was surpassed by that of the F-35A. While the F-22 would remain unquestionably the more manoeuvrable fighter, the F-35A's helmet mounted sights and resulting high off-boresight targeting capabilities, combined with its distributed aperture systems, meant even in visual range engagements the newer aircraft was expected to have a significant advantage. The result of these factors combined meant that the F-35, although designed with air-to-air combat only as a secondary role, emerged as the Western world's most capable fighter for air superiority and missions. While the ideal air superiority fighter

An F-22 (foreground), with F-35A in wing position. Due to early termination of F-22 production, and the growing age of the type's stealth features and avionics, a much greater burden of air superiority missions is expected to be placed on the F-35 fleet, despite the aircraft not having been intended as a premier air superiority fighter. (USAF)

would have paired the F-35's sophisticated airframe materials and avionics with the F-22's flight performance, and with an endurance and radar size comparable to or exceeding those of the F-15, the F-35 was the best the United States and its allies had.

Armament: Electronics

As a highly versatile multirole fighter the F-35 was developed to be compatible with a wide range of armaments, ranging from small gravity bombs and infrared guided air-to-air missiles, to GPS guided cruise missiles and nuclear bombs. While the arsenal of missiles and bombs accommodated in the F-35's internal weapons bays will differ widely between missions, however, one primary weapons system which the F-35 will carry on all missions regardless of its configuration is the AN/ASQ-239 electronic warfare suite, which is one of the most outstanding armaments in its arsenal.

The AN/ASQ-239 pairs with the considerable electronic warfare capabilities of the F-35's radar to provide advanced countermeasures, jamming options, and broadband protection, allowing the aircraft to effectively suppress enemy radars. The system was designed to operate in signal-dense environments, and to provide the F-35 with radio frequency and infrared countermeasures and rapid response capabilities. Its electronics architecture was designed specifically to allow designers to enable new capabilities as these were developed. The AN/ASQ-239 is considered one of the most sensitive systems integrated on the F-35, with the discrepancy in performance between those built for domestic and foreign use reportedly being particularly wide.

With the F-117 and F-22 having lacked comparable electronic warfare suites, the pairing of the F-35's stealth capabilities with the AN/ASQ-239's offensive potential allows the fighter to pose a significantly greater threat. The lack of a need for dedicated electronic warfare aircraft to accompany F-35 operations not only allows services to achieve more with smaller fleets, but also eliminates the possibility of fighters being left vulnerable should the circumstances of a war prevent these supporting aircraft from contributing to operations. A notable example of fighters being left venerable under such circumstances was the shoot-down of an F-15E on 30 January 1991 by an ageing Iraqi S-75 air defence system, which was possible because the supporting EF-111A electronic attack jets had been forced to turn back after encountering MiG-25 interceptors.[70] Even the most capable fighters could be highly vulnerable to relatively basic air defence assets without electronic warfare support, which made the F-35's integration of its own highly potent electronic warfare suite a leading contributor to its survivability. With electronic warfare capabilities being particularly important for air defence suppression, the strong emphasis the F-35 placed from the outset on integrating a world leading electronic warfare suite reflected the performance priorities of the post-Cold War era.

Armament: Air-to-Air

The F-35 deploys three missile types for beyond visual range air-to-air combat, with the vast majority of fighters produced relying on the AIM-120 Advanced Medium-Range Air-to-Air Missile (AMRAAM), which is by far the most widely fielded active radar-guided air-to-air missile type in the world. Upon entering service in the USAF in 1991, the AIM-120 was the third in the world with active radar guidance, meaning it had much prized 'fire and forget' capabilities, could be used to implement a significant range of new tactics, and allowed each fighter to engage many more targets simultaneously. The missile type would be incrementally modernised over more than three decades, culminating in the development of the AIM-120D3 in 2022 with an estimated 180 kilometre engagement range, compared to the 70 kilometre range of the original AIM-120A. The new variant benefitted from comprehensive improvements in areas ranging from guidance capabilities to manoeuvrability.

Developed as a successor to the AIM-120, the AIM-260 Joint Advanced Tactical Missile (JATM) began development in 2017, and represented the first clean sheet air-to-air missile developed in the United States in three decades. Estimated to cost over $2.5 million each, the missile entered service in 2024, had an engagement range exceeding 200 kilometres, and was thought to integrate an AESA radar to improve its ability to lock onto stealth aircraft and reduce its vulnerability to jamming. Little was known regarding the missile, although officials directly referred to the program as a response to China's development of the PL-15 which was seen to outperform the latest AIM-120 variants.[71] The missile was not expected to be affordable in large numbers, and would likely be prioritised to equip F-35 and F-22 units deploying to the Pacific, while the AIM-120D could be relied on to provide superiority in other theatres.

The first launch of an air-to-air missile (an AIM-120C) from an F-35A prototype, on 5 June 2013. (USAF)

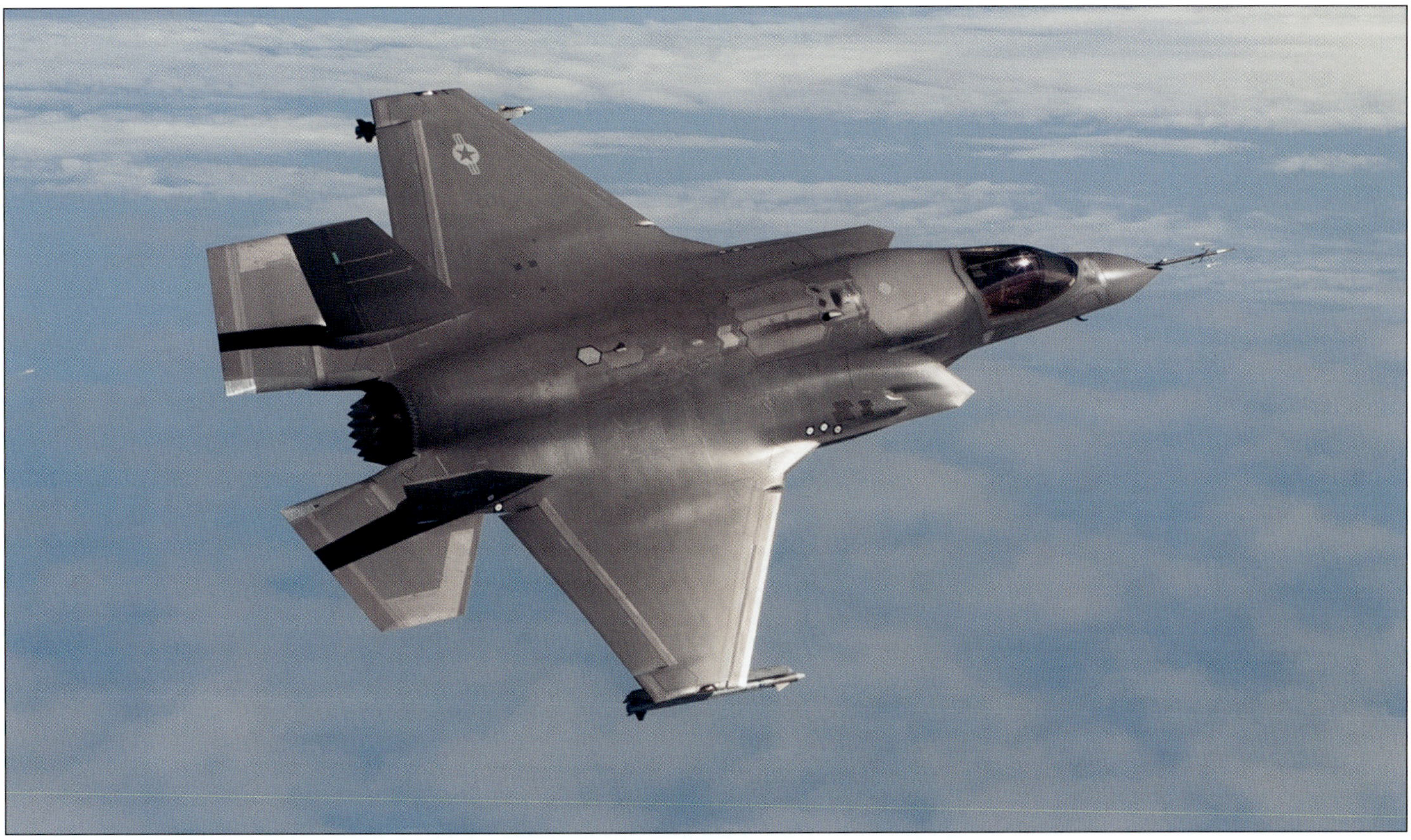

F-35C prototype configured for visual-range air-to-air missiles with externally mounted AIM-9X infrared-guided missiles. (Lockheed Martin)

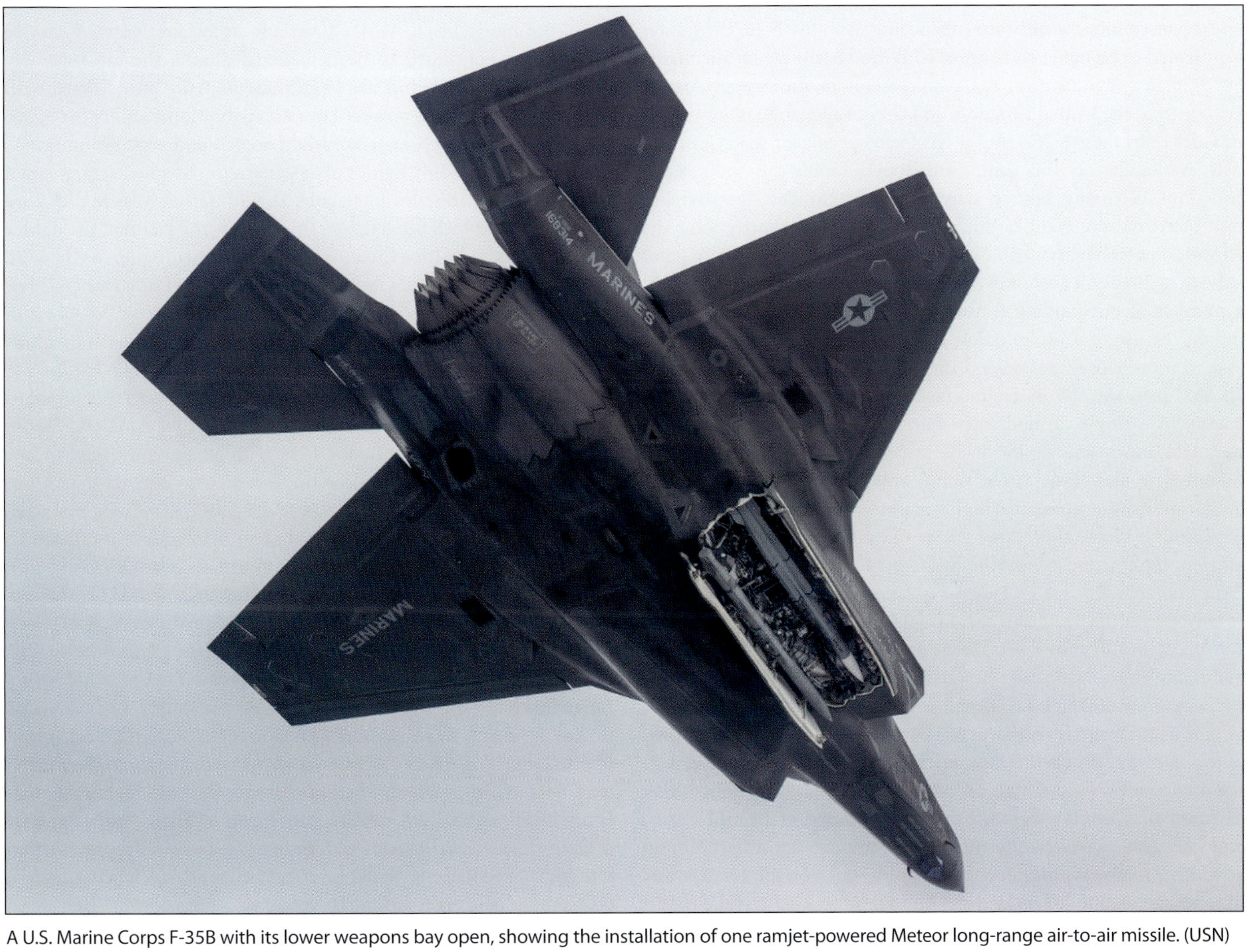

A U.S. Marine Corps F-35B with its lower weapons bay open, showing the installation of one ramjet-powered Meteor long-range air-to-air missile. (USN)

F-35B prototype as seen during a simulated air combat, carrying four laser-guided bombs on underwing hardpoints, in full afterburner, and while firing an AIM-132 Advanced Short-Range Air-to-Air Missile (ASRAAM). (U.S. DoD)

As part of Block 4 software enhancements to the F-35, the fighter is intended to be made compatible with the Meteor air-to-air missile by 2028 in order to meet the requirements of the British Armed Forces. Italy, the United Kingdom and Greece all plan to integrate the missiles onto their F-35s, and it has been speculated that Germany will eventually do the same. Developed jointly by the United Kingdom, Germany, France, Italy, Spain and Sweden, the Meteor's protracted development began in the early 1990s shortly after the AIM-120 entered service in the USAF, although it would only enter service in 2016 at a cost of over $2 million per missile. It introduced a number of outstanding features, and rather than using a rocket motor, the use of a variable flow ducted rocket (ramjet) propulsion system more closely resembled the engine of a cruise missile. This allowed it to throttle its engine in flight rather than expending its energy in a single unmodulated burn cycle. The Meteor can thus maintain more energy for its terminal attack phase to perform manoeuvres and climb faster, significantly increasing the size of its 'no escape zone' even against highly manoeuvrable targets. The ability to modulate thrust also allows the missile's autopilot to use the most efficient flight path, conserving fuel to achieve a much longer range. Other notable features include an advanced data link allowing it to receive course updates from a wide range of assets, from destroyers to AWACSs, and an ability to be re-targeted during flight. The Meteor's competitiveness against the newer AIM-260 remains unknown due to the scarcity of details on the American missile's capabilities.

The F-35's primary armament for visual range air-to-air combat is the AIM-9X Block II Sidewinder, which began development in the 1990s to provide a high off-boresight targeting capability. This capability had been pioneered by the Soviet Union in the mid-1980s, and had proven repeatedly in testing to provide an overwhelming advantage in visual range engagements, although by the 2010s it was ubiquitous to all modern fighters. Although the AIM-9 is the oldest air-to-air missile type in the world, having first entered service in 1956, the modernised AIM-9X variant which first entered service in 2003 has continued to be considered among the most capable weapons of its kind, and has been incrementally modernised with features such as a lock-on after launch capability, the ability to engage targets at more extreme off-boresight angles, and a longer range.

The F-35 is the only fighter of its generation unable to carry visual range air-to-air missiles internally, as its internal missile racks are not compatible with the AIM-9. This reflects the fact that the fighter was not designed with a focus on air superiority missions as the F-22 and J-20 were, and leaves it unable to makes use of its advanced high off-boresight targeting capabilities in visual range combat when in stealth configuration. The F-35 has a hardpoint under each weapons bay for air-to-ground munitions, and a further three hardpoints under each wing to accommodate extra weapons, with the outboard wing hardpoint developed exclusively for the AIM-9X. These external hardpoints provide the F-35 with greater versatility in low threat environments, and allow the F-35A/C to carry a maximum payload of 14 air-to-air missiles and six GBU-31 bombs. External weapons hardpoints are not expected to be frequently utilised in near peer level conflicts due to the importance of the F-35's stealth capabilities, however, meaning under the large majority of likely combat scenarios the F-35 will be one of the very few fighters in the world without any high off-boresight targeting capabilities. This limitation makes it particularly critical for the F-35 to avoid visual range combat.

The sole alternative to the AIM-9X is the AIM-132 Advanced Short Range Air-to-Air Missile (ASRAAM), which was developed by the United Kingdom and equips British F-35Bs. The missile first entered service in 1998, and represented a clean sheet design four decades newer than the AIM-9. It similarly cannot be accommodated internally. Predictions that the Iris-T missile developed under a German-led program would be integrated onto the F-35 failed to materialise, with Italian and German orders for the AIM-9X to equip

A zoomed-in view at the installation of a Meteor long range air-to-air missile next to an AIM-120C in the internal weapons bay on an F-35B. (USMC)

their fleets leaving little possibility of this. A number of unconfirmed reports have indicated that the Israeli Air and Space Force intends to integrate the rival Python-5 onto the F-35, and to eventually market this missile to other F-35 clients.

Armament: Visual Range Air-to-Ground

A decade after entering service, the F-35 in the mid-2020s remains highly constrained in the beyond visual range armaments it can carry for air-to-surface missions, leaving it as one of the most heavily reliant fighters in the world on guided gravity bombs. The F-35A and F-35C's standard configuration for air-to-ground missions is deployment of two GBU-31 Joint Direct Attack Munition (JDAM) 961 kilogram guided bombs, with one being accommodated in each of its main weapons bays alongside a single AIM-120 or AIM-260 missile. The smaller weapons bays on the F-35B restrict it to deploying the GBU-32 461 kilogram JDAM. Benefitting from both inertial and GPS guidance, the JDAM is by far the most ubiquitous weapons class deployed by the F-35, and equips the fleets of all F-35 operators other than the United Kingdom. Providing a smaller option for a GPS-guided weapon, the F-35A can also deploy the GBU-39 Small Diameter Bomb, which weighs just 110 kilograms allowing four to be carried in each weapons bay. Alongside these satellite guided weapons, all F-35 variants can deploy the GBU-12 Paveway II 230 kilogram laser guided bomb which receives guidance from the fighter's Electro-Optical Targeting System. As the only F-35s that do not rely on the JDAM as their primary air-to-ground armament, British F-35Bs deploy the Paveway IV 230 kilogram dual-mode GPS/INS and laser-guided bomb in place of the GBU-32. The Paveway IV can also be deployed by other F-35 operators, and is designated the GBU-49 in the United States.

Alongside conventional bombs, the F-35A became compatible with the B61-12 nuclear bomb in 2024, and is likely to be compatible with one or more types of Israeli nuclear bomb. It is expected to be made compatible with the aforementioned B61-13 and possibly with future B61 variants. The F-35B and F-35C are also expected to become compatible with the B61. The types of guided conventional bombs are also expected to be increased, most notably with the integration of the GBU-54, 261 kilogram Laser Joint Direct Attack Munition (LJDAM), which can provide a means of engaging moving targets.

The F-35's visual range targeting capabilities are expected to be improved significantly in the 2030s with the integration of the AGM-179 Joint Air-to-Ground Missile (JAGM), which was developed to succeed the AGM-114 Hellfire used by drones and helicopters. This is expected to provide a high cost option for precision strikes against targets within approximately 16 kilometres. Not only will the missile be the F-35's only visual-range weapon capable of engaging moving ground targets, but the millimetre wave radar on its onboard tri-mode seeker will allow it to do so without post-launch guidance from the fighter, which has revolutionary implications for the F-35's ability to provide close air support. In November 2023, it was reported that the U.S. Navy intended to also provide the F-35 with compatibility with the AGM-114, which would make it the first fighter type to deploy the missile. This fuelled speculation that a new Hellfire variant could be under development.[72]

Armament: Beyond Visual Range Air-to-Ground

As of the mid-2020s the F-35's options for beyond visual range weaponry for roles other than air-to-air combat remain extremely limited, which restricts its versatility and its ability to operate in a range of roles such as air defence suppression. The fighter's choice of weapons loadouts is set to increase markedly from the early 2030s, however, as it is brought up to the Block 4 standard, and as a number of new missile types enter service.

The longest ranged weapon intended to equip the F-35 is the AGM-158 Joint Air-to-Surface Standoff Missile (JASSM) cruise missile, which first entered service in 2003, and combined a 450kg warhead with a 370km range, and high levels of precision provided by GPS, thermal and inertial guidance. The AGM-158B JASSM-ER variant, which entered service in 2014, extended this engagement range to 925km through use of a more efficient engine and an increased fuel volume. These 1,000 kilogram missiles are rarely deployed due

A prototype F-35B in the process of releasing a GBU-38 JDAM 250kg bomb. (USMC)

One of the F-35C prototypes as seen during separation testing for GBU-38 JDAM with a mock AIM-9X Sidewinder air-to-air missile on its outboard underwing pylon. (USN)

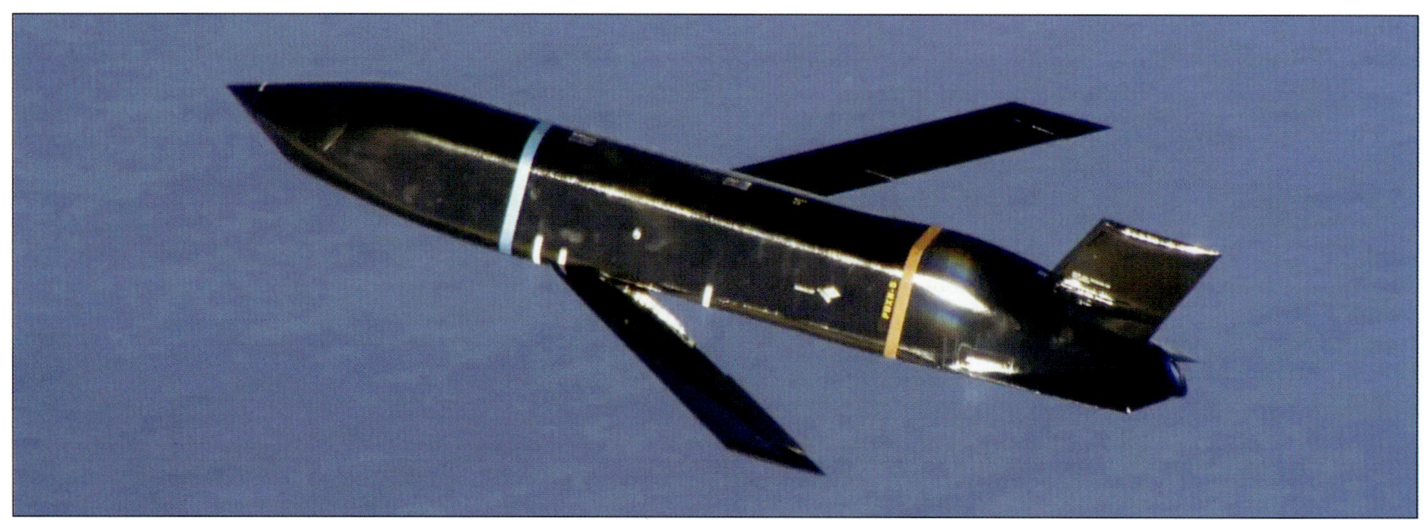

An AGM-158 JASSM – the longest-ranged air-to-ground weapon in F-35's arsenal – as seen in flight. (USAF)

to their inability to be housed in the F-35's internal weapons bays, although their facilitation of strikes from safe distances without needing to rely on the F-35's stealth capabilities is potentially highly valuable against targets in heavily defended airspace.

The JASSM remains as of the mid-2020s the F-35's only operational beyond visual range air-to-ground missile, meaning stealth-configured F-35s can only strike ground targets from close ranges. Among the missiles under development for the fighter, the AGM-88G Advanced Anti-Radiation Guided Missile (AARGM) is designed to target enemy air defence assets by homing in on their radar emissions, and is expected to be among the most widely deployed. Developed as a derivative of the Cold War era AGM-88 High-speed Anti-Radiation Missile (HARM), the AGM-88G replaces the original design's mid-body wings with aerodynamic strakes, and has relocated control surfaces, allowing it to be carried internally by the F-35A and F-35C. In September 2023, Northrop Grumman was selected to complete development of the Stand-in Attack Weapon (SiAW) program to develop a derivative of the AGM-88G able to strike a wider range of targets, and to serve as the F-35's primary air-to-surface missile type. It is specifically designed to be able to neutralise the primary kinds of targets which the F-35 was conceptualised to be able to seek and destroy such as mobile ballistic and cruise missile launch vehicles and mobile electronic warfare and anti-satellite systems. With a speed exceeding Mach 2, and a weight of 361kg, the AGM-88G and its derivative, developed under SiAW, are likely to remain the F-35's only supersonic air-to-surface weapons until the latter half of the 2030s, and to both have ranges of approximately 300 kilometres.

A much shorter ranged air-to-surface missile, the Select Precision Effects At Range (SPEAR), is being developed by the French-based multinational MBDA specifically for the F-35 as a very light short-ranged air-to-surface cruise missile. Weighing under 90kg, the SPEAR's design is intended to allow even the small weapons bays on the F-35B to accommodate up to eight of the missiles, allowing squadrons to saturate enemy air defences. With a range of over 140km, and using a tri-mode seeker with radar, infrared, and laser homing, the missile is optimised to neutralise highly mobile targets such as components from S-400 systems or wheeled Hwasong-11B launchers, and can either prosecute targets autonomously or receive target coordinates via data link. Its small size and low cost will allow it to be used against lower value targets such as armoured vehicles, facilitating entirely new means of providing close air support. The SPEAR's promise is nothing short of revolutionary, making it likely the most significant non-U.S. weapons system confirmed for integration onto the F-35. An electronic attack version of the missile, the SPEAR-EW, is also under development.

On 31 January 2024, the USAF issued a notice for the Extended Range Attack Munition (ERAM), specifying that the missile needed an internal navigation system 'capable of operating in a GPS degraded environment,' as well as a 'terminal accuracy' allowing it to hit within 10 metres of the impact point at least 50 percent of the time including when facing high electromagnetic interference and GPS jamming.[73] Little else was known about the missile type, although the high vulnerability of Western precision guided weapons to Russian jamming demonstrated in the Ukrainian theatre from 2022 was suspected to have influenced the system's emphasis on overcoming such measures.[74]

Armament: Anti-Ship

Although stealth fighters have since the 1980s been expected to pose unique challenges to the safety of enemy surface fleets, as of the mid-2020s a stealth fighter well optimised for such missions has yet to materialise. With the cancellation of the A-12, the F-22's lack of beyond visual range capabilities, and the focus of China's J-20 program on air-to-air combat, the F-35 has the potential to emerge as the first stealth fighter equipped for anti-shipping missions. Although the fighter's deployment from aircraft carriers makes this particularly important, as of the middle of the decade no anti-ship missiles have yet been operationalised.

The longest ranged anti-ship missile developed for the F-35 is the AGM-158C Long Range Anti-Ship Missile (LRASM), a derivative of the JASSM which first entered service in 2018. It is expected to be made compatible with the fighter from around 2030. The LRASM is particularly notable for its use of on-board guidance systems to engage targets autonomously without either GPS or data links. This is expected to significantly reduce its vulnerability to jamming. It

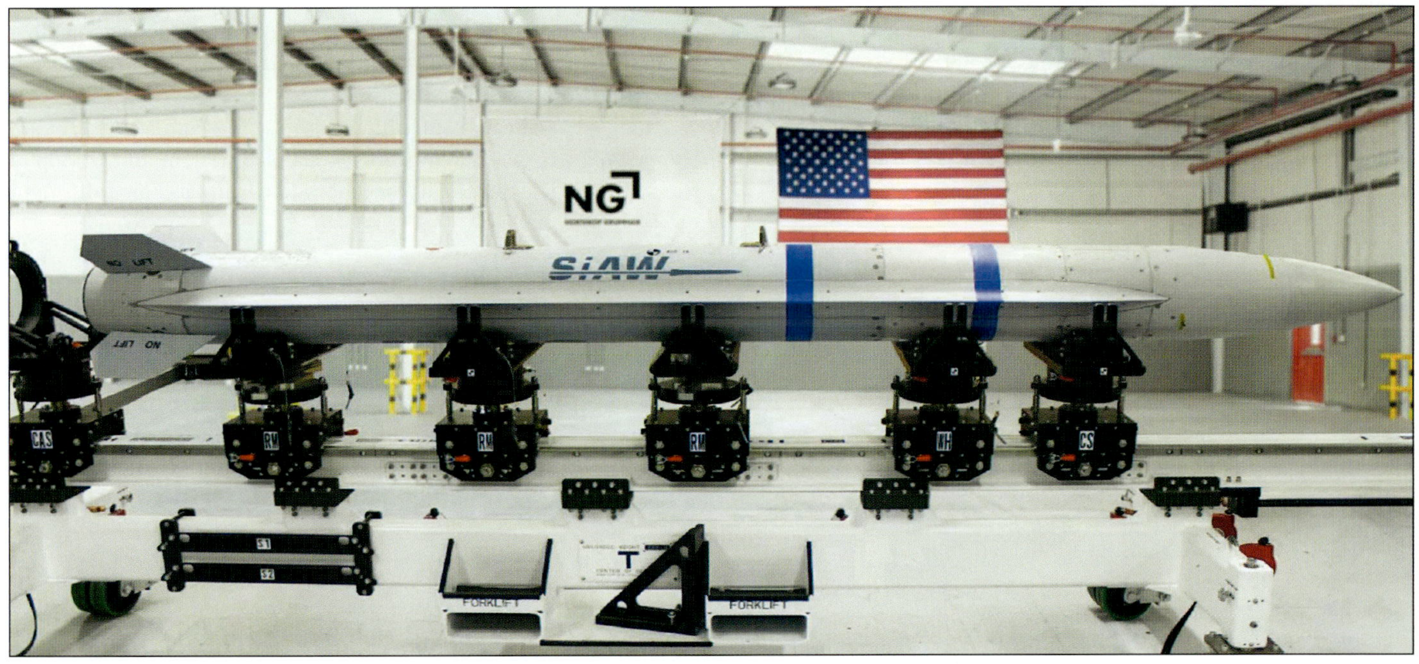

The AGM-88G HARM is the principal anti-radiation missile of the F-35. Notable is the complete removal of the fins of the original design, and their replacement using aerodynamic strakes. (USAF)

A Spear 3 air-to-surface missile, as seen in front of an F-35B of the Naval Air Squadron 809, British Royal Navy. (MOD UK)

also retains an adaptive routing capability, which pairs with its built-in electronic support measures to detect 'pop-up' air defence threats and automatically change flight course in response. Other threat updates can be provided by data link. The missile relies on an imaging infrared seeker for terminal guidance, and has a reported range of 370km and a 450kg warhead. Like the JASSM, it cannot be carried internally. The initiation of LRASM flight tests on the F-35 was announced on 10 September 2024.[75]

On 2 February 2024, Naval Air Systems Command put out a contract notice for the Multi-Mission Affordable Capacity Effector (MACE) system. In contrast to the LRASM, which cost over $3.2 million and weighed over 1,200kg, the MACE is intended to cost under $300,000 and to be accommodated in fours inside F-35A/C's weapons bays. With production planned at 500 missiles per year, the Navy described the MACE as intended to 'provide desired lethality without exposing manned platforms to significant survivability risks and jeopardising mission effectiveness,' specifying the need for only a relatively small 73kg warhead. Its range is expected to be 300-450 kilometres, making it comparable to that of the LRASM but much better suited to saturation strikes.[76] The MACE is expected to have significant commonality with the Extended Range Attack Munition, which the Air Force had issued a notice for just three days before the Navy did for its missile.

The Joint Strike Missile developed by the Norwegian firm Kongsberg in partnership with Raytheon is a derivative of the Naval Strike Missile that had entered service in 2012, and was designed to be accommodated in the F-35's internal weapons bays. It weighs approximately 400kg, carries a 120kg warhead, and has a 555km maximum engagement range, while also being able to deploy on a sea-skimming low trajectory to attack better defended targets at the expense of shortening its range to under 200km. By the end of 2024 Japan, Australia and the United States had all placed orders for the missiles to equip their F-35 fleets.

Alongside dedicated anti-ship missiles, the Mako Multi-Mission Hypersonic Missile, developed by Lockheed Martin and CoAspire from 2017, was expected to have both anti-ship and air-to-ground

The first published image of an F-35C armed with a pair of AGM-158C LRASMs. (USN)

variants. Relatively little is known about the missile, with its weight reported at 590kg, its warhead size of just 60kg, and its speed barely crossing the hypersonic threshold at little over Mach 5. The design from its outset emphasised simplicity as a means to reduce costs, and it is confirmed to be able to fit inside the F-35A/C's weapons bays.

With the F-35 set to form a far greater portion of the Western world's fighter fleets than any other aircraft in history, it is certain that new armaments will continue to be developed to equip it including both enhanced variants of existing weapons, and clean sheet new designs. Weapons programs will be pursued both in the United States, and by the F-35's growing range of foreign operators, with non-U.S. producers of NATO-compatible air-launched weapons expected to attribute growing importance to compatibility with the F-35 due to the size of the client base. While the size of the F-35's internal weapons bays remain a key restriction, and efforts to integrate a more diverse array of armaments have faced very serious delays, the F-35's options for weaponry is expected to become among the most diverse of that of any fighter type in the world.

A U.S. Navy F-35C, as seen while armed with two AGM-158s under its inboard underwing pylons. (USN)

6

THE PENTAGON AND LOCKHEED MARTIN: ACQUISITIONS, SUSTAINMENT, AND FLAWS

Acquisition and Procurement Costs

The F-35's expected procurement costs would change significantly during the program's development, with considerable cost overruns making acquisitions far less affordable than initially envisioned. Between 2001 when systems development began, and 2012 when full-scale production had been scheduled to begin, projected procurement costs had risen from $196.6 billion for a planned 2,852 fighters, to $365.3 billion in 2001 dollars ($395.7 billion at the time) for a planned 2,443 fighters – meaning the cost per fighter was 217 percent as high when accounting for inflation.[1] The estimated program procurement cost would remain stable over the following decade,[2] although as major increases in sustainment costs raised growing questions regarding the armed services' ability to afford the 2,443 fighters planned, the possibility grew that cuts to orders would significantly drive up the procurement costs per aircraft. Significant overruns with both procurement and sustainment costs by the mid-2010s made procurement of the F-35 on the scale initially envisioned appear unlikely and unaffordable.

Although the projected costs of acquiring several thousand F-35s across a decades-long production run would increase, the cost per unit would often fall between production years. Initially, the program had notable successes in reducing costs across the first 14 production lots from 2007-2021, before costs again gradually rose from 2022. The first low rate initial production batches were particularly costly, with the first batch, referred to as Lot 1, costing $221.2 million for each F-35A – excluding the prices of their engines. The batch included just two F-35As, and was ordered in 2007.[3] By Lot 4, which was ordered in 2009, 11 F-35As cost just $111.6 million each, although still excluding their engines.[4] By Lot 6, the contract for which was awarded in December 2012, the price had fallen to $100.8 million for each F-35A including the price of the engine. The lot included 36 fighters (23 F-35As, 6 F-35Bs, and 7 F-35C), with the F-35B and F-35C costing $108.5 million and $120 million respectively. Economies of scale were a primary factor helping to reduce the costs of each variant as production further expanded.

Despite significant progress reducing procurement costs, the Pentagon's relationship with Lockheed Martin would worsen after the F-35's entry into service in 2015, specifically during negotiations for the lots 9 and 10. After months of negotiations failed to realise results, the Joint Program Office on November 2, 2016 was confirmed to have taken the extreme measure of forcing Lockheed Martin to abide by a unilateral contract for Lot 9, which allowed the Pentagon to set the price and the firm's fee without input from the firm. A statement from Lockheed Martin would stress the unilateral nature of the deal, and expressed the firm's 'disappointment.'[5] It was confirmed the following month that the Pentagon was considering issuing a unilateral contract for Lot 10, providing Lockheed Martin with a strong incentive to soften its position in negotiations.[6] Further adding to pressure on the firm, newly elected president, Donald Trump, was quick to publicly criticise the F-35 program, and to raise the possibility of investing in the F-18E/F as an alternative. This was credited by a number of sources with allowing a landmark contract for Lot 10 to be signed in February 2017.[7]

Lot 10 covered the production of 90 fighters (76 F-35As, 12 F-35Bs and 2 F-35Cs), up from just 57 under Lot 9, and for the first time achieved a price of under $100 million – lowering the price of the F-35A to $94.6 million. The F-35B and F-35C cost $122.8 million and $121.8 million respectively, although the price discrepancy between the two would grow considerably in the following years as the F-35C began to benefit from similar economies of scale. In a press statement Lockheed Martin revealed that the increase in annual production to 90 fighters 'enables us to reduce costs by taking advantage of economies of scale and production efficiencies.' 'President Trump's personal involvement in the F-35 program accelerated the negotiations and sharpened our focus on driving down the price. The agreement was reached in a matter of weeks and represents significant savings over previous contracts,' the statement added, in what was widely interpreted by analysts as an attempt to curry favour with the new administration.[8]

The agreement on Lot 10 would not mark the end of the Pentagon's frustrations with Lockheed Martin over procurement costs. In the first week of March 2018 the Pentagon director of the F-35 program Vice Admiral Mat Winter was quoted as having stated regarding negotiations for Lot 11: 'I will tell you I am not as satisfied with the collaboration and the cooperation by Lockheed Martin ... They could be much more cooperative and collaborative. We could seal this deal faster. We could. They choose not to, and that's a negotiating tactic.' Winter by that time had a team investigating 100 of the suppliers in the F-35 supply chain, in order to identify places where production could be improved, reducing issues stemming from the improper manufacturing of parts, and assessing where production could be more streamlined. 'The price is coming down but it's not coming down fast enough,' he stated, adding: 'We don't know to the level of granularity that I want to know, what it actually costs to produce this aircraft.' He conceded that he had hoped to have the deal finalised by the end of 2017.[9]

On 15 July the Pentagon and Lockheed Martin were confirmed to have reached a handshake deal for Lot 11. They would jointly announce on 28 September that the price of the F-35A had for the first time fallen below $90 million, with the $11.5 billion deal covering 141 fighters. The eleventh batch saw the price of the F-35A fall by six percent to $89.2 million, while the prices of the F-35B and F-35C respectively fell to $115.5 million and $107.7 million.

On 28 October 2019, the Pentagon announced the definitisation of a $34 billion contract for the next three batches of F-35s, Lots 12, 13 and 14, which between them included 478 fighters (149 F-35s in Lot 12, 160 in Lot 13 and 169 in Lot 14). The Pentagon reported that the price per aircraft would fall by approximately 12.8 percent across all variants on average from Lot 11 to Lot 14. The deal was a landmark not only due to its size, but also because it for the first time reached the target unit-recurring flyaway cost of under $80 million for each F-35A in Lot 13, which was previously only expected to be achieved in Lot 14. Prices would fall from $89.2 million in Lot 11, to $82.4 million in Lot 12, before falling to $79.2 million in Lot 13, and $77.9 million in Lot 14 – a 13 percent reduction from Lot 10 to Lot 14. The F-35B and F-35C were to cost $101.3 million and $94.4 million in Lot 14. This was the first time the F-35 Joint Program Office awarded a significant F-35 aircraft procurement contract in the same fiscal year as the congressional appropriation year.[10]

The effective lowering of procurement costs to meet targeted levels under Lot 13 and Lot 14 strengthened the consensus that the F-35A had very significant cost effectiveness advantages over other Western fighters, with the price being highly favourable compared to the fourth generation F-15 and F-18E/F, and moreso the lighter Eurofighter and Rafale.[11] This emerging consensus was summarised as follows by the editorial of the *Air & Space Forces Magazine*: 'the $80 million-per-copy cost to acquire these jets is less than some last-generation aircraft — and a bargain considering the combat-multiplying effect of this vastly superior platform.'[12] These reductions placed the Pentagon on track to procure 2,456 F-35s for just $406 billion, averaging $165 million per fighter when factoring in R&D costs. The very high costs of developing the aircraft, which had overrun tremendously, were a primary factor driving this price up significantly higher than the flyaway cost, with this average price also influenced by the higher costs of the F-35B and F-35C variants and the high costs of initial production variants.

On 18 July 2022, the F-35 Joint Program Office and Lockheed Martin announced a handshake agreement on lots 15-17, which covered the production of 375 aircraft. Both the JPO and the firm had long suggested that lots 15-17 would be a turning point in the program, as procurement costs per fighter would cease to fall. This was due to both a surge in inflation, and the growing costs of new variants of the fighter with Technology Refresh 3 upgrades.[13] Former JPO program executive officer retired Lieutenant General Eric Fick had predicted a deal in November 2021, and then in March 2022, with the reaching of a deal in July occurring more than ten months behind schedule. The primary cause for the protraction of negotiations was disagreement over volatile inflation and labour costs in the aftermath of the Covid-19 pandemic. Lockheed Martin stated the parties were 'able to achieve a cost per jet lower than record-breaking inflation trends.'[14] The contract for Lot 15 was finalised on 12 August, while a $30 billion contract for all three lots was finalised on 30 December, covering the production of 398 fighters.[15] Under lots 15-17 the F-35A on average cost $82.5 million, or $4.6 million more than it had under Lot 14.[16]

F-16C, 23rd Fighter Squadron, U.S. Air Force. The F-16 is the primary fighter the F-35A was designed to succeed in service across the fleets of the U.S. Air Force and the majority of foreign operators. Major overruns in the F-35A's sustainment costs to close to double those of its predecessor are considered a primary shortcoming of the fighter program, and has forced the majority of services transitioning between the two aircraft to significantly reduce the number of fighters they field. The F-35A is a considerably larger and longer ranged aircraft that can accommodate a much heavier and more powerful sensor suite, although the two are at opposite ends of the spectrum in the U.S. Air Force fleet in terms of availability rates, with the F-16's maintenance needs remaining far lower. Delays to the F-35A's service entry, and procurements at a fraction of previously intended rates, are expected to continue to force the Air Force to rely more heavily on the F-16 than intended, with modernised F-16s benefitting from refurbishment and life extension expected to serve well into the 2040s in complementary roles to the F-35A. (Artwork by Tom Cooper)

A-10A of the 511th Fighter Squadron, U.S. Air Force. Alongside the F-16, the F-35A was also intended to serve as a direct successor to the A-10 for the provision of close air support. The F-35's lack of armour protection, limited endurance, high cost, and high maintenance requirements were all far removed from the traditional requirements for close air support aircraft, which combined with the significantly lower firepower of its GAU-22 compared to the A-10's GAU-8 made the decision to rely on the new fighter as a replacement highly controversial. This in turn sparked considerable debate regarding the evolving nature of the close air support mission set, with a strong argument in favour of the F-35A being that traditional close air support aircraft have become largely obsolete for peer-on-peer conflicts. Although the A-10 has demonstrated multiple considerable advantages during testing, assessments of the Russian-Ukrainian War have consistently pointed to a limited utility for traditional manned close air support aircraft in medium or high intensity conflicts. (Artwork by Goran Sudar)

AV-8B Harrier II of the Fighter Attack Squadron 231, U.S. Marine Corps. The Harrier provided the Marine Corps with its first combat jet capable of short take-off and vertical landing (STOVL), although its limited combat capabilities for its era and considerable reliability issues reduced its utility even for lower intensity operations. The requirement for a fifth generation successor to the Harrier, and resulting development of the F-35B as a third variant of the aircraft, was a key factor distinguishing the F-35 program from preceding joint programs. The Harrier's limitations meant that Marine Corps fighter units benefitted from the greatest increase in combat capabilities when transitioning to the F-35, which totally transformed the mission scope for amphibious assault ships deploying STOVL fighters, providing viable penetration, air-to-air, reconnaissance, and other capabilities that the Harrier had lacked. (Artwork by Goran Sudar)

F-22 of the 192nd Fighter Wing, Virginia Air National Guard. The F-22 in December 2005 became the world's first operational fifth generation fighter, and was initially envisaged as a successor to the F-15C/D as the Air Force's prime air superiority fighter. Significant issues with the program, however, resulted not only in cuts to over three quarters of planned production numbers, but also to outstandingly low availability rates and limited modernisation of avionics. This placed a significantly greater burden on the Air Force's F-35A fleet for air superiority missions, as despite its shortcomings in areas such as its radar size and manoeuvrability, the newer and much more widely fielded stealth fighter's technological advantages became increasingly significant as it was incrementally modernised. Despite its much larger size, the F-22's range is significantly shorter than that of the F-35, which is considered particularly disadvantageous for operations in the Pacific. Although the F-22 program fell short of expectations, its development was a key stepping stone to work on the more successful F-35 program. (Artwork by Rolando Ugolini)

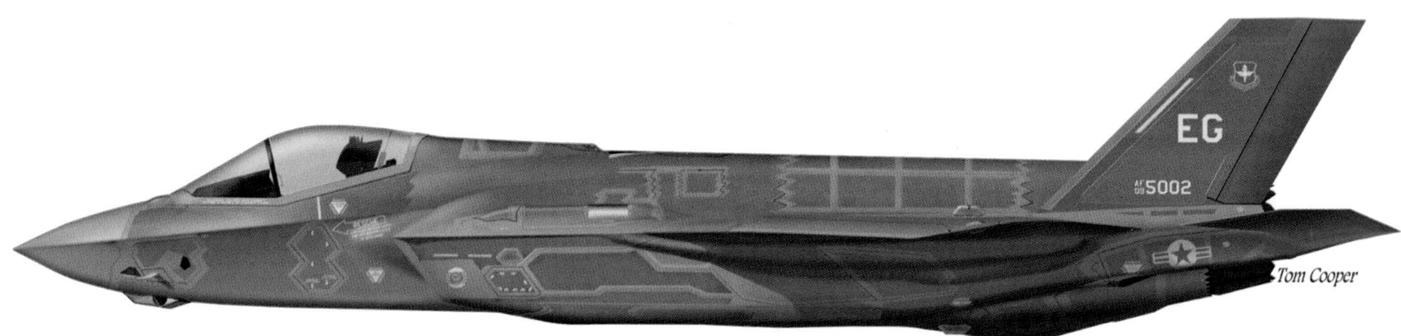

F-35A of the 58th Fighter Squadron, U.S. Air Force. Aircraft 09-5002 was the tenth low rate initial production F-35A, and was first flown on 3 March 2012. The squadron is relied on for graduate flying and maintenance training, both for the Air Force and for the Navy, Marine Corps and foreign operators. The squadron received its first F-35s in 2011, four years before the type entered service in the U.S. Air Force, making it the first training squadron for the aircraft. The significant issues affecting the first 189 F-35s meant they were not expected to be made viable for high intensity combat, and were permanently allocated to such training units. (Artwork by Tom Cooper)

F-35A of the 65th Aggressor Squadron, U.S. Air Force. The aggressor unit was activated in June 2022 at Nellis Air Force Base, the Air Force's leading facility for test training, with the F-35A having been selected specifically to simulate the capabilities of adversary stealth fighters, most significantly the J-20. Reflecting their role, F-35s under the squadron use a colour scheme closely resembling one used on the J-20. The composition of the 65th Aggressor Squadron had long provided an indicator of which adversary fighter types the Air Force considered the most pressing challenge, with the F-35 having been preceded by F-15C/D fighters which was chosen to simulate the capabilities of Russian Su-27s, and before them F-5E/F fighters simulating the capabilities of Soviet MiG-21s. The allocation of scarce F-35s to the squadron highlighted the pressing nature of the challenge posed by the rapid modernisation and expansion of China's own fifth generation fighter fleets. (Artwork by Tom Cooper)

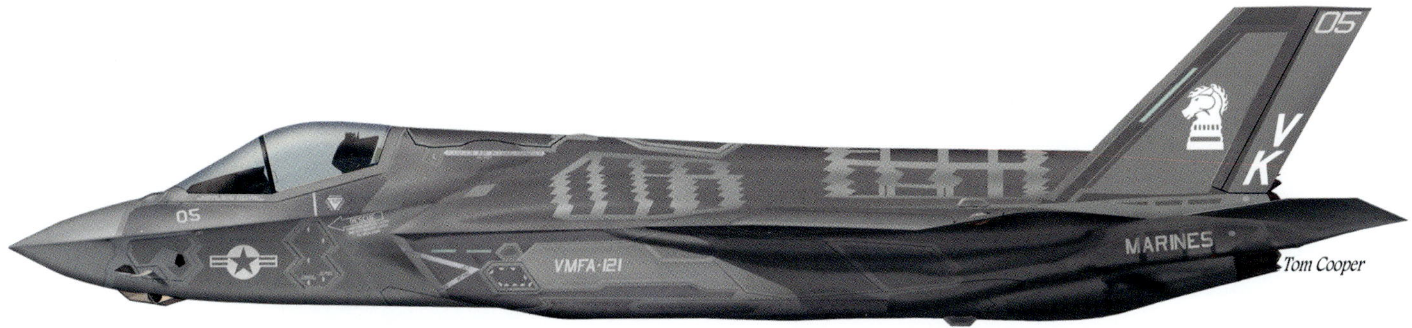

F-35B of the Fighter Attack Squadron 121, U.S. Marine Corps. The squadron was the first in the world to gain an initial operating capability with the F-35, which was announced on 31 July 2015. With the aircraft still reliant on Block 2B software at the time, this caused significant controversy due to the aircraft's performance limitations and low reliability, which were demonstrated during subsequent testing. The squadron in January 2017 became the first in the world to make an operational deployment with the F-35, and crossed the Pacific from Marine Corps Air Station Yuma in Arizona, to Marine Corps Air Station Iwakuni in Japan. This deployment positioned them to contribute to shows of force on the Korean Peninsula that year at a time of high tensions between Washington and Pyongyang. Operations included dropping live GBU-32 Joint Direct Attack Munitions, the largest bomb the F-35B could accommodate internally, at the Pil-sung training range in South Korea, while carrying live AIM-120 air-to-air missiles. (Artwork by Tom Cooper)

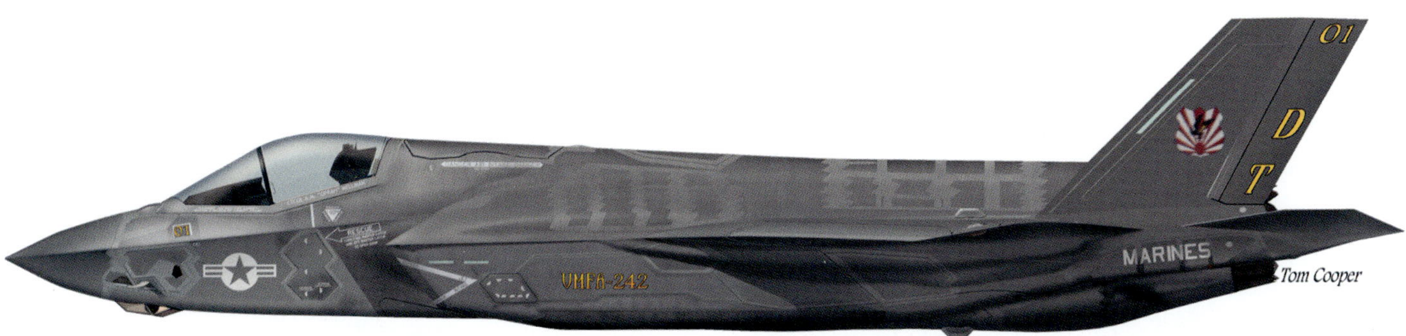

F-35B of the Fighter Attack Squadron 242, U.S. Marine Corps. Squadron 242 was the second F-35B squadron to be permanently based in Japan, and was declared fully operational in May 2022 at Marine Combat Air Station Iwakuni. This reflected part of a broader process of Japan coming to host a greater concentration of F-35s than any other country, as the only country set to host permanent deployments of all three variants by the U.S. Armed Forces, including F-35As under the 35th Fighter Wing at Misawa Air Base, and F-35C fighters under Carrier Air Wing 5. The F-35B's ability to operate from makeshift airfields made it particularly prized for deployments near the territory of peer level potential adversaries due to its ability to continue to operate in the event that major airfields were left non-operational. (Artwork by Tom Cooper)

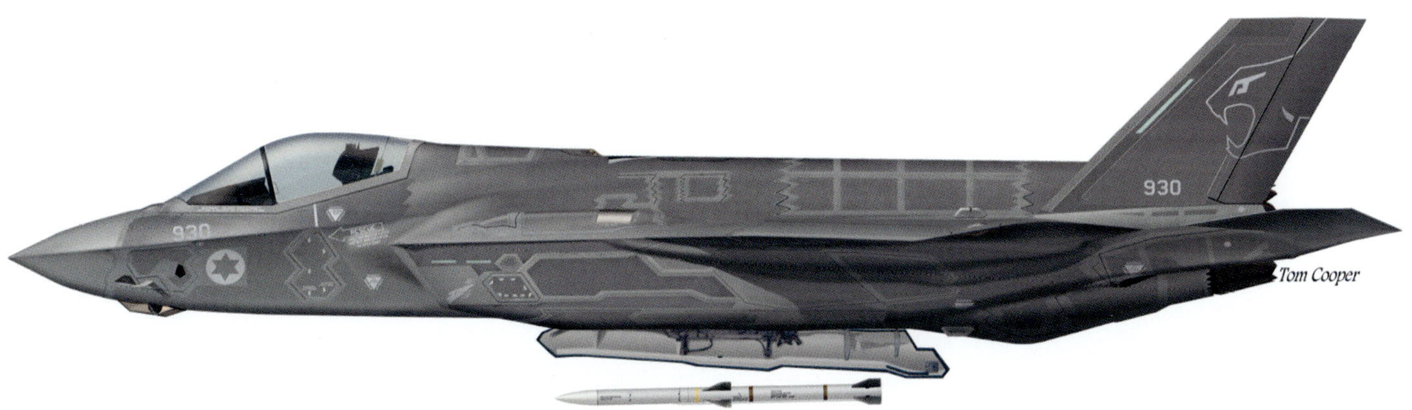

F-35I of the No. 140 Squadron, Israeli Air-Space Force. The Israeli Defence Ministry initially intended to procure a more heavily customised variant of the F-35 by gaining fuller access to source code, more deeply integrating indigenous avionics, and possibly integrating an indigenous radar and ordering a twin seat variant. Although these plans were never realised, Israeli F-35s benefitted from an unmatched level of customisation, which was achieved through the integration of indigenous avionics using open architecture that 'sits on the F-35's central system, much like an application on your iPhone.' A unique sub-variant of the F-35A was supplied to Israel to serve as a testbed for these local modifications. Israel also gained special rights for maintaining, repairing and overhauling both the airframes and the engines domestically, including for depot level maintenance, providing a unique level of autonomy. (Artwork by Tom Cooper)

F-35C of the Strike Fighter Squadron 147, U.S. Navy. The squadron became the first to attain an initial operating capability with the F-35C in February 2019, and in August 2021 made the first-ever operational deployment onboard an aircraft carrier using the new aircraft. The U.S. Navy was significantly less heavily invested in the F-35 program than the Air Force and Marine Corps were with their own respective variants, with the service planning to procure just 273 of the aircraft, while it ordered close to three times as many F-18E/F and E/A-18G advanced fourth generation combat jets. This reflected an expectation that the service would largely leapfrog the F-35C to directly transition the majority of its fighter and electronic attack units from fourth generation aircraft to the sixth generation F/A-XX. As the sixth generation program's future was increasingly brought to question from early 2025, however, there remained a significant possibility that the Navy would be forced to rely much more heavily on the F-35C than expected, and would significantly increase its orders. (Artwork by Tom Cooper)

F-35C of the Strike Fighter Squadron 97, U.S. Navy. The Long Range Anti-Ship Missile (LRASM) seen here is one of a number of missile designs that cannot be carried internally by the F-35, with the need for external carriage compromising the aircraft's low observability. The missile was designed to be launched from safe distances with a reported range of 370 kilometres, and uses on-board guidance systems to engage targets autonomously without either GPS or data links, reducing its vulnerability to jamming. The missile has the potential to revolutionise the long range anti-ship capabilities of carrier air wings, complementing renewed investments in equipping destroyers in carrier battle groups with new anti-ship cruise missiles. (Artwork by Tom Cooper)

F-35C of the Air Test & Evaluation Squadron 9, U.S. Navy. At least three different forms of mirror-like reflective tiles have been applied to three or more different F-35C fighters for testing, each using different patterns and tiles of different size and shape. The coatings could go from appearing mirror-like to matte-like depending on the angle at which the aircraft were viewed. The example here shows 'mirror tiles' have been applied over all of the top fuselage, lower front fuselage, lower side of the intakes and on fins. Developing a means of reducing the impact tail fins have on radar cross section could revolutionise the F-35's detectability, and potentially play a central part in efforts to keep the aircraft viable into an era where new sixth generation fighters dominate the skies. Possible delays or issues with sixth generation programs could potentially lead to a significant increase in the attention and funding for such upgrades to the F-35 fleet. (Artwork by Tom Cooper)

B-2A of the 509th Bomb Wing, U.S. Air Force. The development of the B-2 marked a major leap in the advancement of stealth technologies, with the aircraft retaining a very low radar cross section from all sides and against radars in a much wider range of wavebands, while being able to allocate a proportion of its weight approximately twice as large to weapons carriage as the F-117 had. Between the retirement of the F-117 in 2008, and the F-35A's certification to employ B61 nuclear bombs in 2024, the U.S. Air Force's small fleet of 20 B-2 bombers were the world's only stealth aircraft known to be able to employ nuclear weapons. Compared to a reliance on a very small bomber fleet with ageing stealth capabilities, the operationalisation of the F-35A as a nuclear-capable tactical combat jet fielded in its hundreds across the world totally transforms the threat American adversaries face of penetration strikes for nuclear delivery. (Artwork by Tom Cooper)

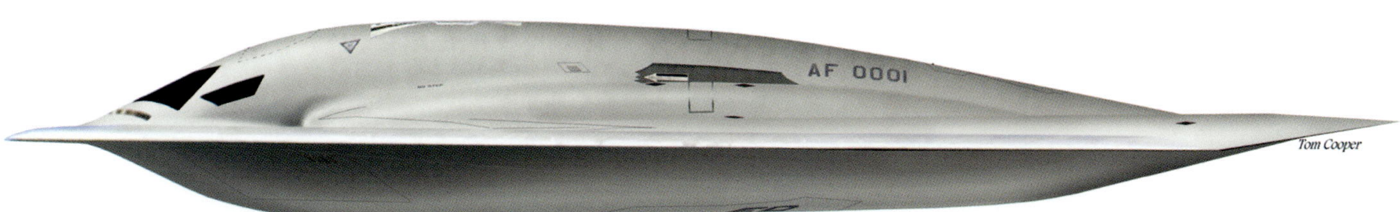

B-21, First Prototype. The B-21 is expected to provide vital support to F-35 operations in the Pacific, and was designed with advanced battle management capabilities, a limited air-to-air capability, and a significant capability for intelligence, surveillance, and reconnaissance including command and control of unmanned air units. The aircraft may also be relied on to compensate for shortfalls in the American fighter fleet by helping to achieve air superiority through attacks on bases hosting enemy fighters, or "breaking eggs in the nest" as it has been referred to by air power theorists. The U.S. Congress Strategic Posture Commission and the Congressional Research Service have been among multiple sources advocating for a larger fleet of over 200 B-21 bombers, raising the possibility that the aircraft will be a direct competitor to the F-35 for increasingly strained procurement funding alongside the F-47. Potential delays to or shortcomings with the F-47 program could see the B-21 relied on much more heavily in the Pacific alongside modernised variants of the F-35, with the possibility of the stealth bomber operating in similar ways to a sixth generation fighter having been highlighted as early as September 2019 by Director of Air and Cyber Operations for Pacific Air Forces General Scott Pleus. (Artwork by Tom Cooper)

E/A-18G of the Air Test & Evaluation Squadron 31, U.S. Navy. Significant delays to the development of the F-35C were a primary factor in the U.S. Navy's gradual extension of production of the E/A-18G and the F-18E/F fighter by 12 years from 2015 to 2027. By the time the first F-35Cs entered service in 2018, the service had already procured 560 F/A-18E/Fs and 131 EA-18Gs, for a total of 691 enhanced fourth generation combat jets. The E/A-18G's capabilities are highly complementary to those of the F-35C, and when the latter began its first-ever operational deployment on an aircraft carrier, the USS *Carl Vinson*, the supporting complement of E/A-18Gs was increased from three to five as part of what was referred to as the "air wing of the future." The commander of the strike group in question, Rear Admiral Dan Martin, would particularly emphasize the value of deploying E/A-18Gs to support F-35C operations, with the electronic attack jets expected to contribute to the stealth fighters' survivability and provide particularly valuable backing when operating against enemy ground-based air defences. (Artwork by Tom Cooper)

G.550 Nachshon Oron of the No. 122 Squadron, Israeli Air-Space Force. An example of unique pairings of F-35s with new types of indigenous support aircraft by foreign clients, the G.550 airborne early warning and control system is used to process and prepare intelligence collected from onboard sensors and all other sources, to jam radars, electronic emissions, and communications, and thus participate in the suppression of enemy air defence operations. The type reportedly played a crucial role in supporting Israeli F-35 operations against Iran in June 2025, and has served as a valuable force multiplier for the fleet. The Israeli G.550 fleet is based at Nevatim Airbase where all F-35Is are permanently based. The U.S. Air Force is acquiring very 10 similar EA-37B Compass Call aircraft to replace the EC-130H Compass Call of the 55th Electronic Combat Group at Davis-Monthan AFB. Italy expressed interest in acquiring two EA-37Bs. (Artwork by Tom Cooper)

E-7 of the No. 2 Squadron, Royal Australian Air Force. The U.S. Air Force selected the E-7 to replace its ageing fleet of E-3 AWACS, with the decision made after officials repeatedly stressed both the extreme limitations of the E-3, and the contrasting high sophistication of the latest rival Chinese aircraft. The E-3 fleet's very low availability rates due to its age, and the inadequate situational awareness its ageing sensors could provide against China's increasingly large and capable stealth fighter fleet, made the E-7 appear particularly vital to revolutionise situational awareness over the Pacific. Funding for the aircraft was an unexpected new addition to the Air Force's budget, with major strain on spending from multiple competing programs in June 2025 bringing the aircraft's future into question. The fielding of modern airborne warning and control systems is considered vital to maximising the combat potential of the F-35 fleet, particularly in the face of peer level competition in the Pacific. (Artwork by Tom Cooper)

KJ-500H of the 26th Special Mission Aircraft Division, PLAAF. The KJ-500 first entered service in 2018, a year after the J-20 fifth generation fighter, after which both were procured at accelerated rates. Facing F-35 fleets deployed by multiple services in the Pacific, the fielding of more modern airborne warning and control systems than of most F-35 operators in the region was seen to provide Chinese air power with an advantage, with support from such aircraft with very large airborne radars considered to increase situational awareness against adversaries' stealth aircraft. The KJ-500 was specifically singled out by U.S. Air Force officials when assessing the J-20's combat potential, highlighting the impressive command and control and missile guidance capabilities provided. By the middle of the 2020s the fleet had come close to 40 aircraft, making it the most numerous system of its kind in the Pacific. (Artwork by Tom Cooper)

J-20A of the 19th Fighter Brigade, PLAAF. Until the service entry of its lighter counterpart, the J-35, which was confirmed in July 2025, the J-20 was considered the F-35's only peer level challenger as a comparably sophisticated fifth generation fighter. In contrast to the F-35, the J-20 was developed as a heavyweight twin engine air superiority fighter, and has a number of significant advantages in areas such as its weapons payload, range, radar size, and flight performance. By the mid-2020s it was being procured on a much greater scale by China's air force than it was by all three American services combined. With the J-20 not being marketed for export, however, the F-35 is likely to retain considerable superiority over enemy fighters in any scenario other than an air war with China itself. (Artwork by Tom Cooper)

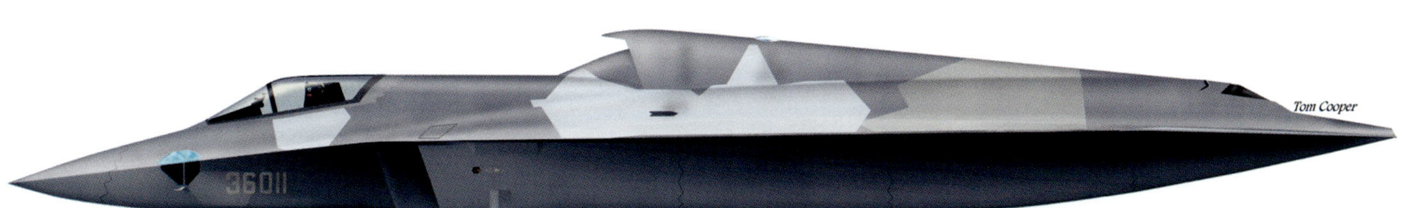

Chengdu Aerospace Corporation Very Heavy Very Long Ranged Sixth Generation Fighter. The first fighter plane of the sixth generation to see images released to open sources, the new tailless aircraft uses a unique tri-engine configuration. The precedent set by the fighter's direct predecessor, the J-20, in the speed at which it could be brought into service after its first flight, indicates that China's defence sector is likely to be able to bring a sixth generation fighter into service around the early 2030s. As the world's largest known fighter plane, it is expected to have a significantly longer range and higher weapons payload and to carry a larger sensor suite than any other tactical combat jet. This is considered particularly vital in the Pacific, and combined with major advances in stealth capabilities has the potential to make it a game changer for the Chinese People's Liberation Army Air Force's ability to interdict enemy aircraft over particularly extreme distances. Its combat radius is estimated to be over four times that of the F-35A. (Artwork by Tom Cooper)

Shenyang Aerospace Corporation Heavy Long-Range Fighter Prototype. The second of two Chinese sixth generation fighter prototypes unveiled on on 26 December 2024, this new aircraft is expected to serve as a lighter counterpart to that developed by Chengdu. The expected introduction of two Chinese sixth generation fighters in the early 2030s has raised serious concerns regarding the future viability of the F-35 as a primary fighter for the American and allied services in the Pacific, and potentially farther afield in the Arctic or near Alaska where operations could realistically reach. The successes of the F-47 and F/A-XX programs are expected to be primary factors determining whether the urgency of the Chinese challenge to American air power will result in cuts to F-35 orders, or in renewed efforts to modernise the F-35 to a '5+ generation' standard. (Artwork by Tom Cooper)

5P85TE2 Transporter-Erector Launcher of the S-400 Long Range Air Defence System, Russian Aerospace Forces. Despite the Russian fighter aviation industry having seen its international standing diminish since the disintegration of the Soviet Union, leaving the country with no peer competitors to the F-35 or J-20 as of the mid-2020s, the country's long range air defence systems such as the S-400 have retained a world leading standing. Reflecting the extent to which the system is depended on for the defence of Russian airspace, the Russian Defence Ministry is estimated to have invested over twice as much in procuring S-400s as it has in procuring all classes of fighter combined from 1992-2022. Responding to the new challenges of the post-Soviet era, the F-35's capabilities are particularly well optimised for operations against ground-based air defence systems like the S-400, contrasting to the F-15, F-16 and F-22 which were developed primarily to counter peer level competition from Soviet air power. This has made the fighter program particularly threatening for Russia and other potential adversaries that rely on such systems. (Artwork by David Bocquelet)

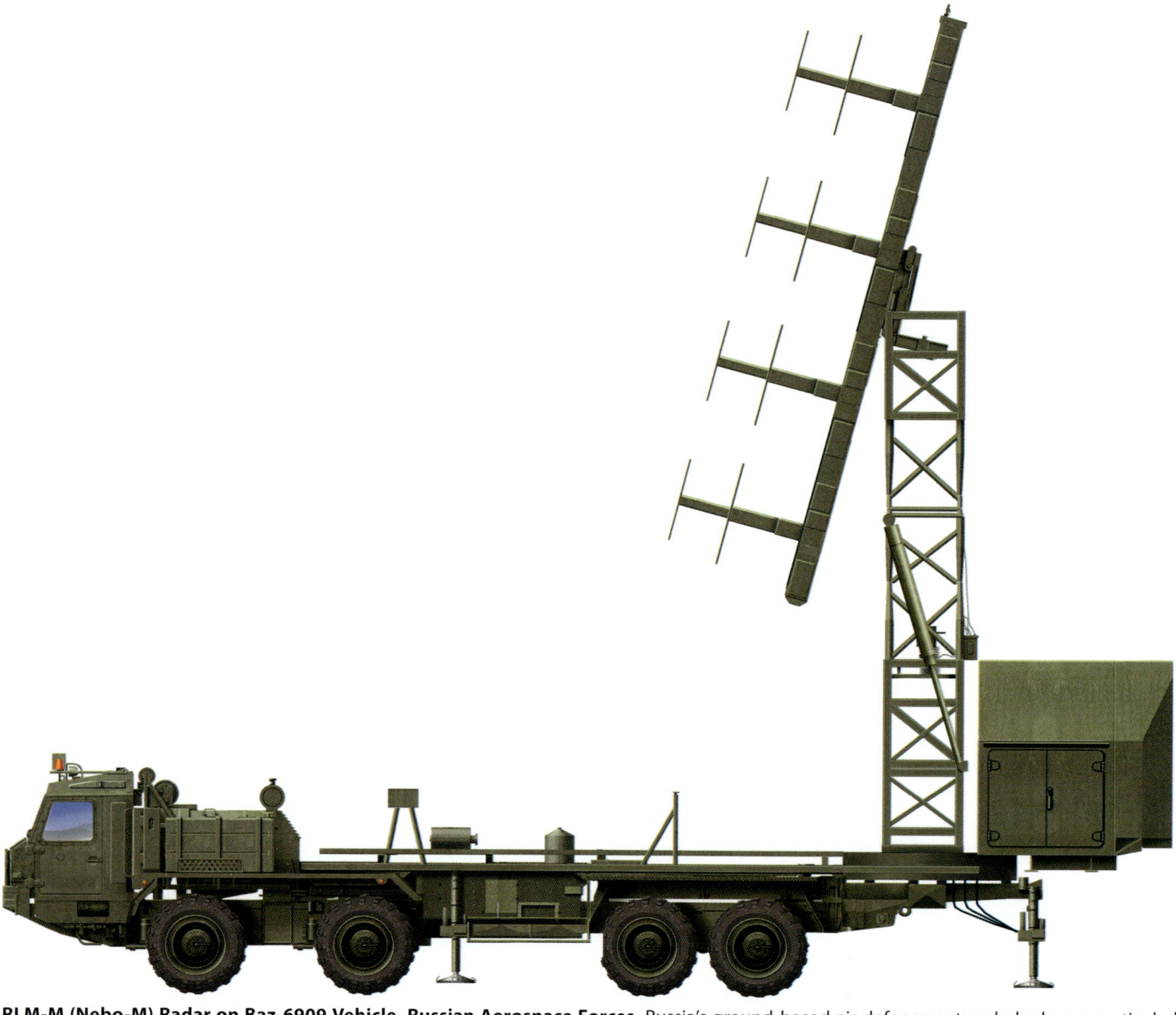

RLM-M (Nebo-M) Radar on Baz-6909 Vehicle, Russian Aerospace Forces. Russia's ground-based air defence network deploys a particularly large array of radars that operate in the L-band, which fighters such as the F-35 are not well optimised to evading detection by. The Nebo-M system in particular was developed specifically to help facilitate engagements with American stealth fighters, primarily the F-35, with its networking with shorter wave targeting radars having the potential to significantly increase their effectiveness for long range targeting of very low observable aircraft. The RLM-M has a reported 600 kilometre tracking range against large non-stealth aircraft, and was designed to be deployed alongside long range surface-to-air missile systems, primarily the S-400. (Artwork by David Bocquelet)

Costs were expected to increase further under next production lots, bringing the cost of the F-35A back up to around $90 million. The combination of the fighter's growing complexity and sophistication, inflation, and a lack of further economies of scale, meant the cost was likely to return to over $100 million in the early 2030s. The development of a new engine for all three variants of the fighter was expected to further increase procurement costs from the late 2020s (see Chapter 8), with the Pentagon's budgets expected to be further strained by the introduction of increasingly complex and costly new generations of weapons such as the AIM-260 air-to-air missile and LRASM cruise missile.

The JPO and Lockheed Martin on 21 November 2024 reached a handshake deal for Lots 18 and 19, with the firm announced two days later to have been awarded a $869 million contract to procure long lead materials, parts, components, and associated support for the production of Lot 20 aircraft.[17] The JPO's unusual decision not to publicise the prices being paid per fighter under the new lots fuelled speculation that inflation rates had driven them considerably higher than under previous lots. The agreement was reached approximately one year later than expected, and after long-lead funding for Lot 18 had run out in the third quarter of the year, Lockheed Martin had been forced to expend significant funds to sustain production. Continuing production in the third quarter incurred expenses of $400 million, while the firm had to cover 'an additional $300 million of impacts across the supply chain.' Officials warned that if F-35 negotiations dragged on into 2025, the firm would be late in booking over $1 billion in sales and revenues from 2024. The date of the completion of Technology Refresh 3 development remained highly uncertain, with the already much delayed projection of between April and June of 2024, which had been announced in December the previous year, appearing likely to be missed by at least six months.[18] In February 2025 the annual report of the Pentagon's Director of Operational Test and Evaluation confirmed that operational testing of F-35s with TR-3 software was not likely to begin before 2026, with the slow maturing of modifications and software being a primary constraint.[19]

Procurement Conflicts

On 21 September 2017, corrosion was found in several fastener holes under the fuselage panels of an F-35A undergoing maintenance at Hill Air Force Base, resulting in the suspension of further F-35 deliveries. A subsequent investigation by Lockheed Martin found that the firm had not been applying the required primer to the fastener holes on F-35 substructures during production, which was essential to preventing corrosion.[20] Although deliveries resumed a month later on 20 October, a dispute subsequently emerged over whether the Pentagon or Lockheed Martin should pay to fix the damage.[21] The necessary repairs cost $119 million, or approximately $600,000 per fighter, with issues affecting close to 200 fighters. Six months after deliveries were suspended, a second suspension occurred on 29 March 2018, after the Pentagon ceased to accept new F-35 deliveries due to prevailing disagreements with Lockheed Martin over repair costs. The issue was announced on 8 May to have been resolved, although the terms of the agreement were not publicised. This would be far from the last or the longest time that deliveries were suspended over a disagreement.

In July 2023 the Joint Program Office placed procurement of the F-35 on hold, with the Defense Contract Management Agency refusing to approve deliveries due to the lack of full development or testing of the hardware and software package for the TR-3 standard. The JPO withheld payments of $7 million per aircraft from Lockheed Martin during this suspension period. The new software build included updates to displays, added computer memory, and increased processing power, and was described as a new 'computer backbone' for the fighter, promising a 25-fold increase in computing power over the preceding TR-2 level. It also provided a number of new capabilities, including allowing F-35s to carry new munition types such as AIM-9X Block II missile and the B61-12 nuclear bomb. It was nevertheless from the outset considered only a stepping-stone to the Block 4 capability milestone, which the services sought to reach before expanding procurement rates.

The F-35's software had long caused serious issues, with efforts to bring it up to the TR-3 standard proving particularly problematic. In January 2022 it was confirmed that a fresh software upgrade was continuing to be installed on the F-35 despite the discovery by the fighter's operators of deficiencies 'in weapons, fusion, communications and navigation, cybersecurity and targeting processes.' A 13-page military testing report highlighted that the upgrade 'does not adhere to the published best practices' and had 'consistently failed to deliver the capabilities contained in their master schedule.'[22] The software's new processes 'often introduced stability problems and/or adversely affected' other functions, as discovered by frontline squadrons that frequently reported 'critical warfighting deficiencies.' Testing had been insufficiently comprehensive to ensure 'unintentional deficiencies [were] not embedded in the software prior to delivery.' The cost of the upgrade by that time had already reached $14 billion.[23]

In March 2024 lawmakers sought to reallocate funding earmarked for F-35 procurement, cutting annual purchases by at least 10 fighters, in order to finance a Cooperative Avionics Test Bed 'digital twin' of the F-35 and set up another Mission Software Integration Laboratory. This was intended to reduce future delays to and performance issues with software upgrades. It followed confirmation by Program Executive Officer for the F-35, Air Force Lieutenant General Michael J. Schmidt, that deficiencies in the number of test assets and programmers had been central factors slowing testing of TR-3 software.[24] With deliveries suspended, Air Force Secretary Frank Kendall on 7 March lamented that the lack of new F-35s was 'hurting' the service. 'Where we expected to replace airplanes, we now are not. So, we've got to carry the existing aircraft, generally speaking, for longer than we had planned,' he stated, adding that 'the operational capability impact is significant.' The suspension resulted in additional unplanned costs for maintenance, spare parts, training, and more, he added. 'We really need the TR-3 hardware and the Block 4 set of upgrades … to stay competitive. And we're going to need them in quantity, so getting on with that is really important to us,' Kendall further stressed.[25]

Faced with a suspension of deliveries that was set to last over 18 months, Kendall noted that there had been debates within the Air Force over whether to resume acquisitions without TR-3.[26] Further elaborating on this possibility, General Schmidt in April called for accepting F-35s before the TR-3 package was complete. 'I am as frustrated as you that I can't nail down a specific date and be extremely clear about exactly when we will deliver,' he stated, stressing that the 'best chance' the program had was to accept fighters with a 'truncated' interim version of the TR-3 software. He added that the Joint Strike Fighter Executive Steering Board had 'agreed to the criteria by which we truncate and when I get a stable, capable, maintainable software version, and terms and conditions of a contract of truncation with industry, then we can truncate it.' Schmidt conceded that a full combat capability with TR-3 software would not materialise for another 12 to 16 months.[27] * He also highlighted issues with 'hardware design maturity,' which 'manifests in low manufacturing yields' of parts required to produce F-35s at the TR-3 standard.[28]

On 16 May 2024, the Government Accountability Office revealed that Lockheed Martin was running out of room to accommodate undelivered F-35s at Fort Worth, Texas, where over 90 undeliverable aircraft were estimated to already be in storage.[29] Delays to the completion of TR-3 software also led a number of foreign clients to express dissatisfaction. This had a range of other repercussions; with a notable example being the delayed integration of Norway's indigenous Joint Strike Missile onto the F-35, as the lack of TR-3 configured aircraft prevented this from going forward.[30]

On 11 July 2024, the suspension of procurement was announced to have ended, after General Schmidt expressed satisfaction that TR-3 software was sufficiently stable and safe for further deliveries. The software package was still far from complete or capable of facilitating high intensity combat, with flight testing which had begun far behind schedule in January 2023 still being ongoing.[31] The Pentagon had again significantly lowered its requirements, requiring only that TR-3 software meet standards required for use in training, with fighters delivered with incomplete software accordingly being reserved for training exclusively. This sparked criticism from lawmakers that the Pentagon had failed to hold Lockheed Martin and its subcontractors accountable for their failure to deliver on their promises, with Representative Matt Gaetz referring to this as 'leav[ing] the American taxpayer on the hook for a broken system.'[32] Concerns were exacerbated by the Joint Program Office's admission that even when full TR-3 software was belatedly delivered, frequent patches might still be needed to correct deficiencies and 'implement critical fixes.'[33]

The delivery of F-35s with incomplete software began on 19 July, with the significant backlog of undelivered fighters, combined with new production aircraft, allowing Lockheed Martin to make deliveries at unprecedentedly high rates. The firm projected at the time that it could deliver at rates of 20 fighters per month. As each stored aircraft required four separate checks before delivery, it was projected that ending the backlog would take close to a year.[34] Although accepting deliveries, the Pentagon would continue to withhold $5 million per aircraft from Lockheed Martin until TR-3 was fully completed, which combined with delays reaching a deal for future production lots proved costly for the firm.[35]

Operational Costs

Far more serious than the issue of development or procurement costs was the issue of overruns in operational expenses, which formed the vast majority of any modern fighter's lifetime costs, and which were a primary factor that made the F-35 unaffordable for acquisitions on a comparable scale to its fourth generation predecessors. Development and procurement costs were by 2021 estimated to amount to just 23.5 percent of the average F-35's total lifetime costs, with sustainment costs accounting for the remaining 76.5 percent.[36] Overruns with the latter were thus a much more serious issue for the program. The F-35A's hourly operational costs originally planned at $25,000 in 2012 dollars, compared to around $16,000 for the F-16C/D, were far from ideal but still somewhat affordable at 56 percent more than its predecessor. By contrast, by the early 2020s despite significant efforts to lower the fighter's operational costs, they still stood at approximately $48,000 in 2016 – close to double those of the F-16. Much as had been the case for the F-22, which was initially intended to cost less to operate than the F-15, the F-35's program's failure to produce a fighter with comparable operational costs to the aircraft it was developed to replace was one of its most serious and consequential shortcomings. It placed the ability to afford F-35A procurements at even half the numbers of its predecessor in serious question, with costs seen to be far from suitable for a primary frontline fighter that could serve as a successor to the F-16 and F-18.

Multiple factors contributed to the F-35's high operational costs, including the complexity of its stealth coatings and its much larger size and greater fuel consumption than originally expected. The panels on its airframe required frequent removal or opening on the flight line for routine maintenance, with more than 5,000 fasteners keeping these in place. As noted by 388th Maintenance Squadron Fabrication Flight Non-commissioned Officer-in-Charge, Master Sergeant Francis Annett: 'all of these, when worn, can potentially limit the jet's stealth capabilities,' with the very high maintenance standards needed to maintain stealth pushing requirements much higher than for fourth generation fighters. The sergeant elaborated: 'maintaining this radar absorbent coating on surface of the F-35 is a job that takes very detail-oriented, sometimes tedious work – masking every small area, properly mixing chemicals, applying them precisely, smoothing, and assessing the smallest imperfections. It's time consuming, but it's vital to get it right.'[37]

Lockheed Martin's general manager of advanced development programs Jeff Babione would himself elaborate regarding the difficulties of maintaining stealth coatings: 'On the other hand, we inadvertently scratch the coating system, and we have to repaint it. Or when the mechanics spray the airplane [with LO coating], not all of it is robotically sprayed. There's some overspray, and they have to go clean that.'[38] The complexity of the aircraft's stealth capabilities not only seriously affected sustainment efforts, but also accounted for approximately half of all failures of quality control for the fighter by the late 2010s.[39]

In December 2017 an Air Force office assessment of the F-35's impact on budgets and operations found that the aircraft's unexpectedly high operational costs could force the service to cut 33.5 percent of planned acquisitions – 590 of a planned 1,763 F-35As. It concluded that this could only be avoided by reducing the fighter's operating and support costs by 38 percent by 2028. The assessment highlighted that the Air Force had 'very limited visibility into how' the funds going to Lockheed Martin for operational support were spent. Approximately half of the funds covering operational costs went to the firm, which according to the Air Force was for 'program management, depot maintenance, part repair, software maintenance, engineering.' With newly delivered fighters already suffering from high operational costs, expenses were only set to increase as flight hours rose and airframes were worn out.[40]

With early efforts to reduce the F-35's operational costs having underwhelming results, on 31 January 2018 Undersecretary of Defense for Acquisition and Sustainment Ellen Lord, the Pentagon's top purchasing officer, said that the Department of Defense would be unable to pay for the planned numbers of F-35s unless these costs were lowered.[41] This followed a statement 13 days prior by recently nominated assistant secretary of the air force for acquisition, Will Roper, that he was 'deeply concerned' about sustainment on the

* Blaming the 'concurrency' approach for the issue, Schmidt added: 'We have signed ourselves up to pipe dreams with concurrent programs and a long set of capabilities for a lot of reasons that we decided, "Well, I have to have it, so it'll be done in this timeframe," without the engineering rigor required to get those capabilities to actually get into the airplane, and all the things that go with that.'

F-35.[42] Lord would continue to stress the F-35's sustainment costs as a primary issue with the program even after leaving office.[43]

Where there were significant successes in lowering the F-35's procurement costs from 2007-2021, there was notably little progress in making the required reductions to operational costs, which remained much more important for the program's affordability. Joint Program Office director Lieutenant General Eric Fick observed, on 13 May 2021: 'I see cost as the program's greatest enemy ... I see high costs as an existential threat to the F-35 as an enterprise. And that cost happens not just in development, not just in production, but in sustainment as well.' 'Eighty percent of the program costs [over the life of the program] … are in that sustainment place. So, that really presents to me both the greatest challenge and the greatest opportunity for us to reduce overall program costs,' Fick stated, adding: 'That's where we really have the biggest mandate … when we look at the services' affordability targets.'[44]

The Government Accountability Office summarised the issue as follows in the title of a July 2021 report: 'DoD Needs to Cut Billions in Estimated Costs to Achieve Affordability.' The office the following month advised the Pentagon and Congress that buying more F-35s should be 'contingent on DoD's progress' in constraining its operating costs. 'There's a substantial and growing gap' between what the services thought they'd be spending on F-35 operations and what they actually were, it observed, projecting that by 2036 the gap would widen to $4.4 billion in the Air Force, and $6 billion in the services combined, unless corrective action was taken quickly. The extent of operational cost overruns varied for each variant of the fighter, but were particularly high for the F-35B, with the 2021 report highlighting that the projected annual sustainment cost of each F-35B would need to be cut by $2.3 million to meet established affordability constraints for the fleet.[45]

The more worn out fighters in service became, the more the total fighter fleet's average maintenance and support requirements grew – barring some unforeseen major surge in procurement rates. This made it particularly difficult to reduce operational costs as the F-35 fleet got older. The fact that the F-35 was already much more costly to operate than the large majority of the Air Force's ageing fourth generation fighters, which were on average over 30 years old, was thus highly concerning. An example of an added cost incurred with age was that as the first F-35s began to approach 2,000 hours of service in the mid-2020s, they would begin to require costly and time consuming overhauls. The Government Accountability Office thus projected in 2021 that the gap between planned annual funding levels for F-35 sustainment, and the expected costs of doing so, would reach a full $6 billion in 2036 alone, with the discrepancy being sharpest in the Air Force. Each F-35A would by then cost the USAF 47 percent more than the service stated it could afford.[46]

The F-35's sustainment costs gained growing attention in the early 2020s, with House Armed Services chair Adam Smith in March 2021 citing the program's chronic sustainment issues to criticise it as a 'rathole' for funding. The F-35's cost per flying hour was at the time estimated at over double that of that F-16. [47] Air Force Chief of Staff General Charles Brown Jr. later that year stated that if F-35A sustainment costs weren't reduced, the service would either have to fly the fighter less often, reserving them just for 'high-end missions,' or would choose to buy fewer of them.[48] As otherwise observed by Director of Defense Capabilities and Management at the GAO Diana Maurer when addressing Congress in April: 'The services have a plane that they cannot afford to fly the way they want to fly,' noting that affordability was a particular issue in the longer term.[49]

Responding to the significant growth in the F-35's costs, internal documents from the Air Force's future war-fighting, first seen by *Aviation Week* in December 2020, indicated a plan to cap orders at just 1,050 F-35As or fewer, down from 1,763 aircraft, which would represent a decline of at least 40 percent.[50] The official target of 1,763 fighters by that time had not been changed for nearly two decades, despite very significant cost increases. The Air Force's procurements decisions appeared to closely align with these plans, with the service in 2014 cutting planned annual procurements from 110 F-35A fighters to just 80, then to 60 in 2016, and finally to just 48 aircraft in the early 2020s – equating to two new squadrons.[51] Even the reduced target of 48 fighters would not be consistently held to, with procurements fluctuating down to 42 fighters in 2025 and just 24-25 in 2026.[52] These cuts to procurement rates allowed production to continue well into the latter half of the 2030s, which was vital to the health of the program and ensured more room for incremental upgrades. Such low procurement rates would have been impractical, however, if the fleet was still planned at over 1,500 fighters. A drawback of these cuts was that the fleet was by the mid-2020s a little over half the size initially projected. Had operational costs not overrun so drastically, there was a high possibility that a larger fleet of over 1,500 fighters would still have been planned, and that procurement rates would have remained at over 60 F-35As per year, resulting in a much larger fleet and less pressure on ageing fourth generation fighter units that had their replacements delayed.

Fleet Availability

Following its entry into service, the significant issues the F-35's operators encountered with its availability rates were expected to gradually be resolved, as the program had the opportunity to address outstanding issues and was able to benefit from greater economies of scale sustaining a larger fleet. Lockheed Martin executive vice president and general manager of the F-35 Program Jeff Babione, for one, projected in March 2018: 'I am certain the F-35 will set records for aircraft availability for a modern fighter in the future, without a doubt.'[53] Only 51 percent of all F-35s were assessed to be flightworthy at the time,[54] with no significant improvements seen since deliveries began in 2014.[55] Such optimistic projections may have appeared ill founded, however, when considering the preceding F-22 program's record of low availability rates. This had only worsened as the fleet matured in service, ensuring that the Raptor was by far the least available of any fighter in the Air Force. The low availability rates of both the F-22 and the F-35 were significantly more serious when considering that availability was closely related to age, and gradually worsened as airframes and engines were worn out with decades of use. Thus the fact that F-15s and F-16s built in the Cold War had availability rates that were tens of percentage points higher than the new stealth aircraft indicated that services operating the F-22 and F-35, already struggling to keep them operational when they were new off production lines, would likely struggle more profoundly as they aged.

A range of factors influenced the F-35's availability rates, including the high maintenance requirements inherent to the aircraft's design which were closely related to its operational costs. The wearing out of the F135 engine at higher rates than expected was another significant example (see Chapter 7), with an investigation in 2022 concluding that taking actions to reduce the non-mission capable due to engine fatigue rate would, in turn, raise the engine's sustainment costs, thus forcing services to choose between availability and affordability.[56] The F-35's unique Autonomic Logistics Information System (ALIS), which was intended to manage training, maintenance, supply chains, and a range of mission functions such as loading mission data, itself suffered from widespread issues. These were considered serious and intractable enough that an entirely new replacement system, the Operational Data Integrated Network (ODIN), needed to be developed. ALIS was designed so that one Standard Operating Unit was deployed on the ground with each F-35 squadron, and was also relied on to prepare data to upload on the aircraft, analyse information downloaded after missions on mobile terminals, and centralise software updates for all F-35s worldwide. ALIS's significant cyber vulnerabilities were a further important factor in this decision, which was made after years of efforts to fix the system fell short of expectations.[57] ALIS proved to be so problematic that Air Force units could spend over 45,000 hours per year performing additional tasks and manual workarounds due entirely to its malfunctions.[58] For training purposes, instructors found ways to cease to use it entirely, although this meant operating less efficiently than if the system been functioning and able to support their operations.[59] Aside from their disruptions to operations, schedule slippage and functionality problems with ALIS also imposed considerable costs on the program, with a Pentagon commissioned plan in 2016 concluding that these had the potential to reach $20-100 billion if unaddressed.[60]

A wide range of contributing issues meant that the F-35 program was unable to achieve the planned swift turnover from ALIS to ODIN, and was forced into a slower 'evolutionary transition.'[61] The lack of a sufficiently capable supply chain management system was an important factor contributing to spare parts shortages across the F-35 fleet, with the 'just-in-time' logistics model increasingly from the mid-2020s demonstrated to be exacerbating issues.[62] This model was intended to use real-time data and predictive analytics to forecast needs for parts, and deliver components to maintenance locations as they were required, rather than creating large stockpiles of spare parts. An unintended result was that any hiccup in the supply chain risked a major fallout, with a persistence of parts shortages often having cascading impacts as fighters left sitting idle became increasingly difficult to return to service.[63] The concurrency approach, and the resulting significant design changes that needed to be made quickly between batches after production began to fix numerous design flaws, meant that spare parts often lacked commonality across the fleet. On the Marine Corps' first F-35B carrier deployments, for example, the spare parts onboard were often not compatible with the specific fighters being hosted.[64]

Supply chain issues were exacerbated by the fact that F-35 operators were limited in the kinds of maintenance and supply chain activities they could perform due to Lockheed Martin's protection of its proprietary data rights, which prohibited many kinds of organic maintenance and repair of aircraft, assemblies or components. This was also an important contributor to the fighter's high operational costs.[65] The impact of supply chain issues on availability rates was expected to significantly worsen in wartime situations, particularly in light of the considerable and growing emphasis placed by all three American services on distributed operations. These supply chain issues were all exacerbated by the F-35 program's limited capacity to produce spare parts,[66] and by qualitative issues with spare parts, with head of the Joint Program Office, Lieutenant Colonel Schmidt, going as far as to refer to the latter in April 2022 as presenting as much of a threat as enemy missiles.[67] Indeed, parts shortages fuelled calls on the House Armed Services Readiness panel in the early 2020s to avoid increasing F-35 procurements specifically because it would spread the limited parts supplies even more thinly.[68] One remaining uncertainty was the extent to which serious issues with the F-35's supply of parts were responsible for the fleet's low availability rates, and to what degree a more robust supply chain would improve availability.

From the 2010s the low availability rates of the F-22 were increasingly overlooked, as the niche and highly specialised fighter was not heavily relied on by the Air Force. The specific threat the F-22 was designed to counter, a high intensity war with an advanced enemy air superiority fleet, appeared unlikely to materialise before

U.S. Air Force personnel perform maintenance on a pair of F-35As. (USAF)

Maintainers of the 421st Fighter Squadron performing maintenance on an F-35A at the Hill AFB. (USAF)

the F-35 had surpassed it in numbers and in air-to-air performance. When serious issues with the F-35's availability rates persisted into the 2020s, however, this became cause for serious concern. Mission capable rates for the fighters would see little improvement, and by early 2022 the Air Force's F-35A fleet was revealed to be only 55 percent mission capable, while the standard rate for fourth generation fighters in the fleet was 75 percent. Furthermore, the portion of the F-35 fleet capable of flying any required mission type, referred to as the fully mission capable rate, stood at only 30-35 percent, compared to a target of 60 percent.[69] These rates would cause considerable shock among lawmakers, with Chairman of the House Armed Services Subcommittee on Tactical Air and Land Forces Representative Rob Wittman in October 2023 reflecting the broad consensus when he rhetorically exclaimed: 'It's a new aircraft — why is it at 55%?'[70] In contrast to the F-15, F-16 and F-18, which when first commissioned had maintained availability rates well over 80 percent, the very poor availability of the F-22 and F-35 served to drive down overall availability rates for America's fighter fleet. The widespread transition of fighter units across the services to the F-35 ensured that availability rates throughout the fleets of the United States and its strategic partners worldwide would decline considerably, which represented one of the most serious drawbacks of the Joint Strike Fighter program.

By the middle of the 2020s, the average maintenance durations of all F-35 variants far exceeded the requirements of the program's Operational Requirements Document. The Director of Operational Test & Evaluation confirmed in February 2025 that there was 'little improvement in these maintainability metrics since FY15 [Fiscal Year 2015], while the mean corrective maintenance time for critical failures remained almost double or more the threshold requirement for each variant.'[71] Efforts led by Defense Secretary James Mattis from October 2018 to raise availability rates in the F-35, F-22, F-18 and F-16 fleets to 80 percent had seen the F-35's very low availability rates represent a leading obstacle,[72] which contributed to forcing the Air Force to officially abandon this target in May 2020.[73] At the beginning of 2023, the Joint Program Office launched a 'War on Readiness' effort intended to raise mission capable rates by 10 percent by the end of March 2024. This also failed, with readiness rising by only 2.6 percent to reach 55.7 percent.[74]

The fallout from the F-35's low availability rates for the American fighter fleet's combat potential exacerbated the issue of the fighter's immense overruns in procurement and operational costs. As a result transitioning to the F-35 not only forced a contraction in the number of fighter units, but also significantly reduced the portions of the fighter units remaining which would be available for combat at any time. As noted by Chairman of the House Armed Services Committee Readiness subcommittee John Garamendi, as the services were 'not able to maintain' those F-35s they did procure adequately, the result for the overall fighter fleet was that 'the more we buy, the worse overall performance has been.'[75] Alongside major overruns in the F-35's operational costs, this emerged as a primary factor stimulating the Air Force in particular to consider options for simpler alternatives to the F-35 which were both less costly to sustain, and could be kept at far higher readiness rates.

Responses to Sustainment Cost and Availability Issues

By the early 2020s, the F-35A's inability to serve as a low maintenance successor to the F-16 with similarly low operational costs and high availability rates appeared poised to force further major contractions in the Air Force's fighter fleet. This fuelled growing interest in the service in procuring a second type of single engine fighter which could be acquired and sustained much more affordably. A major landmark in the shifting of consensus on the matter was revealed in January 2021, when the Air Force's latest review of the tactical aircraft portfolio raised the possibility of orders being placed for the F-16 to make up for shortfalls in the F-35 fleet. This once unthinkable decision would mirror the decision to resume procurements of the F-15 from 2020 to make up for shortfalls in the F-22 program, and boded ill for the future of the F-35.[76] Assistant Secretary of the Air Force for Acquisitions, Technology and Logistics Will Roper on 20 January voiced a degree of support for such procurements a day before his resignation, stating: 'As you look at the new F-16 production line in South Carolina, that system has some wonderful upgraded capabilities that are worth thinking about as part of our capacity solution.'[77]

Responding to growing speculation that F-16 acquisitions would be resumed, Air Force Chief of Staff General Charles Brown Jr. on 17 February stated that it would be preferable to develop a new fighter that was cheaper and simpler than the F-35, but more modern than the F-16. He referred to this as a 'four-and-a-half-gen or fifth-gen-minus' fighter. 'This will help inform the decisions that I think I need to make internal to the Air Force, and what I would recommend that force mix might be,' he stated. 'Now, I will also tell you I don't think that everybody's going to exactly agree with what I say. But I want to actually have a starting point as a point of departure, a point of dialogue.' Brown had opposed further F-16s acquisitions due to the aircraft's lack of open architecture software protocols that would allow it to be rapidly reconfigured, as well as due to the fighter's inability to receive software updates sufficiently quickly. The fleet, he stated, needed 'something new and different, that's not the F-16 – that has some of those capabilities but gets there faster and uses some of our digital approach.'[78]

The traction which the possibility of resumed acquisitions of fourth generation lightweight fighters, including F-16s, had gained in the Air Force, highlighted the F-35's major shortcomings as a successor due primarily to its combination of excessive operational costs and low availability rates. In November 2023 it was reported that the Air Force was considering an even lighter fighter than the F-16, which would be derived from the Boeing T-7 trainer then under development. The development of trainer jets into light fighters had multiple precedents, with the F-16's direct predecessor the F-5 having been a derivative of the T-38 trainer which first flew three months before it. The South Korean T-50 trainer, which the USAF considered leasing due to delays developing the T-7, was itself developed into the FA-50 fighter that proved to have a respectable performance in both simulated and actual combat.[79] Fighters derived from trainers could be into a 'very light' category, smaller than traditional light fighters such as the F-16 and J-10, and had consistently had among the lowest operational costs and highest availability rates in the world as a result of their low maintenance needs.

As the USAF received its first T-7 trainer for fight testing on 8 November 2024, an Air Force official speaking anonymously stated that an 'F-7' fighter derivative was one option to help replace the service's ageing F-16 fleet as F-35A numbers fell short.[80] Unlike the F-16, the T-7 was built with an open architecture and digital design, allowing multiple contractors to integrate new features and subsystems relatively easily. Analysts at *The War Zone* summarised the consensus on the perceived need for an aircraft like the proposed 'F-7': 'For years now it has become increasingly apparent that the service will need new lower-tier combat jets – crewed or uncrewed – to help provide sufficient "affordable mass" to meet all of its future requirements.'[81] As otherwise observed by analysts at *Military Watch Magazine*: 'While the low maintenance F-16 has among the highest availability rates in the fleet, those of the F-35 are among the very worst despite the aircraft being by far the newest, which has seriously limited the fleet's combat readiness as well as pilot training hours.' This 'increased the appeal of acquiring a simpler alternative to the F-35, with an "F-7" fighter based on the T-7, despite its very limited combat potential, being one of very few options currently available to the Air Force.'[82] Despite its simplicity, however, the T-7 would nevertheless face years of unanticipated delays.

As the issues which led F-7 and F-16 procurements to be considered persisted into the second half of the decade, in May 2025 chair of the Senate Intelligence Committee, Senator Thomas Cotton, and Chief of Staff of the Air Force, General David Allvin, discussed the possibility of developing an F-16 Block 80 variant for the USAF, and how the defence industrial base could accommodate it.[83] Although the future of both potential programs remained uncertain, the fact that such options were being seriously considered was a major testament to the shortcomings of the F-35 program.

While the possibility of deep cuts to F-35 acquisitions, and investment in a cheaper lighter non-stealth fighter, gained growing traction from the late 2010s to the mid-2020s, a controversial alternative seriously considered was to make deep cuts to the F-35 fleet's annual flight hours, and thus to pilot training, to facilitate required reductions to operational costs. With the U.S. Air Force having prided itself on its pilots' high flight training hours for decades, this was a potentially revolutionary shift which was favoured for its ability to accommodate the planned F-35 fleet size despite major overruns in sustainment costs. Highlighting that operational costs were 'the place to go in looking for affordability' on the F-35, Joint Program Office director General Fick was one of the earliest officials to publicly repeatedly advocate reducing these by cutting pilot training hours. 'I can fly less, maybe offload some of that work to our full mission simulators, our advanced simulators, which is something we're considering and working with the services on,' he stated. He also noted at the time that the Air Force cancelled some F-35 air show demonstrations to increase the number of training sorties that could be flown.[84]

With major overruns in operational costs being a primary factor raising the projected costs of the F-35 program, the American F-35 fleet's projected lifetime sustainment cost was estimated at $1.1 trillion in 2018, with this figure revised upwards by 44 percent within five years to $1.58 trillion in 2023.[85] It was notable that a primary reason why estimated operational costs had not risen much faster was that the Air Force and Navy had by 2023 reduced their projected annual flying times by 19 percent and 45 percent respectively, meaning that pilots would train considerably less on the aircraft.[86] While USAF fighter pilots in the 1980s flew 200-300 hours a year in new F-15s, F-16s, and A-10s, compared to around 130 hours for Soviet pilots, by the mid-2020s they were flying for less than 130 hours a year, while Chinese fighter pilots were flying for more than 200 hours in aircraft that were on average decades newer.[87]

Reducing training hours as a means to facilitate deep cuts to spending on F-35 sustainment was far from isolated to the U.S. Armed Forced, with such cuts having been planned by multiple European clients for the fighter as a means of making the aircraft affordable. Finland represented a particularly extreme case, and required its F-35A fleet's annual sustainment costs not to exceed 10 percent of the country's peacetime defence budget, placing

A view of the front panel in a F-35A-simulator, revealing details of a major multi-function display that's dominating this type's cockpit. (USAF)

them at around $4.4 million per fighter. This was approximately 60 percent below Switzerland's and a staggering 80 percent below Norway's annual sustainment costs per fighter, and largely reflected discrepancies in planned flight training hours.[88] Reduced flight training was seen as a necessary sacrifice to accommodate the vastly superior capabilities which the F-35 could provide over rival fighters, and allowed for a lowering of sustainment costs without making unacceptable cuts to fleet numbers. This made Finland one of very few countries to order enough F-35s for one-for-one replacements of its fourth generation fighters, with 64 F-35As replacing 64 F-18C/Ds, which would not have been affordable without either significantly increasing sustainment spending or significantly reducing flight hours.

It was hoped that effective use of simulators, combined with the high levels of automation on the F-35, would make reliance on simulators a viable approach with a minimal impact on combat effectiveness. The unprecedented levels of automation achieved made some of the most complex tasks, such as vertical or arrested landings on aircraft carriers, highly straightforward. As observed by U.S. Air Force experimental test pilot in the F-35 Lieutenant Colonel Tucker Hamilton regarding vertical landing of the F-35B, which had been a particularly complex task for pilots to achieve on the Harrier:

> You pretty much could train any pilot in a fairly short amount of time to effectively land that aircraft … it's intuitive in the sense that you, as a pilot, aren't keeping it under control. It is doing all of it by itself with the computers and you're just providing some inputs that totally make sense to you. It's like playing a video game almost. You want to move a little to the left, you just bank a little to the end and then you can roll out. It is so solid that it gets you right where you need to be … it's autonomous for the most part. If I want to slow down I set certain speeds, it does all that for me. Very different, from what I understand, compared to the Harrier.[89]

Regarding the F-35C, Hamilton noted: 'It's so intuitive and easy and nearly, not fully, but nearly autonomous with regard to landing on the carrier.' Speaking regarding the automation of the F-35 more generally, he observed: 'It's really simple to fly, and I think that is step one of the F-35 being a game changer for what it means it be a fighter pilot, is this idea that they've taken the flying aspect of it and made it simpler. So now you can operate the system and be more effective on the battlefield.' 'The F-35, its basically changing what it means to be a fighter pilot ... I truly believe that that's a game changer for what it means to be a fighter pilot, and what our training is all about is going to change dramatically,' he concluded.[90]

To a far greater extent than any previous fighter, the primary challenge for F-35 pilots was managing data rather than actual flight, which meant simulators were expected to do a much better job preparing pilots than they could for other aircraft. As observed by former Royal Canadian Air Force combat commander and F-35 test pilot Billie Flynn: 'there were very few surprises when I finally got to fly the F-35 because our simulators were so realistic that other than the actual feeling of the thrust of the F-35, everything else about the aircraft I had already experienced.' He elaborated:

> [I]t is a remarkably easy aircraft to fly. And flying skills are much less important in F-35 than in any airplane ever before. The massive contrast with previous aircraft is that a pilot has such a significant cognitive workload to manage everything that is displayed on the screens in front of him or her, that the real trick for the F-35 is managing all of the information that is presented, not actually flying the F-35 airframe. It's easy to fly the airplane. It's incredibly difficult to be good, to be great, at managing all the information that's presented. And that's the real job when it comes to operating the F-35 ... you can be a great plot pilot, but that's not what's going to make you amazing in an F-35. It's how well you can manage incredible systems and information that's given to the pilot.[91]

BAE Systems F-35 simulator showing fighter flying alongside a Royal Navy Queen Elizabeth-class aircraft carrier. While carrier landings were considered among the most complex tasks for fighter pilots, advances in automation made this highly straightforward for F-35 pilots. (BAE Systems)

Flynn's assertions were in line with statements from a wide range of informed sources to the effect that the requirements for pilots on the F-35 were very different than other aircraft, and that its high levels of automation allowed them to concentrate on being combat tacticians and managing data, which made simulators much more viable as a substitute for flight time.[92] A number of sources nevertheless raised serious questions regarding the toll which reduced flying hours could take on F-35 units' combat potentials. When F-35 pilots polled were asked whether they believed 'flight time in the simulator is a viable replacement for time in the jet?' only 3.33 percent answered affirmatively, while 87 percent answered that it was not. The remaining ten percent answered that it could be only for 'some things.'[93] Deep cuts to flight hours made the effectiveness, or lack of it, of simulators as substitutes for flight hours a central factor in determining the overall impact the transition to the F-35 would have for the fighter fleets of the United States and its strategic partners.

While cuts to flight training hours were seen to provide a partial solution to the F-35's operational cost issues, another significant factor was that the fighter's superior capabilities could facilitate significant cuts to fleets of supporting aircraft, which would allow services operating F-35s to allocate more funds to covering their sustainment. This was observed as follows by the editorial of the *Air and Space Forces Magazine* in March 2021:

> A pair of F-35s can strike multiple targets in a contested environment with no support save, perhaps, a tanker. To get two conventional fighter jets to a similarly contested target requires 10 to 20 additional aircraft. The strike jets must be accompanied by other planes to jam enemy radar, defend the attackers, and provide situational awareness ... Buying F-35s eliminates the need for other aircraft and the personnel, acquisition, training, and logistics that go with them. No economic argument against the F-35 is viable without that calculus.[94]

This assessment had significant merits, but also a number of caveats. While the F-35's tremendous improvements to situational awareness and electronic warfare capabilities did allow it to operate with far less support from other aircraft, this did come at the expense of performance. Although the fighter's capabilities were a generation ahead of the F-16s and F-18s they replaced, new generations of specialist support aircraft such as the E-7 Wedgetail airborne warning and control system and EA-37B Compass Call electronic attack aircraft also had a far greater potential to serve as force multipliers than their Cold War era predecessors. Although the F-35 could operate much more viably without such support aircraft than F-16s or F-18s could, it was nevertheless without question that the need to cut these aircraft to compensate for the F-35's cost overruns would result in an overall significantly inferior combat capability than if these cuts had not been necessary. This was aside from the fact that compared to rival fighters such as the Chinese J-20 and the F-15EX, the F-35 would be significantly more reliant on tanker and AWACS support due to its far lower endurance and carriage of a much smaller radar.

Major Flaws

Although the first production representative prototype of the F-35 began testing in June 2008, the aircraft continued to suffer from a wide range of considerable issues into the latter half of the 2020s affecting both its hardware and its software. While some of the flaws discovered were relatively straightforward to resolve, others would prove to be far more complex. Solving issues with the aircraft proved to be a highly costly and time-consuming undertaking, and by January 2020 the fighter was confirmed by a report from the Office of the Director of Operational Test and Evaluation to still be suffering from 873 unresolved deficiencies. The continuous discovery of new flaws undermined efforts to reduce the number of problems. 'Although the programme office is working to fix deficiencies, new discoveries are still being made, resulting in only a minor decrease in the overall number,' the report noted.[95] As a result, the number of 'open deficiencies,' which included eight in the most serious Category 1, had not improved significantly since the fighter's development and demonstration phase ended in April 2018.[96]

An additional dimension to the complexity of the F-35's flaws compared to preceding fighters was the far greater size and complexity of its software package. While promising revolutionary increases in combat potential, the writing, validating, debugging, and upgrading of this software would significantly complicate the fighter's development and subsequent modernisation, and was a major contributor to issues with the program including delays, performance deficiencies, and cost overruns. The percentage of the F-35's functionality that was provided by software was unprecedentedly high, and having been under 10 percent for the F-4A introduced in 1960, 35 percent for the F-15A/B introduced in 1975, 65 percent for B-2 bomber introduced in 1997, and 80 percent for the F-22 introduced in 2005, it reached a significantly higher unknown figure for the new aircraft.[97] Software accordingly grew from 1,000 lines of code in the F-4A, to 1.7 million lines on the F-22, and 5.7 million on the F-35.[98]

The F-35 program would increasingly gain a reputation as one overwhelmed by hundreds of bugs and design flaws, with prevailing perceptions summarised in April 2022 by House Armed Service Subcommittee on Readiness Chairman Congressman John Garamendi as follows: 'We're going to go off and buy new bright shiny airplanes and they're going to be flying probably well for a few months and then they're going to wind up with a problem.'[99] While this reputation could partly be attributed to the greater scrutiny which the program received due to its immense scale and cost, and the resulting greater oversight and accountability mechanisms put in place compared to other fighter programs, the extreme nature of the delays, both to bringing the aircraft into service and to implementing upgrades, were among the indicators that the extent of the issues were above and beyond the norm. While a comprehensive assessment of all significant flaws discovered with the fighter would require several volumes, an assessment of a sample of flaws discovered, including both more and less serious examples, is provided below.

Following the considerable scandal surrounding the 'Raptor cough' that had affected F-22 pilots, it had been expected that the resolution of the issue would prevent similar problems from affecting future fighter programs. The emergence of reports of hypoxia-like symptoms suffered by F-35A pilots was thus unexpected, with the fact that such symptoms were found to have been reported as early as 2011, but had gone unresolved, being more concerning still.[100] On 9 June 2017, the 56th Fighter Wing based at Luke Air Force Base, Arizona, cancelled local flying operations for its 55 F-35As after five pilots separately reported symptoms similar to hypoxia, or oxygen deprivation, between 2 May and 8 June. The grounding was initially intended end on 12 June, but was extended indefinitely until 21 June.[101] Hypoxia suffered by F-22 pilots had similarly led the Air Force to ground its fleet for five months in 2011.[102] Finding the cause of the issue affecting the F-35s proved to be challenging, and while some incidents were attributed to more easily identifiable issues such as irregular oxygen valves, the cause of wider issues remained elusive.[103] Although the Joint Program Office on 19 July 2017 announced that it intended to make changes to the F-35's oxygen generation system to optimise oxygen flow to pilots, namely by altering associated algorithms, it made clear that it did not believe this to be related to the symptoms suffered by pilots.[104]

Issues with the F-35's oxygen systems would persist into the next decade, and after the crash of an F-35A on 19 May 2020, the accident investigation considered oxygen systems to be a possible contributor that may have adversely affected the pilot's cognition.[105] In November 2020 a new NASA study found that the F-35 did not continually supply the amount of oxygen needed by pilots, forcing operators to change their breathing rates to compensate. It highlighted that affected pilots 'fault the breathing system for acute

A line-up of F-35As of the 388th and 419th Fighter Wings, as seen at the Hill Air Force Base, during a training sortie in July 2020. At the time, these were the only combat capable Lightning IIs in the entire Air Force. (USAF)

and chronic health conditions that have caused impairment for days, weeks, months, or longer.'[106] The Tactical Air and Land Forces Subcommittee accordingly added provisions to the 2022 defence policy bill requiring an investigation into and implementation of corrective actions for the F-35's pilot breathing system.[107] A congressional aide commented at the time that it was unfortunate that it took an intervention by Congress to press the Department of Defense to act on the issue, stressing that 'the pilot shouldn't have to think about breathing in the airplane. It should just come naturally so that they can focus on the tactical employment.'[108]

While many of the F-35's design flaws hindered the aircraft's combat potential, a not insignificant number also hindered the ability to fly non-combat missions. In June 2019 it was reported that sudden spikes in cockpit pressure had in at least two cases left F-35 pilots with searing ear and sinus pain. Air Force documents revealed that the pain 'has been described as excruciating, causing loss of in-flight situational awareness, with effects lasting for months.' The incidents were attributed to issues which had first been identified in 2014, but had yet to be resolved.[109]

Beyond conditions related to life support, the ability to control the F-35 was itself at times seriously compromised. One of the most extreme examples was the cause of a near fatal F-35A crash at Hill Air Force Base on 19 October 2022. An Air Force investigation published on 27 July the following year showed that the incident had been caused by a software issue, which left the pilot unable to abort the fighter's landing sequence as it stopped responding and sharply banked to the left.[110] One F-35 test pilot who observed the incident from the ground recalled when speaking to investigators that the aircraft 'looked like a totally normal F-35 before obviously going out of control.' 'When the oscillations were happening, I did see really large flight control surface movements, stabs, trailing edge flaps, rudders all seem to be moving pretty rapidly like, probably at their rate limits, and huge deflections,' he stated, with the fighter putting itself in a position with 'virtually no chance of recovering.'[111] Total damage from the incident was evaluated at $166.3 million.[112] Although issues with the F-35 undermined its combat potential in multiple ways, they were in the vast majority of cases insufficient to cause crashes, with the fighter program's crash rate remaining being very low. The October 2022 incident, however, was an exceptional case.

The use of touch screens rather than switches in the F-35's cockpit was intended to reduce pilot's reaction times, but was reported by pilots to be causing a number of issues. The 'click' of switches confirming they were successfully flipped had no equivalent on a touchscreen, and much as was the case for smartphones, it was far from uncommon for a command to be given only for nothing to happen for several seconds. Pilots interviewed anonymously stated in 2021 that the F-35's touch screens failed to give results around 20 percent of the time. One pilot observed to this effect:

> At present I am pressing the wrong part of the screen about 20 [percent] of the time in flight due to either mis-identification, or more commonly by my finger getting jostled around in turbulence or under G. One of the biggest drawbacks is that you can't brace your hand against anything whilst typing — think how much easier it is to type on a smartphone with your thumbs versus trying to stab at a virtual keyboard on a large tablet with just your index finger.[113]

Pilots further noted difficulties interfacing with the F-35's helmet displays, claiming that traditional heads up displays could show information more widely rather than shrinking it to fit the helmet's field of view. One pilot further criticised the voice recognition system, stating: 'Voice input is another feature of the jet, but not once I have found to be useful. It may work well on the ground in a test rig, but under G in flight it's not something I have found to work consistently enough to rely on. I haven't met anyone who uses it.' The extent to which these opinions were widely shared among F-35 pilots remains uncertain, as is the extent of any efforts to remedy the issues raised.[114] The notoriously heavy weight of the helmet itself caused a number of medical issues and forced many pilots to be transitioned to staff jobs.[115] The fact that each helmet had to be heavily customised to the individual pilot mean that issues with any pilot's helmet often left them grounded until it was repaired.[116]

Another notable issue with pilot interface was the emission of horizontal green lines which appeared on the helmet display's night vision camera, and could be particularly dangerous for its obstructing of an aircraft carrier's deck lights during night-time carrier landings. The issue was resolved by updating the design of the display, with new the Generation III OLED Helmet Display Unit significantly reducing the green glow. A separate more serious issue with night vision system persisted, however, namely that their interface with helmet mounted sights was far from smooth, and made even relatively straightforward operations, such as landing the aircraft, highly challenging at night. This led pilots to strongly favour avoiding more complex tasks such as aerial refuelling at times of day when night vision systems were needed. The fact that the large majority of the F-35's combat operations were expected to take place at night made this a particularly serious issue.[117]

While many of the F-35's flaws threatened very general aspects of the aircraft's performance, and undermined its ability to conduct several mission types, some flaws limited more specific functions at times only on a single variant. A notable example were the issues affecting the F-35A's GAU-22/A gun, which although beginning the first phase of testing on 9 June 2015,[118] had been revealed the previous year to only be scheduled to achieve operational status in 2019 at the earliest – a protracted timeline that caused considerable amazement among analysts.[119] A review of the F-35 program by the Office of the Director of Operational Test and Evaluation publicised in early 2019 raised further questions about the accuracy of the gun, with a persistent error causing it to shoot to the right of the pilot's point of aim. This was seen to be one of several significant defects which the Air Force had made few efforts to address, with analysts at *The War Zone* referring to it as 'another well-established issue that the Air Force has, at least implicitly, appeared to ignore over the years.'[120] The annual assessment by the Defense Department's Director of Operational Test and Evaluation provided further details when published in early 2020. 'Investigations into the gun mounts of the F-35A revealed misalignments that result in muzzle alignment errors. As a result, the true alignment of each F-35A gun is not known, so the program is considering options to re-boresight and correct gun alignments,' the report stated. 'Based on F-35A gun testing to date, DOT&E considers the accuracy of the gun, as installed in the F-35A, to be unacceptable,' it concluded.[121]

Moving into the 2020s, the reported issues with the F-35A's gun appeared to only grow more serious, with a further issue emerging of cracking in the outer mold-line coatings and the underlying chine longeron skin near the muzzle. When discovered on newer F-35As, this forced the Air Force to restrict the gun to combat use only for all aircraft from production Lot 9 onwards. Lot 9 aircraft had begun deliveries in 2017.[122] The Government Accountability Office would observe in an April 2022 report that cracking was 'a result of higher than designed for pressure conditions when firing the gun,'[123] with a report by the office in May the following year highlighting the risk that part of a cracked panel could break off and material from it could enter the aircraft's engine.[124] The lack of a functional main gun continued to be a major scandal into the mid-2020s, with the GAU-22/A belatedly confirmed to have been made effective only in March 2024 – 15 years after it had entered production. While accuracy issues were confirmed to have been resolved, the issue of pressure conditions when firing and the resulting cracking of surrounding parts of the airframe remained unresolved.

The GAU-22/A was far from the only subsystem unique to a particular F-35 variant which suffered serious problems, with many requiring extensive redesigns while others proved simpler to resolve. An early example specific to the F-35C was its tail hook. Like all carrier-based fighters without vertical landing capabilities, a tail hook was required to attach to an arresting wire upon landing to help the aircraft decelerate, effectively letting the ship 'catch' the aircraft before it overshot the runway. The F-35C's hook was stowed in a rear bay covered by clamshell doors, and was electronically controlled and moved by hydraulics. Testing the arrestor hook began years behind schedule in 2011, and it quickly emerged that not only was its engagement rate far below what was expected, but that its load carrying capacity was far from sufficient for the F-35. This was hardly unpredictable, with F-35 Test Pilot Tony Wilson recalling being informed by technical experts as early as November 2010, when the first aircraft were delivered: 'This f*cker ain't gonna work. Look at this thing. It's short, it's too close to the wheels, and look at this dumbass hook shoe they got on it. If the wire don't hit it exactly right, it's just gonna go under the hook and you'll bolter.'[125]

Designing the tail hook posed unique challenges, as the F-35C was the first stealth fighter with such a system to reach an advanced development stage. The hook needed to be designed to be concealed when it was not being used, which required fitting it farther forward on the aircraft than on other fighters.[126] Despite the complexities of meeting this challenge, it would prove relatively straightforward to resolve by the standards of the maladies affecting the F-35 program. A key factor in this was that the problem was isolated to the tail hook itself with no secondary effects on the rest of the plane or software-related aspects. On 9-16 January 2014, the F-35 team used a redesigned stronger and better positioned tail hook to accomplish 36 successful roll-in arrestment tests, dispelling remaining concerns regarding the program.[127]

One of the most prominent and controversial hardware related issues affecting the F-35 was that of the B and C variants' tail sections, which were revealed in June 2019 to be at risk of both serious structural damage and a compromising of stealth capabilities if either of the two variants flew at supersonic speeds for more than a short burst of time. A range of antennas on the back of the aircraft were also highly vulnerable to damage if supersonic flight was sustained. The issues were categorised as separate Category 1 deficiencies for each variant. It was revealed at the time that both deficiencies were first observed in late 2011 following flutter tests where the F-35B and F-35C both flew at speeds of Mach 1.3 and Mach 1.4, with 'bubbling [and] blistering' of stealth coatings discovered alongside 'thermal damage' that compromised the structural integrity of the inboard horizontal tail and tail boom.[128]

It was confirmed at the time that beyond the application of improved stealth coatings, the issue would be addressed by changing the operating parameters of the F-35B and F-35C to ensure that neither would fly supersonically other than in very brief bursts. As noted by the JPO: 'This issue was closed on December 17, 2019 with no further actions and concurrence from the U.S. services. The [deficiency report] was closed under the category of "no plan to correct," which is used by the F-35 team when the operator value provided by a complete fix does not justify the estimated cost of that fix.' 'In this case, the solution would require a lengthy development and flight testing of a material coating that can tolerate the flight environment for unlimited time while satisfying the weight and other requirements of a control surface. Instead, the issue is being addressed procedurally by imposing a time limit on high-speed flight,' it added.[129]

With both variants intended to be able to serve as interceptors to protect carrier groups, serious restrictions on supersonic flight were potentially highly detrimental to their capabilities, and further widened the already significant discrepancy in speed between the F-35s and competing fighters. Many rival fighters such as the Chinese J-20 and J-35 could not only fly at well over twice the speed of sound for minutes at a time, but could also cruise at high supersonic speeds. The decision to respond to issues by restricting speed was justified on the basis that the F-35's lack of a supercruise capability limited the utility of supersonic flight, which was 'more of a "break glass in case of emergency" feature' that featured little in prevailing tactics for using the aircraft. Nevertheless, the F-35 was already considered vulnerable in visual range combat, in particular the F-35B which was by far the least manoeuvrable fighter type developed since the Cold War, with the imposition of serious limitations on supersonic flight significantly worsening this. With both variants designed for carrier operations, the fact that damage from supersonic flight would require a depot-level repair was particularly dangerous, with a significant possibility remaining that such repairs would not be possible for several months until their fleets returned to land.[130] The design flaws that limited supersonic flight were far from the only ones which the Joint Program Office would choose to overlook rather than fix.

Another notable flaw that necessitated flight restrictions was the F-35A's inability to fly within 40 kilometres of lightning storms. The fighter's Onboard Inert Gas Generation system responsible for pumping nitrogen-enriched air into fuel tanks to inert them, and thus preventing the aircraft from exploding if struck by lightning, saw tubing and fittings which delivered the nitrogen mix cease to function effectively over time due to vibrations during flight. The issue was discovered in 2020, when maintainers at Hill Air Force Base found tubing damage during depot maintenance, leading to a subsequent inspection which found that 14 of 24 F-35As were affected. With all-weather combat capabilities having been a vital requirement for fighters since the early years of the Cold War, imposing such restrictions on such a widely used fighter could cause serious issues, with some sources speculating that it could even provide adversaries with opportunities to time their operations with thunderstorms.[131] Addressing the issue would prove to be a protracted affair, with efforts to strengthen a number of brackets associated with the affected tubes being far from straightforward. The restriction on flights in lightning was cleared on 19 March 2024, four years after it had been imposed.[132]

Quality control related to the F-35's stealth features continued to be an issue into the 2020s, with Lockheed Martin's general manager of advanced development programs Jeff Babione acknowledging in 2018 'quality escapes that are made around the LO [low observable] system.' 'It's not a human problem; that's just the result of our ability. We're approaching the limits of our ability to build some of these things from precise-enough technology,' he stated, stressing that decreasing the F-35's manufacturing defects was a 'huge, huge

An F-35B from the Marine Fighter Attack Squadron 211, in the process of launching from the Royal Navy's aircraft carrier HMS *Queen Elizabeth*, during cross-deck operations, in August 2021. (U.S. DoD)

priority.'[133] Quality control with the airframe was more generally a major issue particularly in the fighter's initial years in service, with the F-35B and F-35C in particular suffering from very high numbers of cracks during durability testing requiring very considerable repairs and modifications, which would prevent them from coming close to serving their full 8,000 hour service lives.[134]

The F-35 initially faced difficulties operating in cold weather, as cold air entered the aircraft when the doors to the jet's nose landing gear were open, overwhelming the battery heater blanket. Improvements to the battery charger's firmware were made to resolve the issue. The discovery of serious flaws with software was also far from uncommon, and at times grounded entire squadrons. The VMFA-211 Arizona-based F-35B squadron, for example, was temporarily grounded in June 2017 due to problems with the software in its ALIS central cloud-based computer brain, after unspecified 'anomalies' caused by the latest Version 2.0.2 patch.[135]

The discovery of flaws that caused groundings of significant parts of the F-35 fleet was notably far from infrequent, with issues causing temporary groundings having ranged from faulty parts in ejection seats in July 2022,[136] to engine quality issues,[137] among many others. An early example was the grounding of all 97 F-35s worldwide after engine issues started a fire on 23 June 2014. The F-35 had been posed to make its high-profile international debut at two British air shows, but none of the aircraft in the fleet were able to participate due to the engine fracture. The incident occurred not long after an in-flight oil leak had sparked a brief grounding the previous month.

From September to November 2016 an insulation supply defect caused thirteen American and two Norwegian F-35As, to be grounded, and forced the U.S. Air Force, Navy and Marines and international partners to inspect of their F-35 inventories for faulty coolant lines in their F135 engines. These tubes travel through where fuel is stored, although only on the outer tip of the wing, with the insulation placed around that coolant line to keep it from being affected by the warm fuel found to be decomposing into the fuel on several of the aircraft. The cause was delivery of the wrong insulation by one of Lockheed Martin's suppliers. Solving this required a lengthy process involving cutting holes in the wings and removing the bad insulation, as well as cleaning out the potential damage from those pieces floating around. Forty-two fighters in various stages of production had had flawed lines installed, including the first two built for Israel, as well as aircraft on order by Norway, Japan and Italy. The head of the F-35 Joint Program Office Lieutenant General Chris Bogdan stressed at the time that this was 'not a technical issue, it is not a design issue. It is a quality escape from a supplier that supplied us with insulation.'[138]

Qualitative defects with the F-35 would continue to be a major issue into the mid-2020s, with the Pentagon's Defense Contract Management Agency reporting in August 2022 that 'too many quality assurance defects' were not found at initial assembly stations, only to be discovered later on. This remained 'an issue to the user community and a major concern negatively impacting the fleet.'[139] The Agency noted in October 2023 that this was seriously impacting performance after delivery, observing that clients for the aircraft, most recently the Marine Corps, 'are still expressing to us that too many quality assurance defects are escaping to the field,' which remained 'an issue for the user community and a major concern negatively impacting' readiness. The agency further highlighted that 'parts shortages continue to cause production inefficiencies' leading to 'delays for many aircraft,' while even as production increased, in-plant 'scrap, rework and defect' rates 'continue to limit production efficiency during assembly' due to 'workforce turnover and some poor-performing suppliers.'[140] These concerns continued to be raised over the following years.

Production Run

In 2001 Lockheed Martin projected that F-35 production could reach 5,179 fighters, with this figure accounting for the equipping of the United States Armed Forces, program partner countries, and non-partner export clients. This appeared far from unviable at the time. The F-16 (excluding the Japanese F-2 derivative) and F-18 (excluding the enhanced Super Hornet variant), and Harrier were projected to see production runs of around 4,500, 1,500 and 850 – or 6,850

The production line for F-35s at the Lockheed Martin facility in Fort Worth, Texas. (Lockheed Martin)

between them. This was aside from the fact that the F-35 was expected to replace a range of other fighter types due to its unique position as the world's only NATO-compatible fifth generation fighter available to non-U.S. clients, including making unprecedented inroads into European markets to replace Tornados, Eurofighters, MiG-29s and other aircraft. American fourth generation fighters, which had faced somewhat greater local competition, had not been able to dominate European markets as totally as the F-35 was well positioned to do. Thus a combination of factors including the F-35 being a tri-service aircraft and having an unprecedentedly strong advantage over competing NATO-compatible fighters made a production run of close to 5,000, not too much higher than the single service F-16 had alone managed to achieve, far from unthinkable at the time. The F-16 had been one of six American fourth generation fighter types to be serially produced, and one of eleven in the Western world, where the F-35, with the exception of a very small number of F-22s built for the USAF, was the only one of its generation.

The F-35 was produced at United States Air Force Plant 4 in Texas, a massive 17,000 employee facility owned by the Air Force and operated by Lockheed Martin. The factory first opened during the Second World War to build B-24 bombers, before transitioning to production of America's first intercontinental-range bomber, the B-36, followed by the B-58 bomber, the F-111 strike fighter, and eventually the F-16. After the disintegration of the Soviet Union, the facility's position as the largest in the world for fighter production became undisputed, with this only being challenged from 2024-2025 after the Chengdu Aerospace Corporation expanded its production facilities for J-20 fifth generation fighters. The scale of the F-35 production facility made a strong impression on visitors, with Dutch Defence Minister Hans Hillen stating, in January 2012 when visiting: 'It's a kilometre-and-a-half walk from one end to the other. You have no idea how big it is.'[141]

Although the majority of contract work for the F-35 took place at Fort Worth, with the figure standing at 59 percent for Lot 20 aircraft, the facility brought together parts from over 1,650 suppliers worldwide. Fourteen percent of work for Lot 20 aircraft was done at El Segundo, California, with the remainder split between Warton, United Kingdom (9%); Cameri, Italy (4%); Orlando, Florida (4%); Nashua, New Hampshire (3%); Baltimore, Maryland (3%); San Diego, California (2%), and other locations outside of the continental U.S. (2%).[142]

In parallel to F-35 production, Fort Worth continued to produce F-16s for export until 2017, by which time it had manufactured 3,620 of the fighters. Production of the older fighter type was subsequently halted for two years before resuming at a new facility in Greenville, South Carolina, where the new F-16 Block 70/72 was built on a small scale for export. This allowed the Fort Worth facility to accommodate a larger scale of F-35 production. As the facility transitioned to producing the F-35, new moving assembly lines were introduced that pioneered digital processes and automation techniques, with electronic 3D models used to support almost all areas of production.

The Fort Worth production line would continue to be modernised rapidly, with approximately 75 percent of touch labour being phased out by from 2012-2017 alone, while production span time was reduced by approximately 20 percent from 2015-2017.[143] Efficiency improved considerably, with man hours required to build the F-35A falling from 160,000 in 2006, to approximately 110,000 in 2012, and approximately 41,500 in 2017. The F-35B and C variants required 57,000 and 60,000 that year. These figures were very low, with the much lighter F-16C having taken 45,000 man hours to build when the Cold War ended.[144] As observed by Lockheed Martin spokesman Mike Rein regarding the extent of the changes from 2010-2018: 'I came to work here eight years ago ... Nothing in this building right here, apart from the walls and the ceiling, looks the same.'[145] According to the Joint Program Office from 2016-2023 the time associated with scrap, rework, and repair was reduced by 47 percent, while the number of quality escapes from the production line was reduced by 63 percent.[146] The factory had extremely strict security regulations, with even taking out a mobile phone being banned.

Considering that the Western world's entire future investment in the production of fifth generation fighters was so heavily concentrated in this one facility, such measures appeared far from unjustified.

The sharp contraction of the American and allied fighter fleets both in the immediate aftermath of the Cold War, and more gradually over the following three decades, was a primary factor forcing reassessments of the projected size of the global F-35 fleet. The integration of much of the former Warsaw Pact into NATO, the rapid decline of the previously formidable combat aviation capabilities of former potential adversaries such as Syria, Libya, Iraq, Yugoslavia, Belarus and North Korea, and the sharp decline and contraction of the Russian Air Force, combined with subsequent economic decline in the Western world, diminished the prospects for a very large F-35 production run. Further major factors were the significant overruns in the F-35's production and operational costs, which ensured that anything close to one-for-one replacements of F-16s and F-18s would not be affordable. Air Force officials repeatedly warned that if the cost per flight hour was not significantly reduced, this could force the service to buy fewer fighters.[147] A consensus thus began to form from the late 2000s that an F-35 production run of close to 5,000 fighters would not be feasible.

By the late 2000s Lockheed Martin officials projected that production would reach approximately 4,000 F-35s, placing the aircraft's numbers in the same league as those of the F-16. Steve O'Bryan from Lockheed Martin's F-35 business development team specifically referred to 'F-16-like numbers' for production in 2008.[148] Reflecting the growing consensus at the time, in November 2010 analyst Kenneth Epps stated regarding the future of F-35 production: 'The global F-35 market of "up to" 5,000 aircraft ... is outdated and now greatly overstated. Realistically, the likelihood of worldwide F-35 sales is closer to the figure now given as the order total for the program partner countries, that is, "up to" 3,500 aircraft. The uncritical use of F-35 sales projections that are now almost 10 years out of date calls into question other claims made by officials about the F-35 program.'[149]

The U.S. Air Force, Marine Corps and Navy would notably not alter their stated planned procurement numbers of 1,763, 433 and 273 F-35s respectively, bringing total Pentagon procurement to 2,469 fighters. By the late 2010s, however, the Air Force's ambitious procurement goals appeared particularly unlikely to be reached. Aforementioned statements by Air Force and Pentagon officials regarding the unaffordability of procurement due primarily to major overruns in sustainment costs provided one notable indicator, with major reductions to planned annual orders being another.

While annual production of the F-35 was in the late 2000s expected to reach 210 fighters per year as early as 2016,[150] output even a decade after this would fall far short of this figure. As the F-35 first entered service in 2015, Lockheed Martin managed to deliver 45 fighters to the U.S. Armed Forces and to international clients, and would see a rapid increase in the following years to reach 66 fighters in 2017, 91 in 2018, and 134 in 2019 – a 47 percent increase over the previous year. Deliveries fell to 120 in 2020 due to the fallout from the Covid-19 pandemic, which was 21 fighters short of the target of 141 fighters that year. Deliveries would recover to reach 142 fighters in 2021, exceeding the downward revised target of 139 fighters.

From the early 2020s, the Armed Forces and international clients would show a growing degree of reluctance to receive new F-35s, in large part due to major delays to efforts to deliver aircraft built to modernised standards, as well as due to the persistence of wide ranging flaws. Receiving aircraft earlier on with hundreds of flaws and immature software imposed growing costs, as clients would be forced to pay for later modernisation and fixes. Buying and retrofitting all the Block 4 capabilities, for example, and making all the latest necessary fixes to deficiencies, were estimated to cost well over $10 million per aircraft. This was a significant factor leading the Pentagon in April 2022 to officially request the procurement of 61 F-35 fighters for 2023, representing a 35 percent cut from the 94 it had previously projected.[151] Delays to TR-3 software meant that total F-35 deliveries in 2023 reached just 98 fighters, with the fallout from this continuing into 2024 when they reached just 110 fighters, as the Pentagon refused to receive fighters that were below this level.

Lots 15-17, delivered from 2023-2025, saw an average of just 125 aircraft delivered per year, well below the 156 per year that Lockheed Martin CEO James Taiclet had projected in January 2022, six months before the deal for the three batches was made.[152] Acting Chief Financial Officer John Mollard had stated that month that 'the last thing you want is a sawtooth pattern' of up-and-down production rates, although this was exactly what had occurred.[153] Growing frustrations with the program's failure to deliver F-35s at the standards previously expected was a primary factor bringing an end to the gradual rise in production seen in the 2010s.

Production continued to fall well short of even relatively recently set targets, with officials from Lockheed Martin in early 2019 having stated that F-35 output was expected to reach over 160 fighters by 2021.[154] A year later in January 2020 Lockheed Martin projected annual production could reach 180 fighters by 2024,[155] with the firm's vice president of F-35 production Darren Sekiguchi in October 2020 projecting that production would soon reach approximately 168 fighters per year.[156] Despite a surge in foreign orders, with the escalation of conflict in Ukraine from 2022 seen to have played a leading role in stimulating European demand in particular, the target annual production rate by 2024 remained just 156 fighters, with this expected to be achieved in 2025. This figure was to be sustained into the following years, rather than being increased, with prior plans for production of close to 170 or 180 fighters annually, let alone over 200, appearing to have been abandoned.

While the Air Force would publicly continue to claim that procurement of 1,763 F-35As was planned, the contraction of its overall fighter fleet and the relatively low rates of annual F-35 orders brought this increasingly into question. At the rate of procurement seen in the mid-2020s, the service would receive its last F-35s well into the 2040s, approaching half a century after the aircraft's first flight, with the fighter's ability to remain viable and cost effective until such a time remaining in serious question (see Chapter 10). Figures in the Air Force leadership had for years stated privately that discussing a possible reduction in overall F-35A orders was deliberately avoided due to the negative impacts this would have on the unit costs. This was particularly important when considering the program's tremendous development costs, including significant further expenses incurred developing enhancements such as the $16.5 billion for the Block 4 standard. Any reduction to orders would instantly increase the cost that needed to be charged per fighter, as the large projected Air Force orders were key to spreading out development costs to make the F-35 cost effective. 'We learned our lesson with the B-2 and F-22,' one senior Air Force official was quoted as saying by *Air & Space Forces Magazine*, with a spike in unit costs inevitably leading to a reduction in the production run, spurring further unit cost increases which would place the program into 'a death spiral.'[157]

Future F-35 procurements remained highly uncertain, with multiple factors expected to influence this. This included the successes of the separate Air Force and Navy sixth generation fighter programs, the viability of unmanned aircraft both as wingmen and eventually as alternatives, and the impact of the surge in Chinese procurements of the increasingly capable J-20 fighter and successes of its future fifth and sixth generation programs. While USAF procurements were expected to fall significantly below planned numbers, the high likelihood of delays to the service's sixth generation program meant that the amount by which procurements fell could be significantly lower. The Navy, by contrast, had ordered only enough F-35s to equip a small portion of its fighter fleet. Although this may have been intended to allow the service to largely 'leapfrog' the F-35, and transition much of its fleet from fourth generation F-18E/Fs to a sixth generation fighter in the 2030s, the very low number of planned orders left more room for procurements to grow than to decline depending largely on the extent of delays to sixth generation fighter development.

For the Marine Corps, which was unlikely to see another manned STOVL fighter developed for decades, if at all, F-35 procurements could potentially continue for the longest, and likely for as long as manned fighters were seen as viable and production lines could economically be kept open. This was one of the primary factors in the Corps planning to acquire 29 percent more F-35Bs than the Navy planned to acquire F-35Cs (353 vs. 273 aircraft), despite the Navy's overall fighter fleet being 220 percent as large (903 vs. 407) and it thus having more room to accommodate F-35s.[158] Of the three services, the Navy had hedged the most on both sixth and '4+' generation fighters, while the Marines had planned no acquisitions whatsoever of either one and was the most heavily invested in the F-35 as a portion of its total fighter procurement plans.

F-35 production pictured from the crane monorail at Fort Worth. (Lockheed Martin)

The roll-out of the 1,000th F-35 off the production line at Lockheed Martin in January 2024. This was marred by the delay in delivery of the Technology Refresh 3 Upgrade, which was necessary to provide the required computing power to support Block 4 capabilities. (Lockheed Martin)

7

POWERING THE F-35

Competitive Engine Procurement: The F135 and F136 Powerplants

At the outset of the Joint Strike Fighter program in 1996 the procurement strategy called for a competitive engine acquisitions, namely that two separate interchangeable engines would be developed in parallel by competing firms allowing clients for every order to select either one. This had proven highly beneficial during the development of the F-35A's direct predecessor the F-16, with competition between the firms General Electric and Pratt & Whitney having resulted in significant improvements to performance and reductions to price as both bid against one another for contracts. Much as had been the case for the F-16, a primary engine would be developed in the F-35 program's early stages, the Pratt & Whitney F135, with a few years lag time left before development of a competitor began, namely the General Electric and Rolls Royce F136.*

The F135 and F136 would be referred to by some sources as a 'plug in and play' engines due to the simplicity of interchanging them.[1] Fifty percent of the engines were common, namely the augmentor duct module and exhaust nozzle module, while the other 50 percent were fully interchangeable. All the shipping containers, ground handling support equipment, the vertical lift system and hand tools were 100 percent common.[2] Many of the servicing processes were also common to both engines, and no additional manpower was required for a mixed fleet using both, even for more complex aircraft carrier operations.[3] This would mirror the commonality between the F-16's interchangeable F100 and F110 engines.

Although several engines were studied in the initial phases of the program, there was no competition to provide the primary engine for the F-35, with Pratt & Whitney selected due to its prior development of what was at the time the only existing fifth generation fighter engine flying outside Russia, namely the F119 which powered the F-22. With the F135 able to be developed as a close derivative of the F119 using many of the same technologies, Pratt & Whitney had a unique lead in being able to provide a powerplant for the F-35 quickly.

In September 2001 Pratt & Whitney signed a $4.8 billion contract to develop the F135, although it would soon be faced with two major cost increases. The first occurred in 2004 when Lockheed Martin had to redesign the F-35 to reduce its weight to meet program requirements, forcing a redesign of the F135 to achieve a lower weight/thrust ratio. This raised the development cost to an estimated $5.9 billion at the time. Subsequently in 2008 a redesign of both the third-stage turbine and the F-35B specific lift fan required an additional $800 million, bringing costs to $6.7 billion. The Pentagon estimated a further $600 million in additional costs due to program restructuring and a 13-month extension of the development period.

Pratt & Whitney had first begun work developing an engine for a fifth generation fighter in the early 1980s under the Joint Advanced Fighter Engine program, which was intended to provide a powerplant for the Advanced Tactical Fighter Program that produced the F-22. This had been intended to address the challenging requirements for a supercruise capability, which necessitated particularly high levels of dry thrust. The F119 had provided 25 percent more thrust than its predecessor, the F100, that had powered the F-15, which was achieved by leveraging new technologies such as single crystal superalloys, linear-friction welded hollow titanium fan blades and integrally bladed rotors. New technologies also allowed the engine to achieve its performance with only six compressor stages, compared to ten for the F100, and to operate with 40 percent fewer parts. These features were inherited by the F135. The fact that the significant majority of research and development work that distinguished the F135 from fourth generation engines had already been completed for the F119 made the new engine's development cost abnormally high.

The F135 is produced in three primary variants, including the F135-PW-100 variant powering the F-35A, the F135-PW-600 for the F-35B, and the F135-PW-400 for the F-35C, with the latter two using salt-corrosion resistant materials due to their expected primary use for carrier operations. F135s each have four modules: fan, power, augmentor, and nozzle, with a gearbox included in the power module. While variants powering the F-35A and F-35C are near identical, the F-35B's power, augmentor, and nozzle modules have specific parts and features that enable short take-off and vertical landing. The F135 was designed as a two-shaft engine with a three-stage fan low pressure and a six-stage high pressure compressor. The hot section features an annular combustor with a single-stage high-pressure turbine unit and a two-stage low-pressure turbine, while the afterburner features a variable converging-diverging nozzle. It delivers a dry thrust of approximately 12.5 tons, and a maximum thrust with afterburner of approximately 19.2 tons. Primary facilitators of the engine's increased airflow and higher rotor inlet temperature include the incorporation of a new 'superblade' cooling in the high-pressure turbine, use of gamma titanium aluminide blades in the last compressor stage, enhanced cooling airflow pattern in the combustor, and use of high-temperature fuel nozzles to prevent coking.

The F135 as of the mid-2020s remains the most powerful fighter engine in the world, with the F119 generating 17.5 tons of thrust, the Chinese WS-15 built for the J-20 fighter estimated to generate 18.4 tons,[4] and the Russian AL-51F built for the Su-57 fighter 18.7 tons.[5] This was largely achieved by being larger than these rival engines, as the F-35 was the only single engine fighter of its generation and required an enlarged derivative of the F119 approximately eight percent heavier. Although its weight/thrust ratio is superior to that of the F119 at 0.09, it is comparable to the reported ratio for the WS-15 with the two considered the most advanced and efficient in the world. The fact that the F135 entered service a full decade before the WS-15, however, indicated that the American fighter engine industry had maintained the hard won global lead it had gained after the Cold War, despite Chinese industry having very rapidly narrowed the gap in the following 35 years.

* General Electric was responsible for 60 percent of the F136 program, including developing its core compressor and coupled high-pressure/low-pressure turbine system components, controls and accessories, and its augmentor. Rolls Royce was responsible for the remaining 40 percent including the front fan, combustor, stages 2 and 3 of the low-pressure turbine, and gearboxes. Rolls Royce's participation reflected the United Kingdom's position as the only Tier One partner in the fighter program.

The Pratt & Whitney F135 engine, as seen during the Joint Strike Fighter System Development and Demonstration Phase. (USAF)

An F135 built for the Royal Netherlands Air Force. (Pratt & Whitney)

Where the F135 had been closely based on the F119, the rival F136 was more loosely based on the F119's competitor the General Electric F120. Unlike the Joint Strike Fighter, the Advanced Tactical Fighter program had involved genuine competition in the selection of its primary engine, meaning that the YF-22 and YF-23 technology demonstrators that first flew in 1990 were tested with two rival engines from General Electric and Pratt & Whitney, while the X-35 and X-32 had flown with only the F135. The F120 was considered a significantly more advanced and innovative engine design, and pioneered use of a variable cycle where the F119 used a conventional fixed bypass turbofan. Other innovations include the use of one-piece disk and rotor blade assemblies in the fan and compressor stages to increase performance and durability, and reduce weight and parts count. The engine particularly excelled at high-altitude, high speed operations, and allowed the YF-22 and YF-23 to supercruise speeds of Mach 1.58 and Mach 1.72 respectively.[6] Although slightly heavier than the F119, it had much greater room for thrust upgrades. Reflecting broader trends that would shape the Advanced Tactical

Fighter program in the post-Cold War era, the more conservative option seen to present lower risks was selected.[7]

With the risks associated with new variable cycle engine technologies considered to have been a major factor that prevented the F120 from being selected, the F136 instead used a conventional fixed-bypass design much as the F119 and F135 did. The F136 was designed as an augmented turbofan with a twin spool, counter-rotating, axial flow, low aspect ratio compressor and an axial flow counter-rotating turbine. Like the F135, its compressor's architecture including its lower aspect ratio reflected a low emphasis on supersonic performance, contrasting them with the F119 and F120. The F136's integrated high-pressure/low-pressure counter-rotating turbine design was jointly developed by General Electric and Rolls Royce, while Rolls Royce was responsible for the combustor/diffuser system, gearboxes, and an advanced high-pressure-ratio, long-chord, hollow, titanium blisk fan.[8] A primary advantage the F136 had over its rival, however, was that it was designed later on when the F-35's design had undergone significant changes and reached a much more mature stage, leading it to widely be considered a more suitable engine for the aircraft. This advantage was repeatedly highlighted by General Electric.[9]

The most notable example of the advantages which later development conferred the F136 was that it was designed with a larger core than the F135, allowing it to pump significantly more air and run far less hot when generating an equivalent amount of thrust. The F-35 had been planned to have a smaller air inlet at the time when the F135 began development, meaning a larger core the size like that of the F136's had not been considered viable. This changed when Lockheed Martin increased the airflow capacity of the F-35 inlet to 400 lb/sec (181.4 kg/s) in 2005, which was seen as necessary to increase thrust due to the significant increase in the aircraft's weight.[10] Five years later General Electric announced in a press release that its team's decision that year to resize the F136 with a larger core and higher-flow fan was proving fortuitous, as testing has shown that the engine would enter production with cooler running temperatures, which 'will translate into a long-term maintenance cost advantage.'[11] The F136's fan was thus estimated to be able to pump a significantly greater flow of air than the F135.[12] The ability to revise a core part of the engine's design at such an advanced stage in the F-35's System Development and Demonstration phase was a significant advantage, and ensured that the F136's core was better matched to the aircraft's inlet and airflow. It was revealed in 2010 that, largely as a result, the F136 had more than 15 percent thrust margin against specification, significantly exceeding the F135's power, with its thrust expected to exceed the F135's by comfortably over five percent.[13]

While a larger core came at the expense of weight, the fact that the F136 could maintain the same weight as the F135 in spite of this was interpreted by a number of analysts as a significant indicator that it was a more sophisticated design with a higher potential. The F136 had a much higher potential to generate greater thrust with upgrades in future, as the F135's already high temperatures seriously limited the viability of major thrust increases. These greater temperature margins and lower core temperatures, due to the higher air mass flow, were a central factor in increasing hot-section component life. This was a core contributor to the F136's projected lower maintenance needs and longer lifespan if operated the same way as the F135.[14] The engine was projected to have a tremendous 25 percent maintenance-cost advantage over the F135 over its lifetime.[15]

In the year 2000 the F136's core passed a landmark of 75 hours of successful testing. By 2002 its three-stage fan had successfully operated at full speed and pressure ratio while meeting or exceeding all performance targets.[16] The engine first ran on 21 July 2004. In August 2005 the Pentagon awarded the General Electric and Rolls-Royce a $2.4 billion contract for the F136's development and demonstration phase, which was scheduled to conclude in September 2013. The first three months of this period saw the engine pass a Preliminary Design Review led by the F-35 Program Office and Lockheed Martin. The completion of the engine's critical design review was announced in February 2008,[17] and five months later on 16 July the first successful Short Take-off and Vertical Landing Test was completed.[18] Following U.S. Government validation of the design that year, the first complete new-build F136 began testing on 30 January 2009, one month ahead of schedule.

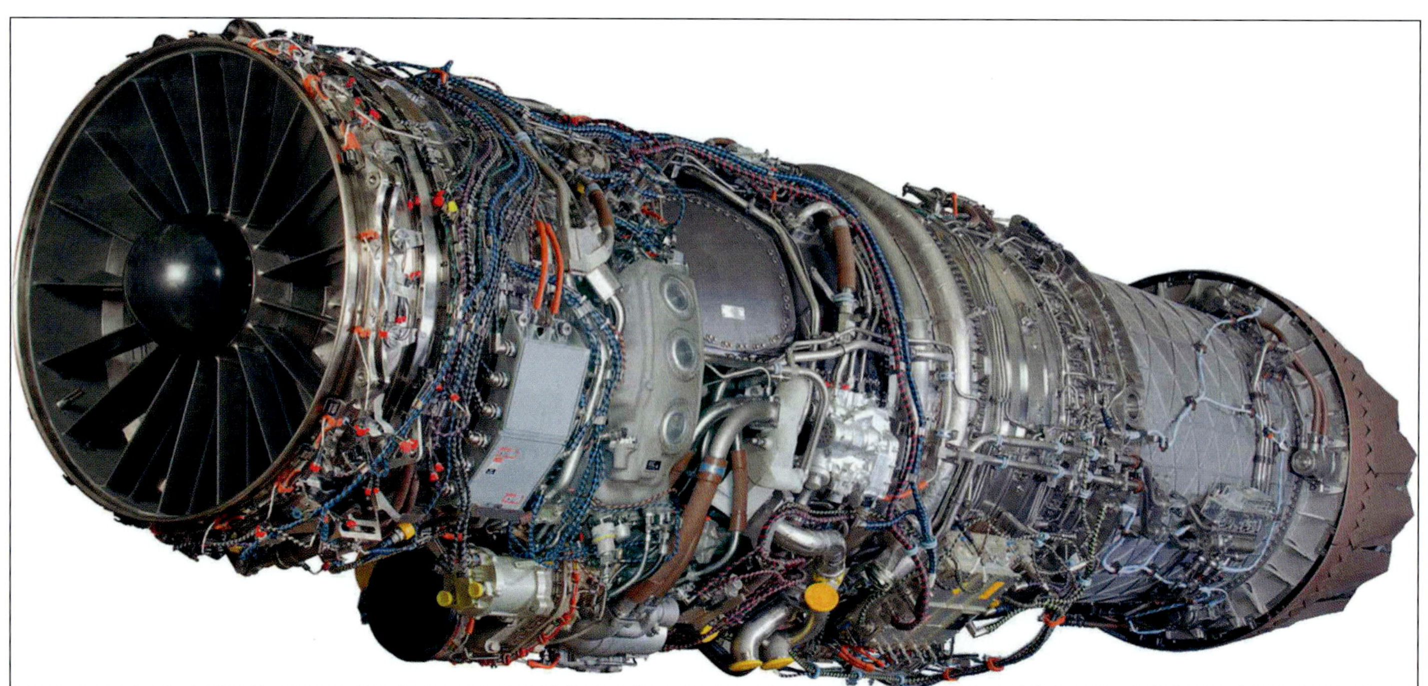

The General Electric/Rolls-Royce F136 engine. (General Electric)

F135 engine powers the F-35 in climb. The engine is the mechanically most-complex part in the development of any modern combat aircraft, and poses particularly significant challenges when operationalising new generations of technologies. (USAF)

Debate Over Ending the F136

Although support appeared near unanimous for the F136's development in the early and mid-2000s, in January 2006 the Pentagon attempted to remove funding for the Fiscal Year 2007 budget, effectively ending development. This occurred amid a worsening budget crisis, and as fighter programs faced particularly high scrutiny for their combination of both high costs and a limited ability to contribute to the ongoing War on Terror. The Department of Defense would for the next five years maintain that the F136's development was an unnecessary expense, although its efforts to terminate development faced opposition across all four congressional defence committees. Efforts to terminate development were particularly controversial as they violated the Weapon Systems Acquisition Reform Act, which mandated competition through the entire life of major defence programs to minimise cost overruns and delays.

Further controversies were raised by a Government Accountability Office report published in May 2006. This found that the Pentagon 'did not conduct an up-to-date, comprehensive analysis of the total life cycle costs, savings, and benefits to support its decision to terminate the JSF's alternate engine development program.' The Pentagon further failed to 'consider the full long-term savings that might accrue from competition for providing support for maintenance and operations over the life cycle of the engine.' The F135 meanwhile had 'completed only a small portion of its ground tests and has not yet been flown,' while the F119 on which it was based had only completed 'about 10 percent of its hours needed for system maturity' and had already fallen short of meeting a number of reliability goals. It thus asserted that commonality with the F119 was of limited benefit for reducing the F135's development risk, which studies had previously concluded, and that there was thus a strong argument for continuing to hedge against overreliance on the F135 with the parallel development of the F136.[19]

Congress was successful in re-inserting funding to the FY 2007 budget, allowing F136 development to continue on schedule. When the Pentagon again attempted to defund the program the following year, Congress similarly prevented this and again gained support from the findings of GAO auditors. This process would be repeated for the next three years. Continued investment in the F136 notably retained some support from within the Pentagon, particularly under the Bush administration. Air Force Secretary Michael Wynne, for example, in February 2008 informed reporters that maintaining the F136 makes sense because, 'like life insurance, you hope that you never need it, but each year you keep buying it.'[20] A year into the next administration, retired Air Force Lieutenant General Stephen Wood reflected the consensus among many in the service when he stated in 2010: 'the risk is too great to allow only one propulsion system for the F-35, which will make up over 85 percent of our nation's fighter force in 20 years.' Wood highlighted that the completion of 80 percent of the F136's development made arguments for its continuation particularly strong, while 'continued competition between F-35 engine makers will force both parties to produce a better engine.'[21]

Pressure to terminate development of the F136 would increase very significantly under the Barack Obama administration, with the new secretary of defense, Robert Gates, from his first months in office consistently making clear his intention to do so.[22] Gates was described as having 'made killing the second engine a centrepiece of his crusade to cut unnecessary defence spending,'[23] and would warn congress that he would urge President Obama to veto any defence bill that provided funding for the program. The new president mentioned the F136 specifically during a 21 August 2009 address to the Veterans of Foreign Wars Convention in Phoenix, during which reforming the acquisition process and cutting waste were central pledges he made. There he stated: 'Think about it, hundreds of millions of dollars for an alternate second engine for the Joint Strike Fighter when one reliable engine will do just fine.'[24] Cancelling the F136 thus quickly became a poster child for the new administration's efforts to demonstrate that it was different to its predecessors and could make major improvements to the efficiency of the defence budget.

In response to arguments on Capitol Hill and from General Electric and that investing in two engines would provide a vital hedge against any problems with either one of them, Secretary Gates asserted that 'my idea of competition is winner takes all.'[25] He would similarly highlight the F136 in his memoir to stress that he pushed for 'real competition, not the kind Congress likes where everybody wins.'[26] The fact that the two engine programs used the same supplier base for 85 percent of their parts, limiting the fallout for the industrial base should one be cancelled, undermined one key economic argument against cancellation.

In a report filed on 18 June 2009, the House Armed Services Committee cited Pratt & Whitney's F135 program cost overruns of $1.872 billion as an important factor in the decision to continue funding the F136.[27] Alongside its particularly strong support in the House, the program also had widespread support in the Senate. Under pressure from the new administration, on 28 September General Electric made an unsolicited fixed-price offer for the F136 covering initial production beginning with the second production lot. This was an apparent effort to assuage key concerns regarding the program, and according to the F136 Fighter Engine Team it would shift significant cost risk from taxpayers to General Electric and Rolls Royce.[28]

As all four congressional defence committees remained staunchly committed to maintaining competition between two rival engine programs, their case was strengthened by a Government Accountability Office report highlighting the significant benefits which maintaining such competition had had for preceding fourth generation fighters. Allowed clients for the F-16, and later the F-15, to choose between the Pratt & Whitney F100 and the General Electric F110 was found to have been a major contributor to driving increased efficiency and performance while reducing costs. The result was nearly 30 percent in cumulative savings for procurement costs, approximately 16 percent in cumulative savings for operational and support costs, and total savings of around 21 percent in overall life cycle costs, while stimulating more rapid improvement to both engines including not only more thrust, but also 'twice the life and much more durability.' Competition also placed pressure on both manufacturers to significantly improve product service, while warranties were enhanced significantly. Denying either firm a monopoly on supplying engines for the F-15 and F-16 also enlarged the industrial base and increased protection against production disruption. The redundancy built into the two fighter programs was not only free, but paid for itself.[29]

In 2010 General Electric and Rolls Royce estimated that another $1 billion would be required to complete development of the F136, in addition to the $3 billion the program had by then already received since 1996. It would cost a further $800 million to bring the engine into production due to the costs of tooling and other required preparations. The total of $1.8 billion was a full $1.1 billion below the Pentagon's estimate of the cost to bring the engine to a competitive procurement stage, representing a reduction of 40 percent. The F135 by contrast had accumulated $3.4 billion in cost overruns and was facing continued very serious delays, although Pratt & Whitney reported that $2.7 billion of these overruns, or 79 percent, were due to changes in the Pentagon's requirements after development had begun.

The House Armed Services Committee on 19 May proceeded to authorise $485 million for the F136 program under the FY 2011

A P&W F135 engine as seen while undergoing testing at Arnold AFB, in Tennessee. (USAF)

budget. The program was subsequently announced on 6 December to have reached a major milestone when tests were launched for a sixth F136, placing development ahead of testing goals for the year. By that year the engines were being tested for close to 1,000 hours annually, with four F136 engines undergoing testing concurrently at three separate locations.[30] By 2011 the F136's development was over 80 percent complete, with six engines having logged more than 1,200 hours of testing since 2009.[31]

On 24 March 2011, the Pentagon issued a 90 day temporary stop work order after Congress failed to pass the FY 2012 defence budget. General Electric at the time declared that it would continue work with its own funds regardless.[32] The order was criticised by House Armed Services Committee Chairman Howard McKeon as failing to follow existing laws, namely the Weapon Systems Acquisition Reform Act, with Secretary Gates lambasted for attempting to 'preempt the congressional deliberation process by yanking funding after a single amendment vote.' Handing Pratt & Whitney a sole-source deal valued at well above $100 billion amounted to 'the largest earmark in the history of the Department of Defence,' he added.[33] Subsequently on 15 April President Obama signed an appropriations bill that defunded the F136 program.[34] Ten days later the Pentagon ended the contract and demanded that all engines built to date be turned over. As observed by the *Wall Street Journal* at the time: 'Gates fought long and hard to stop Congress to kill an alternate engine for the F-35 Joint Strike Fighter. And earlier this month, he got his wish.'[35]

While the Obama administration's at the time controversial decision in 2009 to terminate production of the F-22 would even in hindsight appeared to have been well reasoned, particularly when considering the serious issues the aircraft had, the parallel decision to cancel the F136 program, although gaining less publicity, would as time passed increasing appear to have been a disastrous one. Controversies surrounding the latter decision would increase very significantly throughout the following decade and beyond.

Significant attention was drawn to the dangers posed by excessive reliance on the F135 when on 23 June 2014 a U.S. Air Force F-35A caught fire on Eglin Air Force Base's main runway, with images released a year later showing that the aircraft's skin was badly charred, and its spine was perforated by its F135 engine that tore itself apart from within. After a near year long investigation, the Air Education Training Command found: 'The cause of the mishap was catastrophic engine failure. The engine failed when the third-stage forward integral arm of a rotor fractured and liberated during takeoff ... Pieces of the failed rotor arm cut through the engine's fan case, the engine bay, an internal fuel tank and hydraulic and fuel lines before exiting through the aircraft's upper fuselage.' Friction caused the failure of the third-stage rotor and its integral arm. The engine's liner wasn't ready for prime time, with the issue exacerbated by operational g loads. Two seconds of manoeuvres 'well within the envelope of the airplane' led to the formation of a growing number of microcracks, causing high cycle fatigue that went unnoticed until the day of the fire when the fan-blade system just cracked. The whole circular part of the engine stretched out and went up through the fuel tank causing fire.[36]

The 23 June incident required the entire F-35 fleet to be placed under restrictions, causing serious delays to testing that further stalled the process of bringing the aircraft into service. This was seen to support prior concerns that had been widely raised regarding the vulnerability that overreliance on the F135 could cause. Where the United States had brought six separate fourth generation multirole fighters to readiness for production (or seven if including the F-117), with five of these entering production in their hundreds, the fact that the F-35 was the only fifth generation fighter entering service made the lack of alternative engines particularly dangerous. As observed in a 2009 Heritage Foundation assessment, the fact that the F-35 'will constitute 90 percent of all U.S. fighters in 2035' made the lack of an alternative engine particularly dangerous, as 'if something goes wrong with the engine, it could lead to a system-wide grounding of every aircraft until the problem is identified and fixed – unless there is an alternative available.'[37] The fact that no comparably advanced fifth generation fighters were being developed by allied states only made this more of an issue, as did the fact that the F-35 was a single engine fighter which made any reliability issues significantly more dangerous.

With the incident and subsequent grounding highlighting the vulnerability of the F-35 across three services to any issues with the F135, the Senate Appropriation Committee on July 17 stressed that 'the point about fleet availability has been made,' with reliance on a single engine design leaving it vulnerable. The Committee called on the Pentagon to reconsider the F136's termination, stating:

> Since that time, the F135 engine has experienced numerous problems, including the failure of an oil flow management valve and a pre-take-off fire in the past few weeks, both of which grounded the entire fleet of over 100 aircraft. Further, the F135 engine unit cost has not declined as projected. However, the Committee believes that had the alternate engine program continued, competition would have incentivised the F135 engine manufacturer to find creative methods to drive down prices and ensure timely delivery of a high quality product, which is consistent with current Department preference for competition in acquisitions. Therefore, the Committee recommends the Secretary of Defense reassess the value of an alternate engine program creating competition to improve price, quality, and operational availability.[38]

Nevertheless, the commission noted, Pentagon acquisitions chief Frank Kendall continued to assert that: 'We're not interested in this point in going back several years and opening up to another competitor.'[39]

Following the June 23 incident, Pratt & Whitney's solution to the issue involved breaking in the F135's foam liner in advance, known as 'pre-trenching,' to separate the rubber and the fan blade in a specific part of the engine. As observed by analysts at *Jalopnik*: 'it's a crude fix for such an advanced piece of machinery.' 'The whole affair was and continues to be a stark reminder of just how dumb it was for the Pentagon to give up its General Electric F136 alternative engine program, especially considering it was so far along in its development,' they further noted, reflecting the broad consensus among analysts at the time.[40] The incident with the F135 was far from isolated, and a month before in May 2014 problems with the quality of the titanium used in the engine revealed that Pratt & Whitney subcontractor A&P Alloys had supplied questionable titanium stocks for the machining of components. This caused a temporary pause in production from that month.[41]

Following the beginning of significant deliveries of serial production F-35s in 2015, mounting issues with the F135 would strengthen the growing consensus that a new engine was needed, culminating in widespread and growing support being voiced for such development from 2021 in particular. Growing controversy surrounded the F-35 program's broader cost overruns. The lack of competition, not only to the F135 but also more broadly to the fighter program itself, that could pressure the private sector

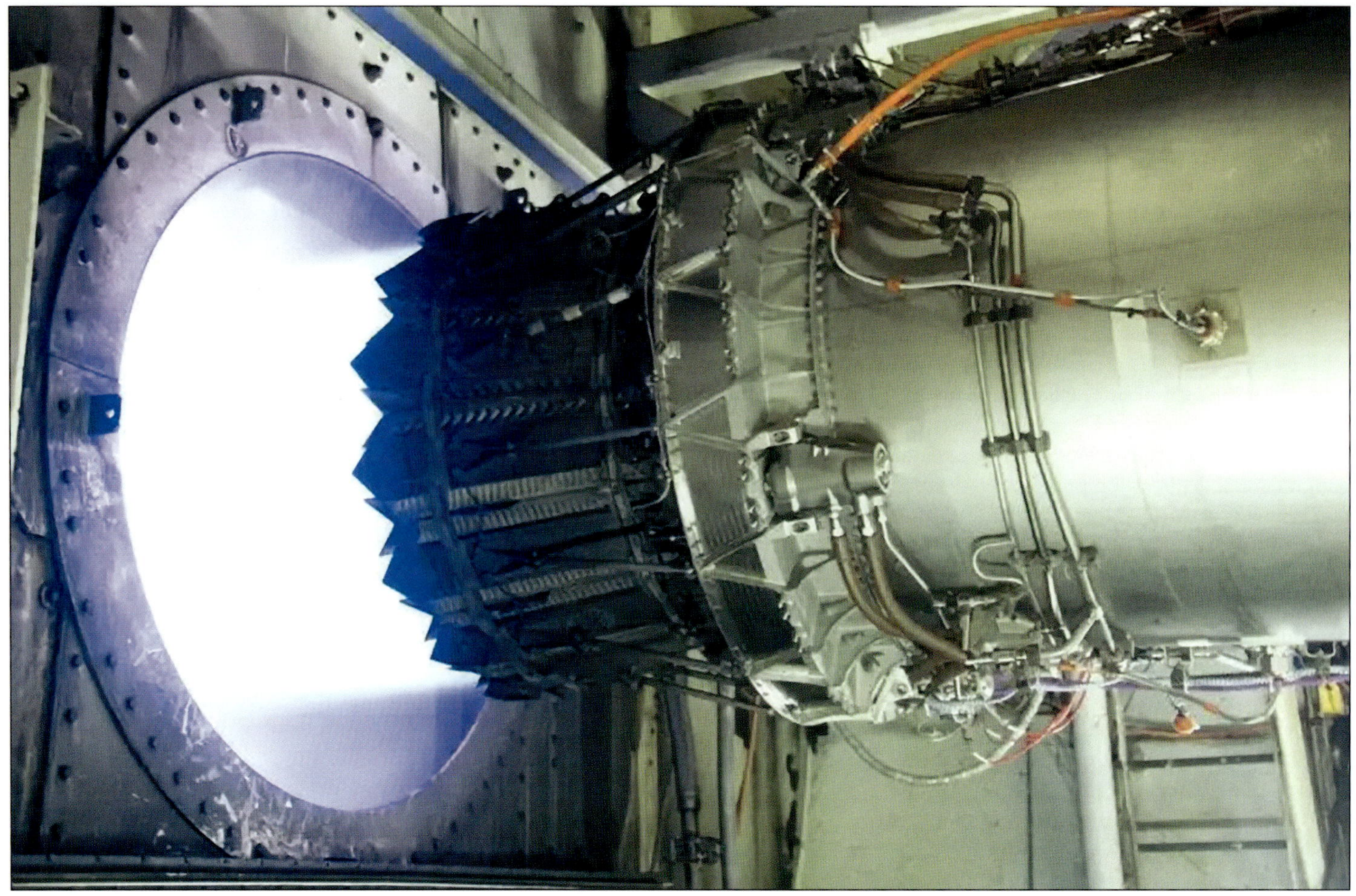

An F136 engine afterburner being tested at the General Electric aviation facility in Evendale, Ohio. (General Electric)

to reduce costs or improve efficiency, led a number of sources to advocate re-introducing engine competition.[42] Six years after the F136's termination this argument was summarised by 25-year veteran of the Air Force and senior defence expert at the Heritage Foundation John Venable as follows: 'World class track and field athletes rarely set personal bests running alone, and no athlete or business reaches its full potential without a competitor in the lane next to them. The history of the F-16 engine program reinforces that point, as does the nearly stagnant pricing history of the F135 engine/propulsion systems to date. Neither has dropped in line with program estimates.'[43] Five years later in 2022, Venable stressed that the F136's cancellation had the effect of 'leaving no compelling reason for the company to compete on price,' which he noted was reflected in the F135 program's less than stellar record.[44]

Engine Disaster

Significant changes to the F-35's design in the 2000s, and the lack of matching adjustments to its engine specifications, were central factors that significantly reduced the aircraft's performance to far below what the program had initially intended. With the aircraft being over 30 percent heavier than initially conceptualised, not only was its flight performance reduced significantly, with acceleration and manoeuvrability remaining relatively poor, but its combat radius was also 15 percent below the program's objectives for all three variants. Other deficiencies ranged from the F135's cooling capacity to its electrical power output, which were barely sufficient for early production blocs and left very little room to accommodate upgrades.[45] While these factors alone provided significant grounds for calls to develop a new engine, and had been central to demands to fund the F136 due to its greater potential, a worsening of issues with the F135 would further strengthen the consensus that a major improvement was needed.

Shortly before leaving office in January 2021, Pentagon Undersecretary for Acquisition and Sustainment Ellen Lord highlighted that a primary cause for the F-35's fully mission capable rates remaining at just 36 percent, well below the 80 percent target, were ongoing issues with the F135's power module.[46] Subsequently on 12 February Pentagon spokesman John Kirby highlighted regarding issues with the F-35's combat readiness rates: 'The leadership team here is focused on a comprehensive recovery plan to mitigate the readiness impact to our F-35 operational units … They don't deem the engine issues right now to be a safety of flight issue, but maintenance inspections are resulting in unscheduled engine removal.' He elaborated that a primary issue 'has to do with the turbine blades of the engine and some malfunctioning that they're experiencing there.'[47] It was confirmed that Air Force F-35As would see the number of planned performance demonstrations cut due to ongoing issues with the powerplant.[48]

In March 2021 the GAO revealed that over 96 percent of F135s delivered by Pratt & Whitney had been delivered behind schedule, which was an issue that would subsequently be raised with concern by lawmakers.[49] Manufacturing issues and parts shortages would continue to cause such delays in the following years, with rates of late deliveries by Pratt & Whitney reaching 100 percent in 2023.[50] On 13 July 2021, officials informed Congress that maintenance issues with the F135 had put 41 F-35As in the Air Force out of service at the time, which amounted to almost 15 percent of the fleet of 272 aircraft. This led lawmakers to voice serious concerns, and to question the rationale of continued production of F-35s with such a problematic powerplant. This included questions regarding whether the Pentagon was considering alternative engine options to the F135.[51] The engine would continue to suffer from a range of issues, with one outstanding flaw being the overheating of a surface coating on its turbine blades, which caused the blades to crack and meant engines needed to be taken out of service earlier than planned and undergo maintenance more frequently.

The state of the F135 program, the wide ranging issues it was causing, and the consensus in opinion towards it, were highlighted at a nearly two-hour hearing on Capitol Hill on 28 April 2022. There House Armed Service Subcommittee on Readiness Chairman Congressman John Garamendi lamented: 'you give us an engine and it doesn't work, well it worked for a little while until it gets some dust around and then it doesn't work. What the hell? What's going on here?' 'Maybe the engine is not working, which is a Pratt & Whitney problem,' Garamendi said, adding: 'They're going to be before this committee soon. If they're in the audience and if they're listening, watch out. I'm coming at you in a very angry mood.'[52]

The possibility was raised at the hearing of issuing a new competition for the engine contract with Pratt & Whitney, or of reviving the competing F136 with General Electric. Garamendi was among several to criticise these suggestions, stating that would likely only result in two different engines that both 'don't work.'[53] This indicated that lawmakers perceived the F135's issues as a symptom of wider issues with the defence sector rather than affecting the specific engine program in isolation. Perceptions of issues with the F-35 and its engine as a symptom of much broader deficiencies in the defence sector were widely highlighted at the hearing, with Representative Jackie Speier observing:

> This reminds me, on a much larger scale, of the debacle of the LCS, [Littoral Combat Ship]. We are incapable of turning off the spigot when something doesn't work. So, this is a $400 billion program to build them [F-35s] and a $1 trillion program to sustain them over the lifecycle. We're asking the American people to pay for the F-35, only 55 percent of which are mission capable when the standard is 75 percent. Only about 30 to 35 percent of the F-35s are fully mission capable compared to a target of 60 percent and maintenance is taking twice as long as originally intended.[54]

Coinciding with the hearing, the Government Accountability Office on 28 April released a report on F-35 sustainment, which highlighted a wide range of issues associated with the F135. 'A leading driver of the F-35 not being mission capable has been engine issues,' it observed, noting that 'an increasing number of F-35 aircraft have not been able to fly because they do not have an operating engine.' Issues were found to affect the power module in particular. 'The engine sustainment strategy's goal is that no more than 6 percent of F-35 aircraft are unable to operate due to engine issues, which DoD has exceeded since April 2021. However, the military services desire outcomes similar to other fighter aircraft, which since 2016 have generally experienced less than 1 percent being unable to operate due to engine issues,' the report added. The F135 was thus causing unavailability at over six times the rates that other fighter engines were. The report projected that without corrective action, the portion of the fleet put out of service by engine issues could rise from over six percent to around 20 percent in 2025, while reaching 43 percent of the fleet in 2030 – which by then would be close to 800 aircraft. A means to mitigate the issue was to use 'a three-level maintenance approach with intermediate maintenance shops that could make minor repairs on the engine, preventing some engine maintenance beyond the most basic repairs from being sent to the depot,' with the two-level maintenance approach for the F135 having contributed to a depot maintenance backlog.[55]

A problem with the heat protective coating on the F135's rotor blades would exacerbate availability issues, and by July 2021 had raised non-availability rates attributable to engine issues to staggering 15 percent of the Air Force's F-35s.[56] Although this specific issue could be isolated and resolved more quickly, more general issues with the F135 continued to have a major detrimental impact on availability rates, with unavailability rates across all variants due to engine issues reaching eight percent in 2022 – placing it at eight times the rate of other American fighter engines.[57] The discovery of premature distress of rotor blade coatings, and the slower than expected rate at which depot maintenance could be performed, were important contributors to the exacerbation of the issue; as was the wearing out of engines significantly more rapidly than expected, in large part due to their need to operate at higher temperatures and provide more power than they were designed to.[58] By mid-2023 the possibility of cutting down the time between major scheduled maintenance of the F135 by one fifth, from 2,000 to 1,600 operating hours, was increasingly raised as a likely necessity.

Beyond the F135's impact on fighter availability rates, the most significant scandal for the engine program was revealed 13 months later on 30 May 2023 when a new Government Accountability Office report concluded that deficiencies with the engine would add $38 billion dollars in unexpected maintenance costs for the American F-35 fleet. To place this in perspective, this was equivalent to the procurement cost of approximately 475 new F-35As, around half the cost of the entire F-22 program, or around 9.2 percent of the originally projected F-35 program cost. The GAO report highlighted the issues that resulted from using an engine that was designed and largely developed when the F-35 had still been intended as a much lighter aircraft with lower power requirements, with the F135's cooling capacity being increasingly unable to meet the power demands of the fighter's avionics suite which were much larger than originally envisioned.[59]

Although the $38 billion figure reported by the GAO drew significant attention to the F135's insufficient power, the issue had previously been widely raised by officials. Two months before the report was published, the head of the F-35 Joint Program Office Lieutenant General Michael Schmidt testified: 'We have been eating into the life of this engine since the beginning of the program, because we did under-spec the engine and its requirements.' 'We are building costs into this program by eating into the life of this engine with additional overhauls that are expected over the life of the program,' he added.[60]

While the F-35 by 2022 had a cooling demand of approximately 30 kilowatts, the F135 was designed to provide just 15 kilowatts. Doubling the power output to meet cooling demands came at a significant cost, and required extracting significantly more bleed air from the engine to run it through heat exchangers. Exceeding the operational parameters which the engine was designed for in such a way not only reduced thrust, but also simultaneously increased both fuel consumption and engine temperatures. These increases respectively resulted in a shorter range for the aircraft and in much greater wear on the engine, which translated into higher maintenance requirements and a shorter lifespan. Not only was the F135's shortfall highly detrimental to the F-35's operations, but continued use of the engine was also unsustainable as the fighter was continually upgraded. F-35s operating at the Block 4 standard were at the most conservative estimate expected to have a cooling demand of 47 kilowatts, with future upgrades expected to raise this to 60 – or four times that which the F135 was built to provide. It was considered totally unfeasible for the engine to meet these requirements.

The GAO report highlighted that Lockheed Martin had discovered the discrepancy between the F-35's cooling requirements and the F135's output as early as 2008, alerting the Pentagon, and had in 2013 requested a design revision to address the issue. The Pentagon had denied the request to avoid further costs and delays to the program. 'Programme officials decided to continue with the F135 engine's original design with the understanding that there would be increased wear and tear, more maintenance, and reduced life on the engine because it would need to provide more air pressure to the PTMS [Power and Thermal Management System] than its design intended,' the report observed.[61] Pratt & Whitney's vice president for the F135 engine program Jen Latka subsequently confirmed that the power thermal management system on the F135 was operating at twice what it was designed for.[62]

Aside from the issue of cooling, the F135's power output was also considered wholly insufficient to meet the F-35's other requirements, particularly as these were set to improve significantly with expected Block 4 upgrades. Subsystems including the new AN/APG-85 radar and new generations of electronic warfare systems would require significantly more power than the engine could generate, with anticipated future subsystems including directed energy weapons expected to only further exacerbate the issue.

The GAO would issue a further report in July highlighting issues with the unique engine sustainment strategy adopted for the F-35, which while seeking to reduce costs, had created significant problems that were not seen on other fighter programs. 'Reliability issues with line replaceable components that have driven increased organizational-level maintenance,' it observed, noting that a 'lack of available power modules was the number one driver of non-mission-capable aircraft. Engine modules sent to depot have taken significantly more time to repair than planned.'[63]

Significant issues with the F135, many of them requiring redesigns, would continue to emerge. Following an F-35B crash on 15 December 2022, in which the aircraft suddenly pitched forward and struck the runway while landing during an acceptance flight, Pratt & Whitney said it identified a 'harmonic resonance' problem with the engine. The firm confirmed that it was a complex 'systems issue' affecting 'multiple parameters,' rather than a problem traceable to a single part of the engine. This not only resulted in a pause to F-35 and F135 deliveries from 27 December, and a grounding of parts of the existing fleet, but also forced the firm to widely implement repairs to engines in the field. Pratt & Whitney elaborated that 'there are several other actions that we will be taking over time' to resolve the issue.[64]

The issues afflicting the F135 would in hindsight vindicate arguments widely made on Capitol Hill to hedge against overreliance on a single powerplant by investing in two separate interchangeable engines. Highlighting the strong consensus that the F136 was 'an essential and stabilising element of a program that was already viewed as extremely high-risk,' aviation analyst Tyler Rogoway in 2014 summarised regarding the seeming absurdity of the decision to cancel it: 'Apparently, the thought that saving a couple billion dollars in the very near term was worth adding massive risk to an already very troubled and risky trillion and a half dollar weapons program.'[65] The next eight years would reveal just how damaging this could be, and made the $1.8 billion needed to complete the engine program when it was cancelled in 2011 – or approximately 0.12 percent of the F-35 program's then projected cost – appear to have been a very cost effective investment.[66]

While a primary argument for cancelling the F136 was that all USAF combat-coded F-16C/Ds were powered by the F110, and 100 percent of its F-15s by the F100, with only export clients fielding either of the aircraft with the alternate engine, this overlooked a number of key issues. The first was that the F-35 would make up a far larger portion of the fleet than either the F-16 or the F-15 ever had, and even if all Air Force F-35s may well have used the F135, the Navy or Marine Corps could have opted for the alternative. More significant, however, was the fact that although the F100 and F110 programs had been relatively unproblematic, it was far from unprecedented for new engines to suffer from major issues, and for these to be devastating for the fleets that operated them if unresolved. A leading example was the problematic TF-30 developed for America's first fourth generation fighter the F-14, which imposed a 'major limitation' on combat capabilities and caused dozens of accidents,[67] with the lack

The construction and series production of the F135-PW-600 engine, which provides the STOVL capability to the F-35B, was one of most significant and complex challenges faced during the Joint Strike Fighter program. The engine consists of the lift fan, drive shaft, two roll posts, and a 'three-bearing swivel module' (3BSM), the latter of which enables the exhaust from the main part of the engine to be deflected downwards at the rear of the aircraft – as illustrated here on an F-35B of the Marine Fighter Attack Squadron 242. (USMC)

of an alternative engine at an early stage limiting the Navy's options to mitigate the issue. Where the F-14 fleet was eventually saved by the integration of F110 engines from the F-15 from 1987, no parallel fifth generation fighter programs existed which could 'lend' their engines to the F-35.

While having the competing F100 and F110 was highly beneficial for the F-15 and F-16 programs for aforementioned reasons of competitive efficiency, the F136's significance was even greater than this because the F135 proved much more problematic than its two fourth generation predecessors. The lack of a competing engine not only removed the impetus for improvements to performance and cost effectiveness, but it also seriously stymied the F-35 fleet's operational potential while imposing significant additional costs.

A New Engine For the Next Generation

Wide ranging deficiencies with the F135, a number of which were set to worsen considerably as the F-35 was modernised to the Block 4 standard and beyond, stimulated a growing consensus in the Pentagon and on Capitol Hill that a new more capable engine was needed. This consensus was strengthened by the central importance which plans for F-35 operations in the Pacific theatre gained, and the severe deficiency in range which the fighter suffered from to wage war over such a vast area. Although the F-22 program was initially intended to provide a long range stealth fighter, its actual range was less than half of what the program had required, making it the shortest ranged fighter of its weight range in the world – significantly shorter than that of the F-15 or even the F-35. China's J-20 fifth generation fighter, by contrast, had over double the range of both its American counterparts, with its performance in this respect being comparable to that originally envisaged for the F-22. A new engine for the F-35 thus not only needed to be more reliable and have greater cooling and power generation capacities, but also needed to facilitate a longer range.

The urgent need for a new engine drew significant attention to the Adaptive Engine Transition Program (AETP), which had the potential to provide a successor to the F135 a full generation ahead in performance. At the centre of the new engine program was the introduction of an adaptive cycle powerplant, the development of which had been announced in 2007. This could facilitate shifts between two modes, one prioritising fuel efficiency and the other thrust, allowing a fighter to use less fuel as it cruised and thereby improving its range, but also affording it the thrust it needed during combat. Announcing the development of this technology on 26 March 2007, the Air Force Research Laboratory stated that it would 'allow pilots to go from high-speed combat maneuvers to long-range persistence mode as smoothly as a bird in flight.'[68]

Alongside an adaptive cycle, the engine developed under the AETP also introduced a 'third stream' of bypass air that served to both cool it and to make it more efficient, which was known as a bypass air system. All prior turbofan engines had used two streams. This was expected to facilitate a 25 percent increase in fuel efficiency, and thus an approximately 36 percent increase to range and significant reductions to operational costs. With cooling capabilities having been a leading shortcoming of the F135, the bypass air system's significantly increased cooling would facilitate easier integration of a growing range of new subsystems ranging from new radars to directed energy weapons. The introduction of the three new technologies was widely perceived to be the most revolutionary change to fighter engines since the shift from turbojet to turbofan engines in the late 1960s. The AETP engine was expected to achieve a 30 percent improvement in fuel efficiency and an improvement of over 10 percent in thrust relative to the F135, reaching approximately 200kN (45,000 pounds), while also being able to provide much more power for the fighter's avionics and weapons systems.

Designing competing engines to meet the requirements of the AETP, General Electric and Pratt & Whitney respectively designated their programs the XA100 and the XA101. The Air Force had previously indicated that the engines could power not only the F-35, but also the Next Generation Air Dominance (NGAD) sixth generation fighter presumably in twin configuration, mirroring the engine commonality in the fourth generation high-low combination between the F-15 and F-16. As observed by *Air Force Magazine* as late as April 2022: 'Air Force and industry officials say the AETP program was always aimed at NGAD. After testing and tweaking, the AETP engines are expected to be available for production around 2027, just in time to equip the first production-representative NGAD test aircraft. Meanwhile, the Air Force is also contemplating applying such technology to power the Block 4 version of the F-35 fighter.'[69] This had been the consensus on the program for several years, before funding was separated under the FY 2021 budget and a distinct Next Generation Adaptive Propulsion engine program for the sixth generation fighter was announced. Subsequently on 11 August 2022, the Air Force confirmed that the AETP engine would not be used on the NGAD, although the two engine programs still shared significant technologies.[70] This separation made the AETP a program exclusively for the F-35.

On 15 September 2021, the head of the Pentagon's F-35 program office Lieutenant General Eric Fick elaborated on the rationale for pursuing the AETP, and for doing so by commissioning offers from two firms: 'I love competition. I'm a big fan of having two viable fighter engine manufacturers in the defence space. What we need to figure out, I think, as an enterprise is: Are we willing to pay the cost associated.' 'We know that beyond Block 4, we are going to need more power' and cooling, he added. 'We know that we need to start [determining a path forward] so that we can put a solution set in place for all aircraft, for all customers.' In contrast to the original requirement for the F-35's first powerplant, there appeared to be genuine competition in the development of a next generation engine. The new engine was expected to cost $6.7 billion to develop, and a choice between two firms' proposals was expected to be made in late 2024.

General Electric anticipated that the XA100 would increase the F-35's range by 30 percent, increase thrust by 10 to 20 percent and improve fuel burn by 25 percent. Its thermal management capability would be doubled due to the third stream of air flowing through it, acting as a heatsink for electronics, avionics and mission systems. This would also significantly increase the F-35's cooling capabilities, comfortably accommodating Block 4 upgrades with a significant margin for expected future increases to power requirements. Alongside the use of an adaptive cycle and the introduction of a third air stream, a third major feature distinguishing the powerplant from preceding engines was the use of new advanced materials and manufacturing technologies. This included a move away from nickel-based superalloy, and the introduction of ceramic matrix composites for the turbines and other components that were one-third the weight and could withstand temperatures several hundred degrees higher. As observed by General Electric's head of advanced combat engines David Tweedie: 'When you run engines hotter, that's how you get more performance out of them. But at the same time, at those higher temperatures and higher performance, [the composites are] providing improved durability versus nickel-based alloys.' Additive manufacturing technologies helped to craft components that could not be made with traditional fabrication techniques, including producing heat exchangers that facilitated significantly greater heat absorption.[71] These material technologies were expected to provide the XA100 with a significant advantage over Pratt & Whitney's XA101.

Under the 2022 National Defense Authorization Act, published in December 2021, Congress mandated that AETP engines needed to be installed in the F-35As starting in 2027. The bill emphasised the need for a 'competitive acquisition strategy,' and also highlighted the need for new engines on the F-35B and F-35C, without specifying whether these aircraft would also use the AETP.[72] In October 2022 49 members of Congress specifically requested that the Defense Department 'fund adaptive propulsion engineering and manufacturing development in the FY24 budget submission and deliver adaptive technology to the services as quickly as possible.'[73]

Despite continuing work on the XA101, Pratt & Whitney would consistently oppose the Adaptive Engine Transition Program, which threatened its monopoly as a supplier of powerplants to the world's largest fighter program. The firm strongly advocated that investment in the AETP be diverted to an upgraded version of the F135 under the more conservative Enhanced Engine Package, which would guarantee its position as the sole supplier. This enhanced F135 variant was pitched as costing as much as the baseline variant, but saving up to $40 billion in sustainment costs over the life of the F-35 program. The firm claimed this approach would entail fewer new factors and less risk than the AETP, while still providing a more than 50 percent improvement in thermal capacity and increases to thrust and range of over 10 percent. Pratt & Whitney's vice president for the F135 engine program Jen Latka asserted that introducing a new engine developed under the AETP would require 'different depots, different support equipment ... two different sustainment engineering organizations ... tooling, support equipment, training, repairs — all of that has to be somewhat duplicated,' which would not be the case for an enhanced variant of the F135. An enhanced F135 would thus be 'a lot easier, less costly, less disruptive.'[74]

In response to pitches for an enhanced F135 as an alternative, General Electric's Vice President and General Manager for Advanced Products David Tweedie said the choice between this and the Adaptive Engine Transition Program came down to the a single question: 'Do you want an incrementalist approach, or do you want a transformational capability improvement that's not just good for the next five or 10 years, but for the next 30 or 40 years?'[75] The XA100, he asserted, would provide a generational-level jump in capabilities.[76] Tweedie otherwise slammed proposals for an enhanced F135 as 'just an incrementalist approach that can solve the next five years' problems.'[77] He added that he had been encouraged by comments made by Air Force Secretary Frank Kendall and other Air Force leaders who had shown interest in developing a clean sheet new engine for the F-35. Tweedie further stated that his program offered 'not only capability, but frankly, the lowest risk approach based on the investment that has been made at this point.'[78] Where doubts had been raised regarding whether the new engine could be fitted onto the F-35B, due to the fighter's downward-rotating rear nozzle, General Electric consistently expressed confidence that this could be done. Pratt & Whitney asserted that this was not possible.[79]

Tweedie further claimed that the AETP engine would over time provide savings of up to $10 billion due to reductions to maintenance requirements and fuel consumption.[80] He later elaborated that this figure did not include significant further savings on aerial refuelling operations due to the aircraft's improved range.[81] 'When you start saving 25% fuel burn and you start moving the needle on durability, that can really translate into life-cycle cost savings over the long term,' he elaborated.[82] Secretary Kendall similarly observed: 'we're going to have a very large inventory of F-35s. So the fuel savings that we could accomplish through that engine would be a significant payoff.' This would augment the benefits of the new engine's increased power, which was vital for future iterations of the aircraft. Kendall made clear when addressing House lawmakers that the AETP engine would entirely replace the F135, rather than serving as an alternative in Air Force's inventory as the F136 had been intended to.[83]

In June 2022 Assistant Secretary of the Air Force for Acquisition, Technology and Logistics Andrew Hunter praised progress made on both the XA100 and the XA101, stating that their early test results were 'very encouraging.' 'The advantages in power, thermal management and fuel efficiency that we were looking for are being demonstrated in the test program,' he stated, adding that the capabilities the engine program were intended to provide were exactly what the F-35 would need in a fight against China in the Pacific. Most notable among these were an increased range and a better ability to manage high temperatures while running advanced electronics.[84] Two months later the director of the Air Force Life Cycle Management Center's propulsion directorate John Sneden praised the program for demonstrating and maturing key technologies, and strongly argued that the cost, and the possibly lack of compatibility with the F-35B, would be justified by the significant improvements to the F-35A/C's performance. 'You can optimise for performance, or you can optimise for tri-variant commonality,' he stated stressing: 'we think the warfighter deserves the performance attributes that AETP can deliver.' He projected that these engines could begin to be integrated around the year 2030.[85]

On 12 September the Air Force and General Electric announced the conclusion of testing on the second XA100 prototype, which represented the end of the AETP's testing and data collection phase. This was referred to by General Electric as 'the culmination of more than a decade of methodical risk reduction and testing,' positioning the firm to transition to the program's Engineering and Manufacturing Development phase.[86] On 7 October 49 lawmakers from both the House and Senate, including leading members of congressional defence committees, sent a letter urging the Pentagon to finance a new phase of development for the AETP, specifically stressing the pressing military competition with China. 'To support the administration's Indo-Pacific Strategy, we must continue to develop and field advanced propulsion systems which will enable our service members to fly into the theatre of operation, complete their mission and return home safely,' they observed. Alluding to major recent advances in the Chinese fighter engine industry, particularly related to the J-20 program, the letter stressed: 'If we do not continue to pursue advanced propulsion systems for our fighter aircraft, we risk opening the door for U.S. adversaries to overtake our advantages in fielded engine technology.'[87] This echoed warnings two months prior by Program Executive Officer for Propulsion at the Air Force Life Cycle Management Center John Sneden, who warned that the United States was 'starting to lose our lead' in engine capabilities, and faced serious risk of being left in 'a place where we have essentially a reduced advanced propulsion industrial base' if the wrong choices were made in next generation programs.[88]

In what at the time appeared to be a major landmark in the F-35 program, and a significant turnaround from previous statements, Secretary Kendall on 10 March 2023 announced the decision not to further develop the Adaptive Engine Technology Program. This was confirmed in the FY 2024 budget. The service cited the program's cost and the strain on funding from a range of other demands, as well as the remaining questions regarding whether the clean sheet new engine could be integrated onto all F-35 variants. It instead favoured Pratt & Whitney's proposed Enhanced Engine Package to develop a conservatively improved F135 variant, which the firm was quick to announce it could begin delivering in 2028. The choice of its enhanced F135, the firm announced, 'saves billions, which ensures a record quantity of F-35s can be procured,' and 'ensures funding will be available to develop 6th generation propulsion for the Air Force's Next Generation Air Dominance Platform' – a program which was placing a high and growing strain on budgets.[89] Mark-ups subsequently released by Senate and House appropriators did not include funding for the AETP, although opinions among lawmakers remained divided.[90] With the decision widely attributed to the AETP's lack of compatibility with the F-35B, this represented one of the most significant cases of sacrifices being made for the STOVL variant with significant detrimental impacts for the performances of the other two variants.

General Electric highlighted that abandonment of the Adaptive Engine Technology Program 'fails to consider rising geopolitical tensions and the need for revolutionary capabilities that only the XA100 engine can provide by 2028. Nearly 50 bipartisan members of Congress wrote in support of advanced engine programs like ours because they recognise these needs, in addition to the role competition can play in reducing past cost overruns.' Mirroring the case for the F136, the firm added that the $4 billion invested in developing AETP technology thus far 'risks being wasted if the program is ended so close to completion.' Much as it had done for the F136, the firm resolved to continue testing and development while pursuing funding support.[91] It would lobby hard for Capitol Hill to keep the program alive, much as it had done successfully for the F136 from 2007-2011.[92]

Addressing concerns that funds already spent on the AETP's development would be wasted, Assistant Secretary of the Air Force for Financial Management Kristyn Jones revealed that work on the program would be leveraged in the development of an engine for the NGAD sixth generation fighter under the Next Generation Advanced Propulsion program. This program saw its budget raised by 166 percent for FY 2024 up to $595 million, which was reported to have been financed largely at the expense of the AETP.[93] Director of the Air Force Life Cycle Management Center's propulsion directorate John Sneden would elaborate: 'This program does leverage off the technology that we've done in AETP, but it is a brand-new system beyond what you see in AETP. So [it's] different in design.'[94] Pratt & Whitney's vice president for the F135 engine program Jen Latka similarly observed of the AETP's significance for sixth generation aviation: 'the AETP program, thank goodness for it, because we need to stay ahead of our adversaries as it relates to propulsion ... that program really matured sixth-gen technology for propulsion, and it will absolutely be used, whether it's GE or Pratt & Whitney. That is what we'll be moving into NGAD.'[95] General Electric would go so far as to announce in May 2023 a third testing phase for the XA100 that collected 'performance-oriented data across different parts of the flight envelope,' which could be used to inform work for the sixth generation fighter powerplant, with the firm's Vice President David Tweedie stressing this engine would 'leverage heavily' from work done on the AETP.[96]

In the year following Secretary Kendall's March 2023 announcement, multiple sources continued to advocate for a reversal of the decision to cancel the AETP. Chairman of the House Armed Subcommittee on Services Tactical Air and Land Forces Rob Wittman was among the supporters of continuing the program to particularly stress its importance.[97] Executive vice president of aeronautics at Lockheed Martin Greg Ulmer stated days later that he continued to 'advocate for' the AETP, stressing: 'I think some of the approaches today are very short-sighted and not considering a longer-term view.' 'Let's put as much margin in the airplane as we can today, such that in the future, I don't have to put another motor in. I don't have to bring new power and thermal management cooling into the airplane,' he said, stressing that the AETP brought further

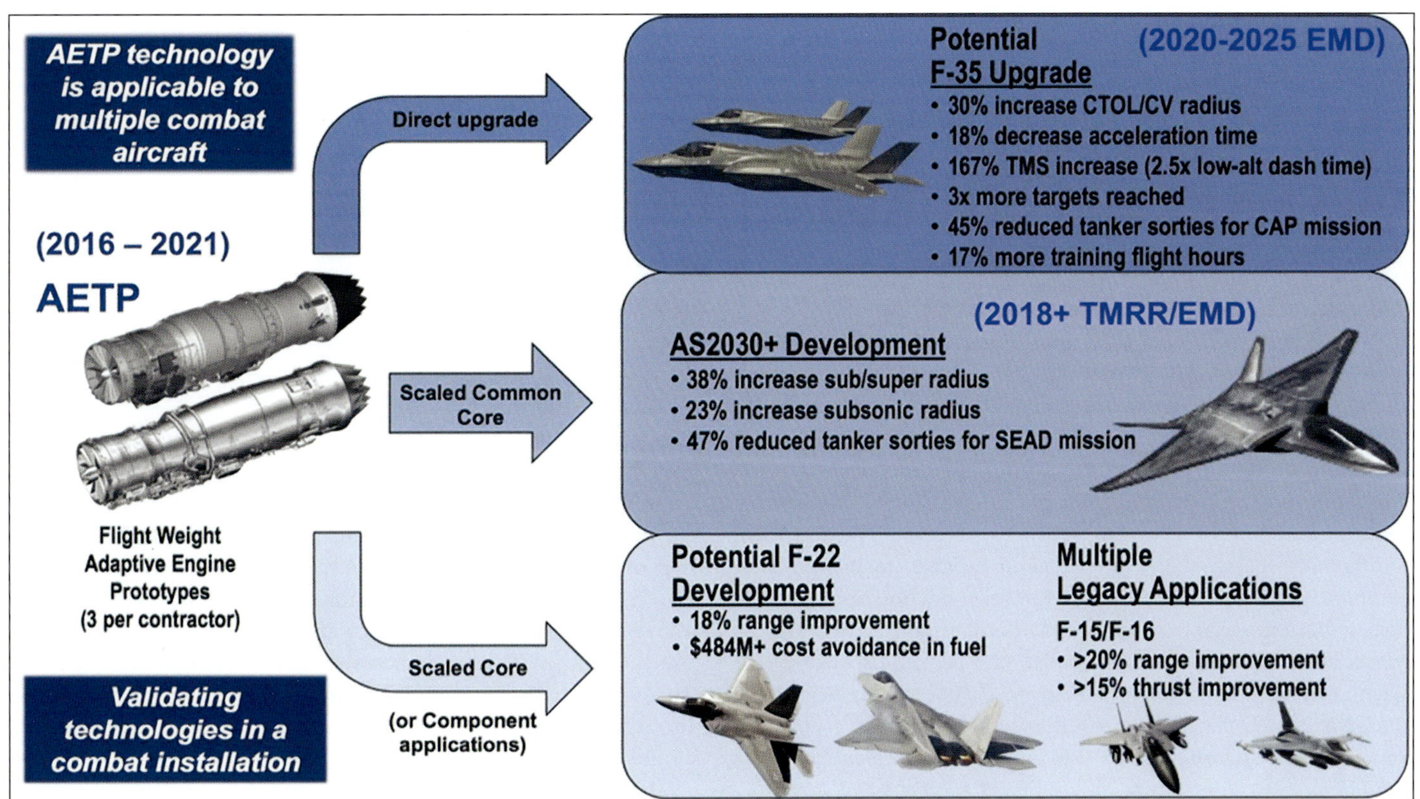

This diagram published by the U.S. Air Force explains the Adaptive Engine Transition Program. (USAF)

improvements beyond power and cooling increases, such as greater thrust and fuel efficiency. 'So you get the benefit of new capability in terms of power and cooling. But you also get aircraft performance improvement with AETP,' he said, adding: 'I'm thinking broader. I'm thinking longer-term.'[98]

Ulmer elaborated regarding why an enhanced F135 was not a sufficient long term solution, particularly when considering how many decades the F-35 would be in service and how many further blocks of upgrades were planned: 'I think they've [Air Force] made a decision informed by Block 4 and the requirements as they understand them today. I think there's elements within the Pentagon talking along the lines that there will be a Block 5 and a Block 6, and there'll be other considerations in the future.' He estimated a future Block 5 upgrade package would require between 20 and 30 percent more cooling capacity than Block 4, highlighting than an enhanced F135 would only be a very temporary solution. Ulmer downplayed concerns regarding the need for additional sustainment infrastructure for an AETP engine, emphasising that capability requirements had to come first. His position highlighted the fact that the F-35's position as America's prime fighter and sole fighter in production in its generation made foregoing a tremendous performance upgrade particularly controversial.[99]

The highly unusual and outspoken statement from a senior representative of Lockheed Martin in favour of the AETP indicated the degree of controversy which the program's cancellation caused, particularly as the Chinese J-20's next generation WS-15 engine showed growing signs of progress towards service entry. The Chinese powerplant was confirmed to use a number of cutting edge technologies including single crystal superalloy turbine blades and powder metallurgy superalloy turbine disks, allowing it to operate with much greater efficiency and at far higher temperatures than previous non-U.S. engines. David Tweedie would himself imply competition from rival programs, of which those in China were by far the most significant, as a reason to sustain the AETP, stressing that this was vital 'to keep the F-35 relevant.'[100] Despite outstanding controversies, however, the cancellation of the AETP was confirmed on 21 March 2024, when legislation released by congressional appropriators prohibited the use of funds to integrate an alternative engine on any F-35 variant.[101]

Despite the AETP's cancellation, the eventual need for a clean sheet successor to the F135 remained inescapable, with the development of the Enhanced Engine Package by Pratt & Whitney representing only a stopgap measure. The fact that many of the same engine technologies would remain under development for the Next Generation Advanced Propulsion program raised the significant possibility that development of a clean sheet engine for the F-35 would be re-initiated once the sixth generation program had further matured, and could be done at a relatively low cost due with a minimal need for R&D. This could be used to power the F-35A and F-35C, while enhanced F135s continued to power the F-35B. The possibility also remained that a common engine with the NGAD or F/A-XX sixth generation fighters could be used by the F-35 with only minor modifications, which would eliminate the need for another engine program. An enhanced F135 variant could thus serve as a stopgap until a sixth generation fighter engine matured.

The fact that the F-35 urgently needed a new engine within just a decade of entering service was almost totally unprecedented, and compared poorly to the F-15 and F-16 which would fly with incrementally modernised variants of the F100 and F110 for over half a century, and even with the F-22 for which the F119 proved sufficient. The mismatch between the F135's performance and the F-35's requirements was a leading shortcoming of the program, which not only had wide ranging consequences for performance, but also imposed significant costs. These included higher than needed operational costs due to greater wear on the engines, the expense of developing new engines after the F135 entered service, and the immense expected costs of upgrading existing F135s to be able to power fighters upgraded to the Block 4 standard. Significant further costs were expected to be incurred when the F-35 was forced to transition away from the F135 in the 2030s.

8

THE F-35 AS PART OF A GLOBAL FIGHTER PROGRAM

International Partnership in the F-35 Program

The development of the F-35 into three variants for the Air Force, Navy and Marine Corps was at the outset of the program intended to ensure 80 percent commonality between the primary fighters of the three services.[1] By 2008, however, expectations for airframe commonality ranged from just 27 percent to 43 percent.[2] Program Executive Officer Lieutenant General Christopher Bogdan confirmed on 10 February 2016 that there was only 20 to 25 percent commonality between the A, B and C variants, mainly in their cockpits. It was 'almost like three separate production lines,' he said, adding that a genuine joint fighter was 'hard' to develop because 'the services were reluctant to compromise' on their requirements.[3] The Senate Arms Service Committee confirmed three months later in the 2017 National Defense Authorization Act that 'despite aspirations for a joint aircraft, the F-35A, F-35B and F-35C are essentially three distinct aircraft, with significantly different missions and capability requirements.'[4] Reporting directly from production facilities at Fort Worth, military aviation journalist Jamie Hunter in 2024 would cite a figure of 'approximately 20 percent parts commonality' between the variants.[5]

To place figures for commonality between F-35 variants in perspective, the F-15C/D built in the late 1970s and the F-15EX built in the early 2020s retained approximately 70 percent parts commonality despite almost half a century separating them,[6] while the French Rafale C's carrier based derivative, the Rafale M, was able to retain appropriately 90 percent commonality (80 percent structural and equipment commonality and 95 percent systems commonality).[7] As summarised by analysts at *The National Interest*: 'the Joint Strike Fighter is actually three different plane designs sharing a basic cockpit, engine and software and a logistical network. The Air Force's F-35A, the Marines' F-35B and the Navy's F-35C should, in all fairness, be the F-35, F-36 and F-37.'[8]

The F-35 program's failure to produce fighters with high levels of commonality not only significantly reduced the benefits of economies of scale, but also had serious operational impacts. It considerably undermined plans for fighter units from different services to share spare parts in campaigns where logistical support was minimal, such as in projected Pacific war scenarios. Limited commonality undermined a primary rationale for pursuing the F-35 as a joint program, and making sacrifices to the F-35A and C variants in particular to meet the F-35B's design requirements. There was a strong argument to be made that had the A and C variants been developed as part of a simpler joint program, much greater commonality could have likely been achieved, much as was seen with other fighters developed into both carrier and ground based variants worldwide. Similar conclusions were widely reached, with a prominent RAND Corporation study in 2013 having concluded that developing three separate fighters would have cost less, provided greater flexibility, and reduced delays than attempting a joint program.[9] Significant avionics commonality between separate programs would still have likely been possible, as was reportedly done between the China's J-11B and J-15, or its J-11BG, J-15B and J-16. Ensuring commonality between variants proved to be one of the areas where the Joint Strike Fighter program fell furthest short of expectations.

Despite shortcomings in efforts to achieve commonality between variants, the F-35 program was nevertheless highly successful in introducing unprecedented levels of commonality between the U.S. Air Force's fighter fleet and those of America's strategic partners around the world due to the very wide proliferation of the F-35A. While the Soviet Air Force had previously had such interoperability with the fighter fleets of a wide range of strategic partners, from the Warsaw Pact and Yugoslavia to Syria and South Yemen, Cuba and Libya, and farther east India, Vietnam and North Korea, as a result of the USSR's disintegration the United States was left totally without compare in its network of partners operating its fighters. Thus while the USSR's most widely produced fighter types of the first, second and third generations had far outnumbered their American counterparts, the state's disintegration in 1991 allowed American industry to for the first time attain this, as production of the fourth generation F-16 far exceeded that of its Soviet rival the MiG-29.

This discrepancy grew wider moving into the fifth generation era, with the F-35 being totally without peer in its generation in how widely it is operated. This provides considerable benefits to the United States, including not only economies of scale and revenues, but also significant political leverage over clients, as well as the benefits of greater efficiency if fighting as part of a coalition. As summarised by Chief of the Air Staff of the Royal Canadian Air Force Lieutenant General André Deschamps: 'We all show up tomorrow with the same kit, the same software, same everything. The procedures are the same, the training's the same. You don't need to bring all the equipment. We can quickly come together with fewer platforms and have a far greater effect.'[10]

The Joint Strike Fighter program was from an early stage envisaged to include a significant number of international partners, with three levels of foreign participation reflecting the size of states' financial stakes in the program, as well as the amount of technology transfer and subcontracts open for bidding by firms from those states. The United Kingdom was the sole Level 1 partner, and had joined the U.S. Marine Corps to develop the Advanced Short Takeoff Vertical Landing in the 1980s before this evolved into part of the Joint Strike Fighter program. The country was formally brought into the program in 1995, and was obliged to contribute $2.5 billion to development. Italy and the Netherlands were both Level 2 partners which respectively contributed $1 billion and $800 million. Level 3 partners included Turkey, which contributed $195 million, Canada $160 million, Australia $144 million, Norway $122 million, and Denmark $110 million. Other than the United Kingdom, where the F-35 was envisaged as a replacement for the Harrier II, and Italy which only briefly leased the F-16, all partners relied on the F-16 or F-18 to form the backbone of their fleets.

A British F-35B from No 617 Squadron takes off from RAF Marham. (British MoD)

The British Armed Forces initially planned to field 138 F-35Bs over the life of the program, although by the middle of the 2020s only 48 had been ordered. These were the first four as seen on delivery flight to RAF Marham in June 2018. In early 2025 a decision was made to procure less costly F-35A fighters, which was likely to further negatively impact the number of F-35Bs ordered. (MOD UK)

Funds contributed by foreign partners to meet the F-35's development costs covered only very small portions of these expenses, with even the United Kingdom's contribution remaining at well under five percent of program development costs, while all other partners contributed significantly under two percent. The five Level 3 partners' contributions were equivalent to around one third of a percentage point or less. A benefit of pursuing the F-35 as a joint program, however, was to better position the fighter to compete in foreign markets by providing potential clients with stakes in development. Partners' industrial contributions were in a small number of cases also significant, with the United Kingdom being a leading example that was particularly valued for its engine technologies and ejection seats. On the opposite end of the spectrum, Turkey's third world level labour costs made it attractive for outsourcing less complex and more labour intensive areas of production, with 817 of the fighter's approximately 24,000 airframe part types and 188 of approximately 3,000 engine part types being built in the country by the early 2020s.[11]

The F-35 itself used over 300,000 parts from over 1,100 suppliers, with the distribution of supply chains not only across almost every U.S. state, but also across multiple partners, providing both constituencies domestically and the governments of strategic partners with important economic incentives to help ensure the program's success. The contracts that foreign partners gained to contribute to the program were in many cases disproportionately greater than their investments in development or procurement. Taking the United Kingdom as an example, British firms were to supply fifteen percent of the content, by value, of all of the over 3,000 planned F-35s, with $12.9 billion in F-35 related orders already received by 2019, despite the country's relatively small financial contribution to development and its orders for just 48 fighters.[12] The country was projected to see between 19,000 and 25,000 jobs created by the program over its duration.[13] Sales of F-35 parts by the late 2010s accounted for well over one fifth of all British defence exports, with Senior Vice-President for the program at BAE Systems Cliff Robson accordingly stating that participation in the program was 'cheap when you look at what that investment is returning to the UK.'[14] Over 500 British firms contributed to supplying the F-35 program, with notable contributions including the aft fuselage and key software provided by BAE Systems, the ejection seat supplied by Martin Baker, and the in-flight refuelling probe supplied by Cobham. The proportion of the F-35B supplied by British firms was significantly greater than other variants, with its STOVL lift fan, roll ducts and bearing swivel nozzle being supplied by Rolls Royce.[15] This was considered an important factor in the Ministry of Defence's reluctance to procure the A or C variants.

Foreign suppliers by some estimates between them made around 40 percent of each F-35. Italy and Japan also both carried out final assembly domestically at their Cameri and Mitsubishi Heavy Industries Komaki South facilities, which also provided extensive maintenance services.[16] Lockheed Martin Vice President for F-35 Business Development and Strategic Integration Jack Crisler observed to this effect in 2016 that the Joint Program Office and partner countries 'deliberately went through a selection process to identify maintenance repair and overhaul facilities in North America, in Europe and in Asia for the airframe and the engines with the expectation that that's where you would go for depot-level capabilities.'[17] The truly international nature of the F-35 program was visible at the main production line at Fort Worth, which defence reporter Marcus Weisgerber reported on as follows in 2018:

> There's already an international feel in Fort Worth. On Tuesday morning, a ceiling crane hoisted the center section of an Israeli jet from one assembly station to the next. Nearby, a robot drilled precise, laser-guided holes into the green wings of Norway's eighth F-35. Farther south, Japan's first F-35A and the U.K. Royal Air Force's seventh F-35B slowly meandered their way northward. Simple printed cards in plastic sheets marked the Air Force's 104th jet and the U.S. Marine Corps' 55th F-35B.[18]

The front of an Italian Navy F-35B, as seen around the time the class obtained the initial operations capability in 2018. As of the mid-2020s, Italy is the only country to have ordered the F-35B to serve separately in two services, the Navy and Air Force, due to the value attributed to short airfield deployments in the latter service. (Lockheed Martin)

While the F-22 and China's J-20 and J-35 programs were developed entirely domestically, Russia would seek to pursue a similar joint program for its own fifth generation fighter the Su-57 by bringing India into a partnership. The structure of the partnership, which proved largely unsuccessful, provided an insightful comparison with that of the F-35. India signed an agreement on joining the program only in 2007, and a preliminary design contract only in 2010, after the fighter had already made its first flight, which was very late for a full partnership. The funds required were substantial and far exceeded those of F-35 clients, including $295 million to fund the initial design and concept-definition phase alone.

The F-35 could succeed as a joint program because it was overwhelmingly clear that the United States was the senior partner, with the technological and defence sector discrepancies, investments in development, and the planned scales of orders leaving little doubt of this. By contrast, although there was a vast technological discrepancy between Russia and India's combat aviation sectors favouring the former, and development was already at a very mature stage by the time India joined, both countries were expected to place similarly sized orders and to finance similar proportions of the development costs. As Sukhoi's director, Mikhail Pogosyan, observed: 'We will share the funding, engineering and intellectual property in a 50-50 proportion.'[19] Considering India's negligible experience in fighter development and very limited relevant technological base, this provided a dubious basis for partnership. The scale of Indian investment, including a stipulated $6.7 billion just to transfer technologies and bring the program to prototype stages, led the Indian Defence Ministry to insist on extensive participation in conceptual development, preliminary design and marketing, and significant technological inputs, all of which were far from viable.[20] This led to the agreement's eventual collapse, and highlighted the difficulties of managing joint programs for very complex and high cost systems. By contrast, foreign partners in the F-35 program placed small orders as portions of total planned production, made small investments in development, and were well aware from the outset that they would be granted only limited technology transfers, and would have only very limited room to influence the fighter's design and the program's evolution.

Foreign partners at times wavered in their public commitment to the F-35 program, usually in protest at what were seen to be overambitious design goals or as a means to lobby for more subcontracts or technology transfers. Only Canada, however, would take active steps to sideline the F-35 from its procurement plans from 2015, albeit only to later place the largest orders of any of the program's foreign partners in 2023. A leading cause for concern was the program's high degree of centralisation and the resulting lack of autonomy over source codes and sensitive data. In the United Kingdom the issue of access to software source code and ensuring operational sovereignty needed to allow 'an unbroken British chain of command' for operations was raised in parliament in the early 2000s, and was seen to be vital. These concerns were addressed by the George W. Bush administration, and by President Bush personally, in 2006.[21] Britain was reported to be one of at least two other partner countries which threatened to leave the program over the issue of extreme centralisation of data in the United States using ALIS, with the subsequent development of the ALIS Sovereign Data Management system being among the concessions made to allow partners to more tightly control and protect their own data.[22]

A notable example of the concerns which issues with the F-35's development raised was British Defence Minister Philip Hammond's statement when visiting Washington in January 2012 that 'of course, if there is any slippage in the program, any reduction in the U.S. numbers required could have impacts on availability and on unit costs.' 'Really, it's a caricaturist's dream – a carrier with no jets to fly on them. So the prospect of any further delays to the carrier variant would be of concern to us,' he added, in reference to the fact that delays to the program would leave the country's new aircraft carrier HMS *Queen Elizabeth* without fighters.[23] Dutch Defence Minister Hans Hillen, who also visited Washington that month, stated that Lockheed Martin would 'have to work hard to keep us on board,' raising the issue of 'the price, the rumours about technical shortcomings' and stressing the prevailing need to 'convince a majority of the Dutch people and of parliament' to select the F-35.[24]

While a detailed overview of the F-35 program's partners and clients' procurements and use of the fighter would require its own separate volume, a number of countries' acquisitions are detailed below to provide case studies of various aspects of the fighter's export profile. These include the cost, capability and interoperability advantages that have allowed the fighter to gain tremendous market share abroad, the requirements some clients have had for customisation, the public relations benefits clients have sought to extract from using the aircraft in combat, the primary security challenges which clients have procured the aircraft to respond to, the controversies surrounding both procurement processes and operational issues once the aircraft enter service, and the means by which exports have been used as leverage demanding policy concessions from clients and to achieve other geopolitical ends.

Belgian Tender: Interoperability Advantages and Market Dominance in Europe

In October 2018 the Belgian Ministry of Defence's selection of the F-35A to replace its F-16A/B fighters marked an important early turning point in the program's position on European markets, with an assessment of the country's procurement decision providing insight into broader trends that allowed the F-35 to gain undisputed dominance over both the F-18E/F and competing local aircraft. Belgian interest in procuring the F-35 was first reported on 12 September 2011, when a leaked diplomatic cable between the U.S. ambassador and Minister of Defence Pieter De Crem was released by Wikileaks.[25] Two years later, on 17 September 2013, *Reuters* reported that U.S. government officials had visited Belgium and briefed local government officials about the fighter's capabilities, citing an unnamed 'source familiar with the matter.' The source stated that Belgium was considering buying 35 to 55 F-35s.[26] On 16 November Chief of Staff Colonel Frederik Vansina confirmed that the Defence Ministry would issue a request for information in early 2014 to potential suppliers of a replacement for its F-16s.

The Eurofighter, Rafale and F-35A were all considered frontrunners to replace Belgium's F-16s, with France being particularly aggressive in marketing its fighter, which had consistently lost when bidding for orders against the F-16, F-15, F-35 and the Russian Su-30. By 2020 only three small foreign orders had been made for the Rafale, while the largest order had been cancelled by the Indian Defence Ministry in 2016. Paris thus offered Brussels €20 billion under the umbrella of a 'strategic and economic partnership' if the Rafale was chosen, and subsequently worked on a more concrete proposal to make the fighter more attractive. The fighter's producer Dassault Aviation promised an economic return of 100 percent of the purchase price, including supporting more than 5,000 high tech jobs in Belgium. With the F-35A boasting significant advantages in almost all of the most important aspects of performance, the offering of economic incentives was seen as vital to allowing the Rafale to compete.

Preceding the conclusion of the fighter tender the Belgian government was in March 2018 widely accused in local press of misleading parliament by hiding the fact that there was a significantly cheaper option to sustain its fighter aviation capabilities, namely that an April 2016 Lockheed Martin study found the country's F-16s could continue see their service lives extended by up to 27

U.S. Air Force Lieutenant Colonel Jason Wall, 312th Fighter Squadron commander, parks the first Belgian Air Component F-35A at Luke Air Force Base on December 3, 2024. This was the first Belgian F-35 at the facility. (USAF)

The first F-35A built for the Royal Netherlands Air Force. (USAF)

years. This fuelled calls to cancel the tender for new fighters, on the basis that this multi-billion dollar investment was no longer urgent. Former Defence Minister André Flahaut, for one, stated: 'since last July, I have been wondering whether our country should replace part or all of its F-16 fighters. In addition to the financial cost, which could durably unbalance defence spending, this replacement begs the question: Do we really need it?' The high sustainment costs of the 34 F-35s, which would collectively set the treasury back by €10 billion over their intended service lives, was another leading point of contention.[27]

On 25 October 2018, the Belgian Defence Ministry formally announced its decision to sign a €4 billion contract for 34 F-35As, making it the thirteenth country to order the aircraft. Defence Minister Steven Vandeput confirmed at the time that 'the offer from the Americans was the best in all our seven evaluation criteria.'[28] The discrepancy between Belgian orders for 160 F-16s during the Cold War, and its procurement of just 34 F-35s in the following generation, reflected a broader trend towards sharp fleet contractions across much of Europe. These cuts were a primary factor fuelling doubts that the F-35 could meet its production goals, despite enjoying a much greater share of U.S. and foreign fighter orders than any previous aircraft, since the quantity of fighters being purchased by most clients were far below Cold War era numbers, and in many cases just a small fraction.

With Brussels having faced considerable political pressure to select a European aircraft, Belgian officials stressed that the choice not to purchase the Eurofighter was due to the difference in price. This again highlighted the significant discrepancy in cost effectiveness between the U.S. and European combat aviation sectors, since the former could produce fighters that were both larger and a generation ahead while still being less expensive. Prime Minister Charles Michel highlighted that the F-35 acquisition and support up to 2030 cost €600 million ($684 million) under the €4.6 billion the government had budgeted for, and over the fleet's 40-year service life would cost €2.6 billion less than the €15 billion previously projected.[29] Emphasising cost aspects, rather than the F-35's tremendous performance superiority, appeared to be a diplomatic attempt to soften the blow to neighbouring states, with Deputy Prime Minister Kris Peeters at the time also stressing that 30 percent of the components for the F-35 would come from Europe.[30*]

The choice of the F-35 nevertheless faced particularly harsh rebuke from France, with French media outlets widely slamming Brussels as betraying the 'European choice.' French President Emanuel Macron took this one step further, claiming Brussels' choice of the F-35 had strategically gone against collective European interests.[31]

Beyond cost and capability advantages, a further notable factor in the choice of the F-35 was the Belgian Air Component's very close operational collaboration with the Royal Netherlands Air Force, which had ordered 37 F-35As. The two services had already agreed to pool the future delivery of air policing cover for their countries and Luxembourg before the tender was launched, and deployed contingents abroad with particularly close integration between them, as seen in Afghanistan. This created a strong incentive to field a common fighter type. While this incentive was specific to Belgium, European states more broadly had a growing incentive to procure the F-35 as more of their allies across the continent acquired the same aircraft to ensure interoperability. Thus the more contracts the Rafale and Eurofighter lost in Europe, the less likely they were to gain future contracts.

Belgium's selection of the F-35 was considered a turning point for the fighter's sales to European states that had not participated in the program, with Switzerland's subsequent selection of the aircraft in June 2021, despite significant controversies that this would undermine the country's official neutrality, seen as a further landmark in its advances across the continent.[32] By 2023 Program Executive Officer for the F-35 Michael Schmidt projected that European states would field 400-500 of the stealth fighters. He highlighted that, alongside the approximately 100 set to be deployed on the continent by the United States, this created 'a huge opportunity that is to leverage each other's logistics and maintenance environments,' which in turn further increased the fighter's attractiveness over less widely used local rivals.[33] By the middle of the 2020s 13 of the 19 foreign countries that had placed orders for the F-35 were located on the continent. The Eurofighter, by contrast, had outside its partner countries gained only one small order from Austria for 18 fighters in 2003, with all remaining orders having been placed by Arab gulf states. The Rafale, meanwhile, saw sales in Europe only on concessional terms, whether to Greece where a portion of aircraft were offered for free as aid, or to Croatia where second-hand aircraft were supplied at significantly reduced prices. Only Serbia would take steps towards procuring the

* The Belgian Defence Ministry would seven years later further placate neighbouring states' demands for industrial support by announcing on 7 May 2025 that future F-35s procured would be assembled in Italy rather than at Fort Worth, which considered very much a political decision.

A French Air Force Rafale and a U.S. Air Force F-35A fly in formation over France. (USAF)

Rafale at full market prices, with the decision heavily influenced by the fact that it was unable to procure American fighters, the Eurofighter, or non-Western fighters, for varying political reasons.

The F-35 was expected to maintain considerable superiority over European fighters for the foreseeable future, with the serious and growing issues that surfaced with the joint Franco-German-Spanish Future Combat Air System stealth fighter program shortly after its announcement in 2018 ensuring that it could not present a serious challenge. CEO of the program's leading contractor Dassault Aviation, Eric Trappier, announced in July 2022 that as a result the fighter would not be ready until the 2050s, ruling it out as a competitor to the F-35 for orders.[34] By the mid-2020s, as France and Spain remained the only major air forces on the continent not to have ordered the F-35, both would face growing pressure to procure the aircraft, even if only as a stopgap until a European successor entered service. Although Trappier and other French sources raised the possibility from the early 2030s of developing a fifth generation fighter domestically, the country's economic situation and the limitations of its tech sector and industrial base made the development of an aircraft competitive with the latest iterations of the F-35 before 2040 appear unlikely.[35]

Finnish Tender: Performance Supremacy

In the autumn of 2015 the Finnish Ministry of Defence's preliminary study working group issued a final report proposing that the country procure a new type of multirole fighter to replace the fleet of F-18C/Ds, which were to be phased out of service by 2030. In October 2019 the cost of the acquisition was capped at €10 billion and the total lifetime cost of the new aircraft at €40 billion. This formed the basis for an advanced invitation for the HX tender, which was sent before the end of the year for 64 fighters. Competing to replace the F-18C/D fleet, the F-35A, F-18E/F, Rafale, Eurofighter and Gripen E/F were all offered to meet the requirements of the tender. Although not part of NATO, growing integration between Finnish forces and those of the alliance meant no non-Western aircraft were considered.

On 5 December 2021, the Finnish newspaper *Iltalehti* reported that the Defence Forces had recommended the F-35 to serve as the country's next fighter, citing 'several foreign and security policy sources.'[36] Five days later the Finnish government confirmed the F-35's selection, marking the latest in a series of successive losses against it for the European fighter types and for the F-18E/F. It was later confirmed that the Rafale and Eurofighter were eliminated in the early stages of the tender, and did not make it to later evaluations.[37] According to Prime Minister Marin Sanna, the decision was unanimous despite some concerns being raised by ministers regarding the F-35's operational costs.[38]

Regarding the F-35's performance advantages, which were the most important factor facilitating its selection, the aircraft was judged to have superior combat and reconnaissance capabilities, with its ability to gather electronic intelligence being particularly outstanding. Its situational awareness, data sharing capabilities, sensors and stealth capabilities were particularly singled out for praise by the Finnish Air Force.[39] Finnish auditors highlighted that the aircraft had a higher development potential up to 2060 than the competing fourth generation fighters. Head of the Finnish Air Force Major General Jokinen Pasi revealed that the aircraft scored 4.47, while the runner up, the F-18E/F, scored just 3.81, when the aircraft were scored in terms of meeting Defence Ministry requirements.[40] Scores evaluated the aircraft's military performance, security of supply, industrial cooperation and costs, with a score of 4.0 was considered the minimum requirement.[41]

Alongside requirements for cost elements of a fighter, the HX Tender had strict requirements for both the security of supply and for industrial participation, namely that the value of industrial cooperation should be at least 30 percent of the contract price. The contract thus included local production of the F-35's front fuselage, including for export, as well as production of structural components, the ability to test and maintain the equipment locally, and an offer for final engine assembly in Finland. This amounted to 4,500 man years of direct domestic employment and 1,500 man years indirect.[42]

The first of Norway's 52 F-35A fighters is lifted by an overhead crane in Lockheed Martin's assembly plant in Fort Worth in April 2015. The Royal Norwegian Air Force in 2022 became the first service in the world to field a fleet comprised entirely of fifth generation fighters. Norwegian fighters were customised with the addition of drogue parachutes to facilitate landings on shorter airfields. (Lockheed Martin)

General manager of the F-35 program at Lockheed Martin Bridget Lauderdale specified that F-35 production in Finland would continue for over 20 years, and that sustainment work would continue into the 2070s.[43] For servicing, the F-35's existing global maintenance system was extensively modified to meet Finnish requirements, which included 'service capabilities to be built in Finland, exclusive spare parts and replacement equipment under Finnish national control and participation in a multinational service network.'[44] Chief of the Finnish Defence Forces Logistics Major General Kari Renko thus reported that Finland would retain the most extensive domestic servicing capability for the F-35 other than the United States.[45]

Despite being a generation ahead of both the F-18E/F and competing European aircraft, and significantly larger than the latter, the F-35 cost at a little over €73 million per aircraft 'was the cheapest in terms of purchase price' according to the Finnish Air Force.[46] A €8.4 billion ($9.4 billion) contract for 64 fighters was formally signed on 11 February 2022, and allocated €4.7 billion (56%) to aircraft acquisitions, €2.9 billion (35%) to maintenance equipment, spare parts, training equipment, and other systems and services from 2025-2030, and just €755 million (9%) to air launched weapons – namely AIM-9s and AIM-120s.[47] This was intended to allow for the procurement of newer air-launched weapons once the fighters began to be delivered, with the Air Force noting: 'the weapon package is refined during the procurement process, taking into account, among other things, the availability of the latest types of weapons and the development of the operating environment.'[48] This fuelled some speculation that the aircraft were planned to deploy the AIM-260, rather than the AIM-120, as their primary air-to-air weapons.[49]

Highlighting the discrepancies between program partners and external clients, Finland's F-35 acquisitions caused a minor controversy in neighbouring Norway, where lawmakers noted that Norwegian F-35As had cost approximately 34 percent more per fighter at 1.74 billion Norwegian krone ($197 million) compared to 1.3 billion krone ($147 million) paid by Finland.[50] The significant cost difference highlighted the benefits which Finland retained both as a latecomer to the program and as a client for acquisitions on a larger scale. The Finnish tender was highly competitive which placed considerable pressure on Lockheed Martin to reduce prices, while the significant fall in production costs meant that Norway, which received its first fighters over a decade earlier than Finland would, had paid for more costly and less capable early production models.[51]

Finland's decision to acquire 64 F-35A Block 4s, matching the 64 F-18C/Ds it had purchased, made it one of very few clients which procured F-35s to make one-for-one replacements of fourth generation fighters. Almost all other clients saw their fleets contract when transitioning to the F-35 in order to accommodate the aircraft's much higher operational costs than its predecessors, with its far superior capabilities more than compensating for this. Each Finnish F-35's projected annual operational costs were very significantly lower than those in neighbouring states, approximately 60 percent below Switzerland's and a staggering 80 percent below Norway's,[52] reflecting the fact that pilots were expected to train more on simulators. Swiss officials had previously confirmed meetings with senior Finnish officials specifically to discuss the F-35's operational costs,[53] with the ability to fly the aircraft much less than those from preceding generations (see Chapter 6) being vital to both countries' ability to afford them within the constraints of their respective tenders.

Israeli Procurement: Customisation of Local Requirements

In June 2006 Israeli Air and Space Force (IASF) chief procurement officer Brigadier General Ze'ev Snir announced that the service would procure over 100 F-35s to replace its F-16s, at a projected cost of just $5 billion dollars.[54] Over the next two years significant increases to the aircraft's procurement cost would emerge as a major obstacle to realising these plans, with an official in the Israel Defense Forces General Staff quoted in November 2008 lamenting: 'It's unbelievable, first it was $40 million to $50 million, and then they [the IASF] told us $70 million to $80 million. Now, we're looking at nearly three times that amount, and who's to say it won't continue to climb?'[55] The significant increases to operational costs ensured that the F-35A could not fully succeed the F-16 as the backbone of the Israeli fleet as originally planned.

The IASF sought to make extensive modifications to the F-35 for domestic use, and initially advocated the development of a twin seat variant to accommodate a weapons systems officer behind the pilot. It required the integration of Israeli avionics, in particular electronic warfare systems, and possibly an indigenous radar, which would require access to the F-35's source code – something that was not provided to program partners other than the United Kingdom. Demands for integration of Israeli subsystems and access to the source code were accordingly firmly rejected,[56] which was described by Israeli sources as a 'take it or leave it' approach to the F-35 program.[57]

As early as 2008, Pentagon officials described the IASF as 'very aggressive' in its negotiations on the F-35,[58] with Defense Secretary Robert Gates recalling that in 2010, following the sale of F-15SAs to Saudi Arabia, it was argued that the United States was obliged to supply F-35s as they were the only fighters that could ensure an Israeli military edge.[59] Procurement of the F-35 faced significant opposition domestically, with three time Israeli Defense Minister, Foreign Minister, Ambassador to the United States and aeronautical engineer Moshe Arens observing:

> The F-35 development program has been plagued by frequent delays and mounting cost overruns. The design compromises that have to be made to accommodate its goal of serving as a joint strike fighter that will be acquired by the U.S. Air Force, Navy and the Marines have limited its performance capabilities. In the meantime, anti-stealth technology is being developed and may yet neutralise what is being advertised as the aircraft's major advantage before delivery or within its operational lifetime.[60]

Concerns were raised repeatedly regarding the F-35's range, payload and flight performance, all of which were significantly inferior to those of the F-15 and at times viewed as insufficient for future Israeli requirements. This fuelled a majority opposition among ministers to further acquisitions in the mid-2010s.[61] Concerns among IASF officers that the F-35's stealth capabilities would be largely nullified by advances in sensor technologies by the 2030s were reportedly a central reason for the insistence on integrating indigenous electronic warfare systems to mitigate this expected vulnerability.[62] The guarantee of high levels of participation from Israeli industry, allowing local contractors produce a number of F-35 parts for the global network of clients, was confirmed by Defense Ministry Director-General Udi Shani to have been key to allowing the deal to be accepted domestically.[63] The fighter's wings, for example, were manufactured by IAI Lahav, which had previously produced F-16 wings, from November 2014.[64]

Although the American position remained unchanged that Israel would not be able to modify anything in the F-35, the country was uniquely permitted to add capabilities and subsystems to the existing infrastructure. These included command, control, communications, computers, and intelligence (C4I) systems, electronic warfare systems, and indigenous weaponry. General manager of IAI's Lahav Division Benni Cohen referred to this as 'open architecture, which sits on the F-35's central system, much like an application on your iPhone.' Accommodating this also required modifications by Lockheed Martin to areas such as power and cooling.[65] U.S. officials had previously rejected the option of 'Israelis sticking boxes in the airplane,' stating that modifications for specific Israeli mission requirements could be made by Lockheed Martin, but that independent modifications by Israeli firms 'is not an option.'[66*]

The Israeli Defense Ministry ordered an initial batch of 19 F-35As on 7 October 2010, followed by 14 more in February 2015. In April 2016 the state-owned defence contractor Israel Aerospace Industries confirmed that it would install an additional suite of command and control software once the first aircraft were received, with Israel being the only country permitted to modify the aircraft to such an extent. F-35As modified with Israeli avionics were referred to as the F-35I Adir – meaning 'Mighty One' in Hebrew. Where all other operators relied on central U.S.-based facilities for the devising of new code packages, Israeli firms could add additional lines of code on top of the aircraft's existing functionality. Benni Cohen highlighted that this 'doesn't change anything in the aircraft itself, but it gives the Israel Air Force the most advanced and adaptable processing capabilities with relative independence of the aircraft manufacturer ... It introduces a new level of freedom for the IAF [Israeli Air Force], as it paves the way for additional advanced capabilities to be embedded in the F-35I in the future.'[67] The addition of indigenous communications and electronic warfare systems were expected to be primary focuses of these modifications, which would also facilitate integration of indigenous armaments including nuclear bombs onto the fighters.

To support customisation efforts, Lockheed Martin was revealed in May 2017 to be building a unique sub-variant of the F-35A for Israel, namely a single aircraft that would serve as a testbed for local modifications. The head of the IASF's main test centre, Lieutenant Colonel Shlomy, elaborated at the time regarding its purpose: 'This unique aircraft, which was not part of any other F-35 contract, will enable us to begin the work of upgrading the capabilities of this aircraft so that it answers our special operational requirements.'[68] Unique levels of access to the F-35's software and mission systems architecture was speculated to potentially allow Israel to keep its aircraft fully operationally capable even if the country was cut off from the fighter program's global Autonomic Logistics Information System (ALIS), cutting dependence on software updates that came through the ALIS cloud-based network. The importance of self reliance and a continued ability to use military assets regardless of positions taken by allies, including arms embargoes and other measures, had been a key factor shaping Israeli thought on defence procurements since the 1970s in particular.[69] This lesson had been

* An Israeli Air and Space Force general speaking to Aviation Week in February 2009 had stated that, at the time, the lack of industry participation had been the second greatest issue with the F-35, with the first being the aircraft's high cost, and the third being the lack of opportunities for customisation and in particular the integration of indigenous electronic warfare systems. The U.S. had thus made concessions, albeit only partial ones, on each of these issues. The issue of cost, however, would be partly addressed in September 2016 by the particularly generous size of the Obama administration's 10-year military aid package to Israel, which while imposing tight limitations on what portions of funding could go to Israeli industries, ensured that funds were more readily available to acquire American equipment. (*Aviation Week*, 25 February 2009).

Israeli Air and Space Force F-35I. Israel received 362 F-16s from the United States beginning in the late 1970s, a figure which dwarfs its orders for just 75 F-35I fighters as of the mid-2020s. The F-35's significant cost overruns were a primary cause for criticism of the aircraft domestically as orders were being discussed in the 2000s, and ensured that it could not be relied on to provide anything close to a one-for-one replacement for the F-16. One of the consequences has been further stimulation for investment in developing and procuring indigenous unmanned aircraft, which can perform a growing range of missions which the F-16 would have been relied on for in the Cold War era. (IASF)

reinforced just two years before the first F-35s arrived, when a fully independent maintenance capability was used to quickly repair bulkhead cracks in F-16s domestically, allowing them to participate in then-ongoing hostilities with Palestinian paramilitaries in the Gaza Strip.[70]

Israel was able to negotiate for a further mitigation of reliance on the United States for its F-35 fleet by gaining special rights for maintaining, repairing and overhauling both the airframes and the engines domestically, rather than at predetermined logistics centres established by Lockheed Martin. This was done at the headquarters for F-35 operations at Nevatim Air Base in southern Israel. Depot-level maintenance was initially planned by the Joint Program Office to be done in Italy, with IASF Lieutenant Colonel Maxim Orgad stating in 2017 regarding the changes negotiated: 'We will not go to Italy or anywhere else. These aircraft will remain in Israel for whatever they need.'[71] Israeli media similarly repeatedly stressed that unlike other clients, the country's F-35s 'will not leave except for combat missions.'[72] The cost of performing depot level maintenance indigenously for a relatively small fleet was nevertheless expected to be higher than doing so alongside other operators under the oversight of the Joint Program Office.

Following the conclusion of a new 10-year aid package from the United States, Israel finalised an order for 17 more F-35s in August 2017, which would bring the fleet up to 50 fighters to equip two squadrons. The first two F-35s built for Israel would land in the country at Nevatim Air Base on 12 December 2016. Compared to F-15s and F-16s using dated mechanically scanned array radars and far less sophisticated avionics, the F-35 represented a very significant technological leap for the IAF which it took time to adjust to. Shortly after the first F-35s were delivered, Air Force Chief of Staff General Tal Kelman observed that the leap in situational awareness provided was 'inconceivable,' and that when flying the fighter 'the whole Middle East is there for you in the cockpit ... the threats, the different players, at both close range and long range.'[73] The F-35's significant intelligence collection and management capabilities had long been seen as valuable to help mitigate Israel's extreme lack of strategic depth,[74] and was repeatedly referred to as a primary factor in the Israeli Air and Space Force's interest in the aircraft.[75]

Commenting on the shift in the service that the F-35's new capabilities caused, retired IASF Brigadier General Ephraim Segoli observed: 'The F-35 is bringing a new culture. It is a big challenge. Not just a technical challenge, like how we talk, but also how airmen and other branches of the military will use information, in what order, and with what aims.' 'The level of uncertainty is very high,' he added, noting: 'It's very difficult to understand the real potential of this system.'[76] Regarding the scope of the new capabilities introduced, Commander of the Air Force Major General Amir Eshel would observe in August 2017:

> I don't look at it just as a plane and capability ... Before the plane was received, we thought about how to change the air force and adapt it to a fifth-generation fighter, and not the opposite. If we'd done the opposite, we would have only diminished the plane's capabilities. You need to look at it at a system-wide level – not of the plane, of the whole air force. How the F-35 makes the other planes far more effective, the information it shares with them and with our information centers, how they can then do so much more thanks to that information. It goes far beyond the fact that it can operate in places that no other plane can.[77]

An F-35I accompanied by an F-16I of the No. 253 Squadron during its first arrival in Israel in December 2016. (IASF)

Israel Takes the F-35 to War

During the Cold War the Israeli Air and Space Force's fighter fleet had faced significant challenges from the Soviet-supplied fighters, interceptors and air defence systems operated by Iraq, Syria, Algeria, Libya, and until the mid-1970s by Egypt. By the 2010s, however, challenges to Israeli primacy in the air were effectively non-existent. Egypt's shift to using heavily downgraded U.S.-supplied equipment in the 1970s, the disarmament of Iraq in the 1990s, and the NATO-led air assault on Libya in 2011, which ended the country's plans to rebuild its obsolete fleet with new Russian equipment, left only distant Algeria as a highly competitive potentially hostile air power in the Arab world. The successful pressuring of post-Soviet Russia to deny Syrian requests to procure advanced equipment such as MiG-29M fighters, MiG-31BM interceptors and S-300 air defence systems ensured a growing Israeli qualitative edge over the formerly cutting edge fleet of its neighbour.[78] Israel's support for an insurgency in the Syria in the 2010s alongside Turkey, Qatar and several countries across the Western world from 2011 devastated the country's economy and its forces.[79] The F-35 thus entered service when the IASF faced far more limited challenges to its power than had been the case when its first fighters of the third and fourth generations were procured in the 1960s and 1970s.

On 6 December 2017 the Israeli Air and Space Force announced it had achieved Initial Operating Capability for the F-35, making it the third service after the U.S. Marine Corps and the U.S. Air Force to do so. Israel had long been expected to be the first to use the F-35 in combat, with frequent air strikes against Palestinian paramilitaries in the Gaza Strip, and against government forces in Syria, providing multiple options to gain the prestige associated with doing so. The first combat mission was confirmed to have been flown in February 2018. Although details on the timing and circumstances were not provided, the F-35 was still unable to hit moving targets on the ground, among other significant limitations, meaning the kinds of targets it may have been used against were limited. Depending on the exact timing that month, it may have also made Israel the first country other than the U.S. to use fifth generation fighters in combat, with the Russian Air Force having first combat tested prototype Su-57 fighters against insurgents in Syria in the final week of February.[80]

Although Syrian government sources claimed multiple shoot-downs of Israeli fighters had been achieved while repelling IASF air strikes in 2016 and 2017,[81] the publication of footage on 10 February 2018 confirming the shoot-down of an F-16I – which had been Israel's most sophisticated fighter before the F-35's delivery – drew increased attention to the new stealth fighter's perceived importance.[82] Uncertainty regarding unconfirmed reports of other Syrian shoot-downs, and the fact that the confirmed shoot-down was achieved using an ageing S-200 system, further illustrated the vulnerability of the IASF's fourth generation fleet, with the reported delivery of much more advanced S-300PMU-2s to Syria near the end of the year further exacerbating concerns.[83]

Israeli F-35 operations in or near Syrian airspace were seen by some analysts to pose risks to the wider program, as the Russian Armed Forces had from 2015 deployed several of its most advanced surface-to-air missiles and electronic warfare systems in the country. These had the potential to collect significant data on the F-35's radar, electronic and heat signatures and on how the aircraft operated. This was confirmed to have been an issue for F-22s operated by the USAF in Syrian airspace, with Air Force Deputy Chief of Staff for Intelligence, Surveillance and Reconnaissance Lieutenant General VeraLinn Jamieson lamenting that the F-22 operations 'have really just been a treasure trove for them to see how we operate. Our adversaries are watching us, they're learning from us … Russia has gained invaluable insights and information with operating in a contested airspace alongside of us in Syria.'[84] The use of F-22s exclusively for low intensity missions against non-state actors, which limited the kinds of intelligence that could be obtained, combined with the USAF's intention to phase the aircraft out of service much earlier, meant this was a far less serious issue than the potential risk of intelligence being collected on F-35s flying against Syrian air defences.

After its combat debut in early 2018, the Israeli F-35 fleet would continue to participate in combat operations at far greater rates than those of any other country. In March 2021 the aircraft shot down two Iranian Shahed 197 stealth drones over Syrian airspace that had been airlifting supplies to Palestinian paramilitary groups in the Gaza Strip, marking the first time fifth generation fighters had ever engaged in air-to-air combat.[85] Following the outbreak of open hostilities between Israel and Palestinian paramilitaries in Gaza in October 2023, the F-35's operations were strongly publicised by Israeli forces as a symbol of military strength and effectiveness. With the country otherwise relying on fighter and tank designs from the 1970s, the F-35 was by far the most prominent 21st century weapons system in service.

An Israeli Air and Space Force F-35I above the Lebanese capital Beirut. The lack of local air defence capabilities allowed Israeli fighter units to operate freely over the country, with missile strikes against Syrian targets often being launched from over Lebanon to maintain a safe distance from Syrian air defences preceding the government's overthrow in December 2024. (IDF)

On 2 November 2023, footage thought to have been taken by an F-35's helmet mounted display showed the fighter's first ever deployment to intercept an enemy missile. An AIM-9X was fired to intercept a cruise missile fired by Yemeni Ansurullah Coalition forces, which closely resembled one of the Quds series. The decision to engage a cruise missile within visual range drew attention to the prevailing uncertainties regarding the F-35's ability to engage such targets at beyond visual ranges, which was expected to eventually be realised after the program further matured.[86]

In December 2023 American lawmakers and defence officials revealed, in a new wide-ranging hearing on the F-35, that the U.S. had surged supplies and accelerated the provision of upgrades to the Israeli stealth fighter fleet. With the F-35 having become notorious for its low mission capable rates, this surge in parts availability allowed Israeli units to maintain a tempo of operations that was highly uncharacteristic of the fighter type.[87] This in turn highlighted the benefits of the global scale of the F-35 program, which meant that if any one operator went to war, others could sacrifice their own supplies and stockpiles to support that operator for the duration of the conflict. A caveat of this for the fighter's foreign operators was that in a full-scale global conflict, states other than the core partners, and potentially all clients other than the United States, could potentially see their supplies deprioritised.

On 1 April 2024, a missile attack on an Iranian diplomatic building in Damascus killed Revolutionary Guard Corps Brigadier General Mohammad Reza Zahedi, his deputy General Haji Rahimi, and nine others, many of them long serving diplomats. The Iranian ambassador in Damascus, Hossein Akbari, subsequently confirmed that the consulate had been struck by six missiles launched by Israeli F-35s, pledging that Tehran's response to the attack would be 'at the same magnitude and harshness.'[88] Use of air-launched missiles had allowed the IASF to engage targets in Syria without placing its aircraft within targeting range of the large majority of local air defence systems. Twelve days later on 13 April the Iranian Islamic Revolutionary Guard Corps launched multiple waves of cruise missile, ballistic missile and drone attacks on Israeli military facilities. In the aftermath of the strikes, the Israel Defense Forces released footage showing F-35s returning from a mission to intercept enemy targets as part of air defence efforts, the nature of which was unconfirmed. As the Iranian-aligned Lebanese paramilitary group Hezbollah launched artillery strikes to support Iranian attacks on 13 April, F-35s were also deployed to strike its installations in Southern Lebanon.[89] While the extent of the F-35's role remains highly uncertain, prominent displays of the aircraft by state media were seen to be central to Israel's efforts to convey an image of strength to the public in the aftermath of the unprecedented attacks.

As tensions between Iran and Israel continued to escalate, an Israeli-organised assassination on the Chairman of the Hamas Political Bureau, Ismail Haniyeh, took place on Tehran on 31 July. While eyewitnesses at the scene recalled a projectile entering the window of Haniyeh's residence, it was speculated that F-35s could have launched such a missile from near Iranian airspace, potentially refuelling in the air and flying over Azerbaijan.[90] After Iranian officials pledged to retaliate, Israeli F-35s were deployed the following month for a major aerial refuelling exercise alongside F-15s and a Boeing 707 tanker. The fighters 'simulated long-range flight deep behind enemy lines,' and were armed with live weapons.[91]

Following Israel's initiation of an invasion of Southern Lebanon on 1 October 2024, in which F-35s were reported to have played important supporting roles, Iran within hours responded with a large-scale missile and drone attack on Israeli targets later that day, with Nevatim Air Base, which hosted the stealth fighter, being among the sites hit. Israel and commercial companies selling satellite imagery blocked the view of the facility for two days after the attack, fuelling speculation that a clean-up operation was underway to mask the extent of the damage. Satellite images made available from

Israeli Air and Space Force F-35I fighters would see a much greater tempo of operations than F-35s fielded by other services, due to both the small size of the fleet and the country's involvement in multiple prolonged conflicts. Israeli F-16 pilots would note that most missions flown by F-35 squadrons during attacks on Iran in June 2025 were for intelligence collection, with the aircraft providing vital information on hostile air defences, including surface-to-air missile launches, to legacy fighter units, serving as a vital force multiplier for the wider fleet. (IDF)

3 October showed significant damage to Nevatim, although Israel claimed no losses in aircraft or personnel, while Iranian government sources claimed the destruction of 'nearly 20' F-35s.[92]

On 26 October the Israeli Air and Space Force launched strikes on Iranian missile and drone manufacturing sites and air defence systems. Reports of the operation's success again varied drastically, with Iranian sources claiming that the large majority of missiles were intercepted, while unnamed U.S. and Israeli officials, speaking to the *Wall Street Journal*, claimed that the attack was a major success and neutralised three full battalions of S-300PMU-2 long range air defence systems, while 'devastating defence manufacturing sites'.[93] The significant publicity given by Israeli sources to the F-35's involvement appeared intended to capitalise on the fighter's reputation for an advanced combat performance to bolster this narrative.

A number of factors made claims that such a large and critical portion of Iran's air defence network had been destroyed in a few hours appear dubious, including the complex multi-layered nature of the network, its demonstrated combat potential in the past, and the fact that F-35s lacked Block 4 software and the AGM-88G anti-radiation missiles that came with it. To place the claims made in perspective, the Russian Aerospace Forces had struggled to destroy Ukraine's network of Soviet-built S-300PS/PT systems in an almost three-year campaign, and while Israel's F-35s were much more advanced than Russian fighters such as the Su-34M, the S-300PMU-2 was also far more sophisticated and more challenging to neutralise, and was protected by more layers of shorter ranged systems than Ukraine's S-300s were. Russian air defence systems such as the S-300PMU-2 and Tor-M2, which Iran operated, had also demonstrated the ability to intercept modern cruise missiles in Ukraine, which made it unlikely that Israel could have achieved such an absolute victory in a few short hours.[94] The participation of components of S-300 systems at an Iranian military parade in April 2025 further undermined claims of a total destruction of the network.[95]

Had the IASF retained the capability to dismantle the core of a network like Iran's in such a short time, it raised the question of why it had not done so during its dozens of engagements in preceding years with Syria's smaller and much less advanced network, launching only limited strikes. Thus while there was little doubt that the F-35 was the world's most capable fighter for air defence suppression missions, the neutralisation of the core of Iran's advanced network by Israel's relatively small fleet of 37 F-35Is, by fighters still using interim software and weaponry, and in such a short time, appeared unlikely. After the October 1 Iranian strikes on Israel, making such a claim had significant public relations value.

Unrealistic and propagandistic stories both claiming major exploits by Israel's F-35s, and claims of successful attacks on the aircraft, began to emerge shortly after they were first received. This reflected the fighter's position as the leading symbol of Israeli military power. Georges Malbrunot, a journalist a *Le Figaro*, claimed that French intelligence sources had informed him that during the night of 12 January 2018, when Israel had fielded just two F-35s, that the aircraft had bombed targets in Damascus. They were reported to have targeted warehouses containing Russian-made Pantsir-S1 air defence systems and destroying an S-300 battery deployed near the Syrian presidential palace on Mount Qassioun, before overflying the palace of Syrian President Bashar Al Assad in a show of force. Other than the fact that these two F-35s lacked even the basic Block 3F software, and that Syria did not field S-300 systems, the likelihood of the aircraft being so quickly deployed for such a high-risk mission remained negligible. The narrative nevertheless had all the hallmarks of a typical propaganda piece, from 'buzzing the dictator's palace,' to rendering advanced Russian equipment useless.[96] Pro-Syrian

Surface-to-air missile launcher from Iranian Air Defence Forces Bavar-373 long range air defence system. (Iranian MoD)

sources had a few months prior claimed that an Israeli F-35 had been damaged by an S-200 system, which was also considered highly unlikely.[97] Israel's deployment of the F-35 highlighted the significant importance that was attributed to perceptions of military power, the conflict between narratives surrounding advanced weapons systems in the information space, and the difficulties posed by the growing dissemination of fake news in judging the performances of various systems. As predicted by analysts at *The National Interest* in October 2017, regarding the 'rumour mill' surrounding Israel's F-35s, unconfirmed and unlikely claims of Syrian air defence successes and Israeli deep penetration strikes were 'just the beginning.'[98]

Unconfirmed reports of F-35I operations against Iran, and of Iranian successes combating the fighters, would again emerge after Israel initiated twelve days of open hostilities between the two countries with a combined air and ground assault on strategic Iranian targets on 13 June 2025. F-35s were claimed by multiple sources to have operated deep inside Iranian airspace to strike vital targets, ranging from underground nuclear facilities, to bunkers housing leadership figures in Tehran. Iranian government sources meanwhile claimed the shootdowns of four F-35s, three of them using the indigenous Bavar-373 long-range surface-to-air missile system. The capabilities of this system were a significant variable regarding which little open source information was available, with Iranian military sources asserting the performances of the latest variants matched or surpassed those of the Russian S-400 – a claim that was widely questioned. Considering the quantities of relatively advanced air defence systems Iran fielded, and the significant time the defenders had to prepare for attacks, even if Iranian claims of four shootdowns were true, it would have represented a remarkably low attrition rate for Israel's small F-35 fleet when required to quickly operate very deeply inside hostile territory without a prior sustained campaign to destroy local air defences. The fact that Israel's fourth generation fleet was largely obsolete, and had not been comparably modernised as those of other major F-35 operators were, only placed more pressure on the stealth fighters. Although only limited verifiable open source information on the engagements was available, they were almost certain to have been closely studied by major militaries across the world, including both operators of the F-35 and other fifth generation fighters, and countries that could potentially face similar attacks by such advanced aircraft.

Japan and Taiwan: Northeast Asia's Stealth Fighter Arms Race

The sudden and unexpected appearance of China's J-20 fifth generation fighter on 21-22 December 2010, followed by its first flight on 11 January 2011, appeared to take the United States and its strategic partners by surprise, and occurred at a time when no countries in East Asia had placed orders for fifth generation fighters. With the futures of other leading regional fleets remaining highly uncertain, unexpectedly rapid progress in the J-20's development was considered a leading factor in stimulating interest from Western-aligned regional actors in procuring the only similarly advanced fighter available, the F-35. Having previously shown little interest in the F-35, eleven months after the J-20's first flight the Japanese government in December 2011 announced its intention to procure 42 F-35As. Lockheed Martin had from July that year offered final assembly of the fighters in Japan and a domestic maintenance, repair and upgrade capability,[99] and had in October been reported to be offering a much greater workshare to Japanese industry including the right to manufacture major components and assemble the F135 engine. It remained uncertain at the time whether the F-35s would be fielded in only a limited number of units, namely to replace Japan's approximately 78 remaining F-4E fighters, or whether they would play a larger role in the fleet.

The F-35's development was reported by a number of sources to have benefitted significantly from U.S. participation in the Japanese F-X program in the 1990s, which produced the F-2 fighter as an enlarged and heavily enhanced derivative of the F-16. The program had leveraged Japan's leadership in electronics, radar and composite materials technologies to pioneer more extensive use of composites in the airframe, and to produce the world's first fighter built with an AESA radar. Washington was reported to have driven a hard bargain to obtain all the new technologies Japan developed for the program in return for American support. As observed by Japanese lawmaker Shintaro Ishihara: '[in the 1990s] our Foreign Ministry and other Government agencies decided it was better to eat humble pie than incur Uncle Sam's wrath on yet another bilateral issue ... we give away our most advanced defense technology to the United States but pay licensing and patent fees for each piece of technology we use.'[100] Although reports on the importance of technologies from the F-2 program to the American fighter aviation sector have varied widely, the technology areas in which the F-2 program helped pioneer the most significant advances were all of central importance to the F-35 program.

Japan had been considered the leading potential client for the F-22 in the 1990s and 2000s, as a direct successor to its large fleets of F-15C/D and F-4E fighters, although with the aircraft suffering from wide ranging issues, and subsequently banned from export, the country was left with no politically viable options for a high-performance long-range air superiority fighter other than procuring newer F-15s. The F-35 had previously not been favoured due to the Japan Air Self-Defense Force's extreme focus on air defence duties, with the aircraft optimised for offensive penetration strikes of enemy airspace, and representing a significant downgrade from the F-15 in terms of its speed, altitude, radar size, weapons carrying capacity and range, while having far lower availability rates. The development of the J-20, however, added considerable urgency to plans for the procurement of a fifth generation fighter, ending the possibility of waiting until an indigenous or joint air superiority fighter could be developed to succeed the F-15, and leaving the F-35 as the country's only option to avoid being left behind once the J-20 entered service.

After the J-20 entered service in February 2017, five or more years ahead of Western projections, Japan's cabinet was on 18 December confirmed to have voted to expand the country's F-35 order to 147 fighters, including 42 F-35Bs. This ensured that the F-35 would replace the F-15C/D to form backbone of Japan's fighter fleet for decades to come.[101] The $23.11 billion order for 105 more F-35s, including 63 F-35As and 42 F-35Bs, was the largest arms export deal in world history, and placed Japan entirely in a league of its own among the F-35's overseas clients in terms of the number ordered. No other foreign client had ordered half as many of the fighters at the time, while by the middle of the next decade the second largest order, namely Canada's order for 88 fighters, was over 40 percent smaller in terms of fighter numbers and was comprised exclusively of the cheaper F-35A variant.

Japan had previously similarly been by far the largest client for the F-15, acquiring 213 aircraft from 1980-1999, of which 199 were produced domestically, and had also been a leading client for the F-15's predecessor the F-4 procuring 140 from 1971-1981, of which 138 were assembled locally. Other than Saudi Arabia, Japan had been the only country that had financed very large procurements of the F-15 to form the backbone of its fleet, rather than part of a high-low combination. This made the Japan Air Self-Defense Force the only service that benefitted from reduced operational costs when transitioning units to the aircraft from its primary fourth generation fighter.

The procurement of 48 F-35Bs was initially expected to facilitate operations on islets in the East China Sea and Sea of Japan, including possibly the Senkaku/Daioyu Islands disputed with China. It was subsequently revealed in February 2018, however, that the country's two 27,000 ton Izumo-class carriers had been built from the outset to be able to accommodate the F-35B, indicating that procuring the aircraft had long been planned.[102] Officials had notably denied such speculation early on in the program, with the ships accordingly referred to as 'helicopter destroyers' to avoid allegations that the country was developing an offensive naval capability.[103] With F-35Bs reported to have been ordered for the Japan Air Self-Defense Force, however, it remained uncertain whether these could be transferred to the Maritime Self-Defense Force or whether they would be jointly operated by the two services.

Alongside Japan, the J-20 program also played a significant role in stimulating interest from the Republic of China Air Force (RoCAF), the official name of the air force of Taiwan, to procure F-35s. With Taipei remaining technically in a state of civil war with the rival Chinese government in Beijing, the Republic of China Ministry of National Defense had as early as the 2000s made multiple attempts to purchase F-35s from the United States, with these intensifying as the J-20 program matured.[104] Eight months after the J-20 made its first flight, Deputy Minister of National Defense Andrew Yang in September 2011 visited the United States and reiterated that Taipei sought to procure F-35s.[105]

Acquiring sophisticated armament from the United States had since 1974 been a far from straightforward process for Taipei, with the Republic of China government having a status close to that of a non-state actor with its territory recognised by the United Nations and all UN member states including the United States as part of China. With the Republic of China's constitution asserting Taipei's jurisdiction over all Chinese territory, rather than over a separate state on Taiwan, this alongside Taipei's lack of any UN

Japan was the only F-35 operator that procured the aircraft primarily to replace a fighter type that was significantly heavier and more costly to sustain, namely the F-15J of which it fielded over 200. This F-15J was photographed while flying next to a KC-135 tanker over the Okinawa area. (USAF)

An F-35A of 302nd Squadron, Japan Air Self-Defense Force. Japan is set to become by far the largest foreign operator of the F-35, with delays to planned procurements of sixth generation fighters in the 2030s reported in early 2025 to have raised interest in further orders for F-35As. (JASDF)

recognition only made arms sales more controversial. Under both the George W. Bush and the Barak Obama administrations, Taipei was thus denied access to the F-16C/D. Although efforts to procure F-35s were renewed almost immediately after the Donald Trump administration's inauguration in January 2017,[106] with this gaining growing support in Washington as rhetoric against Beijing continued to escalate,[107] by April 2018 it was clear that such a sale would not materialise.

The fact that RoCAF pilots had, on multiple occasions, defected to the mainland in Western aircraft, and that strong pro-mainland sentiments remained among much of the population, raised the possibility that any information the service had on the F-35 would quickly be forwarded to Beijing.[108] Unable to procure the F-35 for the RoCAF, efforts were subsequently made to procure the F-16 Block 70/72, with an $8.2 billion contract for 66 aircraft signed in December 2019. Despite the F-16 purchase, there remained several indications that the Taipei would continue to seek to procure the F-35. At the hearing of the legislature's Foreign Affairs and National Defense Committee on 23 September 2019 Minister of National Defense Yen De-fa stated regarding RoCAF modernisation plans: 'according to the military's projected threat assessment, we will need F-35s in the future.'[109] Questions regarding the J-20 and its capabilities largely dominated discussions. Following the second election of Donald Trump as president, Taipei was reported in November 2024 to be planning a renewed effort to procure the F-35 as part of 'a very aggressive package of American hardware.'[110]

One of the requirements of the J-20 program from the 1990s had been to be able to comfortably outperform the F-35 in air-to-air combat, in part due to the expectation that F-35s could be fielded by the RoCAF from around 2015. With mainland China in December 2024 becoming the first country in the world to unveil sixth generation fighter prototypes in flight, however, these aircraft were likely to become operational before any F-35 deliveries to the RoCAF were possible, ensuring that the mainland's significant qualitative edge in the air would be sustained. Indeed, the expected induction of the mainland's first sixth generation fighters into service around 2030 closely coincided with the expected delivery of the last F-16s to the RoCAF, by which the time type would have been operational for 52 years. Thus while the F-35 program had strengthened the standings of the fleets of America's strategic partners across much of the world compared to their potential adversaries, its delays and the restrictions on its export had contributed to moving the RoCAF from a position of technological parity with the mainland in the fourth generation era, to likely falling two generations behind in the 2030s.

South Korea: Shifting the Goalposts in a Controversial Procurement Process

On 18 June 2012, the Republic of Korea Ministry of National Defence's deadline for receiving proposals for the F-X III fighter tender passed, leaving three combat aircraft including the F-15SE,* the F-35A and the Eurofighter Tranche 3 in the 8.3 trillion won ($7.7 billion) competition. Senior South Korean officials claimed that the F-X III was aimed at keeping up with regional states' deployments of fifth generation fighters, following Japan's orders for the F-35A and China's unveiling of the J-20 and J-35.[111] A central focus of the tender was to ensure transfers of technologies for the indigenous KF-X fifth generation fighter program.[112]

From the outset of the tender the U.S.-South Korea alliance, and the benefits of interoperability with American F-15s and F-35s deployed in East Asia, were seen to leave the Eurofighter with little chance of being selected. This was aside from the fact that the medium weight fourth generation fighter was very comfortably behind the competition, with its combination of a comparable cost to the F-35A, higher than that of the F-15, its use of an obsolete mechanically scanned array radar, and its lack of stealth capabilities, seriously limiting its appeal. Airbus Defence and Space, which pitched the fighter, had notably argued for it on the basis that the

* Boeing had sought to make the F-15 more attractive by pitching the enhanced F-15SE variant from 2009. The aircraft integrated a conformal weapons bay, stealth coatings and twin vertical tails canted 15 degrees outward to provide limited stealth capabilities, and while still far less stealthy than the F-35, it combined this with the F-15's inherent significant performance advantages such as an approximately 50 percent larger radar and triple the missile carrying capacity. The aircraft's avionics, including its APG-63 (V)3 AESA radar, new digital flight control and electronic warfare systems sought to narrow key performance gaps with the F-35A.

F-35 was not well optimised for air-to-air combat, and had been developed primarily as a strike fighter, where the Eurofighter was a more well balanced aircraft designed with a greater focus on air superiority missions. 'The U.S. has developed the F-22 as a dominant air superiority fighter and plans the F-35 mainly for strike missions,' Senior Vice President of Eurofighter sales Peter Maute stated to this effect.[113] Despite this difference in specialisation, however, the significant discrepancy in sophistication between the aircraft guaranteed an overwhelming performance advantage in the air-to-air domain for the F-35.

The most significant factor in the F-15SE's favour was that South Korea had recently placed orders for 60 F-15K fighters after Boeing won the preceding F-X I and F-X II tenders, and manufactured 40 percent of the aircraft domestically. Selecting the F-15SE was expected to built on this partnership to provide more benefits to local industry, while the fighter would maintain 80 percent commonality with the F-15K.[114] The perceived need for a fifth generation level capability, however, resulted in the F-35 being strongly favoured from the outset, as it had been in all tenders in which it participated, with the selection of the fighter confirmed on 22 November.

The Republic of Korea Air Force's preference for the F-35 was such that, when Lockheed Martin could not offer the aircraft at a sufficiently low price meet the F-X III's budget, the conditions were changed to cut the number of fighters by one third from 60 to 40. Had this not been done, the F-15SE would have been the de-facto winner as the only fighter that had met the tender's cost requirements. While the F-35A's procurement costs would be lower than those of the F-15 or Eurofighter when it competed in later tenders, in 2013 the fighter's projected production costs to begin early delivery to South Korea were still far higher. Lockheed Martin's agreement to transfer technologies and provide communications satellites were cited as key factors to justify the decision domestically, reversing the de-facto selection of the F-15SE.[115]

The selection of the F-35 caused not insignificant controversies, with details coming to light after the Board of Audit and Inspection of Korea launched a probe into the process in 2017. When summoned, Defense Minister Kim Kwan-jin revealed that the decision to reject the F-15 was influenced by 'political judgement,' with interpretations of this statement varying widely.[116] The government's failure to penalise Lockheed Martin after it failed to implement the launch of five South Korean military satellites as part of F-35 offset deals, or to pay $28 million in owed damages for delivery delays, was a further point of controversy.[117] The U.S. government and Lockheed Martin had also reportedly agreed to transfer 21 key technologies to support the KF-X program. After the contract was concluded, however, Washington in 2017 blocked the transfer of AESA radar, IRST, electro-optical targeting pod and radio frequency jammer technologies, which was yet another point of contention.[118] The handling of the tender was also criticised for making the preference for the F-35 too clear from the outset, and thus failing to place pressure on Lockheed Martin to offer more favourable terms as Boeing had been made to under the F-X I and F-X II tenders.[119]

The nature of domestic politics in South Korea ensured that issues surrounding new weapons programs often received much greater public exposure than they did in other states, with the F-35 being no exception. Controversy surrounding the F-35 grew significantly in October 2022 after Shin Won-min, a member of the National Assembly's National Defense Committee, obtained and publicised data on the fighter's performance. Covering a period of 18 months from January 2021 to June 2022, the data showed that Republic of Korea Air Force F-35As suffered from 234 flaws, including 172 'non-flying status (G-NORS)' and 62 'cannot perform specific mission status (F-NORS)' cases. 117 flightless and 45 mission-specific failures in 2021 saw little improvement in the first half of 2022, with 55 and 17 failures of these respective types occurring over six months.[120]

While F-35s had already caused considerable scandals in the United States for their much lower availability rates than fourth generation fighters worn out by decades of use, in South Korea the F-35's specific mission failure rates were notably more than twice those of the country's Vietnam War era F-4 and F-5 third generation fighters. This had significant implications for the country's warfighting capabilities, with Shin Won-min warning: 'The F-35A was introduced with a very large budget to solve the issue of obsolete fighter jets and strengthen combat effectiveness against North Korea. In the case of the escalation of North Korea's nuclear and missile threats, it cannot be permitted that this core combat force cannot function properly.'[121]

An inspection in June revealed that issues with avionics had forced an immediate cancellation of flights, just one a month after an F-35 was sent to maintenance due to abnormalities in its fire controls. These incidents followed a belly landing in January, after a fighter's landing gear refused to open.[122] These were only a few of several recent cases disclosed. Such issues had taken F-35s out of service for periods ranging from a few days to several months, which according to defence experts 'added to existing questions regarding how viable

A Republic of Korea Air Force F-35A escorting a U.S. Air Force B-2A bomber. (USAF)

the aircraft would be in a wartime situation when high reliability is vital.'[123] 'Although there may be an abnormality in a certain model or a component problem, the F-35A's situation is particularly serious,' a South Korean military official reported anonymously to local media. One Air Force source defended the F-35's record, however, by asserting that operations could become smoother and less problematic over time.[124] Although follow-up orders for 20-25 more F-35As were reported to be imminent multiple times from late 2017, the fact that such an order would only be placed six years later in December 2023 was speculated to be due to the issues the fleet was suffering and the perceived importance of ordering more reliable aircraft from later production batches.

The United Arab Emirates: Fighter Sales as Political Leverage

From the early 2010s the United Arab Emirates (UAE) showed a growing interest in procuring the F-35. The country had emerged as a leading American strategic partner in the Persian Gulf, and was the only Arab state to have participated in six U.S.-led coalition missions since the Gulf War. While the Obama administration from 2011 consistently rebuffed requests for a preliminary briefing on the fighter, under the new Donald Trump administration USAF Vice Chief of Staff Stephen Wilson would confirm in November 2017 that preliminary talks were taking place.[125] Alluding to the widespread deployments of American fifth generation fighters in the country, Assistant Undersecretary for Support Services at the UAE Ministry of Defence Major General Abdullah Al Hashimi at the time commented: 'We in the UAE already live in a fifth generation environment; so acquiring the F-35 fighter jet is only a step forward to cope with the fifth generation mindset.'[126]

The possibility of sales to the UAE highlighted the degrees of control which could be exercised over the F-35 by the United States to ensure that its use did not contravene American interests, which had consistently been a leading requirement when supplying advanced armaments to Arab states. Officials from 2017 raised the possibility that Lockheed Martin could create a new version of both ALIS and the aircraft's on board software with further capability reductions to those currently being offered to other clients, which would ensure a qualitative edge for Israel, Turkey and Western Bloc states.[127] Analysts at *Military Watch Magazine* observed that 'control over software codes, the fighter's extreme reliance on the U.S.-centred Autonomic Logistics Information System, and the maintenance requirements and "just in time" logistics system which leave the F-35 particularly vulnerable to spare parts shortages, all ensure that Washington would have little trouble grounding the fleet.' This would leave the F-35 'effectively useless' for missions seen to be against American interests, with the downgrading of software and limitation of the kinds of weaponry available, such as denying access to the AIM-260, providing options for further insurance.[128] Not only were the risks from making a sale limited, but a further significant point, which was raised by President Trump regarding arms sales to Arab gulf states more generally, was that as they were not locked firmly into Western alliance or trading systems, they could look to Chinese or Russian competitors if Washington was overly restrictive in the armaments it provided.[129] This would not only cost the American defence sector market share, but would also undermine Western, Turkish and Israeli interests, as non-Western fighters would not be downgraded and could thus more seriously challenge these countries' own F-35s.

Although possible sales to the UAE drew attention to the issue, the F-35 program's ability to provide the United States with unprecedented influence over the security situations of clients across the world due to its highly centralised nature had been alluded to for years. As observed in a *Foreign Policy* article by Jonathan Caverley from the U.S. Naval War College and his associates in July 2019: 'Imagine a globe-spanning economic and security project — with a cost of over a trillion dollars and whose members encompass 46 percent of the global economy — designed to advance the interests and influence of the lead state, even as it binds the smaller ones into an asymmetric interdependence.'[130] The F-35 program 'makes a state's very security reliant on the United States for decades— and Washington uses that leverage,' the article noted, citing as an example Washington's suspension of Israel's access to the program in 2005 'in retaliation for Israel selling drone parts to China,' which led Tel Aviv to quickly reverse its position.[131]

ALIS could be used to limit or block clients' access to critical data such as software patches, could be used as a counterintelligence tool to tightly monitor operations such as when, where, and how F-35s were being flown, and provide a range of other advanced safeguards to curtail F-35 operations should these be seen to be against U.S. interests. Analysts at *The War Zone* observed regarding the example of the UAE:

> [I]f the geopolitical environment in the Middle East were to change dramatically, pitting Israel and the UAE against each other for some reason, it would likely be far easier for

A U.S. Air Force F-35A operating from Al Dhafra Air Base in Abu Dhabi alongside a United Arab Emirates Air Force F-16 and Mirage 2000 during the F-35's first deployment to the country in April 2019. (USAF)

> the United States to limit the latter country's ability to use its F-35s. The U.S. government could quickly halt access to vital software updates and logistics support or even launch an active cyber attack on the ALIS terminals in the Emirates to try and disable the aircraft or certain core functions.[132]

On 29 October 2020, following the UAE's establishment of diplomatic ties with Israel, the White House announced the intention to sell 50 F-35As to the country, with a formal notification then sent to Congress on 10 November regarding a $23 billion sale of F-35s and accompanying systems. The UAE signed the deal on 20 January 2021, which reportedly gained final approval from the Trump administration just one hour before its term expired. Having made efforts to procure the F-35 for over a decade, Abu Dhabi would make the highly unexpected decision in December 2021 to withdraw from talks on procurements, which raised questions regarding the terms that had been attached to the sale.

Multiple sources reported that the UAE's withdrawal was a result of Washington's insistence that the country cease its close cooperation with the Chinese telecoms giant Huawei, including ending plans to install the firm's 5G infrastructure, as a precondition for F-35 sales.[133] Analysts at the *National Interest* observed: 'When it came to choosing between the most advanced American fighter jets or China's 5G technology, the United Arab Emirates decided on 5G. After the United States refused to budge on technical requirements and "sovereign operational restrictions," according to one Emirati official, the deal for up to fifty F-35s was cancelled in December 2021.'[134] The choice to sustain ties with Huawei over an opportunity to procure the F-35 was described as a 'fresh blow' to Washington.[135] Although it was claimed that Huawei's infrastructure would place the F-35 program at risk, Huawei 5G infrastructure is widely used in F-35 operating countries such as Germany and South Korea, while USAF F-35s had already been stationed in the UAE and other countries that widely used this infrastructure.

While the F-35 had never lost a tender against a competing fighter, forcing a country to choose between the most prolific product of the world's largest defence contractor, and the most prolific technology of the world's largest telecoms giant, had led to the F-35's rejection. The use of the F-35 to seek to secure concessions from a potential client related to its commercial activities highlighted the diverse political ends that the fighter program often served. Indeed, the fighter was directly referred to by *Foreign Policy* in 2019 as America's direct equivalent to China's Belt and Road initiative, as the program allowed Washington to exert influence internationally in much the same way that China was alleged to be doing with its infrastructure development program.[136] After pulling out of talks for the F-35, the UAE would subsequently show growing signs of looking to Chinese alternatives, and quickly went on to order Chinese L-15 lightweight fighters, before in July 2024 participating in unprecedented joint aerial warfare exercises with the People's Liberation Army Air Force.[137] An image of UAE and Chinese defence officials holding talks with a large image of J-20 fighters in the background in April that year fuelled speculation that discussions regarding fifth generation fighter acquisitions were underway.[138]

After Abu Dhabi's withdrawal from talks, Washington's tremendous leverage over F-35 clients, including its ability to disable their fighters remotely using ALIS among other means, would gain renewed attention in early 2025. Threats by U.S. officials to leverage Ukraine's reliance on American satellites to disable its communications and precision guided weapons fuelled concerns in Germany and other European states that Washington could similarly threaten to disable their F-35s as a means of providing leverage. As observed by former President of the Munich Security Conference Foundation Wolfgang Ischinger, there was a possibility 'that the U.S. could do with future German F-35s what they are

U.S. Air Force F-35A and Russian Su-57 prototype at Aero India 2025. (Aatish Pilai via X)

currently doing with Ukraine.'[139] Head of communications at German defence company Hensoldt informed the local paper Bild at the time: 'The "kill switch" in the F-35 is more than just a rumour,' and could be achieved using its mission planning system to ground the aircraft.[140] Other experts would observe that European states' extreme reliance on the United States for communications support, for electronic warfare support, and for ammunition resupply made a 'kill switch' redundant.[141] Although this had seldom been an issue for countries in the Western world due to their close strategic alignment with Washington, it remains a particularly significant issue for non-Western states which were less fully aligned with the United States.

Unprecedented controls on the export of the F-35 and restrictions on how the aircraft could be utilised were expected to result in a more limited number of international clients compared to its direct predecessors the F-16 or the F-5, despite the lack of any technologically near-peer competitors outside China. Not only were a significant number of clients for the F-16 unwilling or unable to transition to the F-35 as a result, but the stealth fighter's appeal to new clients that had not previously used American fighters was also limited. India was the most notable example, with the limited level of autonomy permitted, and Washington's strong tendency to impose sanctions and arms embargoes that leveraged clients' reliance on its equipment, having been considered leading factors that prevented the F-35 from being seriously considered when it was pitched to the country.[142] The F-35's inability to gain traction in countries that were not fully aligned with the U.S. was a key factor allowing non-American fighters with lower combat potentials and cost effectiveness, such as the French Rafale, to continue to compete for orders, with the fighter being selected by Egypt, Indonesia, the UAE and India, which would all have otherwise likely selected the F-35 had it been offered under similarly non-restrictive terms. This was also considered a leading factor advantaging the Russia Su-57 when both fighters were offered to India in 2025.[143]

9

THREAT ENVIRONMENT: THE F-35 IN A FUTURE WAR

China's J-20 Program: The F-35's Peer Level Challenger

On 14 March 2022, the F-35 was confirmed to have seen its first known encounter with another fifth generation fighter, which marked the first ever encounter between stealth fighters from opposing sides.[1] Commander of the U.S. Pacific Air Forces (PACAF) General Kenneth Wilsbach reported that this had occurred over the East China Sea, and seen F-35s encounter Chinese People's Liberation Army Air Force (PLAAF) J-20s. The Chinese fighters were likely deployed by 1st Air Brigade at Anshan Air Base, which had operationalised them in January 2021.

Providing rare insight into prevailing thought in the USAF on the PLAAF's stealth fighter, Wilsbach recalled regarding J-20 operations: 'What we're noticing is they are flying it pretty well. We recently had – I wouldn't call it an engagement – where we got relatively close to the J-20s along with our F-35s in the East China Sea, and we're relatively impressed with the command and control that was associated with the J-20s.'[2] His assessment followed a Defense Department report to Congress referring to the J-20 as having 'high manoeuvrability, stealth characteristics, and an internal weapons bay, as well as advanced avionics and sensors providing enhanced situational awareness, advanced radar tracking and targeting capabilities, and integrated EW systems.'[3] Speaking to Wislbach at the time, former PACAF Vice Commander Lieutenant General (ret.) David Deptula predicted: 'clearly fifth generation aircraft are going to become increasingly important in the Pacific.'[4] The J-20 had by that time emerged in a league of its own with the F-35 as its only peer level rival in terms of the sophistication of their capabilities, with the development of each program heavily shaping the other.

In the aftermath of the Soviet Union's sale of Su-27 fighters to China in 1990, it had been expected that Beijing would be able to continue to rely on Moscow to provide world leading combat jets. This changed over the following years as the Russian economy, defence sector, and broader tech sector declined rapidly, while work on its fifth generation fighter programs came to a halt. Despite the far more militarised state of the Russian economy, which spent over twice and very often more than three times as great a percentage of GDP on defence as China did, Beijing overtook Moscow in defence spending in 1994-1995, had doubled its defence budget by 1998, and reached close to triple by 2009, while exceeding four times the Russian budget in 2018.[5] The discrepancies in industry and high-tech were far greater still, with Russia largely evolving into a rentier economy heavily reliant on exports of primary goods such as fossil fuels, while China rapidly emerged as a world leader in high tech.[6] Thus although the USSR had enjoyed a lead over China of more than 20 years in its combat aviation sector when the state disintegrated in 1991, by 2000 China already appeared to be in a much stronger long term position to develop a world leading stealth fighter.

Some of the best insights into the early goals of China's first fifth generation fighter program, known in the United States at the time as the J-XX, were provided by a paper titled the *Strategic Study of China's Fighter Aircraft Development.* This appeared to have been written sometime between 1996 and 2003, and highlighted that in the face of American work towards fielding a high-low combination of fifth generation fighters, which later became the F-22 and F-35, the J-XX needed to be able to match the F-22 and comfortably outperform the F-35 in air-to-air combat. The paper made clear that the program was focused on air superiority and beyond visual range engagements.

The first publicly released images of China's fifth generation fighter showed it conducting runway tests on 21-22 December 2010, shortly after the decision to terminate F-22 production. Pentagon sources were quick to downplay its significance, with Director of Naval Intelligence Vice Admiral David Dorsett assuring that China was still a long way from fielding an operational fifth generation fighter.[7] Pentagon spokesman Colonel Dave Lapan asserted that Chinese military aviation was still technologically far behind, and dismissed the program as 'not of concern.'[8] Defense Secretary Robert Gates at the time questioned 'just how stealthy' the fighter really

J-20 from early production batch at the 2018 Zhuhai Airshow. (垂直风行 on Weibo)

The J-20 makes its first public demonstration of high manoeuvrability at the Zhuhai Airshow in 2018. (China Military Online/Wang Weidong)

was,[9] then conceded that 'they may be somewhat further ahead in the development of that aircraft than our intelligence had earlier predicted.'[10]

A number of sources interpreted the J-20's unveiling with greater concern, with a paper in the *Strategic Comments* journal observing, 'The J-20 should be considered within this broader context, rather than as China's riposte to the U.S. Air Force's F-22 Raptor or as an F-35 Joint Strike Fighter "killer."' It concluded: 'It is clear that the West's recent comparative neglect of crewed next-generation combat aircraft has not been mirrored completely by other major powers.'[11] Richard Fisher, a military scholar specialising in China's armed forces, highlighted the significant possibility that the J-20 would be able to outperform the F-22. 'Since World War II, the American military has never gone into battle without the assurance of air superiority. China is a rising power, and it is determined to challenge the American position globally. This fighter will allow them to do that on a military level,' he stated. Fisher highlighted the need for a significant response including 'developing an advanced version of the F-22' and pursuing 'another rework' of the F-35 to make it competitive with the new Chinese jet.[12]

The J-20's first demonstrator airframe made its first flight on 11 January 2011, with the program subsequently surpassing all Western expectations of its performance. While Western analysts widely predicted the aircraft would take another ten years to enter production, indicating a service entry date of around 2022, this would be achieved in under half the time. Following the flight testing of two demonstrators, the first prototype was unveiled in October 2012, and featured redesigned air intakes, a reshaped canopy, an additional inner frame, and an electro-optical targeting system resembling that of the F-35. There were overall eight demonstrator and prototype flight airframes built for the program before serial production began, compared to eighteen for the F-22 and sixteen for the F-35, with all the J-20's pre-production aircraft making their first flights within under five years.[13] Serial production began in 2015,[14] followed by the first flight of a serial production airframe on 18 January 2016, with deliveries to the Air Force then beginning sometime before August,[15] shortly before the first USAF F-35A became operational.[16] The first J-20 unit formally entered service in the People's Liberation Army Air Force in March 2017.[17]

The J-20's development was particularly concerning for the United States when considering the advanced positions of the tech sector and the industrial base which developed it. By 2020, Chinese entities were gaining leads in a growing number of technology areas and filing nearly 50 percent of all patent applications worldwide – over twice as many as those in the United States – with this proportion continuing to expand quickly.[18] The country's technological lead was increasingly widely acknowledged from the late 2010s by experts and policy think tanks in the West,[19] with the country found in an Australia Strategic Policy Institute study in 2023 to be outpacing the rest of the world in 84 percent of technology research areas with critical security applications.[20] Thus while it was open to speculation whether the J-20 or the F-35 was the more advanced fighter, the standing of China's tech sector supported the conclusion that the aircraft by the mid-2020s would be at least comparably advanced to its American counterpart. China's demonstrated ability to operationalise new technologies much more quickly, and to make incremental upgrades much faster, provided a further edge. This also placed the East Asian state in a strong position to potentially gain a distinct advantage in the sixth generation era of fighter aviation, with the Chinese and American combat aviation industries starting work on such aircraft from a far more equal position, in contrast to the fifth generation where the U.S. had started with a technological lead of over 20 years.

The J-20 was designed as a heavyweight twin engine air superiority platform of comparable size to the F-22, and uses a distinctive lift-body leading edge root extension canard configuration, with canards facilitating the use of much smaller wings for significantly reduced supersonic drag, while ensuring a high turn performance by avoiding compromises to transonic lift-to-drag characteristics. The unique canard delta wing design with twin outward canted all-moving fins improved flight performance, including both low-speed agility and supersonic manoeuvrability, providing particularly excellent control over angles of attack, with canards optimised for stealth particularly in the forward sector. While initially hampered by reliance on an enhanced variant of the Russian AL-31 engine as a stopgap, an enhanced supercruise capable variant of the J-20 entered service in January 2021 using the new WS-10C engine. The WS-15 engine was confirmed to have entered serial production in March 2023, and would provide the J-20 by far the highest thrust of any fighter type in the world, a range comfortably exceeding double that of the F-22 or F-35, and a supercruise speed of close to or over Mach 2.[21] The engine would equip a new further enhanced variant of the J-20 with significantly superior stealth capabilities.

As both programs matured in the early 2020s, the J-20 and F-35 were increasingly seen to be each other's sole peer level challengers in terms of production scale, rates of incremental upgrades, and most importantly in their sophistication. The J-20's avionics were considered on par with the F-35's in terms of sophistication, with the use of similar electro-optical distributed aperture systems being among the features that set both apart from other fighters. The J-20's Type 1475 radar was not only considered similarly sophisticated to the AP/APG-81, but was also larger, with between 2,000 and 2,200 transmitting/receiving modules, compared to 1,600 on the American radar. [22] Much like the F-35, the J-20's cockpit design and helmet mounted display were optimised to allow pilots to better process data from onboard and offboard sensors and benefit from information fusion.*

The J-20's service entry just six years and two months after its first demonstrator flight, where the F-22 and F-35 had taken 15 years, was a notable indicator of how quickly the program was progressing. Production reached close to 80 fighters in 2023, 100 in 2024, and 120 in 2025, allowing the PLAAF to procure new J-20s at over twice the rate that any other air force procured any other fighter – 2.5 to 3 times the rate the USAF received F-35s. A separate fifth generation fighter, the J-35, which although lighter than the J-20 was still much heavier and longer ranged than the F-35, was reported to have begun entering service in 2025, and would further widen the gap between China and the United States in the size of their stealth fighter procurements. The program produced both a carrier based fighter for the People's Liberation Army Navy, and a land based variant aimed at export markets, raising the possibility that fighters with cutting edge fifth generation capabilities could begin to proliferate to potential American adversaries.

The challenge posed by the J-20 to the U.S. Armed Forces in the Pacific is particularly significant due to the wide range of advanced supporting assets developed to operate alongside it. The KJ-500 airborne warning and control system provides a significantly more modern counterpart to the USAF's E-3 Sentry, and has been produced on a significant scale and incrementally modernised quickly. The unveiling of a larger system in 2024, the KJ-3000, made the PLAAF the only air force with a high-low combination of such systems. These are complemented by a wide range of other ground based, maritime, and elevated sensor assets with outstanding design features, such as the unique WZ-9 high altitude drone which combines two side-looking conformal radar antenna and an ultra-wide dual-band central radar specifically optimised to countering stealth aircraft.[23] Electronic warfare support is provided by a range of specialist assets such as the J-16D electronic attack jets and WZ-10 electronic reconnaissance drones. While China's lead in AI R&D provide it with advantages in drone autonomation, surveillance and battle management,[24] its lead in quantum technologies also allowed it to form the world's first, and to date the only, major quantum communications network, with the first quantum satellite, Micius, launched in 2016.[25] This provides major advantages for communications security, and a further major edge for J-20 units. Thus not only is the J-20 a fully peer level fighter, but its network of supporting assets in a growing number of areas appears to excel in ways that networks supporting the F-35 do not.

While the F-35 had begun development in the post-Cold War era, when there had been a general consensus in the United States that a peer level challenge to air superiority would not emerge again, the J-20 was developed by an emerging technological and industrial leader which was far less complacent, and which attributed tremendous importance to the ability to defend its airspace from possible Western encroachments. The J-20

* As much as the J-20's very high standing as an air superiority fighter was a result of Chinese advances, it was equally a consequence of the failures in the United States and Russia, with the latter having failed to complete MiG 1.42 and pursued the Su-57 as a far less ambitious program, and the former having failed to develop the F-22 into a fully viable successor to the F-15. This had provided China with a window to develop the J-20 into the world's premier fighter for air-to-air combat. The J-20's entry into service marked the first time since the 1940s that a fighter from outside the United States or Russia could be considered a leading contender for the title of the world's most formidable in an air superiority role.

A close-up view at the wing-tip, centre fuselage section, and the cockpit of an J-20A. Visible in the background are two J-16s. (天砺剑 on Weibo)

A potent and growing threat: cockpit section of a J-20A stealth air superiority fighter of the PLAAF. (空天砺剑 on Weibo)

PL-10 in firing position. Not only is the PL-10 a much newer design that the AIM-9X that is considered more capable, but the F-35's inability when in stealth configuration to carry any visual range air-to-air missiles remains one of its most significant weaknesses if required to operate as an air superiority fighter. (白龙_龙腾四海 on Weibo)

Chinese People's Liberaiton Army Air Force KJ-500 airborne warning and control system. The lack of a comparably modern system in the U.S. Air Force has been a primary factor disadvantaging the F-35A fleet in the Pacific. (China Military Online/Gao Hongwei and Zhang Bin)

A U.S. Air Force Boeing E-3 Sentry AWACS . Despite significant updates, the type's ageing avionics, and its low availability rates as a result of decades of wear on the airframes, led to significant urgency being attributed to the need to field a more capable successor. Delays and uncertainties regarding the financing of a successor have ensured that the discrepancy between the American and Chinese support fleets will continue to grow. (USAF)

epitomises China's emergence as a fully peer level power in combat aviation, and potentially the next global leader, which is a game changer for the F-35 program in terms of what will be required of it going forward. A combination of the J-20's potency, and the F-22 program's very major shortcomings, has forced the F-35 program to increasingly emphasise the provision of an air-to-air combat capability against very high performing fifth generation level challengers – a mission very different from those it had been primarily designed for.

F-35 Training and the Fifth Generation Challenge in the Air

The J-20 program was the central factor stimulating a significant increase in the U.S. Armed Forces' F-35 fleets' focus on preparation for possible engagements with adversary fifth generation fighters. One consequence was the USAF's reactivation of its 65th Aggressor Squadron – a unit intended to simulate the capabilities of enemy fighters to provide dissimilar 'red on blue' air combat training. The announcement of plans to do so in May 2019 followed scathing reports, including a post-audit report in April from the Department of Defense Inspector General, on the state of pilot training and in particular its lack of relevance to facing 21st century challenges.[26] The aggressor unit was activated in June 2022 at Nellis Air Force Base, which was the Air Force's leading facility for test training. The high demand for F-35s elsewhere in the Air Force, however, meant only 11 fighters were allocated to the aggressor squadron, with these coming from deeply flawed early production blocks that were not expected to ever be viable for frontline operations.

The fighters flown by the 65th had long provided an indicator of which fighter types the USAF saw as the most pressing challenge. The aggressor unit had previously flown the F-5E/F to simulate advanced variants of the Soviet MiG-21, before transitioning to the F-15 in 2005 to simulate the capabilities of the Su-27 and its derivatives. The decision to equip the unit with F-35As provided a clear indication that provision of training against fifth generation level threats would be its primary role. The unveiling of the unit's F-35s in a colour scheme closely resembling one used on the J-20 in

June 2022 provided further confirmation of the squadron's purpose, and followed the previous use of a colour scheme closely based on that of Russian Su-27 units to paint the unit's F-15s.

Regarding the use of F-35s to fly red air – a term for the simulation of adversary capabilities in 'red on blue' training engagements – commander of the 65th Aggressor Squadron Lieutenant Colonel Brandon Nauta would reveal that 'F-35s have been flying as red air since the inception of the program,' but that forming a dedicated F-35 aggressor squadron still had important benefits. 'The 65th AGRS [Aggressor Squadron] now allows us to do this professionally and in a more organised manner. We will be able to provide the combat air forces (Joint and Coalition), a standardised replication template so we are all training at the same level,' he stated a month after the squadron's official reactivation. His unit aimed to achieve an Initial Operating Capability around January 2023.[27]

As part of further efforts to train against stealth fighters, the USAF in November 2020 begun using a training program developed by firms Red 6 and EpiSci that projected seemingly real AI-flown J-20s onto pilots' augmented reality helmet-mounted displays.[28] This was intended to prepare pilots before they faced

A F-35A of the 65th Aggressor Squadron in colours mimicking those of the J-20 of the PLAAF. (USAF)

A pair F-35As from the 65th Aggressor Squadron in colours mimicking those used in some J-20 units. (USAF)

USAF 'red air' F-35s in aggressor training. F-35s were used to provide aggressor training for the first time in August 2021 as part of Red Flag exercises at Nellis Air Force Base. Commander of the 64th Aggressor Squadron at Nellis, Lieutenant Colonel Chris Finkenstadt, stated regarding the exercises: 'Based on our focus toward great-power competition, we need to make sure that those [blue air] guys are ready, and we do that by presenting the best possible atmosphere we can.' An Air Force press release indicated that 'red' units won 'a lot of red air victories' in early simulated clashes, which was expected to change as counter-stealth tactics improved.[29] The value of training against stealth aircraft was such that the Head of Air Combat Command Air Force General Mike Holmes in June 2020 raised the possibility of allocating F-22s from older production blocks to aggressor training,[30] while from August 2020 retired F-117s flown by private contractors also began to be used for such training.[31]

F-22s were notably included on 'blue' teams tasked with tackling 'red' F-35s, with Captain Patrick Bowlds, who flew F-22s at Red Flag, stating: 'Having them [F-35s] on red air adds a level of complexity to an already complex scenario.' 'When you have a stealth platform on red air, it makes our job a lot more difficult in terms of knowing where they are, how we are going to protect allied forces or protect points on the ground or whatever the mission set is at that point in time,' he elaborated, adding that 'it is challenging, even flying the Raptor, to have good [situational awareness] on where the F-35s are.'[32] The use of 'red' F-35s to train fighter pilots in counter-stealth tactics, including in 'blue' F-35 units, was notably mirrored in China, where the J-20 was used in

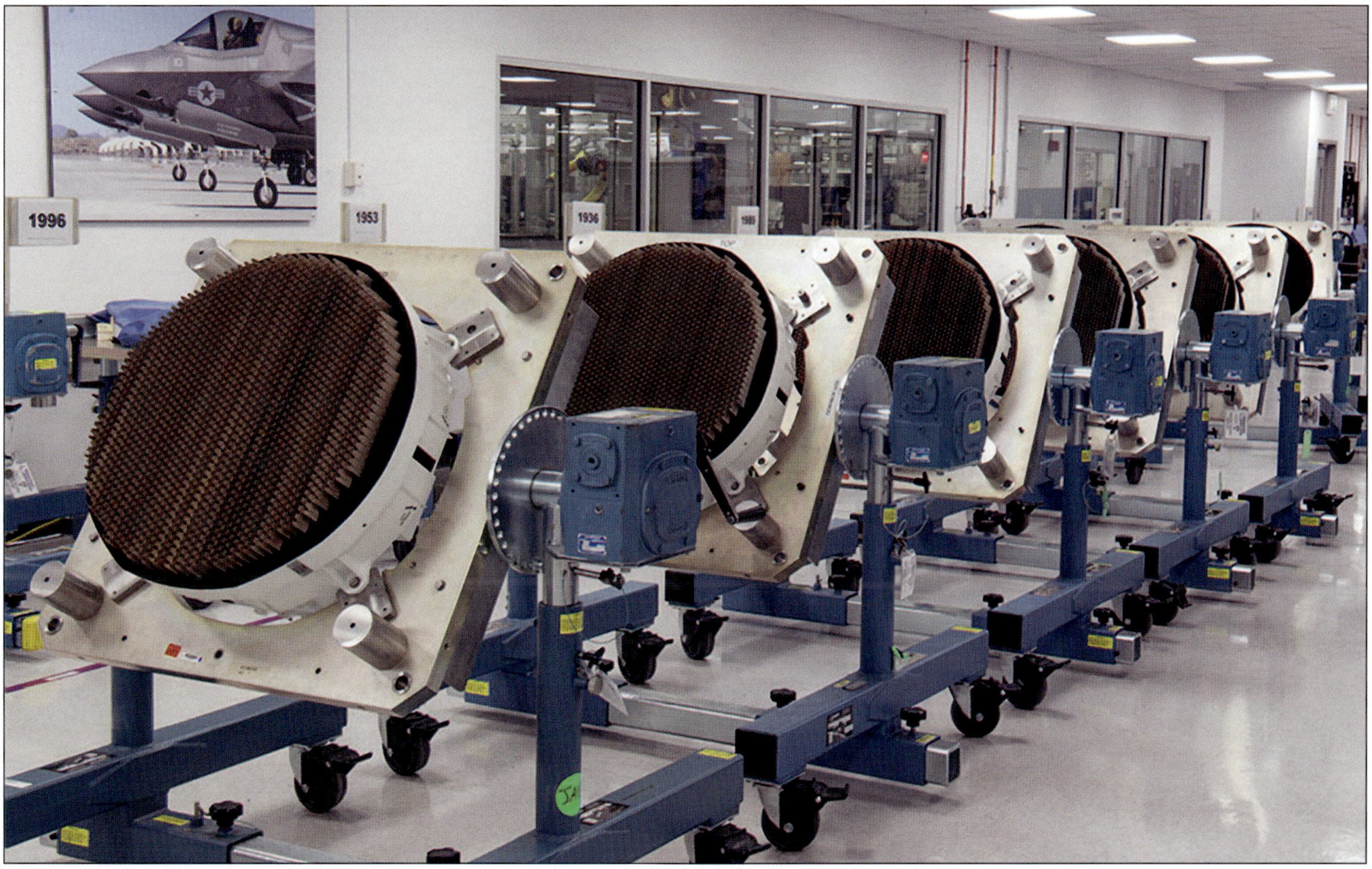

The first batch of AN/APG-85 radars. These advanced multifunction sensors were planned to be compatible with all F-35-variants, and capable of 'defeating all current & projected air & surface threats.' By the middle of the 2020s, problems with their research and development were threatening the entire schedule to upgrade the F-35. (Northrop Grumman)

similar simulated engagements to provide experience in fighting against stealth aircraft.

Responding to Chinese Advances: Accelerated Enhancement of the F-35

The implications of the new perceived threat to American air dominance posed by the J-20 program, and by China's combat aviation sector more broadly, stimulated changes in the F-35 program that went far beyond training. The F-35's much newer airframe design and avionics provided it with greater potential for modernisation than the F-22, with continued production allowing enhancements to be incorporated as part of incremental modernization between production blocks. This made the F-35 the only fighter outside China which appeared to have the potential to keep up with the rapid advances in the J-20 program.

In January 2023 it was confirmed that production of the AN/APG-81 radar, previously planned at over 3,000, would be cut to little over 1,000, and that a new radar, the AN/APG-85, would be put into service in the mid-late 2020s. This was expected to go a long way towards bridging the gap with the J-20's newer and much larger Type 1475 radar. Delays to the F-35's development had allowed many new technologies to mature since its radar was designed, with the AN/APG-85 expected to operationalise many of these to improve reliability, electronic warfare performance and situational awareness. Operationalising a Gallium Nitride based system provided one option to significantly ease conflict between signal strength and power usage. The new radar's developer, Northrop Grumman, described it as one which would 'help ensure air superiority,' providing some indication as to what primary arguments had been made to justify the program.[33] With the J-20 itself benefitting from continuous incremental improvements to its sensor suite, equipping the F-35 with the most capable primary sensor possible was particularly vital.

Concerns in the United States regarding the capabilities of the J-20's primary air-to-air armament, the PL-15 radar-guided missile, were widely reported to be the primary factor stimulating investment in new and more capable air-to-air missile types for the F-35. Operationalised in 2015-2016, the PL-15's range estimated at between 250km and 300km was longer than that of any air-to-air missile in the U.S. Armed Forces service, with this facilitated by a dual-pulse rocket motor.[34] A two-way datalink provided guidance updates to both the PL-15 and the launching fighter. As noted in a 2018 report by the International Institute for Strategic Studies, the PL-15's use of an AESA radar ensured 'improved performance against low-observable targets and greater resistance to countermeasures on target aircraft, such as radio-frequency jammers.'[35] The Chinese missile's apparent superiority over its top American counterpart, the AIM-120D, was met with alarm by U.S. officials, with the head of the Air Force's Air Combat Command Herbert Carlisle remarking in September 2017: 'Look at our adversaries and what they're developing, things like the PL-15 and the range of that weapon … How do we counter that and what are we going to do to continue to meet that threat?' He emphasised in an interview the following day: 'the PL-15 and the range of that missile, we've got to be able to out-stick that missile.'[36] Experts at *Aviation Week* described the PL-15 as having 'quickly provoked the U.S. Air Force to launch a new air-to-air missile program for the for the first time since the 1970s.'[37] Development of a successor to the AIM-120, the AIM-260, was initiated secretly in 2017 and announced in 2019, with officials directly referring to the program's initiation as a response to the PL-15.[38]

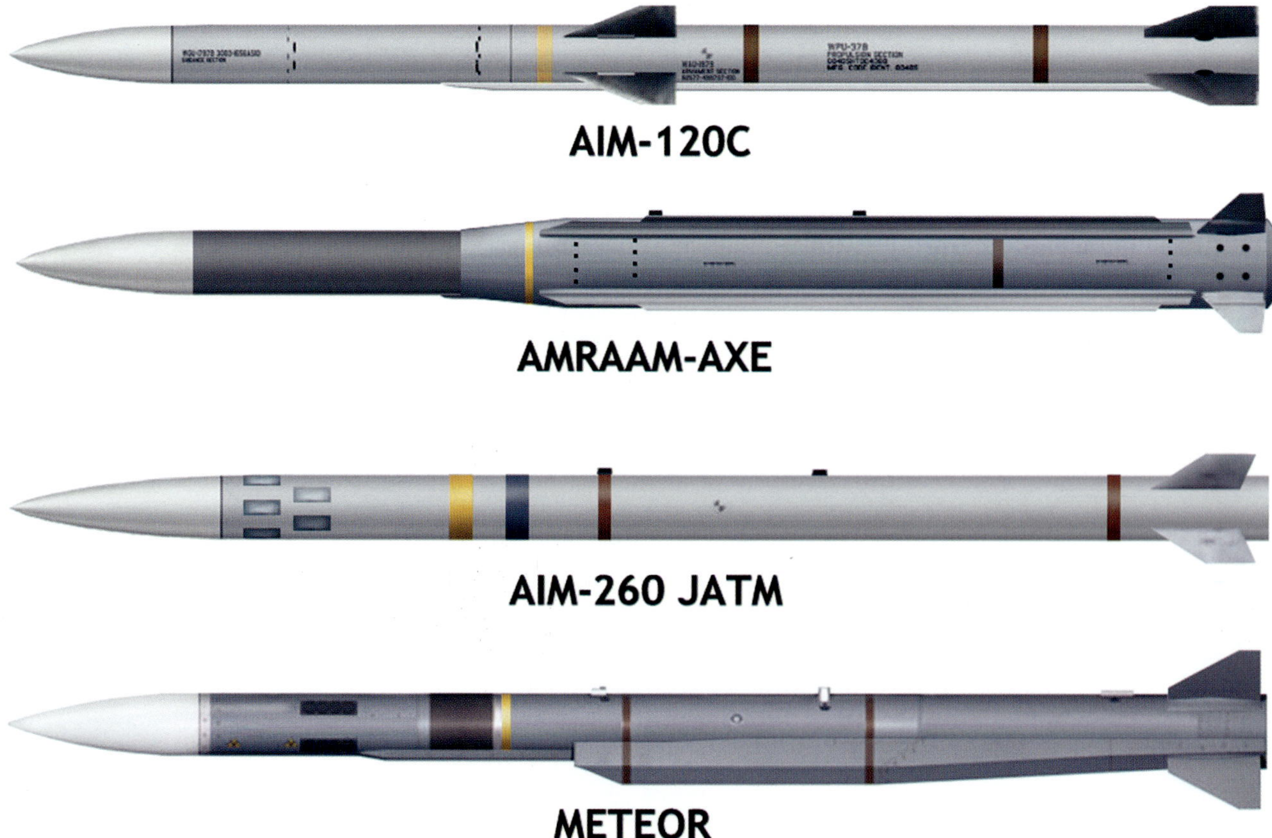

A profile of the AIM-260, in comparison with the proposed AMRAAM-AXE extended range AIM-120 variant, and the F-35's current primary air-to-air missile, the AIM-120C, and the Meteor. The dimensions of each allow them to be accommodated in the F-35's internal weapons bays. (Artwork by Tom Cooper)

While official Air Force statements confirmed that the AIM-260 was 'needed to remain ahead of adversary air threat investments,' it was intended to complement, not replace, the AIM-120, likely due to the unaffordability of acquisitions in comparable numbers.[39] An improved AIM-120D variant, the AIM-120D3, was thus also prioritised for rapid development to help narrow the performance gap with the PL-15. Pressure on the American defence sector to develop more capable primary armaments for the F-35 further increased as China brought a successor to the PL-15, the PL-16, into service in 2024-2025. Senior Fellow for Military Aerospace at the International Institute for Strategic Studies Douglas Barrie projected in early 2025 that alongside an AESA radar, the missile would feature 'Mach 5-plus fly-out, a lot of very capable onboard software, and be very resistant to jamming.'[40]

The J-20's secondary air-to-air armament, the infrared-guided PL-10, was also seen to provide it with an advantage over the F-35, with reports from the British Royal United Services Institute highlighting that the missile had a 'superior kinematic performance to the American AIM-9X Sidewinder,' which was the most capable in the American arsenal.[41] The missile used thrust-vector controls and a gimbaled imaging infrared seeker, and could engage aircraft beyond 90 degrees off-boresight. Its performance was speculated to also stimulate investment in a new visual range missile in the United States, since many aspects of the AIM-9X's design including its rocket motor, fusing system and warhead were several decades old. With the F-35 unable to carry such missiles when configured for stealth, however, its disadvantage within visual ranges would remain overwhelming.

Contrasting to the complacency seen in the F-35 program's first two decades, the J-20 program added considerable urgency to efforts to enhance the American stealth fighter's air-to-air performance, ranging form integrating 'sidekick' missile racks to improve the F-35A and F-35C's internal missile payloads by 50 percent,[42] to further enhancing the fighter's already world leading electronic warfare capabilities.[43] The rate at which upgrades were developed for the F-35 in the mid-2020s bore a sharp contrast to the F-22 program during its own time in production, with the aircraft having seen relatively few changes due to the USAF's far greater complacency in its qualitative edge at a time when no non-American fifth generation fighters were even in their prototype stages. The J-20 program was also seen to be a central factor stimulating efforts to narrow the gap in range and flight performance by developing a successor to the F-35's F135 engine, and in particular in supporting calls for development of an ambitious clean sheet engine design under the Adaptive Engine Transition Program (see Chapter 7).

The F-35 and the AIM-260 were far from the only programs to be heavily influenced by the J-20's progress, with a notable example being the U.S. Navy's decision to integrate infrared search and tracking systems onto its primary fighter the F-18E/F, albeit with not inconsiderable difficulties.[44] The challenge posed by the J-20 was also a primary factor spurring USAF investment in acquiring a new generation of airborne warning and control systems to provide a superior detection capability against the Chinese stealth aircraft. PACAF Commander General Kenneth Wilsbach notably stated in March 2022 regarding the first encounter between F-35s and J-20s that the Air Force's E-3 Sentry AWACS in the region were suffering significant obsolescence issues, strongly implying that as a result during the encounter 'our early warning aircraft could not see the J-20.' 'Those sensors that we rely on [on] the E-3 aren't really capable in the 21st-century especially against a [stealth] platform like the J-20 or something similar to that. It just can't see those platforms far enough out to be able to provide an advantage to the shooters,' Wilsbach elaborated, stressing that 'that's why I would like to have the E-7.' This was aside from maintenance issues which he emphasised seriously affected availability rates, and often meant PACAF had no E-3s available.[45]

The E-7 Wedgtail was selected as the successor within a year of Wilsbach's statement, and integrated far superior electronics and sensors. Funding for the aircraft was an unexpected new addition to the Air Force's budget, with the relatively sudden nature of the decision being interpreted as an indication that it was made as a response to a new perceived threat.[46] After Wilsbach also pointed out the potency of the command and control associated with the J-20, at a time when China was rapidly expanding its fleet of airborne warning and control systems and incrementally enhancing the aircraft at a considerable rate, the continued reliance on the obsolete and often unavailable E-3 threatened to place F-35s in the region at a very significant disadvantage.[47] It was expected that the E-7s procured would be prioritised for deployments to the Pacific, and within reinforcing range in Alaska.

The Russian Air Defence Challenge

By the mid-2020s, the standing of America's top fighter units relative to those of potential adversaries was markedly different from that of the Cold War, and was in many respects more favourable. This was largely due to the advances made by the F-35 program. While medium- and long-term technology and industrial trends were much less favourable vis-a-vis China than they had been vis-a-vis the USSR, and the standing of the F-35 against the J-20 was far from favourable, China did not widely export its advanced fighters. While the USSR proliferated its top fighters widely, from China and Vietnam to Syria and Algeria, Poland and East Germany, and as far west as Cuba, China lacked comparable networks of closely aligned strategic partners with advanced aerial warfare capabilities. As a direct result, in any scenario other than a war with China itself, F-35s were expected to face much lower resistance from enemy aviation than F-104s, F-4s, or F-15s would have in their respective eras serving as America's premier fighters.

While China has not widely proliferated advanced fighter aircraft, modern Russian fighters are relied on by a number of potential adversaries, with derivatives of the Su-30MKI fielded by Algeria, Belarus and Myanmar among others, while the Su-35 and Su-57 were in early 2025 confirmed to have been ordered by Iran and Algeria respectively. Russia's offering of the Su-57 for export, which is expected to find clients across the world including many in potential conflict zones, will also raise the possibility of clashes between these aircraft and F-35s fielded either by the United States or by one of its many clients. Lacking fully peer level capabilities to the most capable Chinese and American competitors, however, Russian fighters have been designed with a strong focus on working alongside and complementing large networks of ground-based air defence systems. The Russian Aerospace Forces and the fleets of many of its security partners will thus seek to engage F-35s on favourable terms in or near friendly airspace where they will work alongside ground based assets. The challenge posed to the F-35 by Russian fighters in the air-to-air domain is thus closely linked to the stealth jet's primary mission of suppressing enemy air defences.

Russia's ground-based air defence network deploys a particularly large array of radars that operate in the L-band, which are optimal for detection of low radar cross section targets. The widespread deployment of F-35s surrounding Russian territory, including in Northeast Asia, the Arctic, and in Eastern Europe, has made the detection of the fighters a primary mission for these systems. They include the Voronezh early warning radar system, which was developed to detect incoming intercontinental range missiles and space targets up to 6,000 kilometres away, and smaller systems including the Rezonans-N, Nebo-M, and the 92N6 from the S-400 system. Russia's Su-35 and Su-57 fighters also respectively integrate N036B-1-01 and N036L-1-01 L-band AESA radars into their wing roots, which are intended to provide a further detection capability against stealth fighters alongside their electronic warfare applications.

L-band and S-band radars are valued for their ability to provide a degree of early warning against stealth targets, including F-35s,

This and next page: Four of the key parts of the Russian ground-based air defence network. RLM-M mobile L-band AESA radar antenna from a Nebo-M radar system (top). 64N6E2 Mobile 3D phased-array long-range surveillance and target acquisition radar system (above). Surface-to-air missile launchers from an S-400 system (above). Surface-to-air missile launcher from an S-500 system (below, next page). (Russian MoD)

and are also particularly difficult to jam. Russian sources have consistently highlighted the capabilities of these radars to claim that their country's air defence network can counter threats from the F-35 and other stealth targets, with an example being the claim by the head of the air defence specialised Almaz-Antey Corporation, Yan Novikov, regarding the Nebo-M L-band system: 'The Nebo-M radar is the menace of stealth technologies. It can see F-22, F-35 and so on perfectly well.'[48] A critical limitation of L-band systems, however, is that they are unable to be used for targeting, with this requiring lower C, X, and Ku band radars which fighters such as F-35s are much better able to evade. Such lower waveband radars can only lock onto very low observable targets like the F-35 at much more limited ranges, with the Russian S-400 system estimated to only be able to lock onto F-22s or F-35s at ranges of 50 kilometres, despite being able to detect them significantly farther away.

A number of factors can improve the ranges at which successful targeting is possible, as well as the reliability of targeting. The use of L-band and S-band radars to maintain awareness of the direction

of the target, and concentrate shorter waveband radars in that direction, can help to improve effectiveness. The use of multiple radars in a range of medium and shorter wavebands, preferably widely spaced out both across the ground and in the air, can very significantly increase detection ranges. The S-400 system, for example, uses the 91N6E S-band panoramic radar with a claimed detection range of 150 kilometres against stealth targets, and can deploy multiple shorter ranged radars such as the I/J-band 92N6 and C-band 96L6. These are all networked with larger radars, such as the L-band Rezonans-N and the S-500's 77T6, and with smaller ones deployed by shorter ranged systems, such as the BuK missile system's H/I-band 9S35M1 or the S-350 missile system's X-band 50N6A. When seeking to lock onto and neutralise stealth fighters, the effectiveness of pairing dispersed advanced radars operating in multiple frequencies with a sophisticated signal processing capability to track and target advanced stealth aircraft at longer ranges remains uncertain, but has been assessed by multiple sources to likely be high.[49]

Although Russia fields a small fleet of airborne warning and control systems, Russian fighters play a greater role in strengthening the broader air defence network's ability to engage stealth aircraft, and on average carry much larger radars than their Western counterparts. The Su-30MKI's N011M radar, for example, weighs approximately 650 kilograms, compared to the around 135kg for the F-16's AN/APG-83 and 220kg for the F-35's AN/APG-81. The MiG-31BM interceptor's N007M radar weighs around 1,000 kilograms, leading the MiG to be referred to by state media as 'its own AWACS', the value of which has been demonstrated in the Ukrainian theatre.[50] These widely deployed large sensors are highly complementary to the ground-based radar network, and may have the potential to facilitate targeting of F-35s at significant ranges when networked together. Russian air defence systems' ability to engage targets at 400 kilometre ranges using targeting data from aircraft has reportedly been demonstrated in the Russian-Ukrainian War,[51] raising the possibility that air defence systems could pose threats to stealth fighters even if missile launch vehicles are at very distant locations.

It remains highly uncertain whether F-35s paired with supporting assets such as E/A-18G electronic warfare aircraft can render Russian air defence networks almost totally ineffective, whether Russian networks can cause extreme attrition among F-35 units leaving them unable to operate in or near the country's airspace, or whether the outcome will be somewhere in between. With the United States having very heavily focused its investments in aerial warfare assets on stealth fighters optimised for air defence suppression, while Russia has focused investments on ground-based air defence networks heavily optimised to neutralise stealth fighters, the consequences of any major kinetic engagement between them will have major strategic implications for both sides.

The potency of the F-35 in air defence suppression has been widely attested to, with the fighter reported in 2021 to have flown 16 simulated offensive counter air missions in which it eliminated 100 surface-to-air missile sites without any losses. The nature of test conditions and of the simulated targets, however, remains unknown.[52] The F-35's electronic warfare systems and sensors, in particular its passive antenna array, are considered to provide it with a significant advantage in this role even compared to other aircraft of its generation.[53] Elaborating on the means by which F-35 units could seek to neutralise Russian and allied ground based networks, former Marine F-35 pilot Marine Major Dan Flatley observed: 'Adversaries have to build a kill chain,' with lower waveband systems relied on to execute the remaining parts of this. 'We're not trying to prevent every aspect of that chain, just snap one of those links ... I don't need to stop everything all the time. I just need to make you unable to finish what you've already invested tons of time and money and effort in trying to shoot me down.'[54] Using the F-35's powerful electronic warfare suite to jam the seekers in Russian surface-to-air missiles, or jamming missiles' data links with ground-based radars guiding them, were among the many options which could be attempted.

The challenges faced by the F-35 in a hypothetical conflict with Russia notably differ significantly by region, and while ground-based air defence systems are heavily concentrated in the country's western regions, their coverage is significantly more limited in the country's vast Arctic and Far Eastern territories. The MiG-31 interceptor was developed by the Soviet Union specifically to protect these regions, which are otherwise almost totally undefended from the air. If facing the F-35, the MiG-31BM has the advantage of deploying a significantly more powerful N007M radar, which although technologically over a decade behind the AN/APG-81 is close to five times the size. The interceptor's primary armament, the R-37M air-to-air missile, is close to three times as large as the AIM-120, which combined with the aircraft's much higher operational altitudes and cruising speeds, provides an engagement range over twice as long at 400 kilometres. The R-37M's 61-kilogram warhead and Mach 6 speed make it particularly difficult to evade.

Even when operating in dispersed flights and sharing data, MiG-31BMs are expected to struggle to detect F-35s at anywhere near

A Russian Aerospace Forces MiG-31BM interceptor, as seen armed with R-77-1 (under the wing) and R-37M air-to-air missiles. Unique aircraft-identification markings have been obscured by the Russian military censor. (Russian MOD)

the distances needed to make use of the R-37M's range advantage, while the aircraft's limited manoeuvrability and very high radar cross sections ensure they will be more vulnerable to radar guided missile targeting by F-35s than vice versa. The Russian interceptors can nevertheless threaten F-35 operations by targeting aerial tankers at well beyond the ranges at which the stealth fighters can retaliate, with the R-37M being particularly well optimised for such roles. Although deployed much more sparsely than in the Soviet era due to severe budgetary restrictions, MiG-31s can thus provide an asymmetric means for Russia to defend its vast northern and eastern territories that exploits the F-35's limited range. The deployment of MiG-31K and MiG-31I strike fighters to the Arctic, which have an air-to-surface engagement range of over 800 kilometres, also raises the possibility that bases hosting F-35s will be singled out for targeting, which again circumvents the need to engage the stealth fighters directly. With plans to develop a successor to the MiG-31 under the MiG-31M and Izdeliye 701 programs cancelled, while the more recent PAK DP program faces consistent delays and an uncertain future, the ageing interceptors are expected to be relied on well into the sixth generation era.

Beyond Russia, significant networks of ground based air defence systems are deployed by other potential adversaries, with some such as Algeria and Belarus making procurements from Russia directly, while China and North Korea have benefitted from significant transfers of Russian technologies to eventually develop systems with comparable sophistication domestically. In China's case, indigenous systems such as the HQ-9B are likely to have a number of performance advantages over their Russian counterparts in areas such as sensors and data links, reflecting the much more advanced position of the country's industry and tech sector. North Korea benefits from a far greater density of air defence system deployments, reflecting the fact that while its peacetime defence spending is estimated at only around 5-10 percent that of Russia, the Russian Aerospace Forces have 140 times as large a territory to defend, while purchasing power factors strongly in the East Asian state's favour. The fact that F-35s have far fewer basing options in the Pacific from which to operate against the country, while North Korea has a wide variety of missiles pointed at all such facilities with options for chemical and nuclear warhead deployment, further complicates the issue.[55]

The Pyongae-6 long range system which forms the backbone of the North Korean air defence network has been assessed to provide a broadly equivalent capability to the S-400, and had demonstrated sophisticated features such as missiles with twin rudder controls and double impulse flight engines.[56] The system's predecessor the Pyongae-5, which entered service in 2017, was credited in an assessment by CSIS that year with having causing 'the loss of the edge the U.S. has enjoyed in the use of air and cruise missile power' in Korea.[57] A particular difficulty F-35 units are expected to face in the event of conflict is that North Korean radar and surface-to-air missile units are heavily fortified underground, and rely on lifts to raise them to surface, and to then withdraw them to relative safety. This has the potential to seriously limit the utility of anti-radiation missiles such as the AGM-88G, which carry only relatively small payloads.[58] Whether North Korea's combination of advanced strike capabilities against bases across the Pacific, with a particularly dense network of heavily fortified and sophisticated ground based air defence systems, will seriously limit the F-35's utility, or whether the American stealth fighter will be capable of sustaining operations from dispersed locations and dismantling the North Korean network, remains highly uncertain.

Tyranny of Distance: Facilitating Long Range Operations

A leading challenge faced by the F-35 fleet, and by Western fighter fleets more generally, is their relatively short ranges, which while adequate in Europe remains highly restrictive in the Pacific, and

Surface-to-air missile launchers from Korean People's Army Air Force Pyongae-6 long range air defence systems. This system, along with the preceding Pyongae-5 introduced in 2017, is considered to have transformed the capabilities of the already extremely dense network of air defences deployed to protect North Korea's small airspace. (Korean Central News Agency)

to lesser extents in the Middle East. Chinese and Russian fighters on average not only carry much larger radars, but also have much longer ranges than their Western counterparts, with comparisons of the Su-30SM, J-11B and J-20 that make up the backbones of the former's fleets, with the F-35, F-18E/F and F-15 in the latter's, effectively illustrating this point. While Western fourth generation fighters have been able to mitigate this issue by frequently deploying with external fuel tanks, which is far more common for Western fighter units than for Chinese or Russian ones, the F-35's stealth profile means this is not possible without seriously compromising its combat potential. The central importance of the Pacific Theatre to U.S. and allied interests, and the strong concentration of F-35s in the region, makes the fighter's limited range a particularly serious deficiency, much as is the case in the Arctic.

To place the ranges of the Pacific in perspective, airbases in Hawaii are located 4,000 kilometres from the American West Coast, with Wake Island another 3,700 kilometres away. The flight from Wake Island to Guam is a further 2,400 kilometres away, while the distance from Guam to the Philippines is another 2,600 kilometres. By contrast, the two leading hubs of the USAF presence in Europe, RAF Lakenheath in the United Kingdom and Ramstein Air Base in Germany, are little over 600 kilometres apart, with the latter facility located little over 1,000 kilometres from nearest Russian border. An abundance of usable airfields between Ramstein and Russian territory provides wide ranging forward basing options, in contrast to the Pacific where friendly airfields are scarce and the large majority are separated from Chinese and North Korean territory by vast seas and oceans.

The first deployment of the F-35 to East Asia provided an extreme example of the difficulties of operating the aircraft in the theatre. To fly ten F-35Bs from Marine Corps Air Station Yuma in Arizona to Marine Corps Air Station Iwakuni in Japan in January 2017, nine tankers were required to provide 250 total mid-air refuellings, or an average of 25 per fighter, despite six overnight stops being made on the way.[59] Although the F-35B had a 29 percent smaller fuel capacity than the Air Force's F-35A, and the new and problematic jets had a particularly safe flight path selected that minimised possible risks, the difficulties of operating F-35s in the Pacific were nevertheless immense.

The F-35 and F-22 were designed around the expectation of near constantly available close proximity aerial refuelling support, much like that which USAF fighters heavily depended on in the Gulf War. Plans for distributed and dispersed operations created additional requirements for aerial tankers to be able to operate particularly far forward from a very limited number of bases. A partial solution to mitigate reliance on tankers was the development of external fuel tanks for the F-35, which could be used to ferry the fighters between bases both in peacetime, and when operating far from adversary positions. Lockheed Martin had originally planned for the F-35A to carry 1,740 litre underwing drop tanks, although development was cancelled at an early stage. In June 2019 the firm was reported to have started engineering studies on the integration of two 2,300 litre underwing drop tanks, which would increase onboard fuel capacity by 40 percent.[60] Israel Aerospace Industries and Cyclone from the mid-2000s had also worked on developing such tanks, and in April 2019 were reported to have completed initial design studies on both a conformal fuel tank and a 1,740 litre underwing drop tank.[61] External tanks could significantly reduce the burden on the tanker fleet, and thus ensure that more tankers would be available to support combat missions in wartime when stealth-configured F-35s operated without external fuel tanks.

A further solution was to develop longer ranged semi-autonomous 'wingman' UAVs for the F-35 under the Collaborative Combat Aircraft program, which could be controlled from F-35s

An F-35B of the Marine Fighter Attack Squadron 121 during its transfer to Japan, supported by KC-135 tankers. (USAF)

loitering hundreds of kilometres away from their targets to engage at closer ranges. The cost effectiveness of such an approach, however, was repeatedly brought to question when compared to investment in a longer ranged manned fighter, with unmanned aircraft with long combat radii, stealth capabilities, and advanced electronic warfare suites needed for high intensity operations in the Pacific projected to have comparable costs to the F-35s themselves.[62] The possibility of developing and reorienting operational plans around longer ranged cruise missiles for the F-35 was also raised, although the limited size of the fighter's internal weapons bay restricted its suitability for such a role, with the longer ranged F-15EX which had a much higher missile carrying capacity being better suited to serve as a missile carrier. If the F-35 was not going to fly close enough to make effective use of its stealth capabilities or its unique sensors, the argument for employing the fighter rather than fourth generation jets largely dissipated.

Not only did a high reliance on tankers to facilitate F-35 operations in East Asia impose considerable additional costs, but their high vulnerability also presented tremendous operational risks. These risks were highlighted as early as 2008 in a RAND Corporation study projecting the outcome of efforts to employ F-22s in a Taiwan Strait conflict scenario. The study found that to sustain operations for 130 combat coded F-22s from Guam over Taiwan, the USAF would need to launch three to four tanker sorties every hour to deliver 2.6 million gallons of fuel. It further observed that even if F-22s had a perfect combat record and sustained no losses to Chinese fighters, they would run out of air-to-air missiles and leave their tankers undefended, with the subsequent destruction of tankers leaving the fighters unable to return to their bases. The result would be extreme losses for the F-22 fleet. Despite much more limited Chinese strike capabilities at the time, Guam was seen as the nearest location where bases had a chance of surviving initial attacks.[63]

The possibility of tanker operations facilitating effective large-scale F-35 operations in the Pacific by the mid-2020s appeared very limited. Not only did the Air Force's top fighter units appear to have largely lost the qualitative edge they had in 2008, whether measured by pilot training hours or by aircraft combat potential, but Chinese capabilities to target tankers had expanded tremendously. The J-16 fighter, which had the highest weapons carrying capacity in the Chinese fighter fleet, was able to deploy PL-XX air-to-air missiles with estimated engagement ranges of 400-500 kilometres. If provided with targeting data either by stealthy forward flying J-20s, or by the country's sizeable KJ-500 and KJ-3000 fleets, the aircraft could represent highly potent 'tanker killers' which could engage well beyond the range of the F-35 to retaliate. The J-20's first appearance with externally deployed missiles in February 2025 indicated that it could also be used for such roles, albeit at the expense of its stealth capabilities.

The People's Liberation Army's ability to threaten tankers was set to continue to grow rapidly, with the surface-to-air capabilities of its destroyers and their numbers continuing to expand, while its sixth generation fighters were expected to pair flight radii of well over 3,000 kilometres with advanced stealth capabilities to be able to engage enemy aircraft far out into the Pacific. As summarised by air power expert at the Royal United Services Institute Justin Bronk in April 2025 regarding the prevailing trend: 'The U.S. will be taking more and more risk to put a small number of tankers even hundreds of nautical miles from the Chinese mainland, or from, say, Taiwan.'[64] Although the U.S. Air Force and Navy would narrow the missile gap with the development of the LRAAM and AIM-174 very long-range air-to-air missiles for the F-15EX and F-18E/F respectively, China until the mid-2020s deployed a negligible fleet of tanker aircraft with just 13 in service, ten of them very small H-6Us, and did not depend on them. The concentration of Chinese forces in East Asia and their focus on regional operations, combined with the much longer ranges of Chinese fighters, meant its fleet was not comparably vulnerable to that of the United States to its tankers being targeted. This was aside from the fact that while China was set to deploy over 400 J-16s, with the fleet surpassing 350 fighters in 2024, deployments of F-15EXs by the USAF remained very limited with just eight fighters in service by the end of the year, while the much older F-15E fleet was scheduled to suffer deep cuts to numbers.

Addressing the issue of the tanker fleet's vulnerability, Air Force Secretary Frank Kendall observed in September 2024: 'During my tenure, we've gone through an evolution in our strategy to recapitalise the tanker fleet ... The threat is now reaching out to longer and longer ranges. That puts both tanker and transport aircraft at risk over ever-increasing ranges. This is a particular problem for aerial refuelling fighters within their combat radius ranges.'[65] He reiterated two months later: 'Essentially the threat, China again, has reached out with new counter-air systems that could threaten our aircraft, especially tankers, at longer ranges, beyond the ranges which we normally would refuel fighter planes.' 'This put our whole tanker acquisition strategy in question. It is still in question, but we are working to resolve the uncertainty as quickly as possible,' he added. Regarding the solution, Kendall stated: 'We must have a more resilient tanking capability. There are a number of ways to accomplish this ... A new design, purpose-built tanker – NGAS [Next Generation Air Refuelling System] – is one of them.' 'Unfortunately, any new design cannot be fielded for several years at best, even if affordable,' he lamented.[66]

While the vulnerability that resulted from dependence on tankers could be reduced by developing longer ranged fighters, which allowed them to refuel farther away from enemy territory, this approach was seen to have serious limitations. As observed by naval analyst and Senior Fellow at the Hudson Institute Bryan Clark in 2020: 'The idea of just continuing to build new manned aircraft with longer ranges to try to overcome the ability of a China or an Iran even or a Russia to shoot long-range missiles at the carrier, it's sort of a losing game because the missiles are cheap ... The airplanes are expensive. So you're in a bad cost exchange situation.'[67] Work was confirmed in March 2024 to be underway in China to develop a surface-to-air missile with an engagement range of up to 2,000 kilometres. A report to Congress by the U.S. Department of the Air Force in January 2025 predicted that anti-aircraft missiles with ranges of up to 1,600 kilometres were likely to enter service in the following decades and pose a particular threat to tankers.[68] It was significantly less costly to develop means of threatening tankers at longer ranges, than it was to develop longer ranged fighters that could allow tankers to operate farther away. This calculus also applied to Chinese and North Korean ballistic missiles' ability to target air bases deeper into the Pacific. While moving planned operations from Okinawa to Guam, or from Guam to Wake Island or even Darwin, could be made possible through major investments in new tankers and in longer ranged combat aircraft, it was far less costly for adversaries to expand their means of targeting these more distant facilities.

In response to the growing vulnerabilities of tanker aircraft, the U.S. Air Force and Navy showed a growing interest in fielding tankers with advanced stealth capabilities. The Navy's primary program, the MQ-25 Stingray, was an unmanned stealth aircraft designed to operate from its aircraft carriers. Although highly survivable, its relatively small size and low endurance limited the number of

First publicly-released photographs showing Chinese People's Liberation Army Air Force J-16 fighters carrying PL-XX long-range air-to-air missiles and associated pylons. The pictures were published in December 2023. (China Military Online)

fighters it could refuel per sortie. The ability to forward deploy from carriers, however, helped compensate for this. The Stingray first flew in September 2019, and as of 2025 it remains under development. The utilisation of valuable space onboard carriers for tankers was considered far from optimal, particularly due to the sheer number of MQ-25s that would be needed to facilitate a long-range operation for even half of a carrier air wing. This was an important argument in the favour of developing a much longer ranged fighter under the F/A-XX program.

On 1 February 2023, the Air Force announced the Next Generation Air-refuelling System (NGAS) program, which was intended to bring a fleet of more survivable aerial tankers in service by 2040. Under this program, the Air Force was willing to consider proposals 'innovative solutions in all size and performance types.'[69] Officials would come to stress a 'strong sense of urgency' in pursuing the program,[70] with Air Force Secretary Frank Kendall observing regarding the need for such aircraft: 'All of our longer-range aircraft based on conventional models of aircraft are increasingly vulnerable to very long-range, even ultra-long-range counter air systems, and we have got to address that survivability issue.'[71] Six days before the program's announcement, Boeing had unveiled a concept for a new tanker and cargo aircraft with advanced stealth capabilities,[72] with further designs having been released by the firm and by Lockheed Martin, McDonnell Douglas and Northrop Grumman, and continuing to be released over the following years.[73] These included a flying wing design by Lockheed Martin, unveiled May 2024, which also integrated a missile defence system to shoot down incoming projectiles.[74] It was followed by another Lockheed Martin stealth design unveiled in November.[75]

Despite its critical importance in the Pacific theatre, the affordability of a next generation tanker program remained in serious question for multiple reasons. A primary issue was the sheer scale of the tanker fleet required to support American air operations, with the U.S. Armed Forces operating a much larger tanker fleet than those of all other countries combined at approximately 470 aircraft. 380 of these were KC-135 Stratotankers which dated back to the 1960s, while the fleet of approximately 40 newer KC-10s dated back to the beginning of the 1980s. With the Pentagon's post-Cold War purchasing power being very significantly lower than it had been before the 1990s, it was likely that the tanker fleet would need to contract very significantly even if only replacing the aircraft with relatively standard modern tankers such as the KC-46, which was based on the Boeing KC-767 and introduced into service from 2019. Significant issues with the KC-46, in particular its mission capable rates and production quality issues, appeared to bode ill for possible efforts to develop a much more complex stealth tanker.[76] With American stealth programs having consistently suffered from immense overruns in their development, production and operational costs, the costs of developing, procuring and operating a stealth tanker could force a much greater contraction of the overall tanker fleet to a fraction of its current size.

A possibility remained that a stealth tanker could be financed for deployment in relatively small numbers, with aircraft being prioritised for the Pacific theatre and reserved for the most high-risk deployments closest to adversary positions. Older tankers could continue to be relied on for the bulk of operations, and potentially receive more funding for integration of advanced electronic and possibly hard kill defences.[77] The possibility of small shorter ranged unmanned stealth tankers being fielded in complementary roles was also significant, with Boeing unveiling a land based variant of the MQ-25 in September 2024 and pitching it to the Air Force.[78]

The significant possibility of major delays to the Air Force or Navy's plans to operationalise a long ranged sixth generation fighter

Lockheed Martin Concept Art Showing Proposed U.S. Navy Carrier Based Unmanned Flying Wing Stealth Tanker Refuelling an F-35C. (Lockheed Martin)

could significantly increase the services' reliance on pairing the F-35 with advanced stealth tankers (see Chapter 10). With the Air Force struggling profusely to afford multiple simultaneous large programs, including the F-35, E-7, B-21, a sixth generation fighter, high performance Collaborative Combat Aircraft 'wingman' drones, and the service's first clean sheet intercontinental range ballistic missile developed in over half a century, it could be forced to make significant cuts. Considering that even the longest ranged envisaged sixth generation fighter and unmanned Collaborative Combat Aircraft designs would struggle to operate in the Pacific without tanker support, with even the B-21 intercontinental range bomber designed to operate with such support due to its shorter range than the older B-2, a stealth tanker is likely to be prioritised as a key enabler both of the F-35 and of any next generation combat jet that would be fielded. It thus appears likely that it will be prioritised for funding.

The vast distances of the Pacific are one of the most valuable defences against the F-35 for China, North Korea and the Russian Far East, with Chinese forces being particularly well positioned to exacerbate difficulties the U.S. Armed Forces have in operating the fighters in the theatre due to its tremendous capabilities to target both bases and aerial tankers. The limited number of airbases available in the region, and the very high vulnerability of bases in Northeast Asia in particular, make it highly possible that F-35s will only be able to operate at scale from Guam, and under worse circumstances be forced to operate from Wake Island, Tinian, or farther afield. Although the F-35's relatively short range exacerbates the issue significantly, it is a problem which any fighter type will encounter if seeking to wage war across the world's widest body of water against a force as capable as the People's Liberation Army. While there are hopes that training for Agile Combat Employment from makeshift bases, or relying more heavily on carrier based F-35B and F-35C fighters, may help mitigate the issue, the fleet's position remained highly unfavourable and increasingly so.

A U.S. Air Force KC-46A Pegasus with its boom in lowered position. (USAF)

10

INTO THE SIXTH GENERATION ERA: THE FUTURE OF THE F-35 AND SUPPORTING PROGRAMS

Enhancements: Block 4 and Beyond

The Block 4 standard was a major milestone in the modernisation of the F-35, and would introduce 53 new capabilities, around 80 percent of which were software related. Although the full list of upgrades as of 2025 remained classified, it includes open mission systems architecture, a next-generation integrated processor with a 25-fold increase in computing power, expanded memory, an enhanced panoramic cockpit display, and superior maintenance diagnostics and communications. The integration of the new AN/APG-85 radar was expected to operationalise several new technologies, and was speculated to use a Gallium Nitride based system to ease conflict between signal strength and power usage. A new variant of the F135 developed under the Engine Core Upgrade program was expected to improve flight performance, increase range, and reduce maintenance requirements and operational costs, while providing significantly more power for onboard systems, including resolving issues with the insufficient cooling capacity. The fighter's AN/AAQ-37 Distributed Aperture System and AN/AAQ-40 Electro-Optical Targeting System would also receive significant enhancements, while its ability to collect, manage and distribute electronic intelligence would be revolutionised. The upgrade would also provide compatibility with a range of new armaments including the AIM-260, the AGM-158C and the SPEAR 3. New missile racks would provide a much needed improvement to firepower for the F-35A and C variants, increasing internal carriage from four to six air-to-air missiles.

Regarding the importance of bringing the F-35 to the Block 4 standard, Pacific Command Director of Strategic Planning and Policy Lieutenant General Steven Rudder would stress that it was vital because of 'how rapidly the threat and the pace of technological developments that [adversaries] are progressing at.' 'There will be some budget decisions that have to be made. If the scope of the work comes in at the level that is proposed ... we are going to be able to handle that.' He stated that bringing the F-35 up to the new standard 'could enable the jet to be more adaptable to threats.'[1] The rapid improvements to China's rival J-20 fighter between production batches was seen to be a leading factor driving the Pentagon to enhance the F-35 quickly. Efforts to achieve major capability improvements for the F-35 would consistently fall years behind schedule, however, with timelines being criticised as unfeasible due to the insufficient number of test aircraft and the lack of sufficient time for flight-testing software changes.[2]

In December 2023 head of the Joint Program Office Lieutenant General Michael Schmidt revealed that 'numerous Block 4 capabilities will not deliver until the 2030s,'[3] years later than a recent estimate by congressional auditors.[4] 'Reimagined Block 4,' as he referred to the new schedule, would prioritise delivering "'must-have" content,' he observed, adding that this 'must consist of "what industry can actually deliver" across the Future Years Defense Program.' Schmidt at the time highlighted the program's history of 'over-promising and under-delivering.'[5]

Among the enhancements that were most strongly emphasised, the F-35's electronic warfare capabilities were expected to gain a particularly significant boost under Block 4. Commander of the USAF Air Combat Command General Mark Kelly emphasised that the new electronic warfare suite was the most important capability improvement for the latest F-35 update, stating: 'Most of what we need the F-35 to do rests on the Block 4 electronic warfare capabilities. Those rest on the suite of hardware and software, Technology Refresh-3, that supports all that Block 4 EW … You've got to have that amount of processing power, transmitting power, speed, and sensors to punch in to truly appear a threat network.' 'If you're gonna go where we need to go, that software, hardware, and EW; all three have to be able to operate in a very, very robust EW environment that our peers will put up that runs the gamut across the electromagnetic spectrum,' he added. 'Single hertz all the way through to kilohertz all the way up to high, high end. It's the only way we can operate. It's processing speed. We've got to have the most current software load, the most current hardware load, current apps, EW, all of that, or we're not going to get as far as we need,' Kelly concluded, stressing 'if we lose the war on the electromagnetic spectrum, we're going to lose the war and lose it quickly.'[6] While the ability to improve the fighter's stealth capabilities remained limited in the face of adversaries' rapidly improving sensor technologies, unlike the F-22 the very large electronic warfare suite on the F-35 placed the program in a stronger position to remain ahead of the curve by ensuring that EW capabilities were sustained at the cutting edge. This would complement procurement of the E-7 system, which had a significant electronic warfare capability, the EC-37 electronic warfare aircraft, and the new Eagle Passive/Active Warning and Survivability System (EPAWSS) electronic warfare suite developed for the F-15.

Although the primary improvements to the F-35's survivability were expected to be achieved through integration of superior electronic warfare capabilities, as well as new generations of armaments that facilitated targeting from greater distances, from the early 2020s there were multiple indications that testing of new stealth coatings were also underway. On 19 November 2021, an F-22 based

An F-35C of the VX-9 flight testing squadron, as seen with 'glass' coating applied. (USN)

An F-35C operated by the Strike Fighter Squadron 125 shown with partial glass coating applied on its fins, as photographed while doing a touch-and-go aboard the aircraft carrier USS *Abraham Lincoln* off the coast of California in December 2023. (USN)

at Nellis Air Force Base was seen for the first time with a tile-like reflective metallic coating, which differed greatly from the fighter type's usual intricate skin coating and delicate composite stealthy structures. The purpose of this coating, including whether it was a realistic option to improve fighters' stealth capabilities, remained wholly unknown.

In January 2022 an F-35C and an F-117 were both seen with very similar reflective metallic coatings. The coatings could go from appearing mirror-like to matte-like depending on the angle at which it the aircraft were viewed, although how they affected radar cross section remained uncertain. Subsequently in March 2022 an F-22 was seen with a new mirror like coating made up of arrays of small rectangular, trapezoidal, and triangular tiles, with a similar coating subsequently seen on an F-35C in August 2022. Mirror coatings were subsequently tested at sea on the outside and inside of an F-35C's tails on the USS *Abraham Lincoln* in December 2023 – two parts of the airframe that increased its radar cross section the most. New mirror like coatings would continue to appear on individual non-deployed F-117, F-22 and F-35 fighters as part of apparent testing efforts, fuelling considerable speculation that they could begin to appear on frontline fighter units.

Challenges in the Sixth Generation Era

Two primary factors shaping the future of the F-35 program would be the state of competition from China as the pacing challenger, and the capabilities of the Air Force's Next Generation Air Dominance (NGAD) and the Navy's F/A-XX sixth generation fighter programs. Throughout the history of fighter aviation, the introduction of more capable new fighters both domestically and abroad has consistently been a central factor in determining the longevity of procurement and production of an aircraft. The introduction of the MiG-23ML and MiG-25P in the Soviet Union, followed by the F-15 and F-16 in the United States, for example, left the F-4 Phantom which had formed the backbone of the American fleet both outmatched by its adversaries, and surpassed by its much more cost-effective successors, leading production to be terminated. Similarly, a key argument for the termination of procurements of F-15s by the USAF was both the development of the F-22, which was intended to be more cost effective and much more capable, as well as the acknowledgment that the older fighter was increasingly outmatched by the Russian Su-27 and its increasingly advanced derivatives such as the Su-35 and Su-37.

For the F-35, while the increasingly advanced capabilities of China's J-20 fighter are credited as a central factor stimulating investment in its modernisation, a perceived inability of the fighter to provide superiority over its Chinese rival may well lead to the early termination of procurements. As China, on 26 December 2024, became the first country in the world to unveil sixth generation fighters at flight prototype stages, against whom it is expected the F-35 to be far outmatched, calls to reduce investment in the Joint Strike Fighter, and to refocus resources towards sixth generation programs, were expected to grow. This was reportedly a primary factor in the downgrading of Lockheed Martin's stock at Deutsche Bank by 14.5 percent near the end of the month. 'We're downgrading Lockheed to Hold as we feel our prior thesis struggles to hold water and we have increased concern on the long-term support for F-35 in the face of China's combat aircraft modernisation efforts,' Deutsche Bank analyst Scott Deuschle stated at the time, adding that he saw 'the reveal of further advancements in combat aircraft capabilities by China as potentially undermining long-term demand for the F-35 aircraft.'[7]

Sixth generation fighters are expected to lack either vertical tails or horizontal stabilisers, both of which significantly increase radar cross section, and to use advanced flight control surfaces to sustain high flight performances at all speeds. This will ensure greater efficiency for sustained high speed cruise and superior stealth capabilities, including very low observability to radars beyond the X, K and Ku bands which fifth generation fighters' stealth features had focused on. Stealth, electronic warfare, artificial intelligence, sensors and network centric capabilities are all expected to be priority features, with all being advanced well beyond what was seen on fifth generation fighters.[8] A significantly improved fuel capacity, and integration of next generation engine technologies are expected to significantly increase range, which is likely to be a priority for

Chinese sixth generation fighter-bomber system, a tri-engine aircraft first unveiled in December 2024 developed by the Chengdu Aerospace Corporation. U.S. Air Force Chief of Staff General David Allvin the following month cited the test flight of the aircraft and its lighter counterpart developed by Shenyang Aerospace Corporation to argue for a major increase in attention and funding for Air Force programs. He expressed his 'sincere hope that this got America's attention and serves as a wakeup call, because we need the nation's assistance advancing the Air Force with the sense of strategic urgency this moment requires,' singling out the need for 'funding a family of medium- and long-range penetrating airframes coupled with modern munitions, survivable refuelling, human-machine teaming, and a hardened warfighting network.' (Chinese Internet)

both Chinese and American designs. Compared to the F-35C's already very large capacity of 9,000 kilograms of internal fuel, the range requirements for the NGAD and F/A-XX fighters and their expected use of twin engines mean they are expected to be required to carry over double this volume, which is a primary factor shaping expectations that they will be particularly large.[9] These features were all seen on the larger of China's two sixth generation fighters developed by the Chengdu Aircraft Corporation, the firm responsible for the J-20, while the smaller of the two aircraft developed by the Shenyang Aircraft Corporation appears intended for operations within the First Island Chain, and to have a similar endurance and weapons payload to the J-20. The aircraft will provide the People's Liberation Army Air Force with a high-low combination, which is not expected to be replicated in any other service worldwide.

China's expected operationalisation of sixth generation fighters by around 2030 had from the early 2020s fuelled calls in the United States to deprioritise the F-35 program and focus on developing a new generation of aircraft. In May 2021, four months after leaving office, former Assistant Secretary of the Air Force for Acquisition, Technology and Logistics Will Roper on this basis recommended a sharp reduction to planned USAF F-35A procurements by approximately 55 percent, from 1,763 fighters to around 800, citing the need for the service to focus on the NGAD sixth generation program.[10] Former Under Secretary of Defense for Acquisition and Sustainment Ellen Lord, who had also left office in January, stated at the time that there remained debate within the Pentagon 'about the degree to which you can reduce the F-35 to put money into NGAD.'[11]

A leading argument against investment in NGAD at the expense of the F-35 was that there remained a significant possibility that the program would face major delays and performance issues. Terminating production of the much delayed and problematic F-22 had been justified largely on the basis that the F-35 program would be able to make up for its deficiencies, only for the F-35 to then face its own major delays and performance issues. Should the F-35 program itself be cut to invest in NGAD, only for the sixth generation program to then face similar issues, the consequences for American air power could be devastating. As America's defence sector and broader industrial base had contracted drastically from the early 1990s, similar issues to those seen on the F-22 had affected all leading weapons programs, from the B-2 bomber to the Littoral Combat Ship and Zumwalt-class destroyer. All entered service many years behind schedule, with serious performance issues, and with costs per unit well over twice as high as intended. Planning for the future of the fighter fleet on the basis that NGAD and its counterpart in the Navy the F/A-XX would bring fighters into service without comparable delays or cost overruns thus posed major risks.

Both Air Force officials and lawmakers would consistently emphasise the vital importance of the NGAD program breaking away from the trends that had affected the country's leading post-Cold War clean sheet weapons programs, avoid the numerous and severe performance bugs, delays and cost overruns which had plagued the B-2, F-22 and F-35. While major delays to the F-22 and F-35 programs had been a key factor allowing Chinese combat aviation to bridge major gaps in performance, the speed at which China had developed and operationalised the J-20 significantly raised the bar for competition. The House Armed Services Committee was accordingly among multiple bodies to emphasise in 2020 that it was imperative for NGAD to avoid the 'unexpected cost growth' and 'run[ning] into problematic issues when they field the capabilities' that had hampered the F-35, going so far as to issue threats to cut off up to 85 percent of funding to ensure this.[12] In May 2023 Air Force Secretary Frank Kendall similarly emphasised that avoiding the 'acquisition malpractice' that had hampered the Joint Strike Fighter – a term he had been using for over a decade to describe the program – was vital to making the NGAD successful.[13] The fact that the F-35 program was widely being referred to primarily as an example of what needed to be avoided, rather than as a precedent to emulate, indicated that it was in hindsight viewed far from positively.

The F-22 and F-35 both took fifteen years between their first demonstrator flights in 1990 and 2000, and their entry into service with a limited Initial Operating Capability in 2005 and 2015. China's defence sector had been able to achieve the same for the J-20 in just six years, placing the program entirely in a league of its own for development speed among aircraft of its generation – the same amount of time taken for the country's first fourth generation fighter the J-10. While America's strong post-Cold War lead in combat aviation related technologies had meant the F-22 and F-35's issues had still left it on a relatively equal footing with China, which was able to bring the J-20 into service within months of the F-35 joining

J-20 first technology demonstrator airframe No. 2001. The aircraft first flew on 11 January 2011, while the first serial production aircraft became operational only six years later in February 2017. The contrast between this and the fifteen year periods required for both the F-22 and the F-35 set a precedent that could have highly unfavourable consequences for American air power as the two countries compete to develop the world's first sixth generation fighters. (top81.cn)

the USAF, should a similar discrepancy in development times be repeated in the sixth generation it would leave the USAF's top fighter units many years behind.

In September 2022 Air Force Secretary Frank Kendall confirmed that the NGAD program had not yet entered its engineering, manufacturing, and development (EMD) phase.[14] Despite not being the first American fighter of its generation, the F-35 had still taken a full fifteen years between the beginning of EMD in 2001, and its attaining of an Initial Operating Capability in the Air Force. A similar timeline for the NGAD fighter would put in on track to enter service close to 2040. The very different speeds at which the F-35 and J-20 were developed thus set a precedent for China to begin fielding sixth generation fighters long before the United States, and for the USAF to be forced to continue to rely on the F-35 as its top fighter until the later half of the 2030s. This had significant potential implications for the F-35's production run as well as for what would be required of the fighters.

Although efforts to see the NGAD through development quickly consistently appeared to fall short, this was not for a lack of emphasis by Air Force officials on expediting the program. In December 2019 USAF Undersecretary Matthew Donovan observed to this effect: 'What we can't afford to do, is get into multidecade programs,' which the F-22 and F-35 had both become due to the major delays they suffered. The F-35, he observed, 19 years after its first demonstrator flight 'still hasn't met full-rate production and still hasn't finished [Initial Operational Test and Evaluation],' which made it 'about a 20-year development program.'[15] In October 2021 Commander of the Air Combat Command General Mark Kelly went as far as to compare the NGAD program to the Manhattan Project in its urgency and importance, stressing: 'I would like to have more of a sense of urgency and a whole-of-nation effort towards it.' The extent to which the U.S. Armed Forces relied on air superiority to operate meant this was hardly an exaggeration, with Kelly warning that failure to prioritise NGAD would leave the USAF 'on the other side of coming in second in air superiority.'[16] Kelly had previously questioned 'if our nation will have the courage and the focus to field this capability before someone like the Chinese fields it and uses it against us,' stressing that the U.S. Armed Forces were not well suited to operating without control of the air.[17]

Kelly's warning was made just days after Secretary Kendall's surprise revelation that NGAD had not yet begun its EMD phase. Having warned nine months prior that China could be the first to make a sixth generation fighter operational,[18] the Air Combat Command chief at the time reiterated this possibility.[19] In September 2022 he again warned: 'I cannot tell you today what's going on in China except they're planning for their 20th National Party Congress [in October]. But I can tell you what's not happening. They're not having a debate over the relevance of six-gen air dominance. And I can also tell you they're on track.' He indicated that China could field such an aircraft before the U.S.[20] The contrast between the F-35's major delays, and the J-20's consistent exceeding of expectations for its development timeline, did much to explain these pessimistic projections for the race to the sixth generation.

Twenty-three days after the unveiling of China's two sixth generation fighter types at flight prototype stages, Air Force Chief of Staff General David Allvin on 17 January 2025 cited this development to argue that his service required significantly more attention and investment. 'Last month, the People's Republic of China released videos of not just one, but two new sixth-generation aircraft,' stressing 'the sense of strategic urgency this moment requires.' He emphasised that China had 'invested in a first-rate Air Force and has instituted realistic training programs rivalling our own,' while 'today, our aircraft fleet is smaller and older than any time in history, and the gap between our high-end combat training and that of our pacing competitors has closed dramatically.'[21] *

While the United States had from the early 1990s been expected to have no pacing challenger in fighter aviation, the J-20 program in particular brought a gradual end to complacency, and was consistently singled out by both analysts and officials as a leading cause for concern in the sixth generation era. In September 2022, when discussing the J-20 specifically, Air Force Chief of Staff Charles Brown emphasised that the aircraft could force the USAF

* Further issues Allvin cited that were impeding the Air Force's ability to compete included 'a force already 20,000-30,000 Airmen short of our requirements,' poor mission readiness rates, and a lack of 'control of our own force structure.' Capitol Hill's refusal to allow divestment of either the A-10 attack jet or of early production F-22s fighters were notable examples of the third point. (Allvin, David W., 'Allvin: It's make or break time. America needs more Air Force.' *Breaking Defense*, 17 January 2025.)

to 'lose sleep' if the service failed to quickly field a sixth generation fighter.[22] As analysts at *The War Zone* similarly observed that year that any confidence the Pentagon had in its ability to tackle the J-20 appeared to have 'less to do with the jet's actual capabilities or how it might be employed,' and instead was based on its confidence in the capabilities which American sixth generation fighters were expected to bring to the field.[23] They had previously warned that an approach to developing NGAD very different to that for the F-22 and F-35 was needed to counter the Chinese challenge, observing: 'The reality is that the sustainability of American air superiority over its peers has become so dire that there really isn't a choice. It's literally become a factor of change or die.'[24]

Similarly singling out the J-20 for mention, the monthly journal of the Air & Space Forces Association would stress that NGAD was needed specifically to counter two threats – the Chinese aircraft and new generations of ground-based air defences.[25] Former Air Force Secretary Deborah Lee James in June 2024 observed that 'the only thing we can say for sure is that China is ruthlessly advancing its NGAD equivalent and does not appear to be slowing down due to budgetary concerns,' stressing on this basis that 'we can't afford to delay NGAD. Doing so would mean risking loss in a future conflict.'[26] Thus not only was the F-35 not seen as a sufficient premier fighter able to ensure air superiority over China's J-20 fleet, but Chinese advances towards a sixth generation capability were set to render the Joint Strike Fighter even more inadequate to control the skies by the early 2030s.

Next Generation Air Dominance: A Sixth Generation Successor

The jet era had multiple precedents of fighter programs falling short of expectations, or failing altogether, and of the preceding fighters they were intended to succeed accordingly being relied on to shoulder far larger burdens and serve in elite units for far longer. The F-15 was one notable example, as not only did delays to the F-22's development leave the F-15C/D serving as the USAF's prime air superiority fighter for over a decade longer than expected, but the F-22's shortcomings and deep cuts to production forced the service to keep over 200 of these older F-15s in service indefinitely, and to eventually procure an enhanced variant of the same aircraft, the F-15EX, to replace them. Post-Soviet Russia faced similar issues on a much larger scale, with the cancellation of the MiG-31M and Izdeliye 701 interceptor programs in the 1990s forcing its MiG-31B/BS fleet to serve on indefinitely, while the cancellation of the MiG 1.42 fighter and serious delays developing the subsequent Su-57 fighter forced it to depend heavily on derivatives of the Su-27 fourth generation fighter for over 40 years.

As America's sole fifth generation fighter produced after 2011, the length of the F-35's production and the extent to which it is relied on will similarly depend heavily on the performance of both the NGAD program, and to a lesser extent the Navy's F/A-XX. Should the programs surpass expectations to quickly produce unproblematic and cost effective fighters, investments in procuring, modernising and operating the F-35 could be cut short. Major shortcomings with the NGAD and F/A-XX programs, however, could extend the F-35's production run, stimulate further funding for modernisation, and ensure a longer time in service. Thus should the two sixth generation programs succeed, the F-35 program's future could mirror that of the F-4 from the 1970s, while should they fail, the program's future could mirror those of the F-15 and Su-27 from the 2000s.

From the early 2020s growing indications emerged of indecisiveness, 'flip flopping' and delays in the NGAD's development. In September 2020 Assistant Secretary of the Air Force for Acquisition, Technology and Logistics Will Roper revealed ambitious plans to leverage new technologies to allow new types of air superiority fighter to enter service every few years, citing the precedent of the Century Series in the 1950s.[27] Two years later in June 2022, however, Air Force Secretary Frank Kendall announced that the NGAD would follow a more traditional development course, with plans for a 'Digital Century Series' having been dropped. The fighter's 'development phase is far too expensive' to pursue such a strategy, he stated, adding that 'the NGAD that we're working on now ... is going to take longer ... It's not a simple design ... [but a] long, hard job to build.'[28] In May 2023 Kendall would reiterate that the NGAD program would produce on a single manned fighter, with plans mentioned in 2021 to potentially develop a high-low combination of fighters with long and medium ranges for the Pacific and Europe respectively thus ruled out.[29] The Air Force was expected to focus on a single top performing long range fighter developed primarily for operations in the Pacific.

In September 2020 Undersecretary Roper stated that digital assembly and testing technologies could revolutionise the time it took to develop new fighters, and hailed the technology for its potential to allow America's defence sector to break away from post-Cold War trends towards highly protracted fighter development. The technology first saw extensive use in an American combat aviation program when used to develop the Boeing T-7 trainer, allowing the aircraft to move from a concept to its first flight in three years.[30] Roper stressed that these technologies could represent a turning point in the industry, reversing the trends of the past five decades towards increasingly prolonged and costly development,* by allowing a new aircraft design to 'fly thousands of hours before it takes off, be laid out and assembled hundreds of times before any metal is even cut.' Future aircraft could 'be designed, built, and tested, not by thousands of people, but by fewer than 200, using leading-edge design tools across a digital landscape, connected virtually across the globe.'[31] Despite its simplicity, the mounting of problems with the T-7 program led Secretary Kendall to conclude in May 2023 that digital assembly and testing had been 'over-hyped,' and at best could cut costs and schedules by only around 20 percent.[32] With hopes for making the NGAD competitive with rival Chinese programs resting heavily on these technologies, particularly in terms of development schedule, this boded ill for its future.

In April 2022, longstanding speculation confirmed that fighters developed under NGAD were projected to cost several hundred million dollars each, making them by far the most expensive tactical combat jets in world history.[33] Secretary Kendall on 7 March 2023 stated that the Air Force projected procurement of approximately 200 of the fighters.[34] When questioned six months later regarding the affordability of the program, Kendall would stress its indispensability, retorting: 'Can the nation afford not to have air superiority? We have to have air superiority.'[35]

* While the world moved from the beginning of the first generation of fighter aircraft in the late 1940s to the beginning of the fourth generation in the early 1970s – a period of 25 years between the introduction of the F-86 in 1949 and F-14 in 1974 which were the first American jets of those generations – fourth generation fighters remain widely in production in the 2020s. The complexity of the fifth generation has made efforts to develop such fighters both slow and scarce, and resulted in only two fighters in production fielded at squadron level strength (F-35 and J-20) by December 2020 – exactly 15 years after the first fifth generation fighter entered service and 50 years after the first fourth generation fighter, the F-14, made its maiden flight.

The second of two Chinese sixth generation fighter-bomber systems unveiled in December 2024. Developed by the Shenayng Aerospace Corporation, it appears to be a heavyweight fighter with comparable dimensions to the J-20, but with a much larger nose cone to accommodate a bigger radar. (@Captain小潇 on Weibo)

Despite an apparent consensus on NGAD's importance, consistent vacillation on the course the program would take culminated in the emergence of an uncertainty as to whether development would be continued at all. This occurred in the context of an emerging consensus that it would be impossible to compete with Chinese programs either on schedule, or in terms of cost effectiveness. On 28 February 2024, Air Force Chief of Staff General David Allvin stated regarding the future of American air superiority that it was 'cost prohibitive to be able to say that we're going to build enough Air Force to do it the way we did before and have air superiority for days and weeks on end,' and that there was a 'cost imposition' to rethink the approach. This provided an early indication of the shift in consensus on the matter.[36] Allvin on 13 June went on to confirm longstanding suspicions that NGAD was facing an uncertain future, and unprecedentedly stated that moving ahead was just one of many 'choices' for the Air Force, rather than a certainty. This contrasted to prior statements from officials that had consistently stressed that the NGAD was vital for the service's future. Allvin emphasised at the time that the Air Force's $200 billion budget, which had been undercut by high inflation rates, was forcing the service to make many difficult choices.[37]

The shift on the NGAD sent shockwaves throughout the Air Force and the analyst community, with military correspondent

Rendering of a Next Generation Air Dominance Fighter during aerial refuelling. An artwork released by Lockheed Martin in 2022 at a time when the firm was still bidding for primary contracts to develop sixth generation fighters to meet both the Air Force and the Navy's requirements. (Lockheed Martin)

David Axe summarising prevailing views on the issue as follows: 'It's a startling development for advocates of American air power. For generations, the whole U.S. military – not to mention the militaries of America's closest allies – have depended on the U.S. Air Force to achieve air superiority against even the most determined and sophisticated foe, affording freedom of action for troops on the ground and ships at sea.' Axe was among many to blame the F-35 program's tremendous cost overruns for seriously depleting Air Force funds, and thus being a leading contributor to placing NGAD's future in jeopardy, observing that the fifth generation program was 'eating the U.S. Air Force's budget – and forcing the service to rethink its next fighter.'[38] It would be confirmed the following month that the Sentinel intercontinental range ballistic missile program's cost overruns by close to $70 billion were a major factor forcing the Air Force to consider terminating the NGAD program, with Secretary Kendall also alluding to 'other programs that are very high-priority that we need to fund.'[39] Although the service had deferred procuring a new ICBM for decades to prioritise other programs, its existing arsenal built from 1970 to 1978, and derived from a 1950s design, had seen its life extended to the absolute maximum, and was the world's oldest by a margin of several decades, leaving no room for further postponement.[40] Former Air Force Secretary Deborah Lee James responded to Allvin's statement by publishing an opinion piece arguing that NGAD was indispensable, and that the service needed to 'explore alternative design and acquisition strategies' to make the program economically viable and operationalisable on a favourable timeline.[41]

On 2 July 2024 Secretary Kendall provided a new estimate for the cost of fighters developed under the NGAD program, stating that it would fall 'three times, roughly, the cost of an F-35,' and thus around $300 million per aircraft.[42] With the fighter not only being technologically a generation ahead, but also being much larger potentially over twice the size, being produced on a much smaller scale, and expected to have well over double the endurance, this cost was far from unexpected, with comparable cost ratios seen between the F-5 and F-15 or the F-16 and F-22. Indeed, this was still viewed as a conservative estimate, and remained below the Congressional Budget Office's prior projection of around $375 million in 2024 for a long-range sixth generation fighter.[43] With only 200 NGAD fighters intended to be procured, confirmation in January 2025 that the program still had $20 billion of expected development costs alone before completion, meaning on average $100 million more spending per fighter before production had even begun, highlighted the conservative nature of the projection of $300 million.[44]

The issue of affordability was expected to be further exacerbated by heretofore unseen sustainment costs. Much as sustainment costs had increased significantly between all previous generations, as seen from the F-4 to the F-15 to the F-22, a similar rise in sustainment costs and maintenance needs relative to the F-22 was expected. As air power expert at the Royal United Services Institute Justin Bronk was among many to observe, the NGAD fighter was expected to cost: 'possibly well north of $300 million per airframe, and it's going to cost multiples of what even an F-22 costs to fly per hour, so probably in somewhere the region of $180,000-$200,000 an hour to fly.' 'However much you need that capability from an operational requirements point of view, and they do seem to need it, it's a pretty tall order to ask how to fit that into a fighter program that is already unaffordable and in crisis – bluntly,' he stated, projecting that this could necessitate deep cuts to other programs, and possibly to operations, should financing NGAD be prioritised.[45]

Kendall confirmed that the Air Force was reassessing requirements for its sixth generation fighter, and that a redesign was seen to be necessary to reduce costs, even if this meant sacrificing some capabilities. This mirrored similar cost cutting which had gradually eroded the Advanced Tactical Fighter's capabilities throughout the 1990s. Kendall specified that one option being explored was to integrate a smaller and less complex engine, indicating that the fighter's range and flight performance could be among the first specifications to which sacrifices were made. Priority would be 'the most cost-effective propulsion system,' he observed, rather than the most capable.[46] Former Air Force Deputy Chief of Staff for Strategy, Integration and Requirements Clint Hinote had on 21 June noted that the Next-Generation Adaptive Propulsion program for the NGAD, a successor to the Adaptive Engine Transition Program considered for the F-35, could be a primary factor driving up NGAD's overall costs.[47]

On 30 July Kendall stated that the pause of several months on developing the NGAD was needed 'to figure out whether we've got the right design and make sure we're on the right course.' He nevertheless expressed confidence that the Air Force was 'still going to do a sixth-generation crewed aircraft.'[48] An Air Force spokesperson that day confirmed that the service was pausing source selection of the program 'as we reconsider the design based on changing threats and affordability,' and would proceed with development after 'concept definition.'[49] Kendall had two years prior announced on 1 June 2022 that the NGAD program had entered its engineering, manufacturing, and development (EMD) phase,[50] before four months later conceding that the program had only entered the EMD phase 'in my colloquial sense,' and that it was not in fact that far along in development.[51] The need for a pause in mid-2024, and re-evaluation of design choices and the course of the program, however, indicated that the program had moved significantly backwards from 'colloquial' EMD.

Following the pause in development, *Breaking Defense* highlighted prevailing uncertainty as to 'how long the service's plans to field the Next Generation Air Dominance fighter may be pushed out.'[52] *Air Force Magazine*, meanwhile, raised the possibility that delays could force the USAF to keep the F-22 in service longer than previously intended.[53] The Air Force subsequently missed its goal of awarding a contract for the fighter in 2024, with Kendall confirming that indecision was driven by two primary factors: budgetary constraints and concerns about the rapid pace of adversaries' technological innovation.[54]

Marking the culmination of years of rising uncertainty regarding the program's future, on 4 September Assistant Secretary of the Air Force for Acquisition, Technology & Logistics Andrew Hunter and Vice Chief of Staff General James Slife confirmed that the pause in NGAD's development would be used to revisit fundamental questions about the aircraft. 'From a requirements perspective, what I would say is we're going back and starting at the beginning with "What is the thing we're trying to do?"' Slife said. He added:

> '"How do we achieve air superiority in a contested environment?" would be one way to frame the question. A different way to frame the question would be, "How do we build a sixth-gen manned fighter platform?" I mean, those are not necessarily the same question ... I don't know exactly how we are going to achieve air superiority in a contested environment,' Slife continued. 'It may involve a manned sixth-gen fighter platform, but we're kind of going back and looking, you know, from the beginning.'[55]

The first official artwork released by a U.S. government source depicting the Next Generation Air Dominance fighter. The image was published in March 2025, as Boeing as declared to have won the contract for designing the crewed fighter in form of the F-47. (USAF)

This was interpreted to imply that alternatives to fielding a sixth generation air superiority fighter were being seriously considered. Secretary Hunter would four months later note that the U.S. may only begin bringing sixth generation fighters into service after China had already done so.[56]

Amid increasingly constrained budgets and growing uncertainty surrounding NGAD's future, General Allvin had in July presented what appeared to be part of a highly concessional attempt at compromise to save the sixth generation program, namely the development of a lightweight fighter.[57] This was corroborated by Secretary Kendall, who in September stated the goal of producing a sixth generation fighter at a comparable or lower cost to the F-35, which would necessitate a much smaller size than previously envisaged.[58] The viability even of a very light sixth generation fighter being procured for under $100 million, however, appeared far from plausible, with fighter costs having consistently risen with each generation, even for aircraft of comparable weight, due to their growing complexity.[59]

A lightweight fighter would inevitably have a far shorter range and carry far smaller sensor and electronic warfare suites than a heavyweight could, but could provide the only means of moving forwards in the face of an inability to afford to compete at the top level in the sixth generation. Such a fighter could potentially pose a greater threat to the F-35 program, as its more affordable procurement and operational costs would allow it to be fielded in greater numbers, thus reducing the need for large numbers of F-35s as part of a high-low combination with a small elite of sixth generation heavyweight fighters. Indeed, Secretary Kendall in January 2025 specifically referred to the possibility of a sixth generation fighter 'that looks more like an F-35 follow-on,' indicating that one option to allow the Air Force to field a sixth generation fighter was to abandon the high-low combination and invest solely in the 'low' end of lighter shorter ranged fighters.[60] This would follow a broader trend of heavier fighters, specifically F-15s and F-22s, forming a smaller portion of the Air Force's fleet after the end of the Cold War, and the Navy's abandonment of heavyweight fighters altogether during this period as available funds contracted. The vast distances fighters were required to operate over in the Pacific made reliance on a lighter fighter particularly disadvantageous.

In November 2024, Secretary Kendall openly raised unprecedented questions regarding the affordability of procuring a combination of sixth generation fighters, and the aerial refuelling tankers and highly autonomous drones needed to operate alongside them in the Pacific, with the three programs confirmed to be closely linked. Reflecting the growing consensus among analysts, in an article titled 'Crisis Brewing Over Air Force's Future Air Dominance Plans Which It Cannot Afford,' writers at *The War Zone* described Kendall's statement as 'deeply concerning pronouncements about the state of the Next Generation Air Dominance (NGAD) initiative.'[61] 'At one point, NGAD's status might have looked all but bulletproof, but developments in recent months have, for the first time, raised the very real prospect of the fighter component, at least, being significantly cut back or even cancelled altogether,' they observed the following month.[62]

In January 2025 it was revealed that the Air Force was considering a greater focus on long range strike capabilities, primarily greater arsenals of modern missiles on older aircraft, as an alternative to NGAD. A watered down fighter that would serve as a 'quarterback' for drone fleets was another lower cost alternative being considered. Secretary Kendall elaborated that the Air Force could procure 'something that's much less expensive, something that's a multi-role aircraft that is designed to be a manager of CCAs [unmanned Collaborative Combat Aircraft] and designed more for that role ... And then there was another option we thought about, which is reliance more on long-range strike.' As another alternative, he stated, 'We could [also] just continue to rely on F-35 and keep it going for [the] foreseeable future and focus on CCAs,' adding 'I'm not quite ready to do that personally.'[63] The course selected, and the success with which it could be pursued, would thus have very significant implications for the F-35 program.

The F-35 in the Sixth Generation Era

Within three months of China's unveiling of its two sixth generation fighters on 26 December 2024, it was confirmed on 21 March that the NGAD program would move ahead, and that Boeing had been selected as the primary contractor to develop a fighter under the designation F-47. The affordability of the program, however, remained in serious question, which further fuelled calls to increase

Digital rendering released by Boeing showing a U.S. Air Force E-7 Wedgetail airborne warning and control system, should the service proceed with procurement. The future of the aircraft and the American AWACS fleet was left highly uncertain in mid-2025, as Congress sought to prevent the Pentagon from cancelling planned procurements, while the Air Force struggled to fund multiple high priority new programs simultaneously. (USAF)

funding for the Air Force and make cuts to other programs. Air Force Chief of Staff General David Allvin, for one, on 16 May stressed that increased investment in air power was vital to America's new focus on preparing for war in the Pacific, and made a highly outspoken call for increases to the Air Force's budget, even if this was done at the expense of other services.[64]

Speculation regarding how the Department of Defense could afford the F-47's immense development, procurement and projected operational costs was widespread, with cuts to programs such as B-52 modernisation being hinted at from May,[65] while some analysts indicated that deep cuts to operations in Africa and other regions could be made specifically for this purpose.[66] On 11 June it was confirmed that the planned procurement of 26 E-7 airborne warning and control systems had been cancelled, despite the aircraft's vital role as force multipliers for the F-35 fleet in the Pacific in particular, and in spite of the considerable value that had been attributed to their ability to track Chinese stealth aircraft. The lack of survivability of such large non-stealth support aircraft was cited as a reason for the decision.[67] With the F-47 being prioritised, cuts to funding for modernisation and sustainment of the F-22 appeared increasingly likely, while the Trump administration's unexpected offer in early June to export the new sixth generation fighter to Japan appeared to be an effort to ensure that foreign sales could help cover development costs and drive down unit production costs. As the USAF's greatest investment in annual procurements, however, it was the F-35A program where some of the greatest savings could potentially be made from cuts.

On 11 June the Department of Defense halved its request to Congress for F-35A procurements for the USAF from 48 to just 24 fighters, which was widely speculated by analysts to be intended to increase the availability of funds for the F-47.[68] It was subsequently confirmed that of the House's $150 billion reconciliation package of additional defence spending, no funding would be allocated to the F-35, despite allocations being made for the F-47 and F-15EX. Todd Harrison, of the American Enterprise Institute, was among the analysts to assess that the decision 'says something about the sentiment around the F-35.'[69] With Lockheed Martin's stock value having been negatively impacted by China's unveiling of its sixth generation fighters six months prior, it had long been expected that an accelerated race to the sixth generation era would negatively impact the F-35 program, as procurements would be increasingly difficult to justify with the aircraft falling a generation behind the cutting edge.[70]

Beyond cuts within the Air Force itself, a Pentagon request to the House and Senate defence policy committees in May highlighted the possibility of making cuts to funding for the Navy's F/A-XX to reallocate investment to the F-47. 'Given the schedule delays and cost growth across numerous airframes, DoD recommends a focus on the F-47, giving the Navy's F/A-XX program time for technical maturity and development,' it observed, adding: 'Phasing the F/A-XX after the Air Force's initial F-47 development will alleviate capacity concerns in the industrial base.'[71] This followed continued delays to award contracts for the F/A-XX's development, with Pentagon officials reported in May to be seeking to delay the program by up to three years. Contracts were initially intended to be announced in March 2025.[72] While in late 2024 it appeared that the F/A-XX had a more certain future among the two sixth generation programs, the Air Force's serious struggles funding its program had the potential to disrupt the one being pursued by the Navy.

The U.S. Air Force's significant cuts to the number of planned operational squadrons in the mid-2010s and early 2020s, plans for further cuts in future, and plans to begin very early retirements of the F-22, were noted by analysts to have left 'a lot riding on' the F-47.[73] As observed by the writer in 2022:

> This made the potential fallout far greater should the program face even half the delays, defects and other performance issues that the F-35 had, leaving the U.S. at risk of ceding a significant

air superiority advantage to China. With the Air Force having given up on plans to expand its fighter fleet, conceded to repeated failure in its effort to raise operational rates, deeply cut the F-22 program, and produced F-35 at a fraction of initially planned rates, the NGAD may well have represented its last chance to reverse the trend towards relative decline in its position.[74]

This situation would only become more extreme as major increases in projected costs for the F-47 itself forced further significant cuts to other programs from early 2025. Should development of the F-47 face major delays or cancellation, it would force the USAF to adapt to the new realities of an era where a peer level competitor had a larger fleet that was similarly if not more advanced. It would require a major shift in thinking towards a focus on tackling adversaries asymmetrically. This could mirror the shift undertaken by the Marine Corps from 2020 under its Force Design 2030 plan. It would also allow the Air Force to avoid major sacrifices to the wider fleet, including to the F-35 program, needed to finance the sixth generation program.

Despite strong signs of renewed resolve from early 2025 to develop a top performing air superiority fighter for the USAF, there remained a significant possibility that the F-47 would face serious delays and even eventual cancellation. This had direct implications for the F-35, with a more problematic F-47 expected to result in more funding for the older aircraft. There were multiple precedents for countries responding to an inability to compete in the latest generation of fighter aviation by investing heavily in developing enhanced variants of last generation fleets, with Russia's reliance on enhanced derivatives of the Su-27, such as the Su-35, to counter NATO's F-35 fleets being a case in point.

The significant benefits which a cancellation of NGAD could have for the F-35 program were highlighted by officials from the F135 engine's primary contractor Pratt and Whitney in 2023, with F135 program chief Jen Latka observing that Lockheed Martin's support for integrating a sixth generation level engine onto the fighter under the Adaptive Engine Transition Program, was intended 'to delay or stop the sixth-gen competition.'[75] Senior vice president of global government relations for Pratt and Whitney's parent company RTX, Jeff Shockey, observed to this effect: 'It's not surprising that Lockheed is attempting to turn the F-35 into a sixth-gen fighter, which it will never be,' with the firm 'trying to negate the need for a sixth-gen fighter competition to extend the longevity of their contract.' 'Maybe their goal isn't to have a sixth-gen platform at all and simply turn the F-35 into something that's close enough.' He criticised such efforts on the basis that 'all Pentagon analysis shows that a sixth-generation fighter is needed to stay ahead of advancing near-peer threats in the INDOPACOM [Indo-Pacific Command] region.'[76] Although work on the Adaptive Engine Transition Program was terminated in 2023, issues with the F-47 could lead to a renewed interest in integrating a clean sheet engine design and other major new subsystems into the F-35.

With Lockheed Martin's sixth generation fighter proposals having been rejected by the Air Force and the Navy, while the F-35's appeal was increasingly limited by questions regarding its viability in a battlespace dominated by sixth generation fighters, the firm redoubled efforts to offer heavily enhanced F-35 variants, leading to the term '5+ generation' fighter to for the first time begin to be widely used. This would position Lockheed Martin to benefit considerably should the F-47 face major difficulties, providing the Air Force with a stopgap to face Chinese sixth generation aircraft until its own fighter units could be equipped with comparably advanced aircraft. Heavily enhanced F-35s also had significant potential to gain orders from clients other than the USAF. In the Pacific in particular, states which either could not afford the F-47, or were unable to procure it for political reasons, could also show a greater interest in a heavily enhanced F-35 as new sixth generation programs set a higher bar for air-to-air combat performance. Similarly enhanced F-35C fighters could also appeal to the Navy and Marine Corps, particularly if prioritisation of funding for the F-47 seriously undercut the F/A-XX program.

On 22 April Lockheed Martin president and CEO Jim Taiclet stated that he believed an enhanced F-35 could deliver 80 percent of the F-47's capability at half its cost. 'We have 70,000 engineers and scientists in the company working on really interesting stuff all the time. Some of the fifth-gen-plus solution set is already being funded by the U.S. government and the F-35 program itself,' he stated, elaborating that upgrades involved 'key techniques, I'll say, and approaches that [the] fighter pilot needs to have to be competitive and win.'[77] He elaborated that '5+ generation' F-35 variants could

Early concept art released by Boeing for the F/A-XX. (Boeing)

pair 'the best radar' with new generations of passive infrared sensors, while noting that it would be possible to alter 'materials ... geometries [and] countermeasures' to increase stealth capabilities, which some sources speculated could involve removing vertical tails.[78] 'We think we can get most of the way to sixth-gen at half the cost,' he concluded.[79] With the F-47 expected to cost well over $300 million to procure, this would provide room to more than double the F-35A's procurement cost with new enhancements. The F-47's sustainment costs were expected to be several times as high as those of the F-35, giving enhanced variants of the older fighter a potentially much greater affordability advantage than Taiclet had indicated, with a just fraction of the newer fighter's lifetime costs.

Speaking on 28 May, Taiclet emphasised that airframe reshaping and use of new radar absorbent coatings could significantly improve the F-35's stealth capabilities. 'There have been some adjustments or learnings, I'll say, on what we call the outer mold line, which is the actual shape of the aircraft itself, especially with regard to engine inlets and outflows of nozzles, that we might be able to again improve on the F-35 without redesigning it,' he stated. 'We could make the F-35 pilot optional over a relatively modest time frame based on a lot of the development we've done' for sixth-generation fighters, he further noted, adding: 'we feel like within two to three years, we could have a meaningful increase of capability for the F-35 by porting some of these technologies over.' He cautioned, however, that efforts to enhance the F-35 needed to be made incrementally, 'because you cannot introduce too much new equipment or too much new software at once, necessarily without interrupting the production flow.'[80]

Should the F-47 fall short of expectations, a larger fleet of F-35s with more funding for ambitious modernisation, and provided with top end support from new generations of stealth tankers and airborne early warning and control systems, had the potential to fill the gap in the fleet. A combination of of stealth tanker support and a sixth generation level three-stream adaptive cycle engine could help to compensate for the fighter's serious deficiencies in range, while a large fleet of E-7s could compensate for the situational awareness limitations imposed by its relatively small radar size. The possibility of the F-47 seeing planned numbers cut, and being reserved almost exclusively for the Pacific, could also lead to more funding for enhancing the F-35 to serve as a premier fighter in other theatres, much as deep cuts to F-22 and F-35 procurements resulted in more funding for F-15 and F-16 modernisation.

Moving into the sixth generation era the F-47, F/A-XX, the F-35 and the B-21 are expected to rely increasingly heavily on unmanned semi-autonomous 'wingman' aircraft, a family of which was developed under the Collaborative Combat Aircraft (CCA) program. Issues with sixth generation programs could see the F-35 re-prioritised to pair with CCAs, allowing the fighters to serve as minor command centres. In January 2025 Lockheed Martin confirmed that the F-35 'has the capability to control drones, including the U.S. Air Force's future fleet of Collaborative Combat Aircraft,' with new technologies allowing pilots 'to direct multiple drones to engage enemies using a touchscreen tablet in the cockpit of their 5th Gen aircraft.' The firm had 'demonstrated end-to-end connectivity including the seamless integration of AI technologies to control a drone in flight utilising the same hardware and software architectures built for future F-35 flight testing.' It noted that 'AI-enabled architectures' allowed it to 'not only prove out piloted-drone teaming capabilities,' but also to incrementally improve.'[81]

Between four and six unmanned aircraft are intended to accompany each fighter. They are expected to use their sensors to maximise situational awareness, their armaments to allow each pilot to direct several times more firepower than a fighter alone can carry, and in some cases their superior stealth capabilities and relative expendability to deploy closer to enemy defences. These accompanying aircraft are also expected to carry supporting equipment such as electronic warfare suites and directed energy weapons, with some also expected to be developed specifically to serve as decoys to draw fire and protect their higher value wingmen. With procurement and sustainment costs of unmanned aircraft expected to be significantly lower than those of fighters such as the

Rendering by Boeing of a Royal Australian Air Force E-7 commanding two MQ-28 Ghost Bat CCAs. It is expected that CCAs will be controlled not only by '5+' and sixth generation fighters, but also by bombers and airborne warning and control systems. Both the E-7 and the MQ-28 are leading contenders to be procured to support American F-35 operations, and have already been selected to do so for the Royal Australian Air Force. (Boeing)

F-35 or F-47, the result would be fleets which are overall significantly larger, but have much smaller numbers of manned fighters. Unmanned aircraft are expected to revolutionise the combat potentials of F-35 units, but also compete with F-35s for funding and potentially significantly reduce the overall number of stealth fighters procured.

The much larger scale at which the United States conducts research and development, and its significantly greater experience developing fighter aircraft, is expected to ensure that the F-35 once modernised and paired with CCAs remains competitive against, and likely boasts a number of significant performance advantages over, the sixth generation fighters developed in Europe and Russia. Indeed, it is likely that aircraft developed under European programs will have performances much closer to a '5+ generation' F-35 than to high performing Chinese and American sixth generation aircraft, with one of the clearest limitations being their use of tail fins. Nevertheless, while unmanned 'wingmen' and new generations of stealth coatings, engines, weaponry, sensors and other avionics may do much to narrow the performance gap between the F-35 and top performing Chinese sixth generation fighters, the Chinese jets are still expected to retain major advantages over anything other than a fully funded iteration of the F-47 or F/A-XX.

Naval Aviation in the Sixth Generation Era

Until the announcement of Boeing's selection as the primary contractor to develop the F-47, a significant possibility had emerged that while the USAF may not field a sixth generation fighter before the late 2030s, the Navy could begin to do so far sooner. The F/A-XX had received far more commitment from the service than the NGAD had from the Air Force, with the small scale of F-35C procurements being among the multiple factors contributing to the sixth generation program's importance to the fleet's future. After development work was confirmed to have commenced in August 2021,[82] the Navy would elaborate two months later regarding program goals: 'specific capabilities and technologies are under development, however analysis shows it must have longer range and greater speed, incorporate passive and active sensor technology, and possess the capability to employ the longer-range weapons programmed for the future.'[83]

Following the end of the Cold War, the Navy had not only ended procurement of the F-14 long range fighter in 1991, but that year also cancelled plans to develop a fifth generation successor to the aircraft. In subsequent years the focus on conflicts in Europe and the Middle East meant that fielding aircraft from the latest generation in the Air Force alone was viewed as sufficient. The 2030s had the potential to see a reversal of this situation, aligning with the shift in the pacing challenge from Europe to the Pacific, where the Navy has traditionally played a far more central role than in other theatres. Air Force fighters remained limited to operating from a small number of bases in the Pacific, with the closest somewhat survivable facility to China being Anderson Air Force Base on Guam, from which a combat radius of well over 3,000 kilometres would be needed to operate effectively. The Navy's carriers were expected to be significantly more survivable at closer distances, with the expected blinding of enemy satellites in a war's initial stages potentially rendering the ships difficult to locate, allowing them to forward deploy sixth generation fighters in ways the Air Force could not. F/A-XX fighters could also see complementary ground-based deployments by the Navy, much as the F-35C had, to complement carrier deployments. Thus if there was a choice between which of the two services ought to be prioritised to see its sixth generation fighter program financed, there were strong argument that the Navy should be the one. This would be far from unprecedented, with the Navy's tactical combat aviation having played a much more central role in the first Pacific War in the 1940s, while the USAF's predecessor, the U.S. Army Air Force, played a central role in strategic bombing.

In October 2024 Chief of Naval Operations Admiral Lisa Franchetti confirmed that the Navy would press ahead with development of a long-range high performance sixth generation fighter, despite the Air Force having suspended work on the NGAD program. The program's timeline for service entry was highly similar

Growing issues of major cost overruns and repeated delays of major armament procurement programs affecting the U.S. Air Force and Navy in the mid-2020s occurred at a time when China's defence sector appeared to be working much more smoothly to bring multiple types of new stealth combat aircraft into service. Pictured above are flight prototypes for two separate Chinese sixth generation fighter programs, both of which were unveiled on 26 December 2024. (Chinese Internet via Military Watch Magazine)

to that previously laid out for the Air Force's fighter. In an apparent response to the issues facing NGAD, Franchetti highlighted that although it was important that the Navy and Air Force's programs were aligned to some degree, this was not the most critical factor for the development of the F/A-XX.[84] Analysts at *The War Zone* were among many to observe that the admiral appeared to be 'making an effort to distance F/A-XX from the current uncertainties around the Air Force's NGAD.'[85] Director of the air warfare division in the Office of the Chief of Naval Operations Rear Admiral Michael Donnelly in November similarly emphasised that the service's F/A-XX program was being pursued independently. 'In totality, they are two unique programs from an acquisition point of view and also going forward, so we're relatively independent of each other at this point,' he stated, adding that the F/A-XX was on track to enter the Engineering and Manufacturing Development phase by October 2025.[86]

As was the case with the NGAD and the F-35A in the Air Force, the course the F/A-XX program took was closely linked to the futures of the F-35C and F-18E/F. In March 2024 Undersecretary of the Navy Erik Raven confirmed that the service was strongly prioritising funding for the F/A-XX at the expense of other programs, stating: 'We knowingly took risks in the schedule for [the] development of those programs in order to prioritise those key investments — whether that's readiness, or investing in our people, or undersea, to make sure that we make those programs whole.'[87] A significant example was the decision in 2020 to reduce planned procurements of F-18E/Fs, which was expected to facilitate the allocation of over $4 billion to developing the F/A-XX.[88] The House Appropriations Committee had notably cautioned against an excessive focus on the F/A-XX at the expense of other fighter programs. It highlighted that, much as the Navy had been forced invest much more heavily than expected in continued procurement of the F-18E/F due specifically to delays with the F-35C, so too should the service be ready to rely more heavily on the F-35C should the F/A-XX face similar delays.[89] Reports that the F-18E/F fleet was deteriorating much faster than the F-18C/D fleet had, with aircraft suffering from lower availability rates when at similar ages, placed further pressure on the F/A-XX program, and increased the likelihood of expanded F-35C orders should the sixth generation program face delays.[90]

The strong prioritization of funding the F-47 from early 2025, the delays to awarding a contract for the F/A-XX, and plans to deprioritise funding for the Navy's program, seriously diminished the possibility of the Navy fielding America's primary fighter capability in the sixth generation era or bringing its fighter into service at an earlier date. With the prioritisation of the F-47's development being potentially devastating for the F/A-XX, while also having the potential to result in deep cuts to F-35A procurements, it was also highly possible that this would significantly increase demand for the F-35C. With F-18E/F production set to conclude in 2027, the Navy's planned F-35C procurements had remained highly conservative primarily due to its plans to quickly operationalise a sixth generation fighter. As the future of the F/A-XX became increasingly uncertain, the possibility of a major expansion in F-35C orders, and of procurement of more capable '5+ generation' variants with extended ranges, appeared increasingly likely.

11

EVALUATION

Program Reception

The discourse surrounding the F-35 from the mid-2010s throughout the following decade has consistently been highly polarised, with the program's supporters often focusing on its impressive next generation technologies while downplaying the very serious performance shortcomings, delays and cost overruns that have hindered it, and vice versa for the program's critics. This is reflected in the books published on the subject, with some such as *F-35: The Inside Story of the Lightning II*, by former Executive Vice President and General Manager of the program Tom Burbage and associates, fitting the pattern of assessments by its supporters, while others such as *American Gripen: The Solution To The F-35 Nightmare*, by David Archibald, provide dedicated critiques. This polarisation contrasts with the F-35's fourth generation predecessors the F-16 and F-18 which were near unanimously seen as major successes, and with other problematic post-Cold War programs such as the Zumwalt-class destroyer and Littoral Combat ship, around which strong consensuses formed that they were resounding failures. Despite wide ranging issues with the program, important factors allowing the F-35 to avoid a negative consensus have included the fact that deep cuts to production, although appearing increasingly inevitable by the mid-2020s, had not been confirmed, as well as the fact that the fighter still proved to have a significantly greater combat potential than any of its predecessors.

Despite a lack of consensus on the F-35, criticisms were significantly harsher than those levelled against any other major weapons program. In January 2021 Defense Secretary Christopher Miller famously stated that 'the F-35 is a piece of ****,' and that by pursuing the program the Pentagon 'have created a monster,'[1] while his predecessor, Patrick Shanahan, referred to it in 2019 as 'f—ed up,' asserting that Lockheed Martin did not know how to run a program properly.[2] A subsequent inquiry by the Pentagon's Office of the Inspector General found that Shanahan's criticisms 'were consistent with other comments about problems in the F-35 program made by other senior DoD officials.'[3] The rejection of the firm's proposals from both sixth generation fighter tenders supported arguments that such a consensus had indeed formed in the DoD.

Reports from the Pentagon and senior officials over more than a decade consistently singled out the F-35 for criticism for its poor reliability, low availability rates, and major overruns in development, procurement and sustainment costs.[4] Reports by the National Security Network,[5] the RAND Corporation,[6] the Project on Government Oversight,[7] the Government Accountability Office,[8] and other think tanks and agencies, were very frequently similarly critical, as were individuals associated with oversight such as the Defense Department's Director of Operational Test and Evaluation Michael Gilmore,[9] and fellow at the Project on Government Oversight Dan Grazier.[10] Grazier, for one, in 2019 observed 'a host of alarming

F-35Cs alongside F/A-18E and F/A-18F Super Hornets during routine carrier operations onboard the USS *Abraham Lincoln*. (USN)

problems' and a 'lack of progress in nearly every essential area' to bring the F-35 closer to being combat ready, including continued malfunctions for 'most combat-crucial computer systems,' major cybersecurity vulnerabilities, and 'so many cracks' requiring 'so many repairs and modifications.' His assessments in both prior and in subsequent years were little more optimistic.[11]

Although the Air Force and Navy did not formally lower their planned F-35 procurement numbers after the 2000s, their procurement-related decisions strongly indicated that accommodations were being made for deep cuts, and that they were far from satisfied with the fighter's performance. The Navy's decision to extend procurements of the F-18E/F and E/A-18G by over a decade, while limiting procurement rates of the F-35C, was one notable example, as was its intention to minimise overall F-35C procurements in order to prioritise the F/A-XX. Air Force officials, from 2021, increasingly highlighted that an alternative fighter to the F-35A was being considered, with possibilities raised including an enhanced F-16, a '5- generation' F-16 sized light fighter, and a derivative of the T-7 trainer. These proposals all highlighted the service's issues with the F-35's high operational costs and low availability rates. The Air Force's resurgence in investment in its fourth generation fleet from the late 2010s, including major modernisation and life extension programs for hundreds of F-16s, provided a further indication that F-35A procurement on the scale previously envisaged was unlikely be materialise.

Despite the significant criticisms directed at the F-35 program, the fighter was consistently praised by its pilots for providing a tremendously greater capability than any of its rivals. Pilots

An F-35A assigned to the U.S. Air Force 48th Fighter Wing next to a Belgian Air Component F-16A. Many aspects of the F-22 and F-35 programs compared highly unfavourably with their fourth generation predecessors, ranging from the extent of delays to their operationalisation, to the number of bugs affecting them years after entering service, and their availability rates which were by far the poorest in the fleet. The F-35 in particular, however, realised tremendous capability advantages over other American fighter classes despite these difficulties. (USAF)

emphasised that the fighter's much greater versatility and sophistication than the F-22 was highly valued, that its situational awareness advantages were difficult for those who had never flown it to comprehend, and that its combination of stealth, electronic warfare and data sharing capabilities was unprecedentedly potent.[12] Evaluations by overseas clients against fourth generation fighters also saw the F-35 consistently favoured by a wide margin, with foreign air forces proving willing to make major sacrifices including deep cuts to flight training hours and the budgeting of tremendous additional operational costs in order to accommodate the aircraft rather than selecting an F-18E/F, Eurofighter or other competitors. Although the F-35's combat performance had a number of significant shortcomings, whether it was its limited flight performance that pilots conceded was 'nowhere near the F-15C or the [F-18] Hornet,'[13] or its lack of off-boresight targeting capabilities when configured for stealth, there was little doubt that once in the air, the fighter's overall combat potential was by far the greatest in the Western world. The unparalleled investments made in the fighter's modernisation ensured that these advantages were set to continue to grow. Thus, while the F-35 program suffered from immense inefficiencies, and produced a much more expensive and maintenance intensive and overall less capable aircraft than envisioned, this far from equated to the F-35 not being a world leader in its performance.

Industrial Trends

Issues with the F-35 program have been widely assessed as symptoms of a general decline in the US defence sector and industrial base following the end of the Cold War, which had resulted in most major programs falling far short of expectations. The F-22 and B-2 programs were notable examples, and suffered from significantly greater shortcomings than the F-35 itself. Founder of Palantir Technologies Peter Thiel summarised in 2021 that the Cold War's end saw 'a shrinking of military budgets, but there was also an incredible consolidation of the defence industry, and the consolidation actually meant the money was spent less efficiently, especially with respect to R&D. And so we spent less money and [with] less efficiency, and so there was some massive decline in the effectiveness of the system in the 90s.'[14] A smaller defence sector left the Pentagon heavily dependent on inputs from abroad, ranging from circuit boards and chemicals to machine tools and infrared detectors, while leaving entire industries near extinction domestically, and aircraft suppliers in states of perpetual financial risk facing bankruptcy threats.[15] Many of the inputs that still came from domestic sources were procured from uncompetitive niche manufacturers, which often had questionable future survivability.[16] Industrial Capabilities reports thus highlighting significant risks from 'dependence on single and sole source suppliers, capacity shortfalls, a lack of competition, a lack of workforce skills, and unstable demand.'[17]

From 2008, as a consequence of both sharper industrial decline and further cuts to defence spending, a significant increase in consolidations among firms supplying military or dual use goods reduced the ability of market forces to raise performance and reduce costs. Contraction of the defence sector had further detrimental impacts on innovation, as while top tier defence contractors such as Lockheed Martin focused on systems integration, they were found to be 'pushing the burden of innovation lower into the supply chain.' The smaller firms relied on to innovate were those that were most vulnerable to the fallout from industrial decline, thus disproportionately harming the defence sector's capacity for innovation. Observing this trend, former analyst at the RAND Corporation Michael Webber highlighted: 'if the manufacturing support base no longer adequately serves the innovative companies, then their ability to be competitive is hindered and innovation does not move up the chain to the top-tier integrators. Consequently, the health of the entire innovation food chain, and thus the entire national innovation system and the defence industrial base, relies on the health of the foundation of the entire system: the manufacturing support base.'[18] These issues were exacerbated by increasingly severe shortages in skilled workers, such as engineers and software developers.[19]

By the early 2020s, issues with the American defence sector had grown sufficiently serious that the possibility of measures as radical as nationalisation began to be openly raised. In July 2020 USAF head of acquisitions William Roper highlighted that this would allow the Air Force to avoid the tremendous inefficiencies in ownership, sustainment and modernisation costs caused by the existing system. This could be necessary 'if our industrial base collapses any more,' he said, concluding that 'everything has to change,' and elaborating that what talent existed was being drawn away from the defence sector.[20] Vice President of Analysis at the Teal Group aviation consulting firm Richard Aboulafia noted that the prospect of nationalising America's military aviation sector was 'an admission that they have failed miserably,'[21] with Army Chief of Staff Mark Milley being among growing numbers to highlight that China's nationalised defence industries were producing armaments far more cost effectively.[22] Many of the most serious shortcomings of the F-35 program were symptomatic of larger issues with the defence sector that were affecting multiple smaller programs, with the program's sheer size allowing it to draw attention to these issues. Senate Armed Services Committee Chairman John McCain accordingly referred to the F-35 program as 'a textbook example' of the country's 'broken defence acquisition system,' which had made it 'both a scandal and a tragedy with respect to cost, schedule and performance.'[23] Beyond the procurement system, however, were deeper maladies with the defence sector and the wider industrial base which would be significantly more difficult to address.

Revolutionary Impacts

By the mid-2020s the fact that the F-35 program had fallen far short of expectations was undisputed, as was the fact that its shortcomings were far from isolated and stemmed from maladies that were more broadly affecting defence sector. The F-35's range, sustainment costs, availability rates and persistent defects, the major delays to bringing the aircraft into service, and the significant troubles with its engine, were among the primary targets for criticism. The structure of the program, and its allowing of the F-35B's STOVL design requirements to seriously undermine the performances of the other two variants, was another serious source of criticism.[24] The February 2025's Marine Corps' de-prioritisation of the STOVL capabilities for which so much had been sacrificed – after reports of major issues employing F-35Bs for Expeditionary Advanced Base Operations – only exacerbated this controversy. Nevertheless, with no serious non-Chinese competition within its generation, the fighter's dominance in combat performance, and consequentially on global markets, was almost unchallenged. The F-35 was entirely in a league of its own for NATO compatible fighters in terms of its combat potential, with its introduction having a revolutionary impact on the aerial warfare capabilities of the United States and its strategic partners across the world.

The F-35's dominance was in large part the product of post-Soviet deterioration of the Russian defence sector and its broader tech sector, industrial base and economy. This ensured that fighter

The front end of an F-35B from the Maine Fighter Attack Squadron 242, as seen while undergoing in-flight refuelling from a Boeing KC-46 tanker. (USAF)

units equipped with F-35s would retain tremendous dominance both over those of the Russian Armed Forces, and those of the vast network of states that relied on Russian fighters. While Soviet and Russian proliferation of advanced third and fourth generation combat jets such as the MiG-25PD, MiG-29, and Su-30 had posed peer level challenges to American F-15s, F-16s, and F-18s across multiple theatres, from South America to Southeast Asia, they had no successor that could compete with the F-35. Thus Australia and Singapore's F-35s would have uncontested dominance over Indonesia and Malaysia's Su-30s that had previously challenged their fleets, Poland's F-35s over Belarus' MiG-29s and Su-30s, South Korea and Japan's F-35s over North Korea's MiG-29s, Israel's F-35s over Syria, Egypt and Iran's MiG-29s, and NATO's F-35s over Algeria and Russia's Su-30s and Su-35s. In all these cases, advanced Soviet and Russian fourth generation fighters had posed serious challenges to U.S. and allied fourth generation fleets, with the balance of power being transformed as these fleets moved into the fifth generation leaving their Russian-equipped competitors behind.

In March 2021 the editorial of the *Air and Space Forces Magazine* observed of the F-35's significance: 'The radar-evading F-35's very presence changes the nature of battle. It's a strategic investment and combat tool, not a tactical one.'[25] References to the deployment of a relatively low level tactical asset as having a strategic impact were not unprecedented, and mirrored Western commentaries on the tremendous implications that the deployment of the Soviet T-64 tank had in the 1960s. With a level of technological sophistication over 15 years ahead of any competition, U.S. Army Four Star General Donn Starry observed to this effect when the T-64 was deployed: 'the Soviets have achieved a technical development at the tactical level of war which has strategic implications. We haven't seen anything like that in Europe since the advent of tactical nuclear weapons.'[26] Much as the T-64 had transformed the strategic balance across the frontlines in Europe, and forced NATO members to adopt a range of asymmetric solutions such as greater reliance on tactical nuclear weapons and man-portable anti-tank missiles, so too did the F-35's deployment across the continent stimulate a similar approach from Russia as it fundamentally transformed the threat it faced from the air. The F-35 was one of very few tactical systems to have so great an impact on the balance of power, with precedents among fighters in the Cold War era being few and far between.

Before the F-35, stealth fighters had been fielded in a small number of niche units, none of which had armaments, sensors or electronic warfare suites optimised for air defence suppression. Top end air defence suppression and electronic intelligence capabilities were similarly relegated to specialist aircraft such as the E/A-18G and EP-3E. The F-35 not only brought these capabilities together in

Italian Air Force F-35A encounters Russian Aerospace Forces Su-30SM over Eastern Europe. (Russian Internet)

an unprecedented way, but did so on a versatile frontline fighter that formed the backbone of the American and allied fleets, thus posing a totally unprecedented threat to adversaries across the world. Its ability to serve as a high performing anti-shipping platform using the AGM-158C, as the world's most dangerous penetration tactical nuclear bomber using the B61, and to provide close air support using a range of guided bombs and short ranged missiles, made it a leading performer in multiple areas.

Although the F-35 was particularly criticised for its limitations in air-to-air combat, the growing discrepancy in avionics between it and the F-22 had by the mid-2020s resulted in a consensus that it was overall much more capable, with distinct advantages over its heavier counterpart in both visual and beyond visual ranges. While Russia invested heavily in fielding a large fleet of dedicated air superiority fighters such as the Su-35, which like the F-22 were much more manoeuvrable, could provide much more energy to their missiles, and carried much larger radars than the F-35, the discrepancy in avionics, combined with the F-35's advanced stealth capabilities, made it highly likely that any engagement would be one-sided in the F-35's favour. Much like the T-64, outside East Asia the F-35 combined an unmatched scale of production and deployments with a technological lead of over a decade.

Shortcomings

An aspect of the F-35 program which drew particularly harsh criticism was the extreme nature of its delays, with almost a quarter of a century passing between the fighter's first flight, and its approval for full-scale production. To put this in perspective, this was a few months short of the time between the service entry of the Korean War era F-86 first generation fighter, and America's first fourth generation fighters the F-14 and F-15. As of 2025 the F-35 had 'shown no improvement in meeting schedule and performance timelines for developing and testing software designed to address deficiencies and add new capabilities,' and was struggling to reach its testing milestones and readiness goals, while testing of TR-3 software 'remained behind schedule throughout 2024.'[27] This followed over two decades of similar difficulties which had become the norm for the program. While such delays and flaws would have had devastating consequences for American air power during the Cold War, however, the fact that post-Soviet Russia had fallen into an even steeper industrial and defence sector decline from 1991, with its plans for a fifth generation fleet by the mid-2020s being around 25 years behind schedule, meant there was room for complacency. The primary shortcoming of the F-35 program in across all theatres was thus not the fighter's performance, which while well below expectations was still far ahead of all non-Chinese competition, nor was it its delays, but rather its major overruns in sustainment costs and abysmally low availability rates.

The F-35 was envisaged as a fighter with low operational costs and maintenance needs, much like the F-5 and F-16 that preceded it, which would make a large fleet highly feasible, while also ensuring that availability rates could be kept high with little difficulty. The program fell very far short of success in this regard, and by the mid-2020s the prospects for remedying these issues appeared slim. High operational costs meant services transitioning to the F-35, other than Japan's air force which transitioned from the large and heavyweight F-15, would need to either contract their fleets significantly, substantially raise spending on fighter fleet sustainment, or make deep cuts to flight training hours. With most services compromising between these three, the result was that fleets which transitioned to the F-35 became smaller, were more strained for funding, and limited pilots to spending fewer hours in the air. The effects of this were exacerbated by the F-35's very low availability rates, as a result of which significantly lower portions of a fleet that had transitioned to the fighter would be mission capable at any time. The result of transitioning from the F-16 to the F-35 could be a halving or less of the number of fully mission capable fighters. The fact that the F-35's availability rates were very significantly worse than those of the F-16, even comparing the former when newly built, and the latter with an operational service life of 30 years, indicated that the issue could worsen considerably as the F-35 fleet began to age, as could the difficulties services faced in funding the sustainment of their fleets.

As the only Western fighter of its generation produced after 2011, and having been developed under a joint program to replace over half a dozen types of older aircraft, the extent of the U.S. Armed Forces' and its strategic partners' reliance on the F-35 remains wholly unprecedented. Its projected production run is eclipsed by those of older fighters such as the F-16 only because the fleets of the United States and U.S.-aligned countries have contracted significantly since the end of the Cold War. Nevertheless, the F-35's major cost overruns and availability issues meant that plans for it to form the vast majority of American and allied fleets by the mid-2010s no longer appeared realistic. In 2010 U.S. Air Force Lieutenant General Stephen Wood had reflected the consensus among many in the service when he stated that the F-35 'will make up over 85 percent of our nation's fighter force in 20 years,'[28] with a Heritage Foundation assessment the previous year having projected that the F-35 'will constitute 90 percent of all U.S. fighters in 2035.'[29] While this would have been highly possible had the fighter retained comparable sustainment costs and availability rates to the F-18 as intended, its failure to achieve this made adoption on such a scale far from viable. Had the F-35 been as cheap to operate and as easy to keep combat ready as the program had intended, it would have transformed U.S. and U.S.-aligned fighter fleets worldwide on a much greater scale, and without significant compromises by the fleets that adopted it, making the program's strategic impact significantly greater.

While the F-35 program's shortcomings in terms of cost, maintainability, and development schedule are primary issues across the majority of the theatres, in the Pacific the much greater challenges which services face both for geographical reasons, and due to the potency of China's own fleet, make the F-35's operational capabilities themselves appear in many ways deficient. Having been developed in an era where peer level challengers to American air superiority were not expected to re-emerge, the F-35 was far less well optimised for air-to-air combat than China's J-20, J-35 and their sixth generation successors. These much longer ranged fighters have significantly more impressive flight performances, carry far larger sensor suites, and are considered to be on a fully peer level technologically. Although the F-35's air-to-air capabilities will improve significantly with the integration of the AN/APG-85 radar, AIM-260 missile, and other upgrades such as sidekick missile racks, it is still far from an ideal aircraft to counter China's J-20 fleet.

Regarding the F-35A's readiness for war, former Air Force Deputy Chief of Staff for Strategy, Integration and Requirements Lieutenant General Clint Hinote observed in April 2021 that there was no value in including the aircraft in war games simulating high-end conflicts due to the low likelihood that it could seriously contribute. 'It wouldn't be worth it,' he said, as 'every [F-35] fighter that rolls off the line today is a fighter that we wouldn't even bother putting into these scenarios.' He further drew attention to the fighter's short range which was a major constraint in the theatre.[30] Although his statement appeared exaggerated, it drew attention to the fact that a

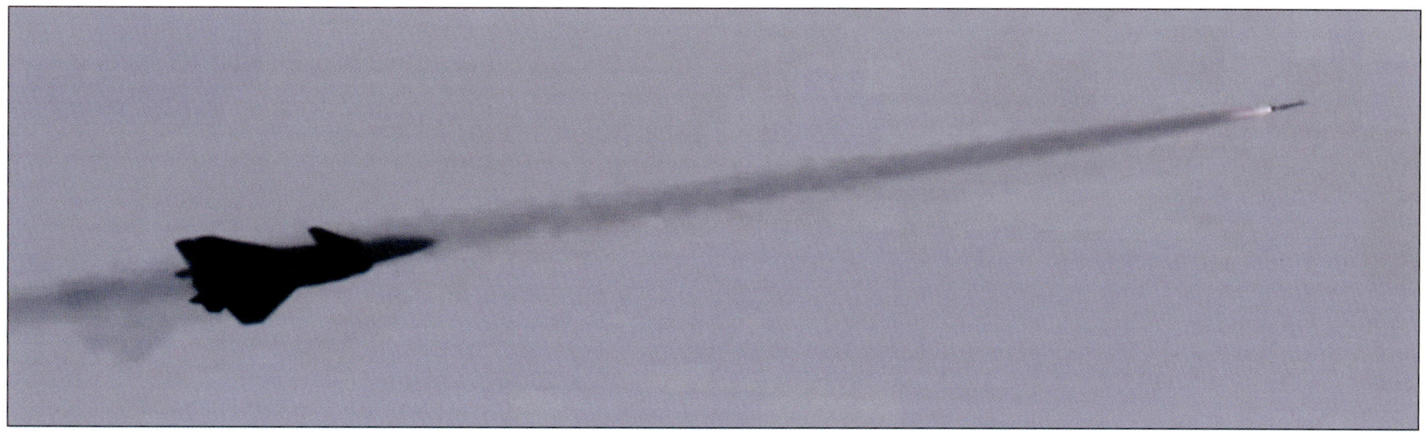

A still from a video showing a J-20 of the PLAAF firing a PL-10 short-range air-to-air missile. (太湖军I名 on Weibo)

combination of persistent flaws, major delays operationalising new hardware and software, and very low availability rates, meant even after F-35s began deliveries, squadrons' combat potentials for years remained highly constrained.

As a result of years long delays, full operationalisation of the F-35 at the Block 4 standard was scheduled to only be achieved at around the same time that China's first sixth generation fighters entered service in the early 2030s. This conclusion was supported by observations of how long upgrades to the program took to apply, and how quickly China could operationalise new generations of combat jets after beginning flight testing. While bringing the F-35 to the Block 4 standard was a primary goal of the program throughout the 2020s, the fact that this would only be achieved as Chinese fighter aviation entered the sixth generation era ensured that even the major performance improvements planned could still leave the American fighter with a disadvantaged standing. This would follow a long trend towards major delays in the F-35 program allowing Chinese aviation to get ahead, with a notable example being the F-35A having entered service just six months before the J-20, despite making its first demonstrator flight 11 years earlier than its Chinese rival had. The fighter's approval for full-scale production only as late as 2024, three years later than the J-20, was a major scandal.

Technology Vulnerabilities

In both operational terms, and as a program, the F-35's success has been staked heavily on the successful utilisation of a number of new technologies. They have the potential to provide revolutionary benefits, but if they fail could also be catastrophic. The expected ability of new computer modelling and other relevant technologies to allow fighters to be put into production while still in early testing stages, which resulted in the concurrency approach, was seen to have the potential to significantly accelerate the F-35 program, but instead had disastrous consequences in terms of cost, performance and timeline. The ability of advanced simulators to substitute for flight training to an unprecedented degree is considered critical to facilitating deep cuts to flight hours to accommodate the F-35's high operational costs and low availability rates, with the fallout should simulators prove less effective than expected potentially being highly detrimental to the fleet's combat potential. Other examples range from ALIS, which was often seen to cause far more issues than it was worth, to the pioneering of a 'just in time' logistics system that had a highly detrimental impact on fleet readiness and caused setbacks far exceeding the benefits of its cost savings. The unprecedented centralisation of ALIS and its successor the ODIN system, while having benefits for intelligence sharing and an ability to exercise

Chinese sixth generation fighter-bomber system, a tri-engine aircraft first unveiled in December 2024 developed by the Chengdu Aerospace Corporation. The precedent set by the J-20 program, which was able to bring a highly capable fighter from a new generation into service just six years after its first flight, fuelled speculation that its sixth generation successor could enter service near the beginning of the 2030s, at around the same time that the F-35 was scheduled to obtain full Block 4 capabilities. The first ever publication of images or footage of a sixth generation fighter raised growing questions regarding the future adequacy of the F-35 as a premier fighter in the Pacific theatre. (Chinese Internet)

control over less reliable clients, also left F-35 fleets worldwide potentially vulnerable to cyber attacks.[31]

As acknowledged by senior military officials the writer has spoken to from multiple countries, while militaries plan high end operations based on the assumption that events do not proceed according to expectations, and thus plan in significant redundancies, reliance on more complex and untested technologies significantly increases the possibilities of failure. The F-35 was on this basis specifically cited as an example of an asset that presented high risks if utilised in high intensity engagements. While many of the technologies related to development, production and sustainment have already been tested, and in many cases have yielded disastrous results, the large majority of those related to the fighter's combat performance remain untested in medium or high intensity engagements. The F-35's extreme emphasis on use of beyond visual range radar guided missiles for air-to-air combat is one notable example, and while potentially providing it with an optimal means of engagement, at the same time presents major potential vulnerabilities if it fails to perform as envisioned.

The performance of radar guided missiles in the U.S. Armed Forces' two previous high intensity conflicts employing them, namely against North Vietnam and Iraq, had both left much to be desired. Although development testing of the AIM-7 missile had indicated 80 to 90 percent kill rates, and operational testing indicated a figure of 71 percent, it achieved a kill rate of just 8.2 percent against North Vietnamese aircraft.[32] Despite significant improvements intended to fix prevailing issues with the missile, and the benefit of detailed studies of the countermeasures of the latest Soviet fighters obtained through East Germany,[33] its performance was assessed to have been 'particularly disappointing' in the Gulf War, with F-15s using the missiles achieving a probability of kill of just 25.8 percent.[34] Although there were high hopes for the new AIM-120 introduced in 1991, in multiple subsequent clashes with Iraqi aircraft it consistently failed to hit its targets, as did the AIM-7.[35] The sole hit achieved was within visual range against a MiG-25 that was flying low, slow, and straight, presenting a particularly soft target.[36] Although the AIM-120 would prove more reliable in later engagements over Yugoslavia and Syria, these were lower intensity clashes with less capable aircraft and saw kills achieved only at shorter ranges.

A similar performance of radar guided missiles to those seen in wars against North Vietnam and Iraq could result in a significant portion of the air-to-air engagements of the future being conducted within visual ranges. Continuing with the example of air-to-air combat, a number of additional factors further raise the possibility that the plan for F-35s using their advanced stealth features and high situational awareness to achieve clean beyond visual range kills could be seriously hampered by the failure of key technologies. During the Gulf War the large majority of engagements occurred within visual ranges due primarily to concerns on both sides of friendly fire and misidentification if targets were not visually identified.[37] The limitations on Russia's long range targeting of aircraft in Ukraine largely due to high incidences of friendly fire indicated that these issues have persisted in at least some services. While Identification Friend or Foe (IFF) systems have improved markedly, they suffer from a number of vulnerabilities, with fighter units having proven capable of mimicking the IFFs of other countries' aircraft.[38] The F-35's capabilities ensure a heavy reliance on fully functional IFF capabilities to be able to perform effectively in the air-to-air domain. The likelihood of F-35s being unable to achieve clean beyond visual range kills is further increased by China's development of aircraft with increasingly advanced stealth technologies, the long range targeting of which is far more complex.

For visual range combat, the F-35 is heavily reliant on the AIM-9X missile's high off-boresight targeting capabilities, which are seen to limit the need to manoeuvre and thus justify the fighter's flight performance limitations. This also presents significant risks, with the AIM-9X's sole air-to-air combat test in June 2017 having seen an ageing and un-manoeuvrable Syrian Su-22 evade the missile using flares – in contrast to all expectations and despite the U.S. having long had access to the aircraft to test its countermeasures.[39] The significant possibility of AIM-9Xs failing when engaging a high performing target leave the F-35, with its limited gun rounds and below average flight performance, potentially vulnerable.

The issue of new technologies being relied on heavily, and presenting a significant risk of failure to meet expectations, was one that affected all pioneering weapons programs to varying extents, but to which the F-35 program was particularly vulnerable due to the design's extreme complexity and multiple compromises to more traditional capabilities. While its advanced precision strike capabilities, for example, were seen to make it sufficiently capable in providing close air support to obviate the need for a large gun or optimisation for strafing, the Russian-Ukrainian War had demonstrated the vulnerability of guided weapons to jamming, raising the possibility that more traditional close air support capabilities could be sorely missed.[40] Considering again the example of high intensity air-to-air engagements, the F-35 could prove to be a world leader in its combat potential should the AIM-120D, AIM-260 and IFF systems prove to be highly reliable, but it may also be left struggling profoundly to counter enemy fighters should these prove to be less dependable.

Into the 2030s

The tremendous costs sunk into the F-35 program meant that by the mid-2010s it was already considered too big to fail, with the lack of any other Western post-fourth generation programs scheduled to bring fighters into service within the next decade, and the major shortcomings of the F-22 program, leaving few options than to continue investment. Despite significant delays, and production on a much smaller scale than originally planned, the F-35's production scale by the mid-2020s far exceeded those of all other Western fighters combined. The scale of the program ensures that considerable investments will continue to be made in further enhancing the F-35, much as was the case for the F-16 which in the mid-2020s retained a respectable performance in its latest variants despite approaching half a century in service. This contrasts to the F-22, with initial expectations for continuous modernisation over a long production run having ended when production was ordered terminated in 2009, while the small size of the fleet was a key factor enabling the Air Force to decide to relegate it to an early retirement.

Much as technologies developed for the F-22 and F-35 facilitated extensive modernisation of the F-15 and F-16 in newer production blocks, so too is the F-35 highly likely to benefit from sixth generation technologies including new generations of engines, data links, stealth coatings, armaments, and sensors, as well as collaborative combat aircraft, to eventually allow it to operate as a '5+ generation' aircraft. The significant possibility of issues and delays to the development of the Air Force's F-47 and the Navy's F/A-XX programs is likely to increase the focus on integrating such upgrades. There remains a significant possibility that with incremental modernisation, the F-35's combat potential will surpass those of the sixth generation fighters being developed in Europe and Russia due to the vast technological discrepancies between their defence and broader tech sectors and those of the United States.

BIBLIOGRAPHY

The information in this book draws on a wide array of sources collected over more than a decade of research into evolving trends in aerial warfare and modern fighter development, and benefits the rapid growth in the number of publications on the F-35 from the early 2010s as it became the world's most prolific and widely analysed single weapons program. The size of the program, its international and multi-service nature, and its duration since development began in the 1990s, has resulted in a particularly large number of publications being available. Sources consulted have include dozens of interviews with pilots, unit commanders, senior officers, program personnel, and defence experts, as well as publications by a range of organisations and agencies such as the Government Accountability Office, the Congressional Research Service and the RAND Corporation. The regular publications on the program's developments by the monthly journal of the Air & Space Forces Association *Air and Space Forces Magazine*, and other publications associated with various services, bases, or units such as the *Air Force Times* and *kadena.af.mil* are among those consulted. Reports and assessments by analysts at sites such as *Defense News* and *The War Zone* are also cited throughout several sections of the book, and provide valuable insight into the evolution of consensus among analysts on various aspects of the program as it has evolved. Parts of the work assessing the program's exports and the F-35's foreign service consult media outlets from relevant countries, for example *Hankyoreh* and the *Chosun Ilbo* for South Korean procurements and operations.

Navigating the tendency among many sources to be either critical of the F-35's shortcomings to the exclusion of its achievements, or vice versa, has been a leading challenge in researching this particularly polarising weapons program, as have the major changes in consensus on important aspects of the program over time. The rapid evolution of the program in its current peak years in production, including the speed at which changes to planned production numbers, investments in competing programs, and funding for various upgrades are made, has represented a further difficulty in researching an producing a book that can make an enduring contribution to understandings of the F-35 and contemporary air power more broadly.

Sources cited on the F-35 have in almost all cases focused on specific events in or aspects of the program, such as test flight achievements, availability rate issues, production contracts, or landmark deployments, or on particular subsystems such as the potentials of bypass air systems for new engines or of the new AN/APG-85 radar. Many sources are thus consulted only once or twice in the book to provide a more comprehensive overview of the program. Rather than compiling a separate bibliography, the author directs readers to the endnotes accompanying each chapter.

ENDNOTES

Chapter 1

1 Trevithick, Joseph and Rogoway, Tyler, 'The SR-71 Blackbird's Predecessor Created "Plasma Stealth" By Burning Cesium-Laced Fuel,' *The War Zone*, 1 December 2019.

2 Pedlow, Gregory W. and Welzenbach, Donald E., *The Central Intelligence Agency and Overhead Reconnaissance: The U-2 and Oxcart Programs, 1954–1974,* Washington, DC, Central Intelligence Agency, 1992.

3 Dabrowski, Krzysztof, *Defending Rodinu: Volume 2 – Build-Up and Operational History of the Soviet Air Defence Force, 1960-1989*, Warwick, Helion, 2023, p.25. Pedlow and Welzenbach, *The Central Intelligence Agency and Overhead Reconnaissance.*

4 Hendrix, Jerry and Price, James, 'Experimentation, High Speeds, High Altitudes, And the Rise of Stealth' in: *'Higher, Heavier, Further, and Now Undetectable? Bombers: Long-Range Force Projection in the 21st Century,'* Center for a New American Security, 2017, p.46.

5 Hendrix and Price, 'Experimentation, High Speeds', p.46.

6 Lynch, David J., 'How the Skunk Works Fielded Stealth,' *Air Force Magazine*, 1 November 1992.

7 Lynch, 'How the Skunk Works Fielded Stealth'.

8 Crickmore, Paul F. and Crickmore, Alison J., *Nighthawk F-117 Stealth Fighter*, St. Paul, Motorbooks, 2003, p.9.

9 Withington, Thomas, *Wild Weasel Fighter Attack: The Story of the Suppression of Enemy Air Defences*, Barnsley, Pen & Sword, 2008, pp.61-62. Sapir, Jacques, *The Soviet Military System*, Cambridge, Polity Press, 1991, p.56.

10 Doyle, Joseph S., *The Yom Kippur War and the Shaping of the United States Air Force,* Maxwell Air Force Base, Air University Press, 2019.

11 'Harold Brown's "Invisible" Aircraft,' *Air and Space Forces Magazine,* 1 August 2006.

12 Hollings, Alex, 'Why the F-117 Nighthawk Is Such a Badass Plane,' *Popular Mechanics*, 12 August 2019.

13 Scott, William B., 'A Shift to Low-Altitude Flight Operations Dictated a Wing Redesign,' *Aviation Week*, 27 March 2006. Withington, Thomas, *B-2A Spirit Units in Combat*, Oxford, Osprey, 2006, p.19.

14 Singh, Mandeep, 'Looking Back at Iraqi Air Defences during Operation DESERT STORM,' *Balloons to Drones*, 19 October 2022.

15 Lambeth, Benjamin S., 'Desert Storm and Its Meaning: The View from Moscow,' Santa Monica, RAND Corporation, 1992, p.23.

16 *Operation Desert Storm: Evaluation of the Air Campaign*, Washington, DC, General Accounting Office, 1997, p.137.

17 Pace, Steve, *F-22 Raptor: America's Next Lethal War Machine*, New York, McGraw Hill, 1999, p.13.

18 Miller, Jay, *Lockheed Martin F/A-22 Raptor Stealth Fighter*, Hinckley, Midland Publishing, 2005, p.9.

19 Miller, *Lockheed Martin F/A-22*, p.10.

20 Pace, Steve, *F-22 Raptor*, p.7.

21 Pace, *F-22 Raptor*, p.39.

22 Tirpak, John A., 'Raptor 01,' *Air Force Magazine*, July 1997, p.48.

23 Rogoway, Tyler, 'Axing The F-35's Alternative Engine Was An Incredibly Stupid Move,' *Jalopnik*, 8 July 2014.

24 '*What's It Like To Fly The F-22? | James "Ammo" Carraway (Part 1)*,' Aircraft Interview (YouTube), 30 December 2024.

25 Younossi, Obaid et al., *Lessons Learned from the F/A-22 and F/A-18E/F Development Programs*, Santa Monica, RAND, 2005, p.4. Niemi, Christopher J., 'The F-22 Acquisition Program: Consequences for the US Air Force's Fighter Fleet,' *Air & Space Power Journal*, vol. 26, no. 6, November-December 2012, pp.53-82.

26 Vartabedian, Ralph and Hennigan, W. J., 'F-22 program produces few planes, soaring costs,' *Los Angeles Times*, 16 June 2013.

27 Vartabedian and Hennigan, 'F-22 program produces few planes'.

28 'Will We Ever Fly Before We Buy? F-22 Doesn't Meet Basic Testing Criteria,' *Project on Government Oversight*, 2 January 2001.

29 *F-22 Pilot Physiological Issues: Hearing Before the Subcommittee on Tactical Air and Land Forces of the Committee on Armed Services House of Representatives*, One Hundred and Twelfth Congress, Second Session, Hearing on 13 September 2012, Washington DC, U.S. Government Printing Office, 2013, p.63.

30 O'Hanlon, Michael E., 'The Plane Truth: Fewer F-22s Mean a Stronger National Defense,' *Brookings Institute*, 1 September 1999. 'F-22 Raptor,' *Battle Stations*, Season 1, Episode 39.

31 Hollings, Alex, 'From High Operating Costs to Low Production Run: all the Shortfalls that Killed the F-22 Raptor Programme,' *The Aviation Geek Club*, 17 March 2021. 'How much cheaper is the F-15EX compared to the F-35?,' *Sandboxx*, 7 February 2022.

32 Axe, David, 'Hangar Queens! The U.S. Air Force's Old F-15s Keep Flying While Newer F-22s Sit Idle,' *Forbes*, 19 May 2020. Everstine, Brian W., 'Breaking Down USAF's 70-Percent Overall Mission Capable Rate,' *Air Force Magazine*, 19 May 2020.
33 Niemi, 'The F-22 Acquisition Program', p.65.
34 'Documents show Air Force neglected concerns about F-22 pilot safety,' *Public Integrity*, 27 September 2012. Axe, David, 'US Stealth Jets Choking Pilots at Record Rates,' *Wired*, 14 June 2012. Axe, David, 'Air Force to Stealth Fighter Pilots: Get Used to Coughing Fits,' *Wired*, 25 February 2013. Fabey, Michael, 'USAF Deciphers "Mosaic" Of F-22 Oxygen Supply Problems,' *Aviation Week*, 1 August 2012. 'Air force pilots describe health problems from flying F-22 jet,' *CBS News* (YouTube), 7 May 2012.
35 'F-22 avionics designers rely on obsolescent electronics, but plan for future upgrades,' *Military Aerospace*, 1 May 2001. Everstine, Brian W., 'The F-22 and the F-35 Are Struggling to Talk to Each Other ... And to the Rest of USAF,' *Air Force Magazine*, 29 January 2018.
36 Vartabedian, Ralph and Hennigan, W.J., 'F-22 program produces few planes, soaring costs,' *Chicago Tribune*, 16 June 2013.
37 Gertler, Jeremiah, *Air Force F-22 Fighter Program*, Washington, DC, Congressional Research Service Report for Congress, 11 July 2013.
38 'Air Force Chief Hints at Retiring the F-22 Raptor in Fighter Downsize,' *Miliary.com*, 12 May 2021. Newdick, Thomas, 'Yes, It's True, The F-22 Isn't In The Air Force Chief's Future Fighter Plans,' *The War Zone*, 13 May 2021.
39 'USAF: F-22 to Be Phased-Out Within Next Decade,' *The Defense Post*, 21 May 2021.
40 Gertler, Jeremiah, *Air Force F-22 Fighter Program*, Washington, DC, Congressional Research Service Report for Congress, 11 July 2013. Tirpak, John A., 'Most USAF Fighter Mission Capable Rates Rise in Fiscal 2020, Led by F-35,' *Air Force Magazine*, 24 May 2021. Rogoway, Tyler, 'F-22 Being Used To Test Next Generation Air Dominance "Fighter" Tech,' *The War Zone*, 26 April 2022.
41 Polmar, Norman, 'The Avenger That Couldn't Avenge,' *Naval History*, vol. 32, no. 1, February 2018.
42 Polmar, 'The Avenger That Couldn't Avenge'.
43 Miller, Jay, *Lockheed Martin F/A-22 Raptor Stealth Fighter*, Hinckley, Midland Publishing, 2005, p.76.
44 Hollings, Alex, 'When Lockheed Tried to Put the F-117 on Aircraft Carriers,' *The National Interest*, 10 October 2021.
45 Wilson, George C., 'The engine that could,' *Government Executive*, 22 January 2002.
46 Whittle, Richard, 'The Ultimate Fighter?,' *Smithsonian Magazine*, March 2012.
47 Stone, I. F., *Hidden History of the Korean War*, Boston, Little, Brown and Company, 1988, p.341.
48 McGill, Earl J., *Black Tuesday Over Namsi: B-29s vs MiGs – The Forgotten Air Battle of the Korean War*, Solihull, Helion, 2012, Chapter 4.
49 McGill, *Black Tuesday Over Namsi*, Chapter 9.
50 Hanley, Charles J., *Ghost in Flames: Life & Death in a Hidden War, Korea 1950-53*, New York, Public Affairs, 2020, p.359. *Associated Press*, 14 February 1952.
51 Didly, Douglas C. and Thompson, Warren E., *F-86 Fabre vs MiG-15: Korea 1950-1953*, Oxford, Osprey, 2013, p.77. Gao, Charlie, 'In 1971, Indian Mig-21's Beat Some American-Built F-104A Starfighters. Was It a Fluke?' *The National Interest*, 5 August 2018.
52 Napier, Michael, *Flashpoints: Air Warfare in the Cold War*, Oxford, Osprey, 2022, Chapter 7.
53 Gordon, Yefim, *Sukhoi Su-27*, Hinckley, Midland Publishing, 2007, p.514.
54 Lake, Jon, *Su-27 Flanker: Sukhoi Superfighter*, London, Osprey, 1992, p.88. Gordon, *Sukhoi Su-27*, p.522.
55 Gordon, *Sukhoi Su-27*, pp.515-516.
56 Gordon, *Sukhoi Su-27*, pp.25, 517, 519.
57 Lilley, James and Shambaugh, David L., *China's Military Faces the Future*, Abingdon, Routledge, 2015, pp.96-99. Lake, *Su-27 Flanker: Sukhoi Superfighter*, Introduction. Ilin, Vladimir, 'Air Bases of Russia: Lipetssk – One of the Aviation Centres of Russia,' Vestnik Vozdushnogo Flota, 14 March 1995, in: Foreign Broadcast Information Service Military Affairs 95-148-S, 14 March 1995.
58 Gordon, *Sukhoi Su-27*, p.524.
59 *Department of Defense Appropriations for 2002: Hearings Before a Subcommittee of the Committee on Appropriations House of Representatives*, One Hundred and Seventh Congress, First Session, Subcommittee on Defense, Washington, DC, U.S. Government Printing Office, 2004, p.813.
60 Lake, *Su-27 Flanker*, Introduction.
61 Gordon, *Sukhoi Su-27*, pp.522-523.
62 Hughes, David, 'Luftwaffe Mig Pilots Effective with Archer,' *Aviation Week and Space Technology*, 20 December 1996, p.83.
63 International Institute for Strategic Studies, *The Military Balance*, Volume 89, 1989, Chapter Two. International Institute for Strategic Studies, *The Military Balance*, Volume 100, 2000, Chapter Three.
64 International Institute for Strategic Studies, *The Military Balance*, Volume 121, 2021, p.198.
65 International Institute for Strategic Studies, *The Military Balance*, Volume 95, 1995, Chapter Four.
66 S-300PMU, *Federation of American Scientists*, 30 June 2000.
67 'China successfully completes trials of S-400s, says source,' *TASS*, 10 January 2019. Strong, Matthew, 'China has tested S400 missile in Taiwan Strait,' *Taiwan News*, 27 December 2018.
68 'Advanced long-range missile for S-400 system accepted for service in Russia,' *TASS*, 18 October 2018.

Chapter 2

1 Tingley, Brett, 'X-32's Test Pilot On Why It Lost To What Became The F-35,' *The War Zone*, 4 February 2022.
2 'Mitchell Institute's Deptula on China's J-20 Stealth Fighter,' *Defense and Aerospace Report* (YouTube), 11 November 2016.
3 Nalty, Bernard C., *The War Against Trucks: Aerial Interdiction in Southern Laos, 1968-1972*, Washington, DC, Air Force History and Museums Program, 2005, pp.294, 301, 302. Cockburn, Andrew, *Kill Chain: The Rise of the High-Tech Assassins*, New York, Henry Holt, 2015, pp.26-31.
4 Westmoreland, William, 'Gen. Westmoreland on the Army of the Future,' *NACLA*, 25 September 2007. Van Staaveren, Jacob, *Interdiction in Southern Laos, 1960–1968*, Washington, DC, Center for Air Force History, 1993, pp.255–69.
5 Venable, John, 'The F-35A Fighter Is the Most Dominant and Lethal Multi-Role Weapons System in the World: Now Is the Time to Ramp Up Production,' *Heritage Foundation*, 14 May 2019.
6 'PAK-FA's New Engines Make It "Easily the Best 5th Gen Fighter in the World",' *Sputnik News*, 25 July 2017.
7 Rogoway, Tyler, 'Infrared Search And Track Systems And The Future Of The US Fighter Force,' *Jalopnik*, 26 March 2015.
8 '078 – F-35 Lightning II,' *Fighter Pilot Podcast*, 13 April 2020.
9 'Department of Defense Press Briefing by Secretary James and Gen. Goldfein on the State of the Air Force in the Pentagon Briefing Room,' *Department of Defense official website*, 10 August 2016.
10 'Aerospace Nation: Gen Luca Goretti,' *Mitchell Institute for Aerospace Studies* (YouTube), 13 October 2023.
11 Altman, Howard, 'The Intricacies Of F-35 Operations Over The Frigid Alaskan Frontier,' *The War Zone*, 11 August 2022.
12 'F-35 Critics Are Completely Wrong. F-16s for Ukraine Were Over-Hyped. | Ep. 44 Prof. Justin Bronk,' *Decoding Geopolitics Podcast* (YouTube), 18 December 2024.
13 Hollings, Alex, 'Why the F-35 Fighter Jet Is Such a Badass Plane,' *Popular Mechanics*, 20 September 2023.
14 '078 – F-35 Lightning II,' *Fighter Pilot Podcast*.
15 Whittle, Richard, 'The Ultimate Fighter?' *The Smithsonian Magazine*, March 2012.
16 Hollings, 'Why the F-35 Fighter Jet Is Such a Badass Plane.'
17 Whittle, 'The Ultimate Fighter?'.
18 Helfrick, Emma, 'New Electronic Warfare Suite Top Feature Of F-35 Block 4, Air Combat Boss Says,' *The War Zone*, 9 March 2023.
19 Hollings, 'Why the F-35 Fighter Jet Is Such a Badass Plane'.
20 '078 – F-35 Lightning II,' *Fighter Pilot Podcast*.
21 Gross, Judah Ari, 'Liberman unveils Israel's future stealth fighter: The F-35,' *Times of Israel*, 22 June 2016.
22 'F-35 Lightning II Program Status and Fast Facts,' Lockheed Martin, 1 April 2020.
23 'F-35 Lightning II Program', Lockheed Martin.
24 'F-35 Lightning II Program', Lockheed Martin.
25 Altman, Howard, 'The Intricacies Of F-35 Operations Over The Frigid Alaskan Frontier,' *The War Zone*, 11 August 2022.
26 '078 – F-35 Lightning II,' *Fighter Pilot Podcast*.
27 Altman, Howard, 'The Intricacies Of F-35 Operations Over The Frigid Alaskan Frontier,' *The War Zone*, 11 August 2022.
28 Majumdar, Dave, 'New U.S. Stealth Jet Can't Fire Its Gun Until 2019,' *The Daily Beast*, 31 December 2014.
29 Venable, John, 'The F-35A Fighter Is the Most Dominant and Lethal Multi-Role Weapons System in the World'.
30 Newdick, Thomas, 'Anonymous F-35 Customer Is Getting A New Variant Of The Stealth Jet,' *The War Zone*, 29 December 2021.
31 Thompson, Roger, *Lessons Not Learned: The U.S. Navy's Status Quo Culture*, Annapolis, Naval Institute Press, 2007, Chapter 10.
32 Harpley, Unshin Lee, 'US and Australia Making "Significant Progress" on New Hypersonic Weapon,' *Air & Space Forces*, 9 August 2024.
33 Newdick, Thomas, 'Ford Class Carrier's EMALS Catapults, AAG Arrester Gear Eyed For Land Bases,' *The War Zone*, 23 July 2024.
34 International Institute for Strategic Studies, *The Military Balance*, Volume 119, 2019, p.52.
35 Finnerty, Ryan, 'Boeing extends Super Hornet production to 2027 with final new-build order from USA,' *Flight Global*, 20 March 2024.
36 Shelbourne, Mallory, 'Navy Questions Future Viability of Super Hornets; Recommends Against New Buy,' *United States Naval Institute News*, 3 August 2021.
37 Miller, Jay, *Lockheed Martin F/A-22 Raptor, Stealth Fighter*, Hinckley, Midland Publishing, 2005, p. 76.
38 Gordon, Yefim, *Yakovlev Yak-36, Yak-38 & Yak-41: The Soviet "Jump Jets"*, Hinckley, Midland Publishing, 2008, pp.1-8.
39 Gordon, *Yakovlev Yak36, Yak-38 & Yak-41*, p.101.
40 Gordon, *Yakovlev Yak36, Yak-38 & Yak-41*, pp.101-120, 130, 131.

41 Gordon, *Yakovlev Yak36, Yak-38 & Yak-41*, p.122.
42 Miller, Alan C. and Sack, Kevin, 'Far From Battlefield, Marines Lose One-Third of Harrier Fleet,' *Los Angeles Times*, 15 December 2002.
43 Bruce Myles, *Jump Jet The Revolutionary V/STOL Fighter*, London, Brassey's Defence Publishers, 1986, p.151. Miller and Sack, 'Far From Battlefield'.
44 Miller and Sack, 'Far From Battlefield'.
45 Miller and Sack, 'Far From Battlefield'.
46 Miller and Sack, 'Far From Battlefield'.
47 Miller and Sack, 'Far From Battlefield'.
48 Miller and Sack, 'Far From Battlefield'.
49 Miller and Sack, 'Far From Battlefield'.
50 Miller and Sack, 'Far From Battlefield'.
51 Miller and Sack, 'Far From Battlefield'.
52 Miller and Sack, 'Far From Battlefield'.
53 Miller and Sack, 'Far From Battlefield'.
54 Trevithick, Joseph, 'New Vision For Lift Fan Aircraft Family Grows From Special Operations X-Plane Program,' *The War Zone*, 9 October 2024.
55 Gordon, Yefim and Komissarov, Dmitry, *Sukhoi Su-57*, Manchester, Hikoki Publications, 2021, p.10.
56 Rogoway, Tyler, 'F-35 Gets the "Pot Of Gold" Treatment After Landing in the UK for the First Time,' *The War Zone*, 30 June 2016.
57 'F-35 Critics Are Completely Wrong. F-16s for Ukraine Were Over-Hyped. | Ep. 44 Prof. Justin Bronk,' *Decoding Geopolitics Podcast* (YouTube), 18 December 2024.
58 Rogoway, Tyler, '7 Things The Marines Have To Do To Make The F-35B Worth The Huge Cost,' *Jalopnik*, 31 May 2014.
59 Ross, Angus, 'Rethinking the U.S. Navy's Carrier Fleet,' *War on the Rocks*, 21 July 2020. Stashwick, Steven, 'US Navy Re-examining the Future of the Aircraft Carrier,' *The Diplomat*, 11 March 2020.
60 Clark, Bryan et al., *Restoring American Seapower: A New Fleet Architecture for the United States Navy*, Washington, DC, Centre for Strategic and Budgetary Assessments, 2017. McCain, John, 'Restoring American Power: Recommendations for the FY 2018-FY 2022 Defense Budget,' United States Congress, Senate Committee on Armed Services, 16 January 2017. Hendrix, Henry J., 'Buy Fords, Not Ferraris,' *Proceedings*. vol. 135, no. 4, issue 1, no.274, April 2009.
61 Ross, 'Rethinking the U.S. Navy's Carrier Fleet'.
62 Morrocco, John D., 'British Aerospace Teams on ASTOVL and Tiger,' *Aviation Week & Space Technology*, 24 February 1992.
63 Fulghum, David, 'Joint Strike Fighter Update,' *Proceedings*, September 1996, p.40. Hancock, Ben D., The STOVL Joint Strike Fighter in Support of the 21st Century Marine Corps, Defense Technical Information Center, November 1996.
64 Hancock, The STOVL Joint Strike Fighter.
65 Prater, Jeffrey C., 'VSTOL and Power Projection,' *Airpower Journal*, Summer 1991, p. 68.
66 'Aerospace Nation: Gen Luca Goretti,' *Mitchell Institute for Aerospace Studies* (YouTube), 13 October 2023.
67 Kass, Harrison, 'The F-35 Has a Range Problem That China Would Love to Exploit,' *The National Interest*, 31 March 2024.
68 Walton, Timothy A. and Shugart, Thomas H., 'Concrete Sky: Air Base Hardening in the Western Pacific,' *Hudson Institute*, 7 January 2025. Watkin, Huw, 'US military's Pacific strategy shifts to survival mode as China gains strength,' *South China Morning Post*, 5 January 2025.

Chapter 3

1 Rogoway, Tyler, 'The Pentagon's "Concurrency Myth" Is Now Available In Supercarrier Size,' *Jalopnik*, 17 June 2015.
2 'F-35 Concurrency was "Acquisition Malpractice",' *Air Force Magazine*, 7 February 2012.
3 Grazier, Dan, '108 U.S. F-35s Won't Be Combat-Capable,' *The National Interest*, 16 October 2017. Trevithick, Joseph, 'USMC's Older F-35Bs May Only Be Able To Fly Around A Quarter Of Their Expected Service Life,' *The War Zone*, 1 February 2019.
4 Pawlyk, Oriana, 'Air Force Could Ditch Oldest F-35 Jets as Part of Fighter Downsizing, General Says,' *Military.com*, 24 May 2021.
5 Capaccio, Tony, 'Stagnant F-35 Reliability Means Fewer Available Jets: Pentagon,' *Bloomberg*, 30 January 2019.
6 Trimble, Stephen, 'US considers non-combat-rated subset of F-35 fleet,' *Flight Global*, 19 September 2017.
7 Shalal, Andrea, 'Engine fire triggers new turbulence for Lockheed's F-35 jet,' *Reuters*, 10 July 2014.
8 F-22 Modernisation: Cost and Schedule Transparency Is Improved, Further Visibility into Reliability Efforts Is Needed, Government Accountability Office, May 2014.
9 Trevithick, Joseph, 'The F-35 Hits A Key Developmental Milestone, But With Watered-Down Requirements,' *The War Zone*, 12 April 2018.
10 Grazier, Dan, 'F-35: Still No Finish Line in Sight,' *Project on Government Oversight*, 19 March 2018.
11 Grazier, 'F-35: Still No Finish Line In Sight'.
12 Insinna, Valerie, 'The F-35 jet might hit full-rate production more than a year late,' *Defense News*, 19 October 2019.
13 Insinna, 'The F-35 jet might hit full-rate production'. Insinna, Valerie, 'F-35 to move into full-rate production later than expected,' *Defense News*, 27 October 2020.
14 'F-35 operational suitability short of expectations, says DoD official,' *Airforce Technology*, 14 November 2019.
15 Capaccio, Anthony, 'Lockheed F-35 Full-Production Decision, Key Test Delayed,' *Bloomberg*, 26 October 2020. Capaccio, Anthony, 'Pentagon Keeps $398 Billion F-35's Full-Rate Production on Hold,' *Bloomberg*, 31 December 2020.
16 Newdick, Thomas, 'It's Official: Pentagon Puts F-35 Full-Rate Production Decision On Hold,' *The War Zone*, 31 December 2020.
17 Insinna, 'F-35 to move into full-rate production'.
18 'U.S. Marines Corps declares the F-35B operational,' *Marines.mil*, 31 July 2015.
19 'Marines: F-35B Squadron Ready for Worldwide Deployment,' *United States Department of Defence Official Website*, 31 July 2015.
20 Grazier,Dan and Smithberger, Mandy, 'Pentagon Testing Office Calls Foul on F-35B "Operational Test",' *Project on Government Oversight*, 14 September 2015.
21 Grazier and Smithberger, 'Pentagon Testing Office Calls Foul'.
22 Grazier and Smithberger, 'Pentagon Testing Office Calls Foul'.
23 Grazier and Smithberger, 'Pentagon Testing Office Calls Foul'.
24 Grazier and Smithberger, 'Pentagon Testing Office Calls Foul'.
25 Grazier and Smithberger, 'Pentagon Testing Office Calls Foul'.
26 Trevithick, Joseph, 'The F-35's Bomb-Dropping Exercise Is a P.R. Stunt,' *War is Boring*, 4 June 2015.
27 'Aerospace Nation: Gen Kenneth S. Wilsbach,' *Mitchell Institute for Aerospace Studies* (YouTube), 15 March 2022. Waldron, Greg, 'E-3 insufficient for timely detection of J-20: Pacific Air Forces chief,' *Flight Global*, 17 March 2022.
28 'VMFA-121 departs for relocation to Japan,' *Marines Official Website*, 10 January 2017.
29 Rogoway, Tyler, 'F-35s Were Carrying Live AIM-120 Missiles During Show Of Force Training Flight Over Korea,' *The War Zone*, 18 September 2017.
30 Rogoway, Tyler, 'Navy Builds Ship For F-35, Ship Needs Months Of Upgrades To Handle F-35,' *Jalopnik*, 13 April 2015.
31 Starr, Barbara and Cohen, Zachary, 'US F-35 fighter jet poised for combat debut,' *CNN*, 26 September 2018.
32 Oprihory, Jennifer-Leigh, 'US Uses F-35 in Combat for First Time in Afghanistan Airstrike,' *Air & Space Forces Magazine*, 27 September 2018.
33 'British Royal Air Force Gains First Air to Air Kill in Over 70 Years With Syria Drone Shootdown,' *Military Watch Magazine*, 17 December 2021.
34 Alert 5 on Twitter: 'The F-22 has a balloon kill marking,' 5 February 2023.
35 Everstine, Brian W., 'F-22s Take Break from Middle East Combat to Increase Readiness, Reassess Basing,' *Air & Space Forces*, 5 March 2019. Pawlyk, Oriana, 'In Syria Strike, F-22 Raptor Once Again Left on Combat Sidelines,' *Military.com*, 16 April 2018. 'What's It Like To Fly The F-22? | James "Ammo" Carraway (Part 1),' *Aircraft Interview* (YouTube), 30 December 2024.
36 '"Stealth" Plane Used in Panama,' *Washington Post*, 24 December 1989.
37 Hancock, The STOVL Joint Strike Fighter.
38 Eckstein, Megan, 'F-35B Allowed Essex ARG to Flex New Blue-Water Capabilities in Absence of Carrier Nearby,' *USNI News*, 11 October 2018.
39 Eckstein, 'F35B Allowed Essex ARG'.
40 'F-35 Aircraft Sustainment: DOD Needs to Address Challenges Affecting Readiness and Cost Transparency,' *United States Government Accountability Office*, 26 October 2017. Grazier, Dan, 'F-35 Far from Ready to Face Current or Future Threats, Testing Data Shows,' *Project on Government Oversight*, 19 March 2019.
41 Garbarino, Micah, 'First operational F-35As arrive at Hill AFB,' *U.S. Air Force Official Website*, 2 September 2015.
42 'We Have Proof the U.S. Air Force Watered Down the F-35 to Avoid Embarrassment,' *War is Boring*, 13 September 2015.
43 'We Have Proof the U.S. Air Force,' *War is Boring*.
44 Rogoway, Tyler, 'The USAF Declares Initial Operating Capability For The F-35A, But it Still Has a Long Way to Go,' *The War Zone*, 3 August 2016.
45 'We Have Proof the U.S. Air Force,' *War is Boring*.
46 Rogoway, 'The USAF Declares Initial Operating Capability For The F-35A'.
47 'U.S. Air Force's F-35A Lightning II Scheduled for First Operational Deployment to Indo-Asia-Pacific,' *U.S. Pacific Air Command*, 23 October 2017.
48 Werner, Ben, 'Schedule at Risk for Navy F-35C Fighters to be Combat Ready by End of Year,' *USNI News*, 29 March 2018.
49 Venable, John, 'Operational Assessment of the F-35A Argues for Full Program Procurement and Concurrent Development Process,' *Heritage Foundation*, Backgrounder No. 3140, 4 August 2016. Venable, John, 'The F-35A Fighter Is the Most Dominant and Lethal Multi-Role Weapons System in the World'.
50 Bennett, Jay, 'First U.S. Air Force F-35s to Receive Full Combat Capability,' *Popular Mechanics*, 28 August 2017.
51 Losey, Stephen and Insinna, Valerie, 'F-35s at Luke Air Force Base grounded after pilots suffered oxygen deprivation,' *Air Force Times*, 10 June 2017.
52 Losey and Insinna, 'F-35s at Luke Air Force Base grounded'.
53 'F-35C achieves Initial Operational Capability,' *United States Pacific Fleet official website*, 28 February 2019.

54 Grazier, 'F-35 Far from Ready to Face Current or Future Threats'.
55 Clark, Colin, 'F-35C Joins Integrated Carrier Ops; Refueling Mishap: Videos Etc.,' *Breaking Defense*, 6 September 2018.
56 Eckstein, Megan, 'Navy's Operational F-35C Squadron Declared "Safe for Flight;" Can Prepare for Evaluations, IOC,' *USNI News*, 12 December 2018.
57 Faram, Mark D., 'This is what's going on with the Navy's F-35C program,' *Navy Times*, 1 March 2019.
58 Eckstein, Megan, 'Three takeaways from the US Navy's first F-35C deployment,' *Defense News*, 15 February 2022.
59 Eckstein, 'Three takeaways from the US Navy's,' *Defense News*.
60 Eckstein, 'Three takeaways from the US Navy's,' *Defense News*.
61 Eckstein, 'Three takeaways from the US Navy's,' *Defense News*.
62 van Brugen, Isabel, 'Video Showing U.S. F-35 Jet Crash in South China Sea Circulates Online,' *Newsweek*, 28 January 2022.
63 'F-35C Lightning II,' *United States Navy Official Website*, 28 September 2021.
64 Schogol, Jeff, 'The Navy's surface fleet is turning into a floating advertisement for Rust-Oleum,' *Task & Purpose*, 2 March 2021. Trevithick, Joseph, 'Warships Caked In Rust Prompting Late Night Trump Texts To Navy Secretary Nominee,' *The War Zone*, 28 February 2025.
65 Rogoway, Tyler, 'The Navy's $9B Stealthy Super Destroyer Is Covered In Rust,' *The War Zone*, 17 December 2021.
66 Venhuizen, Harm, 'Marine Corps' first F-35C squadron ready to deploy on carriers,' *Marine Times*, 7 December 2020.
67 Shelbourne, Mallory, 'USS Abraham Lincoln Return Marks End of Second High-Tempo Carrier Deployment in WESTPAC,' *USNI News*, 10 August 2022.
68 Shelbourne, 'USS Abraham Lincoln Return,' *USNI News*.
69 Shelbourne, 'USS Abraham Lincoln Return,' *USNI News*.
70 O'Hanlon, Michael E., 'The Plane Truth: Fewer F-22s Mean a Stronger National Defense,' *Brookings Institute*, 1 September 1999.
71 International Institute for Strategic Studies, The Military Balance, Volume 120, 2020, Chapter Three.
72 Grazier, Dan, '108 U.S. F-35s Won't Be Combat-Capable,' *The National Interest*, 16 October 2017. Trevithick, Joseph, 'USMC's Older F-35Bs May Only Be Able To Fly Around A Quarter Of Their Expected Service Life,' *The War Zone*, 1 February 2019.
73 Majumdar, Dave, 'Newest U.S. Stealth Fighter "10 Years Behind" Older Jets,' *The Daily Beast*, 25 December 2014. Trevithick, Joseph, 'A-10 Vs F-35 Close Air Support Flyoff Report Finally Emerges,' *The War Zone*, 1 November 2023.
74 Trevithick, Joseph, 'The U.S. Air Force Is Slowly Killing the F-16 — and Leaving Gaps in America's Defenses,' *War is Boring*, 20 August 2015.
75 'F'd: How the U.S. and Its Allies Got Stuck with the World's Worst New Warplane,' *War is Boring*, 13 August 2013.
76 Trevithick, 'The U.S. Air Force Is Slowly Killing the F-16'.
77 Tirpak, John A., 'New Study: USAF Needs Big Cash Infusion to Overcome Aging Fighter Fleet,' *Air Force Magazine*, 29 June 2023. Guastella, Joseph and Birkey, Douglas and Gunzinger, Eric and Poling, Aidan, 'Accelerating 5th Generation Airpower: Bringing Capability and Capacity to the Merge,' *Mitchell Institute*, vol. 43, 29 June 2023.
78 Tirpak, John A., 'Roper's NGAD Bombshell,' *Air Force Magazine*, 1 October 2020.
79 Tirpak, John A., 'New Study: USAF Needs Big Cash Infusion'. Guastella, Birkey, Gunzinger, Poling, 'Accelerating 5th Generation Airpower'.
80 'Upgraded Boeing F-15Cs Arrive at US Air Force's Kadena Air Base,' *Boeing Media Room*, 4 November 2010.
81 'Center Fuselage Rebuild Could Be F-15C/D Achilles' Heel,' *Aviation Week*, 31 March 2017.
82 'Russia's New Su-57 Fighters Cost Just $35 Million Each: Are Fifth Generation Jets Really Cheaper than the Su-35?' *Military Watch Magazine*, 19 May 2019.
83 Peck, Michael, 'Air Force upgrades F-16 radar,' *C4ISR*, 6 July 2017.
84 Tripak, John, 'First Phase of Taiwan F-16V Program Is Complete.' *Air and Space Forces Magazine*, 5 February 2024.
85 Finnerty, Ryan, 'Boeing extends Super Hornet production to 2027 with final new-build order from USA,' *Flight Global*, 21 March 2024.
86 Schogol, Jeff, 'Marines pull aircraft from "boneyard," get used Navy jets amid aviation crisis,' *Marine Times*, 24 June 2016. Clark, Colin, 'Marines Scrounge Yorktown Museum F-18 For Spare Parts; How Bad Is It?,' *Breaking Defense*, 23 March 2016.
87 Schogol, Jeff, 'The Marine Corps' aviation fleet is in peril,' *Marine Times*, 27 April 2016.

Chapter 4

1 Yeo, Mike, 'Another Japan-based F-35 squadron is ready for operations,' *Defense News*, 9 September 2021.
2 Wilson, Alex, 'Marine Corps now has 2 fully operational F-35B stealth fighter squadrons in Japan,' *Stars & Stripes*, 26 May 2022.
3 Young, Dwane, 'Fightin' Fujins soar to Kadena,' *Kadena Air Base*, 21 November 2023.
4 Hadley, Greg, 'F-35s Deploy to Kadena, with No Set Timeline for F-15EX Arrival,' *Air & Space Forces Magazine*, 6 November 2024.
5 Young, Dwane R., 'Vermont Air National Guard deploys to Kadena,' *Kadena Air Base*, 13 January 2025.
6 Tirpak, John A., 'Air Force Mission Capable Rates Fall in 2023, Led by Declines for F-15C and B-1,' *Air and Space Forces Magazine*, 29 May 2024. Tirpak, John A., 'Air Force Mission Capability Rates Reach Lowest Levels in Years,' *Air and Space Forces Magazine*, 18 February 2025.
7 'Aerospace Nation: Gen Kenneth S. Wilsbach,' *Mitchell Institute for Aerospace Studies* (YouTube), 15 March 2022. Waldron, Greg, 'E-3 insufficient for timely detection of J-20: Pacific Air Forces chief,' *Flight Global*, 17 March 2022.
8 Kington, Tom, 'With Italian ship visit, Japanese officials observe F-35 carrier ops,' *Defense News*, 28 August 2024.
9 Dominguez, Gabriel, 'Dutch eyeing F-35 Indo-Pacific deployment in 2026, Japan envoy says,' *The Japan Times*, 18 December 2024.
10 Braaten, Shannon, 'U.S. F-35's Conduct Combined Training with Republic of Korea Air Force,' *U.S. Info-Pacific Command official website*, 19 July 2022.
11 Jeter, Kelley, 'U.S. Air Force and ROK Air Force Conduct Large-Scale Joint Air Training Event Vigilant Storm,' *U.S. Indo-Pacific Command official website*, 31 October 2022.
12 'North Korea claims US has put "nuclear script" into "Final Stage,"' *RT*, 1 November 2022.
13 Smith, Josh, 'North Korea calls South Korea's F-35 jet purchases "extremely dangerous action",' *Reuters*, 11 July 2019.
14 Kristensen, Hans M. and Norris, Robert S., 'A history of U.S. nuclear weapons in South Korea,' *Bulletin of Atomic Scientists*, vol. 73, no. 6, 2017, pp.349–357. Pincus, Walter, 'Neutron Killer Warhead Buried in ERDA Budget,' *The Washington Post*, 6 June 1977. 'Thaw in the Koreas?' *Bulletin of Atomic Scientists*, vol. 48, no. 3, April 1992, p.20. Cushman, John H., Military Options in Korea's End Game, *Nautilus Institute*, 23 May 1994.
15 Kopp, Carlo, 'Operation Odyssey Dawn—the collapse of Libya's relic air defense system,' *Defence Today*, vol. 9, no. 1, 2011.
16 Abrams, A. B., 'North Korea's Leap Forward in Air Defence Modernisation,' *Sino NK*, 5 April 2024. 'Kim Jong Un Watches Test of New-type Anti-Aircraft Guided Weapon System,' *KCNA*, 28 May 2017. 'Anti-aircraft Missile Newly Developed by Academy of Defence Science Test-fired,' *KCNA*, 1 October 2021.
17 Abrams, A. B., 'Legal Barriers to the North Korea-Russia Arms Trade – and the Loophole That Could Allow it to Expand,' *The Diplomat*, 10 January 2024. 'Top Five Potential Clients For the Su-57: Demand For Russia's Fifth Gen. Fighter From Algeria to Vietnam,' *Military Watch Magazine*, 23 November 2024.
18 Deboer, James, 'Marine Corps F-35Cs Make First Arrested Landings At An Expeditionary Airfield,' *The War Zone*, 10 December 2020.
19 Hancock, The STOVL Joint Strike Fighter.
20 Deboer, James, 'Inside How The Marine's Island-Hopping F-35B Playbook Is Being Written,' *The War Zone*, 18 January 2023.
21 Deboer, James, 'We Went With Marine F-35Bs As They Fought A Mock War From A Pacific Island,' *The War Zone*, 22 January 2025.
22 Deboer, 'We Went With Marine F-25Bs'.
23 'Pete Hegseth – Secretary of Defense Nominee | SRS #143,' *Shawn Ryan Shaw* (YouTube), 8 November 2024.
24 Everstine, Brian W., 'F-35s, F-16s to Operate from Austere Airfield on Guam During Cope North,' *Air & Space Forces Magazine*, 26 January 2021.
25 Deboer, 'Marine Corps F-35Cs Make First Arrested Landings'.
26 Newdick, Thomas, 'Ford Class Carrier's EMALS Catapults, AAG Arrester Gear Eyed For Land Bases,' *The War Zone*, 23 July 2024.
27 Katz, Justin and Marrow, Michael, 'Marine Corps cutting F-35B buy for more F-35Cs: New aviation plan,' *Breaking Defense*, 4 February 2025.
28 Common, David, 'Flying just outside Ukraine, NATO's sentinel planes warn of Russia's battlefield moves,' *CBC News*, 22 October 2022. Horton, Alex, 'Whatever the fuss over Elon Musk, Starlink is utterly essential in Ukraine,' *The Washington Post*, 18 September 2023. 'NATO's entire military infrastructure, satellites working against Russia — Kremlin,' *TASS*, 1 February 2023.
29 'Russia's S-400 Missile System Gains First Blood in Ukraine: Su-27 Shot Down 150km Away – Reports,' *Military Watch Magazine*, 6 March 2022.
30 Cohen, Rachel S., 'The US Air Force sent F-35s to defend NATO. Here's what it learned,' *Air Force Times*, 31 March 2023.
31 Cohen, 'The US Air Force sent F-35s to defend NATO'.
32 'F-35's "Electronic Spectrum Duels" with Russian Air Defences in Ukraine Raised to Make Case For Singaporean Acquisitions,' *Military Watch Magazine*, 5 March 2024.
33 Gosselin-Malo, Elisabeth, 'US-Finnish defense pact could bolster Nordic F-35 footprint,' *Defense News*, 9 May 2023.
34 'David's Sling Missile Systems and F-35 Stealth Fighters: An Ideal Pairing to Guard Finland's Long Russian Border,' *Military Watch Magazine*, 7 April 2023.
35 'F-35A touch down on highway demonstrating agility and flexibility,' *NATO Air Command official website*, 22 September 2023.
36 'US Air Force F-35s make historic first on highway in Finland,' *United States Air Force official website*, 4 September 2024.
37 D'Urso, Stefano, 'A Close-Up Look at the F-35's Highway Operations during the Baana 24 Exercise,' *The Aviationist*, 11 October 2024.
38 German, Howard, 'Focus on Pacific Theater and Agile Combat Employment: Exclusive Interviews with F-35 Pilots of Northern Lightning

2024,' *The Aviationist*, 15 August 2024. Rogoway, Tyler, 'Air Force Tests Tiny Personnel Footprint For Operating Fighters In Austere Combat Zones,' *The War Zone*, 14 May 2019.

39 Miller, Amanda, 'F-35 Squadrons in Alaska Shift to Full Operations as "Advanced Threats" Grow "More Lethal",' *Air & Space Forces Magazine*, 10 August 2022.

40 'Arrival of final 2 F-35s completes complement at Alaska base,' *Air Force Times*, 19 April 2022.

41 Woody, Christopher, 'The US Air Force is stocking up on stealth jets in Alaska, and its pilots are learning to thrive in harsh Arctic conditions,' *Business Insider*, 17 August 2022.

42 Altman, Howard, 'The Intricacies Of F-35 Operations Over The Frigid Alaskan Frontier,' *The War Zone*, 11 August 2022.

43 Altman, 'The Intricacies of F-35 Operations'.

44 'US Creates Infrastructure for Nuclear-Capable Jets in Greenland – Russian Ambassador,' *Sputnik News*, 10 January 2025.

45 'Tensions escalating in Arctic – top Russian admiral,' *RT*, 7 December 2023.

46 Marston, James, 'Russia Skirts U.S. Sanctions With $27 Billion Arctic Gas Plant,' *The Wall Street Journal*, 8 December 2017.

47 Hammes, T.X., 'Offshore Control is the Answer,' *Proceedings Magazine*, vol. 138, no. 12, issue 1318, December 2012.

48 Arctic Strategy, United States Department of the Air Force, 21 July 2020.

49 'ПАК ДП в будущем может стать беспилотным' ('PAK DP in the future may become unmanned'), *TASS*, 22 August 2017. Majumdar, Dave, 'Russia's PAK-DP Interceptor: The Unmanned Plane that Could Replace the MiG-31?,' *The National Interest*, 22 August 2017.

50 Everstine, Brian W., 'How F-35 Middle East Deployments Are Shaping Future Ops,' *Air & Space Forces Magazine*, 18 August 2020.

51 Everstine, 'How F-35 Middle East Deployments'.

52 Everstine, 'How F-35 Middle East Deployments'.

53 Everstine, 'How F-35 Middle East Deployments'.

54 Everstine, 'How F-35 Middle East Deployments'.

55 'Iran successfully used Russian-made radar to track US F-35 jets — designer,' *TASS*, 25 August 2022.

56 Gordon, Chris, 'F-35s Leave Middle East After Deployment to Deter Iran and Russia,' *Air & Space Forces Magazine*, 6 October 2023.

57 Gordon, 'F-35s Leave Middle East After Deployment'.

58 'U.S. Air Fleet Redeployment Highlights Close Qatar Ties and Growing Rift with United Arab Emirates,' *Military Watch Magazine*, 6 May 2024.

59 Kass, Harrison, 'The Houthis Almost Shot Down an F-35—and Washington Is Panicked,' *The National Interest*, 16 May 2025.

Chapter 5

1 Hires, Hunter, 'Warren Grove Gunnery Range hosts State Partnership JTAC Training,' *U.S. Air National Guard official website*, 10 December 2020.

2 Golan, John W., *Lavi : The United States, Israel, and a Controversial Fighter Jet*, Sterling, Potomac Books, 2016, pp.134, 162, 191, 192.

3 Grazier, Dan, 'F-35 and A-10 Close Air Support Flyoff Report,' *Project on Government Oversight*, 30 October 2023.

4 Grazier, 'F-35 and A-10 Close Air Support Flyoff Report'.

5 Thomas, Jordan, 'Sen. McCain: B-1s Really Do CAS!' *Breaking Defense*, 1 May 2014. Morgan, Wesley, 'The B-1 bomber: The underappreciated workhorse of America's air wars,' *The Washington Post*, 30 December 2015. Tirpak, John A., 'Repairing Broken Bones,' *Air and Space Forces Magazine*, 25 January 2021. Pawlyk, Oriana, 'B-1B Lancer's Evolving Mission Includes More Close-Air Support,' *Military.com*, 14 January 2018.

6 Liu, Xuanzun, 'China's JH-7A fighter bomber provides close air support in cross-service exercise,' *Global Times*, 25 March 2024.

7 Gosselin-Malo, Elisabeth, 'Are the once-vaunted Bayraktar drones losing their shine in Ukraine?,' *Defense News*, 21 October 2023.

8 D'Urso, Stefano, 'Israeli F-35Is Providing Close Air Support To Troops In Gaza With 2,000-lb Bombs,' *The Aviationist*, 7 November 2023.

9 'The U.S. Air Force Is Trying to Trick Us Into Getting Rid of the A-10,' *War is Boring*, 6 November 2014. Insinna, Valerie and Gould, Joe, 'The A-10 Warthog's biggest advocate lost her bid for the Senate, but does it actually matter?,' *Defense News*, 16 November 2018. Trevithick, Joseph, 'What's To Come Of The A-10 Now That It Has Lost Its Loudest Defenders In Congress?,' *The War Zone*, 15 November 2018.

10 Rogoway, Tyler, 'At What Point Does The USAF's War Against The A-10 Become Sabotage?,' *Jalopnik*, 12 February 2015.

11 Ernst, Douglas, 'Air Force released cherry-picked data to smear A-10 Thunderbolts II: watchdog,' *The Washington Times*, 10 February 2015. Wong, Kristina, 'Watchdog: Air Force "doctored the data" to make A-10 look bad,' *The Hill*, 2 September 2015.

12 Trevithick, Joseph, 'Watch The "Final Cut" Of A Glowing Film About The A-10 That The USAF Tried to Suppress,' *The War Zone*, 30 June 2019.

13 Trevithick, Joseph, 'A-10 Replacement Requirements Do Actually Exist But They're Mired In Bureaucratic Limbo,' *The War Zone*, 30 June 2019.

14 Lamothe, Dan, 'Air Force to move A-10 jets into backup status despite congressional opposition,' *The Washington Post*, 2 March 2015.

15 Trevithick, Joseph, 'The Air Force May Have Managed A Way To Quietly Ground Roughly A Third Of The A-10 Fleet,' *The War Zone*, 13 April 2018.

16 Miller, Alan C. and Sack, Kevin, 'Far From Battlefield, Marines Lose One-Third of Harrier Fleet,' *Los Angeles Times*, 15 December 2002.

17 Axe, David, 'America should unleash its armoured flying Hogs in Ukraine,' *The Telegraph*, 24 January 2024.

18 Naegele, Tobias, 'Editorial: The Best Fighter in the World,' *Air & Space Forces Magazine*, 26 March 2021.

19 Miller, Jay, *Lockheed Martin F/A-22 Raptor Stealth Fighter*, Hinckley, Midland Publishing, 2005, p.3.

20 Wolf, Jim, 'Lockheed F-22 cast as nuclear substitute,' *Reuters*, 17 December 2008.

21 Cushman, John H., 'Military Options in Korea's End Game,' *Nautilus Institute*, 23 May 1994.

22 Marrow, Michael, 'F-35A officially certified to carry nuclear bomb,' *Breaking Defense*, 8 March 2024.

23 Memorandum from the Acronym Institute for Disarmament Diplomacy, Executive Summary, United Kingdom Houses of Parliament, 19 March 2007.

24 Abrams, A.B., 'What Nuclear Weapons Sharing Trends Mean for East Asia,' *The Diplomat*, 4 April 2023.

25 'F-35 to take over nuclear role of the Netherlands within NATO from F-16,' *Netherlands Ministry of Defense official website*, 30 May 2024.

26 Korda, Matt and Kristensen, Hans, 'Increasing Evidence That The US Air Force's Nuclear Mission May Be Returning To UK Soil,' *Federation of American Scientists*, 28 August 2023.

27 Newdick, Thomas, 'USAF Air Base In England Is Nuclear Capable Again: Watchdog Report,' *The War Zone*, 27 February 2025.

28 Barnes, Joe, 'Exclusive: Nato in talks to deploy more nuclear weapons,' *The Telegraph*, 16 June 2024

29 'US ready to consider expansion of number of NATO nuclear missions participants — Pentagon,' *TASS*, 2 April 2025.

30 Vandiver, John, 'RAF Lakenheath lays groundwork for possible return of US nuclear bomb storage, report says,' *Stars and Stripes*, 3 March 2025. Allison, George, 'UK exploring idea of F-35A purchase for NATO strike role,' *UK Defence Journal*, 9 June 2025.

31 'UK to purchase F-35As and join NATO nuclear mission as Government steps up national security and delivers defence dividend,' *GOV.UK*, 24 June, 2025.

32 'Poland's bid to participate in NATO nuclear sharing,' *International Institute For Strategic Studies*, September 2023.

33 Johnson, Jesse, 'Japan should consider hosting U.S. nuclear weapons, Abe says,' *Japan Times*, 27 February 2022.

34 'Kim, Chin-myong, '美 믿고 핵무장 안했는데 돈만 더 내라? "핵공유" 약속 받아내야' ('Trusting the US and not arming ourselves with nuclear weapons, but we just need to pay more? We need to get a promise of "nuclear sharing"'), *Choson Ilbo*, 22 November 2019. Layton, Peter, 'Revitalising Australia's out-of-date US alliance,' *Lowy Institute*, 28 January 2025.

35 'Department of Defense Announces Pursuit of B61 Gravity Bomb Variant,' *U.S. Department of Defense*, 27 October 2023.

36 'Nuclear Bomb Map Shows Impact if Biden's New Weapon Dropped on Russia,' *Newsweek*, 3 November 2023.

37 Keck, Zachary, 'Israel Wants to Add the F-35 to its Nuclear Triad,' *The National Interest*, 29 November 2021.

38 Gordon, Yefim and Komissarov, Dmitriy, *Mikoyan MiG-31: Interceptor*, Barnsley, Pen and Sword, 2015, p.124. Gordon, Yefim, *Mikoyan MiG-31*, Hinckley, Midland Publishing, 2005, pp.134-137.

39 LaGrone, Sam, 'Video: Successful F-35, SM-6 Live Fire Test Points to Expansion in Networked Naval Warfare,' *United States Naval Institute*, 13 September 2016. Abbott, Rich, 'New Demonstration Shows F-35's Data Sharing Capability,' *Aviation Today*, 8 August 2019.

40 Osborn, Kris, 'The F-35 Strengthens Its Role in Missile Defense,' *The National Interest*, 30 November 2021.

41 Freedberg Jr., Sydney J., 'F-35 Ready For Missile Defense By 2025: MDA Chief,' *Breaking Defense*, 11 April 2018.

42 Rogoway, Tyler, 'The Airborne Laser May Rise Again But It Will Look Very Different,' *Jalopnik*, 18 August 2015.

43 Tadjdeh, Yasmin, 'Laser Vision: Special Operations Command Prepares to Test Airborne Directed Energy Weapon,' *National Defense*, 19 April 2017.

44 Bertrand, Natasha and Britzky, Haley, 'American fighter pilots explain how they fought an overwhelming Iranian drone swarm in total darkness,' *CNN*, 15 November 2024. Gordon, Chris, 'USAF Fighters Shoot Down Iranian Drones in Defense of Israel,' *Air & Space Forces Magazine*, 15 April 2024.

45 Keller, Jared, 'Another Dead End for Airborne Lasers: Air Force Scraps Effort to Mount Directed-Energy Weapon on Fighter Jet,' *Military.com*, 17 May 2024.

46 Keller, Jared, 'The Air Force's Dream of Mounting a Laser Weapon on an AC-130J Ghostrider Gunship Is Dead,' *Military.com*, 19 March 2024.

47 'Defence analyst Pierre Sprey on the F-35 (2012),' *The Fifth Estate* (YouTube), 28 December 2016.

48 Mehta, Aaron, 'Boeing Positions F-15 as F-22 Supplement,' *Breaking Defense*, 15 September 2015.

49 Cenciotti, David, '"If we don't keep F-22 Raptor viable, the F-35 fleet will be irrelevant" Air Combat Command says,' *The Aviationist*, 4 February 2014.

50 O'Hanlon, Michael E., 'The Plane Truth: Fewer F-22s Mean a Stronger National Defense,' *Brookings Institute*, 1 September 1999.

51 'F-22 Raptor,' Battle Stations, Season 1, Episode 39.

52 Allison, George, 'No, the F-35 was not beaten by an F-16,' *UK Defense Journal*, 1 July 2015.

53 Cenciotti, David, 'F-35's kill ratio with Aggressors stands at 15:1 during Red Flag 17-1 (most probably thanks to the supporting F-22…),' *The Aviationist*, 5 February 2017.
54 Garbarino, Micah, 'F-35A proving its worth at Red Flag combat exercise,' *388th Fighter Wing official website*, 3 February 2017.
55 Cenciotti, 'F-35's kill ratio with Aggressors stands at 15:1 during Red Flag'.
56 Cenciotti, David, 'F-15E Strike Eagles unable to shoot down the F-35s in 8 dogfights during simulated deployment,' *The Aviationist*, 27 June 2016.
57 Rogoway, Tyler, 'People Are Freaking Out Over Video Of Su-35 Practicing For Moscow Air Show,' *The War Zone*, 22 July 2017.
58 Cenciotti, David, 'The First Reports Of How The F-35 Strutted Its Stuff In Dogfights Against Aggressors At Red Flag Are Starting To Emerge,' *The Aviationist*, 16 February 2019.
59 '媒体披露歼20战机真实空战实力 以"零损伤"击落敌机17架' ('The media disclosed the real air combat strength of the J-20 fighter jets and shot down 17 enemy planes with "zero damage"'), *163*, 25 September 2020. 'Chinese Media Claims J-20 Shot Down 17 "Enemy" Fighters in Exercises – How Reliable Are These Claims?' *Military Watch Magazine*, 16 September 2020.
60 Pickrell, Ryan, 'Air Force F-35s Wrecked Enemies During Mock Air Combat,' *Task and Purpose*, 21 February 2019.
61 Liu, Xuanzun, 'J-20 shows high combat readiness in New Year combat training,' *Global Times*, 9 January 2022. Liu, Xuanzun, 'Newly commissioned J-20 stealth fighters on combat alert,' *Global Times*, 17 January 2022.
62 Liu, Xuanzun, 'J-20 fighters conduct nocturnal battle drill to hone stealth advantages,' *Global Times*, 16 January 2022.
63 'China's J-16 Fleet Surpasses 350 Fighters as Thirteenth Batch Begins Deliveries: Numbers Outstrip All Contemporary Rivals,' *Military Watch Magazine*, 19 August 2024.
64 International Institute for Strategic Studies, *The Military Balance*, Volume 123, 2024, p.47.
65 'NATO's fighter pilots go head-to-head,' *NATO Multimedia*, 20 September 2024.
66 'NATO's fighter pilots go head-to-head'.
67 'Dogfights of the Future,' IMDB, Dogfights, Season 2, Episode 18, 22 May 2008.
68 'Dogfights of the Future.'
69 Pickrell, Ryan, 'A US F-22 Raptor pilot describes the challenge of going up against F-35 red air aggressors,' *Business Insider*, 30 August 2021.
70 Dildy C., Douglas and Cooper, Tom, *F-15C Eagle vs MiG-23/25: Iraq 1991*, New York, Bloomsbury, 2016, p.70.
71 Trimble, Steve, 'The Weekly Debrief: Does Raytheon's New AIM- 120D3 Beat China's Best Missile?' *Aviation Week*, 25 July 2022. Tirpak, John A., 'Piecing Together the NGAD Puzzle,' *Air & Space Forces Magazine*, 29 April 2022.
72 Newdick, Thomas and Rogoway, Tyler, 'Navy Looks To Arm F-35 With Four New Missiles, Including Hellfire,' *The War Zone*, 14 November 2023.
73 Trevithick, Joseph, 'Mini Anti-Ship Cruise Missile That Fits Inside An F-35 Is On The Navy's Wish List,' *The War Zone*, 7 February 2024.
74 Horton, Alex, 'Russian jamming leaves some high-tech U.S. weapons ineffective in Ukraine,' The *Washington Post*, 24 May 2024.
75 'AGM-158 flight testing begins on F-35C,' *dvids*, 10 September 2024.
76 Trevithick, 'Mini Anti-Ship Cruise Missile'.

Chapter 6

1 F-35 Joint Strike Fighter: Current Outlook Is Improved, but Long-Term Affordability Is a Major Concern, Report to Congressional Committees, Government Accountability Office, March 2013, p.5.
2 F-35 Joint Strike Fighter: More Actions Needed to Explain Cost Growth and Support Engine Modernization Decision, Report to Congressional Committees, Government Accountability Office, May 2023, p.7.
3 Reed, John, 'F-35 LRIP-4 Costs Detailed,' *Air International*, 17 December 2010.
4 Reed, 'F-35 LRIP-4 Costs Detailed'.
5 Clark, Colin, 'F-35: DoD Forces Lockheed To Accept Its Price For LRIP 9,' *Breaking Defense*, 2 November 2016.
6 Giangreco, Leigh, 'Unilateral negotiations still in play for F-35 contract,' *Flight Global*, 20 December 2016.
7 Insinna, Valerie, 'Pentagon reaches handshake deal with Lockheed on newest batch of F-35s,' *Defense News*, 15 July 2018.
8 'F-35 Prices Drop Again in Lot 10,' *Air & Space Forces*, 3 February 2017.
9 Werner, Ben, 'F-35 Price Dropping But Not Enough for the Pentagon,' *USNI News*, 1 March 2018.
10 Insinna, Valerie, 'In newly inked deal, F-35 price falls to $78 million a copy,' *Defense News*, 29 October 2019.
11 'Inexpensive F-35: How the World's Most Costly Weapons Program Produced the West's Most Cost Effective Fighter,' *Military Watch Magazine*, 6 October 2023. Emmott, Robin, 'Belgium picks Lockheed's F-35 over Eurofighter on price,' *Reuters*, 26 October 2018.
12 Naegele, Tobias, 'Editorial: The Best Fighter in the World,' *Air and Space Forces Magazine*, 26 March 2021.
13 Tirpak, John A., 'F-35 JPO and Lockheed Martin Reach Handshake Deal for 375 Aircraft,' *Air & Space Forces Magazine*, 19 July 2022.
14 Tirpak, 'F-35 JPO and Lockheed Martin'.
15 'Pentagon and Lockheed Martin Finalize Lot 15-17 Agreement, Capping a Year of International Growth,' *Lockheed Martin Aeronautics*, 30 December 2022.
16 Tirpak, John A., 'Lockheed and F-35 Program Office Have Handshake Deal on Next Two Lots,' *Air & Space Forces Magazine*, 21 November 2024.
17 Jones, Colton, 'Lockheed Martin secures $870M contract for F-35 Lot 20 production,' *Defense Blog*, 23 November 2024.
18 Losey, Stephen and Robertson, Noah, 'Stalled F-35 upgrades will delay next improvements, Wittman warns,' *Defence News*, 7 December 2023.
19 Director, Operational Test & Evaluation, FY2024 Annual Report, February 2025, p.46.
20 Insinna, Valerie, 'Minor quality control issue creates new problem for F-35 enterprise,' *Defense News*, 2 November 2017.
21 Insinnia, Valerie, 'Defense Department halts F-35 deliveries amid repair bill disagreement with Lockheed,' *Defense News*, 12 April 2018.
22 Capaccio, Anthony, 'Lockheed's F-35 Gets Flawed $14 Billion Software Upgrade,' *Bloomberg*, 26 January 2021.
23 Grazier, Dan, 'F-35 Program Stagnated in 2021 but DOD Testing Office Hiding Full Extent of Problem,' *Project on Government Oversight*, 9 March 2022.
24 Tirpak, John A., 'Top Lawmakers Want to Slash F-35 Production, Put Funds Toward Test Capacity,' *Air and Space Forces Magazine*, 14 May 2024.
25 Tirpak, John A., 'Kendall: F-35 Delivery Hold Is "Hurting" the Air Force,' *Air & Space Forces Magazine*, 8 March 2022.
26 Tirpak, 'Kendall: F-35 Delivery Hold is "Hurting"'.
27 Decker, Audrey, 'F-35 deliveries could resume in July, but the new jets won't be combat-ready for a year or more,' *Defense One*, 17 April 2024
28 Marrow, Michael, 'Pentagon delays F-35 retrofits amid upgrade woes,' *Breaking Defense*, 4 April 2024.
29 F-35 Joint Strike Fighter: Program Continues to Encounter Production Issues and Modernization Delays, *Government Accountability Office*, 16 May 2024.
30 Perry, Dominic, 'Norway flags ongoing F-35 delivery delays,' *Flight Global*, 9 October 2024.
31 'Lockheed Martin F-35s delivered with "robust" TR-3 training software,' *Jane's*, 4 September 2024.
32 Losey, Stephen, 'Lockheed feels financial pinch from F-35 upgrade, contract delays,' *Defense News*, 23 October 2024.
33 Tirpak, John A., 'Even After F-35's TR-3 Software is Approved, Frequent Patches May Be Needed,' *Air and Space Forces Magazine*, 30 May 2024.
34 Tirpak, John A., 'Lockheed Ups Pace of F-35 Deliveries to New High to Start Clearing Backlog,' *Air & Space Forces Magazine*, 31 October 2024.
35 Losey, Stephen, 'Lockheed feels financial pinch from F-35 upgrade, contract delays,' *Defense News*, 23 October 2024.
36 The F-35 Lightning II Joint Strike Fighter, Hearing Before the Subcommittee on Tactical Air and Land Forces of the Committee on Armed Services, House of Representatives, One Hundred Fifteenth Congress, Second Session, 7 March 2018. Losey, Stephen, 'Wittman says patience wearing thin on F-35 sustainment plan,' *Defense News*, 3 October 2023.
37 Garbarino, Micah, 'Maintainers help the F-35A remain a "stealthy beast", 388th Fighter Wing Public Affairs, *Hill Air Force Base official website*, 29 October 2019.
38 Insinna, Valerie, 'Stealth features responsible for half of F-35 defects, Lockheed program head states,' *Defense News*, 6 March 2018.
39 Stone, Mike, 'Pentagon stops accepting Lockheed F-35 jets over repair cost dispute,' *Reuters*, 12 April 2018.
40 Capaccio, Anthony, 'Air Force Risks Losing Third of F-35s on Upkeep Costs,' *Bloomberg*, 28 March 2018.
41 Mehta, Aaron, 'Pentagon "can't afford the sustainment costs" on F-35, Lord says,' *Defense News*, 2 February 2018.
42 Insinna, Valerie, 'Air Force acquisition nominee takes aim at F-35 sustainment costs,' *Defense News*, 19 January 2018.
43 Liebermann, Oren, 'Senior Trump Air Force official suggested dramatically slashing F-35 jet numbers,' *CNN*, 15 May 2021.
44 Harper, Jon, 'Program Leader Says High Costs Pose "Existential Threat" to F-35,' *National Defense*, 13 May 2021.
45 F-35 Sustainment: DOD Needs to Cut Billions in Estimated Costs to Achieve Affordability, Government Accountability Office, July 2021.
46 Maurer, Diana, F35 Sustainment: Enhanced Attention to and Oversight of F35 Affordability Are Needed, Testimony Before the Subcommittees on Readiness and Tactical Air and Land Forces, Committee on Armed Services, House of Representatives, 22 April 2021.
47 Gregg, Aaron, 'Powerful lawmaker calls F-35 fighter jet a "rathole," suggests Pentagon should cut its losses,' *Washington Post*, 5 March 2021.
48 Tripak, John A., 'Can a Service Contract Save the F-35? Chronically high operating costs might be tamed with a new deal.,' *Air Force Magazine*, December 2021, p.30.
49 Maurer, Diana, F35 Sustainment: Enhanced Attention to and Oversight of F35 Affordability Are Needed, Testimony Before the Subcommittees on Readiness and Tactical Air and Land Forces, Committee on Armed Services, House of Representatives, 22 April 2021.
50 Trimble, Steve, 'Three Generations Of Fighters Compete For Limited Resources,' *Aviation Week*, 10 December 2020.
51 Selected Acquisition Report (SAR): F-35 Lightning II Joint Strike Fighter (JSF) Program (F-35), United States of American Department of Defense,

December 2016, pp.42-44. Tirpak, John, 'Combat Forces in Peril,' *Air and Space Forces Magazine*, July 2017. Tirpak, John, 'No USAF F-35 Surge in 2018 Budget,' *Air and Space Forces Magazine*, 23 May 2017.

52 Gordon, Chris, 'Air Force Plans to Divest 250 Aircraft in 2025, Shrinking Fleet to New Low,' *Air and Space Forces Magazine*, 11 March 2024. Tirpak, John A., 'Pentagon Report: Air Force to Bed Down Only 25 F-35s in Fiscal 2026,' *Air and Space Forces Magazine*, 7 September 2024. 'Is the Pentagon Halving F-35A Orders to Pay For the F-47? Fighter's Viability in Question as Sixth Generation Era Looms,' *Military Watch Magazine*, 11 June 2025.

53 Pawlyk, Oriana, 'Lockheed Predicts Record-Setting Readiness Rates Soon for F-35,' *Military.com*, 5 March 2018.

54 Pawlyk, 'Lockheed Predicts Record-Setting Readiness'.

55 'Why the Pentagon Isn't Happy With the F-35,' *Bloomberg*, 24 January 2018.

56 F-35 Aircraft: DOD Should Assess and Update Its Engine Sustainment Strategy to Support Desired Outcomes, Government Accountability Office, July 2022.

57 Insinna, Valerie, 'How the US Air Force's Kessel Run team plans to solve one of the F-35 program's biggest headaches,' *Defense News*, 27 February 2019. Grazier, Dan, 'Uncorrected Design Flaws, Cyber-Vulnerabilities, and Unreliability Plague the F-35 Program,' *Project on Government Oversight*, 24 March 2020.

58 Testimony by Diana Maurer, director, defense capabilities and management, U.S. Government Accountability Office, F-35 Aircraft Sustainment: DOD Faces Challenges in Sustaining a Growing Fleet, US House of Representatives Committee on Armed Services Subcommittees on Readiness and Tactical Air and Land Forces, 116th Congress, 13 November 2019.

59 Insinnia, Valerie, 'Key piece of F-35 logistics system unusable by US Air Force students, instructor pilots,' *Defense News*, 9 March 2019.

60 F-35 Sustainment: DOD Needs a Plan to Address Risks Related to Its Central Logistics System, Government Accountability Office, April 2016.

61 Tirpak, John A., 'Can a Service Contract Save the F-35?,'*Air and Space Forces Magazine*, 3 December 2021. Director, Operational Test & Evaluation, FY2024 Annual Report, February 2025, p.48.

62 Insinna, Valerie, 'Government watchdog finds more problems with F-35's spare parts pipeline,' *Defense News*, 26 April 2019. Trevithick, Joseph and Rogoway, Tyler, 'How The F-35's Lack Of Spare Parts Became As Big A Threat As Enemy Missiles,' *The War Zone*, 13 April 2023.

63 Insinna, 'Government watchdog finds more problems with F-35's spare parts pipeline'. Losey, Stephen, ''Just in time' F-35 supply chain too risky for next war, general says,' *Defense News*, 4 April 2023. Trevithick, and Rogoway, 'How The F-35's Lack Of Spare Parts'.

64 F-35 Aircraft Sustainment: DOD Needs to Address Substantial Supply Chain Challenges, Government Accountability Office, April 2019.

65 F-35 Aircraft Sustainment: DOD Needs to Address Substantial Supply Chain Challenges.

66 Tirpak, 'Can a Service Contract Save the F-35?'.

67 'Sea Air Space 2023 Monday (April 3rd) Recap,' *Navy League of the United States* (YouTube), April 4, 2023.

68 Tirpak, 'Can a Service Contract Save the F-35?'.

69 Parsons, Dan, 'Blistering Highlights From The Latest F-35 Sustainment Hearing,' *The War Zone*, 9 May 2022.

70 Losey, Stephen, 'Wittman says patience wearing thin on F-35 sustainment plan,' *Defense News*, 3 October 2023.

71 Director, Operational Test & Evaluation, FY2024 Annual Report, February 2025, p.55.

72 Mehta, Aaron, 'Mattis orders fighter jet readiness to jump to 80 percent — in one year,' *Defense News*, 10 October 2018.

73 Insinna, Valerie and Losey, Stephen, 'US Air Force bails on Mattis-era fighter jet readiness goal,' *Defense News*, 8 May 2020.

74 Decker, Audrey, 'F-35s still missing readiness goals, despite rising spending,' *Defense One*, 21 October 2024.

75 Tirpak, John A., 'Make-or-Break Time for the F-35,' *Air and Space Forces Magazine*, 23 April 2021.

76 Trimble, Steve, 'U.S. Air Force Talks New F-16 Orders In Latest Acquisition Shake-up,' *Aviation Week*, 21 January 2021.

77 Trimble, 'U.S. Air Force Talks New F-16 Orders'.

78 Newdick, Thomas, 'Air Force Boss Wants Clean-Sheet Fighter That's Less Advanced Than F-35 To Replace F-16,' *The War Zone*, 18 February 2021.

79 'South Korean FA-50 vs. Swedish Gripen: Mock Engagement in Australia Highlights Golden Eagle's Superiority,' *Military Watch Magazine*, 24 August 2024. 'More "Effective" Korean T-50 Jets Could Soon Come to the Philippines as President Duterte Slams "Utterly Useless" American F-16 Fighters,' *Military Watch Magazine*, 26 August 2018. Kim, Minseok and Chen, Chuanren, 'KAI Charts Out Single-Seat FA-50 Road Map,' *Aviation Week*, 23 October 2023.

80 Martin, Tim and Marrow, Michael, 'Air Force weighing turning T-7 into F-7 armed light attack jet: Official,' *Breaking Defense*, 8 November 2023.

81 Trevithick, Joseph, 'T-7 Arrives At Edwards, USAF Eyeing Light Fighter Version,' *The War Zone*, 8 November 2023.

82 'Why F-35 Shortcomings Are Forcing the U.S. Air Force to Consider the New "F-7" Fighter,' *Military Watch Magazine*, 10 November 2023.

83 Newdick, Thomas, 'Air Force Chief Responds To Possibility Of Buying New "Block 80" F-16s,' *The War Zone*, 20 May 2025.

84 Harper, Jon, 'Program Leader Says High Costs Pose "Existential Threat" to F-35,' *National Defense*, 13 May 2021.

85 'The F-35 Will Now Exceed $2 Trillion As the Military Plans to Fly It Less,' *Government Accountability Office*, 16 May 2024.

86 'The F-35 Will Now Exceed $2 Trillion As the Military Plans to Fly It Less'.

87 Venable, John, U.S. Air Force, 2024 Index of U.S. Military Strength, 24 January 2024. Allen, Kenneth W. and Garafola, Cristina L., 70 Years of the PLA Air Force, Montgomery, China Aerospace Studies Institute, 2019.

88 Francis Tusa on Twitter: '@CorporalFrisk @iltalehti_fi Re your overall points that a) F-35 cost data is all over the shop, b) that Finnish justification of costs might be insanely optimistic, bordering naive, have a look at this:' 6 December 2021.

89 '078 – F-35 Lightning II,' *Fighter Pilot Podcast* (YouTube), 13 April 2020.

90 '078 – F-35 Lightning II,' *Fighter Pilot Podcast* (YouTube).

91 Epstein, Jake, 'I tested the game-changing F-35 stealth fighter, an incredible jet that demands more than just great flying skills from its pilots,' *Business Insider*, 4 November 2023

92 Whittle, Richard, 'The Ultimate Fighter?,' *The Smithsonian Magazine*, March 2012.

93 Venable, John, 'The F-35A Fighter Is the Most Dominant and Lethal Multi-Role Weapons System in the World: Now Is the Time to Ramp Up Production,' *Heritage Foundation*, 14 May 2019.

94 Naegele, Tobias, 'Editorial: The Best Fighter in the World,' *Air and Space Forces Magazine*, 26 March 2021.

95 F-35 Joint Strike Fighter (JSF), FY19 DoD Programs,Office of the Director of Operational Test & Evaluation, Department of Defence, January 2020.

96 Capaccio, Anthony, 'Lockheed F-35's Tally of Flaws Tops 800 as "New Issues" Surface,' *Bloomberg*, 14 July 2021.

97 Hubinger, Scott, 'Can the F-35 Lightning II Joint Strike Fighter Avoid the Fate of the F-22 Raptor?,' *Joint Forces Quarterly*, vol. 94, Third Quarter 2019, pp.44-52.

98 Dvorak, Daniel L. (ed.), NASA Study on Flight Software Complexity, Final Report, Systems and Software Division Jet Propulsion Laboratory California Institute of Technology, 2009, p.1.

99 Parsons, Dan, 'Blistering Highlights From The Latest F-35 Sustainment Hearing,' *The War Zone*, 9 May 2022.

100 Pawlyk, Oriana, 'F-35A Hypoxia Problems Date Back to 2011, Air Force Reveals,' *Military.com*, 15 June 2017.

101 Losey, Stephen and Insinna, Valerie, 'F-35s at Luke Air Force Base grounded after pilots suffered oxygen deprivation,' *Air Force Times*, 10 June 2017.

102 Church, Aaron, 'Raptor Return,' *Air Force Magazine*, December 2011.

103 Insinna, Valerie, 'Clearing the air: F-35s to get upgrade for oxygen generating system over hypoxia concerns,' *Defense News*, 19 July 2017.

104 Insinna, 'Clearing the air'.

105 Insinna, Valerie, 'House panel demands another investigation into F-35 pilot breathing system problems,' *Defense News*, 3 August 2021.

106 Insinna, 'House panel demands another investigation into F-35 pilot breathing system problems'. Hudson, Lee, 'NASA Study Sheds Light On F-35 Oxygen Deprivation Symptoms,' *Aviation Week*, 14 May 2021.

107 Insinna, 'House panel demands another investigation into F-35 pilot breathing system problems'.

108 Insinna, 'House panel demands another investigation into F-35 pilot breathing system problems'.

109 Insinna, Valerie, 'A fix is coming for a problem that left two F-35 pilots in "excruciating" pain,' *Defense News*, 12 June 2019.

110 United States Air Force Aircraft Accident Investigation Board Report, Department of the Air Force Headquarters Air Combat Command, 25 July 2023.

111 Roza, David, 'F-35 Crashed Due to Computer Glitch Caused by Turbulence: Accident Report,' *Air & Space Forces Magazine*, 28 July 2023.

112 Roza, 'F-35 Crashed Due to Computer Glitch'.

113 'What is good and bad about the F-35 cockpit: A "Panther" pilot's guide to modern cockpits,' *Husk Kit, 21* January 2021.

114 'What is good and bad about the F-35 cockpit'.

115 'F-16s to F-35s to YouTube with "Hasard" (ep. 167),' *Fighter Pilot Podcast*, 20 May 2023.

116 Altman, Howard, 'The Intricacies Of F-35 Operations Over The Frigid Alaskan Frontier,' *The War Zone*, 11 August 2022.

117 Venable, 'The F-35A Fighter Is the Most Dominant and Lethal Multi-Role Weapons System in the World'.

118 Clark, Colin, 'Show And Tell: F-35 Test Fires GAU-22 Gun,' *Breaking Defense*, 20 August 2015.

119 Majumdar, Dave, 'New U.S. Stealth Jet Can't Fire Its Gun Until 2019,' *The Daily Beast*, 31 December 2014.

120 Trevithick, Joseph, 'USMC's Older F-35Bs May Only Be Able To Fly Around A Quarter Of Their Expected Service Life,' *The War Zone*, 1 February 2019.

121 'F-35 Joint Strike Fighter (JSF),' FY19 DoD Programs, U.S. Department of Defense, Director, Operational Test and Evaluation.

122 'F-35 Joint Strike Fighter (JSF)'.

123 F-35 Joint Strike Fighter: Cost Growth and Schedule Delays Continue, Report to Congressional Committees, Government Accountability Office, April 2022.

124 F-35 Joint Strike Fighter: More Actions Needed to Explain Cost Growth and Support Engine Modernization Decision, Report to Congressional Committees, Government Accountability Office, May 2023.

125 'Testing of the F-35C Tailhook,' *The Engi Nerd*, 16 February 2024.
126 Majumdar, Dave, 'Lockheed claims tailhook fix will allow F-35s to land on aircraft carriers,' *Atlantic Council*, 18 January 2012.
127 Clark, Colin, 'Navy's F-35 Tailhook Passes Initial Tests; Carrier Flights In October,' *Breaking Defense*, 5 February 2014.
128 Insinna, Valerie and Larter, David B., 'Supersonic speeds could cause big problems for the F-35's stealth coating,' *Defense News*, 12 June 2019.
129 Insinna and Larter, 'Supersonic speeds could cause big problems for the F-35's stealth coating'. Larter, David B. and Insinna, Valerie and Mehta, Aaron, 'The Pentagon will have to live with limits on F-35's supersonic flights,' *Defense News*, 25 April 2020.
130 Larter, Insinna and Mehta, 'The Pentagon will have to live with limits on F-35's supersonic flights'.
131 Tegler, Eric, 'Air Force F-35 Lightning IIs Still Can't Fly Within 25 Miles Of ... Lightning,' *Forbes*, 23 November 2022.
132 Losey, Stephen, 'F-35A Lightning cleared to fly in lightning for first time in 4 years,' *Defense News*, 2 April 2024.
133 Insinna, Valerie, 'Stealth features responsible for half of F-35 defects, Lockheed program head states,' *Defense News*, 6 March 2018.
134 F-35 Joint Strike Fighter (JSF), FY 2018 DoD Programs, Director, Operational Test and Evaluation. Grazier, Dan, 'F-35 Far from Ready to Face Current or Future Threats, Testing Data Shows,' *Project on Government Oversight*, 19 March 2019.
135 Eckstein, Megan, 'F-35B Operations in Yuma Resume After Temporary Halt Due to Software Update Issues,' *USNI News*, 23 June 2017.
136 Tirpak, John A., 'Air Force F-35s Grounded as Search for Faulty Ejection Seat Parts Widens,' *Air & Space Forces Magazine*, 29 July 2022.
137 Malley, Blaise, 'Failing F-35 fighter grounded once again,' *Responsible Statecraft*, 5 January 2023. Walters, Guy, 'Commentary on Likely Increase in JSF Engine Costs to Increase – Part 1,' *Sir Richard Williams Foundation*, 28 November 2021.
138 Mehta, Aaron, 'Bogdan: F-35 Coolant Line Fix Coming in Weeks,' *Defense News*, 21 September 2016.
139 Capaccio, Anthony, 'Lockheed F-35's factory flaws persist even after 800 are built,' *Bloomberg*, 5 August 2022.
140 Capaccio, Anthony, 'Lockheed's F-35 Quality Flaws Persist as Production Ramps Up,' *Bloomberg*, 16 October 2023.
141 'Dutch Defence Minister In Texas to Discuss Joint Strike Fighter,' *Defence Talk, 13* January 2012.
142 Jones, Colton, 'Lockheed Martin secures $870M contract for F-35 Lot 20 production,' *Defense Blog*, 23 November 2024.
143 'Lockheed Martin Meets 2017 F-35 Delivery Target,' *Lockheed Martin Newsroom*, 18 December 2017.
144 'F-35 Joint Strike Fighter: Development Is Nearly Complete, but Deficiencies Found in Testing Need to Be Resolved,' Government Accountability Office, June 2018.
145 Weisgerber, Marcus, 'F-35 Production Set to Quadruple As Massive Factory Retools,' *Defense One*, 6 May 2019.
146 Director, Operational Test & Evaluation, FY2024 Annual Report, February 2025, p.46.
147 Insinna, Valerie, 'Inside America's Dysfunctional Trillion-Dollar Fighter-Jet Program,' *The New York Times*, 21 August 2019.
148 Jean, Grace V., 'Lockheed Martin Delivers 45 F-35s in 2015,' *National Defense*, vol. 93, no. 656, July 2008, pp.40-44.
149 Epps, Kenneth, 'The Size of The F-35 Market is Overstated,' *Project Ploughshares*, November 2010.
150 Jean, Grace V., 'Lockheed Martin Delivers 45 F-35s in 2015,' *National Defense*, vol. 93, no. 656, July 2008, pp.40-44.
151 Rich, Gillian, 'Pentagon budget 2023: Services desire additional F-35 aircraft,' *Jane's*, 13 April 2022.
152 Tirpak, John A., 'F-35 JPO and Lockheed Martin Reach Handshake Deal for 375 Aircraft,' *Air & Space Forces Magazine*, 19 July 2022.
153 Tirpak, 'F-35 JPO and Lockheed Martin Reach Handshake Deal for 375 Aircraft,'
154 Capaccio, Tony, 'Stagnant F-35 Reliability Means Fewer Available Jets: Pentagon,' *Bloomberg*, 30 January 2019.
155 Reim, Garrett, 'Lockheed Martin sees F-35 production rising to 180 units per year, despite high flying costs,' *Flight Global*, 31 January 2020.
156 Insinna, Valerie, 'F-35 to move into full-rate production later than expected,' *Defense News*, 27 October 2020.
157 Tirpak, John A., 'Strategy & Policy: Thinking Past the F-35,' *Air & Space Forces Magazine*, 1 December 2019.
158 International Institute for Strategic Studies, The Military Balance, Volume 124, 2024, Chapter 2.

Chapter 7

1 'JSF's "plug and play" F136 engine unveiled,' *Flight Global*, 20 July 2004.
2 'GE says F135 and F136 can co-exist on carriers,' *Alert 5*, 12 August 2010. 'GE Pitches Hill on F136's Upkeep,' *Military.com*, 11 August 2010.
3 'GE Pitches Hill on F136's Upkeep'.
4 Waldron, Greg, 'China's enigmatic J-20 powers up for its second decade,' *Flight Global*, 28 December 2020.
5 'PAK-FA's New Engines Make It "Easily the Best 5th Gen Fighter in the World",' *Sputnik News*, 25 July 2017.
6 'YF-22 PAV-1 breaks supercruise speed record,' *Defense Daily*, 19 November 1990. Metz, Paul and Sandberg, Jim, 'YF-23 DEM/VAL Presentation by Test Pilots Paul Metz and Jim Sandberg,' *Western Museum of Flight*, 27 August 2015.
7 Aronstein, David C. and Hirschberg, Michael J., *Advanced Tactical Fighter to F-22 Raptor: Origins of the 21st Century Air Dominance Fighter*, Arlington, American Institute of Aeronautics & Astronomy, 1998, p.227.
8 'JSF-F136 Team Moving Toward Full Engine Design And Development,' *GE Aerospace*, 26 February 2002.
9 Sweetman, Evan, 'F135 Engine Progresses as F136 Alternative for F-35,' *AIN Online*, 16 December 2010.
10 Norris, Guy, 'Alternate JSF Engine Thrust Beats Target,' *Aviation Week*, 13 August 2010. Trimble, Steve, 'Paris Air Show: F136 revs up thrust setting,' *FlightGlobal*, 16 June 2009.
11 'GE Rolls-Royce Fighter Engine Team tests sixth new engine in 2010,' *Rolls Royce*, 3 December 2010.
12 Majumdar, Dave, 'GE, Rolls Royce Stop Funding F-35 Alt Engine,' *Defense News*, 2 December 2011.
13 Norris, Guy, 'Alternate JSF Engine Thrust Beats Target,' *Aviation Week*, 16 August 2010.
14 Norris, 'Alternate JSF Engine Thrust Beats Target'.
15 Norris, 'Alternate JSF Engine Thrust Beats Target'. Majumdar, Dave, 'GE, Rolls Royce Stop Funding F-35 Alt Engine,' *Defense News*, 2 December 2011.
16 'JSF-F136 Team Moving Toward Full Engine Design And Development,' *GE Aerospace*, 26 February 2002.
17 'F136 Passes Major Review,' *Air & Space Forces*, 19 February 2008.
18 Trimble, Stephen, 'F136 engine completes STOVL testing,' *FlightGlobal*, 12 July 2008.
19 Tactical Aircraft: DOD's Cancellation of the Joint Strike Fighter Alternate Engine Program Was Not Based on a Comprehensive Analysis, Government Accountability Office, 22 May 2006.
20 'F136 Passes Major Review,' *Air & Space Forces Magazine*, 19 February 2008.
21 Dorr, Robert F., 'F136 Engine Hitting Milestones in Development Effort,' *Defense Media Network*, 11 December 2010.
22 Miles, Donna, 'Secretary Gates explains opposition to alternate F-35 engine,' *Air Force Times*, 3 September 2009.
23 Norris, Guy, 'Alternate JSF Engine Thrust Beats Target,' *Aviation Week*, 16 August 2010.
24 'Obama's Address to Veterans,' *The New York Times*, 17 August 2009.
25 Dimasico, Jen, 'Gates aims to kill F-35 jet engine,' *Politico*, 21 May 2010.
26 Gates, Robert M., *Duty: Memoirs of a Secretary at War*, New York, Alfred A. Knopf, 2014, Chapter 12.
27 Warwick, Graham, 'The Great Engine Misinformation War,' *Aviation Week*, 1 June 2010.
28 Tiron, Roxana, 'GE, Rolls-Royce to submit fixed-price offer on F-35 Joint Strike Fighter,' *The Hill*, 23 September 2009.
29 Eaglen, Mackenzie, 'Why Congress Cares About Engine Competition for the Joint Strike Fighter,' *Heritage Foundation*, 24 August 2009.
30 'GE Rolls-Royce Fighter Engine Team tests sixth new engine in 2010,' *Rolls Royce*, 3 December 2010.
31 Trimble, Stephen, 'DoD orders F136 termination,' *Flight Global*, 26 April 2011.
32 Shalal-Esa, Andrea, 'Update 2-GE to fund F-35 engine despite stop-work order,' *Reuters*, 24 March 2011.
33 Scully, Megan, 'Pentagon moves to stop work on second engine,' *Government Executive*, 24 March 2011.
34 Trimble, 'DoD orders F136 termination'.
35 Hodge, Nathan, 'A Stake in the Heart for a Fighter Engine?,' *The Wall Street Journal*, 25 April 2011.
36 Mehta, Aaron, 'F-35 head: Delays coming if test planes grounded through September,' *Air Force Times*, 4 September 2014.
37 Eaglen, Mackenzie, 'Why Congress Cares About Engine Competition for the Joint Strike Fighter,' *Heritage Foundation*, 24 August 2009.
38 'The Great Engine War II: Choice or Monopoly for Global F-35 Fleets?,' *Defense Industry Daily*, July 17, 2014.
39 'The Great Engine War II: Choice or Monopoly for Global F-35 Fleets?'.
40 Rogoway, Tyler, 'We Finally Get Our First Look At The Barbecued F-35 Nearly A Year Later,' *Jalopnik*, 5 June 2015
41 Cameron, Doug, 'Pratt & Whitney Delays F-35 Engine Deliveries on Titanium Concerns,' *Wall Street Journal*, 29 August 2014.
42 Venable, John, 'If Trump Wants Lower F-35 Costs, He Should Compete F135 Engine,' *Breaking Defense*, 17 January 2017.
43 Venable, 'If Trump Wants Lower F-35 Costs'.
44 Venable, John, '9 Reasons Why the F-35 Needs a New Engine,' *Heritage Foundation*, 2 November 2022.
45 Venable, '9 Reasons Why the F-35 Needs a New Engine'.
46 Insinna, Valerie, 'The Defense Department still isn't meeting its F-35 readiness goals,' *Defense News*, 21 January 2021.
47 'Pentagon Press Secretary Updates Reporters on DOD Operations,' *U.S. Department of Defense*, 12 February 2021.
48 Pawlyk, Oriana, 'Air Force Cuts Back F-35 Demo Performances Due to Engine Shortage,' *Military.com*, 13 February 2021.
49 F-35 Joint Strike Fighter: DOD Needs to Update Modernization Schedule and Improve Data on Software Development, Government Accountability Office, March 2021.

50 F-35 Joint Strike Fighter: Program Continues to Encounter Production Issues and Modernization Delays, Government Accountability Office, May 2024.
51 Hadley, Greg, 'More than 40 F-35s Without Engines, Air Force Leaders Say,' *Air & Space Forces Magazine*, 14 July 2021.
52 Parsons, Dan, 'Blistering Highlights From The Latest F-35 Sustainment Hearing,' *The War Zone*, 9 May 2022.
53 Parsons, 'Blistering Highlights From The Latest F-35 Sustainment Hearing'.
54 Parsons, 'Blistering Highlights From The Latest F-35 Sustainment Hearing'.
55 F-35 Sustainment: DOD Faces Several Uncertainties and Has Not Met Key Objectives, Government Accountability Office, 28 April 2022.
56 Newdick, Thomas, 'Fifteen Percent Of U.S. Air Force F-35s Don't Have Working Engines,' *The War Zone*, 14 July 2021.
57 Altman, Howard, 'No Engine, No Fly: Ongoing Propulsion Program Problems Are Grounding F-35s,' *The War Zone*, 22 July 2022.
58 Insinna, Valerie, 'An engine shortage is the newest problem to hit the F-35 enterprise,' *Defense News*, 13 February 2021.
59 F-35 Joint Strike Fighter: More Actions Needed to Explain Cost Growth and Support Engine Modernization Decision, U.S. Government Accountability Office, May 2023.
60 Hearing on National Defense Authorization Act for Fiscal Year 2024 and Oversight of Previously Authorized Programs Before the Committee on Armed Services, House of Representatives, One Hundred Eighteenth Congress, First Session—Subcommittee on Tactical Air and Land Forces Hearing on Fiscal Year 2024 Budget Request of the Department of Defense for Fixed-Wing Tactical and Training Aircraft Programs, 29 March 2023.
61 F-35 Joint Strike Fighter: More Actions Needed to Explain Cost Growth and Support Engine Modernization Decision, U.S. Government Accountability Office, May 2023.
62 Losey, Stephen, 'The F-35 engine is at a crossroads, with billions of dollars for industry at stake,' *Defense News*, 15 July 2022.
63 F-35 Aircraft: DOD Should Assess and Update Its Engine Sustainment Strategy to Support Desired Outcomes, Decision, U.S. Government Accountability Office, July 2023.
64 Tripak, John A., 'All F-35, F135 Engine Deliveries Suspended Pending Crash Investigation,' *Air & Space Forces Magazine*, 4 January 2023. Tripak, John A., 'Pratt & Whitney to Resume F-35 Engine Deliveries after 2-Month Hold,' *Air & Space Forces Magazine*, 24 February 2023. Tripak, John A., 'Pratt & Whitney's New Fix for F-35 Engine Issues Will Allow Deliveries to Resume,' *Air & Space Forces Magazine*, 28 February 2023.
65 Rogoway, Tyler, 'Axing The F-35's Alternative Engine Was An Incredibly Stupid Move,' *Jalopnik*, 8 July 2014.
66 Trimble, 'DoD orders F136 termination'.
67 Atkinson, Rick and Pincus, Walter, '"Terrible" F14 Engine Criticized by Lehman,' *Washington Post*, 19 July 1984. Pine, Art and Vartabedian, Ralph, 'F-14 Crashes Raise Questions of Age, Safety,' *Los Angeles Times*, 12 May 1996.
68 'Adaptive Engine Transition Program (AETP)| A revolutionary propulsion mechanism for the F-35,' *100 Knots*, 2 October 2022.
69 Tirpak, John A., 'Piecing Together the NGAD Puzzle,' *Air & Space Forces Magazine*, 29 April 2022.
70 Hadley, Greg, 'Air Force Looks Beyond AETP for Engines to Power NGAD Fighter,' *Air & Space Forces Magazine*, 11 August 2022.
71 Losey, 'The F-35 engine is at a crossroads'. 'GE completes latest adaptive cycle engine tests, successfully concludes Adaptive Engine Transition Program efforts,' *PR Newswire*, 12 September 2022.
72 Tripak, John A., 'Congress Wants AETP Engines to be Installed in All F-35As Starting in 2027,' *Air & Space Forces Magazine*, 8 December 2021.
73 Hadley, Greg, 'Dozens of Lawmakers Urge Pentagon to Move Forward With Adaptive Engines,' *Air & Space Forces Magazine*, 11 October 2022.
74 Losey, 'The F-35 engine is at a crossroads'.
75 Insinna, Valerie, 'F-35 Engine Rivals Prepare For Another Clash,' *Breaking Defense*, 15 October 2021.
76 Hadley, Greg, 'GE, Pratt & Whitney Publicly Pitch F-35 Engine Plans as Decision Looms,' *Air & Space Forces Magazine*, 4 August 2022.
77 Losey, 'The F-35 engine is at a crossroads'.
78 Insinna, 'F-35 Engine Rivals Prepare For Another Clash'.
79 Tirpak, John A., 'Adding New AETP Engine to F-35 Means Air Force Alone Would Pay for It,' *Air & Space Forces Magazine*, 15 September 2021. Losey, 'The F-35 engine is at a crossroads'. Hadley, 'GE, Pratt & Whitney Publicly Pitch F-35 Engine Plans'. Tirpak, John A., 'Air Force Skips AETP Engines for F-35, Presses on with NGAP,' *Air & Space Forces Magazine*, 14 March 2023.
80 Tirpak, 'Air Force Skips AETP Engines for F-35'.
81 Marrow, Michael, 'GE's lobbying message to Congress on F-35 engine: "Take this to the next logical milestone",' *Breaking Defense*, 10 May 2023.
82 Losey, 'The F-35 engine is at a crossroads'.
83 Losey, 'The F-35 engine is at a crossroads'.
84 Losey, 'The F-35 engine is at a crossroads'.
85 Hadley, 'Air Force Looks Beyond AETP'.
86 'GE completes latest adaptive cycle engine tests, successfully concludes Adaptive Engine Transition Program efforts,' *PR Newswire*, 12 September 2022.
87 Hadley, Greg, 'Dozens of Lawmakers Urge Pentagon to Move Forward With Adaptive Engines,' *Air & Space Forces Magazine*, 11 October 2022.
88 Hadley, 'Dozens of Lawmakers Urge Pentagon to Move Forward With Adaptive Engines.' Hadley, Greg, 'Air Force Looks Beyond AETP'.
89 Tirpak, 'Air Force Skips AETP Engines for F-35'.
90 Marrow, Michael, 'HAC-D chair throws cold water on new F-35 engine, won't talk DoD supplemental until budget set,' *Breaking Defense*, 30 June 2023.
91 Tirpak, 'Air Force Skips AETP Engines for F-35'.
92 Marrow, Michael, 'GE's lobbying message to Congress on F-35 engine: "Take this to the next logical milestone",' *Breaking Defense*, 10 May 2023.
93 Tirpak, 'Air Force Skips AETP Engines for F-35'.
94 Hadley, 'Air Force Looks Beyond AETP'.
95 Hadley, 'GE, Pratt & Whitney Publicly Pitch F-35 Engine'.
96 Marrow, Michael, 'GE's lobbying message to Congress on F-35 engine: "Take this to the next logical milestone",' *Breaking Defense*, 10 May 2023.
97 Marrow, Michael, 'Why Wittman wants to save AETP engine while slowing next-gen fighter funding,' *Breaking Defense*, 16 June 2023.
98 Marrow, Michael, 'Lockheed backs new AETP engine for F-35,' *Breaking Defense*, 21 June 2023.
99 Marrow, 'Lockheed backs new AETP engine for F-35'. Everstine, Brian, 'Lockheed Aiming For Maximum "Margin" For F-35 Cooling, Power,' *Aviation Week*, 21 June 2023.
100 Marrow, 'GE's lobbying message to Congress on F-35 engine'.
101 Marrow, Michael, 'It's official: The F-35 will not get a new engine anytime soon,' *Breaking Defense*, 21 March 2024.

Chapter 8

1 Hubinger, Scott, 'Can the F-35 Lightning II Joint Strike Fighter Avoid the Fate of the F-22 Raptor?' *Joint Force Quarterly*, vol. 94, Third Quarter 2019, pp.44-52.
2 Hubinger, 'Can the F-35 Lightning II Joint Strike Fighter Avoid the Fate of the F-22 Raptor?', pp.44-52. Lorell, Mark A. et al., Do Joint Fighter Programs Save Money?, RAND Corporation, December 2013, p.31.
3 Tirpak, John A., 'All For One and All for All,' *Air & Space Forces Magazine*, 14 March 2016.
4 Seligman, Lara, 'McCain Looks To Kill F-35 Joint Program Office,' *Defense News*, 13 May 2016.
5 Hunter, Jamie, 'Building The F-35 – One Of The Most Advanced Machines Ever Made,' *The War Zone*, 1 August 2024.
6 Hoehn, John R., 'Air Force F-15EX Eagle II Fighter Program,' *Congressional Research Service*, 2 May 2022.
7 Forsberg, Randall, ed., *The Arms Production Dilemma: Contraction and Restraint in the World Combat Aircraft Industry*, Cambridge, MIT Press, 1994, p.213. Dassault Rafale, *Jane's All the World's Aircraft* << https://janes.migavia.com/fra/dassault/rafale.html >>
8 'This Is the F-35 Secret No One Wants to Admit,' *The National Interest*, 12 January 2019.
9 Lorell, Mark A. et al., Do Joint Fighter Programs Save Money?, RAND Corporation, December 2013.
10 Whittle, Richard, 'The Ultimate Fighter?,' *Smithsonian Magazine*, March 2012.
11 'Turkey to keep making F-35 parts through 2022: report,' *TRT World*, 30 June 2020.
12 'Evidence on Unclear for take-off? F-35 Procurement,' UK Parliament official website << https://committees.parliament.uk/writtenevidence/83144/html/ >>
13 Allison, George, 'How British is the F-35?,' *UK Defence Journal*, 14 October 2019.
14 Tovey, Alan, 'How BAE is helping make the trillion-dollar jet fighter affordable,' *The Telegraph*, 15 August 2015.
15 'Companies across UK support Lockheed Martin's F-35 programme,' *Institution of Mechanical Engineers*, 27 March 2019. 'MAPPED: All the UK companies manufacturing components for Israel's F35 combat aircraft,' *Campaign Against Arms Trade* << https://caat.org.uk/data/countries/israel/mapped-all-the-uk-companies-manufacturing-components-for-israels-f35-combat-aircraft/ >> (Accessed 19 September 2024).
16 Weisgerber, Marcus, 'F-35 Production Set to Quadruple As Massive Factory Retools,' *Defense One*, 6 May 2019.
17 Opall-Rome, Barbara, 'Israel Seeks Greater Autonomy for F-35 Fighter Force,' *Defense News*, 5 April 2016.
18 Weisgerber, 'F-35 Production Set to Quadruple As Massive Factory Retools'.
19 van der Werf, Mees, 'Part 1. A Longstanding Friendship under Threat,' *Russian International Affairs Council*, 9 August 2018.
20 Gordon, Yefim and Komissarov, Dmitry, *Sukhoi Su-57*, Manchester, Hikoki Publications, 2021, pp.363, 364.
21 'MPs warn over US fighter jet deal,' *BBC News*, 8 December 2006. Fidler, Steven, 'Bush gives way over stealth fighter,' *Financial Times*, 26 March 2006. 'Update 2 – UK signs memo with US on Joint Strike Fighter,' *Reuters*, 12 December 2006.
22 Insinna, Valerie, 'Two F-35 partners threatened to quit the program. Here's why they didn't.,' *Defense News*, 12 June 2019.
23 'UK concern over future of U.S. F-35 fighter jets,' *Agence France-Presse*, 5 January 2012.
24 'Dutch Defence Minister In Texas to Discuss Joint Strike Fighter,' *Defence Talk*, 13 January 2012.

25 Trimble, Stephen, 'Leaked cable spills Belgium's plans to buy F-35s,' *Flight Global*, 12 September 2011.
26 'Exclusive: Belgium considers Lockheed F-35 to replace F-16s – source,' *Reuters*, 17 September 2013.
27 'Calls to Suspend Belgian Fighter Tender After Upgrade Option Is Revealed,' *Defense Aerospace*, 21 March 2018.
28 Emmott, Robin, 'Belgium picks Lockheed's F-35 over Eurofighter on price,' *Reuters*, 25 October 2018.
29 Emmott, 'Belgium picks Lockheed's F-35 over Eurofighter on price'.
30 Emmott, 'Belgium picks Lockheed's F-35 over Eurofighter on price'.
31 'Belgium's purchase of US-made F35 jets "against European interests", Macron says,' *France 24*, 26 October 2018.
32 Tegler, Eric, 'With A "Done Deal" In Switzerland, The F-35 Is Pushing Europe's Fighter Makers Off Their Own Territory,' *Forbes*, 22 September 2022.
33 Losey, Stephen, '"Just in time" F-35 supply chain too risky for next war, general says,' *Defense News*, 4 April 2023.
34 Charpentreau, Clement, 'No FCAS before 2050, says Dassault CEO,' *Aerotime*, 9 June 2022.
35 Charpentreau, 'No FCAS before 2050, says Dassault CEO'.
36 Ristamäki, Juha and Nurmi, Lauri, 'IL:n tiedot: Puolustusvoimat esittää yhdysvaltalaista F-35:ttä Suomen uudeksi hävittäjäksi' ('Information from IL: Defense forces present the US F-35 as Finland's new fighter'), *Iltalehti*, 5 December 2021.
37 C Salonius-Pasternak on Twitter: 'Rafale & EF didn't make it through the gate, so no mil evaluation was done,' 10 December 2021.
38 C Salonius-Pasternak on Twitter: 'In Q&A: PM @MarinSanna says decision was unanimous but Ministers from Left Alliance @liandersson & @ HSarkkinen noted concern about annual use costs,' 10 December 2021.
39 'Lockheed Martin F-35A Lightning II on Suomen seuraava monitoimihävittäjä' ('The Lockheed Martin F-35A Lightning II is Finland's next multirole fighter'), *Ilmavoimat*, 10 December 2021.
40 C Salonius-Pasternak on Twitter: 'Chief of @FinnishAirForce @JokinenPasi says in capability scoring F-35 achieved 4.47 (where 4.0 was requirement), next best got 3.81. 64 jets w tooling, spares, comprehensive weapons package,' 10 December 2021.
41 'Lockheed Martin F-35A Lightning II on Suomen seuraava monitoimihävittäjä'.
42 C Salonius-Pasternak on Twitter: 'Industrial Participation package fulfilled requirements. Incl build and delivery to others of front fuselage- that's huge,' 10 December 2021.
43 'Finland Selects F-35 Lightning II As Its Next Fighter,' *Lockheed Martin*, 10 December 2021.
44 C Salonius-Pasternak on Twitter: 'Industrial Participation package fulfilled requirements'.
45 'Lockheed Martin F-35A Lightning II on Suomen seuraava monitoimihävittäjä'. C Salonius-Pasternak on Twitter: 'Of significant note, per Gen Renko: #Finland will have most extensive domestic servicing capability of F-35, except the United States. THAT IS HUGE. Also highlights how much Finland plans assume having to fight alone – hoping it doesn't have to,' 10 December 2021.
46 'Lockheed Martin F-35A Lightning II on Suomen seuraava monitoimihävittäjä'.
47 'Lockheed Martin F-35A Lightning II on Suomen seuraava monitoimihävittäjä'.
48 'Lockheed Martin F-35A Lightning II on Suomen seuraava monitoimihävittäjä'.
49 C Salonius-Pasternak on Twitter: 'Holy S: out of €8.4Bn deal €4.7 go to F-35, €2.9Bn to service etc, €755m max to A2A weapons (for now), later more A2As and A2Gs as planes come online – avoiding mass obsolescence in the future (and unstated: more advanced weapons, 260 anyone? ;-),' 10 December 2021.
50 'Why is Norway paying more for fighter jets than Finland?' *Norway Today*, 7 January 2022.
51 'Why Do Norway's F-35s Cost 34 Percent More Than Finland's? Explanations for the Controversy,' *Military Watch Magazine*, 10 January 2022.
52 Francis Tusa on Twitter: '@CorporalFrisk @iltalehti_fi Re your overall points that a) F-35 cost data is all over the shop, b) that Finnish justification of costs might be insanely optimistic, bordering naive, have a look at this,' 6 December 2021.
53 Ristamäki, Juha and Nurmi, Lauri, 'IL:n tiedot: Puolustusvoimat esittää yhdysvaltalaista F-35:ttä Suomen uudeksi hävittäjäksi' ('Information from IL: Defense forces present the US F-35 as Finland's new fighter'), *Iltalehti*, 5 December 2021.
54 'Israel Plans to Buy Over 100 F-35s,' *Defense Industry Daily*, 27 June 2006. 'Adir Who? Israel's F-35i Stealth Fighters,' *Defense Industry Daily*, November 2008.
55 'Adir Who? Israel's F-35i Stealth Fighters,'
56 Shapir, Yiftah S., 'The F-35 Deal: An Enlightened Purchase?,' *Strategic Assessment*, vol. 13, no. 4, January 2011, pp.21-38.
57 Arens, Moshe, 'F-35 – take it or leave it,' *Haaretz*, 27 July 2010.
58 Melman, Yossi, 'Pentagon Official Says IAF "Very Aggressive" in Negotiations Over Fighter Jet Purchase,' *Haaretz*, 19 November 2008.
59 Gates, Robert M., *Duty: Memoirs of a Secretary at War*, New York, Alfred A. Knopf, 2014, Chapter 11.
60 Arens, Moshe, 'IDF's Technological Superiority Must Be Defended,' *Haaretz*, 25 January 2011.
61 Williams, Dan, 'Israel may halve second order of F-35 fighters: minister,' *Reuters*, 17 November 2014.
62 'Israel, US Agree to $450 Million in F-35 EW Work,' *Aviation Week*, 10 May 2013.
63 Pfeffer, Anshel, 'Defense Minister Barak approves purchase of 20 F-35 fighters for around $2.75 billion,' *Haaretz*, 16 August 2010.
64 'F-35 Wings Production Line Inaugurated,' *Israeli Air Force official website*, 6 November 2014.
65 Grudo, Gideon, 'The Israeli F-35s,' *Air Force Magazine*, April/May 2017, pp.62-65.
66 'JSF Secrets to Stay Secret,' *Aviation Week*, 10 February 2009.
67 Opall-Rome, Barbara, 'Israel Seeks Greater Autonomy for F-35 Fighter Force,' *Defense News*, 5 April 2016.
68 Egozi, Ari, 'Israeli air force to receive unique test F-35,' *Flight Global*, 24 May 2017.
69 Golan, John W., *Lavi: The United States, Israel, and a Controversial Fighter Jet*, Sterling, Potomac Books, 2016, Chapter 4.
70 Opall-Rome, Barbara, 'Meet the Israel Air Force unit that frankensteined a totaled F-15,' *Defense News*, 15 May 2017.
71 Opall-Rome, Barbara, 'Meet the Israel Air Force unit'.
72 Aronheim, Anna, 'Three F-35 stealth fighter jets to arrive in Israel on Sunday,' *The Jerusalem Post*, 20 April 2017.
73 Gross, Judah Ari, 'Liberman unveils Israel's future stealth fighter: The F-35,' *The Times of Israel*, 22 June 2016.
74 Grudo, 'The Israeli F-35s', pp.62-65.
75 'Israel boosts air force pack of leopards,' *UPI*, 12 April 2013.
76 Grudo, 'The Israeli F-35s', pp.62-65.
77 Harel, Amos, '"We Prevented Israel From Going to War": Outgoing Air Force Chief on Iran, Gaza and the Conflicts Ahead,' *Haaretz*, 25 August 2017.
78 'Истребители двойного назначения: МиГ-31 защитят и Сирию, и Иран' ('Multirole Fighters: MiG-31 Will Protect Both Syria and Iran'), *Kommersant*, 19 June 2007. 'Russia to supply S-300 to Syria within 2 weeks after Il-20 downing during Israeli raid – MoD,' *RT*, 24 September 2018. 'Истребители несирийного применения: МиГи, собиравшиеся для Сирии, будут использованы при реализации других контрактов' ('Non-Syrian Fighters: MiGs Assembled for Syria Will Be Used to Implement Other Contracts'), *Kommersant*, 17 February 2014.
79 Jones, Rory, 'Israel Gives Secret Aid to Syrian Rebels,' *The Wall Street Journal*, 18 June 2017. Tsurkov, Elizabeth, 'Inside Israel's Secret Program to Back Syrian Rebels,' *Foreign Policy*, 6 September 2018. Levy, Daniel J., ' Israel Just Admitted Arming anti-Assad Syrian Rebels. Big Mistake,' *Haaretz*, 3 February 2019.
80 'Новейшие истребители Су-57 прошли боевые испытания в Сирии' ('Latest Su-57 fighters undergo combat tests in Syria – Shoigu'), *TV Zvezda*, 1 March 2018.
81 'IDF dismisses Syria claim it shot down 2 Israeli aircraft,' *The Times of Israel*, 13 September 2016. 'Syrian army says it shot down Israeli jet,' *Sky News*, 17 March 2017.
82 'Netanyahu says Israel undeterred after Syria shoots down F-16,' *Reuters*, 11 February 2018.
83 'Russia to supply S-300 to Syria within 2 weeks after Il-20 downing during Israeli raid – MoD,' *RT*, 24 September 2018.
84 'U.S. General Claims Russia has Obtained a "Treasure Trove" of Data on the F-22 Raptor; Have Operations in Syria Compromised America's Most Capable Fighter?,' *Military Watch Magazine*, 6 January 2018. 'Russia Now Has 'Treasure Trove' of Info About Stealthy F-22s – US General,' *Sputnik News*, 5 January 2018.
85 Frantzman, Seth J., 'Israel reveals first time it used F-35 to shoot down Iranian drone,' *Defense News*, 9 March 2022.
86 'Israeli F-35 Demonstrates Short Range Cruise Missile Defence Capability: Yemeni Strike Intercepted,' *Military Watch Magazine*, 3 November 2023.
87 Marrow, Michael, 'After Hamas attack, US rushed new F-35 capabilities, parts to Israel: Officials,' *Defense News*, 12 December 2023.
88 'Middle East crisis: Iran's Revolutionary Guards Corps says two of its generals killed in Damascus consulate strike – as it happened,' *The Guardian*, 1 April 2024.
89 'Israeli F-35 Fighters Played Central Role in Air Defence Efforts Against Iranian Strikes – Reports,' *Military Watch Magazine*, 14 April 2024.
90 'Israeli Attack Kills Hamas Leader in Tehran: F-35 Precision Strike Suspected,' *Military Watch Magazine*, 31 July 2024. Spencer-Churchill, Julian and Filip, Alexandru, 'Haniyeh Was Killed by an F-35,' *Real Clear Defense*, 21 August 2024
91 Stover, Andrew, 'Israeli Air Force Completes In-Flight Refueling Exercise In Apparent "Show of Force" to Iran,' *The Aviationist*, 18 August 2024.
92 '"No damage..." Israeli Defence Minister visits air base targeted by Iran, flaunts F-35 fighters,' *ANI News*, 7 October 2024. 'Nearly 20 Israeli fighter jets destroyed during Iran's October attack, says IRGC commander,' *Tehran Times*, 9 October 2024.
93 Michaels, Daniel and Roy, Rajesh, 'Israel's Strike on Iran Also Hit Russian Arms Industry's Once-Strong Image,' *Wall Street Journal*, 28 October 2024.

94 'Russian Tor-M2 Air Defense System Destroys Storm Shadow Missile in Kharkiv Oblast.,' *Army Recognition*, 21 July 2024. 'The Tor-M2 SAM system shot down a group of AFU missiles in the sky over Zaporizhzhya region,' *Izvestia*, 24 January 2025.
95 Engel, Richard and Smith, Marc and Aggarwal, Mithil, 'Iran parades missiles through the streets in a show of force as nuclear talks ramp up,' *NBC News*, 18 April 2025.
96 Rogoway, Tyler, 'Has Israel Actually Sent The F-35 Into Combat Already?,' *The War Zone*, 15 March 2017.
97 Rogoway, Tyler, 'The F-35 Rumor Mill Is Spinning After Israeli Counter Strike On Syrian SAM Site,' *The War Zone*, 17 October 2017.
98 Peck, Michael, 'Did a Russian Made S-200 Missile Strike an Israeli F-35 Back in 2017?' *The National Interest*, 18 April 2019.
99 'Lockheed Martin: willing to outsource F-35 production to Japan,' *Reuters*, 3 June 2011. 'Lockheed May Outsource F-35 Final Assembly to Japan,' *Military Aerospace*, 28 June 2011.
100 Lauter, David and Pine, Aart, 'U.S., Japan Agree on FSX Jet Fighter: Bush Announces Accord on $8-Billion Joint Project; Critics Vow Opposition,' *Los Angeles Times*, 29 April 1989. Ishihara, Shintaro, 'FSX – Japan's Last Bad Deal,' *The New York Times*, 14 January 1990.
101 'Japan to build stealth fighter jets by 2014,' *Air Force Times*, 10 December 2007.
102 'Japan's "Izumo" was designed as aircraft carrier from start: Asahi,' *Asia Times*, 24 February 2018.
103 'Japan's "Izumo" was designed as aircraft carrier from start: Asahi,' Yoshida, Reiji, 'MSDF commissions its biggest helicopter carrier yet,' *The Japan Times*, 25 March 2015.
104 'Taiwan seeks advanced U.S. jet fighters,' *RIAN*, 26 March 2009.
105 'Taiwan plans to request F-35s from US,' *Taipei Times*, 20 September 2011.
106 Gady, Franz-Stefan, 'Taiwan Pushes For Sale of F-35 Fighter Jets,' *The Diplomat*, 3 May 2017.
107 Gould, Joe, 'Give Taiwan the F-35 to deter China, top senators tell Trump,' *Defense News*, 26 March 2018.
108 'Taiwan told to boost training for pilots amid F-35 sale doubt,' *Asia Times*, 17 April 2018. 'How Taiwanese Veteran Pilots Defected to China With Their American Jets,' *Military Watch Magazine*, 8 May 2021.
109 'F-16V funding bill passes initial review,' *Taipei Times*, 24 September 2019.
110 Sevastopulo, Demetri and Hille, Kathrin, 'Taiwan considers big US defence purchases as overture to Donald Trump,' *Financial Times*, 11 November 2024.
111 Perrett, Bradley, 'South Korea Nears F-X Phase 3 Decision,' *Aviation Week*, 3 June 2013.
112 Waldron, Greg, 'Seoul weighs options in F-X III fighter contest,' *Flight Global*, 18 January 2013.
113 'EADS proposes Korea buy mix of two fighter jets,' *The Korea Herald*, 11 December 2013.
114 Tae-hoon, Lee, 'Lockheed Martin eager to win Korea's FX-race,' *Korea Times*, 24 October 2011.
115 '이해도 용납도 할 수 없는 "일그러진 엘리트" 김관진' ('Kim Kwan-jin, the "distorted elite" who cannot be understood or tolerated'), *Hankyoreh*, 18 October 2017.
116 Jeong, Jeff, 'South Korea's F-35 purchase under probe,' *Defense News*, 20 April 2018.
117 Jeong, 'South Korea's F-35 purchase under probe'.
118 한국형전투기(KF-X) 사업 추진 현황 ('Status of the Korean Fighter (KF-X) Project'), *Defense Acquisition Program Administration*, 10 July 2017. '국방기술 연구개발 투자 1조 원 시대를 열다' ('Opening the era of 1 trillion won in defense technology research and development investment'), *Defense Acquisition Program Administration*, 6 September 2021.
119 Tae-hoon, Lee, 'Lockheed Martin eager to win Korea's FX-race,' *Korea Times*, 24 October 2011.
120 '价值1000亿韩元的F-35A隐形飞机1年半里出了234次故障' ('The F-35A stealth aircraft, worth 100 billion won, had 234 malfunctions in one and a half years.'), *Chosun Ilbo*, 4 October 2022.
121 Abrams, A.B., 'South Korean Defense Sources Express Concerns About Unreliable F-35 Fighters,' *The Diplomat*, 7 October 2022.
122 Hadley, Greg, 'South Korean F-35 Conducts Emergency "Belly Landing",' *Air & Space Forces Magazine*, 4 January 2022.
123 Abrams, 'South Korean Defense Sources Express'.
124 '价值1000亿韩元的F-35A隐形飞机1年半里出了234次故障' ('The F-35A stealth aircraft, worth 100 billion won, had 234 malfunctions in one and a half years.'), *Chosun Ilbo*, 4 October 2022.
125 Insinna, Valerie, 'US Air Force official confirms rumors of F-35 talks with UAE,' *Defense News*, 11 November 2017.
126 Al Helou, Agnes and Mouchantaf, Chirine, 'Source: UAE wants to buy 24 F-35s,' *Defense News*, 13 November 2017.
127 Opall-Rome, Barbara, 'Trump could let the UAE buy F-35 jets,' *Defense News*, 4 November 2017.
128 'Should the United States Sell F-35s to the UAE? Benefits and Drawback of Proliferating Stealth Fighters,' *Military Watch Magazine*, 25 December 2019.
129 Rodriguez, Jesus and Choi, Matthew, 'Trump: Saudi Arabia would turn to Russia, China if U.S. ends arms sales over missing journalist,' *Politico*, 11 October 2018.
130 Caverley, Jonathan D. and Kapstein, Ethan B. and Vucetic, Srdjan, 'F-35 Sales Are America's Belt and Road,' *Foreign Policy*, 12 July 2019.
131 Caverley, Kapstein, and Vucetic, 'F-35 Sales Are America's Belt and Road'.
132 Trevithick, Joseph, 'UAE Could Become the First Middle Eastern Country After Israel to Get the F-35,' *The War Zone*, 29 June 2019.
133 Lubold, Gordon and Strobel, Warren P., 'United Arab Emirates Threatens to Pull Out of $23 Billion F-35, Drone Deal With U.S.,' *The Wall Street Journal*, 14 December 2021.
134 Hatch, Rhett, 'What the United Arab Emirates Sees in Huawei,' *The National Interest*, 26 March 2022.
135 Helou, Agnes, 'F-35 fighters, 5G networks, and how the UAE is trying to balance relations between the US and China,' *C4ISRNET*, 28 January 2021.
136 Caverley, Kapstein, and Vucetic, 'F-35 Sales Are America's Belt and Road'.
137 Satam, Parth, 'Concerns Over UAE Mirage 2000s Involved In Air Combat Exercise In China,' *The Aviationist*, 28 July 2024.
138 D'Urso, Stefan and Cenciotti, David, 'UAE And China Eye Military Cooperation With J-20 (Literally) In The Background,' *The Aviationist*, 25 April 2024.
139 Watling, Tom, 'Do US F-35 jets have a 'kill switch'? European countries forced to deny claims Trump could cripple air force,' *The Independent*, 10 March 2025.
140 'US-supplied German jets at risk of Trump "kill switch" – Bild,' *RT*, 9 March 2025.
141 'Can the US switch off Europe's weapons?,' *Financial Times*, 9 March 2025.
142 Siddiqui, Huma, 'Is Rafale M the Final Choice for the Indian Navy – Deal Expected to be Announced Soon,' *Financial Express*, 6 January 2023. 'Trump Offers to Export F-35 Stealth Fighters to India: Why Delhi Won't Be Interested,' *Military Watch Magazine*, 14 February 2025.
143 'Trump Offers to Export F-35 Stealth Fighters to India: Why Delhi Won't Be Interested'.

Chapter 9

1 'Aerospace Nation: Gen Kenneth S. Wilsbach,' *Mitchell Institute for Aerospace Studies* (YouTube), 15 March 2022.
2 'Aerospace Nation: Gen Kenneth S. Wilsbach'.
3 Military and Security Developments Involving the People's Republic of China 2020, Annual Report to Congress, United States Department of Defence, 2020, p.75.
4 'Aerospace Nation: Gen Kenneth S. Wilsbach'.
5 'SIPRI Military Expenditure Database,' *Stockholm International Peace Research Institute* << https://milex.sipri.org/sipri >>
6 Mañé Estrada, Aurèlia and de la Cámara Arilla, Carmen, 'Is Russia Drifting toward an Oil-Rentier Economy?,' *Eastern European Economics*, vol. 43, no. 5, September-October 2005, pp.46-73. Wagstyl, Stefan, 'Russia: riding with the rentiers,' *Financial Times*, 8 July 2011.
7 'China stealth plane still "years away", says Pentagon,' *BBC News*, 6 January 2011.
8 Bodeen, Christopher, 'China's stealth fighter photos cause an international stir,' *NBC News*, 6 January 2011.
9 'Gates Comments on Chinese J-20,' *Air Force Magazine*, 10 January 2011.
10 Levine, Adam, 'Gates: Chinese further along than thought on stealth fighter,' *CNN*, 10 January 2011.
11 'China's J-20: future rival for air dominance?,' *Strategic Comments*, vol. 17, issue 1, 2011, pp.1-3.
12 Rizzo, Jennifer and Keyes, Charley, 'Is China closer than thought to matching U.S. fighter jet prowess?,' *CNN*, 6 January 2011.
13 Gertler, Jeremiah, Air Force F-22 Fighter Program, Congressional Research Service Report for Congress, 11 July 2013.
14 Lin, Jeffrey and Singer Peter W., 'Chinese Stealth Fighter J-20 Starts Production,' *Popular Science*, 28 December 2015.
15 Rupprecht, Andreas, *Modern Chinese Warplanes: Chinese Air Force – Combat Aircraft and Units*, Houston, Harpia, 2018, p.40. Joe, Rick, 'China's J-20 Stealth Fighter Today and Into the 2020s,' *The Diplomat*, 16 August 2019.
16 Insinna, Valerie, 'Air Force Declares F-35A Ready for Combat,' *Defense News*, 2 August 2016.
17 'China's first stealth fighter J-20 enters service with Air Force,' *The State Council Information Office of the People's Republic of China*, 13 March 2017.
18 'Vital Signs 2020: The Health and Readiness of the Defense Industrial Base,' *National Defense Industrial Association*. Nebehay, Stephanie, '"Driving force" China accounts for nearly half global patent filings: U.N.,' *Reuters*, 15 October 2019.
19 Allison, Graham, 'The Great Rivalry: China vs. the U.S. in the 21st Century,' *Belfer Centre for Science and International Affairs, Harvard Kennedy School*, 7 December 2021.
20 Gaida, Jamie et. al., 'ASPI's Critical Technology Tracker: The global race for future power,' Australian Strategic Policy Institute, Policy Brief, Report No. 69, 2023.
21 Waldron, Greg, 'Chinese executive hints at progress with J-20's new WS-15 engine,' *Flight Global*, 27 March 2023.
22 '深度：歼20雷达获突破功率比F22高50% 探测范围更远' ('Depth: The breakthrough power of the J-20 radar is 50% higher than that of the F22, and the detection range is farther'), 新浪军事, 31 March 2016.
23 'Exclusive: China Demonstrates WZ-9 Divine Eagle in Flight First Anti-Stealth Drone Detecting Stealth Aircraft.,' *Army Recognition*, 28 December 2024.

24 'The American AI Century: A Blueprint for Action: Transcript,' *Center for a New American Security*, 17 January 2020. 'Artificial Intelligence: How knowledge is created, transferred, and used: Trends in China, Europe, and the United States,' *Elsevier*, December 2018. 'Who Is Winning the AI Race?,' *MIT Technology Review*, 27 June 2017. 2021 AI Index Report, Stanford Institute for Human-Centered Artificial Intelligence, March 2021 << https://aiindex.stanford.edu/report/ >> Shankland, Stephen and Keane, Sean, 'Trump creates American AI Initiative to boost research, train displaced workers,' *Cnet*, 11 February 2019. Chen, Stephen, 'Chinese smart satellite tracks US aircraft carrier in real time, researchers say,' *South China Morning Post*, 10 May 2022.

25 Billings, Lee, 'China Shatters "Spooky Action at a Distance" Record, Preps for Quantum Internet,' *Scientific American*, 15 June 2017. Kania, Elsa B. and Costello, John K., 'Quantum Hegemony: China's Ambitions and the Challenge to U.S. Innovation Leadership,' *Centre for a New American Security*, September 2018. Šiljak, Harun, 'China's quantum satellite enables first totally secure long-range messages,' *Down to Earth*, 18 June 2020. Kwon, Karen, 'China Reaches New Milestone in Space-Based Quantum Communications,' *Scientific American*, 25 June 2020. Yin, J. et al., 'Entanglement-based secure quantum cryptography over 1,120 kilometres,' *Nature*, vol. 582, 2020, pp.501–505. Chen, Stephen, 'China uses quantum satellite to protect world's largest power grid against attacks,' *South China Morning Post*, 10 December 2021.

26 Audit of Training Ranges Supporting Aviation Units in the U.S. Indo-Pacific Command, Department of Defense, Office of the Inspector General, 17 April 2019.

27 Hunter, Jamie, 'F-35 Stealth Fighters Are Revolutionizing The USAF's Aggressor Force,' *The War Zone*, 12 August 2022.

28 Newdick, Thomas, 'Pilot In A Real Aircraft Just Fought An AI-Driven Virtual Enemy Jet For The First Time,' *The War Zone*, 2 December 2020.

29 Vanover, Christie, 'Nellis AFB aggressors, F-35 pilots "punish" blue air to develop unstoppable force,' *United States Air Force official website*, 4 August 2021. Newdick, Thomas, 'F-35s Have Flown Their First "Red Air" Missions As Dedicated Stealth Aggressor,' *The War Zone*, 4 August 2021.

30 Pawlyk, Oriana, 'Air Force's Reforge Plan Could Put Some Older F-22s in "Red Air" Role,' *Military.com*, 23 June 2020.

31 'Mimicking the J-20? America's F-117 Stealth Fighters Joined Red Flag Exercises For Adversary Training,' *Military Watch Magazine*, 20 August 2020.

32 Pickrell, Ryan, 'A US F-22 Raptor pilot describes the challenge of going up against F-35 red air aggressors,' *Business Insider*, 30 August 2021.

33 Helfrich, Emma, 'F-35 Will Get New Radar Under Massive Upgrade Initiative,' *The War Zone*, 3 January 2023.

34 Episkopos, Mark, 'Out of Range: Why China's J-20 Might Have the Tools to Kill an F-35,' *National Interest*, 20 June 2019. '霹雳15在200公里外直取预警机，歼20的优势太大了' ('The Thunderbolt 15 took the early warning aircraft 200 kilometres away, and the advantage of the J-20 is too great'), *Sina*, 16 January 2021. '让美国顾忌的歼20"御用武器"竟然也要出口了' ('The J-20's "Crown Weapon" that Raises American Doubts is About To Be Exported'), *Xinhua*, 28 September 2021,

35 International Institute for Strategic Studies, *The Military Balance*, Volume 119, 2019, p.8.

36 Axe, David, 'New Chinese Missile has USAF Spooked,' *Real Clear Defense*, 24 September 2015.

37 Trimble, Steve, 'The Weekly Debrief: Does Raytheon's New AIM-120D3 Beat China's Best Missile?,' *Aviation Week*, 25 July 2022. Tirpak, John A., 'Piecing Together the NGAD Puzzle,' *Air and Space Forces*, 29 April 2022.

38 Trimble, 'The Weekly Debrief: Does Raytheon's New AIM-120D3 Beat China's Best Missile?'. Tirpak, 'Piecing Together the NGAD Puzzle'.

39 Trimble, 'The Weekly Debrief: Does Raytheon's New AIM-120D3 Beat China's Best Missile?'. 'US Air Force, Raytheon Missiles & Defense execute first live-fire test of AMRAAM F3R,' *Raytheon Missiles and Defense*, 18 July 2022.

40 Newdick, Thomas, 'UK Emphasizes Need To Arm Tempest Stealth Fighter With Larger, Longer Range Air-To-Air Missiles,' *The War Zone*, 14 January 2025.

41 Bronk, Justin, 'Russian and Chinese Combat Air Trends: Current Capabilities and Future Threat Outlook,' *Royal United Services Institute*, October 2020.

42 Cone, Allen, 'Lockheed's Sidekick adds increased firepower to F-35 fighters,' *Lockheed Martin*, 3 May 2019.

43 Helfrich, Emma, 'New Electronic Warfare Suite Top Feature Of F-35 Block 4, Air Combat Boss Says,' *The War Zone*, 9 March 2023.

44 Newdick, Thomas, 'F/A-18's Infrared Search And Track System Plagued By Delays,' *The War Zone*, 9 June 2023. Newdick, Thomas, 'F/A-18's Infrared Search And Track System Has "Significant Reliability Problems",' *The War Zone*, 3 February 2025.

45 'Aerospace Nation: Gen Kenneth S. Wilsbach'. Waldron, Greg, 'E-3 insufficient for timely detection of J-20: Pacific Air Forces chief,' *Flight Global*, 17 March 2022.

46 Tirpak, John A., 'USAF Selects Boeing's E-7A Wedgetail as Successor to AWACS,' *Air & Space Forces Magazine*, 28 February 2023.

47 'Aerospace Nation: Gen Kenneth S. Wilsbach'.

48 'Russia's Nebo-M radars can detect F-22, F-35 warplanes — developer,' *TASS*, 23 May 2021.

49 'Analysis: Russian S-500 Air Defense System Poses New Threat to American F-22 and F-35 Fighter Aircraft.,' *Army Recognition*, 16 December 2024.

50 Dimitri Kornev, '"Длинная рука": ракета Р-37М расширила возможности ВКС РФ по уничтожению воздушных целей' ('"Long Arm": the R-37M missile expanded the capabilities of the Russian Aerospace Forces to destroy air targets'), *Rossiya Gazette*, 11 December 2023.

51 'Ракета ПВО дальностью 400 км: как тандем с "летающим радаром" А-50 повысил точность' ('400 km range air defense missile: how tandem with the A-50 "flying radar" increased accuracy'), *Inosmi*, 9 November 2023.

52 Naegele, Tobias, 'Editorial: The Best Fighter in the World,' *Air and Space Forces Magazine*, 26 March 2021

53 Altman, Howard, 'The Intricacies Of F-35 Operations Over The Frigid Alaskan Frontier,' *The War Zone*, 11 August 2022.

54 Lockie, Alex, 'An F-35 pilot explains why Russia and China's counterstealth can't stop him,' *Business Insider*, 16 May 2017,

55 Abrams, A. B., '4 Ways North Korea Can Counter the F-35,' *The Diplomat*, 19 July 2022.

56 Abrams, A. B., 'North Korea's Leap Forward in Air Defense Modernization,' *SinoNK*, 4 May 2024.

57 Cordesman, Anthony H., 'The Other Side of the North Korean, Iranian, Hezbollah, and Yemeni Missile Threat,' *CSIS*, 30 November 2017.

58 Kopp, Carlo, 'Operation Odyssey Dawn—the collapse of Libya's relic air defense system,' *Defence Today*, vol. 9, no. 1, 2011.

59 'How Often Does The F-35 Need To Refuel?,' *Aviation Week*, 14 February 2017.

60 Trimble, Steve, 'Lockheed Martin Proposes 40% Fuel Capacity Upgrade for F-35A,' *Aviation Week*, 13 June 2019.

61 Trimble, 'Lockheed Martin Proposes 40% Fuel Capacity Upgrade for F-35A'.

62 Luckenbaugh, Josh, 'Air Force Mulls Choice Between Affordability, Capability for Collaborative Combat Aircraft,' *National Defense Magazine*, 10 December 2024. Trevithick, Joseph, 'Crisis Brewing Over Air Force's Future Air Dominance Plans Which It Cannot Afford,' *The War Zone*, 6 November 2024.

63 Stillion, John and Perdue, Scott, 'Air Combat Past, Present and Future,' Project Air Force briefing, August 2008, Unclassified/ FOUO/Sensitive, Slide 29. Watts, Barry, 'The F-22 Program in Retrospect,' *Center for Strategic and Budgetary Assessments*, August 2009.

64 'Why America Is Rethinking Air Power | Justin Bronk,' *Decoding Geopolitics Podcast*, 30 April 2025

65 Trevithick, Joseph, 'Future Stealth Tanker Plans Tied To NGAD 6th Generation Fighter's Fate,' *The War Zone*, 16 September 2024.

66 Trevithick, 'Crisis Brewing Over Air Force's Future Air Dominance Plans Which It Cannot Afford'.

67 Shellbourne, Mallory, 'Navy Quietly Starts Development of Next-Generation Carrier Fighter; Plans Call for Manned, Long-Range Aircraft,' *USNI News*, 18 August 2020.

68 Chen, Stephen, 'Chinese scientists plan surface-to-air missile with 2,000km kill range,' *South China Morning Post,* 28 March 2024. Newdick, Thomas and Rogoway, Tyler and Trevithick, Joseph, 'Air Force Predicts Enemy Anti-Air Missiles With 1000-Mile Range By 2050,' *The War Zone*, 14 January 2025.

69 Trevithick, Joseph, 'Air Force Says It Needs More Survivable Tankers By 2040,' *The War Zone*, 1 February 2023.

70 Trevithick, 'Future Stealth Tanker Plans Tied To NGAD 6th Generation Fighter's Fate'.

71 Trevithick, Joseph, '$20 Billion Price Tag To Complete Development Of USAF's Next Generation Fighter,' *The War Zone*, 13 January 2025.

72 Trevithick, Joseph, 'Stealthy Tanker-Transport Aircraft Concept Unveiled By Boeing,' *The War Zone*, 26 January 2023.

73 Trevithick, Joseph, 'Lockheed Martin Is Crafting New Stealth and Drone Tanker Concepts For The USAF,' *The War Zone*, 20 September 2018. Trevithick, Joseph and Rogoway, Tyler, 'The Mysterious Saga Of America's Hunt For A Stealth Special Operations Transport, Part 2,' *The War Zone*, 1 December 2019.

74 Trimble, Steve, 'Funding Crunch Creates Uncertainty For USAF's Next-Gen Tanker Plans,' *Aviation Week,* 13 May 2024.

75 Everstine, Brian, 'Skunk Works Shows New, Optionally Crewed Tanker Concept,' *The War Zone*, 1 November 2024.

76 Tirpak, John A., 'KC-46 Mission Capable Rates Slipped Further from Goal in 2024,' *Air and Space Forces Magazine*, 7 February 2025. Altman, Howard, 'Cracks In KC-46 Tankers Halt All Deliveries,' *The War Zone*, 1 March 2025.

77 Trevithick, Joseph, 'Navy Eyes "Hard-Kill" Defenses For Transport, Tanker, and Possibly Unmanned Escort Planes,' *The War Zone*, 22 July 2020.

78 Everstine, Brian, 'Boeing Unveils Land-Based MQ-25 Autonomous Tanker Design,' *Aviation Week*, 16 September 2024.

Chapter 10

1 Insinna, Valerie, 'New F-35 modernization plan could come with hefty $16B price tag,' *Defense News*, 9 March 2018.

2 Insinna, Valerie, 'Pentagon's weapons tester slams new F-35 modernization plan as unrealistic,' *Defense News*, 26 January 2018.

3 Marrow, Michael, 'Pentagon delays F-35 retrofits amid upgrade woes,' *Breaking Defense*, 4 April 2024.

4 Marrow, Michael, 'F-35's Block 4 upgrade 55 percent over target costs, up $1.4B since last review: GAO,' *Breaking Defense*, 31 May 2023.
5 Marrow, 'Pentagon delays F-35 retrofits amid upgrade woes'.
6 Helfrich, Emma, 'New Electronic Warfare Suite Top Feature Of F-35 Block 4, Air Combat Boss Says,' *The War Zone*, 9 March 2023.
7 'Lockheed Martin downgraded to Hold from Buy at Deutsche Bank,' *Business Insider*, 2 January 2025.
8 Liu, Xuanzun, 'Next gen fighter jet forthcoming in great power competition: J-20 chief designer,' *Global Times*, 27 July 2020.
9 'Why America Is Rethinking Air Power | Justin Bronk,' *Decoding Geopolitics Podcast*, 30 April 2025
10 Liebermann, Oren, 'Senior Trump Air Force official suggested dramatically slashing F-35 jet numbers,' *CNN*, 15 May 2021.
11 Liebermann, 'Senior Trump Air Force official suggested dramatically slashing F-35 jet numbers'.
12 'U.S. Congress Could Restrict Funding for Ambitious Sixth Generation Fighter Programs,' *Military Watch Magazine*, 25 June 2020.
13 Trevithick, Joseph, 'Avoiding F-35 "Acquisition Malpractice" Aim Of Next Gen Air Dominance Fighter,' *The War Zone*, 23 May 2023.
14 Insinna, Valierie, 'Pentagon inspector general has questions about the Air Force's sixth-gen fighter,' *Breaking Defense*, 27 September 2022.
15 Tirpak, John A., 'Strategy & Policy: Thinking Past the F-35,' *Air & Space Forces*, 1 December 2019.
16 'NGAD: USAF's sixth generation fighter is on schedule, acquisition official says,' *Aerospace Manufacturing*, 11 October 2021.
17 Tirpak, John A., 'Make-or-Break Time for the F-35,' *Air and Space Forces Magazine*, 23 April 2021.
18 Tirpak, John A., 'Kelly Worries F-35 Flying Costs Won't Hit Target, and That China May Get NGAD First,' *Air Force Magazine*, 26 February 2021.
19 'NGAD: USAF's sixth generation fighter is on schedule, acquisition official says,' *Aerospace Manufacturing*, 11 October 2021.
20 Insinna, Valierie, 'China "on track" for 6th-gen fighter, US Air Force needs to get there first: ACC chief,' *Breaking Defense*, 26 September 2022.
21 Allvin, David W., 'Allvin: It's make or break time. America needs more Air Force.,' *Breaking Defense*, 17 January 2025.
22 Trevithick, Joseph, 'Air Force Generals Aren't "Losing Sleep" Over China's J-20 Stealth Fighter,' *The War Zone*, 23 September 2022.
23 Trevithick, 'Air Force Generals Aren't "Losing Sleep" Over China's J-20 Stealth Fighter'.
24 Rogoway, Tyler, 'The Air Force's Secret Next Gen Air Dominance Demonstrator Isn't What You Think It Is,' *The War Zone*, 21 September 2020.
25 Tirpak, John A., 'Piecing Together the NGAD Puzzle,' *Air and Space Forces Magazine*, 29 April 2022.
26 Lee James, Deborah, 'Why the US Air Force should keep Next Generation Air Dominance alive,' *Defense News*, 26 June 2024.
27 Tirpak, John A., 'Roper's NGAD Bombshell,' *Air & Space Forces Magazine*, 1 October 2020.
28 Tirpak, John A., 'Kendall Dispenses with Roper's Quick NGAD Rhythm; System is Too Complex,' *Air and Space Forces Magazine*, 24 June 2022.
29 Newdick, Thomas, 'The Air Force Might Make Two Distinct Versions Of Its Next Multirole Stealth Fighter,' *The War Zone*, 18 June 2021. Tirpak, John A., 'Air Force Will Pick Just One NGAD Design in 2024, Kendall Says,' *Air and Space Forces Magazine*, 22 May 2023.
30 Losey, Stephen, 'T-7 Red Hawk trainer makes its debut,' *Defense News*, 30 April 2022.
31 Cohen, Rachel S., 'Air Force Introduces e-Planes for the Digital Era,' *Air Force Magazine*, 14 September 2020. Tirpak, 'Roper's NGAD Bombshell'.
32 Tirpak, John A., 'Kendall: Digital Engineering Was "Over-Hyped," But Can Save 20 Percent on Time and Cost,' *Air and Space Forces Magazine*, 23 May 2023.
33 'NGAD To Cost "Multiple Hundreds of Millions" Each,' *Aviation Week*, 27 April 2022.
34 Tirpak, John A., 'Kendall Reveals New Details on Air Force Plans: 1,000 CCAs, 200 NGAD Fighters,' *Air and Space Forces Magazine*, 7 March 2023.
35 Losey, Stephen, 'US Air Force eyes NGAD deliveries by 2030. Can it be done?' *Defense News*, 28 September 2022.
36 'Optimizing air power: A conversation with US Air Force Chief of Staff Gen. David Allvin,' *Brookings Institute*, 28 February 2024.
37 Tirpak, John A., 'Allvin Hedges on the Future of Next-Generation Air Dominance Fighter,' *Air and Space Forces Magazine*, 13 June 2024.
38 Axe, David, '"Trillion dollar trainwreck": US super stealth fighter is eating the next generation,' *The Telegraph*, 29 June 2024.
39 Trevithick, Joseph, 'Next Generation Air Dominance Fighter Uncertainty Tied To Sentinel ICBM Woes,' *The War Zone*, 24 July 2024.
40 'U.S. Air Force Secretary Warns Development of Urgently Needed ICBM "Struggling": Program Collapse Possible,' *Military Watch Magazine*, 15 November 2023.
41 Lee James, Deborah, 'Why the US Air Force should keep Next Generation Air Dominance alive,' *Defense News*, 26 June 2024.
42 Losey, Stephen, 'Next-gen fighter not dead, but needs cheaper redesign, Kendall says Engine for US Air Force's NGAD aircraft could be pared down to cut costs,' *Defense News*, 2 July 2024.
43 Insinna, Valerie, 'Budget watchdog warns this fighter could cost three times that of the F-35,' *Defense News*, 15 December 2018.
44 Trevithick, Joseph, '$20 Billion Price Tag To Complete Development Of USAF's Next Generation Fighter,' *The War Zone*, 13 January 2025.
45 'Why America Is Rethinking Air Power | Justin Bronk,' *Decoding Geopolitics Podcast*, 30 April 2025
46 Losey, Stephen, 'Next-gen fighter not dead, but needs cheaper redesign, Kendall says,' *Defense News*, 2 July 2024.
47 Losey, 'Next-gen fighter not dead'.
48 Marrow, Michael, 'Air Force "taking a pause" on NGAD next-gen fighter: Kendall,' *Breaking Defense*, 30 July 2024.
49 Newdick, Thomas, 'Air Force Secretary "Absolutely Confident" 6th Gen Crewed Fighter Will Move Forward,' *The War Zone*, 30 July 2024.
50 Altman, Howard, 'Air Force's Next Generation Air Dominance "Fighter" Program Enters New Stage,' *The War Zone*, 2 June 2022.
51 Insinna, Valierie, 'Pentagon inspector general has questions about the Air Force's sixth-gen fighter,' *Breaking Defense*, 27 September 2022.
52 Marrow, Michael, 'Air Force "taking a pause" on NGAD next-gen fighter: Kendall,' *Breaking Defense*, 30 July 2024.
53 Hadley, Greg, 'USAF Rethinks Whether It Needs a Manned 6th-Gen Fighter for Air Superiority,' *Air and Space Forces Magazine*, 4 September 2024.
54 Marrow, 'Air Force "taking a pause" on NGAD next-gen fighter: Kendall'.
55 'Watch the 2024 Defense News Conference Live,' *Military Times* (YouTube), 4 September 2024.
56 Marrow, Michael, 'China "could beat us to the punch" to a 6th-gen fighter, Air Force official warns,' *Breaking Defense*, 13 January 2025.
57 Satam, Parth, '"Light Fighter" Concept Emerges During US Air Force Chief's Speech at UK's Air and Space Power Association Amid NGAD's Uncertain Future,' *The Aviationist*, 19 August 2024.
58 Tirpak, John A., 'Kendall: New, Re-Imagined NGAD Could Cost Less Than an F-35,' *Air & Space Forces Magazine*, 16 September 2024.
59 Insinna, Valerie, 'Sixth-generation fighter at F-35 costs? "That's not going to happen," industry predicts.,' *Breaking Defense*, 20 September 2024.
60 'A Conversation with Secretary of the Air Force Frank Kendall on The Department of the Air Force in 2050,' *Center For Strategic and International Studies*, 13 January 2025.
61 Trevithick, Joseph, 'Crisis Brewing Over Air Force's Future Air Dominance Plans Which It Cannot Afford,' *The War Zone*, 6 November 2024.
62 Newdick, Thomas and Rogoway, Tyler, 'Future Of NGAD Fighter Punted To Trump Administration,' *The War Zone*, 5 December 2024.
63 Marrow, 'China "could beat us to the punch" to a 6th-gen fighter, Air Force official warns'.
64 Marrow, Michael, 'EXCLUSIVE: Allvin says Air Force must grow, even at "expense" of other services,' *Breaking Defense*, 19 May 2025.
65 'More B-21s May Be Necessary If B-52J Upgrade Goes Awry, Allvin Says,' *Air Force Magazine*, 21 May 2025.
66 'Why America Is Rethinking Air Power | Justin Bronk,' *Decoding Geopolitics Podcast* (YouTube Channel), 30 April 2025.
67 Marrow, Michael and Hitchens, Theresa, 'Not survivable': Hegseth says DoD reviewing E-7 Wedgetail program amid move to space,' *Breaking Defense*, 10 June 2025. 'U.S. Cancels Vital E-7 "Flying Radar" Program Needed to Track Chinese Stealth Planes,' *Military Watch Magazine*, 12 June 2025.
68 'Is the Pentagon Halving F-35A Orders to Pay For the F-47? Fighter's Viability in Question as Sixth Generation Era Looms,' *Military Watch Magazine*, 11 June 2025.
69 Tirpak, John A., 'What Might the Future Hold for the F-35?,' *Air Force Magazine*, 11 June 2025.
70 Peck, Michael, 'China's new stealth fighter spooks Wall Street about Lockheed Martin's F-35,' *Business Insider*, 29 January 2025.
71 Newdick, Thomas, 'Pentagon Wants To Shift Funds From Navy F/A-XX To USAF F-47: Report,' *The War Zone*, 5 June 2025.
72 Stone, Mike, 'US Navy's new fighter jet threatened by funding dispute, sources say,' *Reuters*, 15 May 2025.
73 Altman, Howard, 'Air Force's Next Generation Air Dominance "Fighter" Program Enters New Stage,' The War Zone, 2 June 2022.
74 Abrams, Abraham, *China's Stealth Fighter: The J-20 'Mighty Dragon' and the Growing Challenge to Western Air Dominance*, Barnsley, Pen & Sword, 2024, p.216.
75 Marrow, Michael and Mehta, Aaron, 'Pratt blasts Lockheed's "confusing and misleading" adaptive engine advocacy,' *Breaking Defense*, 22 June 2023.
76 Marrow and Mehta, 'Pratt blasts Lockheed's "confusing and misleading" adaptive engine advocacy'.
77 Tirpak, John A., 'What a 'Ferrari' Version of the F-35 Might Look Like—and What the Pentagon Thinks,' *Air Force Magazine*, 24 April 2025.
78 Tirpak, 'What a 'Ferrari' Version of the F-35 Might Look Like'.
79 Losey, Stephen, 'Lockheed wants to turn F-35 into a "Ferrari" with sixth-gen tech,' *Defense News*, 23 April 2025.
80 Insinna, Valerie, 'Lockheed has path to pilot-optional F-35, CEO says,' *Breaking Defense,* 28 May 2025.
81 'Owning the Skies with Integrated Air Dominance,' *Lockheed Martin,* 22 January 2025.
82 Shelbourne, Mallory, 'Navy Quietly Starts Development of Next-Generation Carrier Fighter; Plans Call for Manned, Long-Range Aircraft,' *USNI News*, 18 August 2020.
83 'US Navy unveils new details about F/A-XX strike fighter.,' *Army Recognition*, 2 November 2021.

84 Gordon, Chris, 'Navy Will Pick a 6th-Gen Fighter as Air Force Pauses NGAD,' *Air and Space Forces Magazine*, 2 October 2024.
85 Newdick, Thomas, 'Navy Making Final Selection For F/A-XX Stealth Fighter, Plans For 2030s Service Entry,' *The War Zone*, 3 October 2024.
86 Trimble, Steve, 'U.S. Navy Carves Independent Path For Future Fighter Design,' *Aviation Week*, 8 November 2024.
87 Eckstein, Megan, 'Navy postpones several modernization programs to pay for operations,' *Defense News*, 12 March 2024.
88 Larter, David B, 'With the future of the US Navy's carrier air wing murky, Congress demands a plan,' *Defense News*, 16 June 2020.
89 Shelbourne, Mallory, 'Navy Questions Future Viability of Super Hornets; Recommends Against New Buy,' *USNI News*, 3 August 2021.
90 Availability and Use of the F/A-18E/F Super Hornet Fighter Aircraft, Congressional Budget Office, February 2023. Shelbourne, Mallory, 'Navy Quietly Starts Development of Next-Generation Carrier Fighter; Plans Call for Manned, Long-Range Aircraft,' *USNI News*, 18 August 2020.

Chapter 11

1 'Transcript: Press Gaggle With Acting Secretary Miller En Route to Washington, D.C.,' *U.S. Department of Defense*, 14 January 2021.
2 Johnson, Eliana and Brown, David, 'New Pentagon chief under scrutiny over perceived Boeing bias,' *Politico*, 9 January 2019.
3 Britzky, Haley, 'Acting SecDef Shanahan thinks the F-35 program is "f–ked up" just like everyone else,' *Task and Purpose*, 25 April 2019.
4 Mehta, Aaron, 'Pentagon "can't afford the sustainment costs" on F-35, Lord says,' *Defense News*, 2 February 2018.
5 'Thunder Without Lightning, The High Costs and Limited Benefits of the F-35 Program,' *National Security Network*, August 2015.
6 Axe, David, 'Pentagon's big budget F-35 fighter "can't turn, can't climb, can't run",' *Reuters*, 14 July 2014.
7 Grazier, Dan, 'F-35 Continues to Stumble,' *Project on Government Oversight*, 30 March 2017.
8 Clark, Collin, 'GAO Draft Slams F-35 On "Unaffordable" Costs: $8.8B Over Legacy Fighters,' *Breaking Defense*, 22 September 2014.
9 Roy, Ananya, 'F-35 jets have over 200 deficiencies, unlikely to be combat ready by 2018-2019, Pentagon report says,' *International Business Times*, 17 January 2017. 'F-35 "scarcely" fit to fly: Pentagon's chief tester,' *Press TV*, 3 April 2017.
10 Grazier, Dan, 'F-35 Far from Ready to Face Current or Future Threats, Testing Data Shows,' *Project on Government Oversight*, 19 March 2019.
11 Grazier, 'F-35 Far from Ready to Face Current or Future Threats'.
12 'Which Stealth Fighter is More Useful? Why U.S. Air Force Pilots May Prefer F-35s to F-22s in a War with Russia,' *Military Watch Magazine*, 16 May 2022. '078 – F-35 Lightning II,' *Fighter Pilot Podcast*, 13 April 2020. '036 – 4th vs 5th Gen Fighters,' *Fighter Pilot Podcast*, 12 January 2019. 'F-16s to F-35s to YouTube with "Hasard" (ep. 167),' *Fighter Pilot Podcast*, 20 May 2023. 'F-35 Critics Are Completely Wrong. F-16s for Ukraine Were Over-Hyped. | Ep. 44 Prof. Justin Bronk,' *Decoding Geopolitics Podcast*, 18 December 2024.
13 '078 – F-35 Lightning II'.
14 The Nixon Seminar on Conservative Realism and National Security, 6 April 2021.
15 Stewart, Phil and Stone, Mike, 'U.S. military comes to grips with over-reliance on Chinese imports,' *Reuters*, 2 October 2018. Assessing and Strengthening the Manufacturing and Defense Industrial Base and Supply Chain Resiliency of the United States, Report to President Donald J. Trump by the Interagency Task Force in Fulfilment of Executive Order 13806, September 2018. Davenport, Christian, 'White House report points to severe shortcomings in U.S. military supply chain,' *Washington Post*, 4 October 2018. Tingley, Brett, 'U.S. "Not Prepared To Defend Or Compete" With China On AI According To Commission Report,' *The War Zone*, 2 March 2021. 'Industrial Capabilities,' Office of Manufacturing and Industrial Base Policy, U.S. Department of Defense, Fiscal Year 2018. 'Industrial Capabilities,' Fiscal Year 2019. 'Industrial Capabilities,' Fiscal Year 2020. 'Industrial Capabilities,' Fiscal Year 2021.
16 Stewart, Phil and Stone, Mike, 'U.S. military comes to grips with over-reliance on Chinese imports,' *Reuters*, 2 October 2018.
17 'Industrial Capabilities,' Office of Manufacturing and Industrial Base Policy, U.S. Department of Defense, Fiscal Year 2018. 'Industrial Capabilities,'Fiscal Year 2019. 'Industrial Capabilities,'Fiscal Year 2020. 'Industrial Capabilities,'Fiscal Year 2021.
18 Webber, Michael, *Erosion of the Defense Industrial Support Base* in: McCormack, Richard, *Manufacturing A Better Future For America*, Washington, DC, The Alliance for American Manufacturing, 2009, pp.245-280.
19 Assessing and Strengthening the Manufacturing and Defense Industrial Base and Supply Chain Resiliency of the United States, Report to President Donald J. Trump by the Interagency Task Force in Fulfilment of Executive Order 13806, September 2018.
20 Weisgerber, Marcus, 'US May Need to Nationalize Military Aircraft Industry, USAF Says,' *Defense One*, 14 July 2020.
21 Weisgerber, 'US May Need to Nationalize Military Aircraft Industry, USAF Says'.
22 Harshaw, Tom, 'China Outspends the U.S. on Defense? Here's the Math,' *Bloomberg*, 3 September 2018.
23 McCain, John, 'U.S. Senator, Arizona, Opening statement by SASC Chairman John McCain on the F-35 Joint Strike Fighter Program,' 26 April 2016.
24 'F'd: How the U.S. and Its Allies Got Stuck with the World's Worst New Warplane,' *War is Boring*, 13 August 2013.
25 Naegele, Tobias, 'Editorial: The Best Fighter in the World,' *Air and Space Forces Magazine*, 26 March 2021
26 Gordon, Mott and Barry, John A., 'A Tank in Shining Armor,' *Newsweek*, 11 April 1988. Barry, John, 'A Failure of Intelligence,' *Newsweek*, 16 May 1988.
27 Director, Operational Test & Evaluation, FY2024 Annual Report, February 2025.
28 Dorr, Robert F., 'F136 Engine Hitting Milestones in Development Effort,' *Defense Media Network*, 11 December 2010.
29 Eaglen, Mackenzie, 'Why Congress Cares About Engine Competition for the Joint Strike Fighter,' *Heritage Foundation*, 24 August 2009.
30 Insinna, Valerie, 'A US Air Force war game shows what the service needs to hold off — or win against — China in 2030,' *Defense News*, 12 April 2021.
31 Grazier, Dan, 'Uncorrected Design Flaws, Cyber-Vulnerabilities, and Unreliability Plague the F-35 Program,' *Project on Government Oversight*, 24 March 2020. 'Back door for hackers? F-35 cyber weaknesses in the spotlight,' *NRI Digital*, 13 March 2019.
32 Michel III, Marshall L., *Clashes: Air Combat over North Vietnam, 1965–72*, Annapolis, Naval Institute Press, 1997, pp.156-157. Angevine, Robert G., 'Adapting to Disruption: Aerial Combat over North Vietnam', *Joint Forces Quarterly*, vol. 96, First Quarter 2020, pp.74-83.
33 'Interview with Robert Hierl on the MiG-29 Fulcrum,' *Aircraft Interview* (YouTube), 4 April 2018.
34 Dildy C., Douglas and Cooper, Tom, *F-15C Eagle vs MiG-23/25: Iraq 1991*, New York, Bloomsbury, 2016, p.74.
35 Priest, Dana, 'U.S. Fires Missiles at Iraqi Jets in "No-Fly Zone",' *The Washington Post*, 6 January 1999. Dudney, Robert S., 'Verbatim,' *Air and Space Forces Magazine*, 1 February 1999.
36 Airframe Details for F-16 #90-0778, F-16 Aircraft Database, *F-16.net* << https://www.f-16.net/aircraft-database/F-16/airframe-profile/3150 >>
37 Leone, Dario, 'MiG-25 pilot who shot down Speicher's F/A-18, could have shot down an A-6 too. But he was ordered to RTB because Iraqi GCI feared he was engaging an IrAF MiG-29.' *The Aviation Geek Club*, 31 May 2019.
38 Trevithick, Joseph, 'Let's Talk About This Rumor That Israeli F-15s Mimicked US Jets To Strike At Iran In Syria,' *The War Zone*, 3 May 2018. Baghai, Christian, 'Understanding the Risks of IFF System Spoofing in the Russian Air Force,' *Medium*, 25 February 2024.
39 'How did a 30 year-old Su-22 defeat a modern AIM-9X?', *Key Aero*, 23 June 2017.
40 Khurshudyan, Isabelle and Horton, Alex, 'Russian jamming leaves some high-tech US weapons ineffective in Ukraine,' *Stars and Stripes*, 24 May 2024. 'Ex-Pentagon Electronic Warfare Specialist Highlights Implications of Russia's EW Advantage,' *Military Watch Magazine*, 29 May 2024.

ABOUT THE AUTHOR

Abraham Abrams is an expert in international security and military affairs specialising in combat aviation. As a long-time analyst of the American defence sector, particularly in the context of its influence on broader global security and geopolitical trends, he has closely studied the F-35 program's development for over a decade. His book draws on a wide range of sources accessed over this period, including various interviews, studies, congressional hearings, and think tank reports among others. Abrams holds a masters degree in War Studies from King's College, London with a dissertation on the post-Cold War modernisation of the Chinese People's Liberation Army, as well as a prior masters in International Relations. He previously authored the book *J-20 Mighty Dragon: Asia's First Stealth Fighter in the Era of China's Military Rise.*